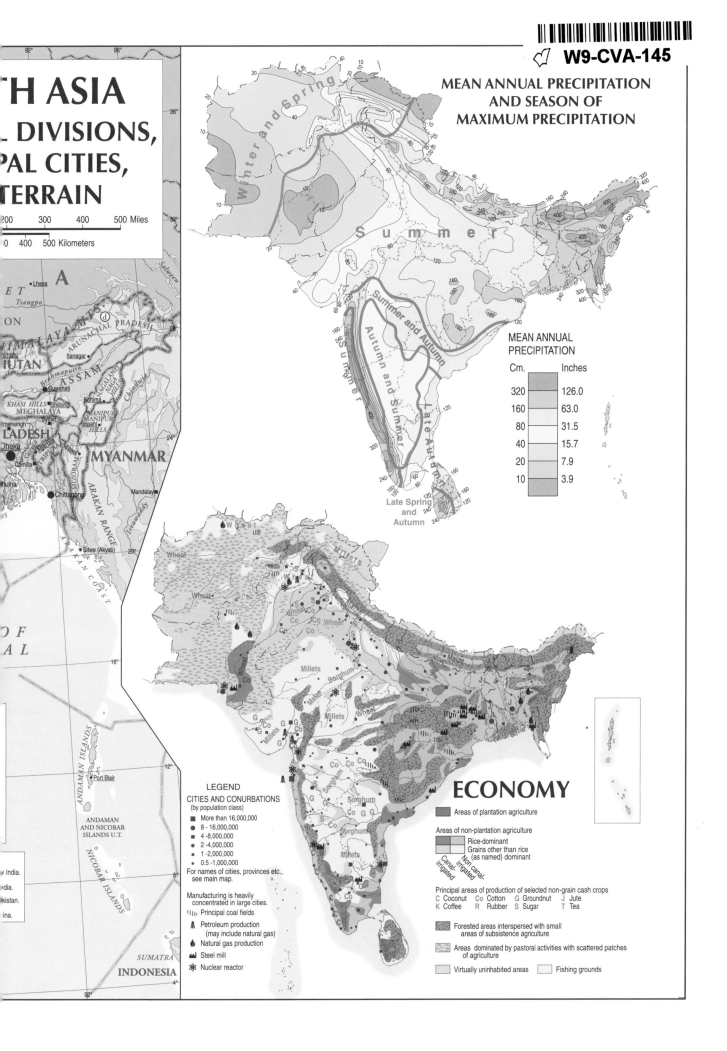

ENCYCLOPEDIA OF *India*

editorial board

ENCYCLOPEDIA OF *India*

VOLUME 4

S–Z

Index

Stanley Wolpert

Editor in Chief

CHARLES SCRIBNER'S SONS
An imprint of Thomson Gale, a part of The Thomson Corporation

Detroit • New York • San Francisco • San Diego • New Haven, Conn. • Waterville, Maine • London • Munich

Encyclopedia of India
Stanley Wolpert, Editor in Chief

For permission to use material from this product, submit your request via Web at http://www.gale-edit.com/permissions, or you may download our Permissions Request form and submit your request by fax or mail to:

Permissions
Thomson Gale
27500 Drake Rd.
Farmington Hills, MI 48331-3535
Permissions Hotline:
248-699-8006 or 800-877-4253 ext. 8006
Fax: 248-699-8074 or 800-762-4058

Since this page cannot legibly accommodate all copyright notices, the acknowledgments constitute an extension of the copyright notice.

LIBRARY OF CONGRESS CATALOGING-IN-PUBLICATION DATA

Encyclopedia of India / Stanley A. Wolpert, editor in chief.
    p. cm.
      Includes bibliographical references and index.
      ISBN 0-684-31349-9 (set hardcover : alk. paper)—ISBN 0-684-31350-2 (v. 1)—ISBN 0-684-31351-0 (v. 2)—ISBN 0-684-31352-9 (v. 3)—ISBN 0-684-31353-7 (v. 4)
      1. India—Encyclopedias.   I. Wolpert, Stanley A., 1927–
DS405.E556 2005
954'.003—dc22
                                        2005019616

This title is also available as an e-book.
ISBN 0-684-31512-2
Contact your Thomson Gale representative for ordering information.

Printed in the United States of America
10 9 8 7 6 5 4 3 2 1

table of contents

list of maps

list of articles

ENCYCLOPEDIA OF *India*

SABARMATI. *See* **Ahmedabad; Gujarat; Gandhi, Mahatma M. K.**

SABHAS AND SAMITIS The term *sabha* occurred eight times in the Rig Veda and seventeen times in the Atharva Veda. In one instance, *sabha* referred to a meeting hall. In other instances, *sabha* referred to a "body of men shining together." The term *sabha* was often linked with the term *samiti* (meeting together), both words referring to a gathering, assembly, or council of people. The Atharva Veda identified *sabha* and *samiti* as two daughters of the high Vedic god Prajāpati. Whenever the terms appeared together, *sabha* preceded *samiti*, leading some scholars to infer that *sabha*s might have existed before *samiti*s. No ancient texts, however, have identified clear differences between *sabha*s and *samiti*s, their sequence in appearance, or their relationships to each other.

Sabha-sthanu (assembly-hall pillar) described a feature of the *sabha*'s physical structure. A variety of additional *sabha*-linked terms suggested actors and activities that may have taken place in the *sabha*: *sabha-vin* (keeper of the gambling/assembly hall); *sabha-saha* (eminent in the assembly); *sabha-pati* (lord of the assembly); *sabheya* and *sabha-yogya* (worthy of the assembly); *sabha-chara*, *sabha-sad*, and *sabhyas* (member of the assembly); *sabha-vati* (woman member of the assembly); and *sabha-pala* (guardian of the assembly). According to the Rig Veda, people in the *sabha* called on the deity Indra to protect the *sabha* and its members and to grant their words effectiveness in the *sabha*.

The term *samiti* occurred nine times in the Rig Veda and thirteen times in the Atharva Veda. The Rig Veda stated that one could not rule without a *samiti*. One Vedic reference described a *rajan*'s (ruler) presence in a *samiti*.

Another reference described several rulers sitting together in a *samiti*. The Rig Veda reported people in a *samiti* discussing their cattle. One Rig Veda prayer called for agreement and unity of thought in the *samiti*. The Atharva Veda included the prayer of a Brahman priest on behalf of a *samiti*.

Despite occasional references to *sabha*s, *samiti*s, and *rajan*s in the Vedas, none of the Vedas provided an unambiguous description of how *sabha*s, *samiti*s, and *rajan*s related to each other. This did not prevent subsequent scholars from suggesting that *sabha*s and *samiti*s engaged in democratic (possibly even unanimous) decision making, served as councils to rulers, elected and removed rulers, collected taxes, and declared war. Nor did it prevent subsequent scholars from suggesting parallels between the Vedic *sabha*s and *samiti*s, anthropological descriptions of clan and tribal gatherings, Homeric agoras, Roman senates, Teuton councils of chiefs, and Anglo-Saxon witenagemots. In view of the scant number of references in the Vedas, all such scholars' suggestions must be recognized as speculative.

The Rig Veda mentioned *jana* 275 times and *vish* 271 times, both terms referring to groups of interrelated families. The *vidatha* was a form of assembly referred to 122 times in the Rig Veda and 22 times in the Atharva Veda. Translated as a "family council," the *vidatha* included women and elders as participants. The *vidatha* collectively worshiped Vedic deities such as Agni and Indra, offering sacred food and singing their praises. Occasionally the *vidatha* selected a priest to sing or lead the singing. The *vidatha* hoped that, in return for the offerings and songs, Agni or Indra would provide wealth and brave sons. Over the centuries, references to the *vidatha* gradually disappeared.

Another form of assembly referred to in the Rig Veda and Atharva Veda was a *parishad* made up of companions

Village Council Meets in a Town near Kutch, Gujarat. Though the *panchayat* is still the main arbiter of justice in rural communities, and many credit it with the relatively low crime rate and harmonious structure of such societies, in certain modern quarters there has been some talk of eliminating the centuries' old tradition (as evidenced by related cases now in India's courts). AMAR TALWAR / FOTOMEDIA.

who collectively owned cattle, worshiped Agni, and shared a common leader. The term *parishadi* implied the inclusion of women as members of the *parishad*. At the end of the fourth century B.C., the Sanskrit grammarian Pānini described a ruler as a *parishad-bala* (one who ruled with a *parishad*, or group of royal associates). Pānini also identified three types of *parishad*s: academic, social, and administrative. Later, in Kautilya's *Arthashastra*, *parishad* referred to a council of royal administrators or advisers—a form of assembly quite different from the *parishad* of the Rig Veda and Atharva Veda.

One of the last times the term *samiti* occurred in Vedic literature was in the Chandogya Upanishad, when the student Shvetaketu visited the Panchala *samiti* and was asked by its *rajanya* (leader) to answer five philosophical questions. Upon Shvetaketu's failure to answer any of the five questions, the *samiti*'s *rajanya* asked how anyone unable to answer those questions could be considered to be educated.

Sabhas and *Samitis* in Post-Vedic Literature

While the term *samiti* gradually fell out of use, the term *sabha* continued to appear in the classical literature. s ti e passed, *sabha* acquired different shades of meaning. The Mahābhārata described a *sabha* in which the legitimacy of Yudhishthira (now a slave) gambling away his and his brothers' noble wife Draupadi was debated before King Dhritarashtra. The Mahābhārata also described three occasions when women entered a *sabha*. The Apastamba Sutra described the construction of a *sabha* to be used as a guest house and recreation hall for the three higher *varṇa*s, the ancient Hindu social ranks: the Brahmans, Kshatriyas, and Vaishyas.

At the end of the fourth century B.C., the grammarian Pānini referred to a religious *sangha* (assembly) that did not separate the high and the low ranks. With the subsequent spread of Buddhism, *sangha* came to refer to orders of Buddhist monks. The Buddhist Mahaparinirbbana Sutta prescribed procedural rules for the *sangha*. These included meeting publicly and regularly, observing established precedents, respecting the advice of elders, making decisions in concord, and supporting the Buddhist sages.

*Sabha*s and *Samiti*s in Post-Independence India

Prior to India's independence in 1947, groups engaged in political, legislative, and social action gave themselves such English titles as committees, councils, associations, leagues, congresses, assemblies, and so on. Independent India's constitution called for two houses of Parliament: an Upper House (the Council of States) and a Lower House (the House of the People). The Hindi terms Rajya Sabha and Lok Sabha were applied to these two Houses, reviving the old Sanskrit word *sabha* and infusing it with new meaning. The government of India established a rural self-government structure called *panchayati raj* (the rule of *panchayat*s). *Panchayat* referred to a council of five elders who were thought to have shaped the affairs of their villages in former times. The government used the Sanskrit terms *samiti* and *parishad* (with no English equivalents) to label components of the *panchayati raj*. These included *gram panchayat*s (village councils), *panchayat samiti*s (executive bodies of all *panchayat*s in the same administrative block), and *zila parishad*s (executive bodies of all *panchayat*s in the same district or *zila*).

Joseph W. Elder

See also **Caste System**

BIBLIOGRAPHY

Basham, Arthur Llewellen. *The Wonder That Was India: A Survey of the Culture of the Indian Sub-Continent before the Coming of the Muslims.* New York: Macmillan, 1954.

Saletore, Bhaskar Anand. *Ancient Indian Political Thought and Institutions.* Mumbai: Asia Publishing House, 1963.

Sharma, Ram Sharan. *Aspects of Political Ideas and Institutions in Ancient India*. Delhi: Motilal Banarsidass, 1959.

Spellman, John W. *Political Theory of Ancient India: A Study of Kingship from the Earliest Times to Circa A.D. 300*. Oxford: Clarendon Press, 1964.

Thapar, Romila. *Cultural Pasts: Essays in Early Indian History*. New Delhi: Oxford University Press, 2000.

SALT MARCH. *See* **Gandhi, Mahatma M. K.**

SAMSKĀRA The life-cycle ceremonies of Hinduism, known as *samskāra*s, carry a sense of gradual perfection, purification, accomplishment, and consecration. Administered ritually to an individual even before birth, they continue to the "last sacrifice," the funeral. *Samskāra*s form a classical ritual system with strong connections to the ideology of Vedic sacrifice, both domestic (*grihya*) and solemn (*shrauta*), and the nurturing presence of *agni*, the sacrificial fire. As many as forty *samskāra*s are listed in ritual literature, but standard rites of passage would limit them to a traditional set of twelve to sixteen concerning birth and childhood, initiation, marriage, and death. More than half apply to the first three years of life. Late Vedic Grihya Sūtras and post-Vedic Dharma Shāstras begin lists with marriage, a ritual that in the ancient period included consummation and the presumed impregnation of the bride as *caturthī karma* on the fourth night. In later times this did not prevail. The following overview presents only the bare essentials of a single life cycle.

Garbhādhāna is the rite of conception, "impregnation," or placement of a *garbha* (embryo). Originally this was marital consummation. Reduction of the age of brides to prepubescence, apparently to safeguard the purity of the lineage, meant postponing this rite until well after marriage.

Pumsavana, "generation of a male," is performed in the third or fourth month to secure a son, particularly during a first pregnancy. The husband feeds his wife two beans and a grain of barley in curds. According to another tradition, he presses into her right nostril a mixture of mashed berries and shoots from the *nyagrodha*, the banyan tree.

Sīmantonnayana is "upward parting of the hair," a rite in which the husband parts his wife's hair from front to back three times with a porcupine quill and *darbha* or *kusha* grass stalks. She looks at a pot of cooked rice and envisions the child to be born. Unripe fruits are involved in this ceremony, which is performed in the fourth or a later month of pregnancy, with the welfare of the mother particularly in mind.

Jātakarma is the "ritual of birth" itself, formerly performed immediately upon delivery, before the umbilical cord was cut. The first part is *medhājanana*, "production of wisdom," in which the father touches the baby's lips with a gold spoon or ring on which curds, honey, and ghee (clarified butter) have been placed. *Vāc* (speech) is whispered into the infant's right ear three times. The second half of the rite, after cutting the umbilical cord, is *āyushya*, with mantras invoking *āyus* (long life) for the infant, who acquires a secret name, known only to the parents, before being given to the mother's breast.

In *nāmakarana*, a name-giving ceremony on the tenth or twelfth day after birth, the child receives the common name by which he or she will be known. This may be determined by the *nakshatra* (constellation) under which birth occurred. Names of gods and goddesses are often employed, including sectarian choices (Vaishnava, Shaiva, Shakta, etc.) special to the family. Ten days of offerings of rice and sesame, with a ritual fire or incense in the birth room, observe a period of ritual impurity due to childbirth. On the tenth or twelfth day, the normal *homa* (offering) fire is resumed, the mother's confinement ends, and ritual purity of house and family is restored.

Nishkramana, "going out," usually in the fourth month, is the occasion for the baby to go out of the birth room for *darshana*, the "sight" of Āditya, the sun, and Candra, the moon. *Karnavedha*, "ear-piercing," most often performed in the seventh month, calls for rings of gold wire, the right ear first for boys, the left ear first for girls. *Annaprāshana* is the first "eating of (solid) food," observed usually in the sixth month. The baby's tongue is touched with cooked rice (*anna*) that will be the lifelong staple of nourishment. Mantras accompany this sacred moment, observed with affection by the entire family. A famous chant about the *ātman* in Taittirīya Upanishad 3.10 concludes repetitively *aham annam*, "I am food."

Cūdakarma (or *cūdakarana*, *caula*), the first "tonsure," usually occurs in the third year. The *cūda* is a tuft of hair that remains on the child's head after a trimming by the father, along with twenty-one stalks of *kusha* grass. The family barber then shaves the head, leaving only the *cūda*. In modern observance, this is often done in the next *samskāra*, the upanayana. *Keshanta* is another "tonsure" after the upanayana, for boys of sixteen or older, similar to *cūdakarana* except that it includes shaving facial hair as well as the head.

Upanayana, the rite of "leading near," is the first approach to a guru for religious instruction. Formerly this was the indispensable second birth for all *dvīja*s, "twice-born" classes, and took place ideally at the ages of eight, eleven, and twelve for Brahman, Kshatriya, and Vaishya boys, respectively. Now it is observed by few castes other than strict Brahmans. Elements that included the reception of a *danda* staff, a *mekhalā* grass belt, and a deerskin as upper garment; a symbolic begging tour for food; offering kindling sticks into the ritual fire; investiture with the *yajñopavīta*, "sacred thread" over the right shoulder; instruction in the sacred Gāyatrī mantra (Rig Veda 3.62.10); and reinforcement of the childhood *medhājanana* were part of what had grown by late Vedic times into an elaborate ceremony of initiation into Vedic learning, the life stage of the *brahmacārin* who lived with or near a guru.

Samāvartana (or *snāna*) is a ritual "bath" to conclude the traditional period of instruction in the Vedas, after which the young man, usually in his late teens, is *snātaka*, "one who has bathed" and made the "return" (*samāvartana*) to his parental home. Expectations are that he will soon marry and advance from the *āshrama* stage of life of *brahmacārin* to that of *grihastha*, a "householder" with a ritual fire, established together with his wife.

Vivāha, "marriage," had many variations in the ancient and classical periods. Since the traditional period of Veda study was twelve years, a groom was ideally twenty-four, and the prepubescent bride eight. Among the many features of the *vivāha* carried into modern times are *pāṇigrahaṇa*, when the groom takes the bride's hand; establishment of fire and an initial *homa* offering to deities by the new couple; circumambulation of the ritual fire; *saptapadī*, taking "seven steps" north of the fire; *pratisarabandha*, tying a thread around the bride's wrist; *parasparasamīkshaṇa*, gazing of bride and groom at one another after removal of a separating cloth; *ashmārohaṇa*, placing of the bride's foot three times on a grindstone; pointing out the pole star Dhruva to the bride, as well as the star Arundhatī, wife of the *rishi* Vasishtha who, like Dhruva, was a model of fidelity. Added after the *sūtra* period was the significant tying of a *mangalasūtra*, auspicious thread, around the bride's neck, one that bears the *tāli* pendant in South India. *Antyeshti*, the "last offering," that is, of the body in the cremation fire, is the final rite of passage to another life.

In the classical period, all *samskāras* required fire, *homa*s, and the presence of learned Brahmans, who were fed in an important closing step. Except for marriage and the funeral, it was the father or father-to-be who performed each ritual, after undergoing several preparations, orienting himself in space and time, and declaring the intention of the rite. In modern times, many *samskāra*s have been bypassed or abbreviated—the *upanayana*, for example, appearing only as the groom's symbolic preliminary to marriage. Ritual manuals always allow for "local practices," an opening for widespread variation. It is noteworthy that appearance of first menstruation (*rajodarshana*, or *samartha*, "readiness" to bear children) is not a *samskāra*, although local customs in

South and eastern India observe this event ritually. Until the time of Manu, compiler of the Mānava Dharma Shāstra at the beginning of the common era, some girls were designated by certain ritualists as *brahmavadinī*, expounders of sacred texts, and received all *samskāra*s, whereas other girls received only *upanayana* and marriage. From Manu on, writers of ritual manuals often observed that marriage should be the basic *samskāra* for females. Nevertheless, many childhood *samskāra*s are common for girls today in different regions of India.

David M. Knipe

See also **Agni; Hindu Ancestor Rituals; Hinduism (Dharma); Shrauta Sūtras**

BIBLIOGRAPHY

Gonda, Jan. "The Sīmantonayyana as Described in the Gṛhyasūtras." In *East and West* 7 (1956): 12–31. An excellent historical and interpretive construction of this ancient prenatal *samskāra*.
———. *Change and Continuity in Indian Religion*. The Hague: Mouton, 1965. Chaps. 8 and 9 detail the significance of the *guru, upanayana*, and *brahmacārin*.
Kaelber, Walter O. *Tapta Marga. Asceticism, and Initiation in Vedic India*. Albany: State University of New York Press, 1989. Useful reflections on the *upanayana, brahmacārin*, spiritual rebirth, and initiatory symbolism.
Kane, P. V. *History of Dharmasāstra*. 2nd ed., vol. 2, part 1. Poona: Bhandarkar Oriental Research Institute, 1974. Chaps. 6–9 are the most authoritative coverage of *samskāra*s as a system and as separate rituals from conception to marriage.
Pandey, Raj Bali. *Hindu Samskāras: Socio-Religious Study of the Hindu Sacraments*. 2nd ed. Delhi: Motilal Banarsidass, 1969. This gives reliable attention to texts and rituals, with occasional discordant comment.
Stevenson, Margaret S. *The Rites of the Twice-Born*. London: Oxford University Press, 1920. Reprint, New Delhi: Oriental Books, 1971. Part 1 is detailed fieldwork coverage of the life of a Brahman in western India from birth to *shrāddha*, accurate although somewhat marred by a missionary bias.

SĀNKHYA The enumeration of categories as they arise in the space of the mind is the concern of the *Sānkhya*. It addresses evolution at the cosmic and the psychological levels.

The legendary systemizer of the *Sānkhya* is the sage Kapila, who lived in the beginning of the first millennium B.C., if not earlier. According to the *Sānkhya*, reality is composed of a number of basic principles (*tattva*), which are taken to be twenty-five in the classical system.

The first principle is *prakriti*, which is taken to be the cause of evolution. From *prakriti* develops intelligence (*buddhi*, also called *mahat*), and thereafter, self-consciousness (*ahamkāra*). From self-consciousness emerge the five subtle elements (*tanmātra*): ether (*ākāsha*), air, light, water, and earth. From the subtle elements emerge the five material elements (*mahābhūta*). Next emerge the five organs of sense (*jnānendriya*): hearing, touch, sight, taste, and smell, and five organs of action (*karmendriya*): speech, grasping, walking, evacuation, and procreation. Finally, self-consciousness produces the twenty-fourth of the basic elements: mind (*manas*), which, as a sixth sense, mediates between the ten organs and the outside world. The last, the twenty-fifth *tattva*, is self (*purusha*).

The emergence from *prakriti* of intelligence and, later, of subtle and gross elements, mind and consciousness, appears to mirror the stages through which a newly conceived individual will pass. Here intelligence, as the second *tattva*, is what endows the newly fertilized cell the ability to organize and grow; self-consciousness represents the stage that allows the organism to sense the environment, and so on.

The doctrine of the three constituent qualities, or *guna*s—transparence (*sattva*), activity (*rajas*), and inertia (*tamas*)—plays a very important role in the system. In its undeveloped state, cosmic matter has these *guna*s in equilibrium. The *guna*s may be viewed at the physical and the psychological levels.

The *Sānkhya* system presupposes a universe that comes into being and then is absorbed back in the substance of reality. This is what we see in the Purāṇic cyclic universe also. Within each cycle, a gradual development of intelligent life is assumed. It is postulated that the plants arose first, followed by animals of various kinds, and finally by man.

There is no ex nihilo creation in the *Sānkhya* but only a progressive manifestation. The *guna*s provide the necessary ingredient for the universe (be it physical or psychological) to evolve.

Cognition cannot be taken to arise out of the sensory organs. The cognitive organs, namely, *ahamkāra, manas* and the ten senses, which are different from one another and which are distinct specifications of the *guna*s, present the whole to the *buddhi*, illuminating it for the *purusha* like a lamp.

Purusha is neither creative nor created. *Purusha* is discriminating, subjective, specific, conscious, and nonproductive. It is the witness—free, indifferent, watchful, and inactive. The *purusha*, in this characterization, does not interfere with *prakriti* and its manifestations. It is transcendent and completely free (*kaivalya*).

The mind is taken to operate in a causal fashion, just as the physical world does. The *Sānkhya* is a sophisticated materialist framework for the laws of nature. There is also a recognition that new enumerative categories are needed in the characterization of empirical world. Thus in *Sānkhya*, we have for the mind eight fundamental predispositions (*bhāva*); eight resultant life trajectories; a set of five breaths that support the embodied condition; and five sources of action. Likewise, the description of the physical world requires categories that go beyond the twenty-five of the basic system.

Subhash Kak

See also **Vedic Aryan India**

BIBLIOGRAPHY

Dasgupta, Surendranath. *A History of Indian Philosophy*. Cambridge, U.K.: Cambridge University Press, 1922–1955.
Mohanty, Jitendranath N. *Classical Indian Philosophy*. Lanham, Md.: Rowman and Littlefield, 2000.

SAROD A lute popular in North Indian classical music, the sarod (Persian, *sarod, sarūd*, "music" or "singing") is constructed from a single piece of wood, with a skin-covered resonating cavity in the base and a hollow metal-covered neck. The fingerboard is fretless so that performers stop strings with the nails or flesh of their fingers, allowing them to slide between notes after plucking with a triangular piece of coconut shell. A characteristic feature of the body is the symmetrical indents that delineate the division between the base and the neck.

Sarods have metal wires: four principal melody strings, two or more drone strings (the highest of which are the *chikārī*), and seven or more sympathetic strings (*tarab*). Like the sitar and the *sārangī*, the sympathetic strings extend from pegs in the side of the neck up through holes in the face of the neck and pass under the melody and drone strings. Both the sarod and the *sārangī* have membranes covering the base of the instrument, and both have holes in their broad, flat bridges through which their sympathetic strings pass. The result of this highly responsive surface is that when a performer plays the melody string, other strings also vibrate, especially if they are tuned to the note played by the melody string.

The sarod is probably a nineteenth-century modification of the central Asian *rabāb*, although similar instrumental traditions in Indian history (e.g., the *dhrupad rabāb* and the *sursingār*) undoubtedly contributed to the sarod's development. The sarod is larger than the Afghani *rabāb*, and the metal fingerboard seems to have been an innovation of Nahamzamatullah Khan (1816–1911) while he was a musician at the Calcutta household of the exiled ruler of Lucknow, Wajid Ali Shah (fl. 1860s). A larger version of the instrument (without the skin-covered base), the *sursingār*, had limited popularity in the late nineteenth and early twentieth centuries.

Sarod Maker at His Workshop. An instrument of Indian classical music, the sonerous sarod possibly originates from the Persian *senya rabāb*, played in India until the mid-nineteenth century. HULTON-DEUTSCH COLLECTION / CORBIS.

Two families have been responsible for the sarod's development and international popularity in the twentieth century. Allaudin Khan and his son, Ali Akbar Khan, have been adventurous innovators and tireless educators, while Amjad Ali Khan represents the Ghulam Ali Khan style of instrument and playing.

Gordon Thompson

See also **Music**

SASSOON, DAVID *(1792–1864), Jewish merchant and philanthropist of British India.* Born into a prominent Jewish family in Baghdad, David S. Sassoon became one of the foremost merchants of British India and a great philanthropist who contributed substantially to the cities of Bombay (Mumbai) and Pune. His descendants include businessmen, British aristocrats, Hebrew scholars, rabbis, and authors. David was the son of Sheikh Sason (later, Sassoon) ben Salah who, as part of a respected and powerful family that had long held the office of banker (*sarraf bashi*) to the local ruler, was the *nasi* (head) of the Baghdadi Jewish community. When the governor of Baghdad was overthrown, the Sassoon family sought another place to live. In 1828 David left for Basra and continued on to Bushire in Persia, where his aged father joined him, bringing David's family with him. After the sheik's death in 1830, David moved his family to India, which was ripe with opportunity for entrepreneurs. Further, Bombay offered a tolerant environment and a safe future for the Sassoon children.

The Sassoons arrived in Bombay in 1832, just as the British East India Company's monopoly on trade was being relaxed. They joined other Iraqi Jewish families—the Ezekiels, the Ezras, and the Gubbays—in the cotton and opium industries that were engaged in burgeoning trade with points east, particularly China. The textile mills built and operated by David Sassoon, Sons and Company were so successful that the company opened a center in Calcutta (Kolkata). Flourishing trade prompted

ENCYCLOPEDIA OF *India*

Sassoon Library in Bombay. Its creation was conceived by a group of mechanics working at the Royal Mint and Government Dockyard in 1847; when the edifice's construction came to a virtual halt during an economic recession, David Sassoon stepped in to donate the funds needed for completion. The innovatively designed library went on to become a landmark, and is still one of the most beautiful spaces in the city. BHARATH RAMAMRUTHAM / FOTOMEDIA.

the creation of Sassoon branches in Rangoon and Shanghai, eventually expanding to Singapore, Hong Kong, and Japan. The U.S. Civil War generated an increased demand for Indian textiles by the British, which led to the creation of the first Sassoon establishment in England.

Sassoon enterprises consistently employed family and community members in their expanding mercantile empire. Wherever Sassoon businesses flourished, the surrounding communities benefited. By the 1850s, David Sassoon had gained vast real estate holdings in Bombay and Pune. In 1861 he built the Magen David (Shield of David) Synagogue as a gift to the community in the then fashionable area of Byculla, Bombay. The complex included a *mikvah* (ritual bath), a religious school, and a rest house for visitors. He also financed the David Sassoon

Benevolent Institution to provide assistance to newly arrived Jews from Arab lands who had come to work in Sassoon businesses. The building, near Bombay University, now houses the Sassoon Library. Beyond tending to the needs of his community, David Sassoon was also a great benefactor of the city of Bombay, for which, among other gifts, he constructed the Sassoon Reformatory and Industrial Institution for Juvenile Offenders and the Sassoon Mechanics Institute. In Pune, his summer home, he financed the David S. Sassoon Hospital, Infirmary, and nearby Leper Home. It was for the Jews of Pune that David Sassoon built the Ohel David (Tent of David) Synagogue in 1863. That structure became a Pune landmark with its tall steeple that long dominated the cityscape; it came to be known locally as the Lal Deul (Red Temple).

From his two marriages (first to Hannah Joseph, who died in 1826, and later to Flora Hyeem, 1812–1886), David Sassoon had eight sons and six daughters. In their mercantile success and wealth as well as their charitable activities, India's Sassoons were often compared to the European Rothschild family. David's grandson, Sir Edward Albert, married a daughter of the house of Rothschild. Their son, Sir Philip Albert (1888–1939), a scion of the house of Sassoon, inherited the prestige of his mother's family along with his father and grandfather's title.

Brenda Ness

BIBLIOGRAPHY

Roland, Joan G. *Jews in British India: Identity in a Colonial Era.* Hanover, N.H., and London: University Press of New England (for Brandeis University Press), 1989.

Roth, Cecil. *The Sassoon Dynasty.* London: Robert Hale, 1941.

SATI. *See* **Devī; Human Rights; Shiva and Shaivism.**

SATYA. *See* **Gandhi, Mahatma M. K.; Vedic Aryan India.**

SATYAGRAHA Mahatma Gandhi developed his revolutionary method of nonviolent noncooperation during his years in South Africa, naming it *satyagraha* (hold fast to the truth). That "truth" (*sat*), ancient Rig Vedic Sanskrit for "the real," was a force in the realm of the "Shining Ones" (*Devas*), Rig Vedic gods whose magic powers could move the world. Gandhi equated *sat* to God and also to nonviolence, or love, as he defined *ahimsa*. Thus reaching back more than three thousand years to the roots of Indian civilization and his own Hindu faith,

Gandhi's Salt March. The Raj long enforced a stiff tax on the sale of salt throughout India. In the spring of 1930, Gandhi led a band of faithful disciples, including Sarojini Naidu to the right, on a 240-mile march to the shore at Dandi. At Gandhi's call, millions of Indians rushed down to the beach to freely take its sea salt: Their action effectively ended the British monopoly. BETTMANN / CORBIS.

Mahatma ("Great Soul") Gandhi offered millions of his unarmed followers the symbols of divine strength and his own passionate yogic powers, launching a mass national revolution against the mightiest "satanic empire" of the modern world, the British Raj.

Though rooted in the past, and drawing upon Hindu religious mantras, Gandhi developed *satyagraha* as a practical technique or method of "action" against social evil, believing it should be universally effective in its power to combat cruel and violent forces of every kind. *Tapasya* (self-suffering) armed Gandhi with yogic strength to endure the most intense physical pain, including food and sleep deprivation, without flinching or fear. His personal struggle throughout life was to achieve perfect *ahimsa* in thought and deed, to "see God" through the truth, or *sat*, of all he did, freeing his "soul" (*ātman*) of all fruits of selfish action (karma) that led to rebirth, thus achieving his Hindu ideal goal of "liberation" (*moksha*). Every *satyagraha* that Gandhi launched began with prayers of self-purification. He often fasted as well, and

he always reminded his followers that in cleansing their own hearts, bodies, and souls, they must pray for those against whom *satyagraha* was launched. He never hated any Boer or Englishman, nor thought of anyone as his enemy, feeling only sorrow and pity for those who lived in deluded realms of violence and falsehood. Before launching his most famous Salt March *satyagraha* in 1930, Gandhi wrote to Viceroy Lord Irwin, notifying him of his intention to break the "unjust" British monopoly on the sale of exorbitantly taxed salt by picking up free salt from the seashore. Gandhi saluted the viceroy, who would soon arrest him, as "Dear Friend." Nearer the end of his life, from his prison cell, he addressed Winston Churchill the same way.

Gandhi always gave clear notice of his specific demands or reasons for launching *satyagraha*. He offered those against whom his action would be launched ample opportunity to remove or rectify the offensive that triggered his action. The "cause" might be a "Black Act" of inherently harsh, or evil legislation, such as the poll tax demanded of every Indian in South Africa, or the cruel extension of martial "law" in India after the end of World War I, or inadequate wages for cotton mill workers in Ahmedabad, or for indigo farmers in Bihar, or exorbitant land revenue demands made in a year of failed rains and famine in Gujarat's Kheda District. There were times when Gandhi led mass national *satyagraha* movements, as he did in 1920 against the Rowlatt Acts, and in 1930 against the salt tax. At other times, *satyagraha* movements were "individual," as in 1940, when Gandhi sent his devoted disciple, Vinoba Bhave, out to be arrested upon his announced intention to break a British "gag order" against "any antiwar speech." Or Gandhi could turn the fiery powers of *satyagraha* against his own body, launching a fast "unto death" or fasting for a "limited period" that he announced before he stopped eating. His last "fast unto death," shortly before he was assassinated at the end of January 1948, was aimed at his two most powerful disciples, Prime Minister Jawaharlal Nehru and Deputy Prime Minister Sardar Vallabhbhai Patel, who were reluctant to release British Raj funds owed to Pakistan in keeping with their promises prior to the 1947 partition. Gandhi also used that most passionate weapon of fasting in the personal *satyagraha* he launched against J. Ramsay MacDonald's "Communal Award" at the end of his London Round Table Conferences, in which Mac-Donald promised to reserve a special number of separate seats for India's "untouchables" on every expanded Council of British India under the new 1935 Constitution. Gandhi viewed that proposal as a lethal attack upon Hinduism and as Britain's meanest attempt to divide upper caste from lower caste Hindus in order more easily to rule over both. So he vowed to starve himself to death rather than quietly accept so nefarious an act. His fast melted the hearts of all who opposed him, or fought one another. Gandhi viewed that as proof positive of the blessed powers of *ahimsa*, its irresistible force. But such thaws rarely lasted much longer than it took Gandhi to leave his fasting bed and resume his regular routine.

Martin Luther King Jr. greatly admired Gandhi's *satyagraha* method, writing that "the Christian doctrine of love, operating through the Gandhian method of nonviolence, is one of the most potent weapons available to an oppressed people in their struggle for freedom." Despite Gandhi's singular successes in waging many passionate *satyagraha*s against tyranny and racism, he himself was the first to admit frankly that his lifelong "experiments with truth" had ultimately failed. It was less his "revolution," Gandhi well knew, that convinced the British to "quit India" half a decade after he had coined that mantra for his last mass *satyagraha* in August 1942, than their own depressed economy and post–World War II fatigue. No matter how hard he tried, moreover, he could not stop the slaughter of Hindu, Muslim, and Sikh refugees that left a million innocents dead following partition in mid-August 1947. Nor could he persuade his own former disciples, who ruled independent India, to stop fighting over Kashmir. "Today mine is a cry in the wilderness," Mahatma Gandhi cried on the eve of his assassination. "I yearn for heart friendship between Hindus, Sikh and Muslims. . . . Today it is nonexistent." For many years he had labored to teach his followers pure "*ahimsa* of the strong," rejecting arms and war entirely, but as soon as India used its armed power against Pakistan in the war over Kashmir, he saw he was wrong. Sadly, Gandhi wrote that "Today we have a larger army. . . . It is a tragedy and a shame. For so long we fought through the *charkha* (spinning wheel) and the moment we have power in our hands we forget it. Today we look up to the army" (Wolpert).

Stanley Wolpert

See also **Gandhi, Mahatma M. K.; Pakistan and India**

BIBLIOGRAPHY

Bondurant, Joan V. *Conquest of Violence: The Gandhian Philosophy of Conflict.* Princeton, N.J.: Princeton University Press, 1988.
Gandhi, Mahatma. *Young India, 1919–1922.* New York: Huebsch, 1924.
———. *An Autobiography: The Story of My Experiments with Truth,* translated by Mahadev Desai. Boston: Beacon Press, 1957.
———. *Satyagraha in South Africa,* translated by V. G. Desai. 1928. Reprint, Stanford, Calif.: Academic Reprints, 1954.
Wolpert, Stanley. *Gandhi's Passion: The Life and Legacy of Mahatma Gandhi.* New York: Oxford University Press, 2001.

SAVING AND INVESTMENT TRENDS SINCE 1950 There has been a consistent increase in the saving rate (gross domestic saving as a ratio of gross domestic product) in India through the post-independence period, from about 10 percent in the early 1950s to 17 percent in the early 1970s, and then to over 25 percent by the dawn of the new millennium (see Table 1). Private saving has accounted for the lion's share of total domestic saving throughout, with public saving declining from the early 1980s. Household saving has remained by far the most important component within private saving, despite the growth of corporate saving. The share of household saving in total private saving declined marginally from over 88 percent in the early 1950s to 84 percent in the late 1990s, reflecting increased corporate saving, from 1 percent to 3.6 percent of India's gross domestic product (GDP) over this period.

India's public saving rate steadily increased from 1.7 percent in the early 1950s to over 4 percent in the late 1970s, then declined persistently to less than 1.5 percent by the late 1990s. Public saving accounted for a mere 7 percent of total saving by the late 1990s, from over 20 percent in the late 1970s, a decline that can be attributed to the increasing fiscal deficits over this period.

An International Comparison

In the early 1960s independent India's saving rate (around 16 percent) was much higher than that of Korea, Taiwan, and Singapore, but from the early 1970s India's saving performance fell behind that of all these high-performing East Asian economies; by the mid-1990s, India's saving rate of 22 percent amounted only to a little over half their average rate. However, India's saving rate remained impressive by comparison to all other South Asian countries.

Differences in saving performance between India and the East Asian high-performing countries is a reflection of differences in overall growth performance. India's success in providing an economic setting conducive to domestic saving and financial deepening is in some measure thanks to the nominal interest rate India has maintained, an administered price, changed only infrequently based on budgetary considerations. Unlike many other developing countries, India has not seen adverse movements in real deposit rates, thanks to the long-standing official commitment to an anti-inflationary macroeconomic policy. Thus, the incentive for saving has remained positive. Perhaps more important, the rapid spread of banking facilities, following the nationalization of commercial banks in 1969, played a pivotal role in increasing private financial saving. Bank density (population per bank branch) declined persistently from over 90,000 in the mid-1950s to around 14,000 in the mid-1990s,

TABLE 1

Gross domestic savings in India and its components as a percent of GDP (in current market prices)						
	Household saving			Private corporate saving	Total private saving	Public saving	Gross domestic saving
Period (1)	Financial	Physical	Total				
1950–1955	1.6	5.1	6.7	1.0	7.7	1.7	9.4
1956–1960	2.5	5.3	7.8	1.2	9.0	2.0	11.0
1961–1965	3.0	4.7	7.7	1.6	9.3	3.2	12.5
1966–1970	2.4	7.2	9.6	1.3	10.9	2.5	13.4
1971–1975	4.1	7.0	11.1	1.6	12.7	3.2	15.9
1976–1980	5.6	8.4	14.0	1.6	15.6	4.3	19.9
1981–1985	6.5	6.8	13.3	1.6	14.9	3.6	18.5
1986–1990	7.6	9.4	17.0	2.1	19.1	2.0	21.1
1991–1995	10.0	8.1	18.1	3.5	21.6	1.6	23.2
1996–2000	10.5	8.4	18.9	4.0	22.9	−0.1	22.8

(1) Annual averages of figures based on the Indian fiscal year, from 1 April in the given year to 31 March of the next year.

SOURCE: Compiled from Economic and Political Weekly Research Foundation, *National Accounts Statistics of India, 1950–51 to 2000–01.*

improving the access of India's average household to banking facilities, reducing the cost of banking transactions.

Investment

Domestic investment in India has been predominantly financed through domestic saving. Foreign capital inflows accounted for less than 1 percent of GDP (compare the last columns in Tables 1 and 2). India has been a significant recipient of foreign aid, but total aid flows have remained negligible relative to the size of the economy. The role of foreign direct investment and other forms of private capital, portfolio investment, and bank-related flows has been even less important, reflecting the Indian government's unwillingness to invite foreign investment uncritically as well as the highly restrictive capital account regime. The saving-investment nexus has not undergone noticeable change, even after the reforms of 1991. The time pattern of the domestic investment rate has virtually mirrored that of the saving rate during the entire period (see Table 2).

The relative contributions of the public and private sectors to gross domestic capital formation have changed considerably from the early 1950s to the early 1980s. Public investment, which increased from about 30 percent to 50 percent, accounted for much of the total increase in investment. However, the rise in the investment rate after the mid-1980s can be attributed primarily to the increase in private investment. Private investment since the 1990s has mostly come from private corporate investment. The share of corporate investment in total private investment increased to over 45 percent in the 1990s. Relative to GDP, private corporate investment increased from 4.3 percent in the second half of 1980s to

7.1 percent by the mid-1990s. (Household investment, on the other hand, fell from 9.3 percent of GDP to 8.5 percent.) Market-oriented reforms since 1991 have begun to play an important role in promoting corporate investment, reflecting the declining cost of capital brought about by import liberalization and favorable changes in investor perception.

Investment-Growth Nexus

As already noted, throughout the postwar period, India has managed to maintain domestic saving and investment rates well above that of many other developing countries—not only those in a low-income category but also most of the middle-income countries in Latin America. However, in terms of growth performance, until the 1990s India remained a typical low-income country, with an average growth rate of around 3 percent. This incompatibility between saving/investment behavior and growth performance can be explained in terms of the nature of overall development policy stance. In the first three decades of the post-independence period and well into the 1980s, a highly interventionist (*dirigiste*) trade and industry policy regime constrained the potential growth effect of domestic investment. Thus, investment levels maintained through macroeconomic stability and financial deepening simply enabled India merely to keep its head above water.

Liberalization reforms since 1991 have set the stage for transforming the investment-growth nexus by lifting import restrictions and dismantling India's industrial "license raj," thus lowering the relative price of capital goods, leading to more investment and the replacement of outdated machinery. Reforms have also contributed to

TABLE 2

Gross investment in India and its components as a percent of GDP (in current market prices)

| Period (1) | Private investment | | | Public investment | Gross investment |
	Household	Private corporate	Total		
1950–1955	5.1	1.5	6.6	3.4	10.0
1956–1960	5.3	2.5	7.8	6.0	13.8
1961–1965	4.7	3.3	8.0	7.6	15.6
1966–1970	7.2	2.0	9.2	6.3	15.5
1971–1975	7.0	2.7	9.7	7.7	17.4
1976–1980	8.4	2.2	10.6	9.1	19.7
1981–1985	6.8	4.7	11.5	10.3	21.8
1986–1990	9.4	4.1	13.5	9.8	23.3
1991–1995	8.2	6.8	15.0	8.4	23.4
1996–2000	8.4	7.1	15.5	6.9	22.4

(1) Annual averages of figures based on the Indian fiscal year, from 1 April in the given year to 31 March of the next year.

SOURCE: Compiled from Economic and Political Weekly Research Foundation, *National Accounts Statistics of India, 1950–51 to 2000–01.*

improved efficiency of investment, shifting business investment to machinery, which has a larger growth effect than structures and inventory investment.

Data Sources

The Indian saving and investment database is relatively good by developing-country standards, and data are available on a comparable basis from 1951. India's Central Statistical Organisation is responsible for generating and disseminating data through its annual publication, *National Account Statistics.* The Economic and Political Weekly Research Foundation of Mumbai has brought together all historical series in its electronic database, *National Accounts Statistics of India, 1950–51 to 2000–01* (<http://www.epwrf.res.in>).

Prema-chandra Athukorala
Kunal Sen

See also **Economic Reforms of 1991; Economy since the 1991 Economic Reforms**

BIBLIOGRAPHY

Athukorala, Prema-chandra, and Kunal Sen. *Saving, Investment and Growth in India.* Oxford and Delhi: Oxford University Press, 2002.

Joshi, Vijay, and I. M. D. Little. *India: Macroeconomics and Political Economy, 1964–1991.* Washington, D.C.: World Bank, 1994.

Lal, Deepak, and I. Nagaraj. "The Virtuous Circle: Savings, Distribution and Growth Interactions in India." In *Trade, Development and Political Economy*, edited by Deepak Lal and Richard Snape. Basingstoke, U.K.: Palgrave, 2001.

Modigliani, Franco. "The Life Cycle Hypothesis of Saving and Inter-country Differences in the Saving Ratio." In *Induction, Growth and Trade*, edited by W. A. Eltis, M. F. G. Scott, and J. N. Wolfe. London: Clarendon Press, 1970.

Sen, Kunal, and Rajendra R. Vaidya. *The Process of Financial Liberalization in India.* Delhi and New York: Oxford University Press, 1997.

SAYYID AHMED KHAN AND THE ALIGARH MOVEMENT After 1857 the Muslims in India significantly responded to the cultural thrust of the West. Sir Sayyid Ahmed Khan (1817–1898) first grasped the challenge of modernization that British rule had brought to India. His intellectual legacy is abiding, though his political tactics are no longer relevant.

Born 17 October 1817 into a prominent family of the later Mughal nobility, Sayyid received a traditional Muslim education, which ended when he was eighteen years old. Subsequently, on his own initiative, he acquired a profound knowledge of Islam. The death of his father and elder brother required him to take a modest job as *sarishtadar* (recorder) in Delhi's criminal court. In 1841 Sayyid was appointed *munsif* (subjudge); the last Mughal king, Bahadur Shah II, granted him the ancestral titles of *Jawad ad-Daulah and Araf Jang* (Supporter of the State and Wise Strategic Thinker). From 1846 to 1854, he remained in Delhi, writing six books on traditional religious themes. In 1847 he published an archaeological survey of Delhi, *Athar Al-Sanadid*, in recognition of which the Royal Asiatic Society of Britain made him an honorary fellow in 1864. In 1855 Sayyid was transferred to Bijnore, where he witnessed the tragic upheavals of 1857.

Sayyid remained loyal to the British government, for which he was rewarded with promotion to the rank of *Principal Sadr Amin*. However, he had emerged from the ordeal of 1857 as a Muslim nationalist as well. He completed in 1859 his *Tarith Sarkashiy-I Dhilla Bijnore* (History of insurrection in Bijnore district) and his critique of the British East India Company's misrule in India, *Asbab Baghawat Hind* (The causes for the revolt of India). To calm the outraged British government, he wrote in his *Risalah Khair Khawahan Musalmanan: An Account of the Loyal Mahomdans of India* that a large number of Muslims, throughout the "Mutiny" of 1857–1858, had remained loyal to the British government. To explore areas of harmony and to foster sympathetic understanding of Christianity among Muslims, Sayyid wrote *Tabiyn al-Kalam fi Tafsir al-Tawrat was al-Injiyl Ala Millat al Islam: The Mohammedan Commentary on the Holy Bible*, publishing it in 1862. In 1864 he established the Scientific Society, translating European scientific works into Urdu and arranging public lectures on scientific subjects. At Aligarh, Sayyid launched his British Indian Association in May 1866 to lobby the British Parliament for the rights of Indians.

Sayyid took a leave of absence from his position of subjudge and sailed to London in 1869, remaining in Britain until October 1870. For his trip he had mortgaged his ancestral home in Delhi and had borrowed 10,000 rupees at a very high interest rate.

Sayyid was enchanted by the dynamism of British society and culture, though he also began to develop a greater awareness of his own cultural identity during that trip abroad. That process of self-realization, called *khudi* (ego) by Indian Islam's poet-philosopher Muhammad Iqbal (1877–1938), was evident as Sayyid wrote from England in 1869: "My faith in the fundamental principles of Islam was strengthened more by exposure to the conditions of Europe . . . than by going on a pilgrimage to Mecca." (Malik 1986, pp. 98–99).

Perceptions of 1857 and the Theory of Participatory Rule

Sayyid's view of the upheavals of 1857 was contrary to the prevalent British view of the events as a "grand mutiny." Sayyid argued that five major causes spawned the revolt: the people's misapprehensions of the intentions of the British East India Company government; the enactment of laws, regulations, and procedures that were not in harmony with Indian mores and their past political systems; the government's lack of information about the peoples' condition, folkways, and other "afflictions," which alienated their subjects from the government; the inefficient management and disaffection of the army; and the government's abandonment of practices that were essential to good government in India.

The Muslim rulers of India, reasoned Sayyid, were once, like the British, alien to India. Differing in faith and culture, the Muslims and the Hindus eventually succeeded in establishing friendship. Initially, and especially during the Turkish and Pathan Delhi Sultanate dynasties, contacts between Hindus and Muslims were minimal. A feeling of cordiality was first established in the reign of the Mughal emperor Akbar (r. 1556–1605), and continued through the reign of Shah Jahan (r. 1628–1658), but unfortunately ceased during the anti-Hindu reign of Aurangzeb (r. 1658–1707). The British could have won the affection and the loyalty of the Indians by inviting the upper classes to attend their viceregal courts. Governors-General Lord Auckland (1836–1842) and Lord Ellenborough (1842–1844) observed this practice, which later fell into disuse. Personal contacts between the ruler and the ruled disappeared, Sayyid noted, and mistrust and suspicions arose.

Reflective of Sayyid's recommendation was the Indian Councils Act of 1861, which added three Indians—the maharaja of Patiala, the raja of Benares, and Sir Dinka Rao—to join the newly created eighteen-person Legislative Council. In 1878 Lord Lytton appointed Sir Sayyid as a member of the Legislative Council, and in 1880 his tenure was extended for two more years by Lord Ripon. Allen Octavian Hume's endeavors for the creation of the All-India National Congress may have been inspired, at least in some measure, by Sir Sayyid's cogent advice to the British Raj.

The All-India Muhammadan Educational Conference

Established in 1886, Sir Sayyid's Muhammadan Educational Congress sought to channel the restless flow of Muslims' energies, accentuated by the rising expectations of educated youth, into a national organization. The organization was to combine the functions of articulation and aggregation of Muslim educational, economic, and political interests, while enabling Muslims to define their role in the polity of British India. Finally, the Educational Congress aimed at the politicization of the Muslim masses. Thus, Sir Sayyid renounced his apolitical role after 1885, recognizing that the establishment of the All-India National Congress that year heralded the dawn of a competitive political environment in British India. In 1890 he persuaded the annual convention of his Educational Congress at Allahabad to adopt "Conference" as its title, instead of "Congress," generating a clearer struggle for power between the National Congress and the Educational Conference, and the ideological successor of the latter, the All-India Muslim League, which was established by the conference's leaders in 1906 in Decca. On 28 December 1887, while the Indian National Congress met in Madras (Chennai), Sir Sayyid utilized a public session of the Educational Congress at Lucknow to oppose Muslim participation in the National Congress. On 16 March 1888, he reiterated more vigorously his opposition to the National Congress at a public meeting in Meerut.

To neutralize the growing power of the National Congress, Sir Sayyid organized a Patriotic Association in 1888. Hindus as well as Muslims of the land-owning classes of Bengal, Bihar, Madras, Bombay (Mumbai), Awadh, the North-West provinces, and Punjab supported the association. The Patriotic Association started sending memoranda to the British Parliament, articulating property owners' interests, which Sayyid believed were in harmony with those of Muslims, adding that the National Congress lacked true "national" representative capacity. However, regional Islamic associations were most conspicuous in the Patriotic Association's system of action, and gradually the role of Hindus virtually disappeared.

Theory of Muslim Nationalism

In the post-1857 period Sir Sayyid was the first to articulate the theory of Muslim Indian nationalism. Other leaders in subsequent generations essentially followed him, embellishing this concept in the light of their own time and erudition. Sir Sayyid, as a scion of Mughal nobility, discussed the concept of nationalism in the terminology of nineteenth-century Europe, and enunciated the creed of Viscount Bolingbroke's aristocratic nationalism. Sayyid believed that nationalism was an instinct, and that national solidarity distinguished man from animal. A mutual feeling of solidarity with those who share many common traits is the quintessence of Sir Sayyid's definition of nationalism. Muslims all over the world were a nationality because of their adherence to the creed of *Shihadeh-La ilaha illa-i Lah Muhammadur Rasula-Allah* ("there is no God whatsoever but Allah; Muhammad is the messenger of Allah"). Sir Sayyid maintained that "to Islam it was irrelevant whether a believer was white or black, Turkish or Tajik, an Arab or a Chinese, a Punjabi or a Hindustani." By Qur'anic dictum, "Muslims all over the world were the progenies of a spiritual father." Sayyid was aware that, despite their allegiance to a common creed, Muslims differed in their geographic locations and historical experiences. Consequently, he maintained that the Muslims' historical encounter with India had molded Indian Muslims into a distinct nationality. Muslim political power in India, from the advent of the Arabs in the eighth century to the heyday of Mughal power in the seventeenth and eighteenth centuries, maintained Muslim preeminence in politics, economics, and education.

In the nineteenth century, Sir Sayyid lamented, the Muslim nation was decaying rapidly from its lack of social solidarity. Sayyid also opposed the Congress's demands for the introduction of elections for the Viceroy's Legislative Council, and for a competitive examination for the covenanted services to be held in India. Relatively backward in acquiring English education, Muslim youth were not yet prepared, in the last two decades of the nineteenth century, to compete with Hindus. For a country like India, where cultural and religious heterogeneity was the rule, competitive examination, Sir Sayyid believed, would introduce elements of tension in the administration. On substantially similar grounds, Sayyid in December 1887 opposed the one-man, one-vote principle of election to the Viceroy's Council.

Framework of Social Reforms

Muslim leadership in India, traditional as well as modern, has always been called upon to define Islamic culture and the limits of its interaction with Hindu culture. Hindu culture has always been assimilative, but Islam in the Indian cultural environment faced the problem of preserving its distinct identity, which greater cultural relations with Hindu society would erode. Striking a balance between the two processes (i.e., cultural identity vs. cultural synthesis) has not been easy; and despite the creation of Pakistan in 1947 the problem for Indic Muslims has remained unsolved.

For Sayyid, Western science and technology strengthened Islamic convictions, since Islam was not dialectically opposed to reason. In fact, he expected modern education to be an ally of Islam, sustaining it with rationalist underpinning. However, Islam needed to be reinterpreted and updated in order to remove irrational accretions added by Muslim theologians. Consequently, for analysis, Sayyid's modernistic interpretations can be divided into three broad categories: the Qur'an and the Apostolic Traditions; the demythologizing of Islam; and finally, the emergence of a modern orientation for Islam.

Sayyid was keenly aware of the need for *ijtahad* (the right of interpreting Islam) in modern times. On this subject he went back to the original sources of Islamic law, the Qur'an and the Hadith (Prophetic Traditions). Essentially, Islamic mythology had developed through the Hadith literature and the Prophet's biographies. Twisting any Qur'anic statement regarding the Prophet, the traditionalists and biographers often allowed their imaginations to take irrational flights. To the believer, these stories became a source of delight, but in the age of reason they embarrassed the educated.

After his return from Europe, Sayyid graduated to the Newtonian view of nature. Consequently, he adopted a rational approach toward fundamental Islamic convictions, including the role of the Prophet, revelation, and the "proofs" of prophecy, the miracles. This intellectual transformation earned him the sobriquet of Nechari, the "naturist." In his scientific approach, Sayyid saw an alliance between science and religion. Like Victorian theologians, he argued that whatever science one chose, it disclosed the power, wisdom, and goodness of God. Moreover, science and religion had two different sets of concerns, but they were not dialectically opposed; while religion dealt with the ultimate cause, science carried out observations and experiments to search for networks of connections.

Sayyid dismissed the traditionally accepted miracles of the prophet Muhammad as fabrications of zealous Muslims, who sought to match Muhammad's "miracles" with those of Moses and Christ. He did accept the Darwinian theory of evolution as a scientific and rational explanation of the descent of man, but refused to accept the alleged superiority of scientific knowledge over the Qur'an. He asserted that scientists interrogated nature objectively in order to yield certain knowledge. This accurate scientific knowledge only served to establish the existence of God, and his rational religion, Islam. In this view, man could scarcely expect to go beyond that level of comprehension. Thus, the theory of evolution was yoked, by Sir Sayyid, to the service of Islam.

Hafeez Malik

See also **All-India Muslim League; Congress Party; Iqbal, Muhammad; Islam; Islam's Impact on India**

BIBLIOGRAPHY

Hussain, M. Hadi. *Syed Ahmed Khan: Pioneer of Muslim Resurgence.* Lahore: Institute of Islamic Culture, 1970.
Lelyveld, David. *Aligarh's First Generation: Muslim Soliarity in British India.* Princeton, N.J.: Princeton University Press, 1978.
Malik, Hafeez. *Sir Sayyid Ahmad Khan and Muslim Modernization in India and Pakistan.* New York: Columbia University Press, 1986.
Malik, Hafeez, ed. *Iqbal, Poet-Philosopher of Pakistan.* New York: Columbia University Press, 1971.
McLane, John R. *Indian Nationalism and the Early Congress.* Princeton, N.J.: Princeton University Press, 1977.
Troll, Christian W. *Sayyid Ahmad Khan.* New Delhi: Vikas, 1978.

SCHEDULED TRIBES India's Constitution, enacted on 26 January 1950, established compensatory benefits for members of India's "scheduled tribes." For centuries, tribes in India had been called "aboriginals," "hill tribes," "forest tribes," "animists," "backward Hindus," "criminal tribes," "primitive tribes," "backward tribes," and "depressed classes." They generally spoke their own languages, observed their own political and cultural patterns, lived in isolated areas, and were regarded as economically and socially "backward."

In the late nineteenth and early twentieth centuries, Indian and European reformers called on the British government of India to do something to improve the lot of India's most disadvantaged groups. The 1935 Government of India Act announced that certain "degraded" groups in India would have special electoral representation in India's forthcoming elections. In anticipation, in 1936 India's provincial governments prepared lists ("schedules") of local groups meeting the "degraded" criteria. Castes considered to be "degraded" because they suffered ritual disabilities (such as denial of admission to Hindu temples) were called scheduled castes (SCs). Tribes considered to be "degraded" were referred to as "backward tribes." The 1941 census recorded 24.5 million tribals (about 6.6% of India's population). In 1950, with the enactment of India's Constitution, these "backward tribes" were referred to as scheduled tribes (STs).

Tribes in India's History

Various terms for human groups appeared in the Vedas and post-Vedic materials. These included *jana* (people), *gana* (originally a nomadic group), and *vish* (a tribelike group). Other terms that might have referred to tribal phenomena included *vidatha* (tribal assembly), *rajan* (tribal ruler), and *purohit* (tribal priest who accompanied a *rajan* into cattle raids and other battles, protecting his *rajan* with prayers). Reference was made to the *sattra*, a sacrifice performed by *yajamana*s (sacrificers) to increase the number of sons and amount of wealth of the entire group. Men and women assembled in *sabha*s and *samiti*s and discussed various topics, including cattle. Buddhist and Jain texts referred to tribal groups living in the Himalayan foothills, including the Shakya tribe into which Siddhartha Gautama (later the Buddha) was born as son of the *rajan*, and the Jnatrika tribe into which Mahavir, the founder of Jainism, was born, also son of the *rajan*. Later narratives referred to the Shakyas and Jnatrikas as Kshatriyas, warriors in the Hindu four-*varna* system. Applicable Sanskrit terms for tribals included *atavika* (forest dweller), *avanyaka* (native), and *atavibala* (forest troops).

The Dharma Shāstra of Manu described certain tribes as the result of the mixing of the four original *varna*s (Brahmans, Kshatriyas, Vaishyas, and Shudras) who emerged from the mouth, shoulders, thighs, and feet of the Cosmic Being when the Cosmic Being immolated itself on the funeral pyre. For example, the Pukkasas and Kshattris who lived in mountains and groves and subsisted by killing animals in holes were produced in turn by Brahman males impregnating Shudra females and Shudra males impregnating Kshatriya females. The

Ugras, who also subsisted by killing animals in holes, were ferocious in manner, and delighted in cruelty, were produced by Kshatriya males impregnating Shudra females. The *Artha Shāstra* (Treatise on material gain) attributed to Kautilya (Chanakya) described how a wild tribe could obstruct a prince's movement and how a prince should use one army of wild tribes to attack another army of wild tribes. The Mauryan emperor Ashoka (3rd century B.C.) referred to the dangers posed in his empire by the forest tribes and to his desire to reform them through compassion rather than violence.

Tribes and forest dwellers appeared in the Mahābhārata and Rāmāyaṇa epics as well as in Purāṇic legends and folktales. Visitors to India also described tribes and forest dwellers. In 1666 M. de Thevenot, a well-educated Frenchman who traveled in Gujarat, described a tribe of Kolies, with no fixed habitation, who migrated from village to village picking and cleaning cotton. In 1676 another Frenchman, Jean Baptiste Tavernier, published a journal in which he described four North Indian tribes of Manari, nomadic tent-living caravaners. Each tribe numbered about a hundred thousand and had its own priests, portable serpent icon, and forehead marks or necklaces applied by priests. Each tribe specialized in the transportation of one kind of product: wheat, rice, pulse (legumes), or salt. Quarrels that interfered with trade occurred so often that the emperor Aurangzeb summoned the chiefs of the wheat and salt caravans and paid them generously—for the benefit of the common good as well as their own interests—not to quarrel.

Tribes and the British

The British East India Company developed a policy for dealing with tribals shortly after it acquired control of the Rajmahal Hills in Assam. To reduce potential resistance, the company paid tribal leaders to provide protection to the company's mail runners and to report any violent outbreaks in their territory. In 1782 the company turned over the administration of justice in the Rajmahal Hills to the hereditary tribal leaders, eventually converting the Rajmahal Hills tract into a rent-free government estate managed by tribal leaders.

In 1871 and 1872, following the military events of 1857 and the transfer of power from the East India Company to the British crown, the British recorded their first all-India census. They noted respondents' caste identities or tribal affiliations. Starting in 1872, M. A. Sherring published his three-volume *Hindu Tribes and Castes*, listing Brahmans and Kshatriyas at the top and continuing down the ranks of the *varna*s to the lowest castes. The first decades of the twentieth century saw major publications describing castes and tribes in different parts of India, including Herbert Risley's two-volume *The Peoples*

Jhabua Tribesman. The state of Madhya Pradesh counts the largest tribal population in India—some 20 percent of the state's population and 23 percent of the nation's total tribal population. The district of Jhabua has the highest density of tribes in that state. AMAR TALWAR / FOTOMEDIA.

of India and other authors' volumes of the castes and tribes of Bombay, the central provinces, South India, and the dominions of the Nizām of Hyderabad. In these publications, and in the district gazetteers, the lines between "castes" and "tribes" were often unclear. "Tribes" were generally considered identifiable because they lived in isolated areas, maintained their own subsistence economies, spoke their own languages, did not use Brahman priests, observed their own religious, cultural, and political customs, and differed from the majority of the populations in physical appearance or dress. Exceptions to these identifying features, however, were frequent.

British authorities differed in their opinions regarding the policies they should implement in territories occupied primarily by tribal groups. They wanted the tribes in these territories to be peaceful, which meant restraining the "criminal tribes." They also wanted to protect tribal groups from rapacious outside traders, moneylenders, and landlords (the British failure to provide sufficient protection led to rebellions by the Santals, Oraons, Kols, Hos, Mundas, and other tribal groups). In 1874, shortly after the British government of India completed its first census, it passed the Scheduled Districts Act, declaring that certain tracts of land in Assam, Bengal, the central provinces, and other areas were "scheduled" for possible exclusion from rules applying to the rest of British India. In fact, in those tracts, laws could be enacted to protect the tribals from invasive outsiders. The Government of India Act of 1919 empowered the governor-general to declare any tract of land in India to be a Backward Tract. Furthermore, some of the Backward Tracts were to be "Wholly Excluded Areas" (in which no laws of British India applied), and other tracts were subject to "Modified Exclusion," with the governor-general in council or the governor in council deciding which British-India laws did or did not apply to those areas.

Prior to the 1931 census, India's tribals were listed as "Animists" rather than "Hindus." Because of the permeability of both categories, it was difficult for census takers to make clear distinctions. The 1941 census abandoned the "Animists" category and referred to people of "tribal origin." This enabled the inclusion of Christians and Muslims of "tribal origin," swelling the census numbers and making it difficult to compare the 1931 and 1941 census figures. The Government of India Act of 1935 called for the first time for representatives of "backward tribes" in provincial assemblies. During the next few years, virtually every province in British India generated its list of "backward tribes," including the names of tribes living in the "Excluded" and "Partially Excluded" areas.

Scheduled Tribes after India's Independence

India's Constitution called for equality of status and opportunity for all citizens. In an effort to improve the socioeconomic conditions of the scheduled castes and tribes, the government of India initiated a policy of affirmative action called "protective discrimination" or "compensatory discrimination." Article 15(4) declared that the state could make "special provision" for the advancement of SCs and STs. Articles 330 and 331 reserved seats in the national Parliament and the state assemblies for members of SCs and STs. The percentages of seats in the legislative bodies were to match as nearly as possible the proportion of SCs and STs living in the represented territory. Article 325 declared that all voters—not just SCs and STs—could participate in the election of candidates for the SC and ST reserved seats. Article 335 reserved jobs in the central and state governments for members of the SCs and STs.

To address the guarantees in Article 16 of equal rights for all Indian citizens, the Constitution stipulated that these reservations of legislative seats and government jobs for SCs and STs would end after ten years. Over subsequent decades, Parliament periodically amended the Constitution to extend the SC and ST reservations another ten years. State governments introduced their own "compensatory discrimination" provisions for scholarships, admissions to colleges and professional schools, low-interest loans, and other benefits. The recipients of these benefits were members of the groups named on the government lists of SCs and STs. In 1960 the government of India published an all-India list of 405 SCs and 225 STs. In 1976 the government of India published an amended state-by-state list of 841 SCs and 510 STs, showing that certain tribes were "scheduled" in some locations but not in neighboring locations, and certain tribes were called by a variety of different names. When designations were unclear, India's Constitution assigned to Parliament and the president the final decisions regarding a group's "scheduled" or "nonscheduled" status. According to the published lists, SCs made up about 17 percent of India's population, STs about 7.5 percent.

The Indian Constitution's fifth schedule, in conjunction with Article 244(1), provided for the administration and control of scheduled areas and STs in parts of India other than Assam. The Constitution's sixth schedule, in conjunction with Article 244(2), provided for the administration of autonomous tribal areas in Assam. The president of India had the authority to declare which areas were or were not scheduled. In most cases, the authority for administering the designated areas rested with the local governor (in consultation with advisory councils) and the central government. The local governor could decide which legislative enactments in the Republic of India applied to the scheduled area under the governor's control. In the most autonomous regions, local councils were authorized to assign and collect taxes, regulate forms of shifting cultivation, manage unreserved forests, deal with inheritance, marriage, and social customs, administer justice, and control money lending and trading with nontribals. During the decades after independence, tribe-inhabited territories north, east, and south of Assam became states within the Republic of India. These included Nagaland (1963), Manipur (1972), Meghalaya (1972), Arunachal Pradesh (1987), and Mizoram (1987).

At the beginning of the twenty-first century, India's largest tribes included the Gonds, Santals, Bhils, Oraons, Khonds, Mundas, Bhuiyas, Hos, Savaras, Kols, Korkus, Malers, and Baigas. Although more than one-third of the STs lived in scheduled areas, the majority lived in parliamentary constituencies where they formed a majority of the population. Chhattisgarh and Jharkhand, two new states formed by redrawing India's state boundaries in 2000, contained concentrations of scheduled tribes. India's scheduled-caste policies have aimed to reduce the socioeconomic differences between SCs and the rest of India's population. In addition, they have sought to preserve some degree of cultural distinctiveness for the STs by granting them considerable autonomy in designated scheduled and tribal areas.

Joseph W. Elder

See also **Caste System; Ethnic Conflict; Tribal Peoples of Eastern India; Tribal Politics**

BIBLIOGRAPHY

Davis, Kingsley. *The Population of India and Pakistan.* Princeton, N.J.: Princeton University Press, 1951.
Galanter, Marc. *Competing Equalities: Law and the Backward Classes in India.* Berkeley: University of California Press, 1984.
Ghurye, G. S. *The Scheduled Tribes of India.* New Brunswick, N.J.: Transaction Books, 1980.
Gomango, Giridhar. *Constitutional Provisions for the Scheduled Castes and the Scheduled Tribes.* Mumbai: Himalaya Publishing House, 1992.
Government of India, Office of the Registrar General. *Census of India, Paper No. 2, Scheduled Castes and Scheduled Tribes Arranged in Alphabetical Order.* New Delhi: Publications Division, 1960.

SCIENCE Indian archaeology and literature provide considerable layered evidence related to the development of science. The chronological time frame for this history is provided by the archaeological record that has been traced, in an unbroken tradition, to about 8000 B.C. Prior to this date, there are records of rock paintings that are believed to be considerably older. The earliest textual source is the Rig Veda, which is a compilation of very ancient material. The astronomical references in the Vedic books recall events of the third or the fourth millennium B.C. and earlier. The recent discovery that Sarasvati, the preeminent river of the Rig Vedic times, went dry around 1900 B.C. due to tectonic upheavals suggests that portions of the Rig Veda may be dated prior to this epoch.

The Harappan period is characterized by a very precise system of weights and monumental architecture using cardinal directions. Indian writing (the so-called Indus script) goes back to the beginning of the third millennium B.C., but it has not yet been deciphered. However, statistical analysis shows that the later historical script called Brahmi evolved from this writing.

Vedic Cosmology

Briefly, the Vedic texts present a tripartite and recursive view of the world. The universe is viewed as three regions of earth, space, and sky that in the human being are mirrored in the physical body, the breath (*prāna*), and mind. The processes in the sky, on earth, and within the mind are assumed to be connected. This connection is a consequence of a binding (*bandhu*) between various inner and outer phenomena. At one level, it is expressed as an awareness that certain biological cycles, such as menstruation, have the same period as the moon. At another level, other equations are postulated, such as the correspondence between the 360 bones of the infant (which fuse into the 206 bones of the adult) and the number of days in the civil year.

The connection between the outer and the inner cosmos is seen most strikingly in the use of the number 108 in Indian religious and artistic expression. It was known that this number is the approximate distance from Earth to the sun and the moon, in sun and moon diameters, respectively. This number was probably obtained by taking a pole of a certain height to a distance 108 times its height and discovering that the angular size of the pole was the same as that of the sun or the moon. The diameter of the sun is also 108 times the diameter of Earth, but that fact is not likely to have been known to the Vedic *rishi*s, or sages.

This number of dance poses (*karana*s) given in the *Nātya Shāstra* is 108, as is the number of beads in a rosary (*japamālā*). The "distance" between the body and the inner sun is also taken to be 108, and thus there are 108 names of the gods and goddesses. The number of *marmas* in Āyurveda is 107, because in a chain 108 units long, the number of weak points would be one less.

The universe was understood to be a living organism, subject to cycles of chaos and order or creation and destruction. The Rig Veda speaks of the universe as infinite in size. A famous mantra speaks of how taking infinity out of infinity leaves it unchanged. The world is also taken to be infinitely old. Beyond the solar system, other similar systems were postulated. An infinite size of the universe logically led to the acceptance of many worlds.

An Atomic World

The knowledge that the mind can connect to only one sense at a time may have led to the conception that it should be atomic. This idea of atomicity was extended to matter. It was postulated that these atoms form molecules of different kinds that appear as different substances.

According to the atomic doctrine of Kanāda, there are nine classes of substances: ether, space, and time, which are continuous; four elementary substances (or particles) called earth, air, water, and fire, which are atomic; and two kinds of mind, one omnipresent and another that is individual. The conscious subject is separate from material reality but is, nevertheless, able to direct its evolution.

Astronomy

Like astronomers in other cultures, Vedic astronomers discovered that the periods of the sun and the moon do not coincide. The Yajurvedic sage Yājnavalkya knew of a ninety-five-year cycle to harmonize the motions of the sun and the moon, and he also knew that the sun's circuit was asymmetric. The second millennium B.C. text Vedānga Jyotisha of Lagadha went beyond the earlier calendrical astronomy to develop a theory for the mean motions of the sun and the moon. An epicycle theory was used to explain planetary motions. Given the different periods of the planets, it became necessary to assume yet longer periods to harmonize their cycles. This led to the notion of *mahāyuga*s and *kalpa*s with periods of billions of years.

Astronomical texts called *siddhānta*s begin appearing sometime in the first millennium B.C. According to tradition there were eighteen early *siddhānta*s, of which only a few have survived. Each *siddhānta* is an astronomical system with its own constants. The great astronomers and mathematicians include Āryabhata (b. 476), who took Earth to spin on its own axis, Brahmagupta (b. 598), Bhāskara (b. 1114), Mādhava (c. 1340–1425), and Nīlakantha (c. 1444–1545). In the Nīlakantha system, which improves upon the system of Āryabhata, the five planets move in eccentric orbits around the mean sun, which in turn goes around Earth.

Evolution of Life

The Mahābhārata and the Purāṇas have material on creation and the rise of humankind. It is said that man arose at the end of a chain that began with plants and various kind of animals. In Vedic evolution the urge to evolve into higher forms is taken to be inherent in nature. A system of an evolution from inanimate to progressively higher life is assumed to be a consequence of the different proportions of the three basic attributes of the *guna*s (qualities): *sattva* ("truth" or "transparence"), *rajas* (activity), and *tamas* ("darkness" or "inertia"). In its undeveloped state, cosmic matter has these qualities in equilibrium. As the world evolves, one or the other of these become preponderant in different objects or beings, giving specific character to each.

Mind and Consciousness

All Indian thought is permeated with questions about the mystery of mind and consciousness. The gods were visualized as points in the inner sky. The Vedas speak of the cognitive centers as individual, whole entities which are, nevertheless, a part of a greater unity.

In the Vedic discourse, the cognitive centers are called the *deva*s (deities or gods). The Atharva Veda calls the human body the city of the *deva*s. In analogy with outer space, the inner space of consciousness is viewed to have three zones: the body (earth), the exchange processes (*prāna*, atmosphere), and the inner sky (heavens).

Limitation of Language

The Vedic texts express the idea that language (as a formal system) cannot describe reality completely. Because of the limitation of language, reality can only be experienced and never described fully. The one category transcending all oppositions was termed Brahman. Understanding the nature of consciousness was of paramount importance.

Knowledge was classified in two ways: the lower or dual; and the higher or unified. The seemingly irreconcilable worlds of the material and the conscious were taken as aspects of the same transcendental reality.

Systems of Philosophy

The idea of complementarity was at the basis of the systematization of Indian philosophic traditions, and complementary approaches were paired together. We have the three groups of: logic (Nyāya) and physics (Vaisheshika), cosmology (Sānkhya) and psychology (Yoga), and language (Mimāmsā) and reality (Vedānta). Although these philosophical schools were formalized in a much later, post-Vedic era, we find the basis of these ideas in the Vedic texts.

The Sānkhya and the Yoga systems take the mind as consisting of five components: *manas* (mind), *ahamkāra* (ego), *chitta* (memory), *buddhi* (intelligence), and *ātman* (self).

Physics and Chemistry

In the Indian atomic theory, the atoms combine to form different kinds of molecules that break up under the influence of heat. The molecules come to have different properties based on the influence of various potentials.

Indian chemistry developed many different alkalis, acids, and metallic salts by processes of calcination and distillation, often motivated by the need to formulate medicines. Metallurgists developed efficient techniques of extraction of metals from ore.

Geometry and Mathematics

Indian geometry began very early in the Vedic period in altar problems, as in the one where the circular altar (earth) is to be made equal in area to a square altar (heavens). Geometric problems are often presented with their algebraic counterparts. The solution to planetary problems also led to the development of algebraic methods.

Bharata's *Nātya Shāstra* has results on combinatorics and discrete mathematics, and Āryabhata's *Āryabhatīya* has material on mathematics. Later source materials include the works of Brahmagupta (seventh century), Lalla (eighth century), Mahāvīra (ninth century), Shrīpati (eleventh century), Bhāskara (twelfth century), and Mādhava (fifteenth century). A noteworthy contribution was by the school of New Logic (Navya Nyāya) of Bengal and Bihar. At its zenith during the time of Raghunātha (1475–1550), this school developed a methodology for a precise semantic analysis of language.

Grammar

Pānini's grammar *Ashtādhyāyī* (Eight chapters) of the fifth century B.C. provides four thousand rules that describe Sanskrit completely. This grammar is acknowledged to be one of the greatest intellectual achievements of all time. The great variety of language mirrors, in many ways, the complexity of nature and, therefore, success in describing a language is as impressive as a complete theory of physics. Scholars have shown that the grammar of Pānini represents a universal grammatical and computing system. From this perspective, it anticipates the logical framework of modern computers.

Medicine

Āyurveda, the Indian medicine system, is a holistic approach to health that builds upon the tripartite Vedic approach to the world. Health is maintained through a balance between three basic humors (*dosha*) of wind (*vāta*), fire (*pitta*), and water (*kapha*). Each of these humors had five varieties. Although literally meaning "air," "bile," and "phlegm," the *dosha*s represented larger principles.

Charaka and Sushruta are two famous early physicians. According to Charaka, health and disease are not predetermined, and life may be prolonged by human effort. Sushruta defines the purpose of medicine to cure the diseases of the sick, to protect the healthy, and to prolong life.

Indian surgery was quite advanced. The cesarian section was known, as was plastic surgery, and bone setting reached a high degree of skill. Sushruta classified surgical operations into eight categories: incision, excision, scarification, puncturing, probing, extraction, evacuation and drainage, and suturing. Sushruta lists 101 blunt and 20 sharp instruments that were used in surgery. The medical system tells us much about the Indian approach to science. There was emphasis on observation and experimentation.

Scientific Imagination in Literature

A remarkable aspect of Indian literature is its scientific speculation. The epic Mahābhārata mentions embryo transplantation, multiple births from the same fetus, battle with extraterrestrials who are wearing airtight suits, and weapons that can destroy the world. The Rāmāyaṇa mentions air travel. The medieval Bhāgavata Purāṇa has episodes related to different passage of time for different observers.

Other texts speak of 8.4 million species and note that the speed of light is 4,404 *yojana*s in a *nimesha*, which when converted to modern units turns out to be close to correct.

The Modern Period

Entering its modern era with the arrival of the English, India in the last two centuries has witnessed a renaissance of its science and a proper appreciation of the past achievements. The most important Indian scientists born in the nineteenth century who achieved international acclaim are Jagadis Bose (1858–1937) in electromagnetics and plant life, Srinivasa Ramanujan (1887–1920) in mathematics, Chandrasekhara Venkata Raman (1888–1970) in physics, Meghnad Saha (1893–1956) in astrophysics, and Satyendra Bose (1894–1974) in quantum theory. More recent contributions of Indian science are part of the story of contemporary world science.

Subhash Kak

See also **Āyurveda; Ashtādhyāyī; Astronomy; Nātya Shāstra; Nyāya; Pānini; Sānkhya**

BIBLIOGRAPHY

Bose, D. M., S. N. Sen, and B. V. Subbarayappa, eds. *A Concise History of Science in India*. New Delhi: Indian National Science Academy, 1971.
Datta, Bibhutibhusan, and Avadhesh N. Singh, *History of Hindu Mathematics*. Mumbai: Asia Publishing House, 1962.
Kak, Subhash. *The Wishing Tree: The Presence and Promise of India*. New Delhi: Munshiram Manoharlal, 2001.
———. *The Gods Within: Mind, Consciousness, and the Vedic Tradition*. New Delhi: Munshiram Manoharlal, 2002.
Srinivasiengar, C. N. *The History of Ancient Indian Mathematics*. Kolkata: World Press, 1967.
Subbarayappa, B. V., and S. R. N. Murthy eds. *Scientific Heritage of India*. Bangalore: Mythic Society, 1988.

SCIENTISTS OF INDIAN ORIGIN AND THEIR CONTRIBUTIONS

Ever since Vedic times, science and scientific inquiry have been integral to Indian intellectual endeavors. It is widely known that Indian mathematicians invented the concept of zero and the decimal system of numbers. It is perhaps not as well

Raja Ramanna. Raja Ramanna, the brains behind India's first nuclear test in the Pokhran Desert of Rajasthan. He was also the scientist primarily responsible for designing and installing the country's first series of nuclear reactors. K. L. KAMAT / KAMAT'S POTPOURRI.

known that the Pythagorean theorem was known in India many centuries before Pythagoras was born; or that the Rig Veda, thousands of years before Isaac Newton, asserted that gravity held the universe together; or that negative numbers, fractions, geometric progressions, simultaneous equations, and quadratic equations were all known to Indian mathematicians thousands of years ago. The Vedic civilization subscribed to a spherical earth, and ancient Indians determined the age of the solar system to be 4.6 billion years. The Indian medical system of Āyurveda reached great heights in Vedic India, its methods including surgery and plastic surgery as well as preventive health maintenance. The Āyurvedic texts of Charaka and Sushruta are still in use today, as are the works of the ancient Indian mathematicians Āryabhata and Bhāskara.

The educational and economic fabric of India was systematically destroyed during modern times by repeated invasions, beginning with the incursions of Mahmud of Ghazni (11th century A.D.), followed by those of the Mughals and the British. The British set up an educational system designed to produce Indians trained primarily for the civil and administrative services. Indian medicine suffered a great setback when the British closed Āyurvedic colleges in areas under their control in 1829. Despite such handicaps, modern India has produced a number of eminent scientists who have made major contributions to science. A significant number of these scientists owe their origins to Presidency College, Kolkata (Calcutta), which was founded by Hindu reformer Ram Mohan Roy in 1817. Among these are Sir Jagadis Chandra Bose (1858–1937), Satyendra Nath Bose (1894–1974), Sir P. C. Ray (1861–1944), Meghnad Saha (1893–1956), and P. C. Mahalanobis (1893–1972). Presidency College of Madras (Chennai) produced two Nobel laureates, Sir C. V. Raman (1888–1970) and his nephew Subrahmanyan Chandrasekhar (1910–1995). Several notable Indian scientists studied at Cambridge University, England, including Homi Bhabha (1909–1966), Srinivasa Ramanujan (1887–1920), Vikram Sarabhai (1919–1971), Hargobind Khorana (1922–), and Harish Chandra (1923–1983). Jawaharlal Nehru (1889–1964), first prime minister of India, studied natural sciences at Cambridge and was largely responsible for the founding of modern scientific institutions, such as the Indian Institutes of Technology, after Indian independence. The institutes continue to spawn large numbers of Indian scientists and engineers, who help fuel modern India's economic expansion.

Jagadis Chandra Bose was a remarkable scientist whose research spanned the fields of microwave physics and botany. He was educated at Presidency College, Calcutta, and also at the University of Cambridge. By 1894, Bose developed the use of galena crystals for receiving short-wavelength radio waves. In 1895 Bose gave a public demonstration of electromagnetic waves, using them to ring a distant bell and to cause gunpowder to explode, predating Guglielmo Marconi's long-distance wireless demonstrations by a year. Indeed, Bose and Marconi knew each other, and Marconi's radio transmitter and receiver used a Bose "iron-mercury-iron coherer." After his work on radio and microwaves, Bose moved on to plant physiology, demonstrating that plants react to electrical stimuli and may feel pain. Honored with a knighthood in 1917 and named a fellow of the Royal Society in 1920, he founded Calcutta's Bose Institute in 1917 and has been acknowledged as one of the pioneers of radio.

One of Bose's students was Satyendra Nath Bose, who became renowned in the field of quantum physics. While a reader in physics at Dacca (Dhaka) University in the 1920s, he wrote a short article on the behavior of quanta of light, which he sent to Albert Einstein; Einstein had the article translated into German and published. Thus developed Bose-Einstein statistics, which describe the behavior of elementary particles of integer spin. Such particles are now called bosons, and Bose statistics, as they have come to be known, explain phenomena such as superconductivity.

Sir Prafulla Chandra Ray was a chemist who began the manufacture of pharmaceuticals in India. He was educated at the University of Edinburgh. On his return, he began manufacturing chemicals at his home, eventually founding the Bengal Chemical and Pharmaceutical Works in 1902. That same year he published his celebrated *History of Hindu Chemistry*, which deals with the knowledge of chemistry in ancient India. He became the first Palit professor of chemistry in the newly founded College of Science of Calcutta University in 1916. He was knighted in 1919, and was the first president of the Indian Chemical Society, founded in 1924.

Meghnad Saha made his name in astrophysics. A contemporary of Satyendra Nath Bose at Calcutta's Presidency College, Saha was taught by Jagadis Chandra Bose and P. C. Ray. In 1919 he published his paper "On Selective Radiation Pressure and Its Applications," about radiation in stars, in the *American Astrophysical Journal*. Saha's "ions theory" explained for the first time the unusual photon line spectra in starlight as being the result of the presence of ions in stellar matter, formed by the removal of various numbers of electrons from radiating atoms. This theory provided a way of estimating the temperatures of stars. In 1927 Saha was made a fellow of the Royal Society. In 1933 he founded the Indian Physical Society, and in 1947 he established the Institute of Nuclear Physics in Calcutta, later renamed the Saha Institute.

Sir Chandrasekhara Venkata Raman was the first Indian scientist to be honored by a Nobel Prize. He won it in 1930, for his discovery (along with K. S. Krishnan) of the Raman effect, which showed that when visible light interacts with matter, the scattered light consists of wavelengths of the incident light as well as degraded wavelengths due to the interaction of the light with matter with molecular energy levels. The Raman effect became an important tool in the hands of chemists and material scientists and is still used to study the properties of materials. Raman was elected a fellow of the Royal Society in 1924 and knighted in 1929. He became director of the new Indian Institutes of Science in Bangalore in 1934, and in 1948 he established the Raman Research Institute in Bangalore. He was awarded the Bharat Ratna, the nation's highest award.

Cambridge University proved influential in turning out scientists of Indian origin. Of these, the most unlikely and astonishing was Srinivasa Ramanujan, who, though

Portrait of Jagadis Chandra Bose. In 1895 Bose publicly demonstrated electromagnetic waves, using them to ring a distant bell and cause gunpowder to explode, predating Marconi's long-distance wireless exhibits by a year. KAMAT'S POTPOURRI.

unable to pass a school examination in India, had an uncanny and intuitive mathematical talent. Ramanujan sent some of his proofs to three mathematicians in England. Of these, only one, G. H. Hardy, along with his colleague J. E. Littlewood of Trinity College, Cambridge, took the trouble to read the proofs. After some time, they decided that Ramanujan was either a crackpot or a genius, finally agreeing that he was the latter and inviting him to Cambridge. Ramanujan came to Cambridge in 1913 and continued to work with Hardy and Littlewood. His mathematical technique was intuitive, not formal, since he had no formal mathematical training. Yet his work continues to be of importance. One remarkable paper that he wrote with Hardy works out the formula (proven asymptotically by Hardy and Ramanujan and later by Hans Rademacher) for the number of partitions "p(n)" that one can make of the integer number "n." He was elected a fellow of the Royal Society in 1918 and later that year was elected the first Indian fellow of Trinity College, Cambridge. Ramanujan's health suffered from his solitary existence in postwar England, and he died upon his return to India in 1920, at the age of thirty-two.

C. V. Raman. Raman, who along with K. S. Krishnan was awarded the Nobel Prize in 1930 for their discovery of the so-called Raman effect. It became an important tool in the hands of chemists and other scientists and is still used to study the properties of materials. K. L. KAMAT / KAMAT'S POTPOURRI.

The second Indian to be elected a fellow of Trinity College, Cambridge, was Subrahmanyan Chandrasekhar, known simply as Chandra. He left India to study under R. H. Fowler at Cambridge at the age of twenty. While on the long sea voyage to England, he deduced that there is a limit to the masses of white dwarf stars (approximately 1.4 times the mass of the sun), now known as the "Chandrasekhar limit." Stars more massive than this will collapse into black holes once their fuel is exhausted. This was so surprising a result in the 1930s that astronomers such as Arthur Eddington refused to believe it, publicly ridiculing Chandrasekhar's theory. As a result, Chandra left Cambridge for the University of Chicago in 1937, where he remained until his death in 1995. Chandrasekhar was a master of mathematical astrophysics, acknowledged as the greatest of his generation. He would take on problems methodically over a span of several years, interspersed with seminal papers and culminating in a text on the subject, such as his *Introduction to the Study of Stellar Structure* (1939), *Principles of Stellar Dynamics* (1942), *Radiative Transfer* (1950), *Hydrodynamics and Hydromagnetic Stability* (1961), *Ellipsoidal Figures of Equilibrium* (1968), and *Mathematical Theory of Black Holes*

(1983). He was awarded the Nobel Prize in 1983 and received numerous medals and awards, including the Copley medal. After his death, the X-ray telescope launched by the U.S. National Aeronautics and Space Administration was named Chandra in his honor.

Prasanta Chandra Mahalanobis completed the Tripos exam in mathematics and physics in 1913 from King's College, Cambridge, and was elected to a research fellowship. Returned to India for a short vacation, he was prevented from traveling to Britain by the outbreak of World War I and was thus unable to accept his fellowship. He became interested in statistics and subsequently engaged in a lifelong collaboration with the Cambridge statistician R. A. Fisher. His work on the "D-squared" statistics that he derived while working in Karl Pearson's laboratory in London and his work on large-scale sample surveys are among his most enduring contributions. He founded the Indian Statistical Institute in 1931, received the Weldon Medal in 1944, was elected a fellow of the Royal Society in 1945, and was chairman of the United Nations Commission on Statistical Sampling in 1947.

Harish Chandra was educated at the University of Allahabad and went to Cambridge to study under Paul Dirac. While there, he met Wolfgang Pauli and pointed out an error in Pauli's work. The two became friends as a result. Harish Chandra obtained his doctorate in 1947 and went to work in the United States at Columbia University and, after 1963, at Princeton. His field of work was in group theory of semisimple Lie algebras. He was made a fellow of the Royal Society and of the National Academy of Sciences, winning the Cole Medal in 1954 and the Ramanujan Medal in 1974. The Mehta Research Institute in Allahabad has recently been renamed the Harish Chandra Institute.

Homi Jehangir Bhabha was renowned as a scientist as well as the founder of scientific institutions. He also possessed a remarkable interest in the arts. In 1927 he joined Gonville and Caius College, where he studied engineering, then physics and mathematics. He joined the Cavendish Laboratory, completing his doctoral degree in theoretical physics. In a seminal paper in 1937, Bhabha, with Walter Heitler, explained the phenomenon of cosmic-ray shower formation. Bhabha also determined the cross sections for electron-positron elastic scattering; such scattered pairs are today known as Bhabhas in particle physics. He returned to India in 1939 to work at the Indian Institute of Science in Bangalore. With the help of the Tata family, to whom he was related, he founded the Tata Institute of Fundamental Research in 1945. He was instrumental in the establishment of the Atomic Energy Commission in India in 1948 and the Atomic Research Center in 1954. Elected a fellow of the Royal Society in 1941, Bhabha won many prizes and honors, including the

Adams prize (1943) and the Padma Bhushan (1954). He died tragically in an air crash in 1966.

Vikram Sarabhai was born in Ahmedabad to an affluent industrial family. He was admitted into St. John's College, Cambridge in 1940, but had to return to India during World War II; he worked with C. V. Raman during this period. After the war Sarabhai earned his doctoral degree at Cambridge and later returned to India to establish the Physical Research Laboratory in Ahmedabad. With the active support of Homi Bhabha, he set up a rocket-launching station at Thumba, near Trivandrum. Their first rocket was launched in 1963. He was instrumental in founding the Satellite Instructional Television Experiment, designed to bring education to the masses, and he embarked on the task of fabricating an indigenous Indian satellite, *Aryabhata I*, which was launched in 1975 with a Soviet rocket. Sarabhai received many awards, including the Padma Bhushan and the Bhatnagar Medal, and can be credited as the architect of India's space program.

Hargobind Khorana was born in Punjab and educated at Punjab University in Lahore and the University of Liverpool. He spent his postdoctoral years at Zürich and Cambridge, where his interest in proteins and nucleic acids was aroused. He spent several years in Canada and the University of Wisconsin before being appointed professor of biology and chemistry at the Massachusetts Institute of Technology (MIT). He shard the 1968 Nobel Prize in medicine and physiology for helping crack the genetic code of deoxyribonucleic acid (DNA).

Jayant Narlikar is a distinguished theoretical astrophysicist who collaborated with Fred Hoyle at Cambridge. He was the first director of the Inter-University Centre for Astronomy and Astrophysics, established in Pune in 1988.

India has also produced scientific administrators who have been instrumental in the research and development institutions of independent India, including M. G. K. Menon, who was educated at the University of Bristol as a cosmic-ray physicist, succeeded Bhabha as the director of the Tata Institute of Fundamental Research, and served as science adviser to the prime minister in the 1980s. P. K. Iyengar and Raja Ramanna played important roles in India's first nuclear test in 1974. They were heads of the Bhabha Atomic Research Centre and the Indian Atomic Energy Commission successively.

The United States has a considerable academic population of expatriate Indians. Over the years, several of them have distinguished themselves in their fields. George Sudarshan's name will always be associated with the V-A theory of weak interactions and quantum optics. Jogesh Pati and Robindra Mohapatra of the University of Maryland are highly respected theoretical particle physicists. Pran Nath of Northeastern University is one of the pioneers of the theory of supergravity. Kumar Patel has become widely known as the inventor of the carbon dioxide laser, and Praveen Chaudhury has recently been appointed director of the Brookhaven National Laboratory.

Indian physicists played an important role in the discovery in 1995 of the "top quark," one of the fundamental particles that form what has come to be known as the standard model of particle interactions. The top quark was jointly discovered by two large teams of experimental physicists working in two separate and competing experiments, called CDF and D-Zero, at the Tevatron, the world's highest-energy particle accelerator, at Fermilab in the United States. Rajendran Raja (Fellow, Trinity College, Cambridge, 1973), the first Indian physicist hired at Fermilab, established collaborative efforts with Indian institutions and served as leader of the top quark search team in D-Zero for four years. The University of Chandigarh, the University of Delhi, and the Tata Institute of Fundamental Research became collaborators in the search. In addition, several Indian postdoctoral fellows and students from U.S. universities were involved in the effort. In 1995 both collaborations announced the discovery of this fundamental particle, making news worldwide.

Rajendran Raja

See also **Indian Institutes of Technology (IITs); Nuclear Programs and Policies**

BIBLIOGRAPHY

Emerson, D. T. "The Works of Jagadis Chandra Bose: 100 Years of MM-Wave Research." National Radio Astronomy Observatory, 1998. Available at <http://www.tuc.nrao.edu/~demerson/bose/bose.html>
Kanigel, Robert. *The Man Who Knew Infinity.* New York: Simon and Schuster, 1991.
Teresi, Dick. *Lost Discoveries: The Ancient Roots of Modern Science—from the Babylonians to the Maya.* New York: Simon and Schuster, 2002.
Tharoor, Shashi. "Why Indian Science Scores." *Hindu,* 8 June 2003.
Wali, Kameshwar C. *Chandra.* Chicago: University of Chicago Press, 1990.

SCULPTURE

This entry consists of the following articles:

BUDDHIST

KUSHANA

MAURYAN AND SHUNGAN

BUDDHIST

Although Buddhism began in approximately the fifth century B.C., the earliest extant Buddhist sculpture can be found in conjunction with the first appearance of stone monastic architecture, dating only to the second century B.C. These earliest monastic complexes are both free-standing (as at Bhārhut) and rock-cut (as at Bhājā), but in all instances the earliest sculptural decoration is composed mainly of deities and spirits associated with popular religious practices. Along with these images of local deities, who seem to have functioned as guardians, we also occasionally find bas-relief narrative scenes depicting moments from the Buddha's life, as well as scenes detailing the events of his many past lives, known collectively as Jataka (birth) tales. However, in none of these sculptures is the Buddha himself ever depicted. In fact, no images of the Buddha were made prior to the late first century A.D. Even when artists sculpted narrative scenes, they would depict all of the major figures with the exception of the Buddha. Often his presence would be implied by the nature of the action in the scene, or would be indicated by the appearance of a symbol, such as a footprint, an empty seat, or an umbrella. Some scholars refer to this period prior to the first appearance of the Buddha's sculptural image as the "aniconic phase."

There has been some debate as to whether the earliest Buddha images were made in the northwestern region of Gandhara (in parts of modern Pakistan and Afghanistan) or in central India near the city of Mathura. The use of Buddha images seems to have become popular in both regions at roughly the same time, the end of the first century and the beginning of the second century A.D. During these centuries, both areas were under the political control of the Kushana dynasty, and the customs of this court may have had a significant influence over this change in religious and artistic practice. Although the Buddha images from these two regions are stylistically quite different, the iconography of the Buddha's image is remarkably uniform and appears to have become standardized very quickly. This iconography includes the presence of the cranial bump or *ushnīsha*, the mark between the eyes called the *ūrnā*, simple monk's robes, and elongated earlobes. The earlobes make reference to the fact that the Buddha gave up his life as a prince, who wore heavy earrings, in order to pursue the life of an ascetic.

Freestanding images of the Buddha became common by the second century, and the practice of depicting narratives continued to remain an important part of the Buddhist sculptural tradition. In particular, scenes of the birth, enlightenment, first sermon, and death were notably popular. It is often possible to identify the event that is being portrayed by examining the iconography of

the sculpture and by recognizing links to textual descriptions of the event. For instance, the presence of deer and a wheel are important indicators of the first sermon because this event took place in the Deer Park at Sarnath, and the sermon itself is referred to as the "Turning of the Wheel of the Law." Additionally, the artists often used specific hand gestures, or *mudrā*s, as visual indications of the event or individual being portrayed. These gestures were taken directly from Indian dance traditions and can be reliably associated with important events in the Buddha's life. For example, the "earth-touching gesture," in which the Buddha's right hand, with the palm turned inward, touches the ground, signifies the moment of the Buddha's enlightenment. These artistic practices form part of an iconographic vocabulary that became a standard part of the Buddhist sculptural tradition, making it possible to easily identify most of the figural imagery associated with Buddhist sites.

Within the Buddhist artistic tradition, the names of individual sculptors are not recorded. Instead, it is the names of the patrons who commissioned these works that have typically been preserved. The vast majority of the sculptures that decorate Buddhist sites were sponsored by individual donors, who paid for these works as acts of personal devotion and then donated the images to the monastery in order to accrue positive merit for themselves and their loved ones. These acts of personal generosity are understood to have a positive karmic result for the person in whose name the work of art is donated. For this reason, standard donative inscriptions will typically give the name of the person who paid for the work, the reasons for the donation, and the names of any other individuals (often deceased loved ones) whom the donation is to benefit. This positive karmic reward, or merit, is believed to help lead to a favorable rebirth and even eventual enlightenment.

As Buddhism spread across the subcontinent and beyond, into Central Asia, China, and Southeast Asia, so did the Buddhist sculptural tradition. Also, as new forms of Buddhism developed within India, the artistic traditions changed to reflect these new sectarian differences. Shortly after the appearance of the first Buddha images, we find sculptural examples of *bodhisattvas* (those who have the essence of enlightenment) associated with the Mahāyāna Buddhist tradition. Within the Mahāyāna tradition, *bodhisattvas* are understood to be compassionate spiritual beings who postpone their own entry into Nirvāna in order to help others reach enlightenment. These beings are described as residing within special heavens, and they are recognizable in the artwork because they are typically adorned with elaborate garments and jewels, rather than the simple monk's robe worn by the Buddha. Likewise, along with the emergence

Sculpture of the "Second Buddha." Sculpture of Guru Rinpoche (the eighth-century tantric master Padmasambhava), at Hemis Gompa in Ladakh. Having brought Buddhism to Tibet, he is considered the "second Buddha." DAVID SAMUEL ROBBINS / CORBIS.

of the Buddhist Tantric (Vajrayāna) tradition (starting as early as the late 4th century A.D.), there develops a tradition of complex sculptural forms and prominent depictions of female divinities.

By the eighth century, Buddhism was beginning to lose ground in India, and new Buddhist projects became scarce in many parts of South Asia. The notable exceptions to this trend can be found in parts of Bihar, Bengal, Kashmir, and Karnataka, where Buddhism continued to enjoy some patronage and support. Eventually, however, even these holdouts began to give way to the mounting influence of first Hinduism and, later, Islam. By the twelfth century, Buddhism was all but absent from the subcontinent. Interestingly, the latest images of the Buddha were created as part of the Hindu tradition, where he is identified as one of the incarnations of the Hindu deity Vishnu. Despite Buddhism's eventual disappearance from South Asia, the Indian Buddhist sculptural tradition established and promoted many of the artistic forms and religious practices that are still known throughout the Buddhist world.

Robert DeCaroli

See also **Buddhism in Ancient India; Buddhist Art in Andhra up to the Fourth Century**

BIBLIOGRAPHY

Coomaraswamy, Ananda. *Elements of Buddhist Iconography.* Cambridge, Mass.: Harvard University Press, 1935.
———. *Origin of the Buddha Image.* 1927. Reprint, New Delhi: Munshiram Manoharlal, 1979.
Huntington, Susan. *The Art and Architecture of Ancient India.* New York: Weatherhill, 1985.
Pal, Pratapaditya, ed. *Light of Asia: Buddha Sakyamuni in Asian Art.* Los Angeles: Los Angeles County Museum of Art, 1984.

KUSHANA

Central Asian Kushana warriors invaded India in the first century of the common era, galloping over the Northwest passes, across the Indus and all of Punjab and Sind, on to Delhi and Banaras (Varanasi). The mightiest Kushana monarch was Kanishka, whose prosperous era probably began in A.D. 78. Kanishka converted to Buddhism and was certainly the most illustrious Kushana king; under his patronage two great schools of sculptural art flourished, one in Mathura, the other around Gandhara.

Coin Depicting Kanishka. Kanishka, the legendary second-century ruler of the Kushan dynasty in India. A major patron of the arts, he authorized the construction of many Buddhist monuments and helped found the Gandharan school of sculpture, thus encouraging the spread of Buddhism to Central Asia. NATIONAL MUSEUM / FOTOMEDIA.

Mathura School

Situated on the right bank of the Yamuna River, southwest of Delhi and northwest of Agra, Mathura has long been a sacred place of pilgrimage in the cultural history of India. Believed to have been the birthplace of Lord Krishna, it is a premier center of ancient Hindu worship. Buddhist texts, moreover, including the Divyavadana, Lalitavistara, and Anguttaranikaya, refer to the Buddha's visits to Mathura; and the twenty-second Tīrthānkara of Jainism, Neminatha, the cousin-brother of Lord Krishna, often visited there as well. The region around Mathura was also sacred to devotees of Shiva; antiquities of Shaivism and Mother Goddess Shaktism, as well as remains of *yaksha*s, *naga*s and other folk deities, are found there.

For the development of Indian sculptural art, the Kushana period may rightly be called the golden age of Mathura. Although the town had functioned as a center of art from earlier Mauryan times, as supported by the tall image from Parkham and its inscription, Mathura emerged as a premier center in the Kushana era. The products of this great manufactory have been recovered in Taxila (Pakistan) in the west, Chandraketugarh (West Bengal) and Mahasthan (Bangladesh) in the east, and Shravasti and Kasia (Uttar Pradesh) in the south. The chance discovery of a stone railing at Sanghol, between Punjab's Chandigarh and Ludhiana in 1885 also indicates that Mathura's art products were exported over long distances.

The Mathura style of sculptural art in the Kushana period had the following distinguishing characteristics: use of spotted red sandstone; the emergence and multiplication of a plethora of images connected with Brahmanical, Buddhist, Jain, and folk sects; a progression from symbolism to anthropomorphism; provision of acolytes with deities; use of the lion pedestal (*simhasana*); depiction of feminine beauty with delicacy, charm, and inviting gestures; introduction of statues of ruling kings; useful Brahmi epigraphs on the pedestals; development of a large number of auspicious and decorative motifs, making India's religious architecture much more attractive; a rich variety of flora and fauna; assimilation of and exchange with Gandhara art; and the pursuit of a policy of eclecticism. Some of the stone masons of the Kushana period have been identified by name, including Rama, Sanghadeva, Jotisa, Dasa, Shivarakshita, Singha, Nayasa, Dehayu, Vishnu, and Jayakula.

Buddhist Images

The most remarkable contribution of the Mathura school of sculpture is the evolution and development of the image of the Buddha. Both Mathura and Gandhara schools are credited with the origin of the Buddha image, but some of the basic elements seem to favor the Mathura school. These elements are: the appearance of a yogi, the concept of *chakravartin* (universal monarch), the lotus seat, the meditating posture, the *urna* (upraised dot of "wisdom" between the eyebrows), and the *ushnisha* (protuberance over the Buddha's head). Already existing Hindu *yaksha* statues had served as a prototype, it seems, of the early Buddha images, which share the *yaksha*s' volume, heaviness, corpulence, and frontal orientation. Early Buddhist texts, Nidanakatha and Majjhimanikaya, note a close resemblance between the *yaksha* and images of later *bodhisattvas*.

Several rudimentary representations may be dated to the pre-Kushana era: the *bodhisattva* figure in the State Museum, Lucknow (B.12b); a slab carved with the scene of conversation between the Buddha and Shuddhodana, also in the Lucknow Museum (J.531); a small Buddha on an architrave along with Buddhist symbols in the Mathura Museum (M.3); and the slab with the Buddha and *lokapalas* (H.12). These experiments paved the way, however, to shape the model Buddha/*bodhisattva*, as demonstrated by examples in the Mathura Museum (A.1, A.2, 76.32) and the Lucknow Museum (B.1, B.18, 66.48) and in Kolkata's Indian Museum (25.524). Stylistically, these belong to the Kanishka phase, that is, the last quarter of the first century A.D.

Seated Buddha. The most notable features of the seated Buddha are: its high relief, uncarved back, and sharp and clear details; a plain halo with a scalloped border; *bodhi* tree foliage at the top; upper corners occupied by celestials hovering in the air with a wreath; acolytes with flywhisks on each side; the Buddha's shaven head with a topknot like a snail shell (*kaparda*), hence called *kapardin*; the right hand raised in *abhaya* mudra (protection) and the left hand resting on the knee, or sometimes clenched, suggesting the commanding attitude befitting a *chakravartin* (universal monarch); the *urna;* wide open almond-shaped eyes, small earlobes, and a somewhat smiling expression; an upper garment covering only the left shoulder; upturned soles in a cross-legged yogic posture, carved with auspicious motifs; and the seat shaped like an altar, with two lions sitting in profile and a central one facing forward. Probably to avoid confrontation with iconoclastic Buddhist sectarians of Hinayana (the "Lesser Vehicle"), the image, though shaped as the Buddha, was often recorded as a *bodhisattva* ("he who has the essence of enlightenment").

Standing Buddha. The standing Buddha/*bodhisattva* images of the same period have similar characteristics in the upper section; the lower half shows the left hand held akimbo, a waistband fastening the lower garment terminating in a double knot, sometimes a bunch of flowers or a turban between the feet, suggesting the superiority of the enlightenment of Buddhahood over kingship. The important citations are to be found in the Mathura Museum (39.2798 and 71.105), the Allahabad Museum (69), the Sarnath Museum (B.1), the State Museum of Lucknow (B.73), and Guimet Museum in Paris (17489). The Allahabad Museum figure is dated in the second Kushana era (A.D. 80), and the Sarnath Museum statue is inscribed with the year three (A.D. 81). Beside Gautama Buddha, the figures of other Mahayana ("Greater Vehicle") Buddhas, such as Dipankara, Kashyapa, Amitabha, and Maitreya, also appear.

The Mathura school came in contact with the Gandharas School in the post-Kushana era, and new traits emerged on the Buddhist icons as a result of interaction: the drapery covering both shoulders (*ubhayamsika sanghati*) with thick pleats; Vajrapani with his thunderbolt as an attendant to the Buddha; other postures, such as *dhyana* (meditation); and a *kusha* grass cushion on the seat. With the passage of time, the drapery becomes thicker, with schematic shutter-type pleats, the lions on pedestal face forward and the central lion disappears or is replaced by a meditating *bodhisattva* or some object of worship. The nimbus gradually becomes elaborate with added bands. By the end of the second century and the beginning of the third century A.D., the Gandharan impact recedes with the disintegration of the Kushana power, and the simpler, earlier traits revive.

Jain Figures

The Jain icons first appeared with the Ayagapatas (tablets of homage) profusely carved with symbols and motifs and sometimes with a tiny figure of a Jina Tirthankara ("ford-crosser" divinity). In the Kushana period, independent Jinas (Tīrthānkaras) were carved and at times four were sculpted in one block of pillar called a *sarvatobhadra* or *sarvatomangala* ("auspicious in all four heavenly directions"). The Tīrthānkaras are naked, either in meditating seated pose (*dhyanastha*) or standing in penance (*danda* or *kayotsarga*), and each bears a mark of Shrivatsa on the chest. In this period, Adinatha (the first Jina) is recognized by the hair falling on shoulders, Neminatha (the twenty-second Jina) with his contemporary Hindu divinities Balarama and Krishna, and Parshvanatha or Suparshvanatha, seen through a snake canopy. A number of Jain images bear Brahmi epigraphs in Buddhist hybrid Sanskrit, furnishing useful historic information about the Jain community in the Kushana age. The carved stone railings around the Jain and Buddhist stupas and *chaitya*s were the most attractive parts of those monuments, and the Mathura railings are full of wonderful details, including charming females from Bhuteshwar and Kankali.

Brahmanical and Folk Deities and Royal Portraits

Brahmanical and folk figures emerged in multiple forms during the Kushana period. Vishnu, Shiva, Surya, Karttikeya, Agni, Divine Mothers, Kubera, *yaksha*s, and *naga*s were the most popular deities. Vishnu was generally sculpted as Vasudeva Krishna, with two arms, four arms, or eight arms. Composite forms depict Balarama and other figures emerging from a central Vasudeva icon (Mathura Museum, 13.392–95). One stela illustrates a scene of the flooded Yamuna reaching Gokula (Mathura Museum, 17.1344). Balarama is seen with a snake hood over his head, right hand raised in the *abhaya* mudra and the left hand holding a cup. Sometimes, he holds a lion-shaped plow, suggesting that he was worshiped as the divinity of agriculture. Surya (the "sun god") is depicted in royal Kushana garb, wearing stitched drapery and boots and driving a chariot.

Shiva is seen in his symbolic lingam as well as in human form. His one, two, or four faces project from the lingam. In complete human form, he is shown with matted hair and erect phallus (*urdhvalingin*). The Arddhanarishvara (androgynous composite form with Pārvatī) was also shaped in the Kushana period. Karttikeya, Shiva's war-god son, is seen as a young man with a lance (Mathura Museum, 42.2949). His brother Ganesha appears as a nude elephant-headed dwarf in the late or post-Kushana period (Mathura Museum, 15.758).

Among the Mother Goddess deities, Mahishasuramardini ("strangling the buffalo demon") was quite popular, generally shown with her powerful four arms.

Other goddesses from this era are Revati, Shashthi, Naigameshi (goat-headed), Pārvatī, Lakshmī, Gajalakshmi, and Ekanamsa (sister of Balarama and Krishna). The composite image of Shakti (female energy) is also seen.

Almost life-size statues of Kushana kings were recovered from a place known as Mat (10 mi [16 km] north of Mathura) where a Devakula (gallery of the statues of the Kushana dynasty) was erected. The sculptures, bearing alien features, represent Wema Kadphises, Kanishka, and Chashtana, and may suggest the indulgence of foreign sculptors.

The folk cults are represented by *yaksha*s and *naga*s. As a result of German archaeological excavations in the region, some beautiful sculptures of a Naga shrine of the Kushana period were recovered from Sonkh in the Mathura district. *Yaksha*s had by then become dwarfish in shape, suggesting a source of amusement rather than divine veneration.

R. C. Sharma

BIBLIOGRAPHY

Agrawala, Vasudeva S. *Indian Art*. Varanasi: Prithiri Prakasham, 1965.

Coomaraswamy, Ananda K. *History of Indian and Indonesian Art*. New York: Dover, 1965.

Gupta, Swarajya P. *The Roots of Indian Art*. Delhi: D. K. Publishers, 1980.

Lohuizen-De Leeuw, J. E. van. *The Scythian Period*. Leiden: E. J. Brill, 1949.

Mukherjee, Bratindra N. *Mathura and Its Society*. Kolkata: Firma K. L. M., 1981.

Ray, Niharranjan R. *Maurya and Post Maurya Art*. Delhi: Thomson, 1975.

Raychaudhuri, Hemchandra C. *Political History of Ancient India*. Delhi and New York: Oxford University Press, 1996.

Saraswati, S. K. *Survey of Indian Sculpture*. New Delhi: Munshiram Manoharlal, 1975.

Sharma, R. C. *Bharhut Sculpture*. New Delhi: Abhinav, 1994.

——. *The Splendour of Mathura Art and Museum*. New Delhi: D. K. Printworld, 1994.

——. *Buddhist Art: Mathura School*. New Delhi: Wiley Eastern Ltd., 1995.

——. "Development of Indian Sculpture from Mauryan to the Kushana Period." In *Life, Thought and Culture in India*, edited by G. C. Pande. New Delhi: Munshiram Manoharlal, 2001.

Smith, Vincent A. *The Jain Stupa and Other Antiquities of Mathura*. 1901. Reprint, Varanasi: Indological Book House, 1969.

MAURYAN AND SHUNGAN

India's Mauryan period (324–185 B.C.), which opened with the martial conquests and diplomatic matrimonial alliances of Chandragupta Maurya (r. 321–297 B.C.), culminated in the creation of a mighty Mauryan empire in the last quarter of the fourth century B.C. India emerged as a vast united continent, thanks to Chandragupta's son Bindusara (reigned c. 297–273 B.C.) and grandson Ashoka (r. 268–231 B.C.), both of whom expanded Mauryan borders and enhanced Mauryan glory in multiple ways.

Ashoka expanded the empire, annexing Kalinga (modern Orissa) after a fierce battle, which proved to be the turning point of Ashoka's life and reign, reflected in edicts he had inscribed on pillars of stone erected throughout India. He aspired to abandon violence and hoped instead to make lasting peace the primary policy of his administration.

There are two distinct forms of Mauryan art: folk art, the tradition of which was handed down through the ages and which manifested itself mainly in clay, timber, early ring stones, and a few statues; and court art, which emerged under the patronage of Emperor Ashoka, and which is represented by monolithic stone columns, crowned by a "Wheel of the Law" or animals, and rock shelters at Barabar and the Nagarjuni hills in Bihar. The so-called Chandragupta Sabha (palace), the remains of which were discovered at Kumrahar, near Patna (Mauryan Pataliputra) was erected followed the earlier Mauryan timber tradition, although several stone fragments were also found there. It may be presumed that the palace and assembly hall constructed by Chandragupta Maurya in the fourth century B.C. served not only the Mauryan dynasty but was probably also used by the succeeding Shunga monarchs. Some of its remains are preserved in the Kolkata's Indian Museum, as well as in Patna's State Museum.

Mauryan Court Art

Rock-cut dwellings. The experiments in architecture by Mauryan stone masons were made in the hills of Barabar and Nagarjuni, in Bihar's Gaya district. These were excavated to provide shelter for Buddhist monks. The Lomasha Rishi Cave is the best preserved of the Barabar group. With its face to the south, the cave has two chambers; the outer chamber, gleaming with lustrous polish, measures about 32 feet by 17 feet (9.86 × 5.18 m); the inner one, measuring about 14 feet by 17 feet (4.33 × 5.18 m), is incomplete. The most striking feature is the facade bearing a fine polish, a hallmark of Mauryan court art, with a frieze in low relief depicting elephants and a Buddhist stupa between a crocodile at each end. The adjacent Sudama Cave bears an inscription, which states that it was carved in the twelfth regnal year of Ashoka. With two chambers, this cave is finished with a high polish.

About .6 mile (1 kilometer) to the east of Barabar are three caves: Gopi, Vapi, and Vadathika of Nagarjuni, which were excavated at the instructions of King Dasharatha, grandson of Ashoka, and gifted to an order of *ajivika*s (Jain monks). Each has a single, highly polished chamber. One other cave is situated at Sitamarhi, 12 miles (20 kilometers) from Rajgir, but it bears neither Mauryan polish nor an inscription.

Aesthetically, the site of Dhauli in Orissa, with an elephant in front, is an outstanding example of Ashoka's rock-cut experiments. Captioned as *seto* in the Brahmi script, meaning "white," it may represent the dream of the Buddha's mother, Mayadevi, in which she saw a white elephant, symbolizing the Buddha, entering her womb. Art historian Nihar Ranjan Ray, on the other hand, speculates that the animal symbolizes the presentation of King Ashoka to the people of Kalinga. The site also has the a number of Ashokan edicts, inscribed in his twelfth regnal year.

Pillars. Ashokan court art is famed for the monolithic columns installed at several places in India and Nepal. The notable features of these columns are the use of light pink Chunar sandstone, tapering shafts, the figure of either a lion or other animals (such as a bull or an elephant) on the capital, auspicious motifs, and messages carved in beautiful calligraphy. Ashokan pillars have been found in the following places:

In Bihar: a lion capital at Basarh, Vaishali; a bull capital at Rampurwa (now in New Delhi, outside Rashtrapati Bhavan); a lion capital at Rampurwa; another lion capital at Lauria Nandangarh; a fragmentary shaft at Lauria Araraja; and some fragments from Patna (now in the Patna Museum).

In Uttar Pradesh: the famous symbol of India, the four-lion capital at Sarnath; an elephant capital at Sankisa; a pillar in the Allahabad Fort (originally from Kaushambi); a fragmentary pillar at Kaushambi; a fragment of an abacus with a lion's paw from Bansi, Basti (now in the State Museum, Lucknow); a pillar from Prahladpur (now in the Sanskrit University, Varanasi); a pillar without capital from Meerut (now on the ridge near Delhi University); a fragment of a pillar reused as a Shivalinga (in the Nageshwaranatha Temple of Ayodhya); and part of a pillar shaft, later shaped as a Surya image (now in the State Museum, Lucknow).

In Madhya Pradesh: a lion capital at Sanchi; and a pillar reused in Umrao Dulla Garden near Bhopal.

In Haryana: a pillar without capital from Topra, Ambala (now at the Firoz Shah Kotla, Delhi); a fragment of a pillar now used as the base of a Minar at Fatehabad; and a fragment of a pillar (now used in Lat Ki Maszid at Hissar).

In Nepal: a pillar at Lumbini; a fragmentary pillar at Nigalisagar; and a fragmentary pillar at Gotihawa.

Turbaned Male Head Sculpture. Sculpture dating to the Shungan epoch, second century B.C., excavated at Bharhut in Northern India. Though the Shungans were adherents of Brahmanism, their rule marked one of the most creative periods of Buddhist art. NATIONAL MUSEUM / FOTOMEDIA.

The erection of such monumental pillars was not only a remarkable aesthetic achievement but a demonstration of great technological and engineering skill, involving the transportation and installation of heavy materials at remote sites. The Ashokan pillars thus attested to India's power, while at the same time spreading the royal message of nonviolence and good conduct. The script used for most inscriptions was Brahmi, with some Kharoshti and Aramaic in the western border areas. The letters are beautiful, sharp and neatly incised, and reflect a meticulous handling and careful supervision. The Ashokan writing presents a highly developed stage of calligraphic art.

These tall, heavy columns were freestanding, requiring no platforms or additional support. The Mauryan sculptors seem to have resolved the problem of harmonizing the pillar shaft with the capital. The lion on the Basarh pillar sits on a square platform projecting from the capital; for this reason, it has been considered pre-Ashokan by some scholars. The Rampurwa bull, Sankisa elephant, and Lauria Nandangarh lion are integrated with the shaft. Further integration is noticed in the Sanchi, Rampurwa, and Sarnath lion capitals.

Sarnath pillar. The Sarnath lion (or wheel) capital pillar, the most remarkable specimen of Mauryan court art, was discovered in 1904. The elegance of its flawless rendering, its soft and lustrous surface, its perfect blend of shaft with abacus, and its majestically seated lions make it a supreme example of Indian sculptural art. The symbolism and rendering of the four lions, the presence of four animals below them (lion, elephant, bull, and horse), and the fluted lotus below the abacus have been universally admired. The "Wheel of Law" (*dharmachakra*) surmounting the four lions suggests the supremacy of *dharma* (right conduct, or Buddha's law) above royalty. It may also indicate the initial turning of the Wheel of Law (*dharmachakrapravartana*) by the Buddha when he first articulated his four noble truths at Sarnath. The four animals symbolize Vedic Brahmanical deities: the lion is Durgā; the bull, Shiva; the elephant, Indra; and the horse, Surya. These may also stand for the four divine guardians of the four quarters of heaven: the lion is Vaishravana in the north; the bull, Virupaksha in the west; the elephant, Dhritarashtra in the east; and the horse, Virudhaka in the south. The major life events of the Buddha may also be symbolized here: the elephant represents his birth; the horse, his renunciation of royal luxury; the bull, his preaching as *munipungava;* and the lion, his clan (Shakyasimha). The four animals may also represent the four wheels of the chariot of a paramount ruler (*chakravartin,* the title of the Mauryan emperors).

Didarganj *yakshi.* The life-size standing female statue—variously described as a *yakshi* (semidivine being), a queen, or a representation of feminine beauty (*striratna*)—recovered from the Didarganj locality of Patna and now exhibited in the Patna Museum is a superb specimen of Mauryan art. This piece may represent both court and folk styles. The female figure, carved in the round, has full and rounded features with prominent breasts, broad hips, and a narrow waist. She wears a head crest, large triple-looped earrings, a pearl necklace, a double-stringed chain *stanahara* (falling between the breasts), five stringed girdles, heavy anklets, and a waist garment (*dhoti*) with schematic pleats. In her right upraised hand, she holds a *chamara* (fly whisk); her facial expression suggests that she is keenly watching or supervising some event. The curves and contours are perfect, and the figure conveys a royal dignity and elegance. The Mauryan polish is noteworthy; the piece may be the product of the late third or early second century B.C.

Lohanipur torso. The torso of a Jina, standing in the *kayotsarga* or *danda* posture while performing penance, was recovered from Lohanipur near Patna, and is now displayed in the State Museum at Patna. This figure in the round bears the Mauryan polish. Some of the kings of the Mauryan dynasty, like Chandragupta, Dasharatha, and Samprati were inclined toward Jainism; hence the possibility of a Tīrthānkara (Jain pontiff) image by the sculptors of the age cannot be ruled out.

Foreign influences. To what extent Mauryan art, particularly its court art, reflected any foreign influence has

been debated. The pillars and polish were supposedly derived from Persian (Achaemenid) imperial influence. An edict of Ashoka mentions the dispatch of his missionaries to the capitals of Antiogonus II of Syria, Ptolemy of Egypt, Antigonus of Macedonia, Alexander of Epirus, and Magas of Syria. With these cultural ties, and the likely exchange of artistic commissions, the services of skilled foreign artists in Mauryan employ may be surmised. Prior styles of Indian architecture had used timber; hence the introduction of stone required specially trained and seasoned Persian artisans. The Hellenistic plastic conventions followed by Greco-Bactrian sculptors may also be traced in some specimens of Mauryan art. There is, however, a basic difference between the Achaemenid and the Mauryan pillars. The former were generally part of some larger architectural scheme, while the Ashokan columns were freestanding monoliths.

Mauryan-Shungan Folk Sculpture

Late Mauryan and early Shungan folk art is represented by a group of *yaksha*s, ring stones, and other pieces.

Yakshas. The term *yaksha* is derived from *yaj,* "to worship," meaning both "wonderful" and "terrible." These semidivine beings are both benevolent and malevolent. Sometimes, the *yaksha* is viewed as the possessor of supreme power, or as a subject of Kubera. The *yaksha*s are generally heavy, dwarfish, and corpulent. With the passage of time, their independent status disappeared, as they became subordinates to the emerging new deities of Vedic Brahmanism, Buddhism, and Jainism. Much the same was true of the *naga*s (snake deities), which were assimilated into the Hindu mainstream. The installation of *yaksha* and *yakshi* statues became a national artistic phenomenon and something of a cult. These figures—of various sizes, from heroic to small—were installed on platforms outside villages as guardian deities. *Yaksha* statues stood at many different places, including Parkham, Basoda, Naglajhinga, Bharnakalan (all in the Mathura district); Rajghat (Varanasi); Noh (Bharatpur); Besnagar (Bhopal) and Pawaya (Gwalior); Patna; Shishupalgarh (Orissa); and Amin (Kurukshetra).

The 8-foot (2.4-m)-tall *yaksha* from Parkham, now in the Mathura Museum (No. C.1) is very important, since its pedestal bears a Brahmi inscription, which informs that it was carved by Gomitaka, the disciple of Kunika. This indicates that Indian sculptural art was practiced in the ancient Mathura tradition of teacher and disciple (*gurushishya parampara*) even before the common era. Similar information is furnished by the *yakshi* statue from Naglajhinga, now in the Mathura Museum (No. 72.5), whose carver is named Naka. *Yaksha*s and *naga*s were frequently carved on the railings of early stupas.

Ring stones. Small circular brown alabaster or soapstone rings, measuring between 3 and 7 inches (7.6–18 cm) with minute carvings, are beautiful specimens of the Mauryan-Shungan period. These were found in India's northern belt from Taxila to Patna, including Ropar, Mathura, Kaushambi, and Rajghat. Specimens bearing a central perforation are known as ring stones; those devoid of holes are termed disks. More rings have been found in the west, more disks in the east, particularly near Patna.

The superb carvings on these specimens depict a female figure, almost nude, who stands majestically with splayed feet and somewhat outstretched arms. A wiglike coiffure, earrings, necklace, and bangles are conspicuous. The waist is narrow and the hips broad. In the complete circle, she is repeated several times, with a tree or honeysuckle motif (*nagapushpaka*), or a pillar, as a divider. Sometimes, the figure is surrounded by birds, animals, and acolytes. The female figure may be recognized as a Mother Goddess (*mahimata*). The pieces were most likely used for religious practicesmeant to ensure progeny, prosperity, and peace.

Caskets. Other items of artistic value from the Mauryan-Shungan age are relic caskets made of soapstone or crystal. The handling of the crystal, shaping it as a fine pot with a lid, demonstrates a high level of craftsmanship. These objects were excavated from the stupa of Piprawah (Basti) on the India-Nepal border in the nineteenth and twentieth centuries. One of these (now in Kolkata's Indian Museum) bears an inscription in old Brahmi recording the deposit of the ash remains of the Shakyamuni Buddha.

Shungan Sculpture

Long after Ashoka, the crumbling Mauryan empire was smashed by Pushyamitra Shunga, who killed the last Mauryan ruler, Brihadratha, and seized power in 185 B.C., ruling for thirty-six years. Shungan art emerged as something of a negation of Mauryan art.

The distinguishing characteristics of Shungan sculptures are: a linear composition; the continuous narration of a story, with different scenes of an episode in one medallion; and an interweaving of religion and art. Shungan sculptors resolved the problem of spatial representation through overlapping figures, which all had a frontal orientation. The narrative sequence of the story was shown by repetition of the main figure at different stages of the episode; past, present, and future were combined in one medallion. An example is the depiction on the Bharut stupa railing of Anathapindaka's gift of the Jetavana monastery to the Buddha. The same formula was adopted in the Shungan depiction of Buddhist Jataka tales.

The major sites of Shungan period (2nd–1st century B.C.) sculpture are: Bharhut (Madhya Pradesh); Kaushambi, Bhita, and Mathura (Uttar Pradesh); and Sanchi (Madhya Pradesh), which is slightly later and may be called Shunga-Kanva. At the same time, there are several other sites from which Shungan sculptures have been recovered or are still seen in situ. These are: Bhaja, Karle, and Pitalkhora in Maharashtra; Jagayapeta, Amaravati, and Nagarjunikonda in Andhra Pradesh; and Udaigiri and Khandagiri in Orissa. *Yaksha* statues belonging to the Mauryan-Shungan phase form an independent group, as do the beautifully carved small ring stones or discs recovered from different sites.

Bharhut stupa. A great monument (stupa) once stood in the vicinity of the village of Bharhut, near Satna in Madhya Pradesh. Its ruins were noticed by A. Cunningham in 1874, and the following year most of the components were moved to Kolkata's Indian Museum. Other remains were later added to the collection of the Allahabad Museum. The Bharhut remains are the best specimens of the sculptural and architectural arts of the Shungan period. An epigraph on the gateway (*torana*) of the stupa states that it was erected in the Shungan reign.

A stupa generally contained some remains of the Buddha, or another venerable enlightened soul. These ashes were carefully kept in a small container (*manjusha*) of stone or metal, covered by earth or encased by bricks or stone. For the protection of the holy spot, a stone railing with gates was erected all around it, and this became a center of attraction for devotees. Though associated with death, the stupa was not a symbol of mourning or grief. It actually signified the enlightened soul's liberation from the bondage of the body and from the painful cycle of rebirth. The Buddha's release (*nirvāna*) from the perishable body was much rejoiced. There are, therefore, many joyful scenes of music, dance, and sports carved onto the railings of Bharhut's stupa. On certain occasions, they are lit with thousands of lamps, appearing as a beacon in the night.

The Bharhut stupa, when complete, was a counterclockwise cross with four gates; the distance between each was covered by sixteen monolithic pillars, which terminated in a return rail, allowing only an indirect entry into the sacred spot. Between the two rail posts, three crossbars were inserted into vertically cut sockets. The gateway (*torana*) in each direction had two tall pillars with a square base, octagonal shaft, and a bell- or vase-shaped capital with lions seated back to back. This motif must have come from Mauryan court art, with the addition of spiral ends representing crocodiles. The space between the two pillars of the gate was filled in by three architraves decorated with animals advancing toward an object of worship. Between the two architraves were set small pillar statues. The uppermost architrave was crowned by an ornamental honeysuckle surmounted by a spoked Wheel of the Law (*dharmachakra*), which was flanked by three-jewel (*triratna*) motifs.

The railing is profusely carved with depictions of a variety of flora, fauna, Jataka narrations, processions, humorous scenes, *yaksha*s, *naga*s (serpent deities), and the Mother Goddess Lakshmī, anointed by two elephants. The Bharhut stupa served as an open-air museum or sculptural gallery, and a number of its scenes have been labeled in Brahmi script. The names of several donors of different components of the monument are also inscribed. The sculptural renderings and the inscriptional evidence suggest that the Bharhut stupa was a national project, supported by donors and pilgrims from distant quarters of the country and emblematic of their Buddhist faith.

Bodh Gayā. Being associated with the attainment of enlightenment (*bodhi*) by the Buddha, Bodh Gayā is held in high esteem in the Buddhist world. Ashoka visited the holy spot and presumably built a temple, but no remains of that shrine have been found. The present temple is the reincarnation of an earlier temple, the fragments of which date back to the late second and early first century B.C., just after Bharhut. A second group of sculptures there were probably created a century later. The original railing of the stupa contained 64 pillars, 10 feet (3 m) high. An inscription notes that it was the gift of Kurangi, wife of King Indragnimitra, and Nagadevata, wife of King Brahmamitra.

Sanchi stupas. In 75 B.C., the tenth king of the Shunga dynasty, Devahuti (also known as Devabhumi) was murdered through a conspiracy by the minister Vasudeva, who founded the short-lived dynasty of Kanvas. Four Kanva kings ruled for only forty-five years; their dynasty's end came at the hands of the Andhras in 30 B.C. The Sanchi stupas near Bhopal in Madhya Pradesh were built during this period, but it is not possible to trace the precise contribution of the Kanva rulers to this building complex.

The Sanchi region is full of stupas, which number 60 in all: 8 in Sonar; 5 in Satadhara; 3 in Andher; 37 in Bhojpur; and 7 in Sanchi. Most of these are miniature; only a few are large. The building of stupas commenced in the third century B.C., when Ashoka, then governor, married Devi, the daughter of a local businessman. He selected the site of the hillock, which after the construction of the great stupa was known as Mahachetiya. The dimensions of the original stupa are known, though the existing stupa was built two centuries later. A portion of the original Ashokan pillar can still be seen near the southern gate.

The Mahachetiya (Stupa I) is 54 feet (16.5 m) high and covers a circular area 120 feet (36.5 m) in diameter. The hemispherical dome has a truncated top, surrounded by a low railing (*harmika*) consisting of a stone shaft topped by umbrellas (*chhatravali*). The body of the stupa is made of bricks surrounded by stone balustrades. At the ground level runs the pathway for clockwise circumambulation around the stupa during worship. This path is surrounded by a railing with 9-foot (2.7 m)-high pillars, placed at an interval of 2 feet (.6 m), with three crossbars. Unlike the Bharhut railing, the Sanchi railing is uncarved.

The four gateways that provide access to the *stupa*, however, are of great aesthetic merit. An inscription on the southern entrance records that it was executed by the guild of ivory carvers of Vidisha. The minute, low-carved renderings vary from gate to gate, although some episodes have been repeated. The representations are of Jatakas (previous births of the Buddha), life events, *yaksha*s, *naga*s, mythical beings, nymphs, flora and fauna, processions, and a number of decorative motifs. Like Bharhut and Bodh Gayā, Sanchi also suggests the presence of the Buddha through symbols. Similarly, Gajalakshmi, the goddess of prosperity, is standing on a lotus, anointed by two elephants. The number of Jataka tales narrated here is only four, while at Bharhut no fewer than thirty are depicted. Nevertheless, the stupa at Sanchi is one of the most impressive examples of ancient Indian art.

R. C. Sharma

BIBLIOGRAPHY

Agrawala, V. S. *Indian Art*. Varanasi: Prithivi Prakasham, 1965.

Arthashastra of Kautilya. Chap. 2. Translated and edited by L. N. Tangarajan. New Delhi and New York: Penguin, 1992.

Coomaraswamy, Ananda K. *History of Indian and Indonesian Art*. New York: Dover, 1965.

Gupta, Swarajya P. *The Roots of Indian Art*. New Delhi: D. K. Publishers, 1980.

Lohuizen-De Leeuw, J. E. van. *The Scythian Period: An Approach to the History, Art, Epigraphy, and Palaeography of North India from the First Century B.C. to the Third Century A.D.* Leiden: A. J. Brill, 1949.

Ray, Niharranjan R. *Maurya and Post Maurya Art: A Study in Social and Formal Contrasts*. New Delhi: Thomson, 1975.

Raychaudhuri, Hemchandra C. *Political History of Ancient India*. Rev. ed. Delhi and New York: Oxford University Press, 1996.

Saraswati, S. K. *Survey of Indian Sculpture*. New Delhi: Munishiram Manoharlal, 1975.

Sharma, R. C. *Bharhut Sculpture*. New Delhi: Abhinav, 1994.

———. *The Splendour of Mathura Art and Museum*. New Delhi: D. K. Printworld, 1994.

———. *Buddhist Art: Mathura School*. 1995.

———. "Development of Indian Sculpture from Mauryan to the Kushana Period." In *Life, Thought, and Culture in*

India: From 600 B.C. to c. A.D. 300, edited by G. C. Pande. New Delhi: Munishiram Manoharlal, 2001.

Smith, Vincent A. *The Jain Stupa and Other Antiquities of Mathura*. 1901. Reprint, Varanasi: Indological Book House, 1969.

SCULPTURE AND BRONZE IMAGES FROM KASHMIR

The ancient kingdom of Kashmir has come to be recognized as the center of a major regional tradition in the history of South Asian art, whose links and influence spread throughout the entire western Himalayan region, as well as to parts of Central Asia and Afghanistan in the post-Gupta and early medieval period. Few material traces of this ancient heritage remain today, which is so well documented by Kalhana in his twelfth-century chronicle of Kashmir, the *Rajatarangini*, since most of its monuments were destroyed during the Muslim conversions of the fourteenth and fifteenth centuries. Initially known from the sumptuous Buddhist bronzes preserved in Tibetan monasteries that came on the international art market in the 1960s and 1970s, following political upheaval in Tibet, the importance and antiquity of the style have been gradually realized through the study of the disparate collection of stone sculpture, much of it fragmentary, preserved in the Sri Pratap Singh Museum in Srinagar, and the relief work of such ruined monuments as Martand and Avantipur elsewhere in the valley. However, documentation prior to the seventh century is hampered by the lack of dated as well as representative material.

Formative Period

The early phase. The earliest evidence of an autonomous Kashmir style lies in a small group of Brahmanical sculptures from Bijbihara, in the south of the valley. They are all carved in the round from gray chlorite, and are notable for their static poses, linear modeling, and squarish faces. Some are of miniature scale, a feature that continues into later styles. Their ornamentation is simple, and the hair is usually bound up in a double-looped topknot. Designated as the early phase of the formative period, it dates from the first half of the fifth century and beyond, during the reign of the Kidarites. Though this is a high point of Gupta art elsewhere in north India—the Udaiyagiri cave sculptures are dated to the beginning of this period—here the influence is late Gandhara Buddhist art, in modeling, ornament, and dress, reflecting the still-flourishing state of that tradition as well as continuity with past centuries.

The most impressive example is the large six-armed Kumara standing with his *vahana* (an animal or bird that served as the mount or vehicle of the deity), the peacock. While the massive frame and arrangement of neck orna-

ments closely resemble those of a Gandharan *bodhisattva* figure, the lower garment reproduces that of a Brahman depicted in that style, while technical features such as the forked string folds and the zigzag and linen folds of the dhoti can be traced directly to the stucco sculpture of Jaulian and Mohra Moradu at Taxila. A Sassanian influence is evident in the corrugated form of the ribbons of the diadem. Two distinguishing masculine features of the formative period are the short single-stranded sacred thread and the garland, formed of overlapping flowers, that clings tightly to the thighs and reaches the knees, both of which are seen on the Kumara. These two accoutrements, though modified in future styles, are almost invariably depicted on Brahmanical and Buddhist deities in Kashmir. Three Mother Goddesses survive from this period, all somewhat stout and wooden in modeling, and clad in Hellenistic garments comprising a short chiton, an ankle-length lower garment, and a himation, of which one finds an almost exact counterpoint on a panel of figures on Stupa A15 at Jaulian.

Around the middle of the fifth century, Gupta features begin to appear in the form of regalia and jewelry, including the ubiquitous annular ear ornament, which is found on the later of the three female figures and on the detached head of a male figure, probably Vishnu, which also has a crown with a large central polygonal panel of Gupta influence. Only a single Buddhist example is known to survive from this period, a headless seated Buddha carved in relief, its robe pleated asymmetrically in ribbed folds, which was found at Baramula at the western entrance to the valley.

The later phase. Sculptures of the later phase of the formative period, carved from both gray chlorite and limestone, of which there are many examples from Bijbihara and Baramula, are notable for a predominantly Gupta influence. This is most evident in the increased volume of the body and limbs, and in the rounded faces and large almond-shaped eyes. The use of the short sacred thread, distinctive floral garland, and simple jewelry continues from the previous phase, but while the feminine attire is still Hellenistic, the masculine lower garment now more closely resembles the Gupta form, clinging tightly to the rounded thighs and tied with a plain belt, the long loose ends falling down the thigh. Images of Shiva retain the double-looped topknot, whereas the Vishnu crown is now of turreted form, derived from depictions of the busts of kings on Sassanian coinage, with a row of corkscrew curls, a Gupta feature, showing along the brow. These eclectic influences were gradually assimilated in the second half of the fifth century and early sixth, at a time when Gandharan art was in sharp decline through lack of patronage, and this phase appears to have reached its zenith around A.D. 525, when the Hephthalite king Mihirakula ruled the kingdom. The Hephthalites, or White Hunas, had earlier defeated the Guptas in their heartland of Malwa, and were probably responsible for the introduction of several Gupta stylistic features to the northwest.

The most important example of the phase, which was found at Fattehgarh, near Baramula, is an addorsed Maheshvara, a form of Shiva, accompanied by his vehicle, the humped bull, in which the placid central Mahadeva head is framed by those of Bhairava and Uma. This iconographical form, in which the reverse figure is Shiva's faithful attendant Nandin, is described as Bhuteshvara in ancient Kashmirian texts. Although earlier examples may yet come to light, it is the first sculpture to combine two features that later become a hallmark of Brahmanical sculptures in the mature Kashmir style, namely, the frequent portrayal of the deity with three lateral heads, and the use of personified weapons in the form of diminutive side attendants. While the former feature has a long earlier history in ancient Gandhara, the depiction of *ayudhapurusha*s is commonly found in Gupta Vaishnava sculpture of the fifth and sixth centuries, including a rock-cut example at Udaiyagiri in Malwa.

The Pandrethan Period: Post-Gupta Influence

The next major stage of development marks the assimilation of post-Gupta influence in the Pandrethan group of sculptures, which probably dates from the second quarter of the seventh century, in the reign of the first Karkota king, Durlabha Vardhana. Most are displayed in the museum in Srinagar. Carved in high relief in large scale from gray limestone, they are distinguished by their exaggerated poses, vigorous modeling and ornamentation, and a new repertoire of dress. Though there are links to the previous style, which seems to have gradually died out, the form and decoration of these sculptures signal an abrupt transition with the past, and they are now in most respects prototypical of the Classical style. A notable feature is the complex detailing of the edges of garments, which was further refined in the following period. The corpus comprises a large group of Buddhist sculpture, much of it fragmentary, which was excavated in 1915 from the site of two stupas and a *vihara* (monastic residence) near the village of Pandrethan (a contracted form of Puranadhishthana, meaning the "old capital"), whence the name of the style derives, and a group of twenty Brahmanical sculptures accidentally discovered in 1926 in the adjacent area of Badamibagh. These comprise Shaivite deities, mostly depictions of Maheshvara, and a group of Mother Goddesses, many in a dancing pose, reflecting a North Indian post-Gupta development that dates from as early as the beginning of the seventh century.

Leaving aside representations of the Buddha, there is little difference between male or female deities of either denomination in dress and ornamentation. The male dhoti now covers the left thigh to the knee, while the outer fold falls to the right ankle, its edge detailed with pleated or plain zigzag folds, which becomes the subsequent standard. The sacred thread, now double-stranded, falls well below the waist, and subsequently never rises above it again. The masculine ornaments consist of a wide, boldly patterned necklace or torque, ear pendants, wide armbands, and a single thick bangle, while the headdress is of tall pentagonal form crowned by a diadem of three triangular leaves with scrolling foliate design and beading around a central gemstone. The centrally parted ribbed hair bulges out beneath the fillet in semicircular bunches around a compartment of pairs of lateral ribs, in what has been described as a "window effect," one of the most distinguishing features of the style, which continues for many centuries, excluding images of Vishnu. The female anatomy now more closely follows the usual Indian form, with pronounced breasts, narrow waist, and large hips, while the standard attire comprises a short-sleeved and tightly waisted long tunic that resembles a modern Punjabi *qamis*, and a diaphanous lower garment falling to the ankles, usually combined with a long floating scarf that covers the hair behind. The jewelry consists of a pair of short necklaces, pendant ear ornaments, wide bangle, and diadem, while the wavy hair is centrally parted beneath the fillet. Depictions of the Buddha are necessarily conservative, but rather than Gandharan influence, Mathura appears to be the main source for the design of the clinging robe, which is invariably asymmetrically pleated in string folds, the neckline treated in several variations. A large standing image already displays a twist to the pelvis, which is partly retracted, and the slightly protruding stomach, so characteristic of the Classical standing Buddha.

The various changes were brought about by a complex combination of borrowing and innovation produced by local and non-Kashmirian artists working together to produce a new dynastic style of sculpture. Artists were almost certainly brought from nearby Simhapura (the Salt Range in modern Pakistan), known to have fallen under the rule of Kashmir in the early seventh century, where there is firm evidence of an earlier Gupta tradition, and where post-Gupta currents must have also reached. Many of the new features can be linked to post-Gupta developments elsewhere in North India, particularly the predominantly Buddhist workshops of Sarnath and Nalanda, from where there was selective borrowing, especially of the window effect and the form of the dhoti. A North Indian influence is most notably lacking in the upper garment of the female figure, since elsewhere in North India in this period the female deity is usually bare-breasted. It is at this stage in its history that Kashmir began to project political power well beyond its borders. One of the effects is a powerful artistic influence on the sculpture of Afghanistan and adjacent territory, which continued until the fall of the Hindu Shahi kingdom to the Yaminids in 1026.

The Classical Style

The Pandrethan features were refined in the Classical Karkota style, which absorbed further influences from mainstream Indian art to produce a rich, vibrant, and varied range of expression. Several of the recorded religious buildings of this period can be identified, the most important being the complex of royal buildings at Parihasapura, the court capital of King Lalitaditya (r. 724–761), the ancient kingdom's most illustrious ruler. Excavations at the site of the stupa built there by his minister Cankuna have yielded several Buddha and Atlas-like *yaksha* figures, which is the earliest datable group from the valley. The surviving sculpture divides into two groups: examples in stone, much of it now carved from green chlorite, terra-cotta, and bronze, mostly Brahmanical, which have been found in Kashmir itself, or its close vicinity; and examples in bronze and ivory, almost exclusively Buddhist, which have been conserved in Tibetan monasteries. Examples of both groups are now in private and public collections worldwide. Among them are several with dedicatory inscriptions in proto-Sharada script, some of which bear the names of the Potala Shahis of Bolur (the region of Gilgit and Baltistan in present-day Pakistan), which has led some scholars to talk of a local school based there.

The dates are in the cyclical Laukika era, of which the century must be inferred, and their interpretation has created disagreement between epigraphists and art historians in the past. However, new evidence demonstrates that the fully developed Buddha type, and thus the entire Classical style, emerged in the seventh century, and not in the eighth century, near the time of Lalitaditya, as previously thought. This takes the form of an inscription in metrical Sanskrit on the pedestal of a standing Buddha in the Potala Palace in Lhasa, which records its dedication during the reign of a King Durlabha. There were two King Durlabhas, who ruled consecutively for almost a century, Durlabhavardhana (r. 626–662) and Durlabhavaka (r. 662–712), and either could have been the king of the inscription. Fortunately, the wide range can be greatly modified by taking into account the date of the Pandrethan sculptures, which cannot be much earlier than the second quarter of the seventh century, and that of a seated Buddha in Classical style in the Norton Simon Museum, which can now be dated with certainty to 696. Until further evidence appears, the most likely date for

the emergence of the Classical style is from between 650 and 680. A slow decline appears to have begun toward the end of the eighth century.

The characteristic and almost invariable features of a Buddha in Classical style, and the standard facial type of the period, can be seen on the standing figure in a private collection, which closely resembles the Potala example, as well as a standing Buddha from Cankuna's stupa. The face is oval with arched eyebrows, an *urna*, large almond-shaped eyes, long nose, compact smiling lips, and small round chin. In profile, the nose and the brow form a continuous line, while the lower half of the face recedes. The robe is symmetrically pleated on the torso, the arms, and the sides, but plain on the legs, and falls from the wrists in two parallel parts, the edges rippled on the proper right, and detailed in a complex design of pleated zigzag folds on the left. A triangular-shaped panel formed on the left shoulder has the same complex pattern, while another on the right is patterned with concentric parallel folds. When the robe covers the left shoulder alone, a single triangular-shaped panel is formed. In the case of a seated image, the same rules apply, apart from the lower part of the garment, where the treatment shows a similar set pattern. Here the Buddha stands on the stamen of a multilayered lotus, which rests on a molded pedestal, as in many examples of this period. However, a wide variety of pedestals is found for the seated Buddha (most frequently depicted in teaching mode or earth-touching mode), ranging from an openwork-type with elaborate cushion, supported by columns, lions and leogrypths (a composite, mythical animal) and a seated *yaksha*; to an even more complex design of a rocky landscape, animals, and deities.

The most outstanding example of Kashmirian bronze Buddhist sculpture is undoubtedly the elaborate composition of the Buddha seated on a stylized mountain with attendants, now in the Norton Simon collection. Many of the more elaborate compositions such as this would have had aureoles, some depicting the various events in the life of the Buddha. A Maradharshana stone group with the Buddha assailed by his daughter Mara and a pair of demons, closely modeled on a Sarnath original, found just outside the confines of the valley and now in the National Museum, New Delhi, has an inscription and date in the year 5, equivalent to A.D. 729. This sculpture, with the Buddha seated on an hourglass pedestal on a rocky podium accompanied by a diminutive Earth Goddess and a mysterious kneeling male figure plucking a stringed instrument, has many of the features of some of the elaborate bronze groups inscribed with the names of the Patola Shahi rulers, which date from around this time; this demonstrates that the full repertoire of design of these so-called Gilgit bronzes was known in Kashmir, and that the sculptures were almost certainly cast by Kashmirian artists.

Many stone sculptures of Brahmanical subjects in Classical style have survived in the valley, mostly fragmentary, of which many are three-headed, a feature peculiar to Kashmir. These were either carved with an integral stepped and molded pedestal, or mounted separately on such a pedestal, usually spouted to the right to drain off libations. These were placed in shrines or set in the niches of the peristyle that enclosed the courtyard of most temples. The most outstanding sculpture in the style is undoubtedly the majestic, richly ornamented three-headed Vishnu, holding his attributes, the lotus and the conch, which must date from the seventh century. It is now in the museum in Srinagar. This iconographical form, incorporating the naturalistically carved lion and boar heads of the *avatāra*s Narasimha and Varaha, but lacking its *ayudhapurusa*s, is often referred to as Vaikuntha Vishnu, though there is ambiguity concerning its exact identification. All the new features of the style can be seen in this image, including the distinctive facial type described above. The pose is now a gentle contraposto, with one foot placed slightly forward, which is common to all depictions of Brahmanical deities with the exception of Surya, and the Buddhist deities Maitreya and Avalokiteshvara. The dhoti is of standard form, and the complex pattern of pleated zigzag folds seen on the Buddha's robe appear on the open edge of the garment, with a characteristic fan-shaped collection of folds below the belt. The multistranded sacred thread now falls to the thigh, and the floral garland is of imbricated leaf pattern design. Among the sumptuous jewelry is a diadem formed of three horned crescents containing foliate designs, a more elaborate alternative to the triangular form, which survives from the previous style.

The Utpala Style

The style underwent a brief revival in the mid-ninth century during the reign of Avantivarman (r. 855–883), as can be seen in the sculptures of the Vishnu and Shiva temples at Avantipura, which are carved from a highly polished black marble. However, though they show new vigor, much stylization has crept in, and the facial features are hardened. The earlier complex patterning of the open edge of the lower garment and the foliate design of the crown is crudely interpreted, and the headdress is out of proportion to the head. Two iconographical changes are evident: the sacred thread is now triple-stranded, and a reverse Kapila (angry) head is added to three-headed images of Vishnu. Sculptures from the Shiva temples erected at Patan by his successor Samkaravarman (r. 883–902) partly reflect influence from the Pala art of northeastern India, and are the last signs of external borrowing. The most important sculpture of the ninth century and one of the largest known castings of the medieval period in India is the almost 6.5 ft. (2-meter) high openwork aureole for a Vishnu image found at Divsar, which contains *avatāra*s of Vishnu and other deities set in scrolling vine roundels. This period is one of pronounced influence on the sculpture of Chamba and adjacent hill regions, and the famous bronze four-headed Vishnu from the Hari Rai temple in Chamba town is closely modeled on the Kashmir type.

The tenth century was a time of political turbulence, economic decline, and increasing isolation, from which the kingdom never really recovered. A silver inlaid bronze of a six-armed Avalokiteshvara group, dated in the reign of Queen Didda in 989, shows a marked decline in the style. Though local demand declined, there was a ready market for stock images of the Buddha from Tibet in the following two centuries. A group of stone sculptures found at Verinag, attributable to the twelfth century, demonstrates that the style had greatly degenerated by that time, but little remains in Kashmir of the intervening period.

John Siudmak

See also **Bronzes: South Indian; Guptan Period Art**

BIBLIOGRAPHY

Barrett, D. "Sculptures of Kashmir." *British Museum Quarterly* 23 (1961): 49–52.
Kak, Ram Chandra. *Ancient Monuments of Kashmir*. London: India Society, 1933.
Pal, Pratapaditya. *Bronzes of Kashmir*. New York: Hacker, 1978.
———. *Himalayas: An Aesthetic Adventure*. Chicago: Art Institute of Chicago, 2003.
Sahni, D. R. "Pre-Mohammadan Monuments of Kashmir." In *Archaeological Survey of India Annual Report* 1915–1916, Delhi (1918): 49–78.
Siudmak, John. "Early Stone and Terracotta Sculpture." In *The Art and Architecture of Ancient Kashmir*, edited by P. Pal. Mumbai: Marg, 1989.

SECULARISM Political secularism may be defined as the separation of religious activities from that of the state, customarily referred to as "the separation of church and state in the West." The state in its governmental capacity will not promote any religion or religious group, or get involved in religious affairs. Freedom of religious belief and practice are confined to the private domain. Following India's independence in 1947, Congress Party governments under Prime Minister Jawaharlal Nehru and his successors declared India to be a secular democratic state, thus distinguishing itself from Pakistan, which they judged to be a theocratic authoritarian state.

As evidence of equality and equal opportunity for Indian citizens of all religions, India points to three Muslim presidents since independence, a Sikh prime minister, a Christian president of the Congress Party, and several non-Hindu central and state government ministers, state governors, and other high-ranking political personalities—in a country in which 82 percent of the population is Hindu.

Interpretations of secularism in India have not, however, been consistent. Nehru's interpretation was that of the West: the state will not engage in religious activities nor promote any religion. Mahatma Gandhi's interpretation suggested that all religions are equal, and that the state should acknowledge and encourage the practice of all religions equally. If one particular religious ceremony were allowed at a state function, then the state must accord that privilege equally to other religions as well. Hence prayers are sometimes offered by all religions on special state occasions and at state funerals. A third position, derived from the Gandhian view, tends to be perceived as more threatening to other religions. In the Hindu nationalist perspective, Hinduism is capable of representing all religions because Hinduism acknowledges different pathways to God. Therefore, all religions are "true," and "all Indians are Hindus." Though all three interpretations of secularism existed concurrently in independent India, it was Nehru's Western concept that prevailed, on the grounds that the separation of state and religion was an essential prerequisite for the conduct of Western democracy. This perspective of secularism in its Western interpretation was disputed in the 1990s with the rise of Hindu nationalism, which advocated the third variant.

The Roots of Indian Democracy and Secularism

The foundations of India's democracy and secularism are drawn from the West, the roots of which may be found in the American and French revolutions of 1776 and 1789. The separation of church and state underlined both democracies. In the United States, the founding fathers wished to shield the fledgling democracy from the religious conflicts and issues that had plagued Europe for centuries. In France, one of the goals of the revolution was to restrict the power of the Catholic Church in political affairs. The fact that France was an overwhelmingly Catholic country was irrelevant in separating religion from the conduct of government.

In Britain, there was no conflict between church and state, except during the Reformation, when England, Wales, and Scotland broke from the Catholic Church in Rome to establish their own churches of England and Scotland. British secularism was embodied in the liberalism of John Stuart Mill and Jeremy Bentham in the late nineteenth century, and in the Fabian socialism of George Bernard Shaw, G. D. H. and Margaret Cole, and Harold Laski of the early twentieth century. The evolution of parliamentary democracy in Britain as a system based on representative government and adult franchise, together with its secular character, was one of British rule's legacies to India.

Unlike India and virtually all other countries of the world, Britain has no written constitution. Its government is based on tradition and prevailing practice. In England, much of the ceremonial affairs of state, especially that of the Crown, involves the Church of England. Hindu nationalist leaders have referred to this aspect of Britain to advocate the primacy of Hinduism and Hindu traditions as the basis of the Indian state, especially since the Indian political system was based on the British political system. However, the British government's activities are strictly secular. Indeed, the formal practice of Christianity itself among the general population has nearly vanished in Britain, with a minority of the population involved in church affairs. A similar situation now prevails in much of western Europe, with the exception of some Catholic countries of postcommunist eastern Europe.

In Western democracies, especially in the United Sates and France, a secular state is considered an essential requisite of a democratic state. The founding fathers of American democracy, including Thomas Jefferson, Benjamin Franklin, and John Adams, were particularly concerned about mixing religion and politics. James Madison, in a private letter, summed up his concerns: "Religion and government will both exist in greater purity, the less they are mixed together." Efforts by right-wing Christian fundamentalists to define the United States as a nation founded upon Christian traditions and values, insisting that Christianity be central to the identity of the state, have thus far been rejected as unconstitutional. Even the reference to "one nation under God" in the American Pledge of Allegiance has been regarded by many as unacceptable in a secular state.

France has gone further. In December 2003, a constitutional committee in France sought to determine whether wearing religious symbols by individuals in public schools constituted a violation of France's secular identity. Such symbols would include the wearing of large crosses by Christians, the yarmulke, or skull cap, by Jewish men, and the head scarf by Muslim women. With a population of 6 million immigrant Muslims and their descendants, France has the largest Muslim population of any state in Europe. According to a preliminary observation of the investigating commission, secularism is not only "the separation of church and state, but it is also the respect of [religious] differences." The flaunting of religious differences in public schools was considered to be provocative and unsecular.

Secularism and India's Constitution

Secularism is not mentioned in the original Constitution of India; nor did the Constitution advocate a religious state, or a state that identifies with one particular religion. In Part III, titled "Fundamental Rights," under the section "Right to Freedom of Religion," all citizens are ensured "freedom of conscience and free profession, practice and propagation of religion." The Indian Constitution did not, however, specify non-involvement by the government in religious practice, as does the Constitution of the United States, nor did it define the government as secular, as does the Constitution of the French republic. The First Amendment of the U.S. Constitution stipulates that "Congress shall make no law respecting an establishment of religion or prohibiting the free exercise thereof." Article One of the French Constitution states that "France is a republic, indivisible, secular, democratic and social; all citizens are equal before the law."

Although the original Indian Constitution made no specific reference to India as a secular state, the Indian constitution was implicitly secular. The post-independence Constituent Assembly was dominated by members of the secular Indian National Congress, led by Jawaharlal Nehru, who was determined that, unlike Pakistan, independent India would be characterized by forward-looking scientific rationalism, not backward-looking religious traditionalism.

A formal declaration that India is a secular state was first introduced in 1976 in the Forty-second Amendment to the Indian Constitution. The amendment was passed by the Congress Party majority in Parliament during the "National Emergency" that Prime Minister Indira Gandhi imposed on India from June 1975 to March 1977. The Emergency suspended the democratic process and introduced twenty-two months of authoritarian rule. Among the several sweeping changes introduced into the Indian Constitution by the Forty-second Amendment, which provided extraordinary authoritarian powers to the government, was a rewording of the Preamble to the Indian Constitution, under Section 2: "In the Preamble to the Constitution, (a) for the words 'SOVEREIGN DEMOCRATIC REPUBLIC' the words 'SOVEREIGN SOCIALIST SECULAR DEMOCRATIC REPUBLIC' shall be substituted; and (b) for the words 'unity of the Nation,' the words 'unity and integrity of the Nation' shall be substituted" [capitalization per the original].

The Forty-second Amendment was swept aside, almost in its entirety, following the defeat of Indira Gandhi and the Congress Party in the March 1977 elections. The new Janata Party coalition government (a motley group of parties that included the Bharatiya Jan Sangh led by Atal Bihari Vajpayee and the Samyukta Socialist Party led by George Fernandes), under Prime Minister Morarji Desai, a former Congress Party finance minister, passed the Forty-fourth Amendment in 1978. While the fundamental rights of all citizens were reinstated and protected from future abuse, the Forty-fourth Amendment reinforced the secular character of the state, noting that:

> Recent experience has shown that the fundamental rights, including those of life and liberty, granted to citizens by the Constitution are capable of being taken away by a transient majority. It is, therefore, necessary to provide adequate safeguards against the recurrence of such a contingency in the future and to ensure to the people themselves an effective voice in determining the form of government under which they are to live. . . . It is, therefore, proposed to provide that certain changes in the Constitution which would have the effect of impairing its secular or democratic character, abridging or taking away fundamental rights prejudicing or impeding free and fair elections on the basis of adult suffrage and compromising the independence of judiciary, can be made only if they are approved by the people of India by a majority of votes at a referendum in which at least fifty-one percent of the electorate participate.

Hindutva and Indian Secularism

Hindu nationalist aspirations, promoted by the Bharatiya Janata Party–led coalition government, which held power from March 1998 to April 2004, revolved around the concept of Hindutva. The idea of Hindutva was used in two separate contexts. First, it implied that all Indians should recognize the essence of being Hindu as a way of life, not just among Hindus in particular, but also by the followers of all other faiths in India. Second, the movement sought the eventual establishment of a political state called "Hindutva," the land of the Hindus, replacing other names such as "India" in English, "Bharat" in Hindi, and "Hindustan" in Urdu.

The name "India" is considered Western, derived from early Persian and Greek references to the land around the Indus River. "Bharat" is the name of the land referred to in Hindu scriptures, and was also the name of the country under Emperor Ashoka's rule (r. 268–231 B.C.), when he and all of his Indian empire became Buddhists. "Hindustan" was the name that represented the "two-nation theory" of the founder of Pakistan, Mohammad Ali Jinnah, who claimed that Muslims and Hindus belonged in two separate states, Pakistan and Hindustan. The partition of India in 1947 carved out Pakistan as the homeland for India's Muslims. Ironically, most Muslims in the Hindu-majority areas, who had demanded the creation of Pakistan because they feared Hindu domination, were left behind in India. With the separation of Bangladesh from Pakistan, there are more Muslims in India than in Pakistan, making the declaration of a "Hindutva" even more problematic. With the flight of all Hindus and Sikhs from West Pakistan at the time of the partition of British India, and following the independence of Bangladesh from Pakistan in 1971 (where some 15 million Bengali Hindus resided), Pakistan is 98 percent Muslim. Pakistan is a nonsecular, nondemocratic Islamic republic.

This demand for Hindutva, in the context of the essence of being Hindu, was controversial even among Hindus. Unlike Christianity and Islam, or even Buddhism and Sikkhism, Hindus do not believe in organized religion. Hinduism makes no specific demands of its followers, either in its beliefs or its worship. Hindutva as a Hindu state would pose problems for India's democracy. A state that is characterized or identified by a particular religion may be incompatible with the concept of a democratic state, even if all or most of its citizens belong to that religion, and even if the electoral process is continued. As illustrated in the French and American practice, secularism is a precondition for democracy. There are other complications in making India into a Hindu state: the sizable numbers of religious minorities; the uncertain religious-ethnic status of the former "untouchables," now known as Dalits, meaning "the oppressed"; and the potential transformation of the traditional practice of Hinduism from what was essentially a secular way of life into a more intense faith.

In a Hindu state, democracy would be undermined in at least two ways. First, a state identified by its dominant religion would imply the rejection of equality for citizens of other religions. The political commitment of religious minorities would probably be deeply eroded. Second, when the religious clergy or religious-minded leaders are able to arouse the passions of citizens on the basis of religion, then the freedom to make choices becomes threatened, given the fear of retribution. The power to coerce citizens by the government, represented by the dominant religion and its religious leaders and clergy, becomes stronger. In a secular state, the government and religious leaders are unlikely to carry such coercive or persuasive powers over the minds of its citizens when the issues and the debate are confined to the secular domain. Thus, secularism would appear essential for the exercise of free choice in any democracy, even if all its citizens belong to the same religion.

The absolute numbers of religious minorities in India make the enforcement of a Hindu state, which would be a counterpart to Islamic Pakistan, difficult. Following the

flight of nearly all Hindus and Sikhs to India, Pakistan's religious minority population is less than 2 percent. In India's population of 1 billion at the beginning of the twenty-first century, 18 percent were non-Hindus, of which 14 percent were Muslims (140 million) and 2 percent Christians (20 million). There are fewer than 100,000 Parsis, who came from Persia in the eighth century to escape Islamic conversions, and who continue to adhere to the pre-Islamic religion of Persia, known as Zorastrianism. The remaining 2 percent religious minorities (about 20 million people) are Sikhs, Buddhists, and Jains, religions that were offshoots of Hinduism, founded in India. Hindu nationalists have declared these groups to be Hindus, but this inclusion is rejected for the most part by Sikhs and Buddhists. Sikhs reject the claim of inclusion for fear of being swallowed up by Hinduism. Some Hindu nationalists have called for the return of Muslims and Christians to their "original" religion, from which they were "converted" during various stages of Indian history, or propose declaring every Indian a Hindu.

There is also the problem of the religious identity of the Dalits, the former "untouchables" at the bottom of the Hindu social order. Some Dalits, including their most famous leader, B. R. Ambedkar, who converted to Buddhism, do not consider themselves Hindus. Dalits number about 250 million and constitute approximately 25 percent of India's population. Hindu nationalists today include them in the Hindu fold, but there is no widespread acceptance of this embrace by the Dalits. Statistically, their exclusion—together with that of Sikhs, Buddhists, and Jains—reduces the Hindu percentage of India's population to about 60 percent.

Hindu Nationalism, Indian Secularism, and the West

The Hindu nationalist movement, led by the Vishwa Hindu Parishad (VHP) and its activist wing, the Rashtriya Swayamsevak Sangh (RSS), argue that secularism is a Western ideology imported from Britain. It was sustained in India after independence by Western-oriented Anglophile Indian intellectuals and political leaders, chief among whom was Prime Minister Nehru. This Western-oriented secularism is perceived by members of the Hindu right wing as anti-Hindu. Those Hindus who continue to advocate a secular Indian state are often branded as "pseudo-secularists," implying a false or phony understanding of secularism. Alternatively, Hindus who oppose the Hindu nationalist agenda and support the secular character of the Indian state are declared to be "godless communists," socialists, or other leftists. Such Hindu "pseudo-secularists," "communists," and "left-wing apologists" are alleged to pander excessively to Muslim and

Christian religious minorities and their religious practice, at the expense of Hindus and the Hindu way of life.

In particular, Hindu nationalist critics of the Nehruvian secular state argue that genuine secularism was not always practiced under Congress Party governments because of "unsecular" concessions to the Muslim minority. Two instances are often cited. First, the Indian government since independence has subsidized the *hajj* pilgrimage to Mecca for Indian Muslims, without similar subsidies to followers of other religions. Second, Muslim law for Muslims is allowed to override civil law that applies to all other Indians. The celebrated case alleging violation of the principles of the secular state is that of the Shah Bano case of 1985; this case involved a Muslim woman with four children, who was divorced by her Muslim husband, who then refused to pay alimony because Muslim law did not require it. The case went to the Supreme Court of India, which overruled Muslim law and granted Shah Bano alimony, thereby undermining the limited legal autonomy granted to the Muslim minority of India. Faced with adverse Muslim reaction, the Congress Party government of Prime Minister Rajiv Gandhi passed legislation reiterating the rights of Muslim law for the husband.

The claims by some Hindu nationalists that secularism in India is a Western import is often countered by the claim India's Constitution and democratic political system are likewise derived from the West. Parliamentary democracy embodied in India's Constitution was based on the British political system; the federal arrangement between the central and state governments was modeled on the Canadian federal system; the list of "Fundamental Rights" was derived from the U.S. Bill of Rights; the "Directive Principles of Social Policy" in the preamble was an idea obtained from the Irish Constitution; and the financial relationship between the central and state governments in India was derived from the Australian system. These states are all secular democracies, even Catholic-majority Ireland, in that there is a separation of the spheres of church and state.

When the Hindu nationalist Bharatiya Janata Party (BJP) gained a pluralist majority in the 1998 national elections and led a coalition government into office, the status of secularism in India became an issue. Perhaps because of the other motley group of parties that formed the coalition, without whose support the BJP could not remain in power, the BJP immediately declared that India would remain a secular state. This did not satisfy the more extreme members of the group of Hindu nationalist parties known together as the Sangh Parivar, which include the RSS, the VHP, and the Shiv Sena. Concerns remain, within the Congress Party and other secular parties, that a clear majority by Hindu nationalist parties in Parliament in future elections could lead to the declaration of Hindutva, ending a secular India. These Hindu aspirations were halted in the April 2004 national elections, when the BJP-led coalition government was defeated by a secular Congress Party–led coalition, which formed a new government. However, the controversy over whether India should be a secular state along the Western model, as embraced by the Congress and left-wing parties, or a Hindutva state, representing Hinduism and Hindus as proposed by the BJP and other Hindu parties, remains unresolved.

Raju G. C. Thomas

See also **Bharatiya Janata Party (BJP); Congress Party; Dalits; Family Law and Cultural Pluralism; Hindutva and Politics; Muslims; Shiv Sena; Vishwa Hindu Parishad (VHP)**

BIBLIOGRAPHY

Hasan, Mushirul. "Secularism in the Time of Hindutva." *Hindu*, 11 May 1997.
Jacobsohn, Gary J. *The Wheel of Law: India's Secularism in Comparative Constitutional Context*. Princeton, N.J.: Princeton University Press, 2003.
Juergensmeyer, Mark. *The New Cold War?: Religious Nationalism Confronts the Secular State*. Berkeley: University of California Press, 1994.
Madan, T. N. *Modern Myths, Locked Minds: Secularism and Fundamentalism in India*. New Delhi: Oxford University Press, 1998.
Mehta, S. M. *Constitution of India and Amendment Acts*. New Delhi: Deep and Deep, 1990.
Misra, R. S. *Hinduism and Secularism: A Critical Study*. Columbia, Mo.: South Asia Books, 1996.
Narain, Iqbal. *Secularism in India*. Columbia, Mo.: South Asia Books, 1996.
Raman, Sunder. *Amending Power under the Constitution of India: A Politico-Legal Study*. Kolkata and New Delhi: Eastern Law House, 1990.
Smith, Donald E. *India as a Secular State*. Princeton, N.J.: Princeton University Press, 1968.

SECURITIES EXCHANGE BOARD OF INDIA (SEBI) The Securities Exchange Board of India (SEBI) was established in April 1988 by order of the government of India to regulate India's securities market, but lacked statutory powers until 1992, when the Securities Exchange Board of India Act was passed. The board has nine members: its chairman and two members are full time; among the part-time members, two are officials of the government ministries of finance and company law matters, and one is from the Reserve Bank of India (RBI), the central bank of the country. The core responsibility of the board is to regulate the securities markets and protect investors' interests. SEBI was given further statutory powers under The Depositories Act of 1996.

SEBI's regulations are statutory in nature, and any infringements are punishable by monetary penalty and/or imprisonment. It has powers to put any market intermediary or participant out of business by suspending or canceling the registration granted to it under its relevant regulations. SEBI can also prosecute the offenders. This serves as an effective deterrent against market manipulation or disruption. SEBI's powers were enhanced significantly in 1995, when it became a quasi-judicial body that can adjudicate breaches to its regulations and impose fines. The affected parties have the freedom to appeal against SEBI's decisions to a three-member tribunal. The verdicts of the tribunal can be challenged only in the Supreme Court.

SEBI regulates stock exchanges, securities markets, stock brokers, subbrokers, share transfer agents, bankers to the issue, trustees of trust deeds, merchant bankers, underwriters, portfolio managers, investment advisers, mutual funds, depositories, depository participants, custodians, foreign institutional investors, and any intermediaries that are connected with the securities markets. Credit rating companies have been brought under SEBI's regulatory oversight to ensure that the rating companies enjoy professional independence and are not subject to unwarranted influence. SEBI enjoys strong powers to prohibit fraudulent and unfair trade practices relating to securities markets. Recently its penal powers have been significantly strengthened to prohibit insider trading in securities. It also regulates substantial acquisitions of shares and the takeover of companies.

Since 1995 the standards of Indian securities markets have improved significantly. Indian markets, once considered risky and inefficient, are now among the best in the world, with state-of-the-art trading and settlement systems. However, only part of the credit for this improvement can go to SEBI. The two most important institutions that have significantly upgraded the quality and safety of the Indian securities markets are the National Stock Exchange of India (NSE) and the National Securities Depository Limited. The record of SEBI in containing market manipulation is also rather patchy. The move to shift to rolling settlement in mid-2001, to avoid manipulation by market players taking advantage of different settlement periods at different exchanges, was taken only at the insistence of the government of India.

Out of the twenty-three stock exchanges, only the NSE and the Bombay Stock Exchange are really functioning, and all others have become practically defunct. The nonfunctioning exchanges are not debarred, however, from listing companies. SEBI has announced the creation of a Central Listing Authority to deal with the competitive devaluation of standards of listing that used to take place, with competition among exchanges to attract companies for listing. The Central Listing Authority has yet to frame its own guidelines and business rules, however. The recent move of SEBI to grant unique identification numbers to all market intermediaries was ill-conceived (attendant complexities were perceived as intrusions into privacy); the intended purpose could have been achieved through an investor database available with the depositories. Therefore, although SEBI has been able to establish itself as the market regulator, it has yet to prove convincingly that it is effective, efficient, and proactive.

R. H. Patil

See also **Capital Market; Stock Exchange Markets**

BIBLIOGRAPHY

There are two web sites that provide exhaustive information on Indian securities markets and the regulative framework: the Securities Exchange Board of India (http://www.sebi.gov.in/) and the National Stock Exchange of India (http://www.nseindia.com/). The following reports and documents are particularly useful: Securities Exchange Board of India, Annual Reports, 1996–1997 to 2002–2003; Government of India: The Securities Exchange Board of India Act (1992), The Depositories Act (1996), The Securities Contracts (Regulations) Act (1956); and The National Stock Exchange of India's annual publication, "Indian Securities Market, An Overview," for the years 1999 to 2003.

SELECTED MACROECONOMIC MODELS A logical explanation of any phenomenon, or a set of mutually interdependent phenomena, is a model. This, referred to as theory, can be purely verbal in nature or mathematical in form. A model is an abstract and simplified picture of a realistic process, given in the form of mathematical equations. It helps in forecasting and policy analysis by government and business. Economists and public policy analysts not only require the direction of the effect of one variable on the other, but also the extent of impact and trade-offs. This necessitates casting theory in the form of mathematical equations, variable measurement, and impact calibration.

Three types of macroeconomic models were developed for India since the early 1950s. They are: input-output (I-O); computable general equilibrium; and econometric models. The objective of all models is structural analysis, forecasting and policy evaluation.

Input-Output Models

With the advent of planning in the early 1950s, focus was on models of plan-variety concerning growth and investment allocation. One aspect central to planning models is the sectoral interdependence and sectoral balance for a given macroeconomic growth rate. Input-output models form a core element of planning exercises.

The economy is viewed as consisting of n producing sectors, each producing ideally a single homogeneous output. The intersectoral flow matrix charts the flow of output of a sector to each of the sectors and to final demand over a specified period, generally one year. The final demand relates to consumers, government, investment, and the foreign sector. It is a two-way table (each sector appearing in a row and in a column) describing the production structure of the economy. The ratio of output of i-th sector used as input by j-th sector, divided by output of j-th sector, represents input-output coefficient. They are technological parameters. The configuration of such n-by-n coefficient matrix represents the I-O table. It is a linear production structure. Inputs bear a fixed proportion to output, constant returns to scale prevail, and no substitution possibilities exist between inputs. The model is static. The intersectoral commodity flow matrix that yields the I-O table is in value terms.

In the intersectoral flow matrix, final demands appear as a column. Imports appear with a negative sign. They balance supply and demand. Imports, which enter as inputs in the production process, appear in a separate row. Rewards for primary inputs, wages, and profits, as well as indirect taxes and subsidies can also be shown as additional rows. If the intersectoral flows are represented at producer prices, the column sums represent the total cost of producing that sector's output. This should be equal to the corresponding row sum, suitably adjusted for taxes and subsidies. The total of row sums should be equal to the total of column sums, and the grand total represents the gross value of goods and services produced in the economy. This represents not only intersectoral flows but also final demand and disposition of total output as inputs and rewards for primary factors. This can be viewed as a social accounting matrix.

The Indian Statistical Institute built an input-output table for 1950–1951 with thirty-six sectors. The Gokhale Institute of Politics and Economics published an input-output model for 1963. The Planning Commission and the Central Statistical Organization constructed the tables for 1968–1969 and subsequently published a new one every five years. The latest table refers to 1993–1994. The various tables differ in the extent of aggregation.

The analytical problem in the solution of the I-O model is one of solving linear simultaneous equations. Planning exercise involves setting an economy-wide growth target, calculating associated final demands, and solving the I-O model to yield sectoral output targets. These output targets aid in calculating sectoral investment requirements, employment, and other related dimensions. In each of the Five-Year Plan exercises in India, these calculations have been made in much detail.

The calculation of forward and backward linkages in an economy is crucial to evaluate alternative strategies of development. Backward linkages reflect the impact of a sectoral output change on all other sectors that supply inputs to it, while forward linkages measure consequent increase in demand for other sectors' output. Key sectors in development are those that have strong backward and forward linkages. These exercises have been made for India with the help of I-O tables. Another application relates to measuring the impact of price changes of primary factors or any other inputs on sectoral prices and overall price level. The estimates represent accounting exercise and do not reflect the effect of many other important factors that underlie price behavior.

Computable General Equilibrium Models

Computable general equilibrium (CGE) models have two facets. First, general equilibrium connotes viewing the economy as a complete system of interdependent economic activities by different agents, for example, producers, households, investors, the government, importers and exporters. The interrelationships are through a web of intersectoral output flows and price connections. The second term, "computable," signifies an empirical system that can be implemented. Rules for the functioning of individual markets and the behavior of agents in the markets, that is, causal links that determine equilibrium mechanisms, are specified. The underlying production structure is the I-O model. CGE models have a close interface both with the I-O and econometric models.

In the early 1980s substantive research on CGE models for India was initiated at the National Council of Applied Economic Research. The model is maintained, frequently updated, and improved over the years. Particularly notable is the recent effort to integrate segments of behavioral macroeconometirc models with the CGE model. The model originally comprised eight sectors, including infrastructure, services, three in agriculture (food, other crops, and livestock), and three in industry (consumer, intermediate, and capital goods). Three income classes (agriculture income recipients, nonagricultural wage income earners, and nonagricultural nonwage income earners) were distinguished. Public finance and money were also later brought into the system. In recent versions, sectoral decomposition has widened. Agricultural output is determined outside the CGE model through an agricultural submodel, treated as exogenous to CGE solutions.

Since the early 1980s, the model is used regularly for making annual forecasts of important macroeconomic indicators, including output, prices, trade, and fiscal and external deficits. Forecasts are made for only one year ahead, and sequential forecast over time do not generally include dynamic interlinks. Many policy simulations have also been made over the years. Policy simulations relevant to the 1990s, which witnessed far-reaching structural adjustments and macroeconomic policy reforms, to name a few, relate to reduction in tariff and nontariff barriers to trade, lower domestic indirect taxes, changes in the exchange rate, reduction in government investment expenditures, and changes in interest rates.

Macroeconometric Models

India has had a history of macroeconometric modeling dating back to the 1950s, unparalleled among developing countries. Many models were constructed, and to date about fifty models, covering different time periods and focusing on issues relevant to those times, have been constructed.

Macroeconometric models for India are based on annual time series data. They are estimated by econometric methods and are subject to statistical inference. They are also subject to in-sample validation, in terms of their ability to replicate historical series. Almost all of them have had a policy focus. Most of the models have had only a short- to medium-run character. They are dynamic in nature. Models have been concerned with the level of economic activity, aggregate and sectoral, price behavior, fiscal and monetary phenomena, intersectoral linkages, private investment and its linkages with public investment, consumption and savings, public sector resource mobilization, current and investment expenditures and their composition, budgetary deficits and pattern of financing, trade flows, balance of payments, exchange rate and nexus between the twin deficits, budgetary and external, among others.

The theoretical approach to macroeconometric modeling in India has been eclectic in character. Specification of components of final demand is Keynesian. Unlike in the simple Keynesian approach, the economy is not entirely driven by effective demand. Supply constraints are well jeweled in the models. Agriculture activity is determined by land, a limiting factor and natural resources. Harnessing these resources is facilitated by capital. In the nonagricultural sectors, output is viewed as constrained by stock of capital, the scarce factor and its utilization. Capital utilization is conditioned by effective demand, which, in turn, is influenced by level of overall economic activity in general, and agriculture in particular, and availability of critical inputs, such as agricultural raw materials, infrastructure and imported materials.

Level of activity in most of the recent models is disaggregated into agriculture, manufacturing, economic infrastructure, and services. Price determination in agriculture is governed by a flex price (supply-demand balance) mechanism, subject to public intervention through procurement and support prices. Price formation in other sectors is based on markup over costs, including wage rate, administered prices of critical intermediates, and imported inputs. Markup is viewed as being influenced by excess demand/liquidity in the economy, proxied by money stock to overall output. This variable is also factored in the agricultural price determination. Money supply is modeled as the outcome of public desire to hold money, government operations, external factors, and monetary policy. Interest rate and exchange rate are also broadly influenced by a similar set of factors. Turning to foreign trade, imports are determined by domestic activity and relative prices, exports by world economic activity, relative prices, and domestic availabilities.

In most of the models large parts of public activity is given. External economic environment is a datum. Most of the recent models are driven by public investment-quantum and composition, current expenditures and their composition, monetary-fiscal policies and external economic environment, among others. In the short run, weather (rainfall) is a decisive factor.

One disappointing aspect of macroeconometric modeling in India has been that each model has turned out to be a one-time exercise. It is only since the early 1990s that sustained ongoing work on a structural macroeconometric model began jointly at the Institute of Economic Growth and the Delhi School of Economics. That model is the single largest macroeconometric model for India. The system has 347 equations. The model has five production sectors: agriculture, manufacturing, economic infrastructure, services, and public administration and defense. Agriculture is further subdivided into food and nonfood segments. Besides output, capital formation, and price behavior relating to each of the sectors, the model includes separate subsystems, dealing with trade and balance of payments, money and banking, public finance, private consumption and savings. The model is a constituent of the Global LINK Model, being operated under the auspices of the United Nations. Biannual (September and March) forecasts for LINK are made regularly, and several policy simulations have been carried out. The forecasts incorporate the dynamics of the model and are made for more than a year ahead. The India model is constantly undergoing revisions to incorporate policy changes, taking advantage of the latest data. The project is now housed at the Centre for Development Economics at the Delhi School of Economics.

Most of the models were subject to policy simulations. They mostly relate to increase in administered prices, enhanced public investment and change in its composition, pattern of financing public deficits, fiscal—monetary policy stances, exchange rate changes, and world economic scenario—world output, trade volume, and international prices. Normal rainfall assumption is invariably a part of counter factual or "what if" simulations for almost all the models.

Conclusion

The trilogy of models—I-O, CGE, and econometric—are complementary to each other. Common to all the three models is the estimation of final demand. Econometric models do not emphasize intermediate demands, as they deal with a net value-added output concept. Behavioral characteristics that underlie consumption, investment, prices, public sector, money, and trade receive more emphasis in macroeconometric models. Sectoral output interdependence is at the core of I-O and CGE models. The data requirements for each of the models are demanding, particularly in the case of developing countries. Whatever model is used, it is essential to maintain it, with refinements in specification, use of the latest data, and use of improved econometric methodologies to keep it relevant for policy analysis and forecasting.

K. Krishnamurty
J. Mahender Reddy

See also **Economy since the 1991 Economic Reforms**

BIBLIOGRAPHY

Desai, Meghnad J. "Macro Econometric Models for India: A Survey." In *A Survey of Research in Economics*. Vol. 7: *Econometrics*. Indian Council of Social Science Research. Mumbai: Allied Publishers, 1978.
IEG-DSE Research Team. "Policies for Stability and Growth with a Comprehensive Structural Model for India." *Journal of Quantitative Economics* 15, no. 2 (July 1999). Edited by V. Pandit and K. Krishnamurty; abridged version of the same under the title *Policy Modeling for India*, edited by V. Pandit and K. Krishnamurty. New Delhi: Oxford University Press, 2004.
Klein, Lawerence R. "Econometric Models, Planning and Developing Countries." In *Development Perspectives* (Silver Jubilee Lectures, 1984), Institute of Economic Growth. New Delhi: B. R. Publishing Corporation, 1988.
Krishna, K. L., K. Krishnamurty, V. N. Pandit, and P. D. Sharma. "Macro-Econometric Modeling in India: A Selective Review of Recent Research." In *Development Papers No. 9: Econometric Modeling and Forecasting in Asia*. Bangkok: Economic and Social Commission for Asia and Pacific, United Nations, 1991.
Krishnamurty, K. "Macroeconometric Models for India: Past, Present and Prospects." *Economic and Political Weekly* 37, no. 42 (October 2000): 19–25.
Krishnamurty, K., and V. Pandit. *Macroeconometric Modelling of the Indian Economy: Studies on Inflation and Growth*. New Delhi: Hindustan Publishing Corporation, 1985.
Mahalanobis, P. C. *The Approach of Operational Research to Planning in India*. Mumbai: Asia Publishing House, 1963.
Narasimham, N. V. A. *A Short Term Planning Model for India*. Amsterdam: North-Holland Publishing Company, 1956.
Pandit, V., and K. Krishnamurty, eds. *Policy Modeling for India*. New Delhi: Oxford University Press, 2004.
Saluja, M. R. *Input-Output Tables for India: Concepts, Construction, and Applications*. New Delhi: Wiley Eastern, 1980.
Sarkar, Hiren, and Manoj Panda. "A Short Term Structural Macroeconomic Model for India: Applications to Policy Analysis." In *Development Papers No. 9, Econometric Modeling and Forecasting in Asia*. Bangkok: Economic and Social Commission for Asia and Pacific, United Nations, 1991.
Taylor, Lance. *Structural Macroeconomics: Applicable Models for the Third World*. New York: Basic Books, 1983.
Taylor, Lance, ed. *Socially Relevant Policy Analysis: Structuralist Computable General Equilibrium Models for the Developing World*. Cambridge, Mass.: MIT Press, 1990.
Venkatramaiah, P., A. R. Kulkarni, and Latika Argade. *Structural Change in the Indian Economy: An Analysis with Input-Output Tables, 1951–1963*. Pune: Gokahale Institute of Politics and Economics, 1984.

SEPOY MUTINY. *See* **British East India Company Raj; History and Historiography.**

SHAH BANO CASE The Shah Bano case resulted in the controversial enactment of the Muslim Women's (Protection of Rights in Divorce) Act of 1986. Introduced by Prime Minister Rajiv Gandhi's Congress ministry, the act jeopardized India's system of secular law, while it circumvented the Shari'a code governing the Muslim community. The priority of minority rights over women's rights was at stake in this important case, which has seriously undermined Muslim women's maintenance rights.

The case began in 1985 in Indore, Madhya Pradesh, where Shah Bano, a sixty-two-year-old destitute woman, filed a suit for nonpayment of alimony against her husband, Ahmed Khan, from whom she had been separated for forty-six years. Shah Bano asked for a monthly alimony of 500 rupees, based on Section 125 of the Criminal Procedure Code, 1973 (CrPC 1973). Citing the Shari'a, Ahmed Khan promptly divorced her, repaid 3,000 rupees of her dowry (*mehr*), and ceased all alimonies. The battle was taken to the Supreme Court, where Chief Justice Y. V. Chandrachud upheld Section 125, as it did not conflict with Qur'anic injunctions (chapter 11, suras 141–142) on women's property and maintenance rights. The chief justice also urged the creation of a uniform Indian civil code that would remove "disparate loyalties to laws which have conflicting ideologies."

Conservative Muslims protested against the Court's authority over the Qur'an, whipping up fears over state encroachment of minority rights. A heated debate ensued over minority rights and women's rights, but the prospect of protracted, expensive legal battles at first daunted many activists. In February 1986, to allay the fears of a nervous Muslim electorate on whom the Congress depended for votes, Rajiv Gandhi shepherded the Muslim Women's (Protection of Rights in Divorce) Act of 1986. Outside Parliament, the leftist All-India Democratic Women's Association and the moderate National Federation of Indian Women joined hands with local Mahila Dakshata Samiti to protest the bill. Arif Mohammad Khan, a Muslim Cabinet minister, resigned in protest, but Muslim Congresswoman Begam Abida Ahmed staunchly defended the bill.

The Act of 1986 redefines the legal grounds for Muslim women's maintenance, while jeopardizing both their secular and religious rights. It thus dilutes Section 125 (CrPC 1973), which stipulates that women are entitled to alimony from ex-spouses. Women have since presented petitions that the act also violates the Indian Constitution, Article 14 on legal equality, and Article 15 prohibiting religious discrimination. Second, the 1986 law also circumvents the Qur'an, which protects women's property and maintenance rights. Third, it places a new legal onus on the largely defunct Muslim welfare board (*waqf*), as it now requires her natal family to support a divorced or separated woman; and if this fails, it requires the *waqf* to do so. Since the *waqf* is governed largely by conservative men, Muslim women's rights have been substantially eroded. The clerical leaders of the All-India Muslim Personal Law Board have frequently resisted government interference in Muslim laws, but they have acceded in this case, despite the act's blatant negation of the Shari'a, which requires the husband to maintain a woman, not the *waqf*. Moreover, if government funds were used by the *waqf*, this would constitute state interference in religion.

Inheritance and marriage customs vary according to region and community. In the nineteenth century, liberal Hindu, Muslim, Parsi, and Christian reformers supported uniform legislation to remedy child marriage, perpetual widowhood, and denial of divorce, resulting in such measures as the 1891 Age of Consent Bill and the Sarda Act of 1930. Muslim law was originally mediated through a Qazi, a judicial expert on Shari'a law, but the abolition of this post in 1864 left legal disputes unsolved. In an era of sectarian and national consciousness, Muslim purists charged that women's Qur'anic rights were forgotten when Muslims adopted Hindu customs. In 1937 the Shari'a Act was passed to protect Qur'anic laws favorable to women, while it helped Muslim jurists (ulama) to weed out non-Hindu practices. The Act of 1986, on the other hand, has eroded women's rights, pitted Muslim liberals against religious leaders, and promoted political opportunism.

Sita Anantha Raman

See also **Family Law and Cultural Pluralism; Women and Political Power**

BIBLIOGRAPHY

Forbes, Geraldine. *Women in Modern India*. Cambridge, U.K.: Cambridge University Press, 1996.

Government of India. *Preamble, the Muslim Personal Law (Shariat) Application Act, 1937*. No. 26 (7 October 1937).

Hasan, Zoya. "Minority Identity, State Policy and the Political Process." In *Forging Identities*, edited by Zoya Hasan. New Delhi: Kali for Women, 1993.

Hasan, Zoya, and Ritu Menon. *Unequal Citizens: A Study of Muslim Women in India*. Delhi: Oxford University Press, 2004.

Keddie, Nikki R. "The New Religious Politics: Where, When, and Why Do 'Fundamentalisms' Appear?" *Comparative Studies in Society and History* 40, no. 4 (1998): 696–723.

Kishwar, Madhu. "Pro Women or Anti-Muslim? The Shah Bano Controversy." *Manushi* 32, v. 6, no. 2 (January–February 1986): 4–13.

———. "Denial of Fundamental Rights to Women." In *In Search of Answers: Indian Women's Voices from Manushi*, edited by Madhu Kishwar and Ruth Vanita. Delhi: Manohar, 1996.

Kumar, Radha. *A History of Doing: An Illustrated Account of Movements for Women's Rights and Feminism in India, 1800–1900*. Delhi: Kali for Women, 1997.

Lateef, Shaheeda. *Muslim Women in India: Political and Private Realities, 1890–1980s*. Delhi: Kali for Women, 1990.

Minault, Gail. *Secluded Scholars: Women's Education and Muslim Social Reform in Colonial India*. Delhi: Oxford University Press, 1999.

SHAH JAHAN (1592–1666), Mughal emperor (1628–1658).

Shah Jahan, whose reign has been dubbed the "Golden Age of the Mughals," was born in 1592 and was named Khurram (Joyous). He was able, ambitious, and ruthless in youth, and was later renowned for opulence and magnificence, a "Great Moghul." He built the Jama Mosque in Delhi, the Pearl Mosque in Agra, and the Shalimar Gardens in Lahore, as well as one of the most renowned buildings in the world, the Taj Mahal in Agra, which was built as a mausoleum for his wife, Mumtaz Mahal, his partner in his government and the mother of fourteen of his sixteen children. Shah Jahan would be buried there next to her. In addition, he built a mausoleum for his father, Jahangir, and a new capital at Delhi, Shahjahanabad, completed in 1648, where he placed the gem-covered Peacock Throne in its Red Fort. Persian literature and art permeated Shah Jahan's court. His reign represents a return to Sunni Muslim orthodoxy, although he continued the Rajput Hindu alliance. He ordered a number of recently completed Hindu temples torn down, and his official court policy conformed to Shari'a laws. Muslim festivals were lavishly celebrated, and he resumed sponsorship of the *hajj* (pilgrimage) to Mecca for his courtiers and faithful servants.

Shah Jahan continued the expansion of the Mughal empire, supervising campaigns, though not leading the armies personally. The Bundela campaign of 1635, led by his third son, Aurangzeb, marked the change of formerly tolerant Mughal religious policy and a reversion to ortho-doxy, as a Hindu temple was demolished and a mosque built in its place, and forced conversions to Islam were ordered. In 1629 rebellion broke out in the south as Shah Jahan attempted to subjugate the Muslim Deccan states of Ahmednagar, Bijapur, and Golconda, remaining in the south until 1631. Ahmednagar was captured in 1632, but the war dragged on and the Mughals were driven out of Bijapur. Shah Jahan returned to the south in 1636, and Bijapur and Golconda were obliged to accept a peace that endured for two decades. The Mughals then aquired four more provinces: Khandesh, Berar, Telingana, and Daulatabad. The Mughals also attacked and defeated a number of states in the north, and Sind was brought more firmly under Mughal control.

In 1638 Shah Jahan captured Afghan Kandahar. From there, the Mughals moved on Balkh in Central Asia, occupying it in 1646. The following year, harassed by Afghan tribal raiders, the Mughal army returned to Hin-dustan, losing thousands in the mountain passes, the expedition a total failure. In 1649 Kandahar fell to the shah of Persia, and three major Mughal campaigns to recover Kandahar all failed.

Shah Jahan then became more retiring, delegating more of the responsibility for governing the empire to his eldest son, Dara Shikoh. In the north, Lesser Tibet was subdued in 1637 and Garhwal in 1656. Turning to the south again, in 1656, the Mughals captured Golconda, and in 1657 Bijapur and Kalyani. In 1657 Shah Jahan became ill, and a murderous war of succession began among his four sons. His third son, Aurangzeb, emerged victorious. He imprisoned Shah Jahan in his Agra palace, where he spent the last year of his life, confined to Agra Fort, from which he could view, but never visit, the Taj Mahal. When he died, he left an expanded and prosper-ous empire with some quarter million men under arms.

Roger D. Long

See also **Akbar; Aurangzeb; Islam's Impact on India; Jahangir**

BIBLIOGRAPHY

Begley, W. E., and Z. A. Desai, eds. *The Shah Jahan Nama of 'Inayat Khan.* Delhi: Oxford University Press, 1990.
Eraly, Abraham. *The Mughal Throne: The Saga of India's Great Emperors.* London: Weidenfeld & Nicolson, 2003.
Richards, John F. *The Mughal Empire.* Cambridge, U.K.: Cambridge University Press, 1993.
Saksena, Banarsi Prasad. *History of Shah Jahan of Dihli.* Allahabad: Indian Press, 1932.

SHAKTI. *See* **Devī.**

SHAKUNTALA. *See* **Kālidāsa.**

SHANKAR, RAVI *(1920–), classical musician and sitar virtuoso.* Born in Varanasi on 7 April 1920, Ravi Shankar's international tours and teaching have con-tributed significantly to the global recognition of Indian classical music. The son of a diplomat/businessman, Ravi Shankar came to music as a boy through his brother Uday's dance troupe in Paris. In 1935 Uday invited Allaudin Khan to Paris to contribute the music for his choreographies drawing upon Indian religious stories, and in this context Ravi Shankar received his first musi-cal training. Shankar continued residential study with Allaudin Khan until the days before partition and inde-pendence, at which time he became a music director for All India Radio. He toured extensively beginning in the 1950s, playing sitar with several popular drummers (including Catur Lal and Allah Rakha), at first primarily for the growing South Asian diaspora, but increasingly for broader European and American audiences.

Ravi Shankar Playing Sitar. *Nada Brahma*: Sound Is God. Photographed here at the 1967 International Pop Festival in Monterey, California, Shankar has traveled the globe to bring Indian music to millions. TED STRESHINSKY.

Ravi Shankar's experiences with Uday Shankar's dance troupe, with experimenter Allaudin Khan, and at All India Radio (where he composed music for an ensemble) uniquely prepared him to be a catalyst for change. He has composed celebrated scores for Satyajit Ray's *Apu Trilogy*, Richard Attenborough's *Gandhi*, and several other films. He championed the use of the bass string on the sitar, has composed new *rāgas*, and has ventured into new forms. His duets with Yehudi Menhuin and his concerti for sitar and orchestra have marked him as both innovator and interlocutor between India and the West. All the while, he has celebrated a reverence for Indian music and culture and for traditional modes of education. His style of playing is at once highly rhythmic (as is that of his brother-in-law and costudent, Ali Akbar Khan) and tuneful, which has contributed greatly to his popular appeal. He is the recipient of numerous national and international awards and honors and is one of the best-known South Asians in the world.

Gordon Thompson

See also **Music; Rāga; Sitar**

BIBLIOGRAPHY

Shankar, Ravi. *My Music, My Life*. New York: Simon & Schuster, 1968.
"Shankar, Ravi." Available at <http://www.ravishankar.org>

SHANKARA (A.D. *788–820), Hindu Vedāntic philosopher.* In the opinion of many, Shankara was India's greatest Vedāntin and one of its greatest philosopher-theologians. He is considered a theologian insofar as he bases much of his thought on revelation (*shruti*) and claims that many fundamental questions are unanswerable by reason alone. But he is also a philosopher because of his claim that his theological standpoint is supported by both reason and experience. What is most remarkable is how much he accomplished in his thirty-two years. Born in Kaladi, Kerala, to devout Shaivite parents, Shankara lived at a time when Buddhist influence in India was still strong—and skeptical of Brahmanic-Hindu orthodoxy. Shankara attempted to thwart this influence by absorbing what he considered useful from Buddhism—hence the ascription "crypto-Buddhist" given by his Vaishnava opponents—and then being fiercely critical of it. His ambition was to reestablish Brahmanism on a sound intellectual and institutional footing. To that end, he established four *mutt*s, or monasteries, in the four corners of India: Badariē in the Himalayas (north), Shringeri in Karnataka (south), Puri in Orissa (east), and Dvārakā in Gujarat (west), plus an additional one at Kanchipuram in Tamil Nadu. The religious ascetics who belong to this order are organized into ten divisions and are known as the *Dashanāmī Samnyasis*, all headed today by Shankaracaryas. He was very concerned with the vitality of these monastic communities, traveling constantly to them, preaching and defending the tenets of his Advaitic (nondualistic) position against opponents from a variety of Hindu and Buddhist schools.

The fundamental reality, according to Shankara's Advaita Vedanta, is Brahman, the name given for timeless, imperishable, immutable Being. Brahman by its very nature is beyond human language, but given the human tendency to describe the indescribable, Advaitins designate Brahman as *saccidānanda*, composed of *sat* (being), *cit* (consciousness), and *ānanda* (bliss). These are not qualities of Brahman, because Brahman as such is quality-less (*nirguṇa*), but rather human ascriptions based on the experience of Brahman. The world has come into being from Brahman and is wholly dependent on it, but since the world is temporal and subject to change, it is "illusory," a product of *māyā*. Shankara does not regard the world as a complete illusion because that would lead to nihilism and would contradict his own intense activity in the world. The world is "illusory" only when seen from the prospective of Brahman, the absolute reality. The "ordinary" human perspective (*vyāvahārika*) for the most part is that of relative, not absolute being but makes the mistake of identifying reality with the world. This congenital ignorance (*avidyā*) of which one is not even aware can be overcome only by the experience of Brahman, when the veil of *māyā* is pushed aside. This view is therefore called *a-dvaita*, or "nondual." God and the world are neither two distinct realities nor one (the latter monistic position would require God to evolve or emanate into the world) but rather nondual, a position different from both dualism and monism. *Avidyā*, or ignorance, applies also to our account of selves. In our "ordinary" experience we are inclined to identify selfhood with our empirical ego, but our true reality is that of *ātman*, which is pure consciousness and not the intentional consciousness of any particular object, including the self. This pure consciousness is identical with Brahman and carries within itself the bliss (*ānanda*) of Brahman.

Shankara's Advaita is thus a philosophical mysticism that takes the reality of the world seriously but attempts to transcend or sublate it into Brahman. Hence the two perspectives, that of the ultimate (*parārthika*) and the penultimate (*vyāvahārika*), and the two levels of Brahman, without qualities (*nirguṇa*) and with qualities (*saguṇa*). In the latter plane, Brahman appears as Īshvara, or God seen as personal, who presides over the world of appearances. Devotion to Īshvara (*bhakti*) is nonetheless seen as subordinate to the contemplative experience (*jnāna*) of Brahman.

Advaita Vedanta is not just a system of thought but a way of self-realization. Disease, says Shankara, is not cured by pronouncing "medicine" but by taking it. In the same spirit, the purpose of philosophical contemplation is not just to know but to be Brahman, or rather to achieve the realization that one "always already" is Brahman. Shankara divides the Vedas into two sections, one dealing with duties and rituals action (*karmakāṇḍa*) and one dealing with right knowledge (*jñānakāṇḍa*). While the former is praiseworthy, it is the latter that leads to the overcoming of ignorance and the achievement of *moksha*, or liberation. This, however, calls for moral and spiritual purification prior to and alongside contemplation of Brahman, specifically for four conditions: discrimination between eternal and noneternal reality, detachment from the fruits of one's actions both here and in the hereafter, rigorous self-control undertaken with serenity, and the desire for liberation. The devout reading of the Vedas is also an essential part of spiritual training, especially given that Shankara claims that his entire philosophy is in fact an exegesis of the Vedas. To that end, he endorses the traditional prescription of *shravaṇa* (hearing the scriptures), *manana* (reflection), and *dhyāsana* (contemplation). It is this combination of profundity of thought and spiritual ardor that makes Shankara so attractive and powerful a figure to philosophers and spiritual aspirants alike.

Joseph Prabhu

See also **Upanishadic Philosophy**

BIBLIOGRAPHY

Mayeda, S., ed. and trans. "Upadesasasahasri." In *A Thousand Teachings: The Upadesasasahasri of Sankara*. Tokyo: University of Tokyo Press, 1979.

Thibaut, George, ed. and trans. "Brahmasutrabhasya." In *The Vedanta Sutras of Badarayana with the Commentary by Sankara*. Sacred Books of the East 34, 38. Reprint, New York: Dover, 1962.

SECONDARY SOURCES

Clooney, F. X. *Theology after Vedanta*. Albany: State University of New York Press, 1993.

Deutsch, Eliot. *Advaita Vedanta*. Honolulu: East-West Center Press, 1969.

Pande, G. C. *Life and Thought of Samkaracarya*. Delhi: Motilal Banarsidass, 1994.

SHIVA AND SHAIVISM Hinduism in the classical, medieval, and modern periods displays two powerful male deities, Shiva and Vishnu, in addition to multiple forms of Devī, the goddess. All have numerous manifestations with various names, mythologies, and rituals. For example, the Sanskrit names of Shiva include, among others, Ardhanārīshvara, Bhava, Bhīma, Hara, Īshāna, Kapardin, Mahādeva, Maheshvara, Naṭarāja, Parameshvara, Shambhu, Shaṅkara, Sharva, and Sthāṇu. Some roots

of Shiva and Vishnu may be traced to the Rig Veda. Although neither is dominant in that seminal text of the mid-second millennium B.C., both emerge to prominence in the post-Vedic period of the Sanskrit epics. Their roles in myths, rituals, and symbols have many intriguing parallels. They evolve, however, in essentially different directions, and their followers, known respectively as Shaivas and Vaishnavas, represent two options for Hindu life and practice. It could be said that all Hindus respect Shiva, Vishnu, and the great goddesses; some worship both Shiva and Vishnu as well as one or more goddesses; while many prefer to concentrate devotion and faithful allegiance to one as supreme deity.

Prehistory and Rudra-Shiva in the Vedas

Recent archaeological and linguistic studies have led historians of religion to new insights into possible prehistoric origins of Shiva. Two areas have drawn attention: the non-Aryan Indus Valley Civilization, centering on Harappa and Mohenjo-Daro around 2600–1800 B.C.; and Indo-Aryan migrations around 2100–1700 B.C. across the Bactria-Margiana Archaeological Complex in present-day Turkmenistan and Afghanistan prior to the early Vedic period. A number of steatite seals from the Indus period depict a powerful male figure with erect phallus and horned animal mask, seated in what the Yoga tradition later calls *padmāsana*, or "lotus posture." Other seals represent various bulls and trifoliate *bilva* leaves. An Indo-Aryan legacy may lie behind myths of an archer deity known as Sharva in the Rig Veda, with a similar name in the Avesta of ancient Iran.

The Rig Veda provides better focus, as hymns addressed to particular deities and references to key rituals supplant speculation about artifacts and language from the deeper prehistory. In a few hymns a mysterious, ferocious, highly dangerous god appears under the name Rudra, perhaps indicating a "Howler" (from *rud*, "to howl, cry, roar") among animals in the mountains and wilderness. Rudra's companion and alter ego is a wild bull (*vrishabha*) that may have replaced an earlier wild water buffalo (*mahisha*). Rudra's weapons are the *vajra* (thunderbolt), a bow, and burning arrows that kill with terror (*ugra*). Here, however, his essentially ambivalent character is revealed. The same missiles that slay can also cool and heal, and strangely enough, "cooling" (*jalāsha*) is a special epithet of this dreaded god. Clearly the poet of Rig Veda 2.33.11 hopes that his verses praising mighty (*bhīma*) Rudra will win his grace. Like a wise physician, Rudra has a thousand remedies (*bheshaja*). Equally fearsome are Rudra's sons and warring companions, the Maruts, also known collectively as the Rudras, born from the cow Prishni. The Maruts, like their father and the great god Indra (whom they also serve), are associated not only with bulls, war, and chariot driving but also with winds and storms that bring fertilizing rain.

Rudra is at times identified with Agni, the Vedic deity of the fire sacrifice (*yajña*). But it is precisely that complex ritual tradition at the core of Rig Vedic religion that separates Rudra from others. At first Rudra is excluded from the soma cult and offerings to dominant deities such as Indra and Varuṇa. Offerings to Rudra (for example, the collected blood and entrails of animal victims) are left to the north, his direction. Over time he is gradually accepted into the pantheon, although his "outsider" status, both as frequenter of untamed space remote from human habitation and as a god of unpredictable behavior, remains integral to his legacy and certainly contributes to his unique appeal.

Somewhat later than the Rig Veda, recensions of the Yajur Veda (Taittirīya Saṃhitā 4.5.1–11 and Shukla Yajur Veda or Vājasaneyi Saṃhitā 16.1–66) contain a litany of a hundred names and forms of Rudra, known as the Shatarudrīya *stotra*. This liturgy accompanied 425 offerings into the sacrificial fire and secured Rudra's place among major deities. The names, which appear as lasting definitions, include: Dweller on Mount Mūjavat; Pashupati, Lord of Animals; Best Physician; Kapardin, Wearer of Braided Hair; Bhava, Existence; Nīlagrīva, Blue-neck; Lord of Thieves; Sharva, the Archer; and many others. In the late Vedic Shvetāshvatara Upanishad 3.4–5, a poet carefully addressed the fearsome, quick-to-anger, death-dealing Rudra as sole sovereign deity, a protector who is "benign, not terrifying, and auspicious (*shiva*)." Shiva is the name by which the god is best known today.

Shiva in Epics and Purāṇas

The post-Vedic Sanskrit literature of the Mahābhārata, Rāmāyana and Purāṇas expanded the many-sided and ambiguous roles of Rudra and generated new myths for the god known more often as Shiva. There also his unruly horde of sons and companions, the Maruts or Rudras, augmented his ferocious appearance. In this period the performance of worship (*pūjā*) to gods, either in homes or temples with permanent resident deities, gradually replaced the centrality of Vedic sacrifice and its temporary altars. In temples housing Shiva, the Shatarudrīya *stotra* became a standard liturgy; worshipers routinely heard his hundred names, and priestly discourses recounted his famous episodes. For personal devotions many ardent Shaivas committed the *stotra* to memory, a practice still prominent today.

Among the many enduring myths of Shiva in epics and Purāṇas, several feature his destructive nature. In myth and iconography a balanced triad of deities known as *trimūrti* appeared: Brahmā as creator, flanked by

Vishnu the preserver, and Shiva the destroyer. In the repetitive eschatology known as *pralaya* (dissolution), it is Shiva who incinerates the cosmos and all its beings, divine, demonic, or human, prior to a long rest and yet another remanifestation of the world in an endless cycle of *yuga*s, or ages. Kāla, the personification of time, is in fact an appellation of this overwhelming god. One myth with roots in the Vedas recounts the demolition of three cosmic cities built by Māyā for the demons. So powerful was the fiery anger of the god that he pierced all three fortresses with a single arrow. In another set of myths he destroyed the Vedic sacrifice of Daksha after Shiva, alone of all the gods, had been excluded. Shiva's wrath is sometimes righteous display, as in the myth of his killing the great god Brahmā (Prajāpati) for attempted incest. In a variant, Shiva in the form of Bhairava cut off Brahmā's fifth head. In retribution for this sin of killing a Brahman, the severed head would not leave the hand of Bhairava. The trident (*trishūla*) is a weapon Shiva employs to dispatch demons, often in his terrible *tāṇḍava* dance of death. Naṭarāja, King of the Dance, another epithet of Shiva, was often rendered in sculpture and painting based on a conception of the sinewy four-armed god poised in elegant mid-dance within a ring of cosmic fire, two hands holding the drum and flame of destruction, another in the "fear not" gesture, one foot planted on the demon of ignorance, as the fourth hand points to the raised foot free of bondage.

The destructive power of Shiva is curiously balanced by his creative nature in many ways. His most visible icon is an erect phallus, the *liṅga*, a ubiquitous symbol in Shaivite temples and homes either as bare pillar or anthropomorphic organ, often with carved faces. Myths describe the *liṅga* as a cosmic center, an endless *axis mundi* penetrating the nether worlds and rising to the highest heaven. It echoes the sacrificial pole of Vedic ritual. With this inexhaustible member, Shiva and his wife Pārvatī famously made love for 36,000 years. But Shiva's unruly sexuality is often chaotic, and his semen, like his celebrated third eye with a capacity to burn someone to ashes, is dangerously fiery. He seduced the wives of the Rishis, the Pine Forest sages, sons of Brahmā, a crime for which he was deprived of his wayward member. The Skanda Purāṇa reports that Kāshī, holiest of cities with its temple of Shiva as Vishvanātha, assembled in acolyte temples vast numbers of *liṅga*s from all over India.

Contradicting his powerful sexuality is Shiva's role as lord of ascetics (*yogin*s), those who renounce marriage, family, and society to meditate, perform austerities (*tapas*) in the wilderness and, scorning tonsure, allow their hair to grow into Shiva's *jaṭā*, or matted locks. The Maitreyi Upanishad stresses the renouncer's identification with the one eternal Shiva. When Pārvatī attempts to distract him from meditation in order to make love, Shiva burns a third eye in his forehead to continue creative insight. The same eye also burns to ashes Kāma, god of love, Shiva's erotic impulse. He is motionless in meditation, earning him the name Sthāṇu, an immovable "post," although his *liṅga*, also postlike, sends a contrary message. The ashes that were Kāma identify a many-layered symbol and paradox: they are the result of Shiva's power to incinerate a being or the entire world, the reduction of every body through cremation, and the remnant of the sacrifice abandoned by a renunciant, whose first act is to internalize his ritual fires. Yet they are also Shiva's semen and therefore regenerative power. As Shiva, Lord of the cremation ground, covered his body with ashes, so do ascetics, and householder devotees touch fire and apply *vibhūti* ash to themselves in his worship.

In the wilderness or high on Mount Kailasa, Shiva, like ancient Rudra, is Lord of animals, often portrayed on or wrapped in a tiger skin, enclosed by *nāga*s (cobras). But his role as Pashupati is sovereign of domestic animals as well, and Shiva's *vāhana* (mount) is the bull Nandin, who lies in placid power as guardian god outside temple doors or serves as decorated processional vehicle in festivals. It would appear that the prehistoric cult of wild buffalo or bull, known in the days of Rudra as "Howler" in the wilderness, was tamed into the docile figure of the Purāṇas as mount or even multiform of Shiva.

Shiva's frequent consort is Pārvatī, also known as Umā or Gaurī, but Satī, Gaṅgā and other goddesses are his spouses in various myths. The marriage of Shiva and Pārvatī, considered a role model in South India, is an elaborate festival in Madurai and other temples. In one striking sense Shiva requires no consort: he has an androgynous form, Ardhanārīshvara, the Lord who is Half Female. Given the number of reconciled polarities in the nature of Shiva, it is not surprising to see him in sculptures and paintings in vertical nonsymmetry, his right side in male attire, left side—properly subordinate in Hindu physiology—with prominent breast and female ornaments. This two-in-one body recalls the Shiva-Shakti pairing that can be either a demonstration of *coincidentia oppositorum*, the transcendence of polarities, or as in Tantra and other Shaiva perspectives, the dominance of female energy (*shakti*). In sexual union with Shakti Shiva is even portrayed as a bloodless corpse, passive and inert under the dynamic female power.

Gaṇesha, also known as Gaṇapati or Vināyaka, became popular as the son of Shiva and Pārvatī, although myths of his origins, perhaps in ancient elephant worship, are varied. One account in the Purāṇas is of his decapitation by his own angry father, his human head then replaced by that of an elephant. Another ancient multifaceted deity drawn into the orbit of Shiva is Skanda, known in various regions and periods as Kārttikeya, Kumāra or Subrahmaṇya, and identified with the Tamil god Murukaṇ. Born from Shiva's fiery semen, this war god is also lord of *graha*s (seizers) who, like numerous ferocious goddesses, attack with diseases. One enduring myth presents him as a six-headed foundling, suckled simultaneously by the Krittikās, six stars in the constellation Pleiades, therefore called Shaṇmukha (six-faced). Other myths celebrate him as the son of Shiva and Pārvatī.

In the Mahā-Nārāyaṇa Upanishad, Shiva is said to have five faces or manifestations (*pañcavaktra*) and in the Mahābhārata eight forms (*ashtamūrti*). Although the *avatāra* doctrine, with *bhakti* (devotion) to, and *prasāda* (grace) from, the several incarnations of Vishnu is perhaps more pronounced, it is in these multiple expressions that Shiva also extends his presence. As cosmic totality, he is simultaneously fivefold and eightfold. One name, Īshāna, declaring him supreme being, is expressed as both manifestation, along with Sadyojāta, Vāmadeva, Aghora, and Tatpurusha, and as form, beside Bhava, Sharva, Pashupati, Vāyu, Ugra, Mahādeva, and Rudra. Variant names occur in some texts, and eventually five mantras came to accompany the five faces. In his elevated role as supreme, Shiva is also frequently called Maheshvara, great Lord, and Parameshvara, Highest Lord.

Shaivas in Faith and Practice

The god with so many contrarities woven into vivid mythologies generated numerous theological perspectives and accompanying means of worship. Just as the god of dreadful habitat and custom was perceived to be an outsider early on, so also were many of his devotees shunned, in particular those Shaivas adopting yogic techniques or Shakta-Tantric worship. Vaishnavas had their clean, comfortable, more respectable god Vishnu and faith in the sufficiency of the householder's path rather than a renunciant's ascetic habits. Traditional expressions of devotion (*bhakti*), however, emerged as similar in both of these major Hindu divisions.

Among the first of many schools or sects devoted to Shiva were the Pāshupatas who recognized him as Pati (Lord) of *pashu*s (creatures). Their faith was in a god who could extend his *prasāda* (grace) in the form of release from bondage (*bandhatva*) to worldly existence and ignorance, just as a cow can be freed from a tether. This spiritual image of the self as *pashu*, the problem as fetter (*pāsha*), and the solution as freedom through divine grace and human effort became the hallmark of Shaiva theology through the centuries. The traditional founder of the Pāshupatas was Lakulīsha in the second century.

Joyous Shaivas at the Kumbh Mela in Allahabad. The Kumbh Mela is a Hindu festival that has been celebrated along the Ganges River for more than four thousand years: The faithful gather to literally wash away their sins. The 2001 Kumbh Mela was the largest gathering of humanity in recorded history, an estimated 70 million people gathered in Allahabad. AMIT PASRICHA.

Both Shiva and Vishnu emerged as principals in the epics and Purāṇas, but in the Guptan period two new and quite different genres appeared, Āgamas and Tantras. Āgamas of the Shaivas and Vaishnavas (those for the latter, usually known as Saṃhitās) were essential liturgical manuals that became known in the fifth and sixth centuries. The ritual texts of the Shaiva tradition eventually reached a collection of 28, with another 108 counted as Upāgamas of secondary authority.

Although the textual and iconographic history of Tantrism does not begin until about the fifth century, some historians of religion have considered deeper, even pre-Vedic roots for Shakta Tantrism in the goddess cults of ancient Mesopotamia. In any case, Tantrism as deciphered from its esoteric texts concerns extreme human quests for transcendence of polarities. No better deity could be found as model than Shiva, master of paradox who overcomes oppositions of the wild and the tamed, male and female, eroticism and asceticism, dynamic energy and silent passivity, creation and destruction. The *vāmācāra* (left-hand) division of Tantrism distinguished itself as a path for heroes (*vīra*s) and transgressive rites and behavior, perhaps a legacy of such communities as the Vrātyas of antiquity. Essential identification with Shiva in unison with Shakti became a liberating ritual technique. Such explorers of the dangerous path considered themselves beyond routine practitioners of yoga in the right-hand division, and certainly above the unknowing herds of *pashu*s.

Among the most horrific and uncontrollable manifestations of Shiva are Bhairava, also known as Vīrabhadra, and Sharabha, an eight-legged, flesh-eating monster. Kāpālikas (Skull-bearers), or Bhairavas, were named for the human skull carried in one hand as begging bowl (remembering Bhairava who could not release the head of Brahmā from his hand for twelve years), with a club in the other. Kālāmukhas were identified by black facial markings. Both were large communities of ascetics from the ninth century until their dissipation in the thirteenth century. Nātha ("protector, lord," a name for Shiva) Siddha was another name for movements eclectically combining Shaiva, yoga, alchemical, and other perspectives in their quest for supernatural powers.

Since a devotee could become one with Shiva, it is not unexpected that great leaders and saints were considered to be incarnations. Such was the case with India's most revered philosopher, Shankara, an eighth-century Kerala Brahman author of commentaries on the Upanishads and Sūtras of Bādarāyaṇa that structured intellectually the nondualist Advaita Vedānta school. Reputed founder of monasteries at the four compass points of India for the ten branches of the Dashanāmi order of ascetics, he was awarded authorship of scores of works, including the beautiful Sanskrit devotional poem, Shivānandalaharī.

In the far north of India there developed from the early ninth century the Kashmir Shaiva or Trika theology, named for its triad of approaches and principles, all recognizing Shiva as universal sovereign, Shakti as cosmic energy, and a finite human self in the bondage of ignorance yet capable of liberation by mystical unison with Shiva. Utpaladeva, a tenth-century Kashmiri poet, composed Sanskrit songs collected in the Shivastotrāvalī and frequently recited today. He shared with others his own pilgrim's spiritual progress, a journey through a stage of personal effort with rituals, recitations, and meditation leading to an acquisition of knowledge, followed by recognition of pure consciousness, then finally by the bliss of becoming one with the cosmic body of Shiva. Such means, said Utpaladeva, who was considered to have become a *siddha*, "perfected being," are available to all without restrictions of age, gender, class, or caste.

At the other extreme of the subcontinent in South India, two important Shaiva sects crystallized in the twelfth century. Tamil Shaivas, known also as Shaiva Siddhāntas, claimed roots in first-century Tamil teachings and included in their heritage such famed poets as Māṇikkavācakar of the ninth century. They stressed the transcendent otherness of God and his boundless love for humans under his protection. Siddhānta texts in Tamil supplanted the Sanskrit texts upon which they were based and brought themes from Tamil devotional poetry into play. Hymns of the 63 Nāyaṉārs, sixth- to tenth-century Shaiva saints (whose legends were collected in the Periyapurāṇm in the eleventh century), were the heart of Tamil Shaivism.

The other quite different and more aggressively independent sect was that of the Vīrashaivas or Liṅgāyats, with texts in the vernacular Kannada and Telugu languages. The iconoclastic founder, Basava, rejected the authority of the Vedas, traditional class and caste hierarchy, the doctrine of transmigration, and standard Brahmanical rites, including cremation. Also abandoned was image worship except for the *liṅga*, worn by devotees as an amulet and focus of devotion.

The names and forms of Shiva gleaned here from epics, Purāṇas, and communities by no means exhaust his presence. Many regional deities and cults that do not bear his name are nevertheless marginally Shaiva. For example, spread across large areas of Maharashtra, Karnataka, and Andhra is the worship of a set of powerful gods known variously as Khaṇḍobā or Mallanna, Mallikārjuna, Mailāra, Mallāri, Malhāri, and Mairāḷ. Here, as in other instances, particular folk deities of indistinct prehistory endure under the umbrella of Purāṇic Shiva.

The worship of Shiva as described in the Āgamas or observed all across the Hindu world today generally centers upon his *liṅga* as altarpiece. Before entering a temple the worshiper greets and touches the nose of the guardian bull Nandin, rings a brass bell to alert the god of a devotee's presence, and proceeds to the *liṅga* positioned in the *yoni* (female genitals) or *pīṭha* (seat) with a northern channel to carry off liquid offerings. Basic offering materials in a temple, home, or roadside shrine are leaves of the *bilva* tree special to Shiva, water, milk, honey, and other items. A Vedic five-syllable mantra, *namaḥ shivāya*, praises him along with the litany of his sacred names, and the worshiper may also transfer powers from the five faces of Shiva to various bodily parts in a rite known as *nyāsa*. Cooked food (*naivedya*) may also be presented in a more elaborate *homa* fire offering.

Meditation upon Shiva as fire, light, and regenerative seed occurs not only in private devotions but also on his special nights when divine favors may be forthcoming. New Moon eve (*amāvāsyā*), the fourteenth of each dark fortnight, is designated Shivarātri, the night of Shiva. Once each solar year, in Māgha (January–February) or Phālguna (February–March), there is Mahāshivarātri, his Great Night. Many Hindus, Vaishnavas as well as Shaivas, fast and remain awake in *jāgara* (vigil) all night in meditation. Monday (Moonday) is the weekday most auspicious for the worship of Shiva, as it has long been connected to soma, the sacred plant of immortality and worship of the dead. The ancient Vedic god Rudra, once considered unfit to attend the sacrifice, sits comfortably today as Shiva, one of the two foremost male deities, the object of devotion and worship from hundreds of millions throughout the Hindu world.

David M. Knipe

See also **Devī; Gaṇesha; Hinduism (Dharma); Shankara; Upanishadic Philosophy; Vishnu and Avatāras; Yoga**

BIBLIOGRAPHY

Bailly, Constantina Rhodes. *Shaiva Devotional Songs of Kashmir: A Translation and Study of Utpaladeva's Shivastotrāvalī*. Albany: State University of New York Press, 1987. Includes romanized text and introduction to this key tenth-century Shaivite hymnal.

Biardeau, Madeleine. *Hinduism: The Anthropology of a Civilization*, translated by Richard Nice. Delhi: Oxford University, 1989. Convincing synthesis explains the transformation of Vedic religion into "a universe of *bhakti*" able to sustain Shaivism along with other options.

Clothey, Fred W., and J. Bruce Long, eds. *Experiencing Siva: Encounters with a Hindu Deity*. New Delhi: Manohar, 1983. Scholars from a variety of disciplines examine Shiva and Shaivas in literature, philosophy, ritual, art, and architecture.

Dasgupta, Surendranath. *A History of Indian Philosophy*. Vol. 5: *The Southern Schools of Śaivism*. 1922. Reprint, Delhi: Motilal Banarsidass, 1975. Survey of Shaiva Āgamas and Purāṇas as well as schools of Pāśupatas, Shaiva Siddhāntas, Vīrashaivas, and others.

Davis, Richard H. *Worshiping Siva in Medieval India: Ritual in an Oscillating Universe*. Princeton, N.J.: Princeton University Press, 1991. A penetrating study of philosophy and ritual, both temple and domestic, in the Shaiva Siddhānta tradition, with excellent illustrations of ritual gestures.

Goldberg, Ellen. *The Lord Who Is Half Woman: Ardhanarisvara in Indian and Feminist Perspective*. Albany: State University of New York Press, 2002. A nuanced feminist analysis of Shiva in his androgynous manifestation; 18 plates of sculptures and paintings.

Gonda, Jan. *Visnuism and Sivaism. A Comparison*. London: Athlone, 1970. A concise, coherent depiction of myth, ritual, theology, and folklore; copious endnotes include further details.

Hiltebeitel, Alf, ed. *Criminal Gods and Demon Devotees: Essays on the Guardians of Popular Hinduism*. Albany: State University of New York Press, 1989. Deities and cults explored in essays from field studies illustrate several regions of the subcontinent.

Kramrisch, Stella. *The Presence of Siva*. Princeton, N.J.: Princeton University Press, 1981. Thirty-two plates of Shaiva sculptures add dimension to this comprehensive study of mythology by an art historian.

Lorenzen, David. *The Kāpālikas and Kālāmukhas: Two Lost Śaivite Sects*. Berkeley: University of California, 1972. Sources, doctrines, cults, priesthoods, and regional centers of two distinctive ascetic movements that were absorbed into others by the fourteenth century.

O'Flaherty, Wendy Doniger. *Asceticism and Eroticism in the Mythology of Siva*. New York: Oxford University Press, 1973. Structural analysis of some 45 motifs in the mythology of Shiva with particular attention to the erotic-ascetic polarity.

Peterson, Indira Viswanathan. *Poems to Siva: The Hymns of the Tamil Saints*. Princeton, N.J.: Princeton University Press, 1989. Translations from Tamil and introduction to the Tēvāram, a collection of 270 hymns of the three primary Nāyanārs; 15 supportive plates.

Ramanujan, A. K. *Speaking of Siva*. Baltimore: Penguin, 1973. Translations of *vacana*s (religious "sayings" in free verse) composed in Kannada by Vīrashaiva saints of the tenth to twelfth centuries.

Shulman, David Dean. *Tamil Temple Myths: Sacrifice and Divine Marriage in the South Indian Śaiva Tradition*. Princeton, N.J.: Princeton University Press, 1980. Detailed analysis of the classical Tamil as well as the Vedic and Sanskrit backgrounds of myths important to specific temple traditions.

SHIVAJI BHONSLE AND HEIRS Shivaji (1630–1680), the father of Maharashtra and the originator of the Maratha polity, which lasted over 150 years from the middle of the seventeenth century until 1818, is more than a historical figure. His legend continued to inspire the Marathas long after his death, into the eighteenth century when Pune's Peshwas established Maratha supremacy over most of the subcontinent. In the late nineteenth century, Shivaji's spirit of independence was recalled in the Shivaji festivals organized by a major early leader of the Indian nationalist movement, Bal Gangadhar Tilak, and by the Bengalis resisting the first partition of their province from 1906 to 1910.

Since its birth as a state of the Indian Union in 1960, Maharashtra has given Shivaji the pride of place by putting his picture in every government office. At least one political party, Shiv Sena, is named for Shivaji, and its Mumbai headquarters are architecturally a replica of one of his fortresses. Shivaji is thus a living legend, who continues to be the subject of biographies, plays, and movies, and whose name is held by millions of Maharashtrians, regardless of their station in life, in a reverence normally reserved for divinities. For them, Shivaji was not just a brave warrior or a great king, but a person of unsullied character and, like Rāma or Krishna, a divine incarnation whose timely appearance on earth not only protected hapless "women, Brahmans, and cows," but protected Hinduism itself from being completely overwhelmed by the advancing tide of Islam.

Shivaji is one of the very few Indian historical figures who are respected outside the region of their activities. Thus, there is much adulatory writing about him in most Indian languages. India's Nobel laureate in literature, Rabindranath Tagore, wrote and set to music two poems in praise of Shivaji's character, military exploits, and administration. In the second quarter of the twentieth century, the celebrated poet of Gujarat, Javerchand Meghani, composed a melodic and inspiring lullaby about Jijabai and the infant Shivaji, which is still sung by thousands of Gujarati mothers while rocking their children's cradles. Akbar and Shivaji were foremost in pre-British Indian history, providing ideal precedents for independent India's polity.

Childhood and Early Years

Born at the Shivneri fort, 40 miles (64 km) north of Pune, on 19 February 1630, Shivaji was the second son of Shahaji Bhonsle. At the time of Shivaji's birth, Shahaji served the nizam of Ahmednagar, holding a prosperous *jagir* (fief) covering Pune and Chakan, which he had inherited from his father, Maloji, who was given the title of raja by Ahmednagar's ruler in 1595. In 1636 Bijapur took advantage of the defeat of Ahmednagar by the

Seventeenth-Century Deccan Miniature Painting by Mir Mohammad. Shivaji is a living legend, far more than a historical, regional hero of the past, whose name is revered by millions of Maharashtrians, rural and urban, regardless of their station in life. K. L. KAMAT / KAMAT'S POTPOURRI.

Mughals to annex portions of the fallen kingdom. After a brief period of service under the Mughals, Shahaji joined the Bijapur ruler, who rewarded him with an extensive *jagir* in Bangalore.

Always on the march and concerned for the safety of his family, Shahaji kept his wife, Jijabai, and Shivaji on his Pune estate under the protection of his trusted lieutenant, Dadoji Konddev, a Brahman. Apart from administrative duties, Dadoji was responsible for educating his young ward in martial arts. Jijabai nourished Shivaji spiritually and instilled in him heroism and ambition by recounting stories from the epics, the Rāmāyaṇa and Mahābhārata. At sixteen, Shivaji was placed in full charge of the *jagir*. By that time, he had rallied the youth of the neighboring Maval region, a 20-mile (32-km) wide mountainous region east of the Sahyadri range, inspiring them with the ideal of an independent kingdom, free of Muslim control.

Many historic accounts—Mughal, Maratha, Portuguese, English, French, Dutch, and Jesuit—establish Shivaji's

astuteness, personal valor, military prowess, and tolerance toward people of all religions. Shivaji began his military exploits on a small scale in the neighboring areas, which were formerly under Ahmednagar but had recently been annexed by Bijapur, his father's current employer. His pretext for taking over those territories was to consolidate them on Bijapur's behalf. Beginning in 1657, however, he attacked and conquered several Bijapur forts. Disturbed by the new threat, the Bijapur court sent a powerful general, Afzal Khan, to destroy Shivaji. On his way, the khan detoured to Tuljapur to desecrate the temple of Bhavani, to whom Shivaji was deeply devoted. Afzal Khan audaciously slaughtered a sacred cow in the temple compound and challenged the goddess to save Shivaji. Afzal Khan also detoured to Pandharpur, where he damaged the temple of Vithoba, the focal point for centuries of an annual pilgrimage by hundreds of thousands of Maharashtrians.

Shivaji and his followers were now determined to avenge the atrocities. Aware that his own small force would be no match for Afzal Khan's well-equipped army of 15,000 in a conventional battle, Shivaji suggested a personal meeting in the thickly wooded region at the foot of Pratapgad fort, where his own knowledge of the terrain and of guerrilla warfare would offer him a distinct advantage. Both leaders came to the meeting armed. In a similar situation a decade earlier, Afzal Khan had used just such a "truce" meeting to imprison a disarmed Hindu general. When the much taller Afzal Khan rushed to embrace the diminutive Maratha leader and smother him, Shivaji used his left hand, armed with *wagh-nakh*s ("tiger-claws"), to dig out the khan's entrails, while his Bhavani sword, concealed under his right-hand sleeve, deftly decapitated Afzal's head from his torso. Shivaji sent the head to the Bhavani temple. As the khan fell, Shivaji signaled his own forces, hiding in the jungle, to attack Afzal's troops.

Following the news of Shivaji's spectacular success against Bijapur, Emperor Aurangzeb, concerned about the fate of his Deccan possessions, sent his own uncle, Shayista Khan, to deal with the "mountain rat." In a surprise nocturnal raid on Shayista Khan's residence, Shivaji cut off his hand, then proceeded to conquer several Mughal fortresses, raiding and looting the well-guarded Mughal port of Surat in 1664. Enraged, Aurangzeb sent a huge army under his most renowned Rajput general, Jaisingh, against Shivaji. Realizing that he would be forced to fight a losing battle against so powerful a force, Shivaji surrendered several forts to Jaisingh, who offered him peace, provided he appear at the emperor's court, and that either he or his son, Sambhaji, accept a court position of *mānsabdār*. Shivaji received Jaisingh's personal guarantee that he would be treated like a "king." Shivaji's later loud remonstrations at court against the humiliating treatment he received led to his imprisonment. Undeterred, he planned a ruse to escape, sending daily presents of baskets laden with sweets, carried by his personal guard, to different Mughal dignitaries including those in charge of security. Both Shivaji and his son then escaped, hiding in two of the "sweets" baskets; adopting various guises, they returned to their homeland in a matter of months.

Shivajis's Military Strategy

Shivaji's spectacular military success was primarily attributed to his brilliant guerrilla warfare and his strategy of keeping nearly one hundred forts, to which his forces could easily withdraw for security. Ninety percent of his fortresses were located in the mountain fastnesses of the Sahyadri range; one of them, Raigad, was his capital.

Shivaji's strength lay in the swift movement of his cavalry, in contrast to the unwieldy Mughal armies, whom the Muslim Deccan rulers emulated. Shivaji's intimate knowledge of Maharashtra's mountainous terrain and fast-flowing rivulets, his dependence on the local population for support, and his ability to cut off the enemy's supply lines also contributed to his many victories. His personal leadership of almost all his military campaigns kept him in close touch with his followers, who were willing to sacrifice their lives for the dream of the *swarajya* (freedom), based on equity and fairness, regardless of religion, caste, or economic status.

Alone among the Indian rulers since the time of Rajendra Chola in the eleventh century, Shivaji realized the importance of maritime defenses—the lack of which, under the land-oriented Delhi sultans, Mughals, and Deccan Muslim rulers, had enabled the minuscule Portuguese navy to control all the coastal commerce from Bassein to Cochin. Shivaji's navy, commanded by the redoubtable Angria family, not only ended the Portuguese control of western India's coastal traffic and commerce, but stopped the early attempts of the English East India Company of Bombay to take over the Portuguese naval role.

Coronation and Administration

In 1674 Shivaji held his own coronation as *chhatrapati* ("lord of the umbrella"), or king, at Raigad, his capital. Consecrated by pandits led by Varanasi's Gaga Bhatt, Shivaji proclaimed a new era, the Raj Shaka, and issued a new gold coin, the Shivarai hon. Unfortunately for his *swarajya*, its illustrious founder did not live long; he died in 1680.

Shivaji's coronation was also marked by his proclamation of the *Kanujabata*, containing basic principles of

government, and *Rajyavyavaharkosh*, detailing instructions for the routine guidance of administrators. The *Kanujabata* provided for the *astapradhana* (eight ministers), with titles in Sanskrit: *mukhya pradhan* (prime minister); *amatya* (minister in charge of land revenues); *sachiv* (records); *sarnobat* (protocol); *senapati* (defense forces); *panditrao* (religion); *nyayadhishr* (judicial); and *sumant* (foreign relations). All ministers were paid cash salaries.

Shivaji's *swarajya* consisted of three large divisions, or provinces, each under a *sarsubhedar*, subdivided into *subhas* (each under a *subhedar* called *deshpande* or *deshmukh*), and further subdivided into *parganas*, *mahals*, and *tarfas*. At each level, there were central government nominees, such as *muzumdar* (accountant), *chitnis* (writer), and *daftardar* (recorder). Each village had a self-governing *gota*, or council, with representatives of the community and of twelve kinds of *balutedar*s, or craftsmen, who were entitled, by tradition, to a portion of the village's agricultural produce in return for their services to the community. With primary jurisdiction in settling land disputes, the *gota*s were respected by Shivaji's central administration and by his successors in the Bhosle line, as well as by Pune's Peshwas.

Shivajis's policy toward Muslims. Shivaji's religious policy reflected respect for all religions, including Islam. None of his wars were religious conflicts. Paralleling the best practices under the Mughals and Deccan's Bahamanis, he employed Muslims in high positions and made grants to mosques and Muslim spiritual leaders. As Khafi Khan, a contemporary chronicler, generally a hostile critic of Shivaji, conceded: "Wherever Shivaji and his army went, they caused no harm to the mosques, the Book of God or the women of anyone." His model was the Mughal emperor Akbar, who had accorded respect to Hindu beliefs and places. The distortion of Shivaji's image as a "founder of a strictly Hindu polity" was, according to Shivaji's latest (2003) biographer, James Laine, the outcome of biographies and ballads during the rule of Pune's Peshwas, who needed such an underpinning for their political agenda in the eighteenth century.

Successors

Sambhaji (1657–1689). Shivaji's elder son, Sambhaji, succeeded his father and was crowned *chhatrapati* at Raigad in 1680. The following year, Aurangzeb came to the Deccan at the head of a huge force, determined to liquidate the Maratha kingdom, which he expected to be in chaos in the wake of Shivaji's death. Instead, he found Sambhaji a valiant defender of his father's *swarajya*, able not only to deal with the Mughals but also with the Siddis of Janjira and the Portuguese in Goa. However, thanks to treachery, Aurangzeb's forces captured Sambhaji in 1689. Brought to the emperor's presence, he was asked to convert to Islam. When he refused, Aurangzeb ordered him blinded, tortured, and killed. Aurangzeb sent Sambhaji's widow, Yesubai, and his son, Shahu, to the imperial harem, where Shahu would be brought up until after Aurangzeb's death in 1707. His successor would then release him, provoking a civil war of succession in Maharashtra.

Rajaram (1670–1700). Before the Maratha capital fell, however, Sambhaji's younger stepbrother, Rajaram, was quickly crowned the *chhatrapati* and was whisked away to the safety of far-off Jinji. The Mughal forces followed him there, besieging the Jinji fort for seven years, as it was ably defended by its loyal Maratha generals. Once again, Rajaram eluded the Mughals, and hurried back to Maharashtra. The ordeal exhausted Rajaram, who died on 2 March 1700 at his Sinhagad ("fortress of the lion") fort.

Tarabai. The leadership of the Maratha "war of independence" was now assumed by Rajaram's widow, the intrepid Tarabai, who crowned her infant son, also named Shivaji, as *chhatrapati* at Panhala, near Kolhapur. The aged and tired Aurangzeb, by then fighting in the Deccan for twenty years, was harassed by her guerrilla forces until his death in 1707. It was at this point that Aurangzeb's successor, Azam Shah, released Shahu, on condition that he would help the Mughal cause.

Shahu (1707–1749). Whether Shahu ever intended to assist the Mughals or not, the Maratha generals and civilian advisers who defected from Tarabai's side to join him did not appear to have any such plans. They helped Shahu to reach Satara, where on 2 January 1708 he crowned himself *chhatrapati*. The two rival claimants to Shivaji's throne at Satara and Kolhapur began an internecine war, which lasted a quarter century and ended with the Treaty of Warna on 13 April 1731, whereby Shahu and his able *peshwa* recognized the "minor" branch of the Bhonsle family as Karweer *chhatrapatis* of Kolhapur. It remained, after the final defeat of the Marathas in 1818, as a princely state under British protection until 1948, when it was integrated into the Indian Union.

Meanwhile, Shahu's state of Satara "lapsed" to the East India Company in 1848 for lack of a biological heir, as Governor-General Dalhousie refused to recognize Shahu's adopted son as heir to the throne.

D. R. SarDesai

See also **Akbar; Aurangzeb; British East India Company Raj; Maharashtra; Peshwai and Pentarchy**

BIBLIOGRAPHY

Bendrey, V. S., ed. *Coronation of Shivaji*. Mumbai: People's Publishing House, 1960.

Desai, Ramesh. *Shivaji, the Last Great Fort Architect*. Mumbai: Government of Maharashtra, 1987.

Deopujari, M. B. *Shivaji and the Maratha Art of War*. Nagpur: Vidarbha Samshodhan Mandal, 1973.

Duff, James Grant. *A History of the Marathas*. 1826. Reprint, 2 vols. New Delhi: Associated Publishing House, 1971.

Gokhale, Kamal. *Chhatrapati Sambhaji*. Poona: Navakamal, 1978.

Gordon, Stewart. *New Cambridge History of India*, vol. II, 4, *The Marathas, 1600–1818*. Cambridge, U.K., and New York: Cambridge University Press, 1993.

Gune, V. T. *The Judicial System of the Marathas*. Poona: Deccan College, 1953.

Kinkaid, Dennis. *The Grand Rebel: An Impression of Shivaji, Founder of the Maratha Empire*. London: Collins, 1937.

Kishore, Brij. *Tara Bai and Her Times*. New York: Asia Publishing House, 1964.

Kulkarni, A. R. *Maharashtra in the Age of Shivaji*. Poona: Deshmukh, 1967.

Laine, James W. *Shivaji, Hindu King in Islamic India*. New York: Oxford University Press, 2003.

Lajpat Rai, Lala. *Shivaji, the Great Patriot*. Translated by R. C. Puri. New Delhi: Metropolitan, 1980.

Pagadi, Setu Madhavrao. *Chhatrapati Shivaji*. Poona: Continental Prakashan, 1976.

Patwardhan, R. P., and H. G. Rawlinson. *Source Book of Maratha History*. 1928. Reprint, Kolkata: K. P. Bagchi, 1978.

Ranade, M. G. *The Rise of the Maratha Power*. 1900. Reprint, New Delhi: Ministry of Information and Broadcasting, 1961.

Samarth, Anil. *Shivaji and the Indian National Movement*. Mumbai: Somaiya, 1975.

Sardesai, G. S. *New History of the Marathas*. 3 vols. Mumbai: Phoenix Publications, 1946–1948.

Sarkar, J. N. *Shivaji and His Times*. Kolkata: Sarkar, 1948.

Sen, S. N. *Administrative System of the Marathas*. 1923. Reprint, Kolkata: K. P. Bagchi, 1976.

———. *Military System of the Marathas*. 1928. 3rd ed. Kolkata: K. P. Bagchi, 1976.

———. *Foreign Biographies of Shivaji*. 1927. 2nd rev. ed. Kolkata: K. P. Bagchi, 1977.

SHIV SENA Founded in 1966, Mumbai's Shiv Sena ("army of Shiva") represents a xenophobic, sons-of-the-soil militant movement that has espoused pan-Indian Hindu nationalism throughout Maharashtra. The Shiv Sena has championed the indigenous Marathis, the "underdogs" of cosmopolitan Mumbai, who have angrily resented the economic success of industrious, better-educated migrants from South India in securing white-collar jobs and running lucrative small businesses. It subsequently articulated similar animosities against Gujarati and other communities in the city, envied for their apparent business acumen. It voiced the frustrations of unemployed Marathi youth and the concerns of older Marathis over law and order and the growing criminalization of Mumbai life. These issues and conflicts of interests were

Bal Thackeray, Ruler of Shiv Sena. His public pronouncements have increasingly labeled Islam (and Pakistan) as India's enemy and appealed to the private convictions of many Hindu nationalists. INDIA TODAY.

accentuated by a severe shortage of land in economically dynamic Mumbai, where housing was the most expensive in India.

The Shiv Sena enjoyed significant control over trade union activity in Mumbai once it aggressively displaced established communist unions. This control is an important factor in its organizational power in Mumbai and a source of involvement with extortion in the city. Recently, the Shiv Sena has reiterated its demand to curtail the entry of new migrants to Mumbai. More recently, it insisted that 90 percent of jobs in Mumbai's premier hotels and local public service employment should be reserved for Maharashtrians as well. However, in 2005, the Shiva Sena's public expressions of hostility toward Hindi-speaking migrants to Mumbai may have been at the cost of success in the politically critical state legislature elections.

The Shiv Sena proved popular with Marathis, especially the urban lower middle class, because it celebrated their proud history of military exploits, articulated genuine grievances, and gratified their sectarian resentments. Their claim on behalf of Marathis for a place under the sun is infused with an evocation of past glories and thus possesses both national and parochial resonance. It recalls the historic role of eighteenth-century Maratha Hindu kingdoms in hastening the decline of Muslim rule in India as well as the glories of the Maratha confederacy. The Shiv Sena itself is named after a remarkable Maratha military leader, Chattrapati Shivaji, revered as an illustrious ruler in the Hindu political pantheon. The Shiv Sena has also identified itself as a "Hindu-first" movement and has been an ardent campaigner for the construction of the Ram temple in Ayodhya, a controversial issue in India. In 1992 it joined in the communal riots that overtook Mumbai in the aftermath of the destruction of the Babri Masjid in Ayodhya. Ugly retaliatory violence against Muslims, following attacks on Hindus, allowed the Shiv Sena to present itself as the defender of Hindu India.

Led by a charismatic former newspaper cartoonist, Balasaheb Thackeray (b. 1927), the Shiv Sena has enjoyed three decades of power in Mumbai, joining a coalition to govern the state of Maharashtra in 1995. Thackeray's authority was absolute, and he has wielded effective organizational power over Shiv Sena's activities. His pronouncements on public issues, such as Indian nationhood and national interests, have increasingly labeled Islam (and Pakistan) as India's enemy; these pronouncements evidently have appealed to the private convictions of many Hindus, which partly accounts for his popularity among nationalists across India. The strong-arm tactics of Shiv Sena cadres, its "Sainiks," over whom Thackeray enjoys remarkable authority, appalls many moderate Indians.

There is widely held conviction that the Shiv Sena's political activities have descended into extortion, and other illicit methods of raising money, such as smuggling and sponsorship of illegal real estate development. There are accusations that the Shiv Sena is competing to supplant the Mumbai criminal underworld in such activities, but the Shiv Sena's policies were not noticeably different from other political parties when it governed the state of Maharashtra between 1995 and 1999 in partnership with the Bharatiya Janata Party.

Gautam Sen

See also **Ayodhya; Bharatiya Janata Party (BJP); Hindu Nationalism; Hindu Nationalist Parties; Hindutva and Politics; Vishwa Hindu Parishad (VHP)**

BIBLIOGRAPHY

Eckert, Julia M. *The Shiv Sena and the Politics of Violence.* Oxford: Oxford University Press, 2002.

Hansen, Thomas Blom. *Wages of Violence: Naming and Identity in Postcolonial Bombay.* Princeton, N. J.: Princeton University Press, 2001.

Katzenstein, Mary Dainsof, et al. "The Re-birth of the Shiv Sena: The Symbiosis of Discursive and Organizational Power." *Journal of Asian Studies* 56, no. 2 (May 1997): 371–390.

SHORE, SIR JOHN *(1751–1834), governor-general of India (1793–1798).* John Shore was born on 8 October 1751. Appointed a writer, the clerical entry level, in the East India Company, he arrived in Bengal in 1769, just as the great trading company was taking over the collection of the land revenues, the key to political control of India. In the next twenty years Shore, through his mastery of how the revenue and judicial systems of Bengal worked, persuaded his superiors that British control of India would only be possible through a just and stable settlement of the land revenue. For Shore, there were three great revenue issues. One was to find out who were the actual owners of the land; the second was to decide how much tax the peasants could reasonably be expected to pay; and third, what kind of revenue system the British should establish in Bengal to ensure the continuance of their rule.

After sixteen years in Bengal, Shore returned to England in 1785; in 1786 he was asked to go back to India as revenue adviser to the new governor-general, Lord Cornwallis, whose mandate was to increase the British government's control over the East India Company. Shore argued that throughout Mughal times the *zamindars*, or great landlords, had been the hereditary proprietors of the soil, and that although the fairest system would be to make a settlement directly with the peasants, the company had neither the knowledge nor the personnel to institute such a drastic change. A ten-year settlement, he was convinced, would give the government time to come to a clear understanding of how the system worked. In the end, however, Cornwallis decided for a permanent settlement, which meant recognizing the *zamindars* as the hereditary owners and guaranteeing that the revenue payment fixed at the beginning would be perpetual.

Shore returned to England in 1790 but went back to India as governor-general from 1793 to 1798. His contemporaries were critical of his preoccupation with revenue reforms, instead of seizing opportunities that might have brought more territory to the British. On his return to England, he was created Lord Teignmouth in the Irish peerage. Shore's organization of the bureaucracy to carry out defined revenue functions, while not glamorous, argues for claiming for him a significant role in shaping India as a modern state.

Ainslie T. Embree

See also **British East India Company Raj**

BIBLIOGRAPHY

The most complete account of Shore's public and private life is *Memoir of the Life and Correspondence of John, Lord Teignmouth* (London: Hatchard, 1843), by his son, Baron Teignmouth. Holden Furber, *Private Record of an Indian Governor-Generalship* (Cambridge: Harvard University Press, 1933) is more critical. Ranajit Guha, *A Rule of Property for Bengal* (Paris: Mouton, 1963) is the best account of the revenue settlement.

SHRAUTA SŪTRAS Around 700 to 300 B.C., many schools or branches (*shākhā*) transmitting oral traditions known as Vedas developed brief ritual manuals called

Shrauta Sūtras. Of the Saṃhitās (anthologies) of the four Vedas, the Yajur Veda in its two main divisions, Krishṇa (Black) and Shukla (White), generated more than half of the extant Shrauta Sūtras. Such manuals were needed as concise guidelines for the four major priests, *adhvaryu*, *hotā*, *udgātā*, and *brahman*, each with three assistants, for increasingly elaborate and sophisticated sacrifices that had been detailed in the Saṃhitās and their respective Brāhmaṇa texts.

For example, the Taittirīya Saṃhitā of the Krishṇa Yajur Veda is matched by the Taittirīya Brāhmaṇa and the later Taittirīya Āraṇyaka and Taittirīya Upanishad. At least nine different Vedic schools preserved the enormous aggregate of Taittirīya texts as an oral tradition, recited by Vedic students who then taught the whole corpus to the next generation of sons and grandsons. For sacrifices known as *shrauta* (from *shruti*, "that which is heard," meaning the Veda) the bulky Saṃhitā and Brāhmaṇa texts were mined to create versatile ritual manuals. Each of the nine schools of the Taittirīya produced its own Shrauta Sūtra in order to systematize the ritual tradition according to its own lights. Therefore, when the Vedic student learns the Shrauta Sūtra of his *shākhā* (for example, the Āpastamba), he is memorizing material on rituals already covered, perhaps years before, in the Taittirīya Saṃhitā, Brāhmaṇa, and Āraṇyaka.

Similarly, various branches of the other Saṃhitās generated Shrauta Sūtras. The names of those extant, listed according to Saṃhitā, are:

Rig Veda: Āshvalāyana, Shāṅkhāyana
Krishṇa (Black) Yajur Veda: Baudhāyana, Vādhūla, Bhāradvāja, Āpastamba, Hiraṇyakeshin, Vaikhānasa, Kāṭhaka, Mānava, Vārāha
Shukla (White) Yajur Veda, also known as Vājasaneyi Saṃhitā: Kātyāyana
Sāma Veda: Lāṭyāyana, Drāhyāyaṇa, Jaiminīya
Atharva Veda: Vaitāna

Although arrangements of rules for *shrauta* sacrifices may vary, the contents of the Sūtras are similar from school to school. For a typical example, the Āshvalāyana Shrauta Sūtra, a guide for the *hotā* priest and his three assistants, all connected to the Rig Veda, begins with *ishṭi* (offerings) on new- and full-moon days and proceeds with the establishment of the fires, the twice-daily milk offering (*agnihotra*), offerings to ancestors, first-fruits offerings and other seasonal sacrifices, animal sacrifice, expiatory offerings, soma sacrifice (*agnishṭoma*), and a lengthy discussion of sacrifices cataloged according to the number of *sutyā* (soma-pressing days) contained in each. The Kātyāyana Shrauta Sūtra, on the other hand, begins with general remarks on *shrauta* rituals before it outlines almost the same list of routine sacrifices with variant order and emphasis, but attention to such sacrifices as *pravargya* (a special rite in a soma sacrifice, an offering of milk poured into boiling ghee) and *purushamedha* (human sacrifice).

The style of Sanskrit is the aphoristic *sūtra* (thread) genre, condensed and formulaic. Gradually, one or more commentaries (*bhāshya*) were attached during transmission of the Sūtras to explain their contents for changing circumstances. Also assembled were indispensable digests (*paddhati*, *prayoga*), often confined to a single type or example of a special ritual. The Vedic schools named here also produced Grihya Sūtras for domestic rituals, including the schedule of life-cycle rites known as *saṃskāra* and household offerings to deities, planets, and the deceased.

David M. Knipe

See also **Hinduism (Dharma); Soma; Vedic Aryan India; Yajña; Yajur Veda**

BIBLIOGRAPHY

Gonda, Jan. *The Ritual Sūtras.* Wiesbaden: Otto Harrassowitz, 1977. Situates the Sūtras in the full compass of Vedic texts.
Kane, P. V. *History of Dharmaśāstra*, vol. II, part II. Poona: Bhandarkar Oriental Research Institute, 1941. As with Gonda's book, Kane masterfully surveys the ritual Sūtra context.
Smith, Brian K. *Reflections on Resemblance, Ritual, and Religion.* New York: Oxford University Press, 1989. Valuable discussion of links between Shrauta and domestic ritual systems.
Staal, Frits. *Agni. The Vedic Ritual of the Fire Altar.* 2 vols. Berkeley, Calif.: Asian Humanities, 1983. Sūtras discussed in context of the Agnicayana.

SHRENI Described in many classical Sanskrit and Pali texts, *shreni*s were occupational groups or guilds. The fourth-century B.C. grammarian Pānini, referred to *shreni*s, though without a clear description. Later Hindu *shastra*s, Buddhist Jataka tales, and other Buddhist literature described *shreni*s as village or town occupational groups that brought together individual workmen as well as associations of workmen in corporate bodies to pursue their common economic interests. Different texts identified *shreni*s of priests, doctors, warriors, farmers, carpenters, makers of irrigation devices, ironworkers, potters, oil pressers, cloth dyers, weavers, gardeners, garland makers, ship pilots, fishermen, betel sellers, ivory sculptors, musicians, courtesans, and even beggars and thieves. Accounts exist of individuals changing their professions (and therefore their *shreni* affiliations) several times. Accounts also exist of members of one family belonging to different *shreni*s.

Communities of *shreni*s sometimes became entire villages or urban neighborhoods. To be close to their work, *shreni*s of foresters lived near forests. *Shreni*s of blacksmiths, carpenters, potters, and weavers would live outside a city's walls in occupational villages or inside a city's walls in trade neighborhoods, located so that clients could find them and obtain their services. Such arrangements have sometimes been interpreted as precursors of India's later *jajmani* system. Where *shreni*s lived in identifiable neighborhoods, a head *shreni* (a *shreshthin*) could find himself functioning as a village headman (*gramika*), with many of the accompanying responsibilities.

As geographical, political, and economic environments changed, *shreni*s and their leaders sometimes chose to move. A fifth-century A.D. inscription described a *shreni* of wealthy Gujarati silk weavers migrating to Mandasor, where they donated enough funds to repair a temple to the Sun God they had endowed more than three decades earlier. After arriving in Mandasor, the *shreni* members entered a variety of different occupations, while still maintaining some consciousness of their earlier guild affiliations as silk weavers.

Accounts indicated that *shreni*s engaged in a broad range of collective activities. Some Buddhist orders required a married woman to receive the approval of her husband and his *shreni* before becoming a nun. Some *shreni*s handled disputes between husbands and wives. Others provided welfare benefits for their members, supporting them during their illnesses and caring for their widows and children after their deaths.

Shreni Organization

Classical texts described *shreni*s as headed by a *shreshthin* (the best, the elder, the most important). The *shreshthin* established his position by heredity or through selection by a *shreni* assembly. According to texts, *shreni* heads were typically aided by a few senior members of the *shreni* and by secretaries (*kayasthas*). On occasion, wealthy and powerful *shreni* heads participated in their ruler's regional councils and sometimes even became their ruler's advisers. *Shreni* heads were also described as participating in elaborate royal horse sacrifices (*ashvamedha*).

According to some accounts, local rulers generally supported a *shreni*'s rights to regulate its members' wages and prices, to make contracts with other *shreni*s and even with private individuals, and to punish (and even expel) members who violated *shreni* regulations. Local rulers also recognized their own responsibilities to uphold and enforce whatever *shreni* contracts had been agreed upon.

Certain *shreni*s adopted or were assigned banners, fly whisks, and other insignia of their corporate life, which they could display on public occasions. *Shreni*s could have their own seals made of terra-cotta, stone, bronze, copper, or ivory, similar to the seals of rulers and ministers. Some *shreni*s collected regular membership fees, to which they added fines collected from delinquent *shreni*

members and donations from contributors. Through the successful management of their funds, some *shreni*s became quite wealthy. They functioned as banks, lending money at lucrative interest rates to local merchants and other *shreni*s. They also lent money to local rulers, thereby gaining political advantages for themselves and their members. Records described *shreni*s organizing militias to protect their caravans and warehouses and then lending their militias (presumably under advantageous terms) to local rulers who wanted additional fighting men. Other records described merchant *shreni*s organizing caravans themselves and commissioning cargo ships for overseas trade.

*Shreni*s did not use their wealth exclusively to produce more wealth. An inscription at the famous Buddhist stupa at Sanchi, Madhya Pradesh, declared that in the first century A.D. an ivory workers' *shreni* donated funds to construct one of the stupa's four main gates. Hundreds of similar inscriptions with donors' names and affiliations gave evidence of *shreni*s' contributions through the centuries to building and renovating monasteries, stupas, temples, and religious communities.

Shrenis and Brahmanical Texts

The Buddhist Jataka tales made frequent references to *shreni*s. Although ostensibly tales of the lives of the Buddha before his final reincarnation in the sixth century B.C., the Jataka tales were not written down until perhaps as many as ten centuries later, during the time of the Guptan empire (4th–6th centuries A.D.). The world of *shreni*s described in the Jataka tales contrasted sharply with the world of ranked hereditary *varna*s and occupations described in then-extant Brahmanical texts like the Laws of Manu. The Brahmanical texts elaborated upon the four *varna*s of humans who emerged from the mouth, shoulders, thighs, and feet of Purusha, the original being. Brahmans, Kshatriyas, Vaishyas, and Shudras were to marry within their *varna*s and to follow their inherited *varna* occupations: Brahmans to teach and perform sacrifices, Kshatriyas to administer and defend the land, Vaishyas to produce and trade wealth, and Shudras to serve the three higher *varna*s.

By contrast, in the Jataka tales a ruler assembled and consulted with eighteen *shreni*s—not Brahmans. Furthermore, the ruler created a new office, head of the *shreni*s, to which he appointed a capable leader. In the Buddhist Jataka tales, a Brahman voluntarily chose to engage in trade (the occupation of Vaishyas) without feeling the need to justify his choice on the Brahmanical basis of hard times. In the Jataka tales, parents discussed what profession their son should enter—unlike the Brahmanical texts, where the profession was preordained. In the Jataka tales, people could change their occupations regardless of birth or background, and could change them again if they so chose. In one Jataka tale, a merchant's slave was brought up so much like a young merchant that he was able to pass himself off as a real merchant and to marry the daughter of a wealthy trader. The first merchant learned of his slave's fraud but revealed it to no one, and the story ended happily for all.

The social and economic life described in the Jataka tales was reflected in such later literary works as the *Panchatantra* (Five treatises) and the *Brihatkatha* (Great story). In these and similar writings, Brahman priests and Buddhist monks and nuns appeared but played a minor role. The leading characters were kings and merchants seeking power, profit, and enjoyment in a world distant from the many constraints of Brahmanical texts. One cannot know to what extent the Jataka tales (with their occupational groups and *shreni*s) or the Brahmanical texts (with their *varṇa*s and Brahman priests) accurately reflected society as it actually existed at any time and place in India's history.

Joseph W. Elder

See also **Caste System**

BIBLIOGRAPHY

Auboyer, Jeannine *Ancient India from 200 B.C. to 700 A.D.* New York: Macmillan, 1965.
Basham, Arthur Llewellen. *The Wonder That Was India: A Survey of the Culture of the Indian Sub-Continent before the Coming of the Muslims.* New York: Macmillan, 1954.
Drekmeier, Charles. *Kingship and Community in Early India.* Stanford, Calif.: Stanford University Press, 1962.
Kosambi, Damodar Dharmanand. *An Introduction to the Study of Indian History.* Mumbai: Popular Book Depot, 1956.
Van Buitenen, J. A. B., trans. *Tales of Ancient India.* Chicago: University of Chicago Press, 1959.

SHULBA SŪTRAS (VEDĀNGAS) The Shulba Sūtras belong to the Vedāngas, or supplementary texts of the Vedas. Although they are part of the Kalpa Sūtras, which deal with ritual, their importance stems from the constructions they provide for building geometric altars. Their contents, written in the condensed *sūtra* style, deal with geometrical propositions and problems related to rectilinear figures and their combinations and transformations, squaring the circle, as well as arithmetical and algebraic solutions to these problems. The root *shulb* means measurement, and the word *shulba* means a cord, rope, or string.

The extant Shulba Sūtras belong to the schools of the Yajurveda. The most important Shulba texts are the ones by Baudhāyana, Āpastamba, Kātyāyana, and Mānava.

They have been generally assigned to the period 800 to 500 B.C. Baudhāyana's text is the oldest, and he is believed to have belonged to the Andhra region. Baudhāyana begins with units of linear measurement and then presents the geometry of rectilinear figures, triangles, and circles, and their transformations from one type to another using differences and combinations of areas. An approximation to the square root of 2 and to p are next given.

Then follow constructions for various kinds of geometric altars in the shapes of the falcon (both rectilinear and with curved wings and extended tail), kite, isosceles triangle, rhombus, chariot wheel with and without spokes, square and circular trough, and tortoise.

In the methods of constructing squares and rectangles, several examples of Pythagorean triples are provided. It is clear from the constructions that both the algebraic and the geometric aspects of the so-called Pythagorean theorem were known. This knowledge precedes its later discovery in Greece. The other theorems in the Shulba include:

The diagonals of a rectangle bisect each other.
The diagonals of a rhombus bisect each other at right angles.
The area of a square formed by joining the middle points of the sides of a square is half of the area of the original one.
A quadrilateral formed by the lines joining the middle points of the sides of a rectangle is a rhombus whose area is half of that of the rectangle.
A parallelogram and rectangle on the same base and within the same parallels have the same area.
If the sum of the squares of two sides of a triangle is equal to the square of the third side, then the triangle is right-angled.

A variety of constructions are listed. Some of the geometric constructions in these texts are based on algebraic solutions of simultaneous equations, both linear and quadratic. It appears that geometric techniques were often used to solve algebraic problems.

The Shulbas are familiar with fractions. Algebraic equations are implicit in many of their rules and operations. For example, the quadratic equation and the indeterminate equation of the first degree are a basis of the solutions presented in the constructions.

The Shulba geometry was used to represent astronomical facts. The altars that were built according to the Shulba rules demonstrated knowledge of the lunar and the solar years.

Subhash Kak

See also **Science; Vedic Aryan India; Yajur Veda**

BIBLIOGRAPHY

Seidenberg, A. "The Origin of Mathematics." *Archive for History of Exact Sciences* 18 (1978): 301–342.

Sen, S. N., and A. K. Bag. *The Sulbasūtras.* New Delhi: Indian National Science Academy, 1983.

SHYĀMA SHĀSTRI *(1762–1827), South Indian poet and composer.* Shyāma Shāstri was the oldest of the three nineteenth-century South Indian poet-composers known as the the "Trinity." His compositions can be recognized by the name Shyāma Krishna, which he inserted in his lyrics as his signature (*mudrā*). Although barely fifty of his songs (*tānavarnam, kriti,* and *svarajati*) have been preserved, they form an important part of the South Indian concert repertoire.

Having grown up in a musical environment, he became an accomplished singer with the help of a visiting musician. Pacchimiriyam Ādiyappayya, a prominent court musician at Tanjāvūr, then became his mentor. (Ādiyappayya's majestic piece in Bhairavi *rāga,* "Viribōni," is widely regarded as the best *tāna varnam* ever composed.)

A hereditary priest, he was entrusted with the responsibility of the Kāmākshi Amman temple in Tiruvārūr, his place of birth, where his ancestors had fled from Kanchipuram in the wake of the fall of Vijayanagar in 1565. The temple idol of Bangāru Kāmākshi, kept in their custody, was installed in a new temple in Tiruvārūr. In his lyrics, Shyāma Shāstri addresses this goddess as Devī, or divine mother.

He chose common as well as rare *rāga*s for his compositions, most of which yield their essence in a rather slow tempo compared to that preferred by Tyāgarāja and most later composers. His pieces are equally appreciated for their subtle rhythmic features and the poetic beauty of his Sanskrit, Telugu, and Tamil lyrics. Ānandabhairavi, an important *rāga,* owes its characteristic form to four of his songs in the concert repertoire. He also developed the *svarajati,* a didactic musical form for which he provided three most impressive examples in the *rāga*s Bhairavi, Tōdi, and Yadukulakāmbhōji.

A specialist in rhythmic intricacies, he employed a technique known as "note-syllables" (*svarākshara*), meaning that some of the sol-fa names (*sā, ri, gā, mā, pā, dhā,* or *ni*), otherwise used to merely represent the notes of a given *rāga,* are so arranged as to coincide with some of the text syllables that constitute his lyrics. Shyāma Shāstri had a predilection for lyrics containing groups of five syllables (e.g., *anudinamu*) that, if articulated through rhythmic syllables (*jati*), mimic a pattern commonly employed by drummers (ta din ki na tom). Another speciality is referred to as dual rhythms, namely the scope he provided for applying two different metric cycles (*tāla*) to some of his compositions.

Although primarily regarded as a scholarly musician and composer, he is also remembered for defeating Kēshavayya, a visiting virtuoso from Andhra who toured the land to challenge musicians patronized by local rulers during musical contests. This episode highlights Shyāma Shāstri's superior mastery of complex musical problems against the backdrop of his secure and uneventful existence, quite unlike the lives led by some his prominent fellow composers. Several of his descendants, including his son Subbarāya Shāstri (a disciple of Tyāgarāja and an important composer in his own right) are regarded as outstanding singers and vina players (*vainika*).

Ludwig Pesch

BIBLIOGRAPHY

Govinda Rao, T. K. *Compositions of* Syāmā Sāstri. Chennai: Ganamandir Publications, 1997.

Sambamoorthy, P. *Great Composers,* vol. 1. Chennai: Indian Music Publishing House, 1978.

Shankar, Vidya. *Subbaraya Sastry's and Annaswamy Sastry's Compositions: Text, Translation, Transliteration, and Notation with Gamaka-Signs.* Chennai: Parampara, 1989.

SIKH INSTITUTIONS AND PARTIES The preoccupation of Sikhs with the political can be traced to Guru Nanak, the founder of Sikhism. His experience of the condition of North Indian society during the fifteenth century inspired his formulation of parallel critiques of the Brahman and the Mulla, the respective representatives of Hindu and Muslim society. Guru Nanak was an eyewitness to the central political event of his time, namely, the change of North Indian power from the Lodi Sultanate to the Mughal empire, initiated by Babur's invasion of India in November 1525. Guru Nanak described this event as having brought inevitable suffering, including the rape and slaughter of innocent people. Although Nanak unambiguously condemned such violence, he was not opposed to violence or to politics, only to that which was unjust, and which stemmed from egoistic desire. He believed that the actions of the ideal ruler had to be grounded in certain norms of behavior derived from spirituality. Nanak translated his ideas into action through the establishment of a commune based on socioethical practices of *simaran* (self-emancipation through remembrance of the divine Name) and *seva* (compassionate service of others), both of which were instituted through the *sadh sangat* (the community of those committed to these principles) and *langar* (free kitchen).

During the reign of Nanak's successors, these early institutions were extended and supplemented with the establishment of the *manji* system run by the *masand*s, an order of territorial deputies who represented the living guru's authority in far-flung places. By the time of the fifth guru, Arjan, it had become common for the Sikhs to refer to the guru as *sacha patshah* (sovereign king) and to the spiritual position of the guru (*gaddi*) as takht (seat of power) and to the congregation as *darbar* (the court), denoting unity between spiritual (*piri*) and political (*miri*) authority. To proclaim Sikhism's fluid synthesis of *miri* and *piri*, the sixth guru, Hargobind, established a platform opposite the Harimandir (Golden Temple) in June 1606, naming it the Akal Takht (Seat of the Timeless). Guru Hargobind thereby inaugurated the tradition of conducting the political affairs of the Sikh community alongside its spiritual and religious development, issuing the first *hukamnama* (edict) asking Sikhs to include in their offerings gifts of weapons and horses. Bhai Gurdas became the first officiant (in contemporary parlance, *jathedar*) of the Akal Takht. Even today, the Akal Takht remains the premier seat of political decision making and the symbol of politico-religious authority, although Sikhs also recognize four other *takht*s: Takht Sri Kesgarh Sahib (Anandpur); Takht Sri Harimandar Sahib (Patna); Takht Sach Khand Hazur Sahib (Nanded); and Takht Sri Damdama Sahib (Talvandi Sabo). All of these four other *takht*s are connected with the life of the tenth guru, Gobind Singh, and the Khalsa, the politico-religious order that he established on the Baisakhi of 1699 and which henceforth became the driving force behind all Sikh politics and institution building.

Post-Guru Period (1708–Present)

During the early decades of the eighteenth century, the Khalsa, as representative of the Sikh body politic and led by the enigmatic figure of Banda Singh Bahadur, was locked in a struggle for its survival against the Mughal state. However, due to the increasing number of invasions by the Afghans during the middle of the eighteenth century, the balance of power in the Punjab had begun to shift in the Khalsa's favor, led at this time by Jassa Singh Ahluwalia. This period also witnessed the emergence of a new and different Sikh collective: the *misl*s, or independent units of Khalsa forces, each with its own *sirdar*, or chieftan. Though they acted independently, the *misl*s would combine and unite under a political configuration known as the Dal Khalsa, or combined Khalsa army, which met twice a year at the Akal Takht in Amritsar. On such occasions the Sikh community would constitute itself as Sarbat Khalsa (literally, the "entire Khalsa"). Collective political decisions taken by the *misl*s were known as *gurmata* (decision according to the guru's will), binding on all members of the Khalsa, even those who were absent at the time the decision was made. Despite the seemingly ad hoc nature of the Sarbat Khalsa and the

Simranjit Singh Mann. President of the Shiromani Akali Dal-Amritsar. In the Sangrur district of Punjab, in early June 2005, the fiery Sikh leader was arrested in connection with four different cases of sedition against the Indian government. INDIA TODAY.

gurmata, this institution nevertheless enabled the Dal Khalsa to act in a united manner, even though it was physically divided into twelve independent *misl*s. Despite the fall of the Mughal empire by the late eighteenth century (an event that also heralded rise to power of the British East India Company) the Sikh *misl*s degenerated into internecine warfare. Eventually the twelve independent *misl*s were superseded by the Sukerchakia *misl*, whose leader, Ranjit Singh, emerged as the supreme ruler or maharajah of the Punjab, establishing his independent Sikh kingdom there. Ranjit Singh ruled as the chief representative of what came to be known as the Sarkar Khalsa, or government of the Khalsa. Although his kingdom was administered from Lahore in the name of the Khalsa, Ranjit Singh also assumed trusteeship of the Harimandar and the Akal Takht, managing the affairs of these two premier religio-political institutions of the Sikhs through his trusted *sirdar*s.

The death of Ranjit Singh in 1839 was followed by a period of conflict and eventual surrender of the Sikh kingdom to the British in 1849; the British also took control of the Akal Takht and Harimandar complex. For the Sikhs this loss of political sovereignty ushered in a period of chaos, confusion, and humiliation. During this period (1850s to early 1870s) the British pushed through radical measures for the economic advancement of the Punjab, bringing about improvements in communication and education. In particular, the creation of a network of English-language mission schools helped to foster a new generation of Western-educated Sikh leaders who made it a priority to revive the pre-colonial Sikh tradition, which they believed had slipped into decadence following the demise of Ranjit Singh's kingdom. In 1873 a group of prominent Sikhs convened a series of meetings in Amritsar that eventually led to the formation of a society called the Singh Sabha, which would lay the foundations for modern Sikh political institutions to emerge in the twentieth century. The founders of the first Singh Sabha were mainly conservative Sikhs, like Baba Khem Singh Bedi, who emphasized caste distinctions, tolerated idol worship, and maintained close ties with Hindus. Such views naturally antagonized reformist Sikhs, who emphasized a more pristine version of Khalsa identity (Tat Khalsa), which also found support with British administrators eager to promote the view that Sikhism was in danger of merging back into Hinduism if it lost its Khalsa identity. By 1879 the more radical members of the Singh Sabha had broken away to form a second branch of the Singh Sabha based at Lahore. Within a few years the radical Lahore Singh Sabha, guided by personalities like Kahn Singh Nabha, Giani Ditt Singh, and Bhai Vir Singh, completely superseded the Amritsar Singh Sabha as the result of a massive campaign of expansion, revivalist teachings, and political canvassing. By the last decade of the nineteenth century, all Punjabi cities and many villages had flourishing Singh Sabhas. However, given the sheer numbers of these organizations and with increasing need to consolidate mainstream Sikh opinion, the Amritsar and Lahore Singh Sabhas were merged in 1902 into a single representative body called the Chief Khalsa Diwan (CKD), whose explicit purpose was to represent all Sikhs in matters of religion and to further their political position in the province at a time of growing political rivalry and separation among Hindu, Muslim, and Sikh communities.

Although one of the CKD's professed objectives was to safeguard the political rights of the Sikh community, its political stance was compromised from the outset by its need to maintain cordial relations with the British rulers. CKD leaders were therefore opposed to the agitational politics that had become the norm during the first decades of the twentieth century. Out of step with the anticolonial stance of the Indian National Congress and the Muslim League, who had successfully campaigned for separate electorates and proportional representation for Hindus and Muslims, respectively, the CKD ended up far short of its expected share of the electoral seats in the Punjab Council. As a consequence, it was eventually superseded by a more strident voice in Sikh politics, the Akali movement.

In 1919 the CKD was dissolved into another organization, the Central Sikh League, which in turn gave rise to two separate organizations in 1920: the Shiromani Akali Dal (SAD) and the Shiromani Gurdwara Parbandhak Committee (SGPC). The SAD was founded on 14 December 1920 in the hope of protecting the political rights of Sikhs, to preserve their religious heritage, and to represent them in public bodies and legislative councils set up by the British. Closely related to the SAD was the SGPC, which was essentially an organization that administered the historical Sikh shrines and under whose control they were to function. Within three years of its formation, the SAD became the premier political party of the Sikhs, and its control over Sikh and Punjabi politics is still powerful today. Soon after its inauguration, the SAD aligned itself with the Indian National Congress and launched a campaign of peaceful agitation against the British, and immediately following, a separate agitation to wrest control of historical Sikh shrines from the *mahants*—the hereditary proprietors of the sacred Sikh shrines, most of whom were descended from the order of Udasis, wandering Hindu ascetics who had taken over the shrines during the time of Ranjit Singh, and many of whom were accused of misappropriating Gurdwara funds for personal gain. This agitation culminated in 1925 with the passing of the Sikh Gurdwaras Act, which, through the SGPC, gave the Sikh community the rights to possess and manage their own shrines through an electoral process. The first leader of the SAD, Baba Kharak Singh, lost the leadership in 1926 to Master Tara Singh, who continued to steer its fortunes for three decades.

Political events and other episodes that have occurred in Punjab since 1925 are a testimony to the influence and longevity of the SAD and SGPC partnership. Key achievements include the reformulation and universal approval of the document called *Sikh Rahit Maryada* (Sikh Code of Conduct) published by the SGPC in the 1950s, and the Indian government's granting of Punjabi Suba (Punjabi state) to the Punjab. The severest test for the SAD and SGPC occurred during the 1980s, a fateful decade that saw a protracted political battle against Indira Gandhi's Congress Party; internal challenges from clerical organizations like the Damdami Taksal, led by the charismatic preacher Sant Jarnail Singh Bhindranwale; the Indian army's assault on the Golden Temple complex; and the destruction of the Akal Takht in June 1984 as part of the army's effort to oust Bhindranwale and his supporters. The assassination of Indira Gandhi by two of her Sikh guards in October 1984 followed, and thereafter Sikh insurgent groups demanded a separatist state called Khalistan. During the 1990s, coinciding with the rise of the Bharatiya Janata Party and the demise of the Congress Party, the SAD split into various factions: Akali Dal (Badal) led by former chief minister of Punjab, Parkash Singh Badal; Akali Dal (Longowal) led by Surjit Singh Barnala; and Akali Dal (Mann) led by former police officer Simranjit Singh Mann. Perhaps the real test for the SAD and SGPC is yet to come, as Sikhs living outside Punjab, constantly growing in numbers and financial strength, seek to articulate a notion of Sikh political sovereignty, derived from the dual sources of Sikhism's supreme authority: Guru Granth Sahib and the lived experience of its Khalsa Panth.

Arvind-Pal S. Mandair

See also **Gandhi, Indira; Sikhism; Singh, Maharaja Ranjit**

BIBLIOGRAPHY

Grewal, J. S. *A Short History of the Akalis.* Chandigarh: Punjab Studies Publications, 1996.
McLeod, W. H. *Sikhism.* London: Penguin, 1997.
Singh, Major Gurmukh. "Akali Dal, Shiromani." In *The Encyclopedia of Sikhism*, vol. 1, edited by Harbans Singh, Patiala: Punjabi University, 1995.
Singh, Mohinder. *The Akali Movement.* Delhi: Macmillan, 1978.

SIKHISM

SIKHISM Sikhism is the religious faith of those who call themselves Sikhs, the followers of Guru Nanak, his nine successors and their teachings, embodied in the Guru Granth Sahib, the sacred scripture of the Sikhs. The Sikh population worldwide at the beginning of the twenty-first century was estimated at 20 million; of these, 17 million reside in India, with 14 million living in Punjab. Of the 2 million or so Sikhs who live outside India, the Sikh diaspora, the majority are in Great Britain, the United States, and Canada.

Origins and Early Sikh History

Sikhism originated in the Punjab region of northwestern India during a time when many religious teachers, known as "Sants," were seeking to reconcile the two opposing dominant faiths, Hinduism and Islam. The Sants expressed their teachings in vernacular poetry based on inner experience. Although the teachings of Guru Nanak were broadly aligned with some of the Sants, his own mission is thought to have emerged out of his direct experience of the divine, initiated with the words *na koi Hindu, na koi Mussalman* . . . ("there is no

Sikh Worshiper. A Sikh pilgrim worshiping at a stream in Anandpur Sahib, the "Holy City of Bliss." It has been a sacred site for centuries, closely linked with Sikhs' religious traditions and history. CHRIS LISLE / CORBIS.

Hindu, there is no Muslim") signaling a third way that was to become the Nanak Panth, or the path of Nanak. The first community of his disciples, those who chose to follow Nanak as their Guru (divine teacher), was composed primarily of former Hindus, who came to call themselves his "Sikhs" (followers).

For the details of Guru Nanak's life Sikh tradition relies on a body of hagiographical literature called the *janamsakhi*s (life testimonies), which appeared a century and a half after Nanak's death, undergoing expansion for sometime until printed editions were made in the nineteenth century. Sikhs today mainly rely on the accounts given in the Puratan Janamsakhi, which expounds four main cycles in Nanak's life story. In the first cycle, Nanak was born in 1469 in Talwandi, a village 40 miles (64 km) from Lahore, and was acclaimed by Muslims and Hindus alike as a future religious leader. In the second cycle, Nanak was married at twelve, his wife joining him at age nineteen; they had two sons. Nanak experienced difficulty settling into any profession, trying his hand as a herdsman, a trader, and finally as an accountant for a local official at Sultanpur. Nanak seemed to be mainly preoccupied with spiritual concerns, preferring the company of holy men and ascetics. Together with his closest associate, a Muslim bard named Mardana, Nanak organized regular nightly singing of devotional hymns, going to bathe in a nearby river before daybreak. During one of these sessions, at age thirty, Nanak underwent his first major mystical experience, in which he received a calling to teach people a path of devotion to the divine Name. According to the Puratan Janamsakhi, shortly after this experience Nanak entered the third phase of his life, in which he spent the next twelve years traveling eastward to Banaras (Varanasi), Bengal, and Orissa, southward to Tamil Nadu and Sri Lanka, northward to Tibet, and finally westward to the Muslim regions as far as Mecca, Medina, and Baghdad. In the final phase of his life at about the age of fifty, Nanak founded a settlement at Kartarpur where he led a community of disciples, instructing them in spiritual practice and study, with *nam simaran* (remembrance of the Name) and *kirtan* (singing hymns of praise) regular features of devotion. At the same time he insisted that his disciples remain fully involved in worldly affairs by doing practical labor (Nanak himself tended his own crops) while maintaining a regular family life.

Shortly before his death in 1539 at age seventy, Guru Nanak's appointment of a successor not only inaugurated a two-centuries long politico-spiritual lineage, with each successor taking the title of Guru, but also marked a break with prior Sant practice of not appointing spiritual successors. During the next two centuries the early Sikh Panth (community) underwent significant expansion and development into a defined and disciplined order, with different steps taking place under successive Gurus. The second Guru, Angad (b. 1504; r. 1539–1552) collected Nanak's hymns, developed the alphabetic script called Gurmukhi ("from the Guru's mouth"), and institutionalized the *langar*, or communal kitchen, to feed disciples who came to visit Nanak's *dharamsala*s. Guru Amardas (b. 1479; r. 1552–1574), the third Guru, encouraged the observance of separate Sikh shrines, pilgrimage traditions and festivals, as well as instituting the *manji* system of supervising distant congregations. The fourth Guru, Ramdas (b. 1534; r. 1574–1581), founded a new center called Ramdaspur (later named Amritsar), where he supervised the excavation of the sacred pool that later became the central site of Sikh pilgrimage. Guru Ramdas appointed *masand*s, or deputies, to represent the Guru's authority in his more dispersed congregations.

Sikhism became more firmly established under the fifth Guru Arjan (b. 1563; r. 1581–1606), who introduced several important innovations. Relying on extant collections, Arjan supervised the compilation and canonization of a scripture, the Adi Granth ("original text"), which contains the compositions of Sikh Gurus and other non-Sikh saints. The completion of the Harimandir temple, and the installation therein of the Adi Granth in 1604, proved to be highly significant for molding Sikh identity. Guru Arjan also founded new towns, such as Tarn Taran, Kartarpur, and Sri Hargobindpur, and extended trading links across India's northwestern frontier into Afghanistan and beyond. The increasing success and expansion of the Sikhs in Punjab inevitably led to confrontation with the Mughal authority under the emperor Jahangir. Guru Arjan was accused of supporting a rebellion led by Jahangir's son Amir Khushru. Charges of sedition were followed by imprisonment and finally execution in Lahore in 1606. Guru Arjan's martyrdom led to increased militarization and overt political involvement under his son and successor, the sixth Guru Hargobind (b. 1595; r. 1606–1644), symbolized by his donning of two swords, one representing spiritual authority (*miri*), the other representing political authority (*piri*). Maintaining a small but effective army, Guru Hargobind consciously prepared the Sikhs to resist willful state oppression. Although confrontation receded during the tenure of his successor Gurus, Har Rai and Har Krishan, they nevertheless maintained a similar style of leadership with a retinue of armed followers. It was the ninth Guru, Tegh Bahadur (b. 1621; r. 1664–1675), who again was forced to confront the increasingly restrictive policies of Jahangir's grandson, the emperor Aurangzeb (r. 1658–1707), which included enforcement of Islamic laws and taxes and the replacement of local Hindu temples by Muslim mosques. Guru Tegh Bahadur's active resistance against such policies, his public defense of Hindus' rights to practice their religion freely, and his own refusal to accept Islam under pain of death led to his imprisonment and execution in Delhi's Chandni Chowk in 1675.

The Sikh Panth's involvement in political resistance came to a climax with the tenth Guru, Gobind Singh (b. 1666; r. 1675–1708). Shortly after the execution of his father, the ninth Guru, the young Gobind Rai moved from Anandpur deeper into the Himalayan foothills. Neighboring hill chieftans, nervous about the young Guru's increasing power, unsuccessfully attacked his men at Bhangani. Following this episode the Guru moved back to Anandpur, where he successfully fought a Mughal force at Nadaun. The Guru built several other fortresses at Anandpur, Lohgarh, Keshgarh, and Fategarh. His best-known contribution to the development of Sikhism was to redefine the very core of the Sikh Panth as a military-cum-spiritual order, the Khalsa ("sovereign" or "free"). According to tradition, he called his followers to assemble for the Baisakhi festival in 1699 at Anandpur.

There he called for five volunteers to pass a test of absolute loyalty. Those who passed the test, the so-called *panj piare* (five beloved ones) were initiated into the new Khalsa order by a ceremonial rite called *khande ka pahul* (baptism of the double-edged sword), thus forming the nucleus of a sovereign, casteless community. Each member of the Khalsa order undertook to wear the five external symbols, or five "K"s (*kesh*, long, uncut hair; *kirpan*, short sword; *kanga*, comb; *kara*, steel bracelet; *kaccha*, breeches), to adhere to a formal code of conduct (*rahit*), and to relinquish family surnames, with males assuming the name Singh (lion) and females assuming the name Kaur (princess), thereby removing sexual inequality while maintaining gender difference. The Guru in turn received the same initiation from the *panj piare*, thereby assuming the name Singh and signifying a merger of identities between Guru and disciples. Many thousands more accepted this initiation. The last nine years of Guru Gobind Singh's life were spent either in protracted battles against the combined forces of Aurangzeb and the hill rajas, in which the Guru lost his four sons and his mother, himself becoming a fugitive relentlessly hunted by the Mughals. Despite these setbacks, the Guru resurrected his army, and upon Aurangzeb's death supported the succession of his son Bahadur Shah to the throne. While at Nander, the Guru commissioned a hermit named Banda Singh to inflict punishment on Wazir Khan, one of Aurangzeb's generals.

The tenth Guru was a prolific writer, composing literature in Braj, Hindi, Persian, and Sanskrit. Much of this literature forms the Dasam Granth (Book of the Tenth Master), which contains devotional hymns such as *Jaap*, *Svaye*, *Chaupas*, mythological treatises such as *Chandi Ki Var* (Tales of the goddess), and a semiautobiographical work *Bachitar Natak* (The wonderful drama). Tradition records that Guru Gobind Singh also recomposed from memory the entire contents of the Adi Granth, since the extant copies were either lost during his battles, or remained in the hands of rival claimants to the Guru's position. Guru Gobind Singh died in 1708 at the hands of an assassin. Before his death, however, he declared the line of living Gurus to be at an end, issuing a command for the Sikh community to look to dual sources of authority, namely, the scriptural text (Adi Granth), which henceforth became known as the Guru Granth Sahib, and the body politic of the Khalsa Panth.

The Post-Guru Period

The Sikhs faced their most difficult period during the first few decades of the eighteenth century, their fortunes depending on the degree to which they could assert themselves against Mughal forces in the southeast and the steadily increasing incursions of the Afghans in the northwest, at the same time jockeying for position with the local Hindu princes in Punjab.

By the middle of the eighteenth century, the Sikhs had forged themselves into twelve independent militia units, or *misl*s, which were instrumental in eventually dislodging the Mughals from power. The twelve *misl*s were finally unified by the most illustrious Sikh ruler, Maharaja Ranjit Singh, who took Lahore and was proclaimed maharaja of the Punjab. After a series of successful campaigns against the Afghans and Pathans, Ranjit Singh had also secured India's northwestern frontier by the 1820s. Among other things, Maharajah Ranjit Singh is celebrated as the benefactor of the Harimandir (Golden Temple) in Amritsar, which he covered in gold leaf. Shortly after the maharaja's death in 1839, however, in-fighting broke out among his successors, the Sikh kingdom fell into disarray, and, after a series of hard-fought battles, was annexed by the British Raj in 1849.

Emergence of Modern Sikhism

The advent of British colonial rule not only marks the entry of Sikhism into Western modernity, but also the emergence of three reform movements (the Nirankaris, the Namdharis, and the Singh Sabha movement), each attempting to revive a sense of separate religious identity among Sikhs at a time when most such traditions were considered to be sects of Hinduism. The Namdharis, founded by Baba Dyal Das (1783–1853), took their name from their condemnation of idolatry and participation in Hindu rituals that had become prevalent among many Sikhs. The Namdharis, founded by Baba Ram Singh (1816–1884), came to be regarded as a separatist movement when they instituted a separate baptismal ritual and code of conduct. Ram Singh advocated strict vegetarianism, the wearing of all-white dress, and loud chanting, which led to their nickname, *kukas* (howlers), because of their spontaneous outbursts during devotional trances. In 1871 the Namdharis came into conflict with the British when they violently opposed the colonial administration's reintroduction of cow slaughter (previously banned by Maharaja Ranjit Singh), and in the process killed Muslim butchers in Amritsar and Ludhiana. The British ruthlessly suppressed the uprising by tying sixty-five Namdharis to the mouths of cannons, blowing them to pieces.

By far the most influential Sikh reformist movement was the Singh Sabha, founded in 1863 under aristocratic patronage. By 1879 the movement had suffered an internal schism that led to the formation of the conservative Amritsar-based faction, led by Baba Khem Singh Bedi, and the more radical (and ultimately far more successful) Lahore-based faction, led initially by Giani Ditt Singh and Principal Gurmukh Singh, and subsequently by

Kahn Singh Nabha, Teja Singh, Vir Singh, and Jodh Singh. Through its political functionary, the Chief Khalsa Diwan (CKD), a body set up in 1902 to jointly conduct the affairs of the Amritsar and Lahore factions, the Singh Sabha movement achieved the most successful reinterpretation of Sikhism adapted to modernity, which has, until recently, exerted a hegemonic influence on Sikh identity. Their reformulation was based on the colonially inspired distinction between, on the one hand, a monotheistic-historical Sikhism centered on the authority of a clearly recognizable scripture and embodied by the Tat (authentic) Khalsa ideal, and on the other hand, a pantheistic ahistorical Hinduism. Crucially the Singh Sabha redefined the means by which the tradition was communicated. Making use of British colonial patronage and new forms of transportation, commerce, and communication (especially the printing press), the Singh Sabhas were able to develop an extensive network of chapters across North India. Through the combined effect of tract publications and more systematic works of theology and history, the leading Singh Sabha scholars redefined the doctrinal foundations of Sikhism. Major political successes include the passing of the Anand Marriage Act in 1909, which prescribed circumambulation of the Guru Granth Sahib in Sikh marriages, replacing circumambulation of the Vedic fire. Under the banner of the Akali Dal Party, political successors to the CKD, a more violent campaign was launched in the early 1920s to wrest control of the Harimandir and other historical *gurdwara*s from the Mahants or traditional custodians, resulting in the Sikh Gurdwaras Act of 1925, which handed administration of these *gurdwara*s back to the Shiromani Gurdwara Parbandhak Committee (SGPC), an elected body dominated by the Akali Dal, which continues to dominate the religious and political affairs of the Sikh Panth. An important milestone for the SGPC was the publication of the *Sikh Rahit Maryada*, or Sikh Code of Conduct, in the 1950's, which guaranteed greater uniformity of Sikh religious practices.

Following British withdrawal in 1947, the partition of India split the traditional Sikh homeland of Punjab into two parts, its western half going to Pakistan, and its eastern to India, with its capital in Amritsar. Amid widescale ethnic and religious violence, approximately 3 million Sikhs were displaced from western Punjab, fleeing across a hastily, ineptly drawn border to India's Punjab. At the time of partition, there were some who called for the creation of a Sikh homeland, to be called Sikhistan or Khalistan, but this suggestion received no official support. However, the desire to create a majority Sikh state in Indian Punjab encouraged the Akali Dal to agitate for a Punjabi-speaking state as part of the Indian Union, which was achieved in 1966 through the separation of Sikh-majority Punjab from Hindu-majority Haryana.

Continuing this tradition of political agitation into the late 1970s and early 1980s (when an increasingly Hindu-dominated India viewed Sikh demands for improving Punjab's economic resources with hostility) resulted in a violent confrontation between the central government of India, led by Indira Gandhi, and groups of Sikh militants. Events culminated in June 1984, when Prime Minister Gandhi ordered India's army to launch its deadly Operation Bluestar, sending tanks into Amritsar's Golden Temple to remove Sikh militants, led by the charismatic preacher Sant Jarnail Singh Bhindranwale, killing over a thousand Sikhs according to government records. In retaliation, Indira Ganhi was assassinated that October by two of her Sikh bodyguards; subsequently Hindu mobs launched reprisals against Sikhs, killing thousands in Delhi alone. More than five thousand innocent Sikhs were killed that November throughout India. Violence escalated throughout the late 1980s and early 1990s as young Sikh militants, supported by Sikhs of the diaspora, revived the demand for a separate Sikh Khalistan.

Sikh Theological Doctrine, Worship, and Customs

The distinctive nature of Sikhism may be traced from Guru Nanak himself, embodied in his hymns that are part of the Adi Granth, and amplified in the lives and works of his nine Guru successors, explained in the exegetical writings of Sikh scholars, such as Bhai Gurdas in the sixteenth century, or Bhai Vir Singh in the twentieth century. For devout Sikhs the most succinct expression of Nanak's thought is encapsulated in the syllable *ik oankar*, which appears at the very beginning of Nanak's *Japji Sahib* (the first and most authoritative hymn in the Adi Granth), and which is often translated in conformity to the rationalized idiom of monotheism as "One God Exists," though it is more accurately translated as "The One Absolute, Manifested through Primal Word-Sound." According to Guru Nanak, the Absolute is non-dual (One). From the conceptual standpoint of the human ego, however, the Absolute is perceived dualistically in terms of either/or distinctions, such as *nirgun/sargun* (without qualities/with qualities; formless/form), or in terms of the difference between God and man. A person limited to mere conceptuality is *manmukh* (ego-centered individual) and therefore unfree, ignorant, limited by a self-generating consciousness. For Guru Nanak, the Absolute cannot be conceptualized or obtained through rituals (*sochai soch na hovi*), through mere silencing of the mind (*chupai chup na hovi*), or by satisfying one's cravings (*bhukhian bhuk na uttari*). The Absolute can only be realized through experience. As such, the nonduality of the Absolute is conceptually inseparable from the notion of freedom (*mukti*) found in the classic mystical themes of separation and fusion between lover and beloved. To realize the One, the individual must be grounded in a state of existence that relinquishes the individuality of the self, so that what remains when ego is abandoned—the *man* (heart/mind/soul)—emerges as the lover and is able to merge with the Other (its Beloved). In this state, one instinctively avoids relating to the One in terms of subject and object. Such a realized individual (*gurmukh*) no longer represents the Absolute to himself, since the conscious distinction between self and other, I and not-I, lover and beloved, disappears, leaving an ecstatic and purely spontaneous form of existence (*sahaj*).

In Sikh tradition, the figure of the *gurmukh* and the spontaneous freedom associated with it are seen as an intensely creative form of existence that is "oriented toward the guru" and aligned with the divine order (*hukam*) yet released from the mechanism of individuation (*haumai*). The transition from duality to nonduality (or, stated otherwise, the transition from *manmukh* to *gurmukh*) turns on the efficacy of *naam* (the Name), which is both the object of love and the means of loving attachment to the beloved. Being the point of contact between transcendence (God) and immanence (world), *naam* is the medium by which the ego loses itself in human communication with others, that is, the medium par excellence for experiencing the condition of nonduality. In Nanak's hymns, *naam* is not a particular word or mantra, but is both written within and yet comprises the vibration of the cosmos. Being the link between mystic interiority and worldly action, *naam* is appropriated by the *gurmukh* through the practice of *simaran* (constant remembrance or repetition of the Name)—a form of meditation in which the One simultaneously becomes the focus of an individual's awareness (*surati*) and his motivation to perform righteous action (*karam kamahe*). However, *naam* cannot be obtained voluntarily. Its attainment depends on grace or the favorable glance of the Guru (*kirpa/nadar*), receiving which the individual can change his predestined nature (*likhia nal*) into the spontaneous being of the *gurmukh*, which no longer generates *samskāras* (the soul passed from one life to another). Sikhs therefore hold a belief in the transmigration of souls, which come and go (*avan jan*) until one is liberated from the bonds of the ego. From the standpoint of the *gurmukh*, the conceptual duality between religion and politics, mysticism and violence, and so on, becomes superfluous, as is evident in the lived experience of the Sikh Gurus, for whom there was no contradiction between mystical experience and the life of a soldier or householder.

As one of the central terms in Sikh doctrine, the term "Guru" takes on theologico-political connotations that go well beyond its meaning and application in Hinduism, where it is limited to a teacher, initially of worldly knowledge, or a conveyor of spiritual insight. In Sikhism

the term "Guru" automatically incorporates this earlier meaning, referring thereby to Guru Nanak and his nine successor Gurus. Metaphorically it refers to the same divine light manifested in all ten Gurus; practically it serves to indicate the authority vested in the name "Nanak." Thus the hymns of the different Gurus in the Adi Granth are cited by referring to their respective composers as sequential locations (*mahala*s) for the manifestation of the name "Nanak." Just before the death of the tenth Nanak, Guru Gobind Singh, authority was jointly vested, on the one hand, in the Adi Granth (henceforth Guru Granth Sahib), leading to the doctrine of scripture or Word as Guru (*shabad-guru*), and on the other hand, in the collective wisdom of the initiated community, the Khalsa, giving the doctrine of Panth as Guru (*guru-panth*). Underpinning all of these notions is the fourth notion of Guru in Sikhism, namely, the *satguru*, or true Guru, which recurs in the hymns as identical to the divine principle itself: that which bestows or gives to those who follow in the way (*hukam*).

Sikh congregational worship takes place in the *gurdwara* (door of the Guru), which is essentially any building in which the Guru Granth Sahib can be appropriately installed. The modern *gurdwara* has evolved out of the *dharamsala*s (resting places) established by Guru Nanak during his travels. The principal congregational activities in the *gurdwara* include *kirtan* (the singing of hymns), *katha vachic* (narrative exposition of Sikh philosophy and history), and more recently, *akhand path* (unbroken recitation of the entire Guru Granth Sahib), funeral services, and marriage ceremonies. Any adult Sikh, male or female, can conduct religious ceremonies. Specialized readers of the sacred texts, called *granthi*s, and professional singers are qualified to perform congregational duties by skill rather than by ritual ordination. In most *gurdwara*s meditational worship begins before dawn with recitals of Guru Nanak's *Asa di Var*, followed at dawn with his *Japji*, and by Guru Gobind Singh's *Jaap*.

Sikh festivals known as *gurpurb*s (the rising of a guru) are associated with an event in the respective Guru's life. The most important *gurpurb*s are Guru Nanak's birthday, celebrated on the full moon in November, Guru Gobind Singh's birthday (December–January), and the martyrdoms of Guru Arjan and Tegh Bahadur (May–June), all of which follow a lunar calendar. Sikh festivals that follow a solar calendar include Baisakhi and Divali. Baisakhi, celebrated as New Year's Day in North India, usually falls on the thirteenth of April. Originally a grain harvest festival for Hindus, it has acquired particular importance for Sikhs due to Guru Gobind Singh's creation of the Khalsa on Baisakhi of 1699. Sikhs today celebrate Baisakhi as a historical birthday for the community. Similarly, while for Hindus Divali is a festival of lights celebrating the return of Ram Chandra to Ayodhya, for Sikhs Divali marks the return of the sixth Guru Hargobind from his imprisonment by the Mughal emperor Jahangir. Another Sikh festival is Hola Mohalla, the day after Holi (which Hindus celebrate by freely throwing colored powder on each other to commemorate an event in the life of Prahlad, a devotee of Vishnu). Sikhs follow the same custom but for different reasons. The emphasis Guru Gobind Singh gave to Sikh observance was to channel people's energies toward military exercises through organized athletic and literary contests.

Arvind-Pal S. Mandair

See also **Amritsar; Bahadur Shah I; Gandhi, Indira; Guru Nanak; Jahangir; Sikh Institutions and Parties; Singh, Maharaja Ranjit**

BIBLIOGRAPHY

Grewal, J. S. *The Sikhs of the Punjab.* New Delhi: Cambridge University Press, 1990.
Macauliffe, Max Arthur. *The Sikh Religion: Its Gurus, Sacred Writings, and Authors.* 6 vols. New Delhi: S. Chand and Co., 1986.
McLeod, W. H. *Textual Sources for the Study of Sikhism.* Manchester, U.K.: Manchester University Press, 1984.
———. *Sikhism.* London: Penguin, 1997.
McLeod, W. H., and Karine Schomer, eds. *The Sants: Studies in a Devotional Tradition of India.* New Delhi: Motilalal Banarsidass, 1987.
Oberoi, Harjot. The *Construction of Religious Boundaries: Culture, Identity, and Diversity in the Sikh Tradition.* New Delhi: Oxford University Press, 1994.
Singh, Harbans, ed. *The Encyclopedia of Sikhism.* 2nd ed. Patiala: Punjabi University, 1996.

SIKKIM. *See* **Geography.**

SIMLA The capital (since 1966) of Himachal Pradesh, Simla had a population of 145,000 in 2001. Its name is derived from the Hindu goddess Shyamali. Located at an altitude of about 7,900 feet (2,400 meters) above sea level, it was built as a "hill station" by the British in 1819 after they had acquired the location in the Gurkha War. From 1865 to 1939 it served as the summer capital of British India. The Kalka-Simla railway, completed in 1903, links Simla with the North Indian plains.

In July 1945 Viceroy Lord Wavell convened the Simla Conference, attended by delegates of the Indian National Congress and the Muslim League. Lord Wavell was eager to install an interim national government, as he was faced with serious postwar problems, among them the demobilization of the large Indian army of about 2 million soldiers.

The conference failed because Mohammad Ali Jinnah, president of the Muslim League, insisted on nominating all Muslim members of the national government, which the National Congress would not accept, even though its president at the time was Maulana Abul Kalam Azad, a prominent Muslim. Jinnah's veto, which Wavell accepted, raised Jinnah's political stature.

Another Simla Conference of historical importance was held in 1972. Indian prime minister Indira Gandhi and the president of Pakistan, Zulfikar Ali Bhutto, met at Simla after Bangladesh seceded from Pakistan in December 1971. During the war of secession, 90,000 Pakistani soldiers had surrendered to the Indian army. Bhutto had to make a number of concessions in order to repatriate them. Gandhi insisted that Pakistan settle all future disputes with India, including Kashmir, solely through bilateral negotiations. Pakistan tried to forget this promise as soon as its prisoners were returned, and Simla thus became a symbol of political frustrations.

Dietmar Rothermund

BIBLIOGRAPHY

Mansegh, N., and E. W. R. Lunby, eds. *Constitutional Relations between Britain and India: The Transfer of Power.* 11 vols. London: Her Majesty's Stationery Office, 1970–1982. Vol. V: *The Simla Conference, Background and Proceedings, 1 September 1944–28 July 1945* (1974).

SIND One of Pakistan's four provinces, Sind occupies the southeastern corner of the country, covering 54,407 square miles (140,913 sq. km), about the area of England. Sind is bounded on the south by the Arabian Sea, on the west and north by Balochistan and Punjab provinces, and on the east by India. Sindi, the native language of the province, is one of the major spoken languages of Pakistan, with a considerable literature.

Sind was conquered by Alexander the Great in 325 B.C. and was one of the first areas on the Indian subcontinent to be influenced by Arab invaders in the early eighth century A.D. During the fifteenth and sixteenth centuries, it came under Mughal Muslim domination. The administrative province of Sind was carved out of the much larger province of Bombay in British India in 1936. Sind's Muslim majority destined that the area would become one of the principal provinces of independent Pakistan after partition in August 1947. Yet unlike the strong identification of Muslim populations in northern and central India with Pakistani nationalism, the political leadership of Sind was not closely aligned with the Muslim League of Pakistan's founder, Mohammad Ali Jinnah. Sind lost its status as an autonomous province when Pakistan's Constituent Assembly in 1955 adopted its "One-Unit Plan" for West Pakistan. Sind's provincial assembly and political identity were restored with the restoration of Pakistan's federal system in 1970.

Sind's population stood at 30 million in 2003, with roughly half its people living in urban centers, the largest being Karachi, Hyderabad, and Sukkur. Sindi society is multiethnic. Sindi identity itself contains different strains historically, but a basic distinction is made between Sindis and Muhajirs ("immigrants"), an urban Urdu-speaking population that traces its origins to immigration from North India after Partition. Subsequently, large numbers of Punjabis and Pathans from the North-West Frontier, as well as Baluchis, migrated to Sind from other provinces within Pakistan. Non-Muslim religious minorities dominated Sind's cities before the Hindu population fled with partition. Only very small Hindu, Christian, and Parsi (Zoroastrian) communities remain in the province.

A strong tradition of Sindi "nationalism" exists. Nationalists have championed greater provincial autonomy and have sought to defend politically and economically those in the population who have their roots in Sind. Sindi nationalists have long resented Pakistan's politically dominant Punjabi community. They chafed at the allotment, after independence, of large tracts of irrigated land to absentee Punjabi landlords, mainly from Pakistan's ruling Punjabi bureaucratic and military elites. Migrating Punjabis are also resented for taking over larger businesses and industries in the province. An unresolved and continuing bone of contention between Sindi nationalists and successive national governments of Pakistan has been the construction of numerous barrages and canals, which divert much of the Indus River's flow to the Punjab.

Muhajirs had been prominent in the national bureaucracy until Pakistan's capital shifted from Karachi to Islamabad in northern Punjab in 1960. Under Zulfikar Ali Bhutto, the first native Sindi prime minister of Pakistan, a quota system was introduced, guaranteeing that 60 percent of jobs and educational admissions provincially would effectively be reserved for rural Sindis, mostly at the expense of Muhajirs. An attempt to impose Sindi as the province's official language incensed the Urdu-speaking Muhajirs and occasioned riots in 1972. The Pakistan army was called in to quell the disturbances. Bhutto's policies of nationalizing industry also fell particularly hard on wealthy Muhajir businessmen.

Dedicated Sindi nationalists have never succeeded in an election. Pakistan's popular People's Party has dominated the province, its strongholds lying particularly in the rural districts of Sind, especially Larkara, the home district of the large landholding Bhutto family. During recent years, the county's religious parties have expanded

their influence in the province, notably in Karachi. Although many Sindis follow a relaxed, though devout, Sufi Islamic tradition, there have been some inroads of more orthodox, rigid Islamic beliefs and practices, especially traceable to the growing number of party-affiliated religious schools.

Another challenge to the Sindi nationalists came in 1984 with the organized political opposition of the Muhajirs, latter called Muttahida Quami Mahaz (MQM), or Immigrant People's Movement. Appealing mostly to urban dwellers from the educated middle and lower middle classes, the MQM has sought to break the political grip of the landlord class in provincial politics. To force attention to their political and economic grievances, the often fractious movement has at times formed alliances with national parties. But the MQM also has a vivid history of confrontation with the central government, which it accuses of using divide-and-rule tactics to disenfranchise Muhajars. In 1995 MQM-instigated interethnic violence, centered in Karachi, was brutally put down by government security forces, and in 1998 Governor's rule was imposed on the province, and military tribunals were introduced.

In human development terms, measured by achievements in health and education and real gross domestic product (GDP) per capita, Sind ranks second among Pakistan's provinces. However, disaggregating the indices presents striking variability. Sind has the highest overall literacy rate at 51 percent of the population, but along with Baluchistan, the lowest school enrollment and the lowest infant survival rate. At the same time, Sind has Pakistan's highest real GDP per capita. This disparity is explained by the province's deep urban-rural divide. While urban Sind comes out highest on combined human development indexes, rural Sind ranks lowest among the four provinces.

Much of Sind is desert. Seasonal rains ordinarily do not exceed 7 inches (18 cm) per annum, and many sections of the province often receive much less. Although Sind contains only 7 million acres of cultivatable land, it is basically an agrarian province. Cropped areas, mostly in cotton, wheat, and rice, are irrigated from the Indus River, which carries water from the Himalayas and Karakoram ranges in the distant north. On 1 April 1948 India had cut off the flow of water from the Indus headwaters under its control. With the intercession of the World Bank, an agreement acceptable to both governments was reached in 1960. That treaty, commonly known as the Indus Water Treaty, is the only major peaceful agreement ever reached by India and Pakistan and, despite subsequent wars and tensions, it remains in force.

Marvin G. Weinbaum

See also **Pakistan and India**

BIBLIOGRAPHY

Blood, Peter R., ed. *Pakistan: A County Study*. Washington, D.C.: Library of Congress, 1994.

Burki, Shahid Javed. *Pakistan under Bhutto, 1971–77*. New York: St. Martin's Press, 1980.

Korejo, M. S. *A Testament of Sindh: Ethnic and Religious Extremism: A Perspective*. Oxford: Oxford University Press, 2003.

Wolpert, Stanley. *Zulfi Bhutto of Pakistan: His Life and Times*. New York: Oxford University Press, 1993.

SINGH. *See* **Sikhism.**

SINGH, BHAGAT *(1907–1931), Indian socialist and revolutionary.* Born in Banga village, Lyallpur district (now Faisalabad, Pakistan), on 27 September 1907, Bhagat Singh represented the radical wing of the Indian freedom movement. Influenced by the Russian revolution and Leninist ideas, particularly toward the end of his brief life, Bhagat Singh differed from mainstream leaders in the Congress Party, both in his advocacy of revolutionary violence and armed struggle and in his belief that national liberation would be incomplete without ending social exploitation.

As a student in Lahore, Singh was inspired by the Ghadar movement and the execution of nineteen-year-old Kartar Singh Sarabha. Drawn to the band of radical young men—influenced by Sachindranath Sanyal and Chandrashekhar Azad—who believed that the only way to force the British out of India was through violence, Singh moved to Kanpur, then a center of revolutionary activity in the United Provinces, to work in the nationalist press run by Ganesh Shankar Vidyarthi. There he joined the Hindustan Republican Association (HRA), whose aim was the establishment of a Federated Republic of the United States of India "by an organised and armed revolution."

Moving back to Lahore, Singh started a youth organization, the Naujawan Bharat Sabha, to further the aims of the HRA, which had been weakened by the execution and arrest of key members following a daring raid on a train near Kakori in Uttar Pradesh (then called United Provinces) in August 1925. On 9 September 1928, Bhagat Singh and other revolutionaries met in Delhi to reestablish the old party, calling it, this time, the Hindustan Socialist Republican Association (HSRA).

Following the police beating—and subsequent death—of Congress leader Lala Lajpat Rai in Lahore in November 1928, the HSRA decided to assassinate the city's police superintendent, J. A. Scott. Singh and Sukh Dev (the HSRA leader) planned and executed the plot,

Portrait of Bhagat Singh. Executed by the British in 1931, Bhagat Singh differed from mainstream leaders in the Congress in both his advocacy of revolutionary violence and in his belief that national liberation would be incomplete without a true end to social exploitation. K. L. KAMAT / KAMAT'S POTPOURRI.

but instead of the intended victim, they ended up killing a young assistant superintendent of police, J. P. Saunders. Singh escaped, but voluntarily surrendered following his next major action, when he and Batukeshwar Dutt threw two bombs and hundreds of leaflets into the chamber of the Central Legislative Assembly while it was in session on 8 April 1929.

Sentenced to life imprisonment for this incident, Singh was subsequently tried, along with Sukh Dev and revolutionary Shivram Rajguru, for the killing of Saunders. Conducted by a special tribunal established by Ordinance and fraught with violations of due process, the trial ended in the imposition of death sentences. Bhagat Singh refused to move a mercy petition and instead demanded he be shot dead rather than hanged, as he had been accused of waging war against the British state. The three young comrades were hanged in Lahore Jail on 23 March 1931.

Despite his youth, Bhagat Singh's politics were surprisingly modern, his commitment to socialism and secularism anticipating by several decades principles that continue to animate independent India's polity. His

Naujawan Bharat Sabha believed religion a matter of personal belief that should not be mixed with politics. In jail, he rejected terrorism, conceding that revolutionary violence had only limited utility, and stressed instead the need to politically mobilize India's millions. Only twenty-three years old at the time of his execution, Bhagat Singh was considered by British intelligence to be as popular a figure nationwide as Mahatma Gandhi.

Siddharth Varadarajan

BIBLIOGRAPHY

Gupta, Manmathnath. *They Lived Dangerously: Reminiscences of a Revolutionary.* New Delhi: People's Publishing House, 1969.

Noorani, A. G. *The Trial of Bhagat Singh: Politics of Justice.* New Delhi: Konark Publishers, 1996.

SINGH, MAHARAJA RANJIT *(1780–1839), Sikh ruler of India.* Maharaja Ranjit Singh ruled a large state in northwestern India that eventually encompassed

the Punjab, Kashmir, several districts to the west of the river Indus, and the region around Multan. Ranjit Singh's grandfather, Charhat Singh, and his father, Mahan Singh, were petty rulers of a Sikh state around Gujranwala, about 30 miles (50 kilometers) north of Lahore. Ranjit Singh was a great warrior who lost an eye on the battlefield and was thereafter called the "one-eyed lion of the Punjab." He conquered Lahore in 1799, Amritsar in 1805, Multan and Peshawar in 1818, and Kashmir in 1819. After the Afghan conqueror Ahmad Shah had defeated the Marathas at the battle of Panipat in 1761 and had then withdrawn, there was a power vacuum in the region, which was filled by a number of Sikh chieftains with their indomitable war bands (*misls*). They rarely acted in concert, proudly maintaining their autonomy. Ranjit Singh subdued them one by one, first compelling them to accept his suzerainty and to pay a tribute (*nazrana*) to him, then annexing their territory. The secret of his success was his devotion to modern warfare. He hired European officers as well as American artillerists and created a large disciplined army. For this he needed a constant flow of land revenue, which he

Indian Postage Stamp. Indian postage stamp bearing images of Maharaja Ranjit Singh, the eighteenth-century ruler who transformed Punjab's Sikhs into "lion-hearted" warriors. KAMAT'S POTPOURRI.

collected more or less in the same manner as the Mughals had done before him. He also followed their example of giving military fiefs (*jagir*) to his commanders. He did not emulate the Mughal system of a hierarchy of ranks (*mānsāb*), yet like the Mughal *mānsabdār*s, his *jagirdar*s received two distinct assignments, one in lieu of their own salary and one to pay for the cavalry troops that they had to maintain. Ranjit strictly inspected these troops and reintroduced the Mughal practice of branding horses so as to make sure that his officers did not deviate from the norms set by him.

As long as Ranjit Singh was alive, he was able to fend off the British, though he knew that he was fighting a rear-guard battle. When he was shown a map of India in which the areas captured by the British were colored red, he remarked that "one day soon" all of India would become "red." Under his weak successors, the control that he had established over the indomitable Sikhs soon lapsed, and the British vanquished them in two bloody Anglo-Sikh wars. This victory was mostly due to the Indian soldiers of the British East India Company's Bengal army, which was therefore hated by the Sikhs. During the mutiny of this army in 1857, irregular Sikh troops helped save the British Raj and thus emerged as one of the "martial races" that were recruited by the British in great numbers. The British thus seemed to be the heirs of Ranjit Singh, organizing Punjab's "lion-hearted" Sikhs as a disciplined force that was rarely matched on the field of battle.

Dietmar Rothermund

BIBLIOGRAPHY

Bakshi, Shri Ram. *History of the Punjab*. New Delhi: Anmol Publishers, 1991.
Banga, Indu. *Agrarian System of the Sikhs*. New Delhi: Manohar, 1978.
Bhatia, Harbans Singh. *Maharaja Ranjit Singh*. Vol. 4 of *Encyclopedic History of the Sikhs*. New Delhi: Deep & Deep Publications, 1999.
Singh, Harbans. *Maharaja Ranjit Singh*. 1952. Reprint, New Delhi: Sterling, 1980.

SINGH, MANMOHAN (1932–), finance minister (1991–1996), prime minister of India (2004–).

Dr. Manmohan Singh, a Sikh, became India's thirteenth prime minister, and its first non-Hindu premier, in May 2004. Additionally, he holds the portfolios of minister of planning and minister of nuclear energy and space. At the time of his appointment, he was not an elected prime minister, having been nominated by the Congress Party in 1991 to India's upper house of Parliament, the Rajya Sabha. Credit for the victory of the Congress Party–led coalition in the 2004 general elections goes to Congress Party president, Sonia Gandhi, the Italian-born wife of the assassinated former prime minister, Rajiv Gandhi. Widespread opposition among extreme Hindu nationalists against the prospect of a foreign-born Italian-Indian Roman Catholic becoming prime minister prompted Sonia Gandhi to deny herself the position of prime minister. Instead, she chose Manmohan Singh to take her place.

Since the Congress Party did not receive enough votes in the 2004 general election to form a majority government, it heads a coalition government, supported by a group of parties called the "Left Front" that includes members of India's Communist parties, the Dravida Munnetra Kazhagam party of the state of Tamil Nadu, the Rashtriya Janata Dal, and other regional parties. Prime Minister Singh's first cabinet of twenty-eight members included eighteen Congress Party ministers. Of the total of sixty-seven Cabinet ministers and ministers of state, the Singh ministry included forty-four Congress Party members.

Manmohan Singh was born on 26 September 1932 in Gah, a village in western Punjab (now in Pakistan). After graduating from Punjab University, Singh went to England to continue his education. He earned a bachelor's degree in economics from Cambridge University, and then moved to Oxford University, where he obtained a doctoral degree in economics. He was subsequently a professor at Punjab University and the prestigious Delhi School of Economics. Singh is the recipient of several honorary doctorates and other awards and honors at home and abroad. Apart from publishing several articles in the field of economics in prominent journals, he is the author of *India's Export Trends and Prospects for Self-Sustained Growth* (1964), an early critique of India's planned economy and inward-looking trade policy.

Singh began his career in the administrative services of the government of India in 1971. He was economic adviser in the Ministry of Commerce, then chief economic adviser in the Ministry of Finance. He has occupied other positions in the Indian government bureaucracy as secretary in the Ministry of Finance, deputy chairman of the Planning Commission, governor of the Reserve Bank of India, and adviser to the prime minister. He was the leader of the Congress Party opposition in the Rajya Sabha between 1998 and 2004. He also worked in Geneva for some years at the United Nations Commission on Trade Development Secretariat and was secretary general of the South Commission in Geneva between 1987 and 1990.

Between 1991 and 1996, Singh was India's finance minister in the Congress Party government of Prime Minister P. V. Narasimha Rao, and during his tenure he spearheaded the economic reform movement in India.

He is credited with the economic transformation of India from socialism to free market capitalism, policies that were continued subsequently by the coalition government led by the Bharatiya Janata Party. His economic initiatives have been continued under his new Congress-led coalition government of 2004. In the early phase of his prime ministership, some questioned whether Dr. Singh would have sufficient political clout to address India's myriad problems, especially given his modest demeanor. But the economic policies underlying the new government bore his stamp of authority and augured well for this future as prime minister.

Raju G. C. Thomas

See also **Economic Reforms of 1991; Gandhi, Sonia**

BIBLIOGRAPHY

Ahluwalia, Isher Judge, et al. *India's Economic Reforms and Development: Essays for Manmohan Singh.* New Delhi: Oxford University Press, 1998.
Venkateswaran, R. J. *Reforming the Indian Economy: The Narasimha Rao and Manmohan Singh Era.* New Delhi: Vikas Publishing, 1996.

SINGH, SADHU SUNDAR *(1889–c. 1929), Christian mystic known for his attempt to "Indianize" Christianity.* Sundar Singh was born to a wealthy Sikh family on 3 September 1889. After converting to Christianity, he devoted his life to mystic preaching, trying as a saffron-robed *sadhu* (Hindu holy man) to present Christianity in a uniquely Indian form.

He studied at a Presbyterian Mission School, and there he first encountered the Christian faith, appealing to God to show him the "way of salvation." He said that the room was flooded with light, "and I saw the form of the Lord Jesus Christ." It was the turning point of his life. Though his family made every effort to dissuade him, he was baptized in Simla on 3 September 1905. Thirty days later, he decided to take up the saffron robes and mendicant life of a *sadhu*, preaching wherever he went.

In 1909 Sadhu Sundar Singh was admitted to St. John's Divinity College, Lahore; because he considered religion a matter of the heart, not the head, he left after eight months. Sadhu Sundar Singh has been described as a Christocentric mystic. By adopting the lifestyle of a *sadhu*, he was attempting to "Indianize" Christianity. He told the story of a Brahman passenger on a train overcome by heat and dehydration. At the station he was offered water in a white cup. He refused, saying, "I will not break my caste." When the water was brought to him in his own brass vessel, he drank it willingly. It is the same with the "Water of Life," said Sundar Singh. "Indians do need the Water of Life, but not in a European cup" (Streeter and Appasamy, p. 228).

For several years he traveled across North India, from village to village, preaching. His fame spread far and wide. In 1918 he visited South India and subsequently went on several trips around the world. After his second trip to Europe, however, his health deteriorated, and he was last seen on 18 April 1929, setting off on a journey across the Himalayas and Tibet.

Many of Sadhu Sundar Singh's sermons and other writings have been published and translated into Indian languages. These include *Reality and Religion; The Search after Reality; Meditations;* and *Soul-Stirring Messages.* He spoke in colorful and descriptive language, coupled with appealing anecdotes. His name is still a household word in thousands of Christian Indian homes.

Graham Houghton

See also **Christian Impact on India, History of**

BIBLIOGRAPHY

Davey, Cyril J. *The Yellow Robe: The Story of Sadhu Sundar Singh.* London: SCM Press, 1957.
Heiler, Friedrich. *The Gospel of Sadhu Sundar Singh.* 1927. Reprint, Delhi: ISCPK, 1989.
Parker, Mrs. E. *Sadhu Sundar Singh.* London: Christian Literature Society, 1948.
Streeter, B. H., and A. J. Appasamy. *The Sadhu: A Study in Mysticism and Practical Religion.* Delhi: Mittal Publications, 1987.

SINO–INDIAN WAR. *See* **China, Relations with.**

SIROHI SCHOOL PAINTING The school of Sirohi painting is synonymous with a Vijnyptipatra, or letter of invitation, which seems to have originated from this town. Until the 1960s the art world of miniature painting was completely unaware of this school. The first reference to Sirohi painting appeared in the Khajanchi Collection (New Delhi) catalog of 1960; its entry 64 is a *vijayptipatra*, titled Rajarthani, Sirohi, dated A.D. 1737. The entry related that "a congregation of citizens from Sirohi sent a letter of invitation to the Vijayadeva Suri (a famous Jain monk) inviting him to visit the city during Paryusana festival." A long descriptive entry appearing in the same catalog reads, in part, "Sirohi, near Mt. Abu, seems to have been one of the centers of painting in southern Rajasthan in the early eighteenth century, and no doubt in the early seventeenth century. The facial types are very similar to another *vijayptipatra* from Sirohi dated A.D. 1725" (p. 48).

According to the Purāṇas, the present state of Sirohi was formerly called Arbutadea. Also, the name "Sirohi" is said to have evolved from the word "Sirnava," a mountain range, at the foothills of which the town of Sirohi was established. The present town of Sirohi is situated in southwest Rajasthan, bounded on the north, northeast, and west by Jodhpur (Marwar), in the south by Palanpur, Danta, and Idar (Gujarat) and on the east by Udaipur (Rajasthan). The physical features of this region include a hilly and rocky region of the Aravalli ranges; the only river that flows is the Banas. It has a varied flora and fauna, though the countryside is mainly arid and dry, with extreme temperatures in summer and winter.

Sanis Mal, son of Rao Sobha, founded Sirohi in A.D. 1425. What seems to have brought renown to Sirohi is its proximity to archaeological and religious sites. It is located near the great Jain temples of Delvada at Mount Abu. The ruins of the ancient temple sites of Chandravati and Vasantgarh (Pindwara, c. 7th century A.D.) indicate socioreligious activities in this region in early times.

The town was situated on the trade route from Abu to Ranakpur and farther to Rajasthan via Pali, Ghanerao, Desuri, and the main Jain seat of learning, Patan. Itinernant Jain monks often demanded certain socioreligious artifacts (such as *vijnaptipatra*s), cloth paintings, and paper manuscripts from time to time. To cater to this demand, a community of scribes known as Laiyas became established in Sirohi. Among them were painters, calligraphers, and teachers who belonged to the Mathen community of painters. They possessed blank letters of invitation, which were long and narrow paper scrolls (often measuring 50 feet × 12 inches [15m × 30.5 cm]), which were used for painting and for writing text in beautiful calligraphy. The themes of the scrolls were often repetitive. The top portion of the scroll contained the eight sacred symbols and the fourteen lucky dreams of the Jains, as well as the depiction of sermons, processions, temples, famous buildings, and marketplaces (represented by a street with shops on either side of the road and people shopping). Stylistically, such scrolls are painted in the established Marwar style, with bold figures and bright color schemes, though a number of them are painted in the distinctive Sirohi style.

Recent scholarship has brought to light a few dated examples with place names that determine the styles at least in the early eighteenth century. Two illustrated manuscripts—the Upadesamala, attributed to Sirohi, of the late seventeenth or early eighteenth century, from the collection of the Deva Sano Pado Bhandar, Ahmedabad; and a Durga-Saptasati, dated 1710, painted at Sirohi, from the collection of the Chhatrapati Shivaji Maharaj Vastu Sangrahalaya (formerly known as the Prince of Wales Museum), Mumbai—help establish the stylistic characteristics of Sirohi painting. There is another complete manuscript of Devi-Mahatmya, dated 1726, painted at Ghanerao (a *thikana*, or smaller feudatory state in rajasthan owing allegiance to the ruling chief, of Marwar), close to Sirohi, which is painted in Sirohi style.

These early examples, though within the known stylistic frame work of the Marwar school, possess certain peculiar features of the Sirohi idiom. In a horizontal Pothi format (of loose folios), they are executed in a refined Kalam style with a number of Mughal mannerisms. Male and female figures are squat and robust. Male costumes consist of a large turban with a broad sash, a long floral Jama, and a broad Patka. Women are clad in Ghaghra (long frilled skirt), *choli* (bodice), and *odhni* (long narrow piece of cloth which is meant to cover the head and the breasts). One of the distinguishing features of the Sirohi style is a kind of shading or modeling that appears on the faces and limbs, an element that is not found in the Marwar and Ghanerao styles. Another noteworthy characteristic of Sirohi style is the depiction of a colorful landscape. Sirohi artists were fond of a variety of flora and fauna, flowing rivers, and scenic waterfronts. The architecture in paintings consists of a domed pavilion with arches, balconies, and *chhajja*s (weather shades). Scenes take place in the middle plane; the foreground is a raised platform with colorful flowering plants and other objects placed below. Trees are often shown in bloom with a variety of foliage. All these elements are rendered in a naturalistic manner. The color palette is predominantly orange, brown, olive green, and brick red. The later paintings of Rāgamālās (garland of melodies) in Indian music are devoid of these subtle qualities. This school seems to have produced at least ten sets of Rāgamālās, dated from the late seventeenth to the early nineteenth centuries. Of these, at least one complete set from the collection of Kumar Sangram Singh of Navalgarh (Jaipur) has been separated; its folios are now in various museums and private collections in India and abroad. Sirohi Rāgamālā paintings do not have text on the top margin, but the name of the Rāga appears in Devanagari (script which has originated from Sanskrit).

Shridhar Andhare

See also **Miniatures: Marwar and Thikanas**

BIBLIOGRAPHY

Andhare, Shridhar. "A Dated Salibhadra Chaupai and the Mathen Painters of Bikaner." *Sri nagabhinandanam*, edited by L. K. Srinivasan and S. Nagaraju. Bangalore: Dr. M. S. Nagaraja Rao Felicitation Committee, 1995.

Ebeling, Klaus. *Ragamala Painting*. Basel: Ravi Kumar, 1973.

Khandalavala, K., M. Chandra, and P. Chandra. *Miniature Painting*. Catalog of the Sri Motichand Khajanchi Collection. New Delhi: Sri Motichand Khajanchi, 1960.

SĪTĀ. *See* **Rāmāyaṇa.**

SITAR The sitar (Persian, *setār*, "three-string") is a long-necked lute popular in North Indian classical music and commonly constructed from a dried gourd base with a hollow wooden neck. The neck of the contemporary sitar has metal frets, which arch over the face of the neck and which are tied from the back so that a single piece of string (made of gut or nylon) loops over indents at the edges of the frets. The advantage of these tied frets is that a musician can move them to adjust the intonation of individual notes. Performers wear a thick piece of twisted wire (*mizrāb*) over the index finger of the right hand as a plectrum.

Sitars have metal wires. The principal melody string (*bāj*, or sometimes, *gayakī*) is steel and is set in the middle of the neck, leaving room for the performer to pull the string over the arched frets (sliding the pitch). The principal drone string (*kharaj*) sits adjacent to the *bāj* (and to the left if facing the instrument) and acts as a secondary melody string. Three or more drone strings (*jorī*) sit next

to the *kharaj*, one or two of which sometimes double as additional melody strings. The highest pitched drone strings (*cikārī*) lie to the far left of the neck and attach to pegs protruding from the side of the neck. Underneath these plucked strings, seven or more "sympathetic" strings (*tarab*), tuned to the notes of the *rāga*, vibrate "in sympathy" without being plucked. Like the sarod and the *sārangī*, the sympathetic strings extend from pegs in the side of the neck, up through holes in the face of the neck, and pass under the melody and drone strings. These *tarab* strings rest on a separate bridge that sits just in front of the higher-sitting platform bridge for the melody and drone strings. The bridges have the distinguishing characteristic of appearing to be flat, although their surfaces actually have a very slight curvature from which the strings gradually leave. This shape produces the instrument's characteristic emphasis on high partials as the very end of the string "buzzes" against the bone or wood platform.

The two best-known sitar performers of the late twentieth century are Vilayat Khan and Ravi Shankar. Vilayat Khan prefers to play sitars with the lowest of the *tarab*

Woman playing Sitar in Jaipur, India, 2000. In a recent interview, Anoushka Shankar (daughter of Ravi Shankar and an accomplished sitar artist herself) commented, "I've never actually come across much prejudice being a female sitar player. Though it's not a common thing, there have been other well-known sitarists who are women." MICHAEL FREEMAN.

strings slightly offset away from the other sympathetic strings. Ravi Shankar prefers a Bengali version of the sitar that features a string one octave lower than the *kharaj*.

The tuning of sitars similarly varies, with some aspects common to all sitars, and others peculiar to the playing tradition and to the particular *rāga* chosen for performance. The *bāj* (melody string) is set to the fourth (*mā*) so that the tonic fret sits midway up the neck. This allows performers to approach the tonic (*sā*) from both above and below. The *kharaj* (principal drone string) is always set to the tonic. The uppermost drone strings (*cikārī*) are also set to the tonic, with other strings set to the fifth or, in some cases the fourth or the fifth (or, sometimes, other notes), depending on the effect the sitarist is attempting to achieve.

The sitar first appears in references in the eighteenth century, and it appears to be related to a class of instruments that include the Persian *setār*, the central Asian *tambur*, and later regional variants such as the Kashmiri *setār*. Characteristics that distinguish the sitar are its lateral and frontal pegs, a gourd body, a nontapering neck, and a flat bridge.

Gordon Thompson

See also **Music; Rāga; Shankar, Ravi**

BIBLIOGRAPHY

Miner, Allyn. *Sitar and Sarod in the Eighteenth and Nineteenth Centuries*. Delhi: Motilal Banarsidass, 1997.

SIZE AND CAPITAL INTENSITY OF INDIAN INDUSTRY SINCE 1950 Conceptually, size and capital intensity have been recognized as important parameters in the evolution of any industry. While the importance of the size of an industry has always been a part of conventional wisdom, analytical growth models have also underscored the importance of capital intensity. Yet, the implementation of these notions is beset with a number of practical difficulties. In both cases, a menu approach is followed in measurement. Industry size is measured, variously, in terms of levels of sales, assets, value added, capital deployed, and employment. Likewise, capital intensity is measured as the amount of fixed capital used in relation to other inputs (especially labor) or to the overall output. Typically, capital-labor ratio and capital-output ratio are seen as alternative measures of the capital intensity of an industry.

Before independence, the British government of India had provided discriminating protection to some selected industries, accompanied by a "most favored nation" clause for British goods. Despite this, a number of domestic industries, including cotton textiles, sugar, paper, and iron and steel, expanded. No effort was made, however, to foster the development of capital goods industry in India. Not surprisingly, on the eve of India's independence in 1947, the Indian industrial sector was characterized by low levels of capital intensity, marked by a high concentration of employment either in the lowest size group (household enterprises and small factories) or in the highest size group (large factories). Medium-size factories were virtually absent from the Indian industrial sector. Low capital intensity in Indian industry was primarily due to the prevalence of low wages and the small size of the domestic market as a result of low per capita income. According to a study by the United Nations in 1958, capital intensity, as measured by capital employed per worker, was substantially lower in India, compared to the United States and other developed economies. Moreover, low capital intensity was reflected not only in consumer goods industries, such as textiles and sugar, but also in capital goods industries, such as iron and steel.

One of the early studies on the size and capital intensity of Indian industry (Rosen) attributed the smaller size and lower capital intensity of Indian industry, compared to that of developed economies, to the difference in the availability of factors and the lack of access to a capital market, which generally encourages the use of capital-intensive methods. Subsequently, on the basis of a comprehensive analysis of twenty-two industries during the period 1953–1958, J. C. Sandesara in 1969 concluded that while small-sized units in some industries were labor intensive, in some others they turned out to be capital intensive. In other words, there was little evidence of a clear and uniform relationship between size and capital intensity.

The average size of factories, in terms of assets, output, and valued added, has increased consistently since the 1970s. Assets increased from 8.7 million rupees in 1970 to 20.2 million rupees in 2002; output increased from 16.7 million rupees in 1970 to 45.9 million rupees in 2002. In contrast, average employment in Indian factories witnessed a decline, from 86 workers per factory during the 1970s to 78 during the 1980s. Clearly, output growth during the 1980s was not accompanied by a corresponding increase in the generation of employment. The declining trend in employment persisted during the 1990s and was further pronounced during 2000–2001 and 2001–2002, when it fell to an average of 60 workers per factory. This was, perhaps, symptomatic of greater use of capital in the production process, leading to higher capital intensity over time. In fact, increases in real wages and job security regulations in the late 1970s seem to have induced entrepreneurs to shift over to capital-intensive techniques. It has also been argued that surplus employment in the 1970s set a limit to the additional employment opportunities in the 1980s and beyond. Structural ratios calculated on the basis of data from the Annual Survey of Industries provide evidence to support this theory.

Almost all the indicators used as proxy for capital intensity show that production processes in Indian industry have increasingly become more capital oriented. Capital employed per worker has increased substantially since the 1970s. Capital-wages ratio increased marginally from 7.3 in the 1970s to 8.3 in the 1980s, but increased substantially following the economic reforms of 1991, to 12.64 by 2000 and to 14.25 in 2002. On the other hand, it should be noted that capital employed per unit of output did not undergo much change during the three decades from 1970 to 2000, reflecting a greater efficiency in the use of capital in the production processes.

A disaggregated industry-wide analysis by J. Thomas in 2002 showed that capital intensity varies widely across different industries. It has been the lowest in jute textiles, and the highest in electricity generation, transmission, and distribution. Basic metals, chemicals, rubber, and petroleum also have high capital intensity, while jute, beverages, textile products, leather, wood products, and food products continue to be the least capital-intensive sectors in Indian manufacturing.

The relationship between size and capital intensity in the Indian industrial sector also seems to have witnessed a noticeable transformation since the 1970s. With the increase in the size of factories (in terms of output), capital per head of worker increased during the 1970s. Correlation coefficients between output (size factor) and capital-labor ratio demonstrate that the covariation strengthened further in the 1980s and in the post-1991 period. In contrast, the capital-labor ratio was inversely related to the size of the labor force in factories. The covariation of capital-output ratio and total output has been negative since the 1970s, probably because growth in output in most of the years since 1980 has been higher than growth in capital, indicating the efficient use of capital by Indian industries.

In retrospect, Indian industry has been undergoing a structural transformation since independence. With the government initially adopting an industrial development strategy that promoted heavy, capital-intensive industries, size indicators in the Indian industrial sector expanded substantially, facilitated by the evolving industrial policy and increased domestic and external demand. Thus, the predominance of primary raw material–based industries in the 1950s was gradually replaced by the emergence and faster growth of metal-based and heavy industries. The industrial policy initiatives since 1991

have led to a diversified Indian industrial structure. While the transition process has led to greater use of capital in relation to the labor force, productivity enhancements have resulted in a gradual decline in the capital-output ratio in recent years.

Narendra Jadhav

See also **Capital Market; Economic Reforms of 1991; Industrial Growth and Diversification; Small-Scale Industry, since 1947**

BIBLIOGRAPHY

Ahluwalia, I. J. *Productivity and Growth in Indian Manufacturing.* Delhi: Oxford University Press, 1991.

Nagaraj, R. "Employment and Wages in Manufacturing Industries: Trends, Hypothesis and Evidence." *Economic and Political Weekly* 29, no. 4 (1994): 177–186.

Rosen, George. *Industrial Change in India: Industrial Growth, Capital Requirements, and Technological Change, 1937–1955.* Glencoe, Ill.: Free Press, 1958.

Sandesara, J. C. *Size and Capital Intensity in Indian Industry.* Economics Series, no. 19. Mumbai: University of Bombay, 1969.

Thomas, J. J. "A Review of Indian Manufacturing." In *India Development Report*, edited by Kirit S. Parikh and R. Radhakrishna. New Delhi: Oxford University Press, 2002.

SKANDA. *See* **Shiva and Shaivism.**

SMALL-SCALE AND COTTAGE INDUSTRY, 1800–1947 In 1800 India had a diversified manufacturing base, employing a significant proportion of the workforce. Textile production was the leading sector, and the weaving of cotton cloth by India's village artisans was a universal occupation. When cloth was produced for the village or local markets, the weavers sold the cloth directly to consumers. In such cases, the capital requirement was low, and the costs of preparatory processes, like spinning and preparation of yarn, were internalized through the labor of the nonweaving members of the household, usually women and children. The organization and relations of production were far more complex when cloth was produced on a commercial scale to produce finer textiles which catered to distant markets, especially for export. Even the preparatory processes of cleaning and carding the cotton were done by specialized workers, and spinning was a distinct and skilled occupation that provided employment to millions of women.

The hinterlands of the three major cloth exporting coastal areas—Gujarat, Coromandel, and Bengal—were best known for their textiles. But textiles were produced for external markets in many other parts of the country. Weaving remained largely a rural activity, though small

Women Spinning Yarn with Wooden *Charkhas*. In India's struggle for self-rule, Mahatma Gandhi forcefully advocated for the revival of this cottage industry as the solution to the nation's economic woes, as the center from which other industries would flow. He declared the wheel "the symbol of the nation's prosperity and, therefore, freedom." AMAR TALWAR / FOTOMEDIA.

towns and even larger cities also had a small population of weavers. The location of weaving itself was less relevant than the markets for which their products were intended, which were predominantly urban and upper-income classes. Weaving was a full-time occupation in most regions. The exception was Bengal and northeastern India, where weavers alternated between cloth production and agriculture. Weaving was also a caste-dominated activity that was carried out by various subcastes of weavers; caste performed a role similar to guilds, providing organizational unity for each activity.

A noteworthy feature of textile production in India was the seemingly endless variety of plain and patterned fabrics produced in every region. Plain, or solid-colored, fabrics were produced in coarse, medium, and fine textures. Patterned fabrics were produced both on the loom, or by using complex dyeing, painting, and printing techniques on woven cloth. The dyeing of cotton was, in fact, India's unique specialty. Because cotton did not absorb dyes directly to achieve a permanent color, Indian dyers used a variety of mordants, resists, astringents, and other products in conjunction with dyes in order to fix a

permanent color to the cloth. Since many dyes were derived from plants, the cultivation of dye crops was an added supporting activity in textile production. With this extensive range of plain, dyed, and patterned cloth, India supplied the textile requirements of most of the world.

Production on a commercial scale, however, increased the requirement of working capital, particularly for purchasing yarn in the market. This capital was provided by merchant capitalists, who played a pivotal role in premodern trading. They advanced working capital to the weavers, usually secured against future deliveries of cloth. For the merchant, this negated a major uncertainty on the supply side by securing a large enough stock of cloth from many individual weavers. The merchant also provided the interface between distant markets and the weavers, ensuring a flow of information on the market so that production could be adjusted to consumer preferences.

The unit of production for this large volume of output was still the weaver, working from home on his own loom. The tools and equipment tended to be rudimentary and the techniques, especially of spinning and dyeing, required a great deal of time. The key factors in maintaining a high level of quality and performance were the highly developed manual skills of the workers, and the empirically evolved intricate techniques of all processes. In such a system, the notions of productivity and wages related to productivity had little relevance. Though data on wages are sketchy, it is evident that wages were by and large pegged to subsistence levels. Low wages were partly the result of controls exercised by the merchants over the weavers, who had no direct access to the market. Textile production was characterized by a high ratio of net output to fixed capital and a low share of wages in the final price.

In crafts like ornamental metalware, master craftsmen worked with apprentices in workshops, which were usually located in urban administrative centers. Since the products were primarily intended for local elite and ruling classes, there were no uncertainties regarding the market or consumer preference, nor were the products traded to distant markets.

Impact of Colonialism

The impact of colonialism on Indian industry has been much debated, but the most widespread view was that the invidious policies of the British colonial government, aimed at protecting the interests of domestic industries in Britain, had destroyed India's handicraft manufactures, especially textiles. This "nationalist view" was first articulated by R. C. Dutt, who also stressed that, in this process, India was transformed from an exporter of manufactured goods to an exporter of raw materials, with most of its population forced into subsistence agriculture for survival. Further, Marxist theories of the world capitalist system cite India as a prime example of the process by which colonized economies were relegated to raw material production to feed the development of the capitalist center. Even where traditional manufacturing survived, this was possible only with the use of zero cost household labor and when the producer depressed his own wages to compete with the cheaper imported goods.

A contending school of thought, which argued that traditional Indian industry had declined because it was unable to compete with mechanized production, was too simplistic, ignoring the unequal power relations that were inherent in colonialism.

Survival of Handicrafts

The incontrovertible evidence of the viable functioning of many crafts, especially hand-loom weaving, well into the twentieth century has led to a reassessment that seeks to understand the dynamics of survival of artisanal industry and the complex processes of adjustment to the

forces of rapidly changing technology and improvements in transportation and communications. The latter integrated India's economy into the global economy at a time when costs were declining internationally.

The sector that was most vulnerable to these forces was the highly export-oriented indigenous textile sector, which had to compete with cheaper cloth in domestic as well as export markets. The general consensus is that textile production did decline during the first half of the nineteenth century, but this impact was both region and product specific, and Bengal as a region and a whole array of medium quality fabrics produced for export were the most affected. However, there was no noticeable decline in the volume of output in most regions.

Until about 1870, hand-spun yarn was still being used extensively, but imports of machine-spun yarn eventually wiped out hand spinning in India, with the resultant loss of employment and income for millions of women. The introduction of chemical dyes toward the end of the nineteenth century similarly pushed out traditional vegetable dyeing techniques. Hand-loom weaving and production of patterned cloth survived, however, by switching to the more cost-effective, though not necessarily better, inputs.

More reliable data are available from 1870 onward. Between 1881 and 1931, the proportion of male workers in industry declined, which happened not merely in textiles, but in many other activities. At the same time, real income per worker rose steadily, indicating that productivity-enhancing technology was being adopted in the crafts, and that nonviable workers were forced to shift to other occupations.

In all crafts, there was a distinct preference for maintaining production within a small, artisanal firm. Imported inputs and new technologies were adopted within the economic rationale of small-scale production. In textiles, a richer class of weavers was emerging, many of whom turned to trade or became entrepreneurs. Such entrepreneurs set up small-scale hand-loom workshops in urban centers in southern and western parts of India. More significant in the long term was the setting up of small power-loom manufactories in towns in western India. Weavers migrated to work in these workshops, shifting from self-employment to wage employment.

The individual weaver, however, remained the mainstay of hand-loom weaving and adjusted to the new macroeconomic environment. The most important reason for the survival of hand-loom cloth was the strong domestic demand for traditional dress materials, designs, and patterns, none of which could be produced through mechanical processes. But the weavers also responded to changing market preferences, producing new fabrics, weaving with silk and manmade yarns, and gradually adopting new technologies, which were economically viable in hand-loom weaving.

Though the Indian mill industry dated back to the 1870s, it did not really compete with the hand looms until the 1920s. The hand-loom sector responded by shifting to higher value products in which it had an advantage. The major problem for hand-loom weaving during the 1930s and 1940s was the shortage of yarn. Weavers had to depend on middlemen merchants for credit to buy yarn and entered into highly disadvantageous tied transactions, which ultimately forced a high percentage of weavers into a debt trap, raising fears about the future of hand-loom weaving.

Kanakalatha Mukund

See also **Large-Scale Industry, 1850–1950; Textiles: Block-Printed; Textiles: Early Painted and Printed**

BIBLIOGRAPHY

Gadgil, D. R. *The Industrial Evolution of India in Recent Times, 1860–1939.* 5th ed. New Delhi: Oxford University Press, 1971. A modern classic on economic transformation in the late colonial period.

Government of India, Fact Finding Committee (Handlooms and Mills). *Report.* Delhi: GOI, 1942.

Haynes, Douglas. "The Dynamics of Continuity in Indian Domestic Industry: *Jari* Manufacture in Surat, 1900–47." *Indian Economic and Social History Review* 33, no. 2 (1986): 127–149. Studies the dynamics of an input in textile production.

Mukund, Kanakalatha. "Indian Textile Industry in the Seventeenth and Eighteenth Centuries: Structure, Organisation and Responses." *Economic and Political Weekly* 27, no. 32 (1992): 2057–2065. Primarily focuses on indigenous techniques in various processes of textile production, and the responses to the changing economic environment.

Roy, Tirthankar. *Artists and Industrialization: Indian Weaving in the Twentieth Century.* New Delhi: Oxford University Press, 1993. A detailed statistical study of the textile industry in the first half of the twentieth century.

———. *Traditional Industry in the Economy of Colonial India.* Cambridge, U.K.: Cambridge University Press, 1999. An unusual study of various nontextile handicrafts between 1870 and 1930.

Roy, Tirthankar, ed. *Cloth and Commerce.* New Delhi: Sage, 1996. Collection of articles reprinted from the *Indian Economic and Social History Review* on the history of the textile industry. The articles by Konrad Specker, Hanaru Yanagisawa, and Sumit Guha dealing with the experience of some textile-producing regions in the first half of the nineteenth century are of special interest.

SMALL-SCALE INDUSTRY, SINCE 1947 India's real gross domestic product (GDP, in 1993–1994 prices) increased from 1,405 billion rupees in 1950–1951 to 11,939 billion rupees in 2000–2001, by 8.5 times. The share of manufacturing in GDP, which was 9 percent in 1950–1951, rose to 18 percent in 2000–2001. Manufacturing is divided into two sectors: registered (factories that use power and employ 10 or more workers, or that do not use power for manufacturing and that employ 20 or more workers) and unregistered (smaller units). In 1950–1951 the two sectors had roughly an equal share; in 2000–2001 the registered sector's share increased to two-thirds and the unregistered sector's share declined to one-third.

Modern and Traditional Industries

Small-scale industries (SSI) are divided into modern and traditional industries. Traditional industries are home-based, use simple tools and equipment, depend on family labor, and are completely manual. Modern SSIs may have a separate workplace, employ outside labor, and use machines and power. Nearly all of the traditional industries and a very large number of modern SSIs fall into the unregistered category, so the GDP of these industries will be roughly equal to the GDP of the unregistered sector. The share of modern SSIs has improved greatly both in production and employment between 1973–1974 and 2002–2003: in production from 68 to 94 percent and in employment from 28 to 43 percent. Over the same period, the share of traditional industries declined: in production from 16 to 6 percent and in employment from 58 to 55 percent.

An SSI is currently defined as an enterprise with investment in plant and machinery up to 10 million rupees (original value). This sector also includes ancillary, export-oriented, and women's enterprises, with an investment limit in each of 10 million rupees and with a special condition for each, and business and service enterprises in specified lines with investment limits of 2.5 million rupees and 0.5 million rupees, respectively, without any condition.

Growth and Change

Production, employment, and exports of SSI increased by 10.0, 5.9, and 12.7 percent per annum from 1973–1974 to 2000–2001. The subperiods 1973–1974, 1980–1981, 1990–1991, and 2000–2001 witnessed deceleration of growth on all the three measures.

In 1972 SSIs producing metals and electrical equipment had the largest share in the number of units, employment, and fixed assets and production, 43–49 percent. Other manufacturing, food, textiles, and services followed, in that order. In 1987–1988, other manufacturing was first in each of the above categories, with a share of 35–42 percent, followed in each category by metals and electricals, food, textiles, and services. The share of food and textiles increased and that of metals and electricals declined, both substantially.

Support and Incentives

SSIs enjoy some advantages, but they also suffer from handicaps relative to large-scale industries in the marketplace. On balance, they are in a weak position. However, they have an appeal in terms of socioeconomic objectives and have, therefore, a strong case for state support. In India, capital is scarce and labor abundant. SSIs are thought to have lower capital-output and capital-labor ratios than large-scale industries, and to therefore better serve growth and employment objectives. Additionally, entrepreneurship has been restricted in India to certain castes, communities, and language groups, and has been male-dominated. It is the policy of the Indian government to widen this base by promoting entrepreneurs from other groups.

It is on these considerations that various assistance programs and incentives have been devised for SSI development. Since independence in 1947, especially since the late 1950s, development has been wide-ranging, both in terms of programs and regions. The programs include information and technology services, entrepreneurship development and training, modernization and technology support, industrial facilities, assistance in procurement of raw materials price preferences, finance, and nursing of "sick" industrial units. To operate these programs and to monitor their progress, new agencies and institutions have been set up, and the existing ones strengthened at the national, regional, state, and lower levels. There is also a special bank for SSIs. The SSIs have their own associations, and are also represented in the national- and state-level associations of large-scale industries.

An attempt was made to estimate the value of incentives on SSI production. The study examined nine programs or incentive schemes for six industries in seven states. It was estimated that the value varied from 70 percent in cosmetics and toiletries to 33 percent in gases.

Policy Issues

There is no doubt that the SSI sector has registered considerable progress. But there are also areas of concern in the policies and programs, arresting further progress. What are these concerns, and how do they influence the outcome? And what is needed by way of corrections?

Overcrowding and failure. The capital and skill required to start and operate an SSI are small, and product is undifferentiated. These easy entry conditions have led to overcrowding of the SSI sector. Assistance programs make

Textile Workers in Rural Rajasthan. Though rich in natural resources, Rajasthan lags behind other states in terms of high poverty and unemployment rates. In recent decades, New Delhi has commissioned numerous studies of small-scale industry in the state (how to make existing businesses more profitable and expand their corresponding markets). The textile industry figures prominently in current initiatives for the region. AMAR TALWAR / FOTOMEDIA.

entry easier. Also, officials administering assistance may tend to be overgenerous, as more assistance improves their service record, adding to overcrowding.

It is therefore not surprising that a substantial number of SSIs close their doors within a short span of operations. The 1987–1988 census reported that of some 300,000 units that closed, one-half were closed within 5 years of the start of operations: 14 percent within 1–2 years and 36 percent within 3–5 years. Evidently, there is a case for a more focused and selective approach to assistance.

A presumption of the SSI policy is that SSIs have low capital-output and low capital-labor ratios relative to large-scale industries. Thus, they are in tune with factor proportions, and thus, they serve growth and employment objectives better. Considerable evidence casts doubt on that presumption, and some studies have pointed to capital-output and capital-labor ratios being higher in SSIs than in large-scale industries.

Definition. The earliest definition of small-scale industries in 1950 had a limit of 0.5 million rupees in fixed investment, with fewer than 50 workers in units using power or fewer than 100 workers in units not using power for manufacturing. The definition has changed several times since then. In 2004 the definition had a limit of 10 million rupees for investment in plant and machinery (original value), without any additional conditions. With this amount one can now buy only an obsolete, low-grade, or secondhand plant and machinery. This limit seems to have more adversely affected the capital-intensive industries like metals and electricals. The SSI censuses show a sharp decline in the shares of this group in number of units, employment, fixed assets, and production between 1972 and 1987–1988. Also, the percentage of closed units to working units in this group was 59, against 52 for all units in 1987–1988.

There is clearly a need for raising the limit. Following the recommendation of the Expert Committee on Small Enterprises, the limit was raised to 30 million rupees in 1997, but in 1999 it was brought down to 10 million rupees. Considering inflation and the availability of better technologies since then, the limit needs to be increased substantially, perhaps to 45 million rupees.

Reservation. The policy of reservation of items for exclusive production in the SSI sector was first introduced in 1967 with 47 items. The number since then has been increasing, reaching a peak of 873 in 1984. Since then, the number is being reduced. As of October 2004, the number of reserved items was 605. Since then, 108 items have been identified for de-reservation, which will bring the number to 497. Under this policy, the production of items in this list by large-scale industries is frozen to their existing capacities, giving protection to small-scale industries in those categories. As a consequence, the SSI sector, especially the reserved part, is expected to improve its efficiency and grow faster.

This policy has been criticized on various grounds such as it has been ad hoc, obstruction of technology and scale up-gradation. Moreover, such evidence as is available on efficiency, profitability, and growth shows that in general the performance of SSI in the reserved items does not outshine that of other SSI, or is it poorer. It would thus seem that the government's policy of gradual de-reservation is moving in the right direction.

J. C. Sandesara

See also **Size and Capital Intensity of Indian Industry, since 1950**

BIBLIOGRAPHY

Hussain, Abid. *Report of the Expert Committee on Small Enterprises.* New Delhi: National Council of Applied Economic Research, 1997.

Mohan, Rakesh. "Small-Scale Industry Policy of India: A Critical Evaluation." In *Economic Policy Reforms and the Indian Economy*, edited by Anne O. Kruegar. New Delhi: Oxford University Press, 2002.

Sandesara, J. C. *Size and Capital Intensity in Indian Industry.* Mumbai: University of Bombay, 1969.

———. *Efficacy of Incentives for Small Industries.* Mumbai: Industrial Development Bank of India, 1982.

———. "Modern Small Industry, 1972 and 1987–88: Aspects of Growth and Structural Change." *Economic and Political Weekly* 28, no. 6 (6 February 1993): 223–229.

Small Industries Development Bank of India. *SIDBI Report on Small-Scale Industries Sector, 2001.* Lucknow: SIDBI, 2002.

Sutcliffe, R. B. *Industry and Underdevelopment.* London: Addison Wesley, 1971.

Tulsi, S. K. *Incentives for Small Industries: An Evaluation.* Delhi: Kunj Publishing House, 1980.

SOMA As a god, Soma is the most prominent deity in the Rig Veda after Indra and Agni; Soma as god and soma as sacrificial substance are one and the same in Vedic tradition. The ninth book of the Rig Veda is devoted solely to Soma, and some 120 hymns address him. The ritual texts of later Saṃhitās, Brāhmaṇas, Āraṇyakas, and Shrauta Sūtras are structured by sacrifices, many featuring two essential offerings: soma and *pashu* (animals). The god's name is also the name of a plant and its "pressed" juice (from *su-* "to press"). *Haoma*, the corresponding name of the plant, juice, and cult in the Avesta, attests to an Indo-Iranian origin, although mythologies of a divine plant or elixir that brings immortality, visions, and insight suggest an even earlier background. Poets of Rig Veda 4.26 and 27 celebrated the theft of soma by an eagle in one of the earliest and most enduring myths concerning a celestial or mountain origin.

Many substitutes for soma were named in Brāhmaṇa texts before 800 B.C. Possibly the plant known to early poet-ritualists became unavailable during migrations from steppe or highland regions onto the Gangetic Plain. Identification of Vedic soma or Avestan *haoma* has been vigorously debated since the late eighteenth century; botanists, archaeologists, and historians have proposed as candidates species of the genus *Ephedra*, as well as *Peganam harmala*, *Amanita muscaria*, *Cannabis sativa*, *Papaver somniferum*, and others. An asclepiad called *soma-lata* or *somatiga*, probably a species of *Sarcostemma*, a bitter-tasting green creeper, not hallucinogenic, is pressed in parts of South India today by small communities of Vedic sacrificers.

The ritual process of extracting juice from plant stems was institutionalized in the soma sacrifice with three pressings each day. The pressings are filtered through wool; the liquid is collected in tubs, sometimes mixing in water, milk, curds, clarified butter, barley flour, or honey. It is then poured into offering fires for designated gods. Soma is served in special carved wooden cups to the sacrificer (*yajamāna*) and ten priests called by heralds (*somapravāka*) to perform the sacrifice. Both sacrificer and wife (*patnī*) are transformed by the rite and entitled to be renamed soma sacrificers. After the initiatory five-day *agnishtoma*, they become eligible to perform other soma rituals of varying magnitude and duration, including the seventeen-day Vājapeya (drink of strength).

Whether from chemical inspiration, or exhaustion and sleep-deprivation during intense sacrificial sessions, an ecstatic response to the drinking of soma juice is clear from ancient poetry and formulas of ritual texts. After offering and drinking soma, a priest may recite Rig Veda 8.48.3, boasting on behalf of all, "We have drunk soma, become immortal, attained the light, reached the gods." A common epithet of soma is *amrita* (not mortal). Several gods receive soma offerings, but none more than Indra. The consequence of his soma-drinking is an enthused battle fury, rendering him invincible in combat.

Associations with immortality led to an important role for Soma in traditions of death, particularly after the Upanishads distinguished the *pitṛyāna* as a "path of the fathers (ancestors)" that recycled an immortal *ātman* (self) down from the moon for rebirth in this world. In Hindu rituals, *amāvāsyā*, new-moon day, is traditionally a time to offer rice as food for ancestors. Soma as the moon—therefore one of the *navagraha* (nine planets)— lends his name to the calendrical weekday Somavaram (Monday is from Old English "moonday"). In Sanskrit epics and Purāṇas, Soma lives on as Oshadhīpati (lord of plants), husband of the *nakshatra* (constellations), and guardian deity of the auspicious northeast.

David M. Knipe

See also **Agni; Hinduism (Dharma); Shrauta Sūtras; Upanishadic Philosophy; Vedic Aryan India; Yajña**

BIBLIOGRAPHY

Gonda, Jan. *Change and Continuity in Indian Religion*. The Hague: Mouton, 1965. Ch. 2 on soma, *amṛta*, and the moon.
Nyberg, Harri. "The Problem of the Āryans and the Soma: The Botanical Evidence." In *The Indo-Āryans of Ancient South Asia*, edited by George Erdosy. Berlin: Walter de Gruyter, 1995. Perspective of a specialist in plant chemistry.
Staal, Frits. *Agni. The Vedic Ritual of the Fire Altar*. 2 vols. Berkeley, Calif.: Asian Humanities, 1983. Soma as used in 1975 Agnicayana sacrifice in Kerala; excellent plates.
Wasson, R. Gordon. *Soma. Divine Mushroom of Immortality*. New York: Harcourt Brace Jovanovich, 1968. Numerous plates and Wendy Doniger O'Flaherty's translations from the Rig Veda build a case for soma as *Amanita muscaria*.

SOUL ("ATMAN"). *See* **Upanishadic Philosophy.**

SOUTH ASIAN ASSOCIATION FOR REGIONAL COOPERATION (SAARC) Regional cooperation in South Asia is a recent phenomenon, even though the idea of regionalism long formed an important element of the foreign policy of India. It took the seven countries—India, Pakistan, Bangladesh, Sri Lanka, Nepal, Bhutan, and Maldives—nearly four decades of the post-colonial era to set up a regional association, the South Asian Association for Regional Cooperation (SAARC). The proposal for SAARC was first made by the president of Bangladesh, Zia ur Rahman, in January 1980. While the smaller countries welcomed the idea, India initially appeared reticent, apprehensive perhaps that the association would bring anti-Indian opinions together to limit its policy options. Similarly, Pakistan suspected the idea to be an Indian ploy to strengthen its regional hegemony. Amid such unfounded fears, diplomatic efforts resulted in a series of consultations and the meeting of foreign secretaries in Colombo, Sri Lanka, in 1981. Foreign ministers of all seven counties then met in New Delhi in 1983 to give a concrete shape to SAARC, which was formally established in December 1985, when the seven heads of South Asia's states and governments held the first summit in Dhaka, Bangladesh.

SAARC has a well-defined charter specifying its objectives, principles, and mechanisms for formulation and execution of policies and programs. One of its principles is that contentious and bilateral issues are excluded from the scope of its deliberations. Decisions must be made unanimously at the summit, based on the recommendations of foreign ministers and a standing committee of foreign secretaries. Technical committees coordinate and monitor the implementation of programs. The overall responsibility for follow-up action on summit decisions is assigned to the SAARC Secretariat, located in Nepal's capital, Kathmandu. Its secretary general is nominated by the member states on the basis of rotation.

Notwithstanding many difficult challenges to its growth, SAARC has begun to evolve a common regional approach to trade and socioeconomic development. Areas of cooperation include agriculture, rural development, poverty alleviation, sports, art and culture, science

South Asian Association for Regional Cooperation Summit. Members of 11th SAARC (South Asian Association for Regional Cooperation) summit, in Kathmandu, Nepal, 5 January 2002. At this meeting, member nation-states pledged their commitment to creating a South Asian Economic Union. INDIA TODAY.

and technology, and women's development. Some of the noteworthy decisions of the member states pertain to the establishment of a food security reserve, the suppression of terrorism, the prevention of trafficking in narcotic drugs and psychotropic substances, the establishment of a SAARC Chamber of Commerce, regional arrangements for preferential trading, and the establishment of a South Asian free trade area. A development fund has also been created. SAARC audiovisual programs seek to foster contacts and interactions among people.

Many laudable objectives of SAARC have not been achieved, however. In the eighteen years of its existence, it has held only twelve summits. Seven summits were postponed, mostly because of rivalry and confrontation between India and Pakistan. There is now a realization that the success of SAARC is contingent upon the resolution of contentious bilateral problems like the Kashmir dispute between the two countries. In addition, a lack of sufficient commitment on the part of some member states to implement summit decisions has contributed to SAARC's sluggish growth. For example, Pakistan still has not ratified a 1987 regional convention on the suppres-

sion of terrorism, thus weakening the association's record of cooperation. Nevertheless, SAARC's formation and its ongoing efforts have created a growing South Asian consciousness and have helped stabilize regional identity, enhancing interactions among the various peoples of South Asia.

Ponmoni Sahadevan

See also **Bangladesh; Maldives and Bhutan, Relations with; Nepal; Pakistan; Sri Lanka**

BIBLIOGRAPHY

Gonsalves, Eric, and Nancy Jetley, eds. *The Dynamics of South Asia: Regional Cooperation and SAARC.* New Delhi: Sage, 1999.
Kanesalingam, V., ed. *Political Dimensions of South Asian Cooperation.* New Delhi: Macmillan, 1991.

SOUTH ASIAN ECONOMIC COOPERATION

India, Pakistan, Sri Lanka, Bangladesh, Bhutan, Maldives, and Nepal agreed in 1980 to form the South Asian

Association for Regional Cooperation (SAARC), which mandated cooperation in a number of areas, including trade and investment, economic development, environmental management and resource sharing, educational enrichment, and poverty alleviation. However, SAARC has yet to achieve its goals of enhancing regional economic cooperation and delivering prosperity to and well-being to its people. Geopolitical analysts may attribute the slow progress to the political tensions between India and Pakistan, but the reality is that South Asia needs to become more actively engaged in the global economy in order to optimize its resources, instead of being left behind in the race for better incomes and jobs.

The new economy has opened up several opportunities for South Asia to move beyond the focus of its traditional commodity trade items, harnessing the economic benefits of business cooperation in high value–adding areas such as natural gas, electricity and power sharing, telecommunications infrastructure, training and manpower development, information technology, and joint projects for foreign investment. The continuing boom in India's economy—especially in high-tech areas like business process outsourcing, information technology (IT) services, computer solutions, biotechnology, consumer call centers, and knowledge-based industries—has added new pressures for enhancing business relations among all South Asian countries.

Traditional Economic Relations: Limited Formats

Traditional trade relations in South Asia have been characterized by the following features:

1. South Asia accounts for less than 1 percent of world income, and its share in total global trade is negligible.
2. All South Asian countries show low volumes of foreign trade as a percentage of their respective gross domestic product (GDP), although South Asia is a major supplier of textiles and garments, raw cotton, rubber, jute, rice, tea, pearls, and precious and semiprecious stones to the rest of the world.
3. Regional trade among the SAARC countries has been a dismal 3 percent for the past decade. This compares poorly with European Union (EU) regional trade, which stands at nearly 65 percent, and trade among the Association of Southeast Asian Nations (ASEAN), which stands at about 35 percent.
4. India is central to South Asian trade, as it accounts for about 80 percent of the combined GDP and population of South Asia. It is also the largest trading partner for Bangladesh, Nepal, and Bhutan, and significant for Sri Lanka. However, India has shown the lowest amount of intraregional trade (5.1%), as

compared to its smaller neighbors Maldives and Nepal (29%), and Sri Lanka (21%), who are trading more intensively within the South Asia region.
5. While intra-SAARC regional trade is low, the South Asian countries do not hesitate to import large quantities of items from the rest of the world, many of which could be imported from within the South Asian region. For example, Pakistan imports tea from China and Kenya, instead of India, despite the availability of better quality, lower price, and geographical proximity of India.
6. The traditional export basket of most South Asian countries is dominated by semimanufactured products, and appears to be quite similar for all the countries, making it difficult for any one country to have a comparative trade advantage over the others. Primary commodities, however, still account for a significant proportion of their trade, which includes jute in the case of Bangladesh, rubber and tea for Sri Lanka and India, rice and raw cotton for India and Pakistan, and iron ore for India. Among manufactured exports, textiles and garments dominate the export basket.
7. All South Asian countries show a high dependence on a few commodities for their export basket. In fact, the top ten export commodities (mainly textile and garment items) account for nearly 82 percent of the total exports of Bangladesh, Maldives, and Nepal; 74 percent for Pakistan, 66 percent for Sri Lanka, and about 42 percent for India. As for imports, all South Asian countries show "industrial intermediates" and crude and processed fuel as major imports. Food deficit countries, such as Bangladesh, Nepal, Bhutan, Pakistan, and Sri Lanka, continued to import food throughout the 1990s.
8. Most South Asian exports are directed toward developed countries. In the case of Pakistan, more than 60 percent of exports are accounted for by the United States, the United Kingdom, Germany, and Japan, while the Middle East constitutes 11 percent of total exports. East Asian countries are providing a growing market for South Asian exports, particularly for India, Pakistan, and Maldives. Bangladesh mainly exports to China; Pakistan to South Korea, Indonesia, and China; and Maldives to Thailand.

Areas of Recent Business Cooperation
SAFTA: South Asian Free Trade Area. The South Asian nations launched a regional economic trade agreement in 1995 that would aim at providing "preferential trade concessions" to each other, under the South Asian Preferential Trade Agreement (SAPTA). After three successive rounds of SAPTA negotiations, a total of 5,550 commodities have been listed for trade under SAPTA.

Although SAPTA showed a high potential for success, its progress has been slow, due mainly to: the bureaucracy's lack of commitment to put aside narrow political interests and support each member state's economic interest; the continuing refusal of Pakistan to grant the most favored nation status to India, which is granted to all other trading partners in South Asia; technical limitations to the implementation of SAPTA, under which negotiating trade concessions on a "product-by-product" basis becomes very tedious.

At the twelfth SAARC Summit meeting in Islamabad in January 2004, it was agreed to initiate the South Asian Free Trade Area (SAFTA), beginning in 2006, to be completed in phases by 2008. However, for the success of any free trade area in South Asia, it will be critical to actively involve the business community in the negotiations as a primary stakeholder, not just as a beneficiary of governmental decisions.

The information technology (IT) sector. The South Asian region has been made aware of the high potential of the information technology and software industry through the recent success of Indian "high-tech" firms in the global market. The Indian software industry has grown consistently at a phenomenal rate of over 50 percent during the 1990s, rising from a modest revenue base of U.S.$195 million in 1989–1990 to an $8.3 billion industry by 2000–2001. India's software industry revenue growth is projected to reach U.S.$85 billion by 2008, of which $50 billion is to come from exports alone.

Software engineers and professionals of Indian origin currently constitute about 10 percent of the employees in the top four global IT companies (Microsoft, IBM, Intel, and Oracle). The Indian industry trains over 1 million people in the country every year in IT, and provides IT-enabled services at one-tenth of the global cost. Thus India has today become a major outsourcing base for businesses all over the world, offering a huge pool of highly qualified, English speaking, analytically strong, and talented professionals.

The South Asian region has the potential for being developed as a regional hub for offshore software development for clients within SAARC and in other countries, with India as its core. The larger challenge will be to attract Indian corporations into doing business with South Asian nations, given that the main markets for their products lie in the United States, Europe, Southeast Asia, and China.

Harnessing the power sector. South Asia is one of the richest sources of hydropower in the world. The estimated hydropower potentials of the countries in the region are: Bangladesh, 52,000 megawatts (MW); Bhutan, 21,000 MW; Nepal, 83,290 MW; India, 75,400 MW; Pakistan, 38,000 MW; and Sri Lanka, 2,000 MW. However, less than 11 percent of this vast regional potential is being exploited so far. Because power generation and supply in South Asia has been a state monopoly over a long period, it has been highly dependent on state subsidies and therefore deprived of a competitive and efficient working environment. A large number of reforms for private sector participation and restructuring in the power sector have been introduced in all the South Asian countries in recent years, which has opened up a valuable potential for private sector collaboration in harnessing the hydropower of South Asia.

India and Bangladesh have an arrangement under which surplus power from the eastern states of India is exported to the deficit western region of Bangladesh. India and Nepal have signed the Treaty for the Integrated Development of the Mahakali Rivers for mutual cooperation in the power sector. Nepal has set up four hydroelectric projects with Indian assistance. India purchases 50 megawatts of power from Nepal, with reliable transmission assured, and provides 70 million units of energy annually free of charge to Nepal from the Tanakpur power plant.

In Bhutan, the 336-megawatt Chukha hydroelectric project was set up with technical and financial assistance from India, and India also constructed a number of micro-hydropower projects in Bhutan. This is a classic case of gains from cross-border trade, built on the basis of common interest and sovereign equality. Bhutan has earned considerable profits from export of this surplus power to India, which is primarily distributed to the Indian power-deficit states of West Bengal, Orissa, and the North-East region.

Conservative estimates made by the government of Pakistan indicate that Pakistan is likely to have surplus power over the next few years. If Pakistan were to export its surplus 200 megawatts of power to India, it could earn U.S.$1.2 billion annually over a period of twenty years. This would be a major nontraditional export item in Pakistan's export basket, and would optimize the use of power plants in Pakistan at 80 percent of their capacity, rather than the current 60 percent levels.

The case for natural gas pipelines. The prospect for the emergence of natural gas pipelines as a key area for South Asian economic cooperation is based on the increasing demand in Indian markets for energy, India becoming one of the fastest-growing energy markets in the world. The prospect for supplying natural gas from neighboring countries like Bangladesh and Pakistan—either through their own resource endowments or as transit points for supply to India—has come up for discussion in recent years. Interest by "third" countries like Iran, Oman, Myanmar, and Turkmenistan to supply their surplus natural gas to India and the region, and the willingness of multilateral funding institutions and foreign multinational corporations to provide insurance guarantees, has generated further expectations for earning revenues from natural gas.

The initiative for an Iran-India gas pipeline began as early as July 1993. Both nations have decided to undertake an offshore feasibility study for laying a pipeline from Iran to India "outside the Exclusive Economic Zone (EEZ) of Pakistan."

Pakistan, on the other hand, has confirmed its willingness for the construction of an onshore gas pipeline from Iran to India, which has the potential for raising a huge revenue from "transit fees," estimated in the range of $500 million annually for Pakistan. However, no decision for an onshore pipeline has yet been made, given the institutional, political, and long-term supply security risks involved in this option for India. A large number of Indian corporates (such as Reliance Industries), foreign multinational companies (such as British Gas, Royal Dutch Shell Group, BHP Australia, and UNOCAL), and multilateral lending institutions (such as the Asian Development Bank), would be key players in supporting active discussions for the construction of a natural gas pipeline in South Asia.

In recent years, major gas reserves have been found in Bangladesh at the Bibiyana Natural Gas Fields. Market studies by UNOCAL and others have confirmed that the Bangladesh market will not be able to utilize such volumes for over fifteen years. An opportunity thus exists for exporting more gas to serve customers along the Hazira-Bijaipur-Jagdhishpur (HBJ) pipeline, on the proposed route between Bangladesh and India. The estimated benefits to Bangladesh are in the range of U.S.$3.5 billion in revenues and tax receipts over a twenty-year period. It would also develop approximately 1,900 jobs for Bangladeshi citizens, and could generate $55 million to $75 million for local procurement during the construction phase. Despite these major benefits, however, Bangladesh has not shown any inclination to export natural gas to the Indian market.

It is clear that the emerging global economy—based on communications, technologies, innovation, and new formats for doing business—will open up several new sectors for economic cooperation in South Asia. It is the responsibility of all the nations of South Asia to find the political will to place high priority on regional economic cooperation, development, and poverty reduction.

Poonam Barua

See also **South Asian Association for Regional Cooperation (SAARC)**

BIBLIOGRAPHY

Barua, Poonam. "RoadMap to SAFTA." New Delhi: SAARC Chamber of Commerce and Industry, 2000.

———. "Towards a Free Trade Arrangement in South Asia." Working report. New Delhi: SAARC Chamber of Commerce, 2001.

"Executive Summary: Water and Security in South Asia (WASSA)." Sponsored by the Carnegie Corporation of New York, and South Asia Program/FPI, School of Advanced International Studies, Johns Hopkins University, Washington, D.C., April 2003.

Kumar, Nagesh. "Indian Software Industry Development: International and National Perspectives." *Economic and Political Weekly*, 10 November 2001.

Lama, Mahendra P. "Economic Reforms and the Energy Sector in South Asia: Scope for Cross-Border Power Trade." *Asian Survey* 2000.

Research and Information Systems. "South Asia Development and Cooperation Report 2003." New Delhi: RIS, 2003.

Schaffer, Teresita A. "Regional Economic Relationships: Trade, Energy, and Water." Washington, D.C.: Center for Strategic Studies, April 2003.

Siddiqi, Toufiq A. "A Natural Gas Pipeline for India and Pakistan." Global Environment and Energy in the Twenty-first Century. Honolulu, 2003.

"South Asian Growth Quadrangles: Emerging Opportunities for Economic Partnership." New Delhi: Federation of Indian Chambers of Commerce and Industry, 2000.

SOUTHEAST ASIA, RELATIONS WITH India's relations with the countries of what is today known as "Southeast Asia" date back to antiquity. Early Indian texts referred to Southeast Asia as Suvarnabhumi (land of gold). Trade and the transmission of the Hindu and Buddhist religions were key elements of India's early interaction with Southeast Asian lands, including Myanmar (Burma), Thailand, the Indochina peninsula, Malaya, and Indonesia. This was not a one-way traffic; Southeast Asians, particularly traders of the Malay world, also sailed west across the Bay of Bengal. The flow of Indian priests, traders, and adventurers, along with intermarriages and cultural assimilation, left a deep and lasting impact on the cultural landscape of Southeast Asia, one of the most impressive examples of acculturation in history. By the eleventh century, a number of strongly "Indianized" kingdoms, such as Funan and Champa, emerged in the Indochina peninsula, as did Nakhon Sri Thammarat in the Malayan peninsula.

Indianization

What historians describe as the "Indianization" of Southeast Asia was "the expansion of an organized culture, founded on the Indian conception of royalty, Hindu or Buddhist beliefs, the mythology of ancient Hindu

Purāṇas, and the observance of the Hindu law codes, expressed in the Sanskrit language." Other features of Indianization included the use of alphabets of Indian origin, the pattern of Indian law and administration and monuments, and architecture and sculpture influenced by the arts of India. But the subject of "Indianization" or "Hinduization" of Southeast Asia has been controversial. The thesis of Indian colonization of Southeast Asia, or Indian views of Southeast Asia as "greater India" or "further India," popularized by nationalist groups, like the Greater India Society of Calcutta, and historians of ancient India, such as R. C. Majumdar, has found less favor among contemporary historians of Southeast Asia.

Archaeological and literary evidence suggests that India's impact on Southeast Asia was achieved largely through peaceful means, by commerce rather than conquest, and by cultural assimilation rather than outright colonization. Nor were Southeast Asians mere passive recipients of Indian ideas, but actively engaged borrowers.

Ideas that suited indigenous traditions, or that could easily be adapted to local interests and practices, were more readily received than those that did not have such potential. The Indian caste system and the practice of according lower status to women were not popular in the Southeast Asia. The temple arts of the Hindu-Buddhist kingdoms of Pagan, Angkor, and Java differ from those of India. The influence of Indian ideas was heavily mediated by indigenous Southeast Asian beliefs and practices; Southeast Asians adapted or localized them to suit their own interests, needs, and values.

The decline of Buddhism in India by the end of the twelfth century and the erosion of Hindu political power with the advent of Muslim rule in India contributed to the decline of Indian influence in Southeast Asia. The conversion of Malacca to Islam in the early fifteenth century saw Islam supplant Hinduism and Buddhism there, although it was Indian Muslim merchants who, ironically, played a key role in the spread of Islam by bringing with them mullahs, Sufi mystics, and Arab preachers. Indians, especially Muslim traders from the Tamil and Gujurati areas of India, played a major role in the rise of Malacca as the premier port city of Southeast Asia. Through intermarriage and commercial power, they became a major force at Malacca's royal court.

The advent of European rule in Asia and the restrictive trade policies of the Dutch and the British severely undermined India's commercial links with Southeast Asia. The Europeans took control of the trade in spices and textiles, the staples of India-Southeast Asia trade. Under the British Raj, the Indian economy was transformed from being an exporter of manufactured goods to

a supplier of raw materials for Britain. The British also actively curbed Indian shipbuilding and shipping. But British rule started a new type of migration from India to Southeast Asia, especially to Malaya, dating from the foundation of Penang in 1786. In contrast to earlier Indian migrants, who tended to be traders and financiers or priests and pandits, the new migration was more regulated and of a larger scale, consisting chiefly of indentured, illiterate laborers. Annual levels of migration from India to Malaya jumped from less than 7,000 in 1880 to over 18,000 in 1889, while migrations to Burma increased from less than 7,000 to over 38,000. In 1910 an estimated 331,100 Indians migrated to Burma, while the figure for Malaya was 91,723. In 1935 the respective figures were 296,600 for Burma and 81,350 for Malaya.

The Post-colonial Period

The Japanese conquest of Southeast Asia and the advance of the Japanese army to the border region between Burma and British India underscored the strategic vulnerability of India to attacks through Southeast Asia. During the Japanese occupation of the region from 1942 to 1945, Southeast Asia also became the launching point of the military campaign led by Netaji Subhash Chandra Bose and his Indian National army, drawn mainly from Indians in Southeast Asia, to oust the British from India.

In the early postwar period, Indian interests in Southeast Asia comprised political, economic, and strategic dimensions. Politically, Indian nationalist leaders viewed the anticolonial struggles in Southeast Asia as being indivisible from their own struggle. India's struggle for independence from British rule was viewed in Southeast Asia with great interest. The second Asian country, after the Philippines, to achieve independence, India after 1947 played an important role in the campaign for self-determination in Southeast Asia. Economically, Southeast Asia was a market for Indian textiles (Burma was an almost exclusive Indian market); and India was heavily dependent on Burma, Indonesia, Malaya, Thailand, and Indochina for oil, rubber, tin, rice, and timber. An estimated 1.3 million to 1.8 million Indian immigrants in Southeast Asia during the immediate postwar period provided another crucial link between India and Southeast Asia; the treatment of Indian migrants in Burma would become an issue in Indian relations with that country. Strategically, Indian diplomat K. M. Panikkar (who is credited with being among the first to use the term "Southeast Asia") suggested the creation of an "Indian security sphere" extending from the Persian Gulf to Burma, Siam (Thailand), the Indochina peninsula, Malaya, and Singapore. Indian leaders like Deputy Prime Minister Sardar Vallabhbhai Patel expressed concern about instability and Communist insurgency in Southeast Asia as potential threats to Indian security. This concern was fueled by the meetings of Asian Communist leaders under the banner of the South Asian Youth Congress in Calcutta (the so-called Calcutta Conference) in February 1948, which was followed by the outbreak of Communist rebellions in both India and Southeast Asia. At the same time, the emergence of China as a major Asian power introduced an important new dimension to India's interest in Southeast Asia.

Despite professing a strong commitment to decolonization in Southeast Asia, Prime Minister Jawaharlal Nehru was prepared only to extend diplomatic support to Southeast Asian struggles. Nehru refused Ho Chi Minh's request for material support against the French, though he took a more active role in supporting Indonesia's struggle against the Dutch. India took the lead in convening the 1949 conference on Indonesia to show support for Indonesian nationalists, though again Indian support was mainly moral rather than material. This affected Nehru's bid to organize a regional grouping of newly independent Asian nations. The unofficial Asian Relations Conference held in New Delhi in 1947 under Nehru's chairmanship attracted delegations from all Southeast Asian countries, but the resulting Asian Relations Organization was moribund and short-lived.

Nehru joined Indonesia's efforts to convene a conference of African and Asian countries, which led to the famous Bandung Conference of 1955. At this time, the regional identity of Southeast Asia remained closely tied to that of India. The Bandung Conference was convened by the Conference of Southeast Asian Prime Ministers (also known as the Colombo Powers), a regional grouping that included the leaders of Pakistan, India, and Sri Lanka, as well as Indonesia and Burma. That conference, though successful in articulating a sense of solidarity among the newly independent countries, revealed serious differences, however, between India and the pro–United States Southeast Asian nations, Thailand and the Philippines. Nehru bitterly condemned military alliances between Asian nations and the superpowers, targeting specifically the Southeast Asia Treaty Organization, antagonizing the leaders of Pakistan, Thailand, and the Philippines.

A highlight of India's involvement in Southeast Asia in the 1950s was its efforts to mediate in the conflict between the French and the North Vietnamese following the Geneva Accords in 1954. Indian diplomacy in the Indochina conflict included Nehru's call for an immediate cease-fire in February 1954. Nehru sought to prevent both Chinese military intervention in support of Ho Chi Minh and large-scale U.S. intervention that might have included nuclear weapons. India's role led to its appointment as chairman of the International Control Commission

(ICC) on Indochina, whose role was to control the flow of armaments into Laos, Cambodia, and Vietnam. But the ICC suffered from a weak mandate and shortage of manpower, and was consumed by the escalation of great power rivalry. China made diplomatic and commercial gains in Southeast Asia at India's expense, while Nehru seemed more preoccupied with domestic issues.

The 1962 war between India and China dashed any remaining hopes of Indian interaction with Southeast Asia within a pan-Asian framework. This was accompanied by a growing divergence of their national economic policies and development strategies: India remained preoccupied with its domestic problems and the conflict with Pakistan over Kashmir, while the Southeast Asian nations remained concerned with the threat of Communist insurgency and potential Chinese and Vietnamese expansionism. Economically, while Southeast Asian countries were experiencing robust economic growth through openness to foreign investment and multinational enterprise, India could muster only what was derisively called the "Hindu" rate of growth of around 5 percent, which was seen in Southeast Asia as the result of its socialist, centrally planned economy. Later, in the 1990s, India's democratic system invited unflattering comments from the likes of Singapore's Lee Kuan Yew, who favored "discipline over democracy." The divergence in strategic outlook was equally pronounced, especially after the formation of the Association of Southeast Asian Nations (ASEAN) in 1967. While India remained somewhat uninterested in joining ASEAN, its leaders also ruled out Indian membership on the ground that it was not "geographically included in Southeast Asia." More importantly, India's nonaligned outlook, albeit with a tilt to Moscow over cold war issues, conflicted with ASEAN's pro–U.S. stance, camouflaged in its doctrine of a "Zone of Peace, Freedom, and Neutrality" in Southeast Asia. The signing of the Indo-Soviet Treaty of Peace, Friendship, and Cooperation in August 1971, intended to deter any Chinese or American intervention in support of Pakistan, was seen in Southeast Asia as compromising India's nonalignment. The Vietnamese invasion of Cambodia in December 1978 led India to recognize the Vietnamese-installed Heng Samarin regime in Cambodia. This was at serious odds with ASEAN's effort to condemn and isolate Hanoi. Moreover, in the 1980s, India's naval modernization program caused some apprehension in Southeast Asia.

India "Looks East"

The coolness and mutual neglect in India-ASEAN relations persisted until the early 1990s. But a major shift occurred in 1994, when Indian prime minister Narashimha Rao outlined India's "look east" policy, whose main thrust was "to draw, as much as possible, investment and cooperation from the Asia-Pacific countries, in consonance with our common concept and solidarity and . . . our common destiny." The "look east" policy was a logical and necessary extension of India's domestic economic liberalization drive, which was dictated by harsh domestic economic and political realities. ASEAN is a key part of the look east policy.

The focus of India's look east policy and India-ASEAN ties has been in the economic arena. According to official Indian figures, India's exports to ASEAN jumped from U.S.$2.9 billion in 1996–1997 to U.S.$4.6 billion in 2002–2003, while imports from ASEAN during the same period rose from U.S.$2.9 billion to U.S.$5.2 billion. Although Southeast Asia accounts for only 8.77 percent of India's total exports and 8.44 percent of India's total imports, and foreign direct investment (FDI) by ASEAN states in India accounted for only 3.4 percent of total FDI flows to India (January 1991–May 2002), India's impressive economic growth portends rising trade with ASEAN. India's leadership position in information technology provides ASEAN with an opportunity to forge stronger economic links with India through greater economic integration.

India's relations with ASEAN have been facilitated by New Delhi's participation in a number of common regional forums. In 1992 India became a sectoral dialogue partner of ASEAN. Although restricted to areas concerning trade, investment, tourism, science, and technology, this represented India's first formal involvement with ASEAN. In 1995 India was made a full dialogue partner by ASEAN, becoming eligible to participate in a much wider range of sectors, including infrastructure, civil aviation, and computer software, as well as in ASEAN Post Ministerial Meetings. India was invited for the first time to summit level talks with ASEAN in Cambodia in November 2002, and at the second ASEAN-India Summit in Bali in October 2003, India signed a Framework Agreement for creating an ASEAN-India free trade agreement (FTA) in a decade. The same year, India also signed a Framework Agreement for creating an FTA with Thailand, and started negotiations for a Comprehensive Economic Cooperation Agreement with Singapore.

In 1996, India joined the ASEAN Regional Forum (ARF), the first multilateral security organization in the Asia-Pacific region under ASEAN leadership. Until then, ASEAN members had opposed Indian membership. India, as with the rest of the South Asian countries, was considered to be outside the geographic scope of the Asia-Pacific region. A more important, if not publicly stated, factor was ASEAN's fear that South Asian membership

would saddle the ARF with the seemingly intractable India-Pakistan rivalry, including the Kashmir problem. ASEAN's motives in inviting India into the ARF was partly determined by ASEAN's perception of the importance of India as a counterweight to China. India's growing links with ASEAN and sub-ASEAN groupings is indicated in its participation in the launching of a new subregional group involving Bangladesh, India, Myanmar, Sri Lanka, and Thailand for Economic Cooperation, whose objectives include regional cooperation in transport and infrastructure. India also engages the newer ASEAN members through the Mekong Ganga Cooperation initiative, which involves building transportation links between India and the newer ASEAN members.

India has no border or land disputes in Southeast Asia and has already marked out its maritime boundary with Indonesia and Thailand. Currently, no Southeast Asian nation considers India to be a threat; nor does India expect any threats to security from any Southeast Asian country. While the situation in Myanmar, especially the growing military ties between Myanmar and China, has been a source of concern to Indian strategists, successive Indian governments have favored a policy of "engaging" China. Like ASEAN, India opposes the isolation of Myanmar. While Indian strategic planners recognize the importance of global trade routes through Southeast Asia, and share a concern over the rise of Chinese military power, India does not appear to have any grand plans for assuming a major security role in the Asia Pacific region, despite its powerful navy.

Nonetheless, the changing strategic climate in Asia appears to favor the development of closer political and security ties between India and the Southeast Asian countries. The 1990s saw increased defense contacts between India and ASEAN countries. The Indian navy has conducted a number of "friendship exercises" with ASEAN navies, including the navies of Singapore, Indonesia, Thailand, and Malaysia. India and Malaysia have cooperated in a program to provide familiarization and maintenance training for Russian-supplied MiG aircraft to Malaysian air force personnel. Since the terrorist attacks of 11 September 2001, Indian has joined the U.S. Navy in providing escort vessels in the Straits of Malacca.

Amitav Acharya

See also **Burma**

BIBLIOGRAPHY

Acharya, Amitav. *Engagement or Estrangement? India and the Asia Pacific Region.* Toronto: University of Toronto–York University Joint Centre for Asia Pacific Studies, 1999.

Focus on "look east" policy and institutional links between India and ASEAN.

Ayoob, Mohammed. *India and Southeast Asia: Indian Perceptions and Policies.* London: Routledge, 1990. A short, insightful study of India-ASEAN relations during the period of the Cambodia conflict.

Coedes, G. *The Indianized States of Southeast Asia*, edited by Walter F. Villa and translated by Sue Brown Cowing. Honolulu: University of Hawaii Press, 1968. A classic study of Indianization by an Indologist.

Majumdar, R. C. *Greater India.* 2nd ed. Mumbai: National Information and Publications, 1948. An Indian nationalist historian's perspective on Indian influence.

Ministry of Commerce and Industry, Government of India. "Export Import Data Bank." Available at <http://commerce.nic.in/eidb/default.asp>

Ministry of External Affairs, Government of India. "ASEAN-India Relations." Available at <http://www.meadev.nic.in/foreign/asian-indrelations.htm>

Sandhu, K. S. *Indians in Malay: Some Aspects of Their Immigration and Settlement (1786–1957).* Cambridge, U.K.: Cambridge University Press, 1969. Pathbreaking and still the most authoritative work.

SarDesai, D. R. "India and Southeast Asia during the Nehru Era." In *The Legacy of Nehru: A Centennial Assessment*, edited by D. R. SarDesai and Anand Mohan. New Delhi: Promilla, 1992.

Sridharan, Kripa. *The ASEAN Region in India's Foreign Policy.* Aldershot, U.K.: Dartmouth, 1996.

Ton-That, Thien. *India and Southeast Asia, 1947–1960: A Study of India's Policy towards the South East Asian Countries in the Period 1947–1960.* Geneva: Librairie Droz, 1963. Comprehensive Southeast Asian perspective.

Van Leur, J. C. *Indonesian Trade and Society: Essays in Asian Social and Economic History.* The Hague: W. van Hoeve, 1955.

Wheatley, Paul. "Presidential Address: India beyond the Ganges; Desultory Reflections on the Origins of Civilization in Southeast Asia." *Journal of Asian Studies* 42, no. 1 (1982): 13–28.

SPACE PROGRAM India's space program undertakes two major activities: it builds satellites used for remote sensing, meteorology, and communications; and it constructs the rockets to launch its satellites. India's space program has passed through two stages. The first stage began in the 1960s, and involved setting up an administrative framework and gaining experience with rocket operations. Initial low-tech space operations commenced in the early 1960s. In 1969 the Indian Space Research Organization (ISRO) was formed to coordinate these activities, and the Indian Department of Space was established in 1972.

ISRO's first chairman, Vikram Sarabhai, planned the gradual evolution and development of the Indian space program. In 1970 Sarabhai noted that in ten years India would have to acquire the capability not only of building telecommunication satellites, such as INSAT-1, but also of launching them into synchronous orbits. His initial goal was the development of a small satellite launcher, such as a Scout rocket, within five years. He noted that once the basic systems were developed, and enough experience acquired in operating them, a further five-year period (from 1975 to 1980) should be adequate for the second stage, the development of larger boosters. India's space program, however, has lagged more than a decade behind Sarabhai's ambitious schedule.

The latter phase of the first stage of India's space program focused mainly on experimental, low capability projects that allowed Indian scientists to gain experience in the construction and operation of satellites and launchers. In this phase, ISRO built (with foreign assistance) the Bhaskara earth observation satellites and the APPLE (Ariane Payload Experiment) communications satellite. From 1979 to 1983, it also conducted four tests of its indigenously built SLV-3 rocket (similar in design to the U.S. Scout rocket). Subsequently, ISRO built an augmented satellite launch vehicle (ASLV).

The second stage of India's space program commenced in the mid-1980s and focused on larger, more powerful, and mission-specific systems. This stage involved building the polar satellite launch vehicle (PSLV) to launch the Indian Remote Sensing (IRS) satellite, and the PSLV's successor, the geostationary satellite launch vehicle (GSLV), to launch a meteorology and telecommunications "Indian National Satellite" (INSAT). With the PSLV commencing operational launches in 1997 after three prior demonstration flights, and the GSLV making its first flight in 2001, India's space program emerged from its developing stages to join the ranks of the world's five advanced space agencies, all of which have geostationary earth orbit (GEO) capability.

The SLV-3 had a single 9-ton solid fuel engine and was only powerful enough to launch a 77–88 pound (35–40 kg) payload to an approximately 186 mile-altitude (300 km) low earth orbit (LEO). Three such engines power the ASLV, enabling it to place a 220–330 pound (100–150 kg) payload in an approximately 280 mile-altitude (450 km) LEO. Such lightweight low-orbit satellites did not have significant military or commercial capabilities. However, the SLV-3 could still be used as an intermediate range ballistic missile, and its first stage was used in the Agni intermediate range missile. The more powerful PSLV and GSLV can launch more capable, heavier satellites into optimal higher altitude orbits.

The PSLV and GSLV utilize two Indian-built propulsion systems: an approximately 130-ton solid fuel engine, and a 37–40 ton liquid fuel engine (whose design is based on the European Space Agency's Viking engine used in the Ariane launch vehicle). They allow the PSLV to launch a 2,645 pound (1,200 kg) payload (the IRS satellite) to an approximately 497 mile-altitude (800 km) polar orbit. The same systems are used on the GSLV, and are supplemented with a 12-ton cryogenic engine, which enables the GSLV to carry a heavier payload to a higher, 22,369 mile (36,000 km) GEO. The 400–414 ton GSLV was designed to launch 2,500 kg INSAT-2 class satellites, but its first three flights carried somewhat lighter satellites weighing 3373 pounds (1,530 kg; 2001), 4023 pounds (1,825 kg; 2003), and 4300 pounds (1,950 kg; 2004). The first three GSLVs also used Russian-supplied cryogenic engines. Later GSLVs will use more powerful, Indian-built, cryogenic engines. ISRO then plans to build a much heavier 630-ton GSLV-Mark 3 that can launch 8,818 pound (4,000 kg) satellites to GEO or 22,000 pound (10,000 kg) satellites to LEO. The rocket will have a 110-ton liquid fuel booster, additional 200-ton solid fuel engines, and a 25-ton cryogenic upper stage.

The IRS satellites have found applications with the Indian Natural Resource Management program, with regional Remote Sensing Service Centers in five Indian cities, and with Remote Sensing Application Centers in twenty Indian states that use IRS images for economic development applications. These include environmental monitoring, analyzing soil erosion and the impact of soil conservation measures, forestry management, determining land cover for wildlife sanctuaries, delineating groundwater potential zones, flood inundation mapping, drought monitoring, estimating crop acreage and deriving agricultural production estimates, fisheries monitoring, mining and geological applications such as surveying metal and mineral deposits, and urban planning. ISRO has also sold its IRS images to international clients; in 2003–2004, it had about 15 percent of the global market share for remote-sensing images. India's early IRS satellites—IRS-1A in March 1988, IRS-1B in August 1991, and IRS-1C in December 1995—were launched aboard Russian rockets. Subsequently, IRS-1D and the IRS-P series were launched on India's PSLV. ISRO thus launched PSLV-C1 with IRS-1D (1997); PSLV-C2 with three satellites—IRS-P4 (an oceanographic satellite), a German Tubsat, and a Korean Kitsat (1999); PSLV-C3 with three satellites—the Indian Technology Experiment Satellite (TES), German Bird, and Belgian Proba (2001); PSLV-C4 carrying a 1-ton meteorology satellite (Kalpana 1) to geosynchronous orbit (2002); and PSLV-C5 with IRS-P6 (2003).

The INSAT-2 and INSAT-3 satellites were launched aboard European Space Agency rockets. INSATs-2A to -2E were launched from 1992 to 1999, and INSAT-3A, -3B, -3C, and -3E were launched between 2000 and 2003. These INSAT satellites have been used to set up a national telecommunications infrastructure. INSAT-1B

extended television coverage to over 75 percent of India's population, and subsequent INSATs have brought television to most of India. The INSAT-2 satellites also provide telephone links to remote areas; data transmission for organizations such as the National Stock Exchange; mobile satellite service communications for private operators, railways, and road transport; and broadcast satellite services, used by India's state-owned television agency as well as commercial television channels. India's Edusat (Educational Satellite), launched aboard the GSLV in 2004, was intended for adult literacy and distance learning applications in rural areas. It augmented and would eventually replace such capabilities already provided by INSAT-3B.

Over time, India's INSAT and IRS satellites have become more sophisticated. For example, the Indian-built 2–2.5-ton INSAT-2 satellite had a greater number of more powerful transponders than the early U.S.-built 1-ton INSAT-1. Further, IRS-1A and -1B sensors had a resolution of 236 feet (72 m) multispectral (in the visible and near-infrared band) and 118 feet (36 m) panchromatic, while IRS-1C and -1D cameras have a better resolution of 75 feet (23 m) multispectral and 20 feet (6 m) panchromatic. ISRO had also planned to launch a mapping and cartography satellite, IRS-P5 (Cartosat-1), with 8.2 feet (2.5 m) panchromatic resolution, but instead launched TES aboard PSLV-C3 in 2001. TES had a panchromatic 3.3–3.6 foot (1–2 m) resolution camera. Subsequently, PSLV-C5 carried IRS-P6 (Resourcesat-1), with sensors of resolution similar to IRS-1D. In 2005, ISRO planned to launch PSLV-C6 with Cartosat-1, after which it will launch Cartosat-2 with a 3.3 foot (1 m) resolution camera, and a radar imaging satellite (Risat) that enables observation at night and under cloudy conditions.

India's satellites and satellite launch vehicles have had military spin-offs. While India's 93–124 mile (150–250 km) range Prithvi missile is not derived from the Indian space program, the intermediate range Agni missile is drawn from the Indian space program's SLV-3. In its early years, when headed by Vikram Sarabhai and Satish Dhawan, ISRO opposed military applications for its dual-use projects such as the SLV-3. Eventually, however, the Defence Research and Development (DRDO)–based missile program borrowed human resources and technology from ISRO. Missile scientist A. P. J. Abdul Kalam (elected president of India in 2002), who had headed the SLV-3 project at ISRO, moved to DRDO to direct India's missile program. About a dozen scientists accompanied Abdul Kalam from ISRO to DRDO, where Abdul Kalam designed the Agni missile using the SLV-3's solid-fuel first stage and a liquid-fuel (Prithvi-missile-derived) second stage. The Agni technology demonstrator flew three times—in 1989, 1992, and 1994—to an estimated range of 621–870 miles (1,000 to 1,400 km). ISRO also built a solid-fuel second stage for the 1,243 miles (2,000 km) range Agni-2, which first flew in 1999.

IRS and INSAT satellites were primarily intended and used for civilian-economic applications, but they also offered military spin-offs. In 1996 New Delhi's Ministry of Defence temporarily blocked the use of IRS-1C by India's environmental and agricultural ministries in order to monitor ballistic missiles near India's borders. In 1997 the Indian air force's "Airpower Doctrine" aspired to use space assets for surveillance and battle management. In 2000 the air force was conceptualizing various programs for an aerospace command and for the military use of space, and a parliamentary committee endorsed the idea. India's space assets provide modest reconnaissance and communications capabilities.

India's IRS and TES satellites have only a moderate military reconnaissance capability, with the drawbacks of poor resolution and limited frequency of coverage. The LISS cameras on IRS-1C, -1D, and -P6 have a 75 foot (23 m) resolution in the visible and near-infrared band, permitting the detection of large military installations. The PAN cameras on these satellites have a resolution of 20 feet (6 m) panchromatic, which can broadly detect surface ships, aircraft, tank formations, and ballistic missile units, but may not precisely identify these objects. India's INSATs can be used for multiple access digital data transmission, teleconferencing, and remote area emergency communications, features useful for a military command and control network and for search and rescue. However, the INSATs are not optimal for military operation due to their inappropriate frequency range.

India's space assets enhance India's military capabilities against Pakistan and China. If New Delhi acquires dedicated reconnaissance satellites that provide better coverage of Pakistan's military installations, it could obtain counterforce capability against Pakistan, since Pakistan's nuclear arsenal is small, and its delivery systems are concentrated at a few airfields and missile bases. If India's satellites can locate these missiles at their bases in real time, they would become vulnerable to an Indian strike. India's satellites also augment its capabilities against China. Once India develops 1,864–3,107 mile (3,000–5000 km) range Agni-3 missiles, it would have countervalue capabilities against major Chinese cities. Further, India's reconnaissance satellites will enable New Delhi to counter Chinese conventional threats. They can detect and track Chinese military forces in Tibet. They also give India's armed forces sufficient early warning about the movement of Chinese military forces from central China toward Tibet and India,

thus facilitating the timely deployment of Indian conventional forces to counter any such Chinese military deployments.

ISRO's annual space budget was approximately $400–500 million in the period 2000-2004 (compared against India's defense budget of approximately $12 billion–15 billion in this period). In the future, as ISRO launches satellites more frequently (two or more times each year) and undertakes new missions, its budgets could increase. ISRO's future plans are to activate its second launch pad, and use it to launch both the PSLV and the GSLV, in 2005. Further, it seeks to send recoverable capsules into space to perform experiments, after which the capsules will land at sea and be reused. ISRO conducted airdrop tests of such a capsule in 2004 and planned a space flight in 2005. In addition, it intends to develop the GSLV Mark-3 to launch 4-ton satellites. Finally, ISRO intends to launch a lunar probe aboard the PSLV in 2007–2008; the probe would orbit and send back high-resolution pictures of the moon.

Dinshaw Mistry

See also **Ballistic and Cruise Missile Development; Nuclear Programs and Policies; Nuclear Weapons Testing and Development; Weapons Production and Procurement**

BIBLIOGRAPHY

Johnson, Nicholas, and David Rodvold. *Europe and Asia in Space, 1993–94.* Kirtland, N. Mex.: USAF Phillips Laboratory, 1994.
Marwah, Onkar. "India's Nuclear and Space Programs: Intent and Policy," *International Security* 2, no. 2 (Fall 1977): 96–121.
Milhollin, Gary. "India's Missiles: With a Little Help from Our Friends." *Bulletin of the Atomic Scientists* 45, no. 9 (November 1989): 31–35.
Mistry, Dinshaw. "The Geostrategic Implications of India's Space Program." *Asian Survey* 41, no. 6 (November–December 2001): 1023–1043.
Sarabhai, Vikram. *Science Policy and National Development.* Delhi: Macmillan, 1974.
Thomas, Raju. "India's Nuclear and Space Programs." *World Politics* 38, no. 2 (January 1986): 315–342.

SRI LANKA A tiny island state, Sri Lanka is separated from South India by a narrow stretch of waters in the Palk Strait. It has a total land area of 25,330 square miles (65,610 sq. km.) and a population of about 19 million, including many ethnic communities with diverse histories, languages, and religions. Sinhalese constitute about two-thirds of the total population of Sri Lanka, while Tamils are the largest minority. Around 90 percent of Sri Lanka's people have Indian ancestors, as their forefathers began migrating from India over a thousand years ago. About 70 percent of Sri Lankans practice Buddhism, which now enjoys special privileges and state patronage. Hinduism, Christianity, and Islam are minority religions. Sinhalese form the majority in seven of Sri Lanka's nine provinces; Sri Lankan Tamils are dominant in the other two northern and eastern provinces, Jaffaa and Trincomalli, which they consider their traditional homeland, temporarily merged under the 1987 India–Sri Lanka accord. Muslims and Indian-origin Tamils live throughout the island, mostly in the eastern and central provinces, respectively.

Sri Lanka's independence from British colonial rule came peacefully in 1948. Given its long colonial experience, the country remained a parliamentary democracy for three decades until the second republican constitution of 1978 introduced its presidential system. A vibrant democracy, it has a multiparty system in which two parties dominate. Elections are held regularly, and participation in the electoral process has been always high. Universal adult franchise was introduced in 1931. Many governments have been coalitions headed by the United National Party or the Sri Lanka Freedom Party.

Plantation agriculture is the mainstay of the Sri Lankan economy. Tea is a major foreign exchange earner. Sri Lanka liberalized its economy in 1977. Over 90 percent of its people are literate, and the average life expectancy of 72.5 years is high.

Despite such impressive social indicators, Sri Lanka has witnessed large-scale death and destruction, especially since 1983, when ethnic riots began in Colombo and a civil war broke out in the Tamil-dominated provinces of the north and east. The root cause of ethnic antagonism lies in the conflicting visions of Sinhalese Buddhist and Sri Lankan Tamil Hindu nationalism, and the Tamil demand for its own nation-state (*eelam*) in the northeastern portion of the island. Successive Sinhalese governments in Colombo, through discriminatory policies regarding language, education, and employment, have alienated Sri Lanka's Tamil minority. The demand for equal linguistic rights and federal autonomy gained momentum in the 1950s, with the Federal Party providing early leadership. Since the mid-1970s, when the Sinhalese leadership failed to redress the Tamils' legitimate grievances, the moderate Tamil United Liberation Front launched a movement for a separate *eelam*. The movement soon took on a violent dimension, as militant organizations were formed to carry on the fight for independence.

The Liberation Tigers of Tamil Eelam (LTTE), led by Velupillai Prabhakaran, has remained the most powerful militant organization. Formed in 1972 as the Tamil

New Tigers (and renamed in 1976), the LTTE has grown strong enough to sustain prolonged insurgency since 1983 in the face of the tremendous military pressure brought upon it by the Sri Lankan state. Ruthlessness is a notable characteristic of the LTTE. By carrying out a systematic campaign of terror, it has created political disorder in the island. Many Sri Lankan leaders, as well as former Indian prime minister Rajiv Gandhi, fell prey to the LTTE's bullets and bombs. Unable to defeat the group militarily, the Sri Lankan government has intermittently offered to negotiate a peace settlement. Peace processes have not been successful, however, due to the LTTE's intransigence regarding their *eelam* goal and the Sinhalese leaders' failure to evolve a bipartisan approach to conflict resolution.

Ponmoni Sahadevan

See also **Sri Lanka, Relations with**

BIBLIOGRAPHY

Manogaran, Chelvadurai. *Ethnic Conflict and Reconciliation in Sri Lanka*. Honolulu: University of Hawaii Press, 1987.
Silva, K. M. de. *Sri Lanka: Problems of Governance*. New Delhi: Konark, 1993.
Wilson, A. Jeyaratnam. *Politics in Sri Lanka, 1947–1979*. London: Macmillan, 1979.

SRI LANKA, RELATIONS WITH Relations between India and Sri Lanka have been shaped by a variety of factors. The close proximity of the two states has encouraged the exchange of people, culture, trade, and hostilities over several millennia. Sri Lanka has also long served as an entrepôt for Indian Ocean commerce extending to West Asia, Africa, and Europe to its west, and Southeast Asia and China to its east. The mixture of diverse cultural influences in Sri Lanka, the relatively greater significance of maritime trade, its small size, and its geographically insular existence gave the island society a distinctive character and complex identity. This situation was reinforced by Sri Lanka's separate experience under British colonialism from the early nineteenth century. The British system of indirect rule through local notables created a commonality, which from the late nineteenth century gave way to nationalist demands by the Westernized elite in both India and Sri Lanka for increased access to representation and power. In Sri Lanka, the establishment and dominance of a colonial plantation export economy contributed to the emergence of a propertied elite with a conservative and accommodating attitude to British colonial power. The Sri Lankan nationalist movement and transfer of power, led by D. S. Senanayake, who was to become the first prime minister of Ceylon (as Sri Lanka was called until 1972), were carried out with little involvement by the masses. The more radical mass movement of India, led by the Indian National Congress under Mahatma Gandhi and Jawaharlal Nehru, backed by the relatively more developed and independent Indian business class, aroused admiration among the more liberal and progressive segments of Ceylonese society while creating great anxiety among the latter's elite. This situation was expressed in the post-independence period in Ceylon by the foreign policy orientations of the two major political blocs that came to dominate Sri Lankan politics. The center-right political party, the United National Party (UNP), remained wary of India, preferring a closer relationship with the capitalist West. In contrast, the center-left party, the Sri Lanka Freedom Party (SLFP) founded by S. W. R. D. Bandaranaike in 1952, favored a more independent, nonaligned stance that was pro-India and the Third World.

Citizenship and Voting Rights of Indian Tamils

A major subject of dispute between the two states in the early post-independence years revolved around the formal status and rights of Indian immigrants to Sri Lanka. The large majority of these immigrants were poor Tamil workers who had come as indentured labor starting from the early nineteenth century to work on Sri Lanka's famous tea plantations in the island's central upcountry. The South Indian Tamils had become the largest ethnic minority on Ceylon by 1911, when they were categorized separately for the first time. Their numbers peaked by 1939, declining thereafter due to discriminatory measures taken against them; by 1946 the census reported there were 857,329 persons of recent Indian origin (PRIOs/ PIOs, officially referred to as "Indian Tamils"). They began to participate in the island's politics in the 1920s by supporting the growing trade union movement and leftist political parties. Though Sri Lanka was bound by agreements with India from the early 1920s to treat the immigrants in a "nondiscriminatory" manner, the competition for votes and power induced Sinhalese political leaders to target immigrant Tamil labor in an exclusionary fashion after 1930, barring them from eligibility to vote and from economic programs. This culminated in the passage in 1948 of the citizenship and franchise acts that stripped the Indian Tamils of their citizenship and voting rights. The Ceylon Citizenship Act of 1948 created two types of citizenship: citizenship by descent and by registration. Citizenship by descent was restricted to persons who could prove that at least two generations (primarily on the male side) had been born on the island. Citizenship by registration would be available to those residents who could prove that either parent had been a citizen by descent, and that the individual had been a resident of Ceylon for seven years, if married, or ten years,

if unmarried. The minister in charge could also register twenty-five persons a year for "distinguished public service." Opposition members of Ceylon's parliament belonging to the left and to the Tamil parties denounced the legislation as having a clear racial and class bias, since it required documentary proof that simply did not exist for the overwhelming majority of poor Tamil workers. In contrast, Indian prime minister Jawaharlal Nehru had suggested a far simpler set of provisions, requiring residence of seven years prior to January 1948, along with a voluntary declaration of the intention and desire to settle in Ceylon. The Indian and Pakistani Residents' (Citizenship) Act of 1949 allowed for citizenship through satisfaction of a more complicated set of conditions: residence of seven years for married persons and ten years for unmarried persons to have been completed by January 1948, applications to be made within two years of the legislation, with proof of adequate means of livelihood and conformance with Ceylonese marriage laws. As events demonstrated, these requirements provided ample scope for the rejection of most applications on technical grounds. The Ceylon (Parliamentary Elections) Amendment of 1949 made the status of citizenship mandatory for franchise rights, stripping most Indian Tamils of the franchise that a number of them had enjoyed in the late colonial period. With India taking the position that all Indian emigrants to other parts of the British Empire were equal "subjects" in, and hence citizens of, their host countries, unless they voluntarily chose Indian citizenship, the Indian-origin population of Sri Lanka were rendered stateless. Not surprisingly, as a vulnerable population, their economic and political situation declined in the following period.

With several rounds of talks failing, and pressed repeatedly by Sri Lanka to help resolve the dispute, India reluctantly stepped away from its earlier position. Under the Sirimavo-Shastri Pact of 1964, signed by Sri Lankan prime minister Sirimavo Bandaranaike and Indian prime minister Lal Bahadur Shastri, Sri Lanka agreed to accept 300,000 persons and their natural increase, and India 525,000 persons with their increase. The status of the 150,000 who remained would be decided later. These numbers were arrived at by the Sri Lankan government without any consultation with its sole appointed Indian Tamil representative and trade union leader in Parliament, S. Thondaman. Nor did the Indian central government seek input from any of its Tamil representatives, arousing strong resentment in the state of Tamil Nadu.

In direct contradiction to the agreed-upon numbers, over 630,000 Indian Tamils applied for Ceylonese citizenship by the end of 1974. Fewer than 439,000 applied for Indian citizenship, many of them reluctantly, after having been rejected for Ceylonese citizenship. A follow-up agreement in 1974, recognizing the nonviability of the proportions in the earlier agreement, decided that each country would accept half of the remaining 150,000, but this agreement was never implemented. By the end of the period of the 1964 pact in October 1981, only 162,000 Indian Tamils had been registered as citizens of Ceylon, while 373,900 had been given Indian citizenship (of whom 284,300 had been repatriated to India). The rest remained stateless and voteless, with few individual and political rights.

In the following period, the Sri Lankan government gradually reversed its previous positions and belatedly granted citizenship to the remaining persons—a process largely undertaken by the UNP as a reward for the political support given by the Tamils in elections in the post-1977 period. The Citizenship (Special Provisions) Act of 1988 granted citizenship to the remaining persons of Indian origin who had not previously applied for Indian citizenship. This benefited 231,849 stateless persons. Further legislation, enacted in March 2003, gave citizenship to a further 200,000 Tamils.

Kachchativu Island

Another subject of dispute between India and Sri Lanka after independence related to the maritime waters and boundaries between them. For the most part, the demarcation of boundaries and areas of countrol over adjacent waters were settled amicably through negotiations in keeping with international law. Kachchativu, a barren island in the Palk Strait, which had traditionally been used by fishermen of both countries to rest and dry their nets while on fishing expeditions and annually for festival observances, acquired importance due to the extended maritime boundary and access to fish, prawns, and other marine resources they would give the possessing country. In the interest of improving relations, India agreed to concede the issue in favor of Sri Lanka's ownership of the island, on the condition that Indian fishermen and pilgrims would be allowed to continue to visit the island as they had in the past.

The Sri Lankan Tamil Separatist Movement

The major issue that has dominated relations between India and Sri Lanka from the early 1980s is the Sri Lankan Tamil movement for the creation of a separate Tamil *eelam* (homeland) in the northeast quarter of Sri Lanka. Differences between the Sinhalese-dominated central government and the Sri Lankan Tamil leadership were rooted in the colonial period. Sri Lankan Tamil fears of marginalization and subordination in the post-independence period grew in reaction to successive discriminatory state policies, including the deprivation of the Indian Tamils of citizenship and representation, the

consequent disproportionate representation of Sinhalese, and the declaration of Sinhala (the language of the Sinhalese) as Sri Lanka's only official language in 1956. The allocation of development funds and projects by Colombo's Sinhalese-led government to majority regions in the southwest, as well as official support of a pro-Sinhalese university admissions policy in the early 1970s, further frustrated and alienated the Sri Lankan Tamils. Militant Tamil youth groups ("The Boys") were soon ready to fight for a separate Tamil state by any means. Efforts by the state to repress these groups through coercion further polarized the situation, culminating in major bouts of ethnic violence in 1977, 1981, and 1983, and ultimately led to civil war.

This trend of events led to an internationalization of the Sri Lankan Tamil issue and drew India into a more active role. India had expressed diplomatic concern in 1977 and 1981 at the impact of the ethnic violence on Indian Tamils, many of whom were Indian citizens. The operations of the Sri Lankan army against the militant Tamil youth groups and the ethnic violence in 1983 sent some 150,000 Sri Lankan Tamils fleeing to seek asylum in Tamil Nadu, the South Indian state in closest proximity, and with which they had the closest historical and cultural ties. The press, people, and political parties in Tamil Nadu, which had its own history of secessionist movements, provided sympathy, support, and funds to the refugees and militants, and demanded action by India's government in New Delhi, led by Indira Gandhi and her Congress Party. This sequence of events coincided with larger concerns in Delhi that had been raised by the growing closeness of the UNP government in Colombo with Western powers, as evidenced by its growing economic dependence and indebtedness, military aid and training to put down the Tamil insurgency, and other concessions having strategic implications. Given the U.S. funds and arms flowing into the region, through the military dictatorship in Pakistan, to support the mujahideen in Afghanistan, India's sensitivities to the presence of an external superpower were exacerbated by the deteriorating situation in neighboring Sri Lanka, a country from which India had traditionally never felt any anxiety and with which it had generally had cordial relations.

India adopted a two-track policy toward Sri Lanka in the subsequent period, under Indira Gandhi and later Rajiv Gandhi. On the one hand, it provided support, training, and funding to Tamil militant groups to help them create pressure on the government in Colombo to desist from its increasing identification with Western interests. On the other hand, India actively sponsored repeated rounds of negotiations between the government in Colombo and the Sri Lankan Tamil parties to further reconciliation, compromise, and the recognition of minority ethnic rights to establish a system of regional Tamil autonomy for Sri Lanka's northeast. The bilateral talks that ensued from 1983 to 1986 compelled a growing recognition and delineation of Tamil rights and demands, providing the basis for the provisions supporting provincial autonomy incorporated into the Indo-Sri Lanka Accord of 1987. Those efforts to effect a reconciliation did not, however, materialize. The many militant youth groups seeking to represent Sri Lankan Tamils suffered from serious individual and political differences among themselves, with the Liberation Tigers of Tamil Eelam (LTTE) maintaining the most militant and intractable separatist position.

Indo-Sri Lanka Accord of 1987. The Indo-Sri Lanka Accord, signed by Indian prime minister Rajiv Gandhi and Sri Lankan president J. R. Jayewardene on 29 July 1987, sought to solve the exploding ethnic conflict by declaring Sri Lanka "a multi-ethnic and multi-lingual plural society" consisting primarily of four main ethnic groups. It recognized that the northern and eastern provinces had been areas of "historical habitation of the Tamil-speaking population." Tamil and English were also proclaimed to be official languages of Sri Lanka, along with Sinhala. The Sri Lankan government promised to devolve power to provincial councils and to allow the adjoining northern and eastern provinces to form one administrative unit, or to remain separate, their preference to be determined by referendum in the Eastern province. As a temporary measure, the two provinces would be merged into a single unit, the North-Eastern Provincial Council, until the referendum could be held. India promised to send a contingent of troops as a peacekeeping force (IPKF), at the invitation of Sri Lanka's president, to be deployed in the northeast of the island to oversee the cease-fire, receive arms to be surrendered by the Tamil militants, and serve as a guarantor of the agreement. In an exchange of letters following the accord, Jayewardene assured Gandhi that specific aspects of Sri Lanka's foreign policy would be modified to accommodate Indian regional security concerns.

The accord set out a tight schedule for the completion of commitments by the various sides but ran into trouble almost immediately, and soon became derailed. Its opponents included a rival faction of Colombo's ruling party, led by Prime Minister Premadasa; the other major Sri Lankan party, the SLFP, and its leader Sirimavo Bandaranaike; the influential Buddhist clergy; and the radical militant Sinhalese youth group, the People's United Liberation Front (JVP). Nor did the accord have the open support of either the leading moderate Tamil party (TULF) or the most militant Tamil Tigers (LTTE). Only several small parties on the left, members of the progressive intelligentsia, and several of the Tamil militant

groups supported the agreement. The surrender of arms was rejected by the LTTE. This and other deliberate actions by the LTTE compelled the IPKF to engage in open armed conflict with them, while the Sri Lankan government withdrew its own armed forces from the northeast.

After Premadasa came to power as president in 1988, he called for a cease-fire with the Tigers, began talks with them, summarily asked the IPKF to leave Sri Lanka (before the accord had been fully implemented), and even clandestinely supplied the LTTE with arms to fight the IPKF, which had already lost 1,500 soldiers. New Delhi began to withdraw all its troops in December 1989. Eight months later the LTTE resumed hostilities against the Sri Lankan government. The LTTE assassinated Rajiv Gandhi in Tamil Nadu in 1991, then Premadasa in Colombo in 1993.

While political opinion in India was divided about the wisdom of sending the IPKF to Sri Lanka, it had remained sympathetic to the Tamil cause. This changed sharply after the LTTE's assassination of Rajiv Gandhi by a suicide bomber in the midst of his campaign to come back to power in India's midterm elections in mid-1991, as demonstrated by popular opinion in Tamil Nadu. India proceeded to try those charged with conspiracy to murder Rajiv Gandhi. It indicted Velupillai Prabhakaran, leader of the Tigers, and three of his closest associates to stand trial for the murder. Request for Prabhakaran's extradition continued to be pending over a decade after conclusion of the trial, given the inability of the Sri Lankan government to catch him in his jungle strongholds in the island's northeast. The LTTE was banned as a terrorist organization by India in 1993, a course later adopted by other states, including Sri Lanka, the United States, Canada, Australia, and the United Kingdom.

Post-accord relations. After withdrawing the IPKF, India continued to stand by the accord, asserting the need for all parties in Sri Lanka to work out a solution among themselves, within the parameters of a united sovereign democratic and pluralistic Sri Lanka. Another round of cease-fire occurred after the changeover of power to the SLFP-led People's Alliance government of Chandrika Bandaranaike Kumaratunge in late 1994. In an effort to compel the LTTE to negotiate a compromise, President Kumaratunge escalated the fighting against the Tigers on the one hand. On the other, she sought to restore trust by working to improve Sri Lanka's record of human rights, offering a package of constitutional reforms instituting a generous degree of regional autonomy to resolve the ethnic conflict. The opposing UNP refused to support the reforms and thereby strengthen Kumaratunge's political position. Rejecting Kumaratunge's peace overtures, the LTTE fought the government forces to a stalemate by 2000, drawing on the globalized network of support, arms, and funds it had built up in its diaspora communities, as well as through overt and covert economic operations.

By December 2000, Sri Lanka's civil war had taken over 65,000 lives and had displaced over a million and a half people. An international coalition, including Norway and other Western powers, Japan, and India, supported a cease-fire and called for a peaceful resolution of the conflict, and were willing to back the effort with funding for reconstruction and development. Sri Lanka's new prime minister, Ranil Wickremasinghe, accepted the offer and the cease-fire was maintained for the next two years, while six rounds of talks were held by representatives of the Sri Lankan government and the LTTE in various capitals in Asia and Europe. The government made numerous concessions to the LTTE in an effort to engage it in the peace process. Over time, these served to enhance the control of the LTTE in the northeast, but the Tigers remained largely unresponsive, raising fears in the south that the unity and security of Sri Lanka was being dangerously compromised. This exacerbated serious political divisions on the issue between President Kumaratunge and Prime Minister Wickremasinghe, a development which only strengthened the separatist leverage of the LTTE.

The deepening political divisions caused opinion on the island about India's role to come full circle in favor of it adopting a more active, and even outright interventionist, role to resolve Sri Lanka's political impasse. India had resisted demands by members of the Sinhalese community and clergy to return in mid-2000, when the Tigers launched a particularly threatening attack on Jaffna. However, by the beginning of 2003, the coalition government led by Prime Minister Atal Bihari Vajpayee's Bharatiya Janata Party exhibited a greater willingness to take a more active role in fashioning a compromise between Sri Lanka's two major parties in the south, while asserting that only a "homegrown" solution with the Tigers themselves could prove durable.

Amita Shastri

See also **Ethnic Conflict; Sri Lanka**

BIBLIOGRAPHY

Bastian, Sunil, ed. *Devolution and Development in Sri Lanka.* Delhi: Konark, 1994.
Dixit, J. N. *Assignment Colombo.* Delhi: Konark, 1998.
Kodikara, Shelton. *Foreign Policy of Sri Lanka.* 2nd ed. Delhi: Chanakya, 1992.
Kodikara, Shelton, ed. *Indo-Sri Lanka Agreement of July 1987.* Dehiwala, Sri Lanka: Sridevi, 1989.
Muni, S. D. *Pangs of Proximity: India and Sri Lanka's Ethnic Crisis.* New Delhi: Sage, 1993.
Phadnis, Urmila. *Ethnicity and Nation-Building in South Asia.* New Delhi: Sage, 1989.
Sahadevan, P. *India and the Overseas Indians: The Case of Sri Lanka.* Delhi: Kalinga, 1995.
Shastri, Amita. "Estate Tamils, the Ceylon Citizenship Act of 1948, and Sri Lankan Politics." *Contemporary South Asia* 8, no. 1 (March 1999): 65–86.
Suryanarayan, V. *Kachchativu and the Problems of Indian Fishermen in the Palk Bay Region.* Chennai: T. R. Publications, 1994.
Tinker, Hugh. *The Banyan Tree: Overseas Emigrants from India, Pakistan and Bangladesh.* Oxford: Oxford University Press, 1977.

SRINAGAR. *See* **Jammu and Kashmir.**

STATE FINANCES SINCE 1952 In order to analyze the trends in state finances in India since the mid-twentieth century, and to identify reform issues that need to be addressed for better macroeconomic management, it is necessary to examine the fiscal role of state governments in India's federal polity and their effectiveness in fulfilling their fiscal roles. As in other important federal fiscal systems, the states play an important role in providing public services in India. The country's 1.2 billion people live in twenty-eight states and seven centrally administered territories (two with their own elected governments). The seventh schedule of India's Constitution demarcates the legislative and fiscal domains of the union and state governments in terms of union, state, and concurrent lists. The states have exclusive authority over the items specified in the state list and coequal powers in regard to those in the concurrent list. While on the one hand the states are required to make substantial investments in providing efficient physical and social infrastructure, they face binding constraints on resources. Restructuring the finances and expenditure priorities to release resources to the desired activities has not been easy. The declining revenues and transfers from the central government have only added to India's woes. The states are faced with challenging times in creating a business-friendly environment.

The Assignment System

The tax and expenditure powers of the central and the state governments are specified in the seventh schedule of the Constitution. The functions required for maintaining macroeconomic stability, international relations, and activities having significant scale economies have been assigned exclusively to the central government, or have to be carried out concurrently with the states. Functions that have a statewide jurisdiction are assigned to the states. Most broad-based and progressive taxes have been assigned to the central government, which also has residual tax powers. A number of tax vehicles have been assigned to the states, but from the viewpoint of revenue productivity, only the sales tax is important. The states can borrow from the central government. They have the powers to borrow from the market, but if a state is indebted to the central government, such borrowing must be approved by the center. The important taxes assigned to the states include the sales tax, excise duties on alcoholic products, stamp duties and registration fees, taxes on motor vehicles and passengers and goods. They can also levy taxes on incomes from agriculture, but none of the states has found this feasible for political reasons. Even land revenue, which contributed significant revenue thirty years ago, has ceased to contribute any worthwhile resources in recent years.

The states play a very important role in the development of agriculture and have a significant role in the provision of infrastructure for industrial development. Even more significant is their role in human development, as they have responsibility for the provision of basic education and health care. The states raise 35 percent of the total revenues and incur 57 percent of total expenditures. Their role in providing social services is particularly significant. In fact, their expenditure share in education, public health, and family welfare is close to 90 percent of public expenditures.

Trends in State Finances: Macroeconomic Implications

The trends in state finances in India since the mid-twentieth century can be examined in two distinct phases. In the first phase, from 1950–1951 to 1986–1987, increased revenue receipts kept pace with revenue (current) expenditures. The emphasis on resource mobilization, particularly to finance large development plans, resulted in the steady increase in both revenues and expenditures, with states' own revenues as well as central transfers steadily increasing. In fact, from 1975–1976 to 1983–1984, revenue receipts exceeded revenue expenditures by a significant margin, enabling the states to finance an appreciable portion of their capital expenditure from savings in the current account.

The second phase in state finances began with the pay revision, following the implementation of the recommendations of the pay commission by the central government. The central government itself had such a significant revenue deficit that it could not increase transfers to meet the additional requirements to finance the pay revision. The states, on their part, did not undertake serious fiscal restructuring, and as the buoyancy of both the states' own revenues and central transfers declined (the latter more than the former), public dissaving at the state level increased steadily. In fact, in the 1990s the states' revenue-gross domestic product (GDP) ratio remained steady at about 5.5 percent, whereas the central tax-GDP ratio declined by two percentage points. The consequence of this has been to reduce transfers to the states by one percentage point. Thus, with stagnant revenues, declining transfers from the center, and ever-increasing pressure on expenditures, revenue deficits in the states widened significantly in the 1990s. Although the states tried to contain their expenditures to adjust for stagnant revenues, the revision of pay scales of state government employees, following the implementation of the fifth central pay commission, did not help matters. Thus, since 1998–1999, the revenue deficits of the states increased sharply, and borrowed resources of over 2.5 percent of GDP were being used to meet states' current expenditures. Correspondingly, fiscal deficit on states' accounts increased from 1.3 percent in 1975–1976 to 2.8 percent in 1985–1986 and accelerated to 4.7 percent in 2001–2002.

The deterioration in state finances since 1987–1988 also marked a sharp deterioration in the quality of deficits as well. Infrastructure spending declined from 3.7 percent of GDP in 1980–1981 and about 3 percent in 1985–1986 to 1.7 percent in 2000–2001. As a ratio of total expenditures, capital expenditure declined from about 27 percent in 1980–1981 to a mere 13 percent in 2001–2002. Sharp increases in expenditures crowded out maintenance expenditures, thereby reducing the productivity of the infrastructure sector as well. Even in labor-intensive social services such as education and health, increases in the pay scales have significantly escalated the input cost of providing these services, and increasing expenditures have not been reflected in the improvement in the standard of these services.

The persistence of large and growing fiscal deficits in India's states over the years has led to a steady accumulation of debt. The states' outstanding debt as a ratio of GDP was steady from 1965–1966 to 1997–1998, but thereafter increased sharply. This deterioration in fiscal imbalances is not just an aggregate phenomenon. It is seen in the case of each of the individual states, particularly after the pay revision in 1998–1999. Even in 1995–1996, some of the states had surpluses in the revenue account, but after the pay revisions in 1998–1999, every state has had revenue deficits of varying magnitude, and capital and maintenance expenditures have been lower than in 1995–1996.

There are a number of reasons for fiscal imbalances at the state level. Since the 1980s, the growth of the states' revenue expenditures has outpaced the growth of revenue receipts mainly because of the two pay revisions, one in the late 1980s and another in the late 1990s. The last one in particular had disastrous effects on state finances. Pay revision was not accompanied with any restructuring plan in public employment, and expenditures on salaries and pensions increased sharply after 1998–1999. The second important reason for the states' imbalances is the decline in transfers from the central government as a ratio of GDP. The central government's own revenues as a ratio of GDP declined by about two percentage points in the 1990s, and this led to the compression of transfers to states by one percentage point. Third, there has also been a significant deceleration in the growth of states' own tax revenue. Fourth, the artificial distinction between plan and nonplan expenditures and an emphasis on increasing the plan size year after year have led to unbridled growth of expenditures. Fifth, increased borrowing, particularly from uncontrolled sources at high interest rates, has caused a sharp increase in the debt service burden. Finally, public enterprises, particularly the power utilities, have continued to be a drain on the states' funds.

The states' fiscal operations have important implications on microeconomic efficiency as well. On the tax side, the structure and operation of sales tax systems has been a major source of distortion. The relative price distortions caused by complicated, cascading type, preretail and partly origin-based sales tax and the impediments to internal trade and distortions and inequity arising from multiple tariff zones (created by interstate sales tax and the tax on the entry of goods into a local area for consumption) are well known. These are only some of the problems in the tax side. On the expenditure side, steady decline in the allocation to the creation and maintenance of infrastructure has adversely affected its quality. Similarly, a significant increase in the input cost due to pay revision has adversely impacted the standards of social services.

Reforming State Finances: Challenges Ahead

Concerned over the perilous condition of their finances, some of the states have taken reform initiatives. A number of states have published white papers on their finances. Some of the states have initiated reforms in their tax and expenditure systems, have tried to quantify contingent liabilities, and have passed fiscal responsibility legislation to cap deficits and impose fiscal discipline. In some cases, reform initiatives have been taken at the instance of multilateral lending agencies as a condition for their lending. The central government also has initiated a fiscal reform program for the states and has linked a portion of its transfers to fiscal performance. However, the design of the program and its implementation leave much to be desired.

In a more open market economy, the state governments will have to provide a higher quality infrastructure.

In particular, their role in human development is critical. This change would require a number of reform initiatives. These initiatives include: restructuring the administrative machinery, improving the buoyancy of the tax system, better cost recovery on the services provided, downsizing of bureaucracy, and prioritizing expenditure allocation to provide quality infrastructure and the creation of a business-friendly environment.

One of the most important areas requiring urgent reform is the power sector. Reform is necessary not only to achieve fiscal consolidation but also to ensure the quality of the infrastructure. Restructuring other public enterprises will also prevent a drain on resources. Reforms in the tax systems are important to ensure that the resources for investment in infrastructure are generated in the least distortionary manner. The states took initiatives to substitute the prevailing cascading sales tax with the value-added tax (VAT) in April 2002. Transition to VAT was necessary not only to impart efficiency to the tax system but also to enhance revenue productivity. The reform journey for the achievement of fiscal consolidation, the improvement of efficiency and productivity, and the creation of a competitive environment will be long and arduous. Political will and administrative competence, along with an awareness of the need for reform among the general public, are the most important ingredients that will be needed in abundance to achieve the desired goals.

M. Govinda Rao

See also **Economic Reforms and Center-State Relations; Public Expenditures**

BIBLIOGRAPHY

Ahluwalia, Montek. "Economic Performance of States in Post-Reforms Period." *Economic and Political Weekly* 35 (6 May 2000): 1637–1648.
Kurian, N. J. "State Government Finances." *Economic and Political Weekly* 34 (8 May 1999): 1115–1125.
Lahiri, Ashok. "Subnational Public Finance in India." *Economic and Political Weekly* 35 (29 April 2000): 1539–1549.
Rao, M. Govinda. "State Finances in India: Issues and Challenges." *Economic and Political Weekly* 37, no. 31 (3 August 2000): 3261–3271.

STATE FORMATION From the dawn of its recorded history, an enduring feature of India's state formation has been the struggle for power between its settled cultures and invading forces. The geographical configuration of the Indian subcontinent also played its part in determining the patterns of invasion and settlement, whether by the "land nomads" from Central Asia, who entered northern India through the invasion corridor of the northwest, or by the "sea nomads" of Europe, who crossed the oceans and penetrated the Indian subcontinent from the coastal areas.

The earliest known population movement was by the Indo-Europeans (Aryans) from the steppe lands of Central Asia, who settled in the Indo-Gangetic Plain and established the North Indian linguistic and cultural tradition. However, the unique configuration of the Indian subcontinent also dictated that most invading forces from Central Asia encountered the barrier of the Hindu Kush Mountains before reaching the plains of northern India. The new waves of invasion that followed—by the Greeks, Kushans, Huns, Turkic and Mongol tribes—were launched as military expeditions that crossed the Indus to conquer the Punjab. Most of them lost their momentum by the time they reached the Gangetic Plain. Thus, while a few established ephemeral dynasties of considerable power, they were not able to change the mass of population or cultural core of the Gangetic region.

The other aspect of the territorial history of the Indian subcontinent is that of the geographical divide between continental and peninsular India. The political concept of India as an "empire state" was first developed during the time of the Mauryas (321–184 B.C.) and defined Bharat (India) as stretching from the northern Himalayas to Kanya Kumari (Cape Comorin) in the south. The ambition of all subsequent Indian rulers has been to achieve the territorial and political unification of the Indian subcontinent. Here again, geography has played a part; the Vindhya Mountains of the Deccan plateau have provided a formidable barrier to the imperial ambitions of the land-based powers of the north.

In the post-Mauryan period, the Indo-Gangetic Plain was subjected to extensive invasions, and periodic attempts at unification were interspersed with long periods of turmoil and conflict. The Gupta dynasty (4th century) was the last North Indian empire to rule from the Gangetic heartland. Their political collapse came in the wake of fresh invasions by Hun nomads in the fifth century.

Muslim rule followed much the same pattern of invasion and conquest, but the introduction of Islam as a new religion and culture proved a critical break in terms of its impact on state and society. The establishment of the Delhi Sultanate in A.D. 1206 changed the political landscape of northern India, the strategically placed capital of Delhi becoming the new seat of central power.

India's next imperial unification, under the Great Mughals, from Babur to Akbar (A.D. 1526–1605). Akbar's rule was renowned for its tolerance, and for his fostering of pluralism and a syncretism of Hindu-Muslim culture and civilization. The Mughal empire was also a warrior

state, administered by a new class of military bureaucratic elites (*mansabdar*s). The Northwest and the Northeast of the Indo-Gangetic belt became Muslim majority areas, the former by invaders who settled there, the latter mostly by Sufi conversions, while the Gangetic Plain retained its Hindu majority. Southern India developed a maritime tradition and a seafaring economy, in contrast to the landlocked economy of the North. The Dravidian culture consolidated its position as the region's major strand of South Indian civilization, and the post-Mughal repository of the Hindu cultural traditions of the North.

The "European epoch" of Indian history dawned as an age of maritime power, of western European authority based on the control of the seas. European expansion to South Asia by sea fundamentally altered the course of Indian history, presenting an entirely new set of challenges to the land-based powers of the North, the Mughals, Rajputs, Marathas, and Sikhs. Not only were the routes, methods of conquest, and patterns of settlement different, but the pressure from the sea had a relentlessness that invasions from land did not possess.

The British, who eventually marginalized all other European contenders (the French, the Dutch, and the Portuguese), penetrated inland from the sea through the two great river valleys: the South's Cauvery valley, and the Ganges valley of the North. Surmounting the Deccan barrier, and in the nineteenth century finally bringing together both continental and peninsular India, the British imperial Raj transformed itself from a sea-based maritime power to a continental empire.

The British Raj emulated and incorporated many of the features of the previous rulers, especially the Mughals, retaining elements of their military and bureaucratic administration. The role of intermediaries (merchants, traders, and moneylenders) and scribal elites, land revenue systems, and mercantile imperatives were common to both empires. Both were warrior states, and the role of the army drawn from the so-called martial races, was crucial for both. The British, however, had to propagate a new theory of martial races after the Great Mutiny of 1857, when Punjab and the tribal Northwest, instead of Bengal, became the new recruiting ground. The induction of Jat Sikhs, Rajputs, Punjabis, and Pathans into the British army changed the sociopolitical history of the Northwest. It has had immense consequences for the successor state of Pakistan, which inherited the strategic "real estate" of the Northwest and the so-called martial races tradition associated with it.

The Unification of British India

The most significant achievement of British colonial rule was the strategic unification of the Indian subcontinent.

It constituted a significant break from the past, as the concept of strategic frontiers and boundaries was introduced to demarcate the sovereign limits of the British Empire. However, the demands of the greater British Empire added an extra dimension to imperial frontier making. The strategic and economic interests of imperial Britain and Tsarist Russia led to the "Great Game" in Central Asia between the two powers. The northwestern frontier became militarized, and Afghanistan emerged as a classic "buffer state."

The colonial enterprise was by no means a unilateral exercise. Interaction as well synthesis were integral to the encounter between India and Britain, whose ideologies and institutions had a profound impact on India. Ideas of nationalism and self-determination were crucial, giving an impetus to India's nationalist movement. Britain's industrial capitalism had its effect as well on the modernization and industrialization of the state. Railways were the great unifiers, both in the strategic and economic sense, helping to extend and consolidate British rule.

Decolonization was a critical juncture in the contemporary history of the Indian subcontinent. In the case of British India, the distinctiveness of the decolonization process lay in the dichotomy that developed between the secular Indian Nationalist Congress's demand for independence and the Indian Muslim League's demand for a Muslim homeland—Pakistan. In the stalemate that followed, the religious separatism of the minority Muslim community became the determinant factor in granting freedom from colonial rule.

In 1947 British power was "transferred" to the two dominions, India and Pakistan, the former as the primary successor state of British India, with Pakistan a secondary successor state. The price of independence was the partitioning of continental India on the basis of the communal majority principle of the "two nation" theory of the Muslim League, which asserted that Hindus and Muslims were two separate nations.

Independence and Partition

British India's partition was both a turning point and a traumatic event in the history of South Asia, as it left many conflicts unresolved and many questions unanswered. One question that has intrigued historians is why independence became conditional on partition. The British policy of creating separate electoral rolls for Hindus and Muslims, which inaugurated modern Indian political communalism in 1909, provides part of the answer. Another part of the answer lies in the genesis of the Pakistan movement and the communal cleavages that developed between the Indian National Congress and the Muslim League over the issue of power sharing and the principle of democratic rule. The notion of parity was an important consideration for the Muslim elite, as was also their concern that the electoral politics of "majoritarian" rule would translate in practice to a "Hindu Raj" in the guise of a "Congress Raj."

One of the paradoxes of the Pakistan demand was that the impetus came not from the Muslim-majority provinces but from a small section of the Muslim elite from the Muslim-minority provinces of North India. North India's Muslim elite were motivated by a complex mix of religious and economic reasons—not the least of which was their apprehension about loss of privilege, status, and economic power under a secular and democratic India. Partition triggered the exodus of these elite Muslims to the promised new state of Pakistan. The decline in status of this Indian Muslim diaspora, from the "creators" of Pakistan to that of refugees (*muhajirs*) in their chosen homeland, is one of the ironies of the Pakistan movement.

The answer to another question has also remained elusive: why did independence and partition give birth to only two nation states in the Indo-Gangetic region, not to many more? Fears of balkanization and the desire for strong centralized state(s) by India's and Pakistan's elites are said to have eliminated those options. The legal and political status of some six hundred autonomous princely states was for the most part resolved by integrating them into the two larger states, India and Pakistan—with the notable exception of the largest state, Jammu and Kashmir.

The application of the communal majority formula as the basis for creating a viable state produced the anomaly of a bifurcated Pakistan, separated by a thousand miles of Indian territory. Geographically, the communal majority formula could be applied only to those regions where Muslims were in a majority, but the provinces of the Northwest, where the Muslims were an absolute majority (North-West Frontier province, Baluchistan, and Sind), constituted only 10 percent of the total Indian Muslim population. Therefore, the two large provinces in which Muslims constituted a bare majority—Punjab (54 percent) and Bengal (57 percent)—were carved up to create the new state of Pakistan.

The legacy of partition. At the time of partition, very little attention was paid to the geopolitical consequences and human dimensions of physically dividing the Indo-Gangetic belt. Once the partition became a reality, however, these traumatic and tragic factors began to impinge on the process of nation building of both fragmented states. The human costs of the partition, the killings and population exchanges that accompanied it, and the refugees and diasporas it created, left a bitter legacy. In effect, the partition produced a divided polity, a divided elite, a divided economy, and divided security.

The geographical aberration of the two wings of Pakistan being separated by a thousand miles of Indian territory created a logistical nightmare for the new state of Pakistan, which ultimately became untenable, both politically and economically, leading to the independence of East Pakistan in 1971, with the creation of Bangladesh, following the third Indo-Pak War. For the Indian state, the near detachment of its Northeast region, which is joined to the Indian mainland by a slender land corridor (the so-called chicken's neck), posed similar problems of marginalization for its inhabitants, which the state has not been able to overcome. The distancing of the northeastern region from the Indian heartland has added to the sense of alienation of the tribal Northeast states and to their depiction as India's "Far East."

The Making of India and Pakistan

In the immediate aftermath of partition, the imperatives of nation building focused on consolidating the state and constructing a central government. The task was relatively easier for the Indian state, which had inherited the mantle of the primary successor state to British India. Post-independent India had a political system and a bureaucratic structure that emphasized continuities with the past, and a national identity imparted to it by the long history of its nationalist movement. The Indian Congress central government in New Delhi stressed the civil base of its rule, underpinned by the ideology of secularism and parliamentary democracy. It soon federated along linguistic lines, seeking to safeguard the multiethnic character of its polity and to accommodate the wishes of the strongly vocal regional units that make up the Indian union. The fear of balkanization, however, made centralization a key requisite, and the Indian model of state making evolved as a federal union with centralized tendencies. In India, it was the political-bureaucratic elite that came to dominate the state structure, with the military kept out of the power equation. That situation has remained a constant in the Indian political system.

In the case of Pakistan, it was the military-bureaucratic nexus that became dominant, with Pakistan's political elite playing the subordinate role. Pakistan not only had to sustain the image of an "equal power" within the regional system, the external thrust of its foreign policy also pushed its elite toward building a military-bureaucratic state. That equation has also remained a constant in Pakistan's domestic and external politics, with its military entrenching itself within the body politic of the Pakistani state.

Regional rivals. The ideological divide created by the particular circumstances of their birth ensured that India

and Pakistan emerged as regional rivals with very different domestic, security, and foreign policy objectives. India's preeminence within the subcontinent was offset by the effort of the smaller Pakistani state to achieve military parity, if necessary, by "borrowing power" from "great and powerful" allies abroad (the United States, China, and several Middle Eastern states). The role of external actors has been vital in maintaining, and reinforcing, the so-called bipolar structure of the South Asian system. The early outbreak of conflict over partition's "unfinished business" of Kashmir soon became internationalized as a symbol of the India-Pakistan adversarial relationship. On this was superimposed the cold war dynamics of the superpower competition, with India developing a "special relationship" with the Soviet Union to counterbalance Pakistan's military alliances with Western powers.

Bangladesh. The dictates of geography, the unequal development of Pakistan's two wings, and elite conflict between the ruling West Pakistani elite and the East Bengali counterelite, all played their roles in sharpening the cleavage between the two wings of Pakistan, leading ultimately to the majority Bengali-state breaking free of Punjabi-Pathan–led Pakistan in 1971. From an international perspective, the birth of Bangladesh was the first instance of the successful culmination of a secessionist movement in the post–World War II period. The liberation of Bangladesh was the result of a conjunction of geography and Bengali linguistic and economic nationalism, supported by India's military intervention.

For South Asia, that second partitioning changed its geopolitical map, though not its political boundaries, since no territorial dispute was involved. The breaking up of Pakistan, however, did challenge the ideological basis of its two-nation theory, since Bengali linguistic nationalism took precedence over its Islamic identity.

Contemporary South Asia

The birth of Bangladesh in 1971 firmly established the centrality and dominance of India in South Asia. Not only is the Indian union now the largest state in South Asia, it is territorially and demographically larger than all the other six states combined. South Asia's geopolitical reality, moreover, is truly bilateral, since all its other states are contiguous to India, but none adjoin each other. The smaller states of South Asia are, therefore, sensitive to being overwhelmed by the enormous power of India.

On the other hand, the new geopolitical configuration has also exposed the vulnerability of the Indian state to its long, porous boundaries. The proliferation of armed secessionist conflicts in its border regions, and the ongoing "proxy war" between India and Pakistan over the disputed state of Kashmir, is an indication that an Indian hegemony is far from an undisputed fact in South Asia. Equally telling is the policy of nuclearization followed by India and Pakistan since 1998. This policy may have enhanced India's great power status, but it has also enabled the weaker Pakistani state to achieve semiparity with the stronger Indian state. But it has certainly not resolved the security dilemma of a fractured subcontinent.

The strongest challenge to the secular identity and pluralist ethos of the Indian state has come from a plethora of ethno-nationalist and subnationalist demands, many with secessionist tendencies. The Sikhs of Punjab, the Nagas and Assamese in the Northeast region, and the Kashmiri Muslims in the state of Jammu and Kashmir have all tested the federal structure of the Indian union. The most serious threat yet to the secular fabric of the Indian state is the rise of transnational religious fundamentalism as a force in the region. The communal passions it has aroused has revived the "Muslim question" in India, and by extension, rekindled a wider debate about minority rights in South Asia.

Post-1971 Pakistan, although more viable as a territorial entity and more cohesive as a political unit, is still beset by internal contradictions, not least of which is the problem of identity among a composite people. The centralization policies of the ruling elite have come into conflict with the demands for provincial autonomy by ethnic Pashtuns, Sindis, and Baluchis. The most striking predicament is that of the *muhajir*s, who are yet to gain their own ethnic and regional identity in the "new" Pakistan. The subordination of Pakistan's domestic politics to its external relations has continued, and the periodic resort to military rule has become the most persistent feature of the Pakistani state.

Pakistan's strategic location in the Northwest and the state's policies of Islamization and an external orientation toward the wider Muslim world have also raised questions about its post-1971 identity: whether it sees itself as part of South Asia, Southwest Asia, or Central Asia. The marrying of Pakistan's Kashmir and Afghanistan policies in the 1990s, and Pakistan's continuing involvement in post-Soviet Afghanistan have kept that question alive.

Bangladesh has charted a zigzag course, reflecting two competing influences on its elites: secular parliamentary democracy and Islamic ideology. The most compelling factor of Bangladesh's security is its geography, as it is surrounded on three sides by India. Conversely, Bangladesh's location at the mouth of the Bay of Bengal and the strategic position it occupies between the Indian mainland and India's Northeast have released new dynamics in Indo-Bangladesh relations. The use of Bangladesh as a sanctuary by separatist movements in India's Northeast

has been an ongoing concern to New Delhi, as have boundary disputes arising from the indeterminate nature of their borders.

Boundary Conflicts

In contrast to the traditional natural frontiers that had developed through custom and usage, British India's colonial boundary making was the product of strategic and economic concerns, which led to the creation of an "outer frontier" that crystallized into the linear boundaries, the Durand Line in the Northwest and the McMahon Line in the Northeast. The partitioning of the subcontinent broke the strategic unity of that frontier, with Pakistan inheriting the northwestern frontier as its outer frontier, and India the northeastern Himalayan frontier. Partition also created a new set of boundaries, or "inner frontiers." Thus, apart from the logistics of maintaining their strategic frontiers, India and Pakistan have had to contend with the irredentist demands of tribal communities that were divided by the linear boundaries. The demand for Pakhtoonistan in the Northwest and the Naga demand for a homeland in the Northeast are but two examples of such transnational claims.

The outer frontier. Recent events have again reinforced the intrinsic importance of the outer frontier to the politics of the Indian subcontinent, with the reemergence of Afghanistan as a "gateway" state between South Asia, Southwest Asia, and Central Asia in the post-Soviet era. The "centrality" of Central Asia has started a new "Great Game" in the region, with its Northwest again being drawn into the calculations of great powers. For India, the destabilization of Afghanistan and Central Asia and the breaching of the Durand Line bring back memories of the Northwest as a corridor of invasion into the Indian heartland. For Pakistan, it represents opportunities to influence events in the wider Muslim world as the inheritor of the strategic "real estate" of the Northwest. The fault lines of religious fundamentalism and the nuclearization of India and Pakistan have further polarized the politics of the region. In that sense, the geopolitical patterns on the Indian subcontinent seem to have turned full circle, with the pressures again coming from the Northwest.

The inner frontier. As for the political borders that separate the modern South Asian system, what stands out most are the "unstable nation state boundaries" that are the legacies of the partition process. In recent years the changing nature of transborder conflicts has added a new dimension to the issue of boundary protection. The porous nature of the boundaries has produced the paradoxical situation of the larger Indian state fencing off its borders to stop armed incursions across the India-Pakistan border (which the Indian state characterizes as cross-border terrorism), and illegal immigrations across the Indo-Bangladesh border (which is threatening to alter the demographic composition of the Northeast region).

Border fencing as the latest phase in boundary making has posed a different set of questions about the security dynamics of the South Asian system. The scourge of cross-border terrorism—including narco-terrorism, arms running, and trafficking in humans—is a manifestation of this phenomenon. The construction of artificial barriers by the Indian state, at enormous cost, has been likened to the modern equivalent of a "Roman Wall" or the Great Wall of China. It is also reminiscent of the ideological divide of the Berlin Wall. The South Asian system has yet to make the transition to a secure regional system, as state formation on the subcontinent still seems hostage to partition's traumatic legacies.

Jayita Ray

See also **Federalism and Center-State Relations; Pakistan and India**

BIBLIOGRAPHY

Bayly, Christopher. *Imperial Meridian: The British Empire and the World 1780–1830*. New York: Longman, 1989.

Jalal, Ayesha. *State of Martial Rule: The Origins of Pakistan's Political Economy of Defence*. Cambridge, U.K.: Cambridge University Press, 1985.

Lattimore, Owen. *Studies in Frontier History: Collected Papers, 1928–1934*. London: Oxford, 1962.

Oomen, T. K. *State and Society in India: Studies in Nation Building*. New Delhi: Sage, 1990.

Panikkar, K. M. *Geographical Factors in Indian History*. Mumbai: Bharatiya Vidya Bhavan, 1959.

Phillips, C. H., and M. D. Wainwright, eds. *The Partition of India: Policies and Perspectives, 1935–1947*. London: Allen & Unwin, 1970.

Sisson, Richard, and Leo Rose. *War and Secession: Pakistan, India and the Creation of Bangladesh*. Berkeley: University of California Press, 1990.

Wilson, J., and Dennis Dalton, eds. *The States of South Asia: Problems of National Integration*. London: C. Hurst, 1982.

STATE-LEVEL PERFORMANCE SINCE REFORMS OF 1991

India is a federal country consisting of twenty-eight states, and the division of responsibilities between the central government and the state governments is set forth in the Constitution. The states vary greatly in the level of per capita income, incidence of poverty, population size, resource endowments, and fiscal capacity, and the promotion of regional balance and equity among states is an acknowledged objective of national development policy. The regionalization of politics in India since the 1980s has focused attention on the performance of Indian states to a much greater extent than before, and the impact of the economic reforms since 1991 on their performance has also been a focus of attention.

Interstate Variations in Growth

While per capita growth in the economy as a whole accelerated in the period after the 1991 reforms, there is considerable variation in the experience of the individual states. Critics of the reforms sometimes present an exaggerated picture of the distributional impact of the reforms, arguing that only the richer states have benefited and that the poorer states have actually become poorer. In fact, none of the states has become poorer in the sense of experiencing negative growth in per capita income. On the contrary, all states have experienced a rise in per capita income, albeit at different rates. Nor is it the case that the richer states have benefited the most from the reforms. The two richest states at the start of the reforms were Punjab and Haryana, and both states actually decelerated in growth in the postreform period. The greatest acceleration in growth was experienced by two of the middle-income states, Maharashtra and Gujarat, while other middle-income states such as Tamil Nadu, Karnataka, and Kerala also accelerated. Two of the poorer states, West Bengal and Madhya Pradesh, also did better than in the prereform period. However, several of the lower-income states that are also very populous (Uttar Pradesh, Bihar, Orissa, and Rajasthan) saw a deceleration in growth compared with the prereform period. This deceleration occurred at a time when the expectation was one of acceleration, and the fact that there was acceleration in many other states produced an understandable sense of not being helped by the reforms.

Various measures of inequality suggest that interstate inequality, that is, inequality due solely to differences in per capita incomes across states, ignoring intrastate inequality, increased in the postreform period. This is an interesting finding, since available measures of inequality for the country as a whole (which are based on the distribution of consumption) do not show a significant increase in inequality in the postreform period.

Explanations for Growth Variation

Growth outcomes are obviously the result of initial endowments, investment rates, and economic policies, which determine the productivity of investment. Since the economic reforms were designed to promote economic efficiency, and were also applied to the entire country rather than to selected regions as in China, one might expect that they would improve growth performance in every state, which should lead to an acceleration in all states. The fact that some states actually decelerated calls for an explanation.

One possible explanation lies in the weakening of one of the two mechanisms traditionally used for promoting regional balance in India. One of these mechanisms, which was not affected by the reforms, was transfers from the central government to the state governments. These transfers took the form of distribution of a share of central government tax revenues to the states, with the proportion to be transferred and its distribution among the states being determined every five years by the Finance Commission; and distribution of central assistance to state finance plans, with the amount of the transfer and the distribution among states being determined by the Planning Commission. In each case, the formula used for interstate distribution explicitly favored states with lower per capita incomes. The second mechanism used to promote regional balance in the prereform period, which was affected by the reforms, was the direction of investments toward the poorer states. This was achieved either by deliberately locating public sector projects in these states, or by using the industrial licensing mechanism to push private investments toward these states.

The scale of public sector investment relative to private sector investments declined as a consequence of the economic reforms, making this option less effective. It also became impossible to direct private investment to particular regions following the abolition of industrial licensing in 1991. Thereafter, the location of private investment was driven by competitive considerations, and these were bound to redistribute investment toward better endowed states with favorable infrastructure—states that already had a faster rate of growth.

More generally, liberalization has meant an increase in the role of the state government in determining the investment climate in each state, and the individual states have varied greatly in the way they have responded. To the extent that the low-income states have responded less or more slowly than other states to the new challenges, it is likely that investment resources have moved away from these states to those that are seen as more investor-friendly. Such a process of reallocation of investment across states could lead to an actual deceleration in growth in some states even if the "investment climate" and "productivity" indicators in these states are no worse in absolute terms than before. This is simply because the relative position of other states has improved, attracting investment toward them. It is not possible to test whether this has happened in a rigorous fashion because investment data are not available at the state level, but anecdotal evidence suggests that some such factor has been at work.

Human Development

The picture of state performance presented by the gross domestic product (GDP) growth numbers needs to be supplemented by considering performance in other dimensions, especially human development indicators, and particularly the adult literacy rate and the infant mortality rate.

The performance regarding literacy suggests broad-based improvement in the postreform period. The nationwide adult literacy figure increased from around 52 percent in 1991 to about 65 percent in 2001, an increase of 13 percent in that decade, compared with an increase of only 9 percent in the decade from 1981 to 1991. The literacy rate has also risen substantially in most of the poorer states though the comparison with the 1980s presents a mixed picture. In Rajasthan there was an increase of 22 percent in the 1990s, compared with only about 14 percent in the 1980s. In Uttar Pradesh, the increase in the 1990s was just under 15 percent, marginally higher than in the 1980s. In Orissa, it was about 1 percent lower than the almost 15 percent increase in the 1980s. The least encouraging performance was in Bihar, which had an increase in the literacy rate of only 8.5 percent in the 1990s, which was actually lower than the increase of over 12 percent in the 1980s.

The infant mortality rate (IMR) is generally regarded as a robust indicator of the well-being and health status of the population, especially of the poorer sections. There were large differences in the IMR across states at the start of the reforms, with Kerala being the best performer with an IMR of 16, while Orissa was the worst with an IMR as high as 124. There is evidence of progress in almost all states in the postreform period, but in this dimension the rate of progress in the 1990s is much less than in the 1980s. The IMR for India as a whole declined from 110 in 1981 to 80 in 1991, but in the subsequent decade, the decline was much slower, reaching 66 in 2001. The picture for individual states shows considerable variation. Kerala was able to reduce the IMR from 16 to 11 over the decade, and many states (Maharashtra, Madhya Pradesh, West Bengal, Uttar Pradesh, Karnataka, Gujarat, Orissa) also showed a significant improvement. However, there was relatively little improvement or even a small deterioration in Bihar, Punjab, Haryana, and Rajasthan.

The Role of the States in the Postreform Period

One consequence of the economic reforms has been an increase in the role of the private sector, which in turn implies that the role of government must shift to delivering essential public services, such as health and education, as well as the creation of infrastructure and an environment of good governance, which would improve the investment climate and increase productivity. In all these areas, it is the state governments that have a major role. Health, education, the creation of rural infrastructure related to irrigation, watershed development, all roads except the national highways, and the supply of electric power are all within the domain of the states, and the administrative instruments for delivering these services are controlled by the state governments. The central government can only help fund programs in the areas that are implemented by state administrative structures.

Although substantial financial resources are being devoted to various types of development programs in these areas, especially education, health, and rural development, their effectiveness in achieving expected objectives is low. In education, for example, enrollment rates indicate that 93 percent of children in the relevant age groups are enrolled in primary schools, but a very large proportion drop out before completing primary school, and the quality of education provided is often inadequate. Similar problems exist in health and other sectors.

There is a growing consensus that public service delivery in India could be greatly improved by shifting from top-down systems of planning and managing programs toward greater involvement of local communities in the design of programs, with prioritization among different programs delegated to lower levels of government to reflect the priorities of the local communities, and also to ensure more active involvement of the local community in monitoring and accountability. One way of achieving this objective is to empower the elected local government institutions, the so-called *panchayati raj* institutions, which consist of an elected village council (*gram panchayat*) at the village level, the block *panchayat* at the next higher level, and the *zilla parishad* at the district level (the last two being composed largely of representatives from the lower-level bodies). In 1994 the Constitution was amended to establish a regular system of election to these institutions and to identify subjects that would be their responsibility. The system of electing representatives to these local bodies has been put in place, and their areas of responsibility have also been determined. However, some of the other steps needed, notably financial devolution of resources from the state to *panchayat* level, and the transfer of control over functionaries to the local level, has yet to be achieved. Some states—notably the southern states—have made greater progress than others, but a great deal more remains to be done in all parts of the country. Genuine empowerment of the *panchayati raj* institutions will make a major contribution to the effectiveness of service delivery programs in the states, and differences in this dimension of performance are likely to contribute to interstate variations in the future.

One of the most important determinants of economic growth in individual states will be the quality of the electric power supply, as this will affect not only industrial and commercial growth but also agricultural development, especially the diversification of agriculture. Reform of

the power sector is perhaps the most important unfinished reform in India, and the key to success lies in improvements in electricity distribution. At present, the state-run electricity distribution systems suffer from losses ranging from 35 to 40 percent in most states. This partly reflects technical losses in transmission, but mainly represents theft of electricity through underbilling, usually in connivance with the utility staff. Tariff structures are also uneconomical, with some categories of consumers (farmers and households) obtaining power at unrealistically low rates. The result is that the state utilities are financially unviable and unable to undertake the large investments needed to ensure an adequate supply of good-quality power. Reform of the power sector requires a gradual move toward rational user charges in which cross-subsidies are kept to a reasonable level and improvements are achieved in collection efficiency, either through improved management of the public sector system or through privatization. Thus far, only Orissa and Delhi have opted for privatization, and it is too early to pronounce whether the initiative is successful.

Progress in all these areas will depend upon how energetically state governments address these problems. As in other areas, performance will vary, but hopefully the diversity of experience will generate lessons on what works and what does not. A very hopeful development in the postreform period is the growth of awareness in the states that the state governments must work to create a favorable investment climate. Several nongovernmental bodies routinely engage in rating states regarding this issue, and the publicity given these ratings is generating healthy competition.

Montek S. Ahluwalia

See also **Economic Reforms of 1991; Economy since the 1991 Economic Reforms; State Finances since 1952**

BIBLIOGRAPHY

Ahluwalia, Montek S. "State Level Performance and Economic Reforms in India." In *Economic Policy Reforms and the Indian Economy*, edited by Anne O. Krueger. Chicago: University of Chicago Press, 2002.
Bajpai, N., and Jeffrey Sachs. "Trends in Inequality of Income in India." *Harvard Institute for International Development Discussion Paper*, no. 528.
Cashin P., and Ratna Sahay. "Regional Economic Growth and Convergence in India." *Finance and Development* (March 1996).

STEP-WELLS OF INDIA Step-wells are wells with underground flights of stairs leading down to the level of the water. They were built in all parts of South Asia, but in especially great numbers in the states of Gujarat and Rajasthan, in western India, which have a dry climate and sandy soil. Since it was also considered an act of religious merit to dedicate watering places in memory of the dead, thousands of step-wells, ponds, and tanks came to be built. In its fully developed form, a step-well consists of an ornate entrance gateway at ground level, an underground stepped passage punctuated by a series of pillared pavilions, and a well at the far end. There may even be a small reservoir to collect any surplus water flowing out of the well.

Forms

There are step-wells proper (those with a stepped corridor and a well at the far end), and there are others that should be more correctly described as stepped tanks, though sometimes such tanks were also combined with wells. The step-wells proper are laid along one long axis; the staircase usually starts at one end, and there is in most instances only a single entrance. A step-well may have more entrances, but this is the exception rather than the rule; also, the well at the far end may be rectangular or circular. The more evolved examples, however, are always circular.

In addition to the Hindu step-wells, there are others built by Muslim rulers after the thirteenth century. Their character and purpose, however, were altogether different; while the Hindu step-wells were religious undertakings as well as useful watering places for men and for agriculture, those built under Muslim rule were essentially for pleasure, as a retreat from the hot weather.

Many inscriptions record how step-wells were built as pious acts in memory of the dead. A stone slab from Mandasor of A.D. 532 commemorates the deceased relative of a nobleman, Daksha, employing the imagery of the myth of the descent of Gaṅgā (Ganges) from heaven to liberate the spirits of an ancient king's ancestors. Another, of A.D. 1042, from Vasantgarh in Rajasthan, records that a queen, Lahini, repaired the stairs of a step-well which were to provide a stepped ascent to heaven for her husband. The reference to the world of the departed is explicit in the imagery in the records of both Mandasor and Vasantgarh.

Structure

Step-wells involve both excavation and construction in the sandy soil. It took their builders a long time to overcome all the engineering problems, but in due course they created a remarkably efficient structural form. The earliest step-wells consisted of a short flight of steps down a pit whose sides were protected only by dressed stone, and the well at the end of the corridor was at right angles to it, that is, the two parts of the step-well formed an L shape. This was decidedly unsatisfactory, since it lacked an impressive facade, and it also involved an awkward sharp turn for someone bearing pitchers of water on the head. By the end of the tenth century, however, the structural constraints had been understood and resolved. Then followed a long series of step-wells in which the architectural potential of their basic form was perfectly realized.

In a "complete" example, a *toraṇa* (arch) built at the ground level stands at the head of the stepped corridor. At the first landing of the steps there is an open structure or pavilion whose top reaches the ground level. At the second landing, deeper down, another pillared pavilion is introduced, of two, or even three stories, its top again reaching the ground level, and likewise at every stage of the descent. As the depth of the trench increased with the increasing length of the corridor, it became necessary to stabilize the deep walls, which might have collapsed if kept vertical; therefore, terraces were introduced, corresponding to the height of the stories of the pavilions. Finally, in order to further strengthen the walls, a retaining structure of bricks came to be constructed behind the stone facade of the walls.

By far the largest number of step-wells is concentrated in the two western Indian states of Gujarat and Rajasthan, but such watering places were built all over the country. Step-wells dug by Hindu donors, and those by Muslims as well, are in Delhi (Gandhak ki Baoli, Rani ki Bain), in central India (Vidisha), and even in the southern states (Bagali in Karnataka).

The Ranki Vav Step-Well at Patan

By far the most ornate step-well is the seven-storied Ranki Vav, "the Queen's Step-well," at Patan, the capital of the Solankis from the tenth century. It was built by the widowed queen Udayamati in memory of her husband, Bhima I, in the second half of the eleventh century. Two hundred twenty feet (67 m) long, it is 60 feet (18 m) wide, and the well is 100 feet (30 m) deep.

The long stepped corridor commences at ground level and, interrupted at four increasingly deeper levels, leads down to where the well water stayed in the driest period of the year. There are multistoried pillared pavilions on the landings, the number of the stories progressively increasing as the depth increases, to reach the ground level above. In addition to the main steps, supplementary staircases are introduced for quick access to different parts of the step-well. Deep niches and projecting panels, with hundreds of nearly life-size sculptures of gods, goddesses, and *apsarā*s (semidivine female beings, nymphs) decorate the walls. The inner surface of the well is also lined with the same kind of images. The Hindu pantheon is present in force, with Shiva, Vishnu and his incarnations, the Seven Mothers, and other divinities. But images of Pārvatī performing the harsh penance by standing "surrounded by five fires" predominate. For just as the goddess performed austerities in order to win Shiva as a husband, Udayamati by building her well was performing a religious act in order to be reunited with her departed husband in her next life.

Other Important Step-Wells

There is an early seventh-century rock-cut step-well at Mandor, in Rajasthan, that has an L shape. Though quite bare, it is important for its "architecture" because it reproduces the form of the earliest structural step-wells in living rock, before the builders had discovered how to build a corridor and a well on one axis. A more ornate example, at Chhoti Khatu, also in Rajasthan, of the ninth century, also has an L shape, and its statuary of river goddesses and *nāga*s, or anthropomorphized snakes, clearly evoke its aquatic character.

The tradition that culminated in the Ranki Vav in the eleventh century continued in the later centuries as well, but by then Muslim power had been established in Gujarat, with far-reaching changes. First, hardly any human figures were used in their decorative elements. And, more importantly, the step-wells built by the sultans functioned not as religious structures but as pleasure retreats to escape the heat of summer.

The two step-wells at Ahmedabad and Adalaj, only a few miles apart, were both built at the end of the fifteenth century. Bai Harir, a rich eunuch at the court of Sultan Mahmud Begda, built the first in a suburb of Ahmedabad. It is over 240 feet (73 m) long. A raised pavilion, supported on twelve columns, stands at the head of the long corridor in the east, and by means of graded stairs reaches first an octagonal well, then a circular well at the western end. Balconies with low parapets look down into the octagonal well. In addition to the main stairs, there are two spiral staircases on the sides that provide access to the four stories.

The consort of a local chief built the step-well at Adalaj, called Ruda Bai's Step-Well after her name, about 12 miles (19 km) north of Ahmedabad. It is planned on a south-north axis. In addition to the main approach at the southern end, there are two more stairs at right angles to it, on the two sides, all three meeting at the first landing, in a sort of foyer with elegant balconies and richly crafted columns.

Sacred Tanks

The reservoirs described above are proper step-wells, but the sacred tank, or *kuṇḍa*, is a monument of comparable character. These are deep pools of water, mostly square or rectangular, which are reached through steps built on three or all four sides, sometimes with a shrine in the middle. Their perfect geometry, the miniature shrines built at intervals along the stairs, and the well-proportioned supplementary stairs create a pleasing appearance.

Such sacred tanks may be of modest size, as is the seventh-century *pushkarin* (lotus pool) at Mahakuta in Karnataka. Or they may be planned on a more impressive scale, such as those at Osian (eighth century), Abhaneri (ninth century), and Baroli (tenth century), all in Rajasthan; and at Modhera in Gujarat (early eleventh century). The Osian and Abhaneri examples have steps on three sides, while a well placed on the fourth side feeds the tank; that at Modhera has long flights of steps on all four sides. The tank at Baroli is built over a natural spring that flows on a rocky bed; on an elevated natural rock in the center, a holy man in the tenth century built a shrine to Shiva, characterizing the god as Jhareshvara, "lord of the Stream."

Kirit Mankodi

See also **Hinduism (Dharma)**

BIBLIOGRAPHY

Jain-Neubauer, Jutta. *The Stepwells of Gujarat.* New Delhi: Abhinav Publications, 1981.
Livingston, Morna. *Steps to Water: The Ancient Stepwells of India.* New York: Princeton Architectural Press, 2002.
Mankodi, Kirit. *The Queen's Stepwell at Patan.* Mumbai: Project for Indian Cultural Studies, 1991.

STOCK EXCHANGE MARKETS India established the first stock exchange in Asia in Bombay in 1875. Given the large geographical size of the country and the typical floor-based trading system prevalent until 1994, a total of twenty-two stock exchanges were eventually created to cater to the needs of investors in every part of India. Three basic models were adopted: associations of individuals, limited liability companies (without profit sharing), and companies limited by guarantees. Regardless of the form of organization, all were recognized by the tax authorities as nonprofit entities, or entities in which their members had no claim to operating surpluses. Although the generated surpluses were not explicitly distributed, exchanges provided various services to their members invariably below cost, with the subsidy element varying from exchange to exchange.

Exchanges enjoyed subsidies in many forms. The respective state governments allotted land for constructing the buildings for exchange operations and brokers' offices on nominal terms. Until recently, the government of India had adopted the concept of regional stock

Bombay Stock Exchange. Site of today's Bombay Stock Exchange, which was the first stock exchange in Asia. In the era of reform after the financial reverses of the early 1990s, the BSE has followed the lead of India's NSE in providing fully modernized systems and services. BHARATH RAMAMRUTHAM.

exchanges (RSEs) defining the operating area of each exchange. A public company was required to list its stock on the RSE nearest its registered office.

A listed company has to pay listing fees, both initial and annual and such fees were linked to the size of its issued capital. For most RSEs listing fees were the main source of income. Each exchange enjoyed monopoly rights in securities trading in the city of its location. Investors had no mechanism to protect themselves from collusive behavior by the stock brokers. This monopoly also led to the creation of fragmented markets that were shallow, inefficient, and cost ineffective. Brokers generally dealt with investors through a multilayered chain of intermediaries increasing cost of transaction.

Since exchanges prohibited corporate membership, all brokerage entities were either proprietary or partnership concerns. Although the liability of a brokerage firm was unlimited, this did not mean much to investors, as almost all the brokerage firms were poorly capitalized. Brokerage firms distributed most of the profits at the end of each accounting year, transferring them to their family members. Thus, in the event of a firm's insolvency, investors were the main losers.

Reforms since 1991

Capital market reforms process launched in 1992 was in response to a major financial scam that shook the banking system and the capital markets. Some prominent stock brokers defrauded several Indian banks (both government-owned and private) as well as prominent foreign banks. They diverted bank funds to their personal accounts for artificially increasing the prices of their favorite stocks. This became possible due to severe deficiencies in trading and settlement systems for sovereign bonds and bonds issued by public sector units. The resultant boom in equity markets attracted thousands of gullible investors who hoped to make quick gains. The bubble burst after some investigative journalists exposed the frauds perpetrated by unscrupulous stockbrokers. When the banks demanded funds back from the brokers, the market collapsed. The banks lost an estimated U.S.$2 billion in this scam. For the Indian government, which had just launched a series of reforms in the securities markets, the crisis was a major embarrassment.

The government promptly introduced a number of measures with far reaching consequences in the securities markets. A significant component of this reform package was the need for setting up a new Indian stock exchange, which would be operated in accord with globally accepted best practices, both in trading and settlement systems. The National Stock Exchange (NSE) was thus born. It was initially conceived to be a model exchange to exert pressure on the other twenty-two stock exchanges, inducing them to improve their functioning styles. Within six years, its impact on Indian capital markets was so overwhelming that all the other exchanges, except for Bombay Stock Exchange (BSE), became virtually defunct. As a survival strategy, ten regional exchanges set up subsidiary companies that became members of NSE and BSE. The systems and procedures introduced by the NSE have been accepted by the market regulator, the Securities Exchange Board of India (SEBI), and were made applicable to the other exchanges, all of which look to the NSE for further initiatives in market reforms.

The Design of the National Stock Exchange

The NSE was set up as a limited liability pro-profit company by twenty-one leading financial institutions in 1993. Its executive board includes senior bankers, lawyers, and financial executives. To avoid any possible conflict of interests, the day-to-day management of the exchange is handled by professionals, who do not have proprietary trading positions in the stock market.

India's NSE is patterned on the U.S. Nasdaq model, extending its trading facilities to all parts of the country, and providing trading facilities only in large stocks, like the New York Stock Exchange. It has adopted an anonymous order-driven trading system, with orders originating from all its members being matched automatically by the computer as per the price time priority trading algorithm. Thus there is no human intervention in the deal-matching process. India's NSE is the first exchange in the world to set up a captive satellite communications network, connecting its members spread across a vast geographical area in the country to its centralized trading and settlement hub. All members enjoy a response time of less than 1.5 seconds; orders originating from any part of the country are matched, and trade confirmed on the respective trading terminals, in this short time span. This highly transparent system gives investors instant information about traded prices and quantities as well as unmatched bids and offers in all stocks on a real time basis. To start with, NSE enforced on its trading members (stock brokers) certain minimum stringent disclosure norms that provided a clean audit trail of a trade at the investor level. The trading members were forced to provide automatically generated trade and order confirmation notes to all investors. This unique system of disclosure became the standard regulatory requirement subsequently.

India's NSE also started guaranteeing the settlement of members' net obligations, at a time when guaranteed settlement was unheard of in India, by establishing a subsidiary National Securities Clearing Corporation Limited, which developed unique software to monitor each member's net exposure in each stock as well as members' aggregate exposure in all stocks. Each member was required to trade within the overall exposure limits, based on the concept of initial margin adopted globally by the futures exchanges. The moment a member exceeds the exposure level, all its trading terminals are automatically disconnected from the trading system. The trading terminals are reactivated only when additional funds are brought in. If a member fails to honor its settlement obligations, member margins are usually adequate to close out positions. The BSE took more than a year to adopt its own settlement guarantee program, but later developed its own exposure monitoring mechanism based on the national model.

Impact on Other Exchanges

The impact of the major investor-friendly trading and settlement systems was so decisive that the NSE emerged as India's largest exchange before it completed its first

year in November 1995. Business losses then forced the BSE to launch computerized trading as well. Later, all RSEs computerized their operations. But since their response was slow and halting, they lost much of their business to the large exchanges.

Options and Futures

In June 2000, India's two major exchanges, the NSE and the BSE, offered futures and options products on their main indexes, with one-, two-, and three-month expiration contracts. Options on indexes on these exchanges began in June 2001, options on select stocks in July 2001, and futures on select stocks in November 2001. As of December 2004, stock options and futures were available on fifty-three highly liquid stocks. Based on certain objective criteria, the regulator approves inclusion of stocks in the list of equities eligible for futures and options trading. Stock futures and options have proved to be very popular among investors.

As of December 2004, average trading turnover in futures and options (both in stocks and the indices) was twice the turnover in the cash market for equities. The Indian futures and options market has become vibrant; from April to December 2004, the daily average of contracts traded on the NSE was 288,616. The average contract size was, however, small. India is among the few countries to have introduced stock futures, as they are feared to be highly risky. Unless stringent regulations and tight surveillance are in place, stock futures may be misused to manipulate individual stock prices. In India, stock futures account for over 60 percent of trading in the entire futures segment. The daily turnover in stock futures in December 2004 was about 155 percent of the NSE's turnover in the cash market for all traded equities. The Indian experience proves that even relatively backward capital markets can quickly and successfully absorb globally accepted trading and settlement systems.

India's new trading system has encouraged price competition and has helped in the significant decline in bid/offer spreads. As a result, transaction costs are estimated to have declined by a factor of eight to ten after the NSE came to dominate the Indian market.

R. H. Patil

See also **Capital Market; Securities Exchange Board of India (SEBI)**

BIBLIOGRAPHY

There are three web sites that provide useful information on the Indian securities markets, including the functioning of the Indian stock exchanges: the Securities Exchange Board of India at <http://www.sebi.gov.in/>; the National Stock Exchange at <http://www.nseindia.com/>; and the

Bombay Stock Exchange at <http://www.bseindia.com>. The following reports and publications are particularly useful: Securities Exchange Board of India, *Annual Report,* 1996–1997 to 2002–2003; National Stock Exchange of India's annual publication *Indian Securities Market: A Review,* 1999 to 2004; National Stock Exchange of India's annual publication *Fact Book,* 1998 to 2004; Reserve Bank of India, *Report on Currency and Finance,* 1999–2000.

STRATEGIC THOUGHT

Carl von Clausewitz (1780–1831), modern Europe's great strategist, considered the purpose of war to be the imposition of the victor's will over the enemy (strategy), and the destruction of the adversary's main force in decisive battle (tactics). Clausewitz also postulated that strategy was neither an art nor a science but an act of human intercourse. Furthermore, he emphasized that successful war was waged by the trinitarian structure of the state: its government, its people, and its armed forces. India, as a dependency of the rising British Empire, had a government that was alien and an army that was selectively recruited. Accordingly, neither was representative of the people of India. Earlier, the Mughals had understood the strategic significance of India's mountain passes in the northwest, but were oblivious to sea power. Even the great Mughal emperor Akbar remained unmindful of the Portuguese embargo of his main seaport, Surat. Though the fatal weakening of the Mughals followed the invasion by the Turcoman adventurer, Nadir Shah (1739), the coup de grâce was rendered by a British mercantile company that took control of the Indian sea trade. By its conquest of India, Britain became a great power, and London used India's central position and resources to control "any point either of Asia or Africa," as asserted by the Viceroy Lord Curzon.

The *Artha Shāstra*

Ancient India's greatest strategist, Kautilya (also known as Chanakya or Vishnugupta, c. 320 B.C.), prime minister to Emperor Chandragupta Maurya, wrote his great work on statecraft, the *Artha Shāstra,* which focused on the duties of a king and military affairs. Kautilya considered the *dharma* (sacred duty) of a king to expand the resources of his state by employing varying combinations of *sam* (amity or treaty), *dam* (rewards), *dand* (retribution), and *bhed* (discord). However, if war became necessary, Kautilya considered employing the following seven principles and three "controls" before hostilities were undertaken: an efficient system of governance; capable royal councilors and other officials (*amatyas*); firm control over one's own territory (*janapada*); a fortified city (*durg*) within the king's domain; a full war-chest (*kosha*); an adequate army (*danda*); and allies, either equals (*mitra* or *sandhi*) or stronger ones (*samasraj*). The three "controls" were equally timeless: to examine the morale and motivation of the opposing leaders; to calculate the material resources, numerical strength, and level of training of the two states; and to consider the strengths and weaknesses of the two kings' advisers, generals, ministers, and diplomats.

As his overall strategy, Kautilya based *vijigishu* (victory) on the concept of the *mandala* (circle), whereby one's neighboring state was always a real or potential enemy, and the state next to one's immediate neighbor was a natural ally. Among other related topics, the *Artha Shāstra* covered battlefield dispositions, tactics, peace treaties (a weak enemy should be crushed, whereas the stronger one should be negotiated with), and methods of combat, ranging from coercive diplomacy to clandestine warfare.

Kautilya used legends and mythology to buttress his analysis. For instance, he quoted Brihaspati, the legendary sage of sages, as saying that "three to one" superiority over the enemy was necessary for victory. This still widely quoted maxim (without attribution to either Brihaspati or Kautilya) was to make caution the strategic imperative in India, since such overwhelming military superiority was rarely achieved. Kautilya also prescribed responsibilities of the *navadhyaksha* (superintendent of ships) and analyzed sea trade but paid little attention to maritime strategy. Perhaps it was his North Indian outlook and the influence of another Indian epic, the Rāmāyaṇa, in which Lord Ram invades the island of Sri Lanka by building a bridge, not ships, to cross the sea. Kautilya also limited his wars of conquest to the Indian subcontinent. Hence, over the next millennium, his towering but flawed work created a defensive and introspective Indian military mindset. Muslim invasions and conquests from the twelfth to the sixteenth centuries consigned Kautilya to obscurity, only to be resurrected after 1907, when his *Artha Shāstra* was first published in English.

Independent India

Forty years after the rediscovery of Kautilya's *Artha Shāstra,* India became independent. However, freedom was accompanied by South Asia's partition and the destruction of the geographical unity visualized by Kautilya. The leadership of newly independent India had little experience in governance, foreign policy, or strategic planning, and was wary of the military, as postcolonial armies seized power in most newly independent states. Moreover, India's new leaders considered British India's military, which had remained aloof during the struggle for freedom, as little more than mercenaries. The organization and mindset of the army (by far the largest of the defense services) was based on static, not operational, considerations. Hence, a few high-ranking Indian officers had some administrative experience, but little knowledge of strategy. Furthermore, India's first prime minister, Jawaharlal Nehru, was determined to avoid entangling foreign alliances and believed that Indian security was enhanced by reduced militarization of the planet. These perspectives were in consonance with the Gandhian strategies of nonviolence and economic self-sufficiency. The latter stifled modernization of the military, as the country's industrial base was small and imports were restricted. Consequently, senior officers, busy husbanding scarce resources, had little time for prospective planning or post-colonial strategy. The Gandhian precept of nonviolence had its own ramifications on the military. For instance, the navy was discouraged from acquiring submarines, since they were perceived as offensive warships and therefore unsuitable for a country advocating disarmament and nonviolence. The electorate, too, was little concerned about defense issues. Accordingly, few members of Parliament wished to serve on the forty-four-member Standing Committee on Defence. Even forty years after independence, fewer than half of the committee's members attended its meetings; apart from the chairman, only seven others were present at all its sessions. Not unexpectedly, strategic thought evolved fitfully, yet incrementally under the influence of the following major factors.

History. The assimilation of non-Hindu cultures and religions is integral to the modern Indian identity. Hence, symbols of the Indian Republic are of Ashokan Buddhist origin, the link-language of the country remained English, and the Muslim Mughals epitomized Indian cuisine and many forms of the arts and architecture. History also reminded India that the country's lag in military science had led to repeated defeats in the past. Therefore, independent India made a conscious effort to keep abreast of modern technology. The sudden emergence of India as a powerhouse in the software industry may be an unintended but fortunate consequence of this commitment.

Geography. India's continental geographical contours were drawn 2,400 years ago by Kautilya. Indians were largely isolationist, for they considered their land secure behind the mountain chains stretching along their eastern, northern, and western borders. The ocean toward the south was not understood in military terms but only as a means of trade, travel, and proselytization. Neither the limited Chinese foray through the Himalayas in the seventh century nor the successive raids from the northwest altered the Indian perception of living in a safe, insular, and prosperous continental nation, though given to fissiparous tendencies that led to piecemeal conquests of the country. Hence, national consolidation of the country was a major security issue for New Delhi, whereas the legacy of insularity contributed to India's attempts to minimize the presence of outside powers in the six-country subcontinent of South Asia.

Culture. Though concerned about divisive tendencies, New Delhi considered the distinctive Indian culture compelling enough to keep the country united, despite the centrifugal effects of well-defined regional subcultures. Furthermore, the Hindu concepts of *dharma*, karma, and reincarnation were integral to this belief. *Dharma*, as Kautilya instructed, was sacred law, requiring all members of society to perform their various duties. Karma enjoined that individual action and performance was the basis for future incarnations. The concept of reincarnation gave Indians a cyclical rather than a linear perspective on time. Hence, as the universe itself goes through the phases of birth, growth, decay, and rebirth, so must individual countries and living beings. Therefore, in a sense, Kautilya's India was basically eternal, going through cycles from birth to rebirth. Accordingly, Indians appear to possess a capacity for timeless endurance and tolerance.

Colonialism. During the colonial period, strategic responsibility for the defense of India shifted to London. Hence, Indians had little say or understanding of those issues. The net result was material poverty and numerous other losses, including confidence and management skills.

Partition. To Indians, the geographical unity of the country was torn by the creation of Pakistan, a hostile neighbor, across a newly created border that was devoid of natural barriers. Consequently, India was preoccupied by the defense of this new frontier and paid scant attention to its ill-defined border with China. In addition, New Delhi was concerned about the further instigation of Indian Muslims by fundamentalists. Accordingly, internal security became another issue. The conflict over Kashmir became India's major security and diplomatic challenge. Three Indo-Pakistan Wars were fought over Kashmir. Furthermore, the Pakistani-supported, though indigenous, insurgency (since 1987) in Indian Kashmir remains an ongoing conundrum for New Delhi.

Nuclear weapons. Despite the abhorrent nature of nuclear weapons, there was clear recognition in New Delhi of nuclear weapons as a deterrent against aggression or coercion by other countries, especially Pakistan and China. In addition, nuclear weapons came to symbolize political maturity, ultimate sovereignty, and technological prowess. Foreign military interventions in Yugoslavia and in the Gulf have added further relevance to the importance of nuclear deterrence.

Strategically, some of these factors led India to focus on the subcontinent and on its immediate neighbors. The neighbors were dealt with as minor "enemies," whereas the transneighbors, especially the Kingdom of Afghanistan and the Soviet Union, were treated as natural allies. The United States became an incipient opponent, an outsider intruding into the subcontinent as

Pakistan's partner in collective security arrangements and with its own military base on the British-owned island of Diego Garcia in the Indian Ocean.

India had, perhaps intuitively, followed the *mandala* theory as visualized by Kautilya, antagonizing its neighbors, accommodating the strong (China on Tibet), and overwhelming the weak (Nepal and Bhutan). Buffer states, a European concept, were overlooked. Ironically, it was the loss of the largest buffer state, Tibet, that compelled India to move from vague strategic concepts to threat assessment and defense planning, especially after the reverses suffered in the border war with China in 1962. However, it took another thirty years before the factors mentioned above led India to form a cohesive national security perspective. The stimuli were many: the collapse of the Soviet Union with the attendant rise of the United States as an interventionist sole superpower; the global rise in Islamic fundamentalism; the ongoing Sino-Pakistani collaboration, especially in nuclear weapons and missile technology; cross-border terrorism as part of an insurgency in Indian Kashmir; and a compelling study by an American think-tank, the Rand Corporation. Rand's main inference was that India had no long-range strategic perspectives, as evidenced by the country's reactive approach to international affairs and the absence of the military's participation in policy making. The study had its shortcomings, the most obvious being its failure to recognize the sense of mission and commitment of the scientific community to the successful development of nuclear devices, chemical weapons, and missile systems. The unusual group of scientist-strategists received such high public acclaim that one of them, Dr. K. Santhanam, was appointed director of the Ministry of Defence's leading think tank, the Institute of Defence Studies and Analysis in New Delhi. Another eminent scientist, Dr. A. P. J. Abdul Kalam, was elected president of India in 2002.

Consensus on the country's strategic imperatives was reached by the new millennium during the several years of the rightist coalition government led by the Bharatiya Janata Party (BJP). The process was invigorated by nuclear tests, accelerated missile development, and military ties with the United States and Israel. Under these circumstances, bureaucrats, scientists, politicians, and perhaps military officers set the strategic vision for the country. Hence, the contours of New Delhi's nuclear policy were already in the public domain before a draft nuclear doctrine, framed by eminent strategic thinkers, declared that India would maintain a minimal credible and survivable deterrence, based on a triad of delivery systems (missiles, aircraft, and submarines) with adequate command and control facilities. The draft also affirmed a no-first-use policy and a commitment not to threaten or use atomic weapons against a nonnuclear country.

The army, bearing nuclear weapons in mind, posited the operational strategy of a limited "hyperwar." The limits were defined as time, geographical area, force levels, and war objectives. Hyperwar meant the use of intense firepower, long-range sensors, precision-guided munitions, and the elimination of the front and the rear of battle. Such a battle could be fought continuously, regardless of day and night, and through all weather. The air force preempted the others by publishing its Air Power Doctrine in 1997. The doctrine gave equal priority to both offensive and defensive operations, and accepted the possibility of reduction in force levels if compensated by induction of high technology equipment and acquisition of force-multipliers like airborne warning and control systems, multirole war planes, and midair refueling capabilities. By implication, it distanced itself from the subsidiary role as the tactical air arm of the army. Its doctrine acquired greater relevance, as it was the only service with the means to deliver nuclear weapons. Hence, it automatically became the preeminent strategic force in the country. The smallest service, the navy, potentially has the largest strategic role through sea-denial, sea-control, power projection, management of the Indian Exclusive Economic Zone of 1.08 million square miles (2.8 million sq. km.), and as a part of the triad of nuclear deterrence. Like other navies, it acquired land-attack missile capabilities. However, its sea control and blue-water potential remains limited. The pursuit of a nuclear submarine arm as a part of the triad of nuclear deterrence, raises concerns among some admirals, as they fear that nuclear submarines would divert funds from the surface ships necessary to fulfill the navy's other tactical and strategic ambitions. Like the rest of India, the armed forces are engaging with the world. Indo–U.S. cooperation ranges from joint exercises to Indian political support for various U.S. ballistic missile defense programs.

In general, India's wider strategic goals remain constrained by an inadequate indigenous military-industrial complex, the constricted strategy of managing domestic conflicts and insurgencies by attrition and co-option, and sudden outbursts of ethnic and communal violence in the country. Furthermore, for forty years, Indians were Pakistan-centric and reactive in the acquisition of weapons and military systems. Submarines, supersonic fighters, and reconnaissance and support battalions were Pakistani initiatives with India following suit. In addition, American strategists continue to find that serving senior Indian military officers still had little exposure to the outside world and insufficient training in such strategic subjects as geopolitics, military history, and patterns of organization.

Nevertheless, the 1990s brought economic liberalization and an unfolding of talents, self-confidence, and more pragmatic international relationships. India was no longer the hungry country of the 1943 Bengal famine trying to keep Nehru's "tryst with destiny," by espousing global peace, prosperity, freedom, and social justice. Instead, newly confident of its ancient civilization, and a vibrant, stable democracy, India sought new paradigms: self-reliance rather than self-sufficiency, and participative growth instead of a command economy. As India has no territorial ambitions, the pattern of past politico-military engagements is likely to persist. Hence, India will militarily intervene only at the request of a friendly government and withdraw its forces as soon as possible, as in Sri Lanka (1971, 1987), Bangladesh (1971), and Maldives (1988). At present, for the uniformed services and security-related establishments, the new imperatives are greater integration of command, control, modernization with triservice compatibility of acquisitions, and intelligence sharing. Still, fourteen different ministries and departments in New Delhi exercise overlapping authority over the country's maritime affairs. Howsoever slowly, a holistic approach toward strategic affairs appears to be evolving in New Delhi as India develops tangible political, economic, and military ties with countries in Southeast Asia, Central Asia, the Middle East (including Israel), Africa, and the United States. Hence, India's strategic perspective appears to have completed yet another cycle of reincarnation, from Kautilyan back to Curzonian concerns.

Rajesh Kadian

See also **Armed Forces; Artha Shāstra; Civil-Military Relations; Pakistan and India; Wars, Modern**

BIBLIOGRAPHY

Clausewitz, Carl von. *On War*. Translated by Michael Howard and Peter Paret. Princeton, N.J.: Princeton University Press, 1976.

Curzon of Kedleston, Lord. *The Place of India in the Empire*. London: John Murray, 1909.

Mohan, C. Raja. *Crossing the Rubicon: The Shaping of India's New Foreign Policy*. New Delhi: Viking, 2003.

Sengupta, Prasun K. "India's Armed Forces in the New Millennium." *Asian Defense Journal* 26 (June 2002): 13–16.

Shamasastry, R. *Kautilya's Arthashastra*. 5th ed. Mysore: Sri Raghuvir Printing Press, 1956. Shamasastry's first tentative translation was published in *Indian Antiquary* in 1905.

Singh, Jasjit. Foreword to *India's Maritime Security*, edited by Rahul Roy Chaudhury. New Delhi: Knowledge World, 2000.

Singh, Ravinder Pal, ed. *Arms Procurement Decision Making*, Vol. I: *China, India, Israel, Japan, South Korea and Thailand*. New York: Oxford University Press, 1998.

Tanham, George K. *Indian Strategic Thought: An Interpretive Essay*. Santa Monica, Calif.: Rand, 1992.

STUPAS. *See* **Buddhism in Ancient India.**

SUBBALAKSHMI AMMAL, R. S. *(1886–1969), educator and activist for women's education.* R. S. Subbalakshmi Ammal, a pioneer in the education of upper-caste widows in colonial Madras presidency, was born in July 1886 into a Brahman family. Her students affectionately called her Sahōodarii, or Sister Subbalakshmi. In an era when upper caste girls' schooling was haphazard, her father, a college professor, supervised her education, supported by her mother and a widowed aunt. In accordance with upper caste custom in that era, Subbalakshmi was married before puberty, but the early death of her bridegroom left her a virgin widow at the age of eleven. Widows were often shunned as inauspicious blights, languishing in perpetual celibacy, clothed in drab mourning, their heads tonsured. In most cases, they remained illiterate and were dependent on family charity. However, Subbalakshmi's family defied tradition by educating her, moving to Madras (Chennai) to facilitate her attendance at the Presidency Convent Higher Secondary School. She won gold medals for academic achievement, then joined Madras Presidency College, where she majored in mathematics and botany. She graduated in 1912, the first Hindu widow in Madras to receive a bachelor's degree.

In 1910 Subbalakshmi had started an informal home to educate young widows whose grieving parents had approached her for this purpose. She also simultaneously taught at her former high school for a minimum wage, respecting the nuns who had been her own teachers, but disliking their attempts to convert her. She remained a devout Hindu, committed to the ideals of Upanishadic humanism. Though critical of misogynist traditions, she avoided alienating Hindu traditionalists whose widowed daughters she wished to educate. This pragmatism enabled her to succeed in promoting the education of widows. Her success attracted the attention of Christina Lynch, the progressive inspector of Government Girls' Schools. The two women soon planned to start a government teachers' training institute for widows. On 1 July 1912, their Sārada Widows' Ashram opened, named for the Hindu goddess of learning.

In an age when prepuberty marriages were the norm, Subbalakshmi became a beacon for women whose education had been curtailed by early marriage. In January 1912 she started her Sārada Ladies Union to promote intellectual inquiry among women. As a colonial government employee, Subbalakshmi could not openly join the nationalist Women's Indian Association (WIA), although she worked with feminist members like Muthulakshmi Reddi in an unofficial capacity.

In 1919 Subbalakshmi opened the Sārada Vidyālaya Higher Secondary School for destitute unmarried girls. In 1921 she addressed the Indian Women's Conference delegates on the need for establishing more teachers' training institutes for women, and on the inclusion of occupational programs in the curriculum. She was respected by conservatives and reformers, colonials and nationalists, men and women. In 1947 Sāradā Ladies' Union was finally affiliated with the WIA. After independence, Subbalakshmi served as a member of the Madras Legislative Council. Denied children of her own, she lavished her maternal love and wisdom upon countless students, nieces, and nephews to whom she became an icon.

Sita Anantha Raman

See also **Women's Education; Women's Indian Association**

BIBLIOGRAPHY

Primary sources include Government of Madras educational records; Subbalakshmi Ammal's private diary; and Sāradā Ladies' Union commemorative journals in her honor.

Chellammal, S. "Sister Subbalakshmi Ammal." In *Sister Subbalakshmi Ammal: First Anniversary Commemoration Souvenir.* Tamil: Sāradā Ladies' Union, 1970.

Felton, Monica. *A Child Widow's Story.* London: Gollancz, 1966.

Krishnaveni, K. *Sahodari Subbalakshmi.* Tamil: Sāradā Ladies' Union, 1962.

Raman, Sita Anantha. *Getting Girls to School.* Kolkata: Stree Press, 1996.

———. "Crossing Cultural Boundaries: Indian Matriarchs and Sisters in Service." *Journal of Third World Studies* 18, no. 2 (Fall 2001): 131–148.

Ramanathan, Malathi. *Sister Subbalakshmi Ammal: Birth Centenary Souvenir.* Tamil: Sāradā Ladies' Union, 1986.

Sastri, Kokila. "Sister R. S. Subbalakshmi." In *Women Pioneers in Education (Tamil Nadu),* edited by T. M. Narayanaswamy Pillai. Chennai: National Seminar on the Role of Women in Education in India, 1975.

SUBBULAKSHMI, M. S. *(1916–2004), Indian vocalist.*

Madurai Shanmugavadivu Subbulakshmi, a charismatic singer from South India, was venerated as an outstanding exponent of Karnātak vocal music. "M. S.," as she was popularly known to her millions of fans around the world, was considered the "embodiment of music." Her music appealed to both the uninitiated and the learned with its sophistication and profundity.

Born into a family of professional musicians on 16 September 1916, Subbulakshmi was a child prodigy. Her mother, Shanmugavadivu, was a competent vina player, and Subbulakshmi took her initial lessons on the vina from her mother. Shrinivas Iyengar and M. Subraminiya Iyer taught her vocal music, as did Dakshinamurthy Pillai and veteran Karnātak singer Semangudi Srinivas Iyer.

Total concentration on the alignment of microtones, caressing diction, and purity of *swarasthanams*, or note

positions, are some of the hallmarks of Subbulakshmi's music. Her dignified stage presence, enchanting voice, versatility, and humility enhanced her career, as did her linguistic ability. She did not indulge in showmanship. Devotion was her main driving force, and her vocal communication tended to transcend words. She could simultaneously cater to the most exacting demands of an orthodox Mylapur Madras audience and also touch the heartstrings of a mammoth gathering at the Harvallbh Mela (a musical soiree held annually in the precincts of a temple in Julunder).

Subbulakshmi also acted in films in the 1940s; her portrayal of the poet-saint Mīrabai catapulted her to fame throughout India, and even Mahatma Gandhi became her fan. Thanks to her husband Sadashivam, who was a close associate of Chakravarty Rajagopalachari, Subbulakshmi was exposed to the ideals of the national movement. She enjoyed a rapport with leaders like Sarojini Naidu, Jawaharlal Nehru, and Indira Gandhi. Nehru called her "Queen of Song" and Naidu surrendered her poetic title, "The Nightingale," to her. Since Karnātak music has its origins in the ancient temples, in whose precincts the ecstatic Hindu saints sang their songs to the gods, a devout singer like Subbulakshmi built her musical interpretation on devotion to God.

The peak of her long career was her performance before the United Nations General Assembly in 1966, at the invitation of Secretary General U Thant. On this occasion she urged all nations to give up aggression and cultivate friendship. The government of India decorated her with Bharat Ratna, its highest civilian honor. Subbulakshmi died on 11 December 2004.

Amarendra Dhaneshwar

See also **Music: Karnātak**

BIBLIOGRAPHY

Gangadhar, V. *M. S. Subbulakshmi: The Voice Divine.* Kolkata: Rupa and Co., 2002.

George, T. J. S. *M. S. Subbulakshmi: A Biography.* New Delhi: HarperCollins India, 2004.

Raghuvanshi, Alka. *A Moment in Time with Legends of Indian Arts.* New Delhi: Government of India, 1996.

Ramnarayan, Gowri. *Past Forward: Six Artists in Search of Their Childhood.* Delhi and New York: Oxford University Press, 1997.

SUBSIDIES IN THE FEDERAL BUDGET

Subsidies, like taxes, have been considered legitimate tools of government intervention. Before the 1990s, Indian government intervention over a wide spectrum of private decisions about production and consumption brought extensive use of tax subsidies, designed to achieve given objectives of its socialist approach to economic development. These subsidies took various forms, including:

standard consumer subsidies, for example food subsidies; interest or credit subsidies on priority sector lending by public sector banks; tax subsidies or tax "expenditures"; free public supply of certain services, like primary education and some health services; procurement subsidies for food grains and some other agricultural products; and regulatory subsidies arising from administered prices pegged below market prices, as for iron and steel.

Rationale

All subsidies add to public expenditure and must be financed from general revenues. In a balanced budget framework, this requires an equivalent rise in taxes or other sources of income whenever subsidies are given. Under normal circumstances, subsidies must be justified in specific benefits, and comparison of these benefits with the costs, both private and social, associated with such revenues is implied.

The basic economic rationale for subsidies is to bridge the gap between private returns and social returns of goods and services that have large externalities. Examples would include inoculation against communicable diseases, elementary education, social forestry and water conservation. In India, however, government subsidization has gone well beyond this primary reason, and widespread subsidies have been justified on several grounds, including self-sufficiency in production, supporting infant industries, poverty alleviation, or sometimes for distributional reasons (e.g., food subsidies).

The main problem with the subsidy regime in India is that much of it is nontransparent because subsidies are given in the form of unrecovered costs. As such, they are not really mandated by the empowered legislature, nor are their costs fully appreciated in general. The explicit subsidies are large but form only a fraction of the total amount of subsidies. Large implicit and explicit subsidies have been responsible to a considerable extent for the high fiscal deficits now observed at all levels of government in India. This has resulted in absorption of nongovernment savings to finance the deficits, leading to high interest rates, lower private investment, and consequent adverse effects on growth. Subsidies also change relative prices, and the resultant price distortions have led to resource misallocation.

Estimates

In India, official figures of subsidies either relate to only explicit subsidies or those including a small part of the implicit ones. After more comprehensive estimates of subsidies were unofficially made and widely accepted, official acceptance also followed. An official white paper on the subject that used the wider concept and its methodology for estimation of subsidies has tried to take

TABLE 1

Goods and services

Merit goods and services	Nonmerit goods and services
Elementary education	Education, sports, arts and
Public health	culture (other than
Sewerage and sanitation	elementary education)
Welfare of scheduled castes, scheduled tribes, and other "Backward" castes	Medical and family welfare
	Water supply and sanitation
	Housing
Labor	Urban development
Social welfare	Social security and welfare
Nutrition	Other social services
Soil and water conservation	Agricultural and allied activities
Environmental forestry and wildlife	Cooperation
Agricultural research and education	Rural development
Flood control and drainage	Special area programs
Roads and bridges	Irrigation
Space research	Power
Oceanographic research	Industries
Other scientific research	Transport
Ecology and environment	Civil supplies
Meteorology	Other economic services

SOURCE: Courtesy of author.

into account the justification for various kinds of subsidies by classifying subsidized services into merit and nonmerit goods based on subjective judgments regarding the degree of externalities involved (see Table 1). There are several difficult problems encountered in measuring this concept on the basis of available information. The stock of accumulated capital is given in nominal terms at heterogeneous prices that vitiate the computation of depreciation. The life of the assets concerned is also not uniform, and therefore the rates of economic depreciation. There is also the problem of change in value of some of the assets, particularly land, which cannot be taken into account, but which are extremely important for understanding the opportunity costs involved.

Another important problem relates to the issue of efficiency costs as opposed to actual costs, and the conceptual need to eliminate the excess of actual over efficiency costs from the estimate of subsidies. This is an intractable problem that has not yet been tackled. There is also the problem of lags between investment and the generation of service flow, and hence the need to abstract from the associated capital costs during this lag, but the informational requirements for this are not readily available.

Table 2 presents the four discrete estimates of aggregate budgetary subsidies, all of which put the total at around 12 percent of the gross domestic produce (GDP) or more. About one-third of these constitute the share of the central government, the rest being provided at the state level. The state governments provide the bulk of the subsidies, mostly in the areas of education, medical and public health, agriculture and allied services, energy,

TABLE 2

Comprehensive estimates of all India budget subsidies: Estimates for selected years

(Rs. Crore)

Study	Year	Estimated subsidies	GDP at market prices	Combined revenue receipts	Combined fiscal deficit	Subsidy as percentage of		
						GDP	Revenue receipts	Fiscal deficit
Mundle-Rao (1991)	1987–1988	42,324	355,417	66,838	32,182	11.91	63.32	131.51
Tiwari (1996)	1992–1993	95,373	747,387	135,422	50,726	12.76	70.43	188.02
NIPFP (1997)	1994–1995	136,843	1,009,906	178,012	70,062	13.55	76.87	195.32
NIPFP (2003)	1998–1999	235,752	1,740,935	274,769	155,760	13.54	85.80	151.36

Note: One crore = ten million rupees

SOURCE: Compiled from Mundle, Sudipto, and M. Govinda Rao, "The Volume and Composition of Government Subsidies in India," *Economic and Political Weekly* (4 May 1991), pp. 1157–1172; Tiwari, A.C., *Volume and Composition of Subsidies in the Government:1992–1993*, New Delhi: ICRIER, 1996; Srivastava, D. K., et al., *Government Subsidies in India*, New Delhi: National Institute of Public Finance and Policy (NIPFP), 1997; Srivastava, D. K., C. Bhujanga Rao, Pinaki Chakraborty, and T. S. Rangamannar, *Budgetary Subsidies in India*, New Delhi: National Institute of Public Finance and Policy (NIPFP), 2003; *Indian Public Finance Statistics* (various issues), and *National Accounts Statistics* (various issues).

TABLE 3

Explicit subsidies at the central level

Year	Amount (in Rs. Crore)	As percentage of GDP
1971–1972	140	0.286
1980–1981	2,028	1.411
1985–1986	4,796	1.725
1990–1991	12,158	2.138
1995–1996	12,666	1.066
2000–2001	26,838	1.275
2001–2002	31,207	1.359

SOURCE: Compiled from Srivastava, D. K., C. Bhujanga Rao, Pinaki Chakraborty, and T. S. Rangamannar, *Budgetary Subsidies in India*, New Delhi: National Institute of Public Finance and Policy, 2003.

irrigation, and transport. At the central level, about a third of the total subsidies are explicit, the rest given through low or nonrecovery costs of public services. In fact, the overwhelming bulk of explicit subsidies are at the central level. Aggregate estimates of subsidies rose as a ratio of revenue receipts, but fell as a ratio of fiscal deficits. The implication is that subsidies are being financed less by current income of the government, and more by borrowed resources that push up the fiscal deficit, which creates problems of sustainability.

Table 3 shows the growth of explicit subsidies given by the central government, and the clear deceleration in growth during the 1990s. The deceleration would have been much larger had the trends suddenly not reversed direction in the second half of the 1990s, possibly caused by the increase in current costs of service provision due to upward wage revisions.

Assessment

The targeting of subsidies leaves much to be desired, due to design faults as well as implementation problems. Food subsidies, through the public distribution system, are good examples. Most input-based subsidies (like fertilizer or power subsidies) are ill-designed, so that they are not properly targeted and are often regressive. Subsidies at the intermediate stage of production always carry the risk of getting dispersed to all consumers simply in proportion to their consumption.

In the long-term perspective, unnecessary subsidies, coupled with persistent deficits in the public sectors, can actually have the opposite effect of that intended. Provision of many basic services by the government is now facing this paradox, since large subsidies divorce price and output decisions and breed indifference to cost recovery. With growing pressure of population increase and no built-in controls on costs, implicit subsidies keep rising until they hit a budget constraint, and the subsequent adjustments affect both quality and quantity. Poor quality confers an inferior status on such services.

Reforms

A reform that is gradually gaining ground is that of re-establishing the link between price and supply of services, by allowing some autonomy to service units in user charges and allowing use of the proceeds at the same unit for improving the quality of the services concerned. Another reform that is becoming popular concerns collection of charges for irrigation. Water user associations are being set up in some states to take care of distribution of water and collection of appropriate user charges. But proper pricing for piped water supply, particularly in urban areas, still awaits effective reform. Similarly, problems of major power theft raise the issue of who exactly benefits from the huge subsidies in this area.

Several products actually receive unmerited subsidies, as does jute, long subsidized despite a clear worldwide trend of lower demand. This distorts cropping patterns and prevents market orientation of agriculture.

Tapas K. Sen

BIBLIOGRAPHY

Mundle, Sudipto, and M. Govinda Rao. "The Volume and Composition of Government Subsidies in India." *Economic and Political Weekly* (4 May 1991): 1157–1172.

Rao, M. Govinda, and Sudipto Mundle. "An Analysis of Changes in State Government Subsidies: 1977–1987." In *State Finances in India*, edited by A. Bagchi, J. L. Bajaj, and W. A. Byrd. New Delhi: National Institute of Public Finance and Policy, 1992.

Srivastava, D. K., et al. *Government Subsidies in India.* New Delhi: National Institute of Public Finance and Policy, 1997.

Srivastava, D. K., C. Bhujanga Rao, Pinaki Chakraborty, and T. S. Rangamannar. *Budgetary Subsidies in India.* New Delhi: National Institute of Public Finance and Policy, 2003.

Tiwari, A. C. *Volume and Composition of Subsidies in the Government: 1992–1993.* New Delhi: ICRIER, 1996.

SULTANATE OF DELHI. *See* **History and Historiography.**

SULTANATE PAINTING The term "Sultanate painting" should refer to manuscript illustrations or murals commissioned by Muslim patrons in the regions of India ruled by sultans before the founding of the imperial Mughal atelier in 1556. Though the so-called Sultanate period began in 1206, manuscript painting cannot be traced back much earlier than about 1450. Thus, most Sultanate painting dates between about 1450 and 1550, and the centers of production seem to be primarily Mandu in central India and Jaunpur in eastern India, with some work being done in the Delhi region and in Gujarat in western India. The succession of Muslim sultans ruling from Delhi in the thirteenth and fourteenth centuries were more concerned with public building projects, and many of them were opposed to figural painting for religious reasons. Several examples of the Qur'an with calligraphy and ornamentation distinctive to India have survived from this period, but they include no figural illumination. Several passages in literature refer to the existence of wall paintings during the time of the early Delhi sultanates, but little survives.

In 1398 Timur, the Turkic warrior from Central Asia (known in the West as Tamerlane), sacked Delhi and defeated the ruling sultan, Firuz Shah Tughluq. The ensuing decentralization of political power led to changes in the history of Indian art. Provincial governors in outlying regions gained greater independence and became self-proclaimed sultans. Over the course of the fifteenth century, these provincial sultans strove to take on the trappings of kingship, following the Persian model. These trappings included the building of fortifications, palaces, mosques, schools for the study of the Qur'an (*madrasa*), and libraries. The libraries were for the use of scholars of the court and for the personal enjoyment of the patrons. They required books, and the rulers and wealthy Muslims on the eastern fringes of the Islamic world began to commission illustrated versions of the classics of Persian literature.

As a rule the works commissioned during the fifteenth and early sixteenth centuries were epics and lyric romances. Most popular were the *Shah Nāma*, a history of the kings of the Islamic world; the *Hamza Nāma*, which relates the fantastic adventures of Hamza, uncle of the prophet Muhammad; and the *Khamsa* of Nizāmī, or its retelling by the Indian author Amir Khusrau Dihlavī, which contains five distinct books of poetry, including the *Sikandar Nāma*, which recounts the exploits of Alexander the Great. The *Chandāyana* (also called the *Laur Chandā*) was evidently the most popular among the lyric romances; five fully illustrated editions survive in more or less fragmentary condition, painted in different styles.

Styles of Sultanate Painting

The illustrated manuscripts made for Muslim patrons between 1450 and 1550 vary considerably in style, as there was no unifying force in the production of these works. Some of the early works were heavily reliant on Turkman prototypes, namely paintings made in Shiraz in eastern Iran, or in Herat in Central Asia. It appears that the painters themselves were typically Indian, trained in the stylized and highly conservative indigenous styles exemplified by illuminations of devotional manuscripts commissioned especially by Jains in western India, but also by Buddhists in eastern India, and by Hindus. These Indian artists were apparently charged with adopting the Turkman style, and different artists produced works with greater or lesser fidelity to their foreign sources. Most of the surviving examples of fifteenth-century Sultanate painting are significant more for historical than aesthetic reasons. Among the more visually engaging works is a *Shah Nāma* of about 1450, now dispersed primarily among museum and private collections in Europe. The manuscript is arranged in a vertical format with horizontal illustrations and four columns of Persian text. The paintings are closely related to the indigenous western or central Indian styles of paintings in non-Muslim sacred texts of the time.

A remarkable manuscript called the *Ni'mat Nāma*, painted in Mandu in central India around 1500, is a book of recipes, which shows the sultan surrounded by attendants preparing foods, medicines, and aphrodisiacs. The painters of the pictures were Indian, but they drew heavily from Shirazi models, with much use of thick green swards, pastel background colors, and provincial Persian figural types. Indian elements are especially noticeable in the renditions of the Indian ladies, who were part of his extensive, multicultural harem.

By the mid-sixteenth century a harmonious fusion of Persian and Indian styles was achieved, seen especially in the paintings illustrating the adventures of the lovers Chandā and Laurak in the *Chandāyana* of about 1540. The text was composed by a Muslim poet in India, written in the northeastern dialect of Hindi known as Avadhi, in Persian script, and the paintings were painted by a Hindu artist. Artists working in this unique hybrid style, characterized by bright pastel colors, repeated ground patterns, delicate line drawing, and exquisite arabesques, were particularly influential in the early decades of the imperial Mughal atelier.

Sonya Quintanilla

See also **Miniatures**

BIBLIOGRAPHY

Digby, Simon. "The Literary Evidence for Painting in the Delhi Sultanate." *Bulletin of the American Academy of Benares* (Varanasi) 1 (1967): 47–58.

Goswamy, B. N. *A Jainesque Sultanate Shahnama and the Context of Pre-Mughal Painting in India.* Zürich: Museum Rietberg Zürich, 1988.

Khandalavala, Karl, and Moti Chandra. *New Documents of Indian Painting: A Reappraisal.* Mumbai: Prince of Wales Museum, 1969.

Losty, Jeremiah P. *The Art of the Book in India.* London: British Library, 1982.

Skelton, Robert. "The *Ni'mat nama*: A Landmark in Malwa Painting." *Marg* 12, no. 3 (June 1959): 44–50.

SULTANATE-PERIOD ARCHITECTURE OF SOUTH ASIA Scholars frequently refer to the years 1192–1526 as the Delhi Sultanate period, defined by the establishment and proliferation of a series of Islamic states in South Asia. After the numerous Afghan Ghaznavid raids into the Indus Valley in the late tenth to twelfth centuries, the Afghan Ghurids and their Mamluk deputies, also from Afghanistan, founded the first enduring Islamic dynasty in northern India, spanning 1192–1290. Thereafter, several other Islamic dynasties with varying territorial holdings appeared in Delhi and in other regions of India. Finally, in 1526, the Timurid prince Babur was victorious at the first Battle of Panipat, launching the great Mughal dynasty with pan-Indic ambitions. During the Sultanate period, the Islamic dynastic patronage of the many building styles of South Asia—firmly rooted in regionally based traditions—produced a plethora of Islamic architecture.

Muslim communities had settled in Sind before the late twelfth-century rise of a lasting Islamic power. Architectural remains from Banbhore in Sind (c. 711), Gwalior in central India (8th century), and Bhadresvar in Kachh, Gujarat (c. 1160) indicate that Muslim groups settled at these sites probably for mercantile purposes. The Gwalior mihrab and Bhadresvar mosques particularly demonstrate that these communities employed local craftsmen for their religious buildings. Indeed, the high quality of those remains indicate that the craftsmen had worked on Islamic architecture before, thereby pushing the presence of Muslims in central India and Kachh to earlier than the eighth and mid-twelfth centuries, respectively.

The Ghurid annexation of northern India underpinned innovations in the building tradition indigenous to the plains by introducing new architectural practices and forms from the Iranian ambit, the latter of which were executed according to local methods. Delhi's well-known Qutb Mosque (Quwwat al-Islam, 1192–1193) exhibits extensive recycling of materials from earlier buildings, a practice comparatively little documented in Hindu and Buddhist foundations of the first millennium A.D. These older fragments were integrated with others contemporaneous with the complex's foundation, meaning that Ghurid deputies also patronized local building traditions. Continuity in style and method is underscored by the arched facades, elements imported from eastern Iran-Afghanistan but constructed using corbelled arches, and iconography from the pan-Indic water cosmology. Ghurid foundations west of the Indus, such as the Ribat of Al-ibn Karmakh, also evince continuity and innovation: While the fortified grave is a conflation of forms imported from Islamized lands, the iconography shows a direct relationship to the region's earlier temples.

The architecture of the Delhi-based powers succeeding the Ghurids and Mamluks emphasized a military aesthetic of heavy proportions, battered walls, and overall austerity. Dynastic Khalji (1290–1320) and Tughluq (1320–1401) architectural patronage, seen in the Ala-i Darwaza (1311) and the Hauz Khass Complex (1388), show that brick was the preferred building material and arcuation the favored articulation of interiors. This architectural style originated in these dynasties' homeland of

Qutb Minar Complex, Delhi. With its first stones laid in 1199, the red sandstone tower of Qutb Minar. Built by Qutb-ud-din Aibak, the founder and first sultan of the Islamic city of Delhi, who applied his own name (*qutb* meaning "axis") to the tower to mark it as a new symbol of Islamic sovereignty. AMAR TALWAR / FOTOMEDIA.

Multan, where Sufi mausoleums like the Tomb of Shah Rukn-i Din Rukn-i 'Alam (c. 1300) were abundant. The Lodi sultans (1451–1526) of Delhi continued in a similar aesthetic vein (Tomb of Sikandar Lodi), though these buildings were more decorative, with niches puncturing their surfaces.

Throughout the fifteenth and early sixteenth centuries, two sultanates neighbored Delhi, the Sharqis (1394–1483) holding sway at Jaunpur to the east, and the Ghuris (1391–1436) and eventually the Khaljis (1436–1531) at Mandu to the west. Both sultanates dedicated much of their financial and labor resources to architectural patronage, studding their urban centers with several large mosque, tomb, and *madrassa* complexes. The influence of the Delhi-based architectural style seemed to radiate east and west: Jaunpur's Atala Mosque (1408) raised what had originally been a military aesthetic to a monumental scale. Mandu's Congregational Mosque (1454), with its heavy proportions, evokes the earlier Delhi buildings, though their characteristic austerity was relieved here by means of blue-glazed tile decoration applied on selected surfaces.

The architecture of the Delhi-based dynasties, derived from traditions originating west of the Indus, was adopted and further developed by the nearby sultanates. However, the architectures of many other Muslim states in South Asia, which were more removed from Delhi than Jaunpur and Mandu, stylistically and technically ensued from, and even rejuvenated, their respective indigenous building practices.

Various sultanates appropriated pockets of territories in the Deccan, and some of them maintained control of their holdings for over three centuries (1347–1686) until Mughal conquest. Indeed, the flourishing of South India's Hindu kingdom of Vijayanagar until 1565 reminds us that the "Sultanate period" is something of a misnomer, since the dynasties of this powerful state were not Muslims but Brahmanical Hindus. Architectural patronage throughout the Deccan can be characterized by the application of old building principles to new purposes, often resulting in unprecedented spatial solutions. The Bahmanids' Mosque at Gulbarga (latter half of the 14th century) presents a case in point: The covered prayer area and open courtyard of the archetypal mosque was covered with corbelled domes. The arched facade, known since the late twelfth century, was here transferred to the exterior to create monumental entrances. Ibrahim Adilshahi's Tomb at Bijapur (c. 1626) relied heavily on indigenous architectural and iconographic traditions, including South Indian column orders and ornament.

Architectural patronage in the Bengal (1339–1576) and Gujarat (1411–1573) sultanates emerged from and rejuvenated those regions' local building practices. Bengal had within its borders a well-entrenched tradition of brick construction, including the use of voussoir arches to span short distances. Moreover, the local craftsmen excelled at terra-cotta and molded brick surface decoration. Thus, Gaur's Qadm-i Rasul Mosque of about 1525 is decorated with terra-cotta plaques as well as tilework, and the arch here rose to the challenge of spanning considerably larger interior spaces than before.

The religious architecture of Gujarat was primarily of trabeate construction in stone, with exteriors profusely decorated with stone sculpture. Both of these practices were productively adapted to Islamic buildings, as seen at Ahmedabad's Congregational Mosque of 1424. The monumental entrance facade shows that, rather than the teeming exteriors of the region's medieval temples, local stone-carving methods were applied toward the creation of a surface well balanced in its proportions of ornament and austerity. The interior demonstrates that trabeation did not produce only low, dark interiors, but could also be successfully employed to create lofty spaces with natural light. The introduction of Islamic ritual and social demands, then, were beneficial for the local styles of building.

Alka Patel

See also **Babur; Islam**

BIBLIOGRAPHY

Al-Akbar, Siddiq, Abdul Rehman, and Muhammad Ali Tirmizi, eds. *Architectural Heritage of Pakistan*, vol. II: *Sultanate Period Architecture*. Lahore: Anjuman-e Mimaran, 1991.

Blair, Sheila S., and Jonathan M. Bloom. *The Art and Architecture of Islam 1250–1800*. New Haven, Conn.: Yale University Press; London: Pelican History of Art, 1994.

Hasan, Perween. "Sultanate Mosques and Continuity in Bengal Architecture." *Muqarnas* 6 (1989): 58–74.

Hillenbrand, Robert. "Turco-Iranian Elements in the Medieval Architecture of Pakistan: The Case of the Tomb of Rukn-i ʿAlam at Multan." *Muqarnas* 9 (1992): 148–174.

Jackson, Peter. *The Delhi Sultanate: A Political and Military History*. Cambridge, U.K.: Cambridge University Press, 1999.

Patel, Alka. *Building Communities in Gujarat: Architecture and Society during the Twelfth through Fourteenth Centuries*. Leiden: E. J. Brill, 2004.

Tadgell, Christopher. *The History of Architecture in India*. London: Phaidon, 1998.

Welch, Anthony, and Howard Crane. "The Tughluqs: Master Builders of the Delhi Sultanate." *Muqarnas* 1 (1983): 123–166.

SURYA. *See* **Vedic Aryan India.**

SWADESHI. *See* **Gandhi, Mahatma M. K.**

SWARAJ. *See* **Gandhi, Mahatma M. K.**

TABLA Tabla (Arabic), a pair of kettle drums with "loaded" drumheads played with the fingers, are the most important rhythmic accompaniment for North Indian classical, religious, popular, and folk music. They are probably a combination of a Central or Western Asian kettledrum tradition (played in pairs with sticks) and South Asian drums such as the *mrdangam* (played with the fingers, tuned, and with rice paste applied to the head), although the *dholak* tradition (a barrel-shaped drum) may also have contributed. Documentation of the

Zakir Hussain Playing the Tabla. World-renowned tabla virtuoso Zakir Hussain (left) performing in New Delhi, 1988. After the eighteenth century, the instrument slowly became the primary drum for both the classical and popular music of northern India. NEAL PRESTON.

origins of the tabla (or at least drums appearing to be tabla) does not appear until the eighteenth century in North India.

The higher-pitched right-hand drum (*dāyan* or, more simply, *tablā*) has a hollowed wooden shell. The most important feature of the goatskin heads is the weighted center, a circular patch of a specially applied and modified rice paste. The drummer usually tunes an overtone of this drumhead to the tonic pitch of the music. The drummer obtains this overtone (a result of the weighted center) by damping the head's fundamental with the ring finger of the right hand while striking the edges of the head with his or her index finger.

The lower-pitched left-hand drum (*bāyan* or *duggī*) is usually a metal vessel, although some musicians still play clay drums. This drum too has a weighted head, although the pitching of this drum is often less specific than the *dāyan*, and the drummer does not manipulate the overtones. The patch on this head has the function of helping to focus the sound and pitch so that the drummer has more control over the relative pitch of the drumhead. By pressing the heel of the left hand into the drumhead while striking the drum, the drummer can raise (or alternatively lower) the pitch of the drum.

Drummers learn and remember drum patterns through a system of mnemonic syllables (*bols*) representing drum strokes: dental sounds represent right-hand strokes, guttural sounds represent left-hand strokes, and aspirated sounds represent simultaneous strokes on both the left and right drumheads.

When the drummer solos, he or she uses a number of different forms. For example, a *kāydā* (Persian-Hindustani, "rule"; Urdu, *qā'idā*) is a composition that shows the shape of the *tal* and *theka* and serves as the basis for a number of other subcompositions and extemporizations. These include both the *dohrā* (Persian-Hindustani, "twofold," "compound," or "couplet"), a variation of a rhythmic musical idea (such as a *kāydā*) in which sections of the original theme repeat, and the *paltā* (Hindustani, "turn" or "exchange"), a variation (often a *dohrā*) of a rhythmic musical idea manipulating individual strokes or groups of strokes.

Gordon Thompson

See also **Music; Tāla**

BIBLIOGRAPHY

Kippen, James. *The Tabla of Lucknow: A Cultural Analysis of a Musical Tradition.* Cambridge, U.K., and New York: Cambridge University Press, 1988.

TAGORE, RABINDRANATH (1861–1941), renowned Bengali poet.

Author, activist, artist, choreographer, dramatist, educator, musician, and philosopher, Rabindranath Tagore was primarily a poet. He was called a "universal man," which he certainly was. His roots, both cultural and creative, were set deeply in his beloved Bengal. His talents blossomed from the dusty and wet plains of Bengal in over a thousand poems, two and a half thousand songs, a sizable number of short stories, novels, and discursive essays on education, history, literature, rural reconstruction, politics, philosophy, and science. He became a painter rather late in his life, when he turned seventy. In ten years, he produced some three thousand paintings.

Tagore was born in the Jorasanko district of Kolkata (Calcutta) on 7 May 1861. He was the youngest child of Debendranath Tagore (1817–1905) and Sarada Devi (1826–1875). Originally from Jessore, now in Bangladesh, the Tagore (Thakur in Bengali) family belonged to a Brahman subcaste known as Pirali. Orthodox Brahmans refused to have any social contact with the Tagores and other Piralis due to their closeness to Muslim rulers. The family moved to Kolkata around the time the city was founded, in the 1690s. The Tagores prospered working for the East India Company. Rabindranath's grandfather, Dwarkanath Tagore (1794–1846), known as "the Prince," built the family fortune with his great industrial enterprises, which included banking, insurance, agency houses, mining, shipping, and real estate. A contemporary of Ram Mohan Roy (1772–1833) and a close associate in the reform movement, Dwarkanath was arguably India's first modern and global entrepreneur. His industrial enterprises collapsed soon after he passed away, but the extensive landed estates he had built up in East Bengal continued to comfortably support the extended family in the next generation.

Debendranath Tagore's large family lived in a commodious mansion in Jorasanko. All of his children distinguished themselves in some way or another. Dwijendranath Tagore (1840–1926) was a poet and philosopher, Satyendranath Tagore (1842–1923) was the first Indian to join the Indian Civil Service, Jyotirindranath Tagore (1849–1925) was a playwright and translator, and Swarnakumari Devi (1855–1925) was India's first woman novelist.

As a child, Rabindranath had trouble studying in school. He disliked the set currriculum, the strict discipline, and the restrictive atmosphere of the four schools he attended until he was thirteen. He was withdrawn from the St. Xavier's School in 1874. Thereafter he received home schooling from his brother Jyotirindranath and his wife Kadambari Devi. Both of them exercised great influence on Rabindranath's literary pursuits in his adolescence and early adult life.

Tagore started to publish verse, narrative poetry, short fiction, and translations from 1876 onward in the family's literary journal *Bharati*. He also started to act on the family stage. He appeared, for example, in the title role of Molière's *Le Bourgeois Gentihomme*, adapted to a Bengali farce by his brother Jyotirindranath. The following year, he traveled to London with his brother Satyendranath. He enrolled at the University College, London, to read English literature. His frankly explicit "letters" sent from London alarmed his elders, concerned about his youthful waywardness. He received urgent summons to return home. Upon reaching Kolkata, he began to publish in earnest. His opera *Valmiki Pratibha* (The genius of Valmiki), modeled after the European operas he saw in London, impressed Kolkata's literary elites, especially those engaged in experimenting with Western literary genres and music. Tagore scored the music for the opera and cast himself in the title role. He recorded his first major poetic inspiration in a passionate work that he titled "The Awakening of the Waterfall." A plethora of new works followed, including a series of devotional songs in the tradition of the medieval Mithila Vaishnava poet Vidyapati. He composed these songs in the company of Kadambari Devi, his talented sister-in-law.

Tagore had an arranged marriage in 1883 with Mrinalini Devi. The next year, Kadambari Devi committed suicide, apparently due to her unrequited love for Rabindranath. The tragedy shattered Tagore and arguably created the emotional impetus for his novella *Nashtanir* (The broken nest), which Satyajit Ray adapted for his film *Charulata* (1964). By 1890, when Tagore revisited England, he was considered a top literary talent in Bengal by no less than Bankim Chandra Chatterji.

Tagore spent the next decade (1890–1900) supervising the family's extensive landed estates in what is now Bangladesh. The experience brought him in close and intimate contact with Bengal's countryside and its people. He wrote scores of short stories showing the dark side of Bengal's village life while celebrating in exquisite verse the beauty and bounty of the land. The first decade of the twentieth century saw the emergence of two diametrically opposed profiles of Tagore: the first was that of a dedicated patriot and political activist, and the second that of a deeply mystical poet searching for unity and oneness in the complexity and diversity of the universe.

Tagore's political involvement began in 1886, when he composed and sang at the inauguration of the Indian

Portrait of Rabindranath Tagore. The master of countless intellectual and artistic pursuits, Tagore lifted Indian culture—and even more significant, the Indian psyche—to a new sphere of revitalization. FOTOMEDIA ARCHIVE.

National Congress. The next year, he participated in the public protest against the blatantly discriminatory policies of Lord Cross, the secretary of state for India. One sees Tagore's fully formed political personality and activism in the wake of Lord Curzon's decision in 1905 to partition the province of Bengal in two halves, roughly corresponding to the Hindu and Muslim populations. The *swadeshi* (self-rule) movement (1905–1911) was the first major "militant" agitation against colonial rule. During the first phase, Tagore led the protestors in the streets of Kolkata, singing patriotic songs he had composed for the movement. He gave music to Bankim Chatterji's famous hymn to the motherland, *Bande Mataram*. The hymn soon became the battle cry of the antipartition patriots as well as the name of a fiery journal edited by Aurobindo Ghose (later Sri Aurobindo). Terror and violence marked the extremist challenge against the Raj in Bengal. Unable to accept the narrow nationalism and its destructive divisiveness, Tagore withdrew himself from the movement. He was quickly condemned and criticized; some called him a "lackey" of the British. A decade later, in 1915, Tagore published *Ghare Baire* (The home and the world), a major novel (also later adapted to film by Satyajit Ray) in which he articulated his theses on nationalism.

This period of intense public activism was followed by private withdrawal, which coincided with great personal tragedies in Tagore's life. His wife Mrinalini passed away in 1902, his daughter Renuka died in 1903, his father Debendranath died in 1905, and in 1907 his youngest son Samindranath died of cholera. It appears that Tagore attempted to negotiate the crises in a series of profoundly moving poems, also songs, uniting humanity to nature and nature to humanity. His own elegant yet simple prose translation of *Gitanjali* took the English literary circles by storm in 1912. Among Tagore's admirers in England were Mez Sinclair, Evelyn Underhill, Ezra Pound, Bertrand Russell, and most importantly, W. B. Yeats, the Irish poet. "These prose translations from Rabindranath Tagore have stirred my blood as nothing has for years," Yeats wrote in his introduction to *Gitanjali* (p. ix). In 1912 and 1913 Tagore was in the United States, lecturing at the University of Chicago, University of Illinois at Urbana, and Harvard University. Soon after his return to India, Tagore received the news that he had been awarded the Nobel Prize for literature.

Yeats lamented that even though the poetry of Tagore stirred sublime emotions in him, he knew nothing about "his life, and of the movements of thought that have made them possible." At once unique to Bengal and universal, Tagore's work was the product of the Anglo-Bengali, East-West encounters of the nineteenth century. The colonial world that Tagore inhabited, and the asymmetrical power relations among the colonizers and the colonized, prompted him to seek new and novel pathways to express his autonomy and creativity.

From 1913 to 1941, one can locate this dialectical process in three areas of Tagore's life. The first was the project of building a utopian community in Santiniketan, 100 miles (160 km) outside Kolkata in the saffron-colored soil of southern Bengal. In 1863 his father Debendranath had bought the land, built a guest house, and named it Santiniketan (Abode of Peace). A prayer hall was built in 1891. In 1901 Rabindranath established an academic institution to provide an "overall development of the students amidst close contact with nature . . . classes were to be held in open air under the shades of the trees." In 1918 Tagore transformed the institution into Visva Bharati (World University). Although the atmosphere and environment reminded one of the intentional communities of the Upanishadic age of the pre-Christian

era, Visva Bharati was purportedly a twentieth-century academy. Tagore invited scholars and students from the East and the West to occupy an academic and creative space that was, by design and intent, outside the baneful influences of colonialism, industrialism, and nationalism. To raise funds for Visva Bharati and to speak about its mission, he traveled the globe: to China and Japan (1924), South America (1925), Europe and Egypt (1926), Southeast Asia (1927), and Canada (1929). He delivered the Hibbert Lectures at Oxford in 1930, which were published as *Religion of Man*.

Tagore attempted to provide a practical and material foundation to his vision of the World University. At the adjacent Sriniketan, he established the Center for Rural Reconstruction in 1922. Its first director was Leonard K. Elmhirt, an English agricultural expert. Experimental research activities accompanied agronomy and rural development. Chemical fertilizers and modern medical facilities were introduced. The focus at Sriniketan was, and still is, on vocational education: leather craft, wood craft, clay craft, lacquer work, embroidery, bookbinding, carpet weaving, and block carving and printing. Along with the Art School (Kala Bhavan) and the Music School (Sangit Bhavana), the Santiniketan-Sriniketan complex combined the practice of the traditional arts with contemporary and modern elements.

The second project that preoccupied Tagore during this period concerned his scrupulous spurning of forms of colonial knowledge, and his staunch anti-imperialist and antinationalist positions. He rejected, for example, "academic histories" that are narrowly focused on political and public policies of the state. In numerous poems, plays, and novels, he attempted to capture what Ranajit Guha has called the "historicality" of everyday life.

Tagore surrendered his knighthood in an angry protest against the Amritsar Massacre of 1919. Although he disagreed with Mahatma Gandhi about some aspects of the nationalist movement, his harshest critique was directed to the West, sundered as it was by the Holocaust and World War II. In his last address and testament to the world before he passed on in 1941, he stated, "Perhaps the new dawn will come from this horizon, from the East where the sun rises."

The third area of Tagore's involvement was his continued creative effort. He remained magnificently innovative and profusely productive to his last day. He started experimenting with *verse libre* in 1933; he invented a new play form combining music, mime, and dance. He took up painting at seventy, and the three thousand paintings he completed are considered among the best of modern Indian art.

William Radice, arguably the best translator of Tagore in English, divides Tagore's life and work in a series of paired oppositions borrowed from *Isha Upanishad*: he moves, he moves not; he is far, he is near; he is within all, and he is outside all. Tagore moved away from the orthodox Brahmo church founded by his father; he also moved away from the Hindu revivalism and nationalism. Tagore was quite a radical in more ways than one, but he remained tradition-bound in some key areas. For example, he married a ten-year-old semiliterate from his own caste; he followed the family custom by giving his two daughters in marriage when they were only twelve and fourteen. He can seem utterly foreign to non-Bengali readers. Although there are some good translations, most of Tagore's poetry is inadequate if not inaccessible in translation. Tagore's songs are equally inaccessible to non-Bengalis. There are over two and a half thousand of them, sung and listened to every day by Bengalis everywhere. As a composer of songs, Satyajit Ray says, Tagore has no equal, even in the West (quoted in Dutta and Robinson, p. 385). Most non-Bengalis, however, are denied the pleasure of enjoying Tagore's songs. Yet Tagore proves—in his fervent idealism, in his spiritual reality, in his romanticism—close to all of humankind. Tagore's modernity as a poet, thinker, and activist is accessible to most, as are his antimaterialist, feminist, and educational ideals. Most important is the agency or autonomy of Tagore the artist and poet, and its expression in his creative work. His personality and life are present in his poetry, plays, stories, and novels. He is within all. Yet he is outside all—human creativity is, in his own words, "amoral, arbitrary, fanciful, whimsical, unreal," and the natural artist in him "is naughty, good for nothing, separate from the man of a hundred good intentions" (quoted in Radice, pp. 36–37).

Is it possible to overcome the translational problems to appreciate Tagore, the poet? Anna Akhmatova, who translated Tagore into Russian, offers an insight: "He is a great poet, I can see that now. It's not only a matter of individual lines which have real genius, or individual poems . . . but that mighty flow of poetry which takes its strength from Hinduism as from the Ganges, and is called Rabindranath Tagore" (quoted in Dutta and Robinson, p. 1).

Dilip K. Basu

BIBLIOGRAPHY

Dutta, Krishna, and Andrew Robinson. *Rabindranath Tagore: An Anthology*. New York: St. Martin's, 1999.
Guha, Ranajit. *History at the Limit of World-History*. New York: Columbia University Press, 2002.
Kripalini, Krishna. *Tagore: A Biography*. London: Oxford University Press, 1982.
Radice, William. *Rabindranath Tagore: Selected Poems*. London: Penguin Books, 1993.
Tagore, Rabindranath. *Gitanjali*. 1912. Reprint, New York: Dover, 2000.
———. *Crisis in Civilization*. Kolkata: Visva Bharati Press, 1942.

TAJ MAHAL. *See* **Shah Jahan.**

TĀLA In the classical music traditions of India, *tāla* (Sanskrit, "palm of the hand," or "clap") is the combined concept of rhythm and meter. Analytically, a *tāla* is a cyclic and additive measure of musical time. That is, unlike the approach to musical time that has prevailed in Euro-American culture (which has parsed pulses into linear duple and triple patterns and then has subdivided the pulses), South Asian musicians have constructed time by cyclically patterning added subsections of pulses and subdividing the beats. The conceptual categories for *tāla* stem from South Asia's language and poetics, in which verses consist of patterned long and short syllable combinations. Cyclical musical time parallels other Indian conceptualizations of time, such as the agricultural rhythm of the seasons, the cycle of birth, death, and rebirth, and notions of cosmic time.

As with *rāga*, musicians in North and South India understand *tāla* similarly, while differing on the specifics. The common concepts are those of cycle (*āvarta/ āvartanam* in the South and *āvarta/āvard* in the North), structural subsection (*anga* in the South and *vibhāg* in the North), and beat (*mātra* in both cultures), as well as the notion that these beats can have subdivisions. Similarly, the North and the South generally pattern performances from open, pulseless, and meterless beginnings (*ālāpana/ ālāp*) to the microsubdivision of the mensural musical moment. Finally, both systems think of tempo in three

TABLE 1

Common *tāla*s					
Laghu/Jāti Tāla	Caturashra 4	Tishra 3	Mishra 7	Khanda 5	Sankīrna 9
Dhruva $\mid_n$O $\mid_n\mid_n$	$\mid_4$O $\mid_4\mid_4$				
Mathya $\mid_n$O $\mid_n$	$\mid_4$O $\mid_4$				
Rūpaka O $\mid_n$	O $\mid_4$				
Jhampa $\mid_n$UO			$\mid_7$UO		
Triputa $\mid_n$OO	$\mid_4$OO	$\mid_3$OO			
Āta $\mid_n\mid_n$OO				$\mid_5\mid_5$OO	
Eka $\mid_n$	$\mid_4$	$\mid_3$	$\mid_7$	$\mid_5$	

SOURCE: Courtesy of author.

broad (but modifiable) tempi: *vilambita-laya* (slow tempo), *madhyama* or *madhya-laya* (medium tempo), and *druta-laya* (fast tempo). The differences derive in large part from the historical and cultural contexts of music performance, but also from the cultural disposition of the cultures.

As with scale types, southern traditions have systematic structures for generating and categorizing musical time that inform and have been informed by performance practice. Northern traditions, on the other hand, derive heavily from performance practice, so that *tāla* structure emerges from an ecological evolution of practical forms.

South India

Musical time plays a prominent role in Karnātak music practice and is an integral part of South Indian musical instruction, while functioning as an underlying, albeit often unstated, principle. That is, in South Indian musical practice, performance reflects the underlying structures of *tāla* (the patterning of sections and relative points of importance), but no specific musical part has the charge of keeping and showing the *tāla*. Musicians will often reveal the *tāla* in which they are performing through standardized gestures (and the audience may also "keep time" in this fashion), but no musical part has the specific charge of keeping or showing the time for the other musicians.

South Indian musicians and music scholars have developed systematic formulas for generating time patterns. The overarching idea is that of cycle. An *āvarta/āvarttanam* (Sanskrit/Telegu, "cycle" or "a return to the beginning") is the span of one cycle of a *tāla*. Once established, the pattern of an *āvarta*—the *tāla*—remains consistent until the end of the composition.

This pattern derives principally from the arrangement of the subsections. Each subsection, or *anga* (Sanskrit, "member" or "part"), can consist of 1, 2, 3, 4, 5, 7, or 9 beats or *mātra*s (Sanskrit, "syllable"). Karnātak musicians and scholars have developed ways to symbolically represent *anga*s both by a physical gesture and/or a written symbol. The two most common physical gestures employed today are the *tattu* (Telegu, "beat" or "clap") and *vīccu* (Telegu, "wave") with smaller articulations of the fingers to help in the counting of longer *anga*s.

Karnātak practice recognizes three different kinds of *anga* and represents them with written symbols. The *drutam* is a two-*mātra anga* marked by a clap (*tattu*) and a wave (*vīccu*) and symbolically indicated as a circle (O). The *anudrutam* is a one-*mātra anga* marked by a clap (*tattu*) and indicated as an upwardly opening circle (U).

The *laghu* is a multiple-*mātra anga* marked by a clap (*tattu*) and a number of additional silent beats to complete an *anga*. Musicians represent the *laghu* with a vertical bar and a number indicating its duration ($|n$). A *laghu* can be *tishra* (triple) with 3 *mātra*s ($|_3$); *caturashra* (quadratic) with 4 *mātra*s ($|_4$); *khanda* (broken) with 5 *mātra*s ($|_5$); *mishra* (mixed) with 7 *mātra*s ($|_7$); or *sankīrna* (composite) with 9 *mātra*s ($|_9$).

Practice also allows the subdivision or *laya* (Sanskrit, *layate*, "to go"; *laya*, "the act of sticking or clinging to") of each *mātra* in several ways. The single count pulse division is *gati* or *natai* (Sanskrit and Tamil, "pace"), *tishra natai* is a triple submetric division of the beat, *caturashra gati/natai* is quadruple (also known as *sarva-laghu*), *khanda natai* is quintuple, and *mishra natai* is septuple. That is, each *mātra* at *tishra natai* can have triplets at *tishra natai*, quadruplets at *caturashra natia*, and so on.

Sūlādī Tālas.
The devotional singer Purandara Dasa (1480–1564) established a musical time system based on seven *sūlādī tāla*s for use in formal compositions by combining the *laghu* ($|$), *drutam* (O), and *anudrutam* (U) in ways that reflect the performance practice of his time. The most commonly used of these *tāla*s appear in Table 1.

When naming the different versions of these *tāla*s, one first names the quality of the *laghu* followed by the name of the *tāla*; however, particular versions of these *tāla*s have special recognition. For example, *caturashra* Triputa *tāla* (that is, the eight-*mātra* version of Triputa *tāla* with a *laghu* of four *mātra*s followed by two *drutam*s) more commonly carries the name Ādi *tāla* (first), as this is one of the most common *tāla*s in South Indian music. However, some *tāla*s are common in particular contexts and yet have no special name. For example, *khanda* Āta *tāla* (the 14-*mātra* version of Āta *tāla* with two five-*mātra laghu*s and two *drutam*s) is particularly important in *tana varnam* compositions, but has no separate appellation.

Capu Tālas.
While the *sūlādī tāla*s have been the choice of composers for the most complex compositions of the repertoire, the *cāpu tāla*s are common in lighter works and occur most often in fast *laya*. A characteristic of the *cāpu tāla*s is that each *tāla* has two parts, with the second part one beat longer than the first. The most important of these are (a) *mishra cāpu* (3 + 4; sometimes known only as *cāpu*) which often acts as an up-tempo version of *tishra triputa* (3 + 2 + 2); (b) *khanda cāpu* (2 + 3; often called *ara Jhampa* [half Jhampa]) which similarly functions as an up-tempo version of *mishra jhampa* (7 + 1 + 2); (c) *tisra capu* (1 + 2 and a slightly different emphasis than *tishra* Eka *tāla*); and (d) *sankīrna cāpu* (4 + 5).

FIGURES 1–3

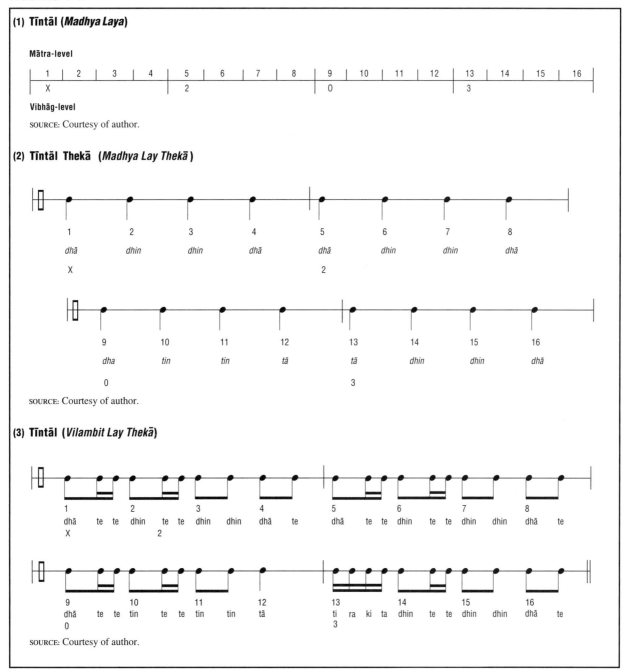

(1) Tīntāl (*Madhya Laya*)

Mātra-level

1	2	3	4	5	6	7	8	9	10	11	12	13	14	15	16
X				2				0				3			

Vibhāg-level

SOURCE: Courtesy of author.

(2) Tīntāl Thekā (*Madhya Lay Thekā*)

1	2	3	4	5	6	7	8
dhā	dhin	dhin	dhā	dhā	dhin	dhin	dhā
X				2			

9	10	11	12	13	14	15	16
dha	tin	tin	tā	tā	dhin	dhin	dhā
0				3			

SOURCE: Courtesy of author.

(3) Tīntāl (*Vilambit Lay Thekā*)

1			2			3		4		5			6			7		8	
dhā	te	te	dhin	te	te	dhin	dhin	dhā	te	dhā	te	te	dhin	te	te	dhin	dhin	dhā	te
X			2																

9			10			11		12		13				14		15		16	
dhā	te	te	tin	te	te	tin	tin	tā		ti	ra	ki	ta	dhin	te	te	dhin	dhin	dhā	te
0										3									

SOURCE: Courtesy of author.

North India

Again, North and South India share conceptions of *tal*. Each cycle or *āvarta* (or sometimes *āvard*) consists of one or several *vibhāg*s (Sanskrit/Hindi, "partition" or "breakdown"), which in turn usually consist of two, three, or four *mātra*s. A clap (*tāli* [Sanskrit-Hindustani diminutive of *tal*, "beat" or "clap"]) or wave (*khālī* [Hindustani "empty"])

marks the beginning of each *vibhāg*. The most important *vibhāg* marker is the *sam* (Hindustani, "together"), the first beat of an *āvarta* and the point at which the end of the time cycle comes back and joins the beginning.

North Indian musicians and scholars use a schematic system to describe the structure of *tāla*. An "X"

FIGURES 4–6

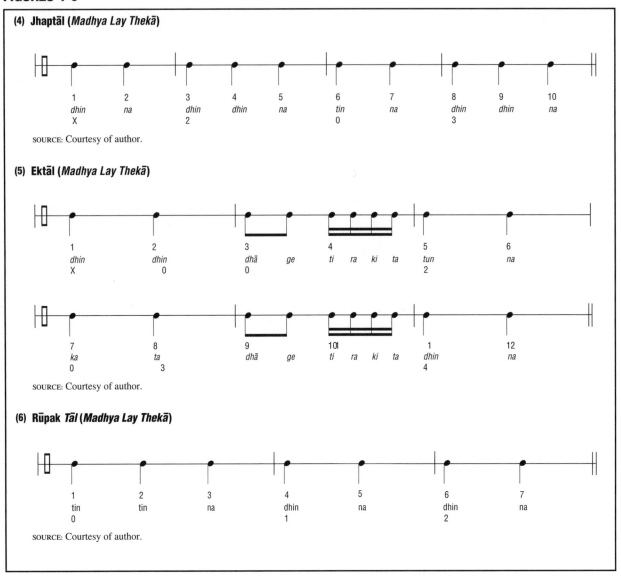

(4) Jhaptāl (*Madhya Lay Thekā*)

1	2	3	4	5	6	7	8	9	10
dhin	na	dhin	dhin	na	tin	na	dhin	dhin	na
X		2			0		3		

SOURCE: Courtesy of author.

(5) Ektāl (*Madhya Lay Thekā*)

1	2	3	4				5	6
dhin	dhin	dhā	ge	ti	ra	ki	ta	tun	na
X	0	0					2	

7	8	9	10				1	12
ka	ta	dhā	ge	ti	ra	ki	ta	dhin	na
0	3						4	

SOURCE: Courtesy of author.

(6) Rūpak *Tāl* (*Madhya Lay Thekā*)

1	2	3	4	5	6	7
tin	tin	na	dhin	na	dhin	na
0			1		2	

SOURCE: Courtesy of author.

marks the *sam*. *Tāli*s are numbered (with the exception of when the *sam* is a *tāli*—which is true of most *tāl*s). An "O" marks the *khāli* or beginning of an "empty" *vibhāg*. Figure 1 illustrates these parts in the context of one *āvarta* (cycle) of the most common *tāl* in the Hindustani *sangīt paddhati* (North Indian classical music tradition): *Tīntāl*.

In Figure 1 the *āvarta* consists of 16 *mātra*s divided into four *vibhāg*s of four *mātra*s each, with the first, second, and fourth *vibhāg*s marked by *tāli*s and the third *vibhāg* marked by a *khāli*. (Note that an X marks the first *tāli*, the *sam*. The number "1" appears only when the *sam* is *khāli*.)

The Hindustani *sangīt paddhati* sense of *lay* (subdivision, tempo) parallels that of the Karnātak *sangīt paddhati* in that the metric subdivision of *mātra*s can be *caturasra* (quadratic, 4 subbeats), *tisra* (triple, 3 subbeats), *misra* (mixed, 7 subbeats), *khanda* (broken, 5 subbeats), and *sankīrna* (composite, 9 subbeats). Thus, the above schematic of *Tīntāl* could have *mātra*s further divided into triplets, quadruplets, quintuplets, or groups of nine. And, as in South India, the terms *vilambit* (slow), *madhya* (medium), and *drut* (fast) describe tempo, with the prefix *ati* (very) modifying the slow and fast extremes.

North Indian time, like that of South India, is conceptually additive. However, rather than a standard set of formulas modified through a grid of metrical options (like the *sūlādī tāla*s) or meters, which follow a standard mathematical function (like the *cāpu tāla*s), North Indian *tāl*s derive almost entirely from performance practice. Hindustani musicians generally describe *tāl*s not as a series of *laghu*s, *drutam*s, and *anudrutam*s, but rather as a stylized series of drum strokes. These drum strokes most often come from the performance practice of *tabla* and sometimes, the *pakhāwaj*.

Figures 2 through 6 illustrate the most common *tāla*s, beginning with the aforementioned *Tīntāl*. In general, syllables beginning with a "dh" sound indicate "open" strokes played by both drums in a pair of *tabla* (or drumheads, in the case of the *pakhāwaj*), with the lower-pitched drum resonating or ringing. A syllable beginning with a "t" represents a stroke played only on the higher-pitched head. A syllable beginning with a "k" or "g" represents a stroke played only on the lower-pitched drum. (Note: the use of Western notation to represent these drum strokes is for the convenience of those familiar with this mode of musical representation.)

In Figure 2, note how "open" strokes (*dhā*, *dhin*) predominate in the first, second, and fourth *vibhāg*s—marked by *tālī*s (claps)—and how "closed" strokes (*tā*, *tin*) predominate in the third *vibhāg*—which begins with a *khālī* (wave). This example is in medium tempo (*madhya lay*). Figure 3 is an example of the same *tāl* in slow tempo (*vilambit lay*). The structure remains on the principle of *mātra*s, but each *mātra* has an underlying quadratic (*caturashra*) subdivision (represented by the sixteenth notes).

In Figure 4, the same pattern of *tālī*s and *khālī* is manifested in the ten-*mātra tāla*, Jhaptāl; however, this time the *vibhāg*s consist of alternating patterns of two and three *mātra*s.

Not all *tāla*s follow this pattern, however. Some treatises list tens if not hundreds of possible *tāla*s; but in performance practice, one commonly hears only around a dozen *tāla*s, some of which occur only in special circumstances. Figure 5 represents a realization of Ektāl, a *tāla* that is commonly associated with both vocal and instrumental music. The twelve beats divide into six *vibhāg*s of two *mātra*s each. In contrast to the other examples (but imitating them), not all "open" *vibhāg*s have claps, nor are "closed" *vibhāg*s dominated by "closed" strokes. The resulting pattern has the curious complementary and overlapping arrangements of *mātra*s into three groups of four (clap-wave + clap-wave + clap-clap) and two groups of six (as defined by the rhythm: clap-wave-clap + wave-clap-clap).

Finally, not all *tāl*s begin with a clapped *sam*. The popular Rūpak tāl (Figure 6)—a seven-beat *tāl*—begins with

a *khālī* and a *vibhāg* of three *mātra*s, followed by two *tālī*-marked *vibhāg*s of two *mātra*s.

Gordon Thompson

See also **Music**; *Rāga*; **Tabla**

BIBLIOGRAPHY

Kippen, James. *The Tabla of Lucknow: A Cultural Analysis of a Musical Tradition.* Cambridge, U.K., and New York: Cambridge University Press, 1988.

TAMIL LITERATURE. *See* **Literature: Tamil.**

TAMIL TIGERS. *See* **Sri Lanka.**

TANCHOI A distinct style of textile developed in the nineteenth century, *tanchoi* was favored among the Parsi women of India. The Chinese opium trade had brought affluence to the Parsis, and a display of this Chinese connection became a status symbol. Two distinctly Indo-Chinese, or "Parsi," textiles resulted from these interactions: the *tanchoi* and the *garo*, which was a plain fabric with embroidery. These have as much ethnic association with the Parsis, as the *bandhani* with the Gujaratis and the Paithani with the Maharashtrians. *Tanchoi* saris were so popular among the Parsis that practically every home possessed at least one, and they were an essential part of the marriage trousseau of the Parsi bride.

The *tanchoi* is woven with both the twill, and the sateen weave, which can produce an unbroken surface of color while retaining structural strength. The twill weaving produces a much more tightly woven fabric than the plain weave, and was used for the *pallu* (decorative endpiece of the sari) of the *tanchoi*. The rest of the sari was woven using a sateen weave. The most important quality of the *tanchoi* is the complete absence of loose long floats (loose threads of the weft on the reverse of the fabric, not interwoven with the warp) on the back of the fabric, even if they are required at long intervals in the pattern. In the most intricate designs too these kinds of floats are not permissible in *tanchoi* weaving.

The earliest *tanchoi*s seem to be only two colors, generally the color of the warp for the ground, with that of the weft creating the design on the right side of the cloth. The other side of the material appeared exactly opposite: the weft color became the ground, and the design appeared in the color of the warp. In a multicolored sari the warp as well as the weft formed the design. *Tanchoi*s of the nineteenth century generally had a large *pallu* with a combination of large and small paisley motifs at both ends, while the ground designs vary from *buti*s (small decorative motifs) to lozenges in an all-over pattern. *Jari* (gold or silver) was also used at times to highlight part of the motif, which required cutting off the extra weft float of *jari*. In addition to its use for saris, the *tanchoi* was also available as a fabric by the yard and was used for various decorative purposes. Parsi women preferred blouses of this material.

With the introduction of the power loom and changes in fashion, *tanchoi* weaving went out of vogue soon after the first quarter of the twentieth century. The way of life of the Parsis, who had been the chief patrons of *tanchoi*, had changed, and Chinese styles were replaced by British and European fashions. Clothing changed, and georgettes and lacy materials replaced materials like *tanchoi*. Surat has long ceased to manufacture *tanchoi*s, but Benaras (Varanasi) weavers have now revived the art.

Kalpana Desai

BIBLIOGRAPHY

Godrej, Pheroza J., and Punthakey Mistree Firoza, eds. *A Zoroastrian Tapestry: Art, Religion and Culture*. Ahmedabad: Mapin, 2002.
Stein, Aurel. *Serindia*. Vol. II. Delhi: Motilal Banarasidass, 1980.
Trivedi, A. B. "The Silk Weaving Industry of Surat." *Journal of the University of Bombay* 10 (1941–1942): 109.
Wardwell, Anne E., and C. Y. James Watt. *When Silk Was Gold*. New York: Metropolitan Museum of Art, 1997.

TANSEN *(1506–1589), Indian musician.* Tansen, also known Miyan Tansen, was a legendary Indian musician. His father, Markand Pandey, was a poet who lived in a village near Gwalior. Tansen displayed an intense interest in music from an early age, and he was sent to Vrindavan, near Mathura, to study under a famous musician saint, Swami Haridas. After completting his training, Tansen was appointed court musician at Gwalior; he later went to Rewa (in Central India) as court musician of Raja Ramsingh, a musician himself. When Emperor Akbar (r. 1556–1605) heard of Tansen, he invited him to his court and honored him as one of the Navaratna, or "Nine Gems" of the Mughal empire. Abul Fazl, the chronicler of Akbar's reign, wrote of Tansen, "A singer like him has not been in India for the last thousand years." Tansen enjoyed considerable influence in the imperial court and was an exponent of *gaurhar bani*, one of the four known styles of *dhruva-pada* music, prevalent in North India during that era.

Tansen is credited with reshaping *dhruva-pada* music by introducing such Persian nuances as *meend* and *gamaka*. Tansen created new *rāga*s, some of which are still regarded as the foremost *rāga*s in North Indian music, such as "Darbari Kanada," "Darbari Todi," "Miyan ki Malhar," and "Miyan ki Sarang." Tansen was also known to be a musical codifier, studying the structure of *rāga*s, listing about four hundred. His *Sangeeta Sara* and *Rāgāmalā* are important documents on music. He is, moreover, credited with introducing certain developments in the *rabab* and *rudra-veena*. The Dhrupad singers of the *seniya gharana* attribute their lineage to Tansen.

There are many legends about the miraculous powers of Tansen's music. The most famous legend recounts how Tansen sang "Rāga Dipaka" at a royal request, even though that *rāga* was known to generate "unbearable heat" in its singer's body. His victorious competition with the great Baiju Bawra is another legend often narrated by music lovers. The achievements of Tansen are referred to in detail in the work *Virabhanudaya Kavya* by Madhava, written in A.D. 1555, in which his music is decribed as "immortal."

Tansen and his wife Hussaini had four sons and a daughter, Sarasvati, a vina player. His sons—Suratsen, Saratsen, Tarang sen, and Bilas Khan—all played *rabab*. His son-in-law, Misri Khan, was also a vina player. Tansen died at the age of eithty-three, around 1589, and was buried at Gwalior next to the tomb of Mohammad Ghaus. Many musicians make pilgrimages to his tomb to seek his blessings.

Kalpana Desai

BIBLIOGRAPHY

Fazl, Abul. *Ain i-Akbari*, translated by R. Blochmann. Lahore: Qausain, 1975.
Kuppuswamy, Gowri, and M. Hariharan. *Royal Patronage of Indian Music*. Delhi: Sundeep, 1984.
Massey, Reginald, and Jamila Massey. *The Music of India*. New York: Crescendo, 1977.

TANTRIC BUDDHIST IMAGES With the introduction of the Bodhisatvayana (commonly known as Mahayana, the "Greater Vehicle"), the monastic form of early Buddhism, Shravakayana (popularly called Hinayana, the "Lesser Vehicle") underwent a radical change in the theological concept of Buddhist doctrine. In place of the wise teacher, Shakyamuni Buddha, who had already attained *bodhi* (enlightenment) and Nirvāna (literally, "extinction" or "salvation"), emerged various groups of *bodhisattva*s, both male and female, who had attained *bodhi* but had postponed Nirvāna to help others reach enlightenment. Five transcendent, or cosmic Buddhas appeared, dominating the heavenly quarters and the whole Buddhist pantheon. These are: Akshobya, Buddha of the eastern direction; Amitabha, Buddha of the western direction; Amoghasiddhi, Buddha of the northern direction; Ratnasambhava, Buddha of the southern direction; and Vairocana, Buddha of the central direction. Of these five, Amitabha played an important role at an early date, while Akshobya was very significant in eastern India, and Vairocana, mostly as the Buddha at the center of a *mandala* in Nepal. Multiple *bodhisattva*s were ascribed to each of the cosmic Buddhas, as each of them represented a different *kula*, or family, and hence were called *kulesha*, or lord of the family. Each cosmic Buddha shows a different hand gesture (*mudrā*), each has a different complexion, a different vehicle (*vahana*) and a different female companion, Prajna or Shakti. They complete the Tantric form of Buddhism.

The noted Buddhist iconographic text, Sadhanamala (Garland of Meditation) describes the Buddhist divinities, most of them with Tantric affinities. The worship of the Tantric divinities in a diagram in the shape of a circle (*mandala*) originated a later phase; an important addition, it was very popular with the Tantric Buddhist priests. The Buddhist text Nishpannayogavali of the "great scholar" (*mahapandita*) Abhayakaragupta (12th century) gives elaborate descriptions of such *mandala*s dedicated to several Buddhist divinities, the last being Kalacakra. The Nishpannayogavali is basically a Tantric text describing the Tantric divinities Heruka, Sambara, and Yogambara. The *dharani*s, or esoteric descriptive formulas of each Buddhist divinity, were muttered in a mechanical way. At the time of Bengal's Pala ruler Devapala (9th century) the *dharani* of the popular Buddhist goddess Tara was well-known in eastern India. Abhayakaragupta selected twelve principal *dharani*s and deified them with human shapes, colors, and weapons. Of these goddesses, Ushnishavijaya, Parnashabari, Janguli, and Cunda were especially well-known.

In a later develoment, Vajrasatva holding a *vajra* (masculine principle) and *ghanta* (female principle) was considered the Adi-Buddha, along with the other five cosmic Buddhas. Another Buddha, Vajradhara, holds two *vajra*s or *vajra* and *ghanta*, embracing his Prajna, is sometimes considered the Adi-Buddha, and is confused with Vajrasatva. Together with parts of eastern India, Kashmir and the adjoining areas were imortant sources for Tantric Buddhism, and many manuscripts of important Tantric texts have been recovered from Kashmir. Among the specifically Buddhist Tantric deities represented in Kashmir bronzes are Vajrasatva, Vajrapani, Manjushri, Yamantaka, Sambara, and Kalacakra.

Stone Sculpture of Aparajita. Aparajita, defiant Tantric Buddhist deity. Stone, perhaps from Ganga, c. eleventh century. PHOTO COURTESY OF GOURISWAR BHATTACHARYA.

In Tantric Buddhism, the union of *upaya* (means) and *prajna* (knowledge), represented by the masculine and feminine personages, leads to *bodhicitta* (mind of awakening). Many Buddhist deities in Tantric Buddhism are therefore shown in the *yab-yum* (intercourse) position. The Hevajra-tantra, Kriyasamgraha, Advayavajrasamgraha, and Guhyasamaja-tantra are the special texts for this concept. Another Tantric manuscript of importance, especially in Nepal, is the manuscript describing the five "protectresses," or Pancarakshas: Mahapratisara, Mahasahasrapramardini, Mahamantranusarini, Mahashitavati, and Mahamayuri. The female deities are of different complexions, many-headed and many-armed, and all seated in various sitting positions. Both the Sadhanamala and Nishpannayogavali texts describe the Pancaraksha *mandala*, in which Mahamantranusarini is in the south, Mahashitavati in the west, and Mahamayuri in the north. These Pancaraksha deities are mostly shown in the manuscripts. Tara, two-armed and of green or dark (*shyama*) complexion, is

Marici. Carved image of Marici (or Marichi), revered Buddhist goddess. Her name is still invoked by the lamas of Tibet at sunrise. From Bhimpur, c. eleventh century. Collection of Varendra Research Museum. PHOTO COURTESY OF GOURISWAR BHATTACHARYA.

the Tantric rite of *vashikarana*, which brings success by enchanting men, women, ministers, and even kings. In the Uddiyana form, the goddess is four-armed, red in color, and fierce in appearance, and she sits in *ardha-paryanka* position (one leg hanging down) on a human corpse.

Goddess Cunda is the embodiment of the Cunda *dharani*. She has one face but two, four, sixteen, eighteen, or twenty-six arms. As Cunda-vajri she is mentioned in one of the earliest Tantric works, the Gukyasamaja-tantra. That the worship of Cunda was popular in southwest Bengal (Bangladesh) is mentioned in a Prajnaparamita manuscript of the Cambridge University Library of A.D. 1015 as "Cunda in the excellent temple of Cunda at Pattikera" (present-day Mainamati in Comilla).

Mention should be made here of two other Tantric female deities, Ekajata and Bhrkuti, who are often illustrated in sculptures from Bihar-Bengal. Ekajata, four-armed, wearing a tiger skin and holding an elephant skin above her head, accompanies Tara, a description of whom is not to be found in the Sadhanamala.

There are some Tantric Buddhist deities who are antagonistic to some Hindu gods and goddesses. Apara-jita, one such deity, tramples upon Ganesha and slaps him. Similarly, the four-faced, eight-armed male deity Trailokyavijaya, displaying anger, tramples upon the head of Shiva with his left leg and with his right leg presses upon the bosom of Gauri. Heruka, the well-known Buddhist Tantric deity of the Heruka-tantra, is known as Hevajra when two-armed and embracing his Prajna, Nairatma, but when four-armed he embraces Vajravarahi. The union of Vajravarahi with Heruka is the cult of the celebrated Cakrasambara-tantra. Vajravarahi is a *dakini*. Vajravarahi resembles Marici, who has a sow-like face, but she has a natural sowlike excrescence just near the right ear and she dances in the *ardhaparyanka* pose. Marici is more well-known as a Buddhist goddess. Marici is invoked by the lamas of Tibet at sunrise. Like the Hindu Sun god, she rides on a chariot (drawn by seven pigs, not seven horses). Recent scholars have identified her with the *bodhi* of Shakyamuni. Marici is the principal deity in the Marici *mandala* of the Nishpan-nayogavali. She has different forms, but her main symbols are needle and string. As three-faced and eight-armed Maricipicuva, she is attended by four sow-faced goddesses called Varttali, Vadali, Varali, and Varihamukhi. The cosmic Buddha, Vairocana, is her mate. With six faces and twelve arms she is called Vajradhatvishvari marici. The three-faced goddess, of which two are sow faces, is called Ubhayavarahanana. In this form she tramples under her feet the Hindu gods Hari, Hara,

the most popular goddess of the Buddhist pantheon, but her four-faced and eight-armed form, called Vajratara, is a Tantric form shown in the *mandala*. Two other Tantric female deities are Kurukulla (a form of Tara) and the popular deity Cunda. Kurukulla is one-faced but may have two, four, six, or eight arms. Kurukulla is associated with

Hiranyagarbha (Brahmā), and others. With six faces and twelve arms she is called Vajradhatvishvarimarici and is the Prajna of Vairocana.

Vajrayogini, in eastern Bengal (now Bangladesh), near Vikrampur, was a seat of Vajrayana (Tantrayana) Buddhism, and many images of Tantric deities were found there, including that of the strange goddess Parnashabari. The worship of this deity was believed to prevent outbreaks of epidemics. The pot-bellied, three-faced, six-armed deity wearing leaves (hence Parna-shabari) tramples in *pratyalidha* attitude upon a couple, the elephant-headed ram below, accompanied by an animal-headed male figure and the smallpox goddess Shitala riding on a donkey. In her six hands she holds, clockwise, an elephant goad, an arrow, a *vajra*, a branch, *tarjani-mudrā* (warning gesture), and a bow.

The prominent Buddhist male deity Kalacakra is the principal deity of the Kalacakra *mandala* and of the famous Kalacakra-tantra. With four faces and twelve eyes and twenty-four arms, he dances on the bodies of the Hindu god of love Amanga (Kama) and Rudra, who are lying on their backs. In one of his hands he holds the severed head of Brahmā. He holds various weapons, including a *vajra*, in other hands of different colors.

Avalokiteshvara was a sublime *bodhisattva* in the early Buddhist pantheon, but with the influence of the Hindu god Shiva he assumed a form called Simhanada-Lokeshvara, seated on a lion, wearing a crown of matted hair, a tiger skin, and having three eyes. In his right hand he has a white trident, entwined by a white snake, and in the left hand a sword burning like fire.

Another important (especially in Tibet) manifestation of Avalokiteshvara is his Shadakshari, or six-syllabic form. In this form he is four-armed and is attended upon by the male deity Manidhara and the female deity Shadakshari-Mahavidya. In this four-armed form Avalokiteshvara is seated, showing *sarvarajendra-mudrā* (actually *namaskara-mudrā*) with the main two hands, while the back right hand holds the rosary (*akshamala*) and the back left hand a full-blown lotus (*padma*). The six syllables are the famous mantra, *om manipadme hum*, which is uttered daily by the Nepalese and Tibetan Buddhists and which is engraved on the votive stones, popularly called Manistones. Unfortunately the mantra is often incorrectly translated and is therefore commonly misunderstood. This mantra invokes the female form of Avalokiteshvara as Manipadma.

The other well-known *bodhisattva* is Manjushri, the god of learning. He is shown brandishing a sword, which removes ignorance, and holding a blue water lily (*nilotpala*)

Painting of Vaishravana. Also known as the "Guardian King of the North," the Buddhist god of wealth, date unknown. With the development of Tantric Buddhism in the seventh century came the images of magnificent gods and goddesses, all portrayed in paradise-like settings. In time the archetypal imagery delved more deeply into the unconscious. LINDSAY HEBBERD / CORBIS.

or a manuscript (*Prajnaparamita* text) on it. In an esoteric form he is shown riding a tiger and showing with two hands the *vyakhyana-mudrā* (gesture of explanation). An extremely important Tantric form of Manjushri is Manjuvajra, with three faces and six arms. With the principal arms he makes the gesture of embracing his Prajna, and he holds a sword (*khadga*) and an arrow in the right hands and the stalk of a blue water lily (*nilotpala*) and a bow (*capa*) in the left hands. The deity is sometimes shown with other similar images in a *mandala*.

Southeast Bengal (*vanga-samatata*), now Bangladesh, was the home of learned Tantric Buddhist pandits, one of whom, the famous Atisha Shrijnana Dipankara (11th century), went to Tibet to preach Tantric Buddhism there.

Gourishwar Bhattacharya

See also **Buddhism in Ancient India; Buddhist Art in Andhra up to the Fourth Century; Sculpture: Buddhist**

BIBLIOGRAPHY

Bhattacharyya, Bentoytosh. *The Indian Buddhist Iconography.* 1958. Reprint, Kolkata: Firma K. L. Mukhopadhyay, 1968.

Bhattacharyya, Benoytosh, ed. *Sadhanamala,* I and II. Baroda: Oriental Institute, 1968.

———. *Nispannayogavati of Mahapandita Abhayakaragupta.* 1949. Reprint, Baroda, 1972.

Mevissen, Gerd J. R. "Studies in Pancaraksa Manuscript Painting." *Berliner Indologische Studien* 4–5 (1989): 339–374.

Saraswati, S. K. *Tantrayana Art: An Album.* Kolkata: Asiatic Society, 1977.

TAPAS Although the root meaning of *tapas* is "heat," this versatile term can indicate creative cosmic energy, sexual fervor and chastity, ecstasy and pain, contemplative ardor and austerity, self-promotion and self-mortification. It held diverse meanings already in the Rig Veda and Atharva Veda before becoming the key feature of asceticism in Hinduism, Jainism, Buddhism, yoga, other philosophical systems, and in regional epics beyond the Mahābhārata and Rāmāyaṇa. Ecstatic and shamanic experiences associated with fire and heat in West and South Asia may be far older than the Vedas, as are Proto-Indo-European mythic and epic motifs of heated battle fury that rises in warrior gods and heroes. In the Rig Veda, Indra defeats Vritra with the weapon of *tapas;* ritual soma is empowered by *tapas;* ancient Rishis first envisioned the Vedas by cultivating *tapas;* ancestor-fathers (*pitris*) gained heaven by *tapas;* and the great gods of fire and sun, Agni and Sūrya, are natural reservoirs of *tapas.* In the tenth and latest book of the Rig Veda, hymns 129 and 190 separately diagram cosmogony: precosmic *tapas* is succeeded by desire (*kāma*), mind (*manas*), order (*rita*), and truth (*satya*). A famous passage in Atharva Veda 11.5 proclaims that a student learning the Vedas generates *tapas* that infuses the universe, including all its gods. Like the sun, he is a reservoir of productive *tapas.*

Brāhmaṇas that follow the earliest Vedas feature Prajāpati, famous as source of creation, Lord of Creatures, and successor to self-sacrificing Purusha, conceiving by desire born of heat. Giving up his body, as did Purusha, Prajāpati exhausts himself through self-heating in order to create by repeated emission. His *tapas* may last for a millennium. The human sacrificer identifies with both Prajāpati and his sacrificial fire (*Agni*) in a similar ritualized striving that simultaneously maintains the world and transcends it. The Upanishads provide further nuances to these homologies between inner and cosmic heat. With the emergence of the Sanskrit epics and Purāṇas, and developing traditions of yoga and tantra, a wide-ranging pattern of ascetic practices is apparent. A *tapasvin,* one who cultivates *tapas,* usually through a solitary forest or mountain vigil, may be a celibate yogin or *yoginī,* god or goddess, *rishi* or his wife, king, demon, child, or even an animal. *Tapas* can be positive, yielding drought-ending rains, for example, or negative, producing heat that melts mountains and dries up oceans. Countless myths begin with a world threatened by an uncontrollable ascetic, demon, or deity whose silent *tapas* has the destructive power of a raging forest fire.

Tapas has a considerable role to play in Patañjali's Yoga Sūtras, its commentaries, and succeeding traditions. Three practices in *kriyā-yoga* are necessary to gain *samādhi*: self-study, devotion, and *tapas* that yields perfection (*siddhi*) of the body and senses. Perhaps it is in Jainism that *tapas* has its most vigorous adepts today. Both lay and monastic disciplines declare an increasingly rigorous program of austerities—fasting, meditation, chastity—necessary to burn off the impurities of existing karma, as in the burning of sin (*pāpman*) by *tapas* recommended in the Upanishads more than twenty-five centuries ago.

David M. Knipe

See also **Agni; Hinduism (Dharma); Indra; Jainism; Soma; Yoga**

BIBLIOGRAPHY

Blair, Chauncey J. *Heat in the Rig Veda and the Atharva Veda.* New Haven, Conn.: Yale University Press, 1961. Philological study of the root *tap-,* its derivatives, and other words for heat in the two texts.

Eliade, Mircea. *Yoga: Immortality and Freedom.* 2nd ed. Princeton, N.J.: Princeton University Press, 1969. Links shamanic techniques, Brahmanic speculation, and the interior sacrifice, magical inner heat and light of yoga and tantra.

Kaelber, Walter O. *Tapta Mārga. Asceticism and Initiation in Vedic India.* Albany: State University of New York Press, 1989. Particularly useful on the initiatory symbolism of *tapas.*

Knipe, David M. *In the Image of Fire. Vedic Experiences of Heat.* Delhi: Motilal Banarsidass, 1975. Reviews *tapas* from Vedic correspondences to Dharma Shāstras in the context of symbols of fire and the dynamics of heating and cooling in the history of religions.

O'Flaherty, Wendy Doniger. *Asceticism and Eroticism in the Mythology of Śiva.* London: Oxford University Press, 1973. Analyzes Purāṇic and other motifs on creative and destructive *tapas* and related terms; see motifs 8, 10, 18, 25, 36, 39, 45.

TATA, JAMSETJI N. *(1839–1904), Indian industrialist.* A Parsi pioneer of Indian trade and commerce, Jamsetji Nusserwanji Tata emerged as a beacon of hope in the early phase of industrialization in India. He was born on 3 March 1839 in the town of Navsari in Gujarat, the son of Nusserwanji Tata, whose father was a Parsi (Zoroastrian) priest. Jamsetji is also known for his nationalist ideals and his humanitarian efforts to alleviate poverty in Indian society, pursuing what could be called "strategic philanthropy."

Tata's early education was in form of verbal instruction in the Zoroastrian prayers and scriptures. Later he attended Elphistone College in Bombay (Mumbai), graduating in 1858. He acquired his business acumen from his father, starting a trading company with a capital of 21,000 rupees in 1868. Jamsetji went on to establish a cotton mill, the Central India Spinning, Wearing and Manufacturing Company, in Nagpur, Maharashtra, in 1874. This was followed by his establishment of the Empress Mills in Bombay on 1 January 1877, coinciding with the proclamation of Queen Victoria as the empress of India.

The last two decades of his life helped shape the course of industrialization and modernization in India, in terms of the iron and steel industries, hydroelectric power generation, and the establishment of educational institutions to promote science and technology. Though steel production started in 1912 and hydroelectric power generation in 1915, almost a decade after his death, they were visualized during his lifetime; in 1901 he had begun organizing the first large-scale ironworks in India. His son Dorabji J. Tata expanded the business under the name Tata and Sons.

Jamsetji Tata is also considered a forerunner in ushering in a professional code of conduct in the management of industries, including a provident fund for employees, decent working conditions, and management by a managing director and a board in an age of family oligarchs. Tata's city of Jamshedpur remains a classic example of the realization of his concept of capital-intensive heavy industries, blended with a modern industrial township.

Tata's Indian Institute of Science at Bangalore (Karnataka), which was established with his endowment, remains an outstanding symbol of corporate philosophy and citizenship. It was set up after an ideological battle with the colonial regime under Viceroy Lord Curzon, who questioned the academic credentials of Indian students. Jamsetji Tata was deeply concerned about British colonial rule and its impact on India's economy, and he supported self-rule under British paramountcy. He attended the first session of the Indian National Congress Party in Bombay and remained committed to its cause until his death in May 1904.

R. Radhakrishnan

See also **Jamshedpur**

BIBLIOGRAPHY

"The Giant Who Touched Tomorrow." Available at <http://www.tata.com/0_b_drivers/lasting_legacies/20040811_jnt.htm>

Harris, F. R. *J. N. Tata: A Chronicle of His Life.* Mumbai: Blackie & Son Limited, 1958.

"The Jamshedji Who Trounced Lord Curzon." *Financial Express*, 15 August 2004. Available at <http://www.tata.com/tata_sons/media/20040815.htm>

Tripathi, Dwijendra. "Ahead of His Times: The Uncommon Vision of J. N. Tata." *Times of India* (New Delhi), 3 March 2004.

TAXATION POLICY SINCE 1991 ECONOMIC REFORMS A comparison of the current structures of India's main central government taxes with those prevailing before 1991 indicates that, following international trends, there has been a sizable scaling back of rates in income, excise, and trade taxes. During this period, states also attempted to harmonize their sales tax rates and, most importantly, introduced a value-added tax (VAT) on 1 April 2005, comprising perhaps the most important subnational tax reform since the formation of the Indian Republic in 1950. The base of the central government's service tax has been expanded steadily, though its full coordination into a national VAT remains to be accomplished. At the subnational level, an agreement among states to cut back incentives and exemptions met with partial success. The VAT should improve its adherence.

Before 1991 India's overall tax structure had been broadly inefficient and quite inequitable. By international standards, the income tax rates had been high, and there was no VAT at the central level, except on a selective basis from the mid-1980s. The consumption tax base was narrow, with services excluded from the tax base, and customs duties were very high yet riddled with complex exemptions. Selected export duties reduced the international competitiveness of traditional exports. At the subnational level, state sales taxes caused heavy excess burdens due to input taxes getting built into the prices of final commodities, resulting in tax-on-tax, or cascading. The changes in India's tax structure are generally agreed to have led to improvements in its efficiency and equity.

Nevertheless, one cost of the improvements has been the government's inability to make up for revenue loss from rate decreases because of insufficient base expansion. The central government's tax revenue collected since 1994 declined by 1 percent of gross domestic product (GDP) from what had been collected previously. Declines in customs and excise revenues were not compensated by the increase in income tax revenues. Some sunset tax exemption clauses were extended and new incentives crept in, despite the scaling back of central tax

TABLE 1

Corporate tax rates in India for selected years

(in percent)

	1990–1991	1992–1993	1995–1996	1997–1998	2001–2002	2004–2005[1]
Domestic company	50	45	40	35	35	35
Foreign company	65	65	55	48	45	40

(1) Subject to a surcharge of 2.5 percent. Capital gains are taxed at 20 percent plus a surcharge of 2.5 percent (which is exempted if reinvested in primary securities).

SOURCE: Ministry of Finance, Government of India.

incentives in the newly emerging economy. Attempts by the tax administration to expand the taxpayer net through registration drives and a new set of requirements for filing tax returns were initially successful. But further improvements would depend on the efficiency with which newly legislated information returns from third-parties is utilized and associated computer techniques implemented.

Though the states' tax collections improved somewhat, they could not fully compensate for the central government's tax revenue decline, so that the combined central and states tax/GDP ratio fell during the decade. Overall, the ramifications for the consolidated fiscal deficit and, in turn, for public debt could be significant. There are expectations that the VAT will be revenue enhancing. However, there may be an initial period of revenue loss since the VAT rates for all states are the same and, for some high-revenue states, the VAT rates are not revenue-neutral when compared to their earlier sales tax rates. As a result, the central government has agreed to compensate states for revenue loss in the initial three years.

Major Changes in Central Tax Structure

Income tax. By the mid-1990s, many developing countries had emerged from the reform process with much lower and fewer individual income tax rates, typically 15, 25, and 35 percent. Even India legislated comparable rates of 10, 20, and 30 percent in 1997–1998. Both the rates, and their number and dispersion, were reduced on efficiency grounds. Across the developing world, for example in East Asia and Latin America, corporate income tax rates were slashed. The scaling back of corporate income tax rates reflected, to some extent, the twin objectives of administrative feasibility and better tax compliance, but was motivated in particular by the forces of globalization and the increased international movement of capital. In India, corporate income tax rates for both domestic and foreign companies have been

reduced to 35 percent and 40 percent respectively (see Table 1).

Insufficiency in streamlining exemptions and incentives has adversely affected the full potential of revenue productivity in both the individual and corporate income tax. The coverage of tax incentives includes savings generation, regional development, capital investment, labor employment, research and technology, infrastructure development, exports, and charities, among others. The outcome has been a thinning out of the overall income tax base. However, income tax revenue in terms of GDP has steadily improved, reflecting administrative improvements, an expansion in the taxpayer net, and, possibly, favorable supply-side effects.

While industry tends to favor income tax incentives, these incentives have tended to benefit large entities, resulting in inequity within the corporate sector. The effective corporate tax rate is, therefore, skewed among companies. Highly generous depreciation rates were scaled back in 2005–2006 and that should correct for some of this problem. There is little doubt that without base broadening, income tax revenue is unlikely to be able to make up fully for the revenue losses emanating from structural reforms of production and trade taxes.

Central excises and customs. Central excises essentially operate as a VAT that has evolved over almost two decades, with a small beginning in 1986–1987, when a VAT-type credit mechanism for selected raw materials was introduced for the production of specified goods. In 1994–1995, capital goods were made creditable. The emerging quasi-VAT structure was termed Modified VAT or MODVAT. With a further effort to reduce the main rates to only two—8 and 16 percent—it was renamed the Central VAT, or CENVAT, in 2001.

Thus, the excises have been transformed to a VAT structure that is comparable to the successes and foibles of the VATs of most countries, with its administration carried out by the Customs and Excises Department of the Ministry of Finance. The main, and quite important, difference is that while most countries that have introduced the VAT have tended to do so as a one-shot preparation and implementation package, India has done so in a seemingly deliberate, learning-by-doing approach. This provides an interesting alternative to the usual rapid approach to VAT introduction that has sometimes entailed strong opposition from the representative taxpayer in many parts of the world. Another crucial difference from other countries is that the base of CENVAT is truncated to manufacturing, given the taxation assignment of manufacturing only (and not sales) to the central government by the Constitution of India. This has led to much litigation by businesses on the definition of manufacturing to truncate its definition to avoid tax. The CENVAT base also gets eroded by various exemptions. More than 200 pages of the standard excise tariff, of some 700 pages, comprise exemptions. Each exemption has many entries, conditions, and lists, in turn containing hundreds of items in each list.

The rate structure of customs duties is widely recognized to have been rapidly scaled back over the last decade, the peak rate declining from 150 percent in 1991–1992 to 15 percent in 2005–2006. Nevertheless, the tendency to tinker with incentives and exemptions remains alive. This inherently leads to much complexity in interpretation and administration, let alone economic distortions.

State-Level Taxes

Multiple taxes and low buoyancy. The taxing powers of Indian states include a plethora of minor taxes and one major source of tax revenue, the sales tax, recently replaced by the VAT. In the major states (14 out of a total of 25), tax revenue has represented approximately 7 percent of the state domestic product in recent years. Indirect taxes include state excise duties, taxes on vehicles, purchase tax, entertainment tax, and some surcharges. The sales tax represents approximately 60 percent of total tax revenue, while excises are the second most important revenue source, in particular, on potable alcohol. Thus, Indian states have been assigned mainly indirect taxes by the Constitution. Direct tax powers include stamp duty and registration fee, profession tax, and an income tax on agriculture. The last is usually viewed as insufficiently exploited, while the profession tax is basically a fee with a low nominal ceiling imposed by the central government. Only the stamp duty and registration fee could be said to have been revenue productive among the direct taxes.

A disturbing factor has been the low buoyancy of revenue (i.e., the percentage response of tax revenue, including discretionary changes, to a percentage change in

GDP) from these various taxes. A tax-reform commission of the Government of Karnataka (2001) estimated that the buoyancies of various taxes fell sharply during the 1990s. Recommendations made in selected state-level tax reform studies—including Government of Karnataka (2000), Government of Madhya Pradesh (2001), Government of Maharashtra (2000), and Government of West Bengal (2001)—offer many ideas and directions in which structural reform could be undertaken, with a focus on extending the tax base.

Replacing sales tax with a VAT. Given the primary importance of the sales tax in revenue generation and its recent conversion to a state-level VAT, the main concerns and prospects are examined here. The general dilemma for a subnational VAT is that introducing a VAT at the central level is far easier than at the state level. Countries with the intention of introducing a subnational VAT have grappled with one main problem, that of structuring the VAT as a consumption tax, generally without an appropriate solution. Either they have introduced a VAT that is not a fully consumption-type (Brazil), or one that is administratively complex (Canada); or they have desisted from introducing it at all (United States), or have been debating its appropriate form for a considerable time (Argentina).

In India, all states—through an empowered committee of state finance ministers—have agreed to have the same rate structure—4 and 12.5 percent—for the VAT and the same exemptions. However, each state is allowed to have ten additional exempted items of local importance from a list of about forty items. Some goods such as petroleum products are outside the VAT base with a floor rate of 20 percent. Immediately after the VAT's introduction, however, the states felt compelled to add to the exemption list reflecting popular demand. This was especially to counterbalance the opposition-ruled states that decided not to introduce the VAT at the last moment. Out of a total of thirty-five, twenty-three states (and centrally administered Union Territories [UTs]) have introduced the VAT. Two UTs should introduce them soon, while two did not even have a sales tax. The remaining eight states that did not introduce the VAT are states with opposition governments.

The states have gone halfway in their attempt to move to a destination based VAT, though interstate trade continues to be taxed at 4 percent as before. Under the VAT, states will not give input tax credit in their own states for inputs bought in another state. However, when a good is exported to another state, input tax credit will be given against such export. It is anticipated that input tax credit for inputs imported from another state should be in place in 2006 or 2007. However, a solution would need to be found regarding how to capture the lost revenue currently collected from this source. A computerized system for exchange of information among states, under development, would also need to be operational prior to implementation.

In sum, the states have made an impressive beginning in the introduction of their VAT, and as in the case of the central government's CENVAT, future evolution in its structure should result in its sophistication. The central government, in its catalytic role, has demonstrated its willingness to participate in the states' tax reform process. The combination demonstrates exemplary fiscal federal cooperation.

Tax Administration

Three issues in tax administration are closely connected to the success of any tax policy reform: expanding the taxpayer register; computerization; and implementation of the state-level VAT. Arguably the most successful action that has been undertaken in the area of central tax administration has been an impressive expansion of the taxpayer net for the income tax. In the mid-1990s, the taxpayer roll included some 14 million taxpayers, of which 10 million to 11 million were current. However, a rudimentary calculation of the potential number of taxpayers would be as follows. Of the total population of 1 billion, the taxable population is approximately 300 million. With an average household size of 5, that would imply 60 million potential taxpayers. Discounting 10 million for taxable agricultural households would result finally in a net 50 million taxable households. Thus only about 20 percent of potential taxpayers were within the taxpayer net.

In the second half of the 1990s, a voluntary disclosure program required individual income earners who possessed certain characteristics, such as ownership of property and telephones, and trips undertaken abroad, to register even if their taxable income was nil. The characteristics were further expanded with time so that more individuals would be required to register. By 2000 the taxpayer register had increased to over 20 million. Thus, within a relatively short period, the number of potential taxpayers doubled, an objective that had been unattainable for decades. In 2005 the register contained approximately 30 million, of which about 25 million are understood to be current.

While it has been found that the number of assessees has not constrained tax collection, nevertheless there is a need to allocate adequate administrative resources to bring the medium to small taxpayer into the tax net. The strategy must include a credible threat of audits for all taxpayers. This draws attention to the second issue of the extent of resources the tax administration can devote to administering the returns of relatively small taxpayers. If the taxpayers that were rapidly brought into the tax net

realized that their chances of being assessed or audited were very small, then having a larger taxpayer register may not result in any significant increase in revenue collection in the long run. Needless to say, having a large taxpayer unit (LTU), which facilitates payment of all taxes by large taxpayers through a single window, is also important. India does not yet have an LTU but the intention to set one up has been announced.

In order to more effectively tackle the problem of tax evasion in a modern tax administration, a computerized information system needs to be quickly developed. For example, the income tax department collects a wide array of evidence during the course of any investigation. In addition to information from taxpayers' returns and other information returns, a large volume of information is collected during assessment, searches and seizures, and survey operations. Third-party information has been legislated from various sources, but this could lead to revenue enhancement only if such information is successfully collated, disseminated, and verified. Currently the income tax department has initiated massive information-technology transformation that is experiencing teething problems. Complete implementation will take a year or two. Customs operations, on the other hand, are focused specifically at import-export points, catering mainly to businesses, so computerization of customs procedures has moved further on. Excise or CENVAT entails cross-checks of invoices among buyer and seller. It poses more difficult challenges, and systems development is in a nascent, discussion stage regarding alternative models of computerization.

The success of implementation of the state VAT is dependent on the computerization of VAT procedures of various states. States have progressed at differing speeds in this area. The central government is lending a helping hand to some of the smaller states in the form of turnkey projects through computer training, installation, and implementation. A further challenge remains in the development of a comprehensive information exchange system among states that should enable the states to cross-check tax data across state borders, once the VAT evolves to the destination principle. The cost of developing such a system is being shared between the center and the states.

The loss in the tax/GDP ratio could be made up and further resource mobilization successfully achieved only through an expansion of the tax base. Thus exemptions and incentives for both direct and indirect taxes at the central level need to be scaled back significantly. On the administration side, computerization is imperative. At the state level, there is generally a high expectation that, through a broad tax base, and by its extension to the retail arena, the VAT would be revenue productive in the medium term.

In the long term, the goal for the reform of consumption taxation must be a national VAT. Many strides have been made, though much remains to be done. The process should not stop with the introduction of the state level VAT operating side by side with the central CEN-VAT. A national two-tier VAT, based on the destination principle, would comprise both the central and state levels. The center and states would appropriately share services as a tax base, reflecting cross-border or intraborder consumption, respectively. The challenge would be to achieve cooperation in information sharing between the central government and the states, and among the states themselves, for the concurrent VAT to operate successfully. Only then could the national VAT comprise a comprehensive consumption tax that would cover both goods and services at all subnational levels.

Parthasarathi Shome

See also **Economic Reforms of 1991; Economy since the 1991 Economic Reforms; Fiscal System and Policy since 1952**

BIBLIOGRAPHY

Dasgupta, Arindam, and Dilip Mookherjee. *Incentives and Institutional Reform in Tax Enforcement.* New Delhi: Oxford University Press, 1998.

Ebrill, Liam, Michael Keen, Jean-Paul Bodin, and Victoria Summers. *The Modern VAT.* Washington D.C.: International Monetary Fund, 2001.

Government of India. *Report of the Group of Officials and Experts on Taxation of Interstate Sales.* New Delhi: Ministry of Finance, 1996.

———. *Report of Expert Group on Service Tax.* New Delhi: Ministry of Finance, 1999.

———. *Tax Policy and Tax Administration for the Tenth Plan.* Report of Advisory Group. New Delhi: Planning Commission, 2001.

Mukhopadhyay, Sukumar. *Manufacturing in Central Excises.* New Delhi: Centax Publications, 1995.

Ponniah, Aurobindo. "India: Budget for 2004/2005." *Asia Pacific Tax Bulletin* 10, no. 4 (2004): 210–211.

Shome, Parthasarathi. *India's Fiscal Matters.* New Delhi: Oxford University Press, 2002.

Shome, Parthasarathi, ed. *Tax Policy Handbook.* Washington, D.C.: International Monetary Fund, 1995.

———. *Value Added Tax in India: A Progress Report.* New Delhi: National Institute of Public Finance and Policy, Centax Publications, 1997.

Shome, Parthasarathi, Pawan K. Aggarwal, and Kanwarjit Singh. "Tax Evasion and Tax Administration: A Focus on Tax Deduction at Source." In *Fiscal Policy, Public Policy and Governance,* edited by Parthasarathi Shome. New Delhi: National Institute of Public Finance and Policy, Centax Publications, 1997.

Tait, Alan A. *Value Added Tax: International Practice and Problems.* Washington, D.C.: International Monetary Fund, 1988.

TECHNICAL CHANGE IN AGRICULTURE, 1952–2000

The fragility of the Indian food production and distribution system was exposed after the disastrous Bengal famine in 1943. Then, following partition, about 32 percent of total irrigated land went to Pakistan. Consequently, food production in India had fallen short of demand and the prices of food grains surged significantly. In order to increase the food grain production levels, the cultivated area under food crops was expanded through special programs, even in the early 1940s, with such initiatives as the Grow More Food Campaign. Further, on the basis of the recommendations of the Food Grain Policy Committee in 1947, the reclamation of 25 million acres (10 million hectares) of land was undertaken to expand the cultivated area under food crops. But this singular focus on food grain production led to an acute shortage in cotton and other fiber production in the late 1940s, and this problem was addressed through an Integrated Production Programme initiated in 1950. The consequent increase in food production was largely achieved through expansion of cultivated area during the 1950s (see Table 1). However, due to the limited scope for further expansion in cultivated area, agricultural production soon became stagnant and even declined during the subsequent drought years. At this stage, the vital role of technology was realized, particularly the land-augmenting technology that enhances the yield per unit of land. The introduction of technical changes through improved seed, fertilizer, irrigation, mechanization, and plant protection have brought dramatic changes in agricultural production since the 1950s. These technical changes in agriculture have proceeded in a step-by-step manner; initially, the focus was on the development of land, irrigation, and other inputs; subsequently, the emphasis was on high-yielding varieties (HYVs) and improved "package of practices"; and finally, postharvest and marketing aspects were explored. Following this progression, technical developments in agriculture from 1952 to 2000 can be spread across three distinct phases, based on the nature and progress of technical changes: the pre-"revolution" period, the period of production revolution, and the period of market reforms.

Pre-Revolution Period (1952–1966)

Though the major breakthrough in agricultural production had come through the "Green Revolution," which introduced HYVs, steps toward land-augmenting technical changes were actually initiated in the 1950s. In order to address the problems of food shortage and the resultant rise in food prices, the agriculture sector was given the highest priority in India's first Five-Year Plan. Focus was placed on expansion of irrigation, land reclamation, and the domestic production of inorganic fertilizers.

Rose Cultivation for Export. In recent years, rose cultivation—which once seemed a secure industry in states like Karnataka, Tamil Nadu, West Bengal, Andhra Pradesh, and Maharashtra—has faced stiff competition in the form of cheaper imports from Africa. With many small growers being driven out of business, others are trying to survive by exploring new overseas markets. DINESH KHANNA.

Land reclamation and development. As a part of the Grow More Food Campaign, the reclamation of nearly 25 million acres (10 million hectares) of land was set as a target, and land reclamation was undertaken on a large scale across India. Nearly 188,000 acres (76,000 hectares) of land was reclaimed in the Tarai region itself, through a process of mechanized jungle clearing and provision of drainage, between 1948 and 1960. Consequently, the net area sown had gone up from about 297 million acres (120 million hectares) in 1952–1953 to about 341 million acres (138 million hectares) in 1966–1967, and the respective annual average growth rates (net as well as gross area sown) were the maximum during the 1950s, compared to any other period (see Table 1).

Irrigation. A number of major irrigation projects were completed during the first Five-Year Plan, including the Tungabhadra Project (1956), Maithon (1957), Konar (1955), Kakarpara (1957), Gandhi Sagar (1960), Lower Bhawani (1955), Ghataprabha Left Bank (1956), and Hirakud Dam (1956). In addition to surface irrigation, groundwater irrigation through tube wells gained popularity in the 1950s. Further, mechanization of irrigation operations, as reflected by the steep increase in number of diesel engines and electric pumps, picked up momentum in the late 1950s. As a result, the extent of irrigated area in the total cultivated area had gone up from about 17 percent in the 1950s to about 20 percent in the 1960s (see Table 1).

Mechanization and rural electrification. The mechanization of agriculture was also initiated in the early 1950s but was largely restricted to irrigation operation (diesel engines and electric motors) and included to a

TABLE 1

Growth trends in land utilization from 1950 to 2000

(percent per year)

	Net area sown	Gross area sown	Net irrigated area	Gross irrigated area	Percent area irrigated
1950s	1.2	1.6	1.6	2.3	17.4
1960s	0.4	0.5	2.0	3.0	20.0
1970s	0.1	0.5	2.6	3.1	25.4
1980s	−0.1	0.4	1.8	2.2	31.1
1990s	−0.1	0.5	1.9	2.4	37.6

SOURCE: Compiled from *Agricultural Statistics at a Glance*, Department of Economics and Statistics, Ministry of Agriculture, Government of India, New Delhi, August 2004.

limited extent the use of tractors. The number of electric pumps for irrigation purposes increased steeply, from about 56,000 at the end of first plan period to more than 500,000 by the end of third plan period, as a result of the expansion in rural electrification launched during the first plan period.

Fertilizer use. Though the role of fertilizers as an important source of nutrients and a substitute for organic manures was recognized, their use was not widespread and was restricted to commercial crops in southern regions of the country until 1950. In order to create awareness among farmers about the importance and methods of fertilizer application, a number of programs were created, such as the Agricultural Technical Assistance Programme (1951) and the Fertilizer Demonstration Programme (1954–1956). Soil-testing laboratories were also established to collect and analyze soil samples and to prepare a nutrient status map of the villages. As a result, the application of fertilizers increased, with an average annual growth rate of about 20 percent in the 1950s and 25 percent in the 1960s. The consumption of phosphatic and potashic fertilizers was almost negligible until the 1950s but started rising in the subsequent period; the growth in phosphatic and potashic fertilizer application outpaced that of nitrogenous fertilizers during the 1950s and 1960s, although the use was judicious in absolute quantities.

Package of practices. Following an increase in the first plan period, the food grain output actually declined in the second plan period as the result of successive drought years. As a result, the gap between the targeted and actual production became more pronounced. In view of the serious food deficit situation, the government of India invited the Ford Foundation Team to study India's food production problems and to help in shaping proposals for a coordinated effort to increase food production on an emergency basis. Based on the recommendations of the team, the Intensive Agricultural Development Programme (IADP) was initiated, which featured a "package of practices" for each crop, based on recent research findings. According to the team, the package of practices, which included irrigation, improved seed, mechanization, fertilizers, and pesticides, could lead to a remarkable increase in crop production only if all practices were adopted in particular combination with one another. Though the program was successful in increasing yields to some extent during the early 1960s, the success was restricted to resource-endowed areas that accounted for only 5 percent of the total cultivated area in the country. Further, severe drought in 1965–1966 and 1966–1967 led to a sharp fall in food grains, to 71 million tons (72 million tonnes) from 87 million tons (89 million tonnes) in 1964–1965. Consequently, food grain imports reached more than 9.8 million tons (10 million tonnes) in 1966–1967.

Period of Production Revolution (1966–1990)

The IADP program, or package of practices, could not, however, solve the problem of shortage in food grain production completely, despite the hope for increasing yield levels through better practices. The reason for the program's limited success was recognized to be an inherent problem associated with the traditional improved varieties of wheat and rice. After the application of high doses of fertilizers, those varieties grew taller, with slim stems, and had a tendency to fall over at the time of maturity, notwithstanding the grain weight. Hence, the immediate focus was to find a technology through which vertical growth of improved varieties could be restricted.

Green Revolution (1966–1980). During the same period, U.S. agronomist Norman E. Borlaug (often called the "father of the Green Revolution"), director of the Cooperative Wheat Research and Production Program in Mexico, was successfully incorporating dwarfing

TABLE 2

Area under High Yielding Varieties (HYVs)

(million hectares)

	Paddy	Wheat	*Jowar*	*Bajra*	Maize
1966–1967	2.5	4.2	1.1	0.5	4.1
1969–1970	11.5	29.5	3.0	9.2	7.7
1979–1980	40.6	67.8	18.3	28.0	23.6
1990–1991	64.2	86.8	49.1	54.4	44.2
1998–1999	73.7	87.2	95.0	76.9	58.1

SOURCE: Compiled from *Fertilizer Statistics of India,* Fertilizers Association of India, New Delhi, 2004.

genes in high-yielding wheat varieties by crossing the short-stemmed germ plasm from Norin 10 with high-yielding Mexican wheat varieties capable of responding to high doses of fertilizers and irrigation. The Mexican dwarf wheat varieties recorded increases as high as 400 percent in their yields in 1965 over that in 1950. Soon, India had imported the dwarf germ plasm (Lerma Rojo 64 and Sonara 64) from Mexico, and Indian scientists developed high-yielding, pest-resistant, and input-responsive dwarf wheat varieties by crossing these lines with local high-yielding varieties.

Similarly, the first semidwarf *indica* rice variety, Taichung Native 1, was developed by crossing a semi-dwarf *indica* variety, Dee-gee-woo-gen, with a drought-resistant variety, 'sai-Yuan-Chung, at the Taichung District Agricultural Improvement Station in Taiwan in 1956. Subsequently, the rice breeders at the International Rice Research Institute made several crosses of Dee-gee-woo-gen and ultimately developed new semi-dwarf rice varieties (IR 8, IR 5, IR 20, IR 22, and IR 24) with heavy stalks, responsive to high fertilizer doses and capable of maturing in 100 days instead of 160 days. India, being the world's largest source of rice germ plasm, had actively participated and cooperated in developing the new rice varieties. The high-yielding semidwarf rice breeding lines were introduced, and numerous improved varieties were developed with the active participation of the Central Rice Research Institute, the All-India Coordinated Rice Improvement Programme, and various state agricultural universities. Finally, high-yielding rice varieties were released for large-scale commercial cultivation all over India in 1966. In addition, high-yielding varieties of coarse cereals, including sorghum, *bajra*, and maize, were also developed through hybridization and were released for large-scale commercial cultivation during the late 1960s.

With an established network through IADP, the cultivation of high-yielding varieties spread rapidly across the country. Technological changes in the form of high-yielding dwarf wheat varieties became an instant success in India. Thus began the golden period in Indian agriculture called the "Green Revolution." The spread of HYVs of rice was relatively slow compared to that of wheat. The area under HYVs of wheat reached more than 60 percent of total wheat cultivated by the mid-1970s, while it took fifteen more years (until 1990–1991) to reach the same level (64 percent) for rice (see Table 2). The expansion in cultivated area under HYVs led to a steep increase in rice production in the subsequent years, from about 31.5 million tons (32 million tonnes) in the triennium ending in 1968 to about 49 million tons (50 million tonnes) in the triennium ending in 1980. However, the increase in production was much steeper in the 1980s, rising to 71.8 million tons (73 million tonnes) in the triennium ending in 1991 (see Table 3). Adoption of HYVs of *jowar*, *bajra*, and maize was slow, and most of the expansion took place after the mid-1980s. Consequently, the growth of food grain production was the highest during the 1980s, compared to any other period.

Considering the frequency of drought, a characteristic of Indian agriculture, assured irrigation has become a prerequisite for intensifying agricultural production in India, particularly following the introduction of HYVs. A number of major irrigation projects were completed, and the area under irrigation expanded rapidly in the 1960s and 1970s (see Table 1). Apart from major irrigation projects, emphasis was also placed on increasing minor irrigation projects through groundwater exploitation. Consequently, the total area under irrigation grew from about 55.8 million acres (22.6 million hectares) in 1950–1951 to about 123 million acres (50 million hectares) in 1979–1980. Most of this increase was brought about through minor irrigation projects that tapped groundwater to provide assured irrigation.

Considering the limitations to expanding irrigation through canals as well as groundwater, agricultural scientists and planners started promoting rain-fed agriculture through a promising "watershed" technology during the 1980s. A number of watershed projects emerged in the subsequent period, sponsored by domestic as well as external sources. The amount invested in watershed development reached U.S.$500 million by the late 1990s. Further, in order to conserve soil and water, particularly in rain-fed areas, technical changes in the form of sprinklers and drip irrigation methods were also promoted through the provision of subsidies in the 1980s and 1990s.

Plant protection, though practiced in Indian agriculture since ancient times, became more vital with the introduction of HYVs. The HYVs, due to their responsiveness to fertilizers, particularly to nitrogenous fertilizers, have a tendency to grow succulent and become susceptible to pests and diseases. With increasing irrigation and fertilizer application, the growth of weeds also increased. As a measure of plant protection, the first Pest and Disease Surveillance Service was organized in 1969 in selected districts of the IADP. The service was extended to other parts of the country in the subsequent period. With the growing awareness of pests and their control, the application of chemicals for plant protection increased sharply, from about 13,800 tons (14,000 tonnes) in 1960–1961 to about 59,000 tons (60,000 tonnes) in 1978–1979. Application of pesticides became an important component of crop production, particularly in the case of commercial crops like cotton, tobacco, and sugarcane.

Similar to the other inputs, a steep increase in farm mechanization was observed in the production revolution period. Mechanization of irrigation operation expanded rapidly and resulted in a multiplier effect on crop production through crop intensification. This led to the mechanization of other farm operations to ensure timeliness. A steep growth in the number of tractors and other major farm machinery was evident during late 1960s and 1970s.

Yellow (Oilseed) Revolution (1986–1990). The Green Revolution could be called a "cereal revolution," as the thrust was to increase food production to meet the domestic consumption demand. As a result, other crops (oilseeds and pulses [legumes]) were left untouched, and their output levels remained stagnant in the 1970s. In view of the dismal performance of oilseeds during the 1960s and 1970s, the government of India created the Technology Mission on Oilseeds (TMO) in May 1986. The objective of the TMO was to achieve self-sufficiency in edible oils; to achieve this, the TMO implemented the introduction of HYVs of oilseeds, together with the adoption of improved production technology, a better supply of inputs, and extension services and postharvest technologies. Consequently, a major increase in oilseed production was achieved; the production of oilseeds increased from 10.7 million tons (10.83 million tonnes) in 1985–1986 to 24.6 million tons (25 million tonnes) in the late 1990s. Following the success in oilseed production, other crops, including pulses, oil palm, and maize, were brought under the TMO in 1990, 1992–1993, and 1995–1996, respectively.

White Revolution (1970–1996). Technical changes in the livestock sector, including cross-breeding, frozen semen technology, and artificial insemination, were initiated in the 1950s. But the performance of livestock as a whole, and the dairy subsector in particular, was disappointing, with near zero growth during the 1960s. In light of this, the government initiated a massive dairy development program, popularly know as Operation

TABLE 3

Trends in output of various crops

(millions of metric tons)

	Paddy	Wheat	*Jowar*	*Bajra*	Maize
1966–1967	30.4	11.4	9.2	4.5	4.9
1969–1970	40.4	20.1	9.7	5.3	5.7
1979–1980	42.3	31.8	11.7	4.0	5.6
1989–1990	73.6	49.9	12.9	6.7	9.7
1999–2000	89.7	76.4	8.7	5.8	11.5

SOURCE: Compiled from *Agricultural Statistics at a Glance*, Department of Economics and Statistics, Ministry of Agriculture, Government of India, New Delhi, August 2004.

Flood, in 1970. Veghese Kurien was the principal architect of the program, which was implemented in three phases from 1971 to 1996, with support from the European Economic Community, the World Food Programme, and a soft loan from the World Bank.

The aim of the program was to expand milk production through processing and marketing facilities. Toward this objective, milk producers' cooperatives were organized to collect, process, and sell milk to achieve a secured market and remunerative prices. Further, in order to enhance milk production, inputs such as better feed and fodder, breed improvement through artificial insemination, and disease control measures were also arranged through cooperatives. This coordinated effort led to an increase in milk production and ushered in an era of "White Revolution." During this period, milk production increased at an annual average growth of about 5 percent. Consequently, milk production in India increased from 21.6 million tons (22 million tonnes) in 1970 to 29.6 million tons (30.1 million tonnes) in 1980–1981 (first phase) and to 78.7 million tons (80 million tonnes) in 2000–2001 (following the second and third phases).

Blue Revolution. Fishing has been practiced traditionally in the coastal states of India since ancient times. The importance of introducing scientific fishing to increase productivity was recognized, and the Indian Council of Agricultural Research (ICAR) implemented an All India Coordinated Research Project on Brackishwater Fish Farming (1973–1984). The objective of the program was to develop and test various farming technologies under different agro-climatic conditions of the country. The main center of the project was located in West Bengal; other centers were located in Orissa, Andhra Pradesh, Tamil Nadu, Kerala, and Goa for demonstrating the technologies to small-scale farmers. In addition, shrimp hatchery technology was also introduced into the country, and two commercial hatcheries were established in the late 1980s with an initiative from the Marine Products Export Development Authority. As a result, the production of fisheries, particularly of inland fisheries, increased significantly, at an average annual growth rate of 7.1 percent and 6.2 percent during the 1980s and 1990s, respectively. By 2002 India had become the third largest producer of fish. The growth of inland fisheries outpaced the growth in marine fisheries, primarily due to a rapid expansion of shrimp farming in the coastal states of the country.

Period of Market Reforms (1991–2000)

There were no significant economic reforms directed toward agriculture, except the removal of the quota system with the inception of the World Trade Organization. However, the devaluation of the rupee in 1991, as part of the financial reforms, triggered the growth of agricultural exports. Among agricultural products, exports of fruits and vegetables, meat, and marine products recorded a significant increase throughout the 1990s as a result of growing international trade in these products, underscoring the significance of postharvest and agro-processing technology in promoting exports.

Agro-processing. The growing market reforms and commercialization of agriculture has created a need for processing and postharvest handling of agricultural produce. Processing adds value, enhances shelf life, and minimizes losses. As the productivity levels of almost all crops reached near stagnation in the 1990s, processing technology emerged as an alternative for increasing the availability of food products through minimizing losses and enhancing shelf life. In addition, growing urbanization has also led to a significant increase in domestic demand for processed and packaged agricultural products. In order to encourage food processing, the government of India has taken a number of steps, first creating the Ministry for Food Processing Industries in 1988. The ministry has taken many initiatives, such as integrated food law, the creation of cold storage facilities, and the establishment of food parks (centers for distribution of all the processed grains and horticultural products across the country). As a result, the food processing industry expanded significantly in 1990s. Recognizing the potential and comparative advantage that India has in the agro-processing industry, a number of agro-export zones were established across the country. Thus, it is the changes in postharvest technology that have dominated Indian agriculture since the 1990s.

Genetically engineered crop varieties. Near stagnation in yields of all field crops in the 1990s created the need to look for alternative technology that can further boost crop yields. In this context, genetic engineering appeared to be a promising choice. Genetically engineering has been widely used in the pharmaceutical industry, but its entry into the agriculture sector has been surrounded by apprehensions. In India, the efforts initiated in the late 1990s to release the first genetically engineered crop, "Bt cotton," were not successful until 2002, due to strong protests from environmentalists. On the other hand, several research units under ICAR and state agricultural universities have been working to develop genetically modified crops suitable for Indian conditions. However, the dilemmas concerning the commercial cultivation of genetically engineered crop varieties still persist, owing to the serious concerns of biosafety and biodiversity.

See also **Agricultural Growth and Diversification since 1991; Agricultural Labor and Wages since 1950; Economic Reforms of 1991**

L. Thulasamma

BIBLIOGRAPHY

Economic and Political Weekly Research Foundation. *National Accounts Statistics of India 2003–04*. Mumbai: EPWRF, 2004.

Fertilizers Association of India. *Fertilizer Statistics of India*. New Delhi: FAI, 2004.

Government of India. Department of Economics and Statistics. Ministry of Agriculture. *Agricultural Statistics at a Glance*. New Delhi: GOI, August 2004.

Government of India. Economic Division. Ministry of Finance. *Economic Survey 2004–05*. New Delhi: GOI, February 2005.

Kerr, John, Ganesh Pangare, and Vasudha L. Pangare. "Watershed Development Projects in India: An Evaluation." Research Report 127. Washington, D.C.: International Food Policy Research Institute, December 2002.

Randhawa, M. S. *A History of Agriculture in India*, vol. IV. New Delhi: Indian Council of Agricultural Research, 1986.

Socolofsky, H. E. "The World Food Crisis and Progress in Wheat Breeding." *Agricultural History* 43 (October 1969).

TEMPLE TYPES (STYLES) OF INDIA The forms of the Hindu temple are based on a rich blending of imageries, including most significantly those drawn from the ritual requirements of Vedic sacrifice and the hierarchical arrangements and towered forms of the royal palace. The geographic spread of the styles through which this imagery is expressed roughly parallels that of India's numerous languages, in a wide range of local vernaculars that fit generally into northern, Nāgara, and southern, Dravida, regional traditions. Their chronological development is framed by the regnal eras of the dynastic powers governing their patronage.

Though we may consider any Indian shrine for icon worship a Hindu temple, the elite, refined (*samskrita*) temples constructed in brick and stone, or excavated from the living rock of a promontory, have received the most prestigious patronage over the centuries and—because they have survived—the greatest recognition by modern cultural historians. The vast majority of these *devasthāna* or *prāsāda* (places or palaces of the gods) are Brahmanical, but Jains, Buddhists, and other sects have had closely comparable temples constructed or excavated by the same communities of artisans and more or less according to the same quasi-textual principles. Their remains in the ancient period extend beyond the borders of modern India to the historical limits of Indic culture, reaching as far north and west as Afghanistan, as far east as Bangladesh, south to the island of Sri Lanka.

The oldest evidence of these temples can be traced to the emergence of monumental arts in stone of the Maurya period of the third century B.C. The rock-cut Lomas Rishi and Sudhama excavations of the Barabar Hills in Bihar preserve in their outlines the essential form that has lasted to this day, of inner and outer chambers, constructed on carefully proportioned, symmetrical, geometric layouts, oriented to the celestial axes, and crowned with domed or vaulted ceilings. The Barabar Hills excavations were created for the Ajivika sect. Among the earliest representations we have of a Brahmanical temple is the stone relief depiction of the domed Sudhammā Deva Sabhā (the Holy Assembly Hall of the Gods) enshrining the Buddha's turban as an object of veneration, attached to the multistoried Vijayanta Pasāde (Victorious Palace) of Indra, on a railing pillar from the Buddhist stupa at Bharhut, from about 100 B.C. It shows a design quite similar to the Barabar Hills pair, of a rectilinear hall connecting to a domed chamber. As the palace of a Brahmanical deity enshrining an object of worship, it is quite literally a Hindu temple. Both designs represent wood-framed structures, carefully articulated to display refined carpentry and joinery, as contrasted with the less refined wattle and daub constructions represented for common, vernacular dwellings in early Buddhist reliefs.

The oldest texts referring to the construction of Hindu temples, such as the sixth-century A.D. Brihat Saṃhitā, and the later Vāstu Shāstras, like the Mayamata, explain the devotional temple for the worship of Purāṇic deities as the equivalent of a Vedic sacrifice, both in the process by which the metaphysical (*sūkshma*) significance is implanted in its physical (*sthūla*) structure and in the benefits its construction achieves for its *yajamana* (sacrificer) patron. Prior to the construction of the temple, the metaphysical design was inscribed upon the chosen site as a *vāstu mandala* (sacred grid) with its various *pada* (squares) assigned to different deities. The main deity occupies the central squares of the grid, with subordinate

Mahabodhi temple complex in Bodh Gayā. Dating from the late Gupta period (fifth or sixth century), it is one of the earliest Buddhist temples built entirely in brick still standing in India. LINDSAY HEBBERD / CORBIS.

deities occupying the separate *pada*, cells of the inner and outer surrounding bands of the grid. These geometric forms are not a ground plan for the temple, but a conceptual model for the *parivārālaya-prākīra*, the concentric cloisters of chambers surrounding the *deva* (king or deity), which is the ideal form of both the royal palace and the refined Hindu temple.

Unlike the architectural systems of Europe or East Asia, where structures are conceptualized as being assembled from bays, measuring the space from one support column to the next, Hindu temples are conceived as assemblages of compartments. Even more distinctively, the Brahmanical temple is conceived as a transcendental entity. Once consecrated, it is as much the body of the gods it enshrines as the sanctum icons that represent them in figurative and symbolic form. As the worshipers pass through the temple's halls on their way to the witness the deity in its sanctum, they pass within the cloister

Gangotri Temple. In the hinterlands of the Himalayas, in Uttar Pradesh, the River Ganges, the "stream of life," begins its flow. Built in the eighteenth century, the Gangotri temple marks this spot and is the destination of many Hindu pilgrims who often perform rituals in the surrounding cascading waters. CHRIS LISLE / CORBIS.

of compartments inhabited by the main god's surrounding divinities.

The forms of the Vedic altars, ritual *mandalas*, cosmic mountains, and gods' chariots are all models for the stone temple, but it is the imagery of the royal palace that dominates the temple's visible forms and ritual operation. The temple is the god's palace, constructed as a handsome, domed and turreted mansion of inner and outer quarters, where the deity is represented in human (as well as symbolic) form, surrounded by its court of subordinate beings and served by its human priests and worshipers. Though they are mural structures of brick or stone masonry, these celestial mansions are articulated to represent the wood frame construction, with plaster walls and thatched roofs, of contemporaneous palaces. The hierarchy of the central deity surrounded by ranges of demigods and lesser beings, protected by walls excluding

those of the lowest castes, proclaims the social hierarchy of the *varṇa* system.

The simplest temples are (usually though not necessarily) square sanctums (*garbha griha*) covered by vaulted towers, oriented toward one of the cardinal directions. Normally the sanctum is preceded by a porch or a hall where worshipers can go to approach the god, and the temple sanctum carries a tower representing multiple stories, to signify the enclosing rings of encircling deities, the *parivāra-devatā*, of the god's retinue, described in the Shāstras.

Textual references to these temples go back to Pānini, in the fourth century B.C. The earliest structural temple remains are archaeological fragments, and inscriptions on structures that have long since disintegrated. The earliest preserved of these sites, like Nagari and Nagarjunakonda, show elongated halls on rectilinear and apsidal plans, located within walled compounds more or less in the forms seen more fully in the interiors of the Buddhist *caitya griha* at the contemporaneous rock-hewn sites of Bhaja, Nasik, and Ajanta.

Historic Remains

The most striking element of temple form, from the earliest examples to the present, have been the towers—called *vimāna* in the south, *shikhara* in the north—that reach over their sanctums, indicating the location of the deity, and symbolically depicting the deity as surrounded by its numerous subordinate deities. The ornate forms of these towers are the most prominent displays of their distinctive styles.

The Shilpa Shāstra texts divide the myriad temple types into Nāgara (northern), Dravida (southern), and Vesera (mixed), according to the shapes of their towers. The full scope of these traditions extends beyond the tower forms to their entire structural and ornamental vocabularies, including pillar, doorway, wall niche, architrave, and molding orders. The great majority of fine stone temples can be classed into local varieties of northern or southern regional traditions, or a combination of the two.

The locations of the Nāgara and Dravida traditions coincide roughly with the regions associated with Indo-European and Dravidian language use, upon which much Indic culture is organized, expressing a conscious alignment with that pattern. The Dravida traditions, with their additive combination of fully formed miniature *kūta* (sanctum depictions) are in accord with the agglutinative nature of Dravidian languages, much as the highly elided, nonagglutinative form of the Nāgara traditions suit Indo-European languages. Geographically the Nāgara style extends farther south than the concentration of Indo-

European language use, beyond the Krishna and Tungabhadra rivers, which are more or less the northern limit of the Dravida style. Many sorts of Vesera (mixed) style temples can be found in the upper Krishna and Tungabhadra basins, where the two macroregions overlap.

The earliest surviving Brahmanical temple remains, such as the brick temple at Bhitargaon and the rock-cut shrines of Udayagiri Vidisa, come from the fifth century A.D. and display the gradual emergence of the two style traditions. By the sixth century, temples in a number of places show them in their distinctive forms.

The Dravida Style

The mid-sixth century A.D. South Temple of the Rāvaṇa Phadi complex at Aihole offers us what is likely the simplest and possibly the earliest surviving example of the Dravida style. It is a cubical sanctum, raised on a molded basement, crowned by a four-sided cupola, and preceded by a porch. It is a simple *ekatala vimāna* (single-story sanctum). The Dravida style is characterized by the crowning of every significant element with a domed superstructure, if not such a square vault then a round, apsidal, eight-sided, or oblong (barrel) vault.

A glance toward the contemporaneous rock-cut shrine beside the South Temple shows a facade representing a pair of comparable domed pavilions flanking its entrance. As with other rock-cut temples of South Asia, the promontory into which the temple is excavated expresses its tower. A difference between the Nidhi (wealth deity) shrines, represented in relief on the cave facade, and the freestanding South Temple is the presence of a dormer window, *gavāksha*, in the center of these domes.

The addition and multiplication of such architectural details as this *gavāksha* dormer is one of the key means of developing temple design from the earliest period to this one. The other is the more subtle contouring, proportion, and ornamentation of these forms. The two-story Banantigudi, at nearby Mahakuta, adds a *gavāksha* to the dome and raises it over a pilaster-articulated second story. The subsequent Chalukya Dravida temple on the north fort at Badami raises this simple four-sided dome to a third story, articulates its supporting stories as a *hāra* (cloister) of *kūta* (cells), and sets the entire multistoried tower within a hall articulated to represent a *parivārālaya-prākāra* ring of miniature chambers set in a connecting gallery. By the early eighth century, Dravida temples, like the Malegitti at Badami and the Kailasanatha at Kanchipuram, display eight-sided domes, buttressed by miniature *kūta* and raised over multiple *parivārālaya* stories and surrounding halls.

In the Kailasanatha we can see this essential Dravida prototype articulated spatially in a towered sanctum buttressed by surrounding chambers, set within a courtyard ringed by a free-standing *parivārālaya-prākāra* (courtyard wall of subdeity sanctums). The Virupaksha and Mallikarjuna temples at Pattadakal both display *parivārālaya-prākāra*. This is not because, as was once believed, they were copied from the Kailasanatha, but because this multiplication and elaboration of vaulted pavilions in concentric hierarchies is the essential pattern of the Dravida temple, recognizable in the decorative imagery of its towers, wall entablatures, and door and window pediments.

As the northern and southern style regions coincide roughly with the linguistic-cultural macroregions, the individual Dravida traditions in stone were developed within the vernacular-linguistic regions represented roughly by the modern states of Tamil Nadu, Kerala, Karnataka, and Andhra Pradesh. Within each region they have been most effectively distinguished by the dynasties that have patronized their creation. The imperial Chalukya developed the earliest Dravida tradition of the Kannada-speaking Deccan, and the imperial Pallava the earliest of the Tamil coastal plain. The subsequent traditions in the Tamil region, associated with the patronage of the earlier and later Chola dynasties (ninth to thirteenth centuries), carry on directly from the Pallava in relatively similar forms, enriching some decorative and structural elements and adding others. In the Chola's royal Brihadesvara temple at Tanjavur, the Dravida temple *vimāna* reaches its greatest height, at 216 feet (66 m), and begins to display the multiplication of concentric *prākāra* enclosures and barrel-vaulted *gōpura* (gateways) that become characteristic of larger second-millennium complexes.

We can see an example of this later, developed Dravida temple complex in the multiple sanctums, halls, and enclosing courtyards, of the Bhaktavatsaleshvara at Tirukkalukkundram. The Bhaktavatsaleshvara, which includes structures from as early as the ninth century at its core, reached its present size in the seventeenth century. Though early temple texts require the tower of the main deity to be the tallest structure at a site, it is interesting to note that with the multiplication of concentric temple walls and gateways, we find *gōpura* towers increasing in height as one moves away from the main temple, in a reversal of previously established hierarchy.

With the Vijayanagara dynasties from the fourteenth to the mid-sixteenth centuries, the Tamil regional formula of vast walled compounds was spread to the Deccan, and there is a multiplication of broad, open, multipillared pavilions with elaborate figurative piers. The Kannada Dravida traditions of the Chalukya of Kalyani in the eleventh and twelfth centuries are mostly, though not always, characterized by increasingly profuse decorative detail, and a multiplication of sanctums off a common hall. From the twelfth century on, decorative *kūta* of a distinctively Nāgara type are incorporated in these designs. Thus an essentially Dravida tradition becomes subtly Vesera.

In the Telugu-speaking regions of the Deccan are found styles quite comparable to, but distinct from, those in the Kannada regions. The earliest surviving structural temples there were created under an eastern branch of the Chalukya, carrying a similarly simple, early Dravida style into the ninth and tenth centuries with a growing profusion of ornamentation. The Kalyani Chalukya tradition of Karnataka crossed into Andhra with the spread of that dynasty's power. The progressively enriched and elaborated Deccan Dravida temples of the Telugu Choda, Kakatiya, and Reddi, from the eleventh through the mid-fourteenth centuries, are marked by increasingly elaborate architectural articulation and the development of finely stylized, large-scale figurative imagery.

The most striking variations within the Dravida tradition are found in the styles of the western coastal plain of Kerala and Karnataka, where expansive wood frame roofs crown the designs and wood details take over important elements of the internal decoration as well. That these are essentially Dravida style designs can be seen from the domed pavilions depicted in its stone niche pediments and entablatures, though the dramatic visual impact of its wooden roofs leave much of these walls in shadow, obscuring this element at first glance. The temples of coastal Karnataka combine the wooden superstructures and ornamentation of the southwest coast with Deccan Dravida stone articulation.

While the conservative Dravida traditions of Tamil Nadu have been maintained within a relatively narrow range up to the modern period, changing in proportion, elaboration, and ornamentation but relatively little in their basic forms, the styles of the west coast and the Deccan have continued to create a wide range of local variation.

The Nāgara Style

The Nāgara style articulates the same underlying symbolic forms seen in Dravida temples, in an alternative stylistic tradition. Its distinctive curvilinear *latina* tower presents a more vertical and compactly unified representation of these forms than the layered, horizontal, and segmental display of the Dravida style. It is not as obvious at first glance that the rings of miniature chambers set in concentric hierarchies, raised one story above the other, are depicted on the Nāgara tower, as they are relatively obscured by the abbreviations and fusions of its decorative vocabulary and their subordination to the curvilinear outline and vertical ribs. Where Dravida

forms are composed of separate *kūta* chambers lined up in distinct rows, the *latina shikhara* represents its collection of miniature chambers more subtly, through contractions and combinations, subordinated to the commanding unity of its parabolic silhouette.

The famous Kumrahar plaque of the second century, apparently depicting an early incarnation of the Mahabodhi temple at Bodh Gayā, reveals that this variation existed from an early period. It represents a *shikhara* temple, with four stories rising over its sanctum, the miniature chambers of the upper levels represented not by fully articulated *kūta* but by the abbreviation of *gavāksha* dormers.

At Mahakuta, where eighth-century Nāgara and Dravida temples stand side by side, we can see a clear example of the *latina* tower on the Sangamesvara temple. The wall of the Sangamesvara has a raised central image niche at its center, and subordinated *udgama* (interconnected *gavāksha*) pediments on either side, representing smaller, flanking chambers. The Nāgara tower above continues this imagery with a raised central rib crowning the central niche, flanked by corner ribs over the subordinate bays. Within its curvilinear outline, the Nāgara tower blends its horizontal layers and vertical ribs into a complex unity, capped by the cogged wheel of the crowning *āmalaka*, which is the Nāgara's equivalent of the domical cupola of the Dravida style. (Both traditions add a *kalasha*, a ritual water vessel, above the crown, to signify the temple's ritual consecration.) A continuous *udgama* network blends the central rib into a single unit. The corner ribs, however, are divided into Nāgara *kūta* formed out of two *udgama* layers capped by a corner *āmalaka*. Thus, like the Dravida's *vimāna* tower, the Nāgara's *shikhara* tower represents a palatial, skyscraper crown for the sanctum, composed of story upon story of cloistered chambers.

If we shift our gaze from the Deccan-Nāgara to the Kalinga-Nāgara of Mukhalingam, in coastal Andhra, we can see the *parivārālaya-prākāra* represented on the *mandapa* of the ninth-century Madhukesvara. The Madhukesvara's hall has enlarged replicas of its curvilinear tower at its four corners, linked by a row of miniature towers in reliefs, representing a cloister of Nāgara cells. Comparable *parivārālaya* of cells are represented on most Nāgara sanctums and halls, though this may be obscured by the richness of the ornamentation, depicting the abbreviations and elaborations of the underlying forms.

Nāgara temple designers employed an impressive creativity in devising the bewildering variety of rich decorative schemes to express the uniqueness of each subregional style and each individual temple. The visual emphasis of the tenth-century Lakshmaṇa temple at Khajuraho, in central India, stresses its horizontal layers of molded basements, and walls with figures stacked one over the other, before taking off vertically in its rippling towers. Here too every element is organized into a distinguishable sequence of linked cells, each crowned with an appropriate tower of its own.

The Lakshmaṇa temple shows an evolutionary variation of the Nāgara's curvilinear tower, where the *latina* core is buttressed by *urahshringa* (half-tower) forms on each side, and smaller quarter and three-quarter *shikhara* representations below. Each of these abbreviated towers represents the chamber of an attendant deity. But, in the nonagglutinative northern fashion, the individual cells are integrated into the compound whole through the abbreviations and elisions of modules ambiguously alluded to, rather than literally enunciated.

Preceding the Lakshmaṇa's compound tower, we can see lower, pyramidal roofs, covering its hall and two porches. These layered roofs complement the dramatic verticality of sanctum towers while distinguishing the spaces they cover as less exhalted. There are smaller, subordinate temples standing at the corners of the Lakshmaṇa's subbasement, forming a conventional five-altar (*pañcāyatana*) worship complex.

As North India was divided among a larger number of local dynasties, spread over a wider geographic expanse than in the South, a greater number and variety of local styles were developed. The most widely spread variation of the curvilinear tower is found in the rudimentary-seeming *phāmsanā latina*, seen on the Madukesvara, where the horizontal tiers, visible beneath the *udgama* networks of the usual *latina*, are represented without ornamentation, within the characteristic curvilinear silhouette and crowned by *āmalaka*. We can see one of these towers on the temple beside the Sangamesvara at Mahakuta in the Deccan. Others are found from Gujarat to the Himachal foothills and to coastal Andhra. The Nāgara also makes occasional use of the barrel-vaulted form (called *valabhi* in the North), as seen in the eighth-century Teli-ka-mandir at Gwalior or the Vaital Deul at Bhuvaneswar. Unlike the usual square sanctum, the oblong sanctum is associated with particular deities, the Seven Mothers (Sapta Matrika), or the reclining Anantasayana Vishnu, or the similarly lateral Trivikrama Vishnu.

The later Jain temples of western India represent a variation in which the cloister of exterior chambers is fully developed into discrete sanctums, as can be seen in the fifteenth-century temple of Adinatha at Ranakpur. The Yogini temple layout presents a variant in which the cloister of goddess cells surrounds a Bhairava temple or altar open to the sky, and so usually without a central tower at all. The Buddhist *vihara* layout presents a variant in which the cloister of cells, inhabited by monks, stood alone, without a central structure. In the Mahayana phase, central cells of the cloister were enlarged to situate images of the Buddha.

Regional variations of the Nāgara grew progressively distinct over time, even appropriating a few West Asian decorative elements during the course of the second millennium. The incorporation of domes in Western India, as seen on the entrance pavilions at Ranakpur, provide an example of this appropriation.

The Vesera Style

There are a good number of temples that fit the textual reference to Vesera, or mixed traditions, in the region where the northern and southern traditions overlap, between the upper Krishna and Tungabhadra basins, and as far south as the Kaveri in Karnataka. Early Chalukya temples, from the seventh century on, incorporate distinctive elements from the Nāgara tradition into structures that are essentially Dravida, such as the Nāgara tower on the otherwise Dravida-style Durgā temple at Aihole. More rarely, Dravida elements appear on Nāgara structures, as in the wall entablatures of the Papanatha temple at Pattadakal.

Beginning with Kalyani Chalukya of the later eleventh century, there are temples that go beyond mixing, to blend elements of the two traditions together. The Hoysala, Kesava temple at Somnathpur is the most well-known example of this blending. Its crowning cupola is carved into so many wedge-shaped facets that it approaches the form of the *āmalaka*; its towers are difficult to classify into one style or the other; its niche pediments and miniature decorative elements mix northern-looking elements with southern-looking ones.

In a manner that parallels the spread of northern, Indo-European, elements into the essentially Dravidian languages of Kannada, Telugu, and Tamil, this is essentially a Dravida architectural tradition, incorporating Nāgara elements. The same combination is visible in the Deccan style of capping straight-sided *phāmsanā* towers with domical cupolas at Papanasi and Vijayanagar.

Temple Complexes

From their earliest remains, Hindu temples are found in hierarchical complexes, both as planned ensembles and as irregular assemblages, with smaller and peripheral, subordinated structures, surrounding primary shrines. From the earliest remains onward, we have evidence of enclosing *prākāra* walls and gateways. Nearly all temples of any size include a hall for worshipers attached to the sanctum. Many Shaiva temples in the South and some in the North include a Nandi *mandapa*, for the god's alter-ego, the bull Nandi, who is located facing the sanctum on the longitudinal axis to the east. As time went on, the number of such halls increased. Dancing or offering pavilions are regularly located along the axis leading to the main sanctum in Orissa.

A number of temples were planned in pairs and in ritual or symbolic combinations. Major South Indian temples of the second millennium regularly have *amman* (goddess) shrines beside those of the god. Shiva shrines have separate temples for Chandesa, who is the custodian of Shiva's temple. *Pañcāyatana* arrangements of four subordinate sanctums surrounding a central sanctum are a conventional worship set. Tanks for ritual bathing are a common part of temple complexes. Halls without sanctums normally have flat or relatively lower pyramidal roofs, distinguishing them from the towering *vimāna* or *shikhara* over the deities.

Wherever there are temples of any importance, subordinate temples are likely to be added subsequently, by those wishing to share in the prestige of the original builder or in devotion to the god to whom the temple is dedicated. In many cases these appear to be the temples built by the courtiers or descendants of those who built the primary temples. At prosperous sites, such structures may be added at any time and often in the most irregular of manners, revealing the power of the later patrons rather than any original plan.

The Modern Period

With the Arab, Turkish, and Iranian invasions of the later twelfth century, the patronage of masonry temples declined precipitously in most of northern India. The more cosmopolitan traditions that continued exhibit the impact of new sources and the diminution of earlier continuities. An example of this can be seen in the seventeenth-to nineteenth-century brick temples of Bengal in eastern India, which preserve distinct references to the curvilinear forms of the Nāgara, while evolving a distinctly original new local style. The seventeenth-century temples at Brindaban display a style that blends traditional central Indian Nāgara forms with Mughal and west Indian architectural elements.

Nineteenth- and twentieth-century India saw three notable developments in Hindu temple style. The first was a response to the gradual emergence of a subcontinentally expansive Indian state and enhanced communications, which have resulted in the regional styles of one locale appearing in distant sites through the movement of patrons and artisans. Thus Gujarati temple designs have appeared in Varanasi, Pune, and Chennai, and Dravida style *gōpura* have arisen in New Delhi and Brindaban. The second has been a conscious historicism, based on

traditionalist, and in some cases nationalist, political goals. Large temples in this mode have been patronized by the Birla industrial families in important North Indian cities, like the Lakshminarayana temple in New Delhi and the Sri Venkatesvara temple in Hyderabad. There have also been contrasting modernist structures attempting to transcend previous traditions, in structures like the Anandamayi Ma temple at Varanasi.

Gary Michael Tartakov

See also **Ajanta; Hinduism (Dharma)**

BIBLIOGRAPHY

Bhat, M. Ramakrishna, trans. *Brhatsamhitā: Varāmahira's Brihat Samhitā*. Delhi: Motilal Banarsidass, 1982.
Dagens, Bruno, ed. and trans. *Mayamata*. Delhi: Motilal Banarsidass, 1994.
Kramrisch, Stella. *The Hindu Temple*. 1946. Reprint, Delhi: Motilal Banarsidass, 1976.
Michell, George. *The Hindu Temple: An Introduction to Its Meaning and Forms*. New York: Harper & Row, 1977.
Tartakov, Gary Michael. "The Beginning of Dravidian Temple Architecture in Stone." *Artibus Asiae* 42, no. 4 (1980): 33–99.

TEXTILES

This entry consists of the following articles:

BLOCK-PRINTED

EARLY PAINTED AND PRINTED

KARUPPUR

BLOCK-PRINTED

A practical difficulty in tracing the history of technological processes in India is the paucity of archaeological evidence. Ethnological evidence based on an extremely efficient method of transmission, however, helps to bridge this gap. Added to this is the strong element of social continuity engendered through the workings of caste and *jati* (the endogamous group into which a person is born within which marriages can take place) in the Indian social fabric. India has a great tradition in wool and silk, but the fabric that has received the greatest degree of commercial exploitation is cotton. Cotton, being a cellulose fiber, has not only a lesser affinity to dye than silk, but its light reflection capacity is also inferior. Ornamentation can thus be introduced more through variation in color and, to a lesser extent, through diversity in weave. The presence of a fragment of mordanted cotton yarn in Mohenjo-Daro, circa 3500–2500 B.C., attests to the mastery in dye chemistry achieved in South Asia since early times. It is evident that once the dye process had been understood it would be easy to embark

Worker Imprints a Bolt of Cotton, Jaiphur, 1987. In India the expanding middle classes and a Westernized lifestyle have widened the market in block-printed textiles, in spite of growing competition from other emergent forms and materials. ZEN ICKNOW / CORBIS.

on the next step, that of selective application of mordant and resist through block or pen to control the range in color and pattern. When the term "block printing" is used in relation to natural dyes, it is important to remember that the block controls the application of resist and mordant on the material. It is on the basis of the application of mordant and resist that the desired color spectrum is developed. Turmeric and saffron, for yellow, and indigo, for blue, do not require the imposition of mordant.

Tradition

Merutunga, who recorded conditions in Gujarat (c. 884–1194), suggests that block printing was by then well established in the area. Hemachandra, born 1089 and hailing from the same region, also supports this. However, the earliest block-printed fragments of western Indian provenance found in Quseir al-Qadim, Egypt, have been dated to the thirteenth to fourteenth centuries.

The practice of block-printed textiles is spread over a large area in northern, western, and central India, inclusive

of the Gangetic belt. The northern belt includes the Jammu region and Punjab. The printing is unrefined and shares the characteristics of the tradition of Tajikistan, Uzbekistan, and Georgia. The Gangetic belt is represented in Mathura, Tanda, Lucknow, and Farrukhabad. Jafarganj, near Fatehpur in Uttar Pradesh, was a celebrated center of printing in 1908. Its characteristic feature was color: vibrant red and striking blue. Mathura, being a pilgrim center, catered to an all-India market; a specialty was the *nāmavalī*, a printed shoulder cloth for ritual use. The background color ranged between yellow and ocher, and the names of deities and sacred symbols were printed on this. Tanda reflected the Mathura tradition and had markets in Nepal and Bhutan. Lucknow and Farrukhabad specialized in the "tree of life" motif and were influenced by the Persian style in ornamentation. West Bengal, having a superlative tradition in weaving, diversified into printing only in the nineteenth century. A description of cotton manufacture in Dhaka, dated to 1851, refers to the community of *chipigur,* who printed lines or passages from the Vedas on cloth for the Hindu community. The Muslim community utilized their services for the printing of appropriate Qur'anic texts on their winding sheets, or *kuffan*.

The western Indian belt, characterized by the use of mud resist, comprises printing centers in Gujarat, Rajasthan, and Madhya Pradesh. Individual centers, each having variations in technique, comprise the Ajrakh (a type of mud resist printing practiced on the western part of the subcontinent) printing centers of Kutch (Gujarat) and Barmer (Rajasthan); ritual cloth (dedicated to the Mother Goddess, the *Māthāji ne Pacheī*) is printed in Ahmedabad; Bagru, Sanganer (Rajasthan), and Rajapur-Deesa (Gujarat) share a common technique, while Bagh and Bhairongarh represent two variants in Madhya Pradesh. Mud and lime resist are well suited to somewhat coarsely woven cotton. However, if more delicate work is required, wax resist is preferred. Georges Roques, of the French East Indian Company, noted the printing of wax resist in Ahmedabad in 1678. Wax resist was the dominant mode in South India, but it was *kalam* (brush) painted rather than block printed. The practice of *kalamkari* block printing in Masulipatam is a nineteenth-century innovation.

There is also evidence of clamp-resist printing on silk in Gujarat. This technique is also practiced in Nepal and Tibet for decorating the mounting of Buddhist ritual paintings, or *thankha*. A characteristic feature of this form is the outlining of motifs in a white aura, rather than defining the outline in black. The sumptuous textiles depicted in Jain Kalpa Sūtra manuscripts share the former characteristic and could be taken as depictions of silk ornamentation through the procedure of clamp resist.

Technique

There are several stages in cloth printing. These include initial preparation of cloth by removal of impurities, smoothening the texture, bleaching by dunging, a natural agent, and preparation of the fiber for enhanced penetration of the mordant. There is no application of the block at this stage. The cloth is then thoroughly washed, preferably in the flowing waters of a river or stream.

The next stage is that of mordanting. Mordant is a chemical substance that enables cotton to absorb and retain certain dyes. Mordants can either be acid or basic (alkaline). Acid mordants are tannin based. The most common source in India is either myrobalam (*Terminalia chebula*) or catechu (Hindi, *katha*; *Acacia catechu*). Basic mordants are derived from salts of various metals, particularly aluminum, chromium, iron, copper, zinc, or tin. Alum is the one most commonly used in India. Alkali from *surti kar* (saltpeter) or *sapan kar* (carbonate of soda)

has been used for *al* (*Morinda citrifolia*) dyeing in Berar. After mordanting, the fabric is boiled in a cauldron along with the dyestuff. The vessel can be of earthenware, copper, or iron. In the latter two cases, the metal containers themselves contribute an element to the mordanting process, thereby introducing variations in shade and hue.

Other aspects of the dyeing procedure include the use of items such as *jajakku* (*Memecylon edule*) in Tamil Nadu, or *padvas* (*Narigama alta*) in Gujarat, which act as carriers during the dyeing operation. In the case of *al*, on termination of the dyeing process alum or *dhā* (*Woodfordia floribunda*), is used as a fixing agent.

The application of resist is associated with indigo dyeing. The resist is derived from wax, mud, or lime. The dye is reconstituted in the vat through a process of fermentation. A cold vat is used. Although indigo blue is a stable color, it tends to rub off. Rubbing fastness can be improved by a final soaking in catechu. The technology of indigo printing had also been developed and practiced in India. Jean Ryhiner in 1766 referred to the Indian method of indigo printing with the use of orpiment, sulfur of arsenic, the liquid being further thickened with gum.

Design and Use

Although there is some congruity between woven and printed design, the latter offers a much greater degree of freedom in terms of layout and pattern. The costume of traditional India has been the multifunctional unstitched garment. It remains so in many sections of rural India. The patterning, whether woven or printed, is composed of two borders along the horizontal edges and crossborders defining the two vertical end alignments. In the female costume, the sari, the cross-border at the exposed terminal end can be elaborately designed to set it off from the inner field.

The *Mānasōllāsa*, authored by the Chalukyan king Sōmeshvara III (r. 1127–1139), provides comprehensive coverage of textile design in the section titled *Vastrōpabhōga* (using or enjoying of clothes by the king). In addition to geometrical motifs, floral, vegetal, animal, bird, and fish motifs could be used. *Ikat* and *plangi* motifs (which indicate the method by which the yarn to be used in weaving is tied according to pattern and dyed) could also be duplicated in block print. With the introduction of Islam, stitched garments became popular, leading to more elaborate all-over patterning. The *buteh* and the *badam* (popularly known as paisley) now emerged in a more distinctive manner. Tinsel printing, in which gum was applied with the block, was another innovation. Draperies began to emerge as a separate category. The forest was a place of retreat and contemplation in Hindu imagery, while the hunt had symbolic overtones in Islamic culture. The palace was no longer fixed in location, and the roving camp of the king became the shifting imperial capital, with tent hangings providing much play to the imagination in the area of block printing. It was against this background that block-printed chintz design materialized with the advent of the Europeans, heralded by the arrival of Vasco da Gama on the Malabar coast.

Today the impact of the export market, accompanied by the onset of globalization, has led to many changes. Masulipatam has managed to sustain an export market without a total loss of identity. Screen printing has begun to make considerable inroads. The expanding middle classes and a Westernized lifestyle have widened the market in block-printed textiles, despite severe competition from other emergent forms and materials.

Lotika Varadarajan

BIBLIOGRAPHY

Barnes, Ruth. *Indian Block Printed Textiles in Egypt: The Newberry Collection in the Ashmolean Museum, Oxford*. New York: Clarendon Press, 1997.

Berinstain, Valérie, ed. *La manière de négocier aux Indes par Georges Roques*. Paris: Maisonneuve & Larose, 1997.

Bühler, A., and E. Fischer. *Clamp Resist Dyeing of Fabrics*. Ahmedabad: Calico Museum of Textiles, 1977.

Chandramouli, K. V. *Natural Dyes of India*. Mimeograph. Bangalore: Regional Design and Technical Development Centre, 1980.

A Former Resident of Dacca. A *Descriptive and Historical Account of the Cotton Manufacture of Dacca, in Bengal*. London: British Museum, 1851.

Loubo-Lesnitchenko, E. "La Technique du 'Jan-Kie' dans la Chine du Moyen-Age." *Bulletin de liaison du CIETA* 11 (1971): 75–96.

Mohanty, B. C., K. V. Chandramouli, and H. D. Naik. *Natural Dyeing Processes of India*. Ahmedabad: Calico Museum of Textiles, 1987.

Technical Objects from India and High Asia Collected by Hermann, Adolphe and Robert Schlagintweit, 1854–1858. London: British Museum.

Varadarajan, Lotika. *South Indian Traditions of Kalamkari*. Mumbai: Perennial Press, 1982.

———. *Traditions of Textile Printing in Kutch, Ajrakh and Related Techniques*. Ahmedabad: New Order Book Company, 1983.

EARLY PAINTED AND PRINTED

India's mastery over permanent dyes can be traced back to Harappan civilization (3000 B.C.) with the discovery of a fine cotton fragment dyed with mordants, attached to a silver vase. The export of dyed cotton must have been carried out during this period, as dye vats were found at Lothal, a Harappan port in Gujarat. There are hardly any fragments of printed and dyed cloth except for tie-dyed fabric (c. 1000 B.C.) found in Central Asia by Sir Auriel

Antique *ghagra* Skirt. In the state of Rajasthan, an often barren and colorless landscape, villagers and royalty alike commonly wear brightly colored, brilliantly detailed clothing. ADITYA PATANKAR / FOTOMEDIA.

Stien. Fragments were later found in Fostat and at Red Sea ports, dating to the thirteenth century A.D. The latest carbon dating has dated some fragments to the tenth century A.D.

Early literary sources mention the importance of the printing and dyeing industry. The Greek physician Ktesias (fl. 500 B.C.), while visiting Persia, mentioned "flowered cottons with glowing colors," greatly coveted by Persian women and imported from India. *The Periplus of the Erytherian Sea*, a first-century Roman record, gives a list of printing centers of western India, and Pliny commented that Roman coffers of gold were being depleted by the import of Indian cottons to satisfy the vanity of Roman women. It was the durability and brilliance of Indian cottons that made them renowned throughout the world.

Traditional Block-Printed Fabric from Sanganer, Rajasthan. Sanganer remains a center for textile dyeing and printing that utilize centuries-old techniques. In the printing process, cloth is spread on wax-coated tables and color in the form of a paste is applied through screens. AMAR TALWAR / FOTOMEDIA.

The eastern coast had ancient links with Southeast Asia. Kalinga (present-day Orissa) had been greatly enriched by Southeast Asian trade during the pre-Buddhist era. Southeast Asia must also have had contacts with the west coast, as early examples of semiprecious agate stone beads excavated at Lothal were found in Indonesian grave sites dating to 500 B.C. Indian as well as Arab traders used printed Indian cottons as currency, exchanging them for spices, as Indonesian islanders were not interested in bullion. Carbon dating of recent discoveries of fine Indian printed and painted cottons from Indonesia, especially from Toraja in Sulawesi, has given an accurate early date not only to these textiles, but also to printed cottons found in Fostat and Red Sea ports.

Europeans entered the trade in printed textiles much later, while Indians, Chinese, and Arabs had been trading from prehistoric times. The Portuguese were the earliest Europeans, followed by the Dutch, the French, and the English. They traded with the Spice Islands, as well as carrying printed cloth (which came to be known as chintz) to Europe.

The finest centers for Indian printing were in Sind, Gujarat, Rajasthan, Madhya Pradesh, Bengal, Delhi, Farrukhabad, Golconda, Masalipatnam, Madras (Chennai), Pulicat, and Tanjore. The printers, *chipa*, were of a separate community from the dyers, *rangrez*. In Kalamkari, also known as *vartapani*, all three techniques—painting, printing and dyeing—were done by one community.

The block makers came from the carpenters' community, but many were dedicated solely to the creation of printing blocks, requiring great skill. An old family of block makers survives in Pethapur, Gujarat. For generations they prepared the fine blocks for printed cloth exported to Thailand, known as Sodagiri, trade cloth. Farrukhabad, an important center for printing the large Tree of Life known as *palampore* during the nineteenth century, also had specialized block carvers.

Printing Technique

The hand printing of traditional textiles prepared with the use of wooden blocks was of three kinds: direct printing, resist printing, and outline block printing augmented by hand painting. Direct printing was done on bleached cloth prepared with mordants for dye absorption; on this surface the outline block was printed, followed by a fill-in block for coloring both the outlined motif and the background. In resist printing, blocks were used to create the outline; the motif was then printed with another color, then covered with a resist material, either mud or wax, and dyed. Indigo dyed cloths were prepared using this technique, as indigo could not be used for printing with blocks. Fragments found at Fostat and Red Sea sites followed these techniques and were made in Western India. Recent finds in Indonesia have the same patterns and have been carbon dated to the tenth century. Printing carried out in large quantities in Southeast Asia especially for the Spice Islands was done at Masalipatnam using a combination of printing and painting while very fine cloths were hand painted.

Hangings from South India, known as *kalamkari* or *varatapani*, were entirely hand painted. The finest were prepared at the court ateliers of Golconda and appear to be the work of master painters working with dyes. They were like large-scale murals, similar in style to the Persian murals of the Saffavid period in Isfahan, but using Indian imagery. The large hangings created for temples were of a different style, generally using themes taken from the Rāmāyaṇa. Episodes were painted and enclosed within a frame in narrative form, with verses describing the scene painted below. These were of ritual importance in Hindu temples. Special cloths of *kalamkari* with the battle scene from the Rāmāyaṇa, showing the victory of good over evil, were made for export to Indonesia.

Gujarat produced elaborate hangings with large female figures created in western Indian style with a three-quarter face and a protruding eye. Some of these were created with blocks and then colored by hand, while others were entirely hand painted, with each figure appearing to be a portrait. These examples have all been discovered in the family "treasure chests" in Toraja. Some have been dated to the fourteenth century A.D. The tradition of figurative hangings existed from ancient times. The older Pechwais of Shrī Nath cult were printed and painted.

Consumption and Export

The printing centers produced a range of textiles for local consumption and a different style for export. Local production carried the distinctive designs and colors of each caste. There were also different designs for rites of passage, as well as for different age groups. Ritual cloths with the attributes of different deities accompanied by a printed *sloka*, or litany, such as "victory to Durgā," were for use by priests as well as householders performing rituals.

During the Sultanate period (13th–15th centuries), royal ateliers produced cloths for the court, particularly printed tents and canopies. Printed and painted tent walls of very fine quality have survived from the Mughal period (late 16th–18th centuries). Ain-e-Akbari gives a detailed description of the tented Mughal court (created while on the move), which used the richest fabrics, among which printed and painted fabrics were prominent. The Jaipur court atelier produced very fine printed cloths for use by the royalty and the courtiers, and examples from the seventeenth century are maintained in the City Palace Museum at Jaipur. The detailed "account books," *bahi khata*, of the ateliers are preserved in the archives at Bikaner.

The export of textiles from India to Europe had been carried out from a very early period through Fostat, which had become the major port center for the distribution of printed cotton (thus the name given to these cloths, "fustian"). The records of an Anglo-Saxon Synod Calcyth of the eighth century A.D. mentions that priests were discouraged from using Indian dyed cloth. Agnes Geijner (1951) mentions references to fustian cloth as a luxury item, hence forbidden for use by clergy in Scandinavia.

At the end of the fifteenth century, Vasco da Gama landed on the southeastern coast at Calicut, which later gave its name to "calico." The Portuguese seized power from the local Muslim ruler, the *zamorin*, winning their first base in India. They controlled trade from the area; among the commodities they took back were printed fabrics, which they called *pintadoes*. These later found their way into the European market.

In the early sixteenth century, regular trade in printed and painted cloth began to be developed with Europe, after the Dutch, French, and English set up their "factories" along India's coasts, creating a more organized system of Indian ocean trade. By the early seventeenth century, the resident European representatives began to exert a stronger influence; elaborate detailed patterns began coming from Europe, and Indian printers and dyers began creating textiles for the lucrative European market. The Indian word for a fabric printed with a sprinkling of flowers was *chint* (sprinkled), transformed in the West into "chintz." English patterns combined Indian motifs with chinoiserie as well as motifs taken from the Balkans. Trailing flowing patterns with subtle color combinations were developed. These created so great a demand that by 1664 the English alone imported 250,000 "calicoes." The French, who had entered the scene with La Compaigne des Indes Orientales with factors on the western and eastern coast near Kolkota (Calcutta), became competitors of the British East India Company, until their defeat by the English army under Robert Clive.

The craze for Indian printed goods reached its zenith by the last quarter of the seventeenth century, when British and French textile producers exerted influence on their own governments to ban the import of Indian cotton. Indian cotton of all kinds was banned in France in 1686 and in England in 1700. India continued to export cloth to Holland, but the demand for Indian cottons decreased considerably.

The import of printed textiles into Southeast Asia continued until the nineteenth century but decreased considerably because of the growth of the local Indonesian batik and printing industry. By the twentieth century, the import of mill-printed wax prints from Holland captured that market. World War I broke whatever links had existed between Indonesia, Malaysia, and Thailand with India's Masalipatnam and Gujarat, and printed cotton ceased to be exported to Southeast Asia.

The printers continued to supply the local market with printed yardage for skirts, saris, and veils, as well as quilt covers and floor spreads. However, they faced severe competition from mill-made printed fabrics from Manchester, as well as from Bombay's machine-made prints. The loss of major overseas export markets and dwindling local markets created great hardship for the Indian printers, who began producing crude, cheaper prints to compete with the machine-made goods, selling them at very low prices. By the mid-twentieth century, the All-India Handicrafts Board began a special project for research, design, and promotion of hand prints, and a number of centers throughout India were revived. Exhibitions were conducted in India and abroad, and the printing industry soon revived. Today many of the centers, which had previously stagnated, are producing very fine quality printed fabrics, using both synthetic and vegetable dyes.

Jasleen Dhamija

See also **Bandhani**

BIBLIOGRAPHY

Barnes, Ruth. *Indian Block Printed Textiles in Egypt: The Newberry Collection in the Ashmolean Museum, Oxford*, New York: Clarendon Press, 1997.
Dhamija, Jasleen. *Indian Folk Arts and Crafts.* New Delhi: National Book Trust, 1970.
———. *Woven Magic*. Jakarta: Dina Rakyat, 2002.
Geijner, Agnes. *Oriental Textiles in Sweden*. Copenhagen: Rosenkilde and Bagger, 1951.
Gittinger, Mattibelle. *Master Dyers to the World: Technique and Trade in Early Indian Dyed Cotton Textiles*. Washington, D.C.: Textile Museum, 1982.
Guy, John. *Woven Cargoes: Indian Textiles in the East*. London: Thames & Hudson, 1998.
Irwin, John. "Indian Textile Trade in the Seventeenth Century." *Journal of Indian Textile History* 1–4 (1955–1958).
———. "Golconda Cotton Painting of the Early Seventeenth Century." *Lalit Kala* 5 (1959).
Irwin, John, and Katherine B. Brett. *Origins of Chintz, with a Catalogue of Indo-European Cotton-Paintings in the Victoria and Albert Museum*. London: H. M. Stationery Office, 1970.
Irwin, John, and Margaret Hall. *Indian Painted and Printed Fabrics*. Ahmedabad: Calico Museum of Textiles, 1971.
Maxwell, Robyn. *Textiles of South East Asia: Traditions, Trade, and Transformation*. New York: Oxford University Press, 1990.
Singh, Chandramani. *Textiles and Costumes from the Maharaj Sawai Man Singh II Museum*. Jaipur: Maharaj Sawai Man Singh II Museum Trust, 1979.
Varadarajan, Lotika. *South Indian Traditions of Kalamkari*. Mumbai: Perennial Press, 1982.

KARUPPUR

Relatively unknown among ancient textiles, the exquisite textiles of Karuppur can be understood only from existing masterpieces of saris, dhotis (loincloths), and turbans in museum collections, and from written accounts that appear in travelogues from India and abroad. Skilled craftsmen using special techniques appear to have made these textiles only for the royal courts of Tanjore (now known as Thanjavur), and no distribution elsewhere was recorded beyond this lineage, which does not extend past the nineteenth century.

The rulers of Tanjore, particularly Raja Sarfoji (r. 1799–1833), were strongly influenced by British taste and admired Western art in its contemporary neoclassical phase. Under Sarfoji there was a close integration of ancient tradition and European taste, which continued under his successor, Shivaji. There is no way of knowing with any degree of certainty the date at which the village craftsmen of Karuppur began to supply garments to the royal court of Tanjore. No records are available to indicate whether the fine robes had been provided from ancient times or whether they were introduced during the Maratha dynasty. It is certain, however, that the technique itself persisted from early times. Early cotton paintings of South India depict the dyeing technique, in which fine patterns are drawn with molten wax to appear white on the colored ground. The Karuppur textiles use the same technique, and early examples approach the skill of India's greatest craftsmen of the seventeenth century. The saris were still known to have been made in 1855; after that, the craft declined.

One can observe from museum pieces the fine workmanship of Karuppur textiles, which combine richness of pattern with simplicity and elegance, using a technique of resist dyeing and gold brocading. Each textile contains several shades of red and black and, in some pieces, a touch of blue, with hints of gold and the warm ecru color of the natural cotton outlining the design configurations.

The nuances of color and texture change as the cloth is moved slightly. Though the predominant designs of Karuppur textiles tend to be geometrical forms arranged within framing borders and large central fields, the repertoire was not confined to these forms but included other motifs, such as delicate vines, deer, birds, and sometimes stolid elephants arranged in a grid pattern.

In Karuppur textiles, the patterns of gold yarn were worked in the ground, on the cotton warp, using the tapestry technique. The areas that became the centers of the configurations, as well as the lines of borders and panels, were woven in gold, and the rest were in plain weave. The design forms, freely drawn using a *kalam*, or pen, were created using a wax-resist technique; the mordant for red and black was applied, and the cloth dyed a deep red. For perfecting the shades of red and black, two important mordants, alum and iron, were used in varying concentrations. Alum in association with red dye (*rubia tintorium, oldenlandia umbelleta*) created shades of red. Iron, steeped in a sour acidic substance, yielded a mordant that, in conjunction with tannin, produced the black shades. To further enhance the depth of the design forms, selected outlines were enriched with a deeper red, immediately at the edge of the gold. With the exception of the wax-resist areas, the dye was absorbed all over the cloth, including the yarn that formed the core of the loosely wrapped woven gold. This resulted in a graceful blend of texture, with subtle hints of gold embedded in shades of deep red. Some superb samples had the resist applied on both sides, and both faces of the textile have been worked. Certain examples indicate that blocks may also have been used to apply the mordants.

The patterns and the format of the Karuppur textiles resemble features in classic Southeast Asian textiles, indicating that textiles for the Tanjore court were a refinement of existing South Indian traditions of textile design, which had profoundly influenced the East through trade to East Asia as early as the sixteenth and seventeenth centuries. During the late eighteenth and early nineteenth centuries, the patterns of Karuppur textiles seem to have been made in a modest mordant-painted and dyed version, without the wax-resist pattern and gold yarns. The Tanjore book wrappers who used this style of textile without gold, provide additional evidence of hand-painted textiles being made in the area, though the use of carved blocks (to stamp the design) began to displace the hand-painting technique in the early nineteenth century.

During the same period, in the contiguous areas of Kumbakonam and Pudukkotai, artisans appear to have employed the Karuppur technique with slight variations. The Kumbakonam cloth seems to have been prepared first with a red dye mordant, completely covering it and making it gray in color. The design was both hand painted and stamped, using copper perforated blocks dipped in a solution of oxalic acid and sometimes wax, which produced a pattern of white forms on the gray mordant ground. Then the cloth was dyed red.

The intrinsic beauty of the Karuppur textiles is difficult to reproduce today. The existing photographs of these textiles only raise intriguing questions about the techniques used, and their origin continues to be shrouded in the mists of time. Answers may perhaps be found by further study of ancient records in and around Tanjore.

Jagada Rajappa

BIBLIOGRAPHY

Gittinger, Mattiebelle. *Master Dyers to the World.* Washington, D.C.: Textile Museum, 1982.
Hadaway. William S. *Cotton Painting and Printing in the Madras Presidency.* Chennai: Government Press, 1971.
Holder, Edwin. "Dyes and Dyeing in the Madras Presidency." Monographs from School of Arts (Chennai), 28 February 1896: 1–9.
Irwin, John, and Margaret Hall. *Indian Painted and Printed Fabrics.* Ahmedabad: Calico Museum of Textiles, 1971.

THEATER In traditional India, theater is explicitly associated with one deity or another, and the act of performance is an act of worship for performer and congregation alike. Many forms are still staged inside or next to temple precincts, or during religious festivals and holidays on common village grounds. Folk theater often dramatizes episodes from myth and legend pertaining to divinities or devotion. The aesthetics of Indian theater, originating in Bharata's *Nātya Shāstra* (Theater treatise), prioritize performance, inner life, and emotional moods in expressing that life. *Rasa* (literally, "juice" or "flavor") forms the nucleus of this aesthetic. A play must evoke the *rasa*s, of which there are nine, in complementary combinations, with one of them predominant. The nine *rasa*s comprise the erotic, comic, pathetic, heroic, furious, fearful, odious, wondrous, and peaceful. In order to arouse these *rasa*s in the "sympathetic connoisseur," performers must emote appropriate *bhava*s (feelings) throughout. The importance given to emotions causes many non-Indians, preconditioned by their own artistic heritage, to react adversely to Indian drama as being too sentimental and devoid of action.

History

Indian theater history can be classified under three rubrics: classical, traditional, and modern, by no means mutually exclusive or chronologically sequential. Indeed, all three coexist at present. Folk and traditional theater takes place in villages and religious contexts, while

Man Performing in a Hindu Dance Play. Contemporary performance (c. 1972) of *Kathakali*, literally "dance story," in Kerala. CHARLES & JOSETTE LENARS / CORBIS.

modern theater is the preferred urban idiom. Classical theater, strictly speaking, refers to the courtly Sanskrit drama that flowered in the first millennium A.D. It is extinct, like the classical language in which it was written. But some scholars correctly argue that a couple of genres (Kutiyattam and Krishnattam) still use Sanskrit as a living medium, and directly link Kutiyattam to classical Sanskrit theater, pushing back Kutiyattam's conjectural origins because it seems to have preserved the texts and accompanying production manuals of plays by the earliest known Sanskrit dramatist, Bhasa, in apparently unbroken continuity.

Classical. The sources of Indian theater are shrouded in obscurity, though Vedic rituals and recited duologue may have given birth to it in the first millennium B.C. A small cave amphitheater at Sitabenga, in Chhattisgarh state, possibly dates to the third century B.C., while an outdoor arena, perhaps used by Buddhist monks in the second or third century A.D., exists in Nagarjunakonda, in Andhra Pradesh. Bhasa may have composed his works around the turn of the common era, but we have no documents to

prove it. Later writers mentioned his name, but it was only in 1911–1912 that his plays came to light, discovered among manuscripts in a library in Kerala, and identified with texts performed for centuries by Kutiyattam troupes in Kerala temples. Thirteen such scripts were attributed to him, the largest number to have survived by a Sanskrit author. They reveal a wide range, from full-length seven-act plays to one-act miniatures, covering tales from the epics, and always theatrical, rather than simply literary.

Judged by the *Nātya Shāstra* (c. 2nd century B.C. to 4th century A.D.), Bhasa would have either failed its prescriptions or deliberately flouted them. For instance, he shows a hero dying on stage, though the *Nātya Shāstra* forbids such scenes. Other possibilities are that he preceded the *Nātya Shāstra*, or wrote when its principles had not fully crystallized—many authorities consider it to be a compendium accumulated over time. Besides expounding on *rasa*, its thirty-odd chapters offer methodological categorizations of the types of drama; guidelines on music, dance, and architecture; and details of a highly semiotic system of gestures and expression, dividing acting into four components—verbal, physical, internal (emotional), and external (costumes and makeup). We can thus safely deduce that Sanskrit theater, composed by court poets and staged in royal durbars for aristocratic audiences, was uncommonly refined and artistic, with grace, beauty, suggestion, and idealism given primary importance.

Kālidāsa (fifth century) is unanimously acknowledged as the pinnacle among Indian authors in any language, for his masterpiece *Abhijñāna-Sakuntala* (Recognition of Sakuntala). Two of his other plays have survived, but the lyrical romanticism and spiritual intensity of *Sakuntala* gave it an uncontested primacy in Indian drama. The four verses in act 4 when the pregnant Sakuntala bids farewell to her ashram home and her foster father, to leave for her husband who seems to have forgotten her, are regarded as the zenith of *rasa* in Sanskrit poetry. Rediscovered by European Indologists in the late eighteenth century, *Sakuntala* persuaded them to reassess Indian literature and to elevate Sanskrit to levels previously reserved for the Greek and Latin classics.

Sudraka's *Mricchakatika* (Little clay cart, c. 2nd century A.D.) is probably the most revived play in the canon because of its social consciousness; it depicts a successful revolution that overthrows an unpopular ruler. Among later Sanskrit works, Visakhadatta's *Mudrā-Rākshasa* (Rakshasa's ring, 5th century) is an unusual historical drama of realpolitik, with the astute Chanakya, Chandragupta Maurya's minister, as protagonist. The famous king Harsha (r. 606–648) has three romantic plays ascribed to him, of which *Ratnāvali* is the finest. Bhavabhuti (7th–8th centuries), considered by some to be Kalidasa's equal, is best known for *Uttara-Rāmacarita* (Later story of Rāma), a moving and powerful narrative of the epic hero Rāma. A slow degeneration of standards characterized subsequent Sanskrit theater, and for all practical purposes it had ceased to be a creative force by the tenth century. Theater in the colloquial idiom of Prakrit briefly occupied a transitional phase, notably in the output of Rajasekhara (9th–10th centuries).

Traditional. As Sanskrit theater declined, the first indications of performance in the regional languages appeared, coinciding with the formalization of those tongues, descended from the various Prakrits and Apabhramsa. Popular forms unknown to us must have previously entertained the lower castes, parallel to the Sanskrit theater meant for the upper castes. Ancient texts in Tamil make cryptic reference to dance-drama genres and stage preparations, from the beginning of the common era. Certainly, several varieties of Indian puppetry (particularly shadow puppetry) have a long history; the striking similarities between leather puppets in Orissa and Andhra Pradesh and those in Indonesia point to acculturation via mariners from the eastern seaboard who settled in Southeast Asia.

The major influence in the invention of many traditional (formerly known as "folk") forms was the *bhakti* (devotional) movement that spread throughout the subcontinent. Advocating faith in a personal god rather than the institutionalized, priesthood-dominated ceremonies that had accumulated around Brahmanism, reformers needed to propagate their message, and opted for theater as the most effective medium of communication. Between the fourteenth and seventeenth centuries, these Vaishnava forms proliferated, telling stories of Vishnu's avatars, mainly Rāma and Krishna. One of the first, Kirtaniya, was created in the rich literary language of Maithili in northern Bihar by the poets Jyotiriswara (1280–1360) and Vidyapati (1360–1440). By the end of the fifteenth century, Raslila (based on Krishna's *rās* dance) arose in Braj, in western Uttar Pradesh, in a local dialect of Hindi. In the fifteenth and sixteenth centuries, the elaborately accoutred Terukkuttu and Yakshagana developed in Tamil and Kannada, the languages of Tamil Nadu and Karnataka, respectively, followed by Kuchipudi dance-drama in Telugu (Andhra Pradesh), credited to Siddhendra Yogi. The sixteenth century saw *bhakti* theater take shape in eastern India with the active participation of two saints: Jatra (originally called Krishna-jatra) in Bengali received the enthusiastic support of Chaitanya (1486–1533), and Sankaradeva (1449–1568) invented Ankiya Nat in Assamese. Ramlila emerged in Hindi in North India by the seventeenth century, while the Konkani Dasavatar (literally, "ten avatars") in Goa and coastal Maharashtra imitated Yakshagana from neighboring Karnataka. In Kerala, two forms were created: the delicate Krishnattam in Sanskrit by the Zamorin (ruler) of Kozhikode in 1653, and the vigorous Kathakali (initially Ramanattam) in Malayalam by the raja of Kottarakkara in 1661. The former, because of its elite language, remains cloistered in the Guruvayur temple, whereas Kathakali's choice of the mother tongue saw it flourish, into currently the most recognizable face of Indian theater worldwide. After Vaishnavism reached the far eastern state of Manipur, Maharaja Chingthangkhomba sponsored the lyrical Manipuri Ras Lila in 1779. The tribal-cum-martial arts form of Chhau, in Orissa, Jharkhand, and Bengal, also adopted mythical tales for presentation.

It seems useful to distinguish two strains of traditional theater, the temple styles (of worship) from the worldly ones (of comedy and social satire), but considerable overlap occurs. Notwithstanding the intensely spiritual aim, horseplay and frightening scenes are integral to the religious forms, keeping the entire family, especially children, entertained. A few of the originally devotional forms, like

Jatra, gradually metamorphosed into secular ones, though others like Ankiya Nat or Manipuri Ras Lila retained their pristine purity. Some nominally associated with worship appear to have crossed over into subversive comic modes fairly early in their history, and became even more boisterous down the centuries. These include the Bhavai in Gujarati (ascribed to Asaita Thakar, 14th century) and Tamasha in Marathi (probably intended as a diversion for soldiers, from the 18th century). Another major form, the Nautanki in Hindi/Urdu, which evolved in the nineteenth century out of and alongside the Swang in Hindi and Punjabi, may have had tenuous sacred links to begin with, but achieved renown for exquisitely musical renderings of heroic romances. The Bandi Pethir in Kashmiri, whose records go back to the tenth century, is exclusively farcical, its clowns' routines recalling the slapstick of Italian commedia dell'arte.

With the exception of Kirtaniya, all these genres remain alive. Besides, dozens of less popular, but not inferior, forms inhabit the Indian landscape, all increasingly threatened by the incursion of film and television into rural lifestyle in the late twentieth and early twenty-first centuries. They range from ritualistic possession, such as Teyyam and Bhuta on the southwestern coast, to diverse storytelling modes (many of them orally keeping alive the Mahābhārata and Rāmāyaṇa) that incorporate substantial elements of dance and music. This multiplicity of theater is endangered, ironically, by the homogeneity of performance manufactured in the electronic media, whatever the language, which attract mass viewership by their glamour and pretensions to modernity. Villagers prefer to watch the dream-factory-generated pictures of supposedly greener urban pastures, instead of their local entertainers, whom they consider rustic and backward. Their livelihood thereby imperiled, these performers turn to other careers. Also ironically, interculturalists come to India to study these very genres, seeking the secrets of exotic techniques; renowned directors such as Jerzy Grotowski and Peter Brook have borrowed methods from Kathakali or Chhau for their own work.

Modern. The British introduced the proscenium arch auditorium to India, and with it modern (Western) theatrical concepts. Initially, the expatriate communities in the port cities of Calcutta (Kolkata), Bombay (Mumbai), and Madras (Chennai) built playhouses for their own recreation in English, in the eighteenth century. The Bengally Theater (Calcutta, 1795) established by a Russian bandmaster and adventurer, Herasim Lebedeff, pioneered the use of an Indian language on a European-style stage for Indian audiences. The next century witnessed further inroads: the formal reading of English literature by Indian students under Thomas B. Macaulay's education policy; their first amateur attempts at representation

of English drama; their translations of this canon into Indian languages; their emulation of Western models in writing and staging original plays; and, finally, the arrival of full-blown professional theater in every major language. Some regions started earlier—Bengali, Marathi, and Hindi have particularly long lineages of modern theater—whereas in others (Dogri, Konkani, Maithili, Nepali, Rajasthani) modernism began only around the time of India's independence.

The first modern Indian play was composed in English by Krishna Mohan Banerjea in 1831, but was never performed. Titled *The Persecuted, or Dramatic Scenes Illustrative of the Present State of Hindoo Society in Calcutta*, it had a modern topic: for the first time, an Indian dramatist censured living conditions. In 1853, at the Grant Road Theater in Bombay, Vishnudas Bhave produced the first ticketed shows in Marathi, soon followed by Gujarati theater from companies owned by the Parsi (Zoroastrian) community. The same year, Urdu theater commenced in Lucknow with Amanat's *Indarsabhā* (Indra's court) at Wajid Ali Shah's durbar. While these primarily comprised mythological stories, within the next ten years, eastern India contributed much original social drama. In Bengali, Ramnarayan Tarkaratna castigated Brahman polygamy, and Michael Madhusudan Dutt lampooned upper-class affectations. In Assamese, Gunabhiram Barua criticized child marriages, and Hemchandra Barua, opium addiction.

In 1872 Bengali theater turned professional as well as political. Dinabandhu Mitra's *Nildarpan* (Indigo mirror) condemned British indigo planters' ruthless oppression of peasants. Anti-British productions increased to the extent that the government clamped down with the Dramatic Performances Act (1876), banning seditious material. However, playwrights like Girish Ghosh (1844–1912) in Bengali and Bharatendu Harishchandra (1850–1885) in Hindi circumvented that law, allegorizing familiar tales of repression and rebellion under the guise of seemingly innocuous mythical or historical inspiration. Meanwhile, the spectacular commercial fare of Parsi troupes and Marathi Sangitnatak succeeded in making theater a favorite of the public. Parsi companies toured across India and even abroad, performing in easily understood Hindustani with attractive sets and special effects, the first pan-Indian theater since Sanskrit times. Sangitnatak (musical drama), created by B. P. Kirloskar in 1880, became so much the rage in Maharashtra that spectators went mainly to hear star actors deliver the songs, sometimes as many as a hundred in a show, in exquisite compositions derived from classical, devotional, and folk melodies. Bal Gandharva (1886–1967), singer and female impersonator, commanded a huge following, and women devotedly copied his fashions.

The major innovator in modern Indian theater, Rabindranath Tagore (1861–1941), authored, directed, scored, choreographed, and acted in over sixty Bengali plays, which were stylistically lyrical and symbolic. They critiqued orthodox Hinduism and dramatized spiritual quest, celebrated nature, pleaded for ecological consciousness, and foresaw the dangers of exploiting mineral resources and damming rivers indiscriminately. Tagore gave importance to women's issues and encouraged girls from respectable families to act (taboo at the time); he initiated open-air children's theater at the school he established in Santiniketan (Abode of Peace), Bengal. He experimented with the musical and dance-drama as forms, and traveled with these productions to large Indian cities. His other plays, translated internationally after he became the first non-European to win the Nobel Prize for literature (1913), were staged all over the world, bringing modern Indian drama to the attention of a global audience.

Theater's halcyon days at the box office began to fade with the arrival in 1931 of the "talkies," which cleverly appropriated the escapist formulas that had enticed viewers to the professional companies, which never recovered. In their place, new theater arose, avowedly amateur to protect itself from the demands of popular taste, overtly socialistic in its politics, and realistic in its technique. The founding of the Indian People's Theater Association (1943) signaled this change, with Bijon Bhattacharya's Bengali *Nabānna* (New harvest, 1944) revolutionizing theater by its stark radicalism (using no scenery or makeup) on the subject of the horrendous Bengal famine of 1943. The movement grew rapidly. In 1944 Prithvi Theaters' Hindustani plays took social awareness across India, and the Dravida Kazhagam Party's Tamil productions opposed Brahmanical dominance in the south. The Praja Natya Mandali (1946) and the Jammu and Kashmir Cultural Front (1953) employed folk forms to advocate their messages in Telugu and Kashmiri, respectively; the Kerala People's Arts Club (1952) espoused the Communist cause in Malayalam. Most serious groups since independence have owed allegiance to leftist ideologies, covering a wide gamut from strident Marxist activism to simple social awareness. Technically amateur, their members hold full-time jobs in other professions.

Contemporary urban theater shows great variety, though three broad currents have emerged: the above-mentioned political, the poetic-symbolical, and the folk nativistic. In Bengali, actor-director Sombhu Mitra (1915–1997) earned respect for his poetic grandeur; Utpal Dutt (1929–1993) regaled with witty plays that expressed an agitprop Communist line; and Badal Sircar (1925–) abandoned the proscenium for free street theater and informal spaces, literally a poor theater with a

conscience. Hindi theater was galvanized by the directorial visions of Ebrahim Alkazi (1925–) at the government-funded National School of Drama, the works of Habib Tanvir (1923–), who heads a troupe of Chhattisgarhi village artists, and the unusual psychological dramas of Mohan Rakesh (1925–1972). Marathi drama introduced three noted playwrights: Vijay Tendulkar (1928–), drawn to controversial topics; Mahesh Elkunchwar (1939–), sensitive to domestic relationships; and Satish Alekar (1949–), often absurdist or meta-theatrical in his themes. Tamil theater ranged from the outrageous political satires of Cho Ramaswamy (1934–) to the symbolism and folk-based work of Na Muthuswamy (1936–). Kannada brought the dramatists Chandrasekhar Kambar (1938–) and Girish Karnad (1938–), and the director B. V. Karanth (1929–2002), to the national limelight, reinterpreting folkloric material. In Malayalam (and Sanskrit), Kavalam Narayana Panikkar (1928–) revived traditional genres in modern contexts. Acharya Atreya (1921–1989), Manoranjan Das (1921–), and Arun Sarma (1931–) were the leading playwrights in Telugu, Oriya, and Assamese, respectively. Heisnam Kanhailal (1941–) gave to Manipur a theater of protest and resistance against mainstream culture from India. Gursharan Singh (1929–) bravely preached nonviolence in the Punjabi countryside during the peak of separatist extremism there. A minority English-language theater also exists in the metropolises, its most arresting authors including Asif Currimbhoy (1928–1994) and Mahesh Dattani (1958–).

Ananda Lal

See also **Literature**

BIBLIOGRAPHY

Deshpande, G. P., ed. *Modern Indian Drama*. New Delhi: Sahitya Akademi, 2000. An anthology of fifteen post-independence plays.
Lal, P., trans. *Great Sanskrit Plays*. New York: New Directions, 1964. The widest selection of classical drama in a single volume.
Tagore, Rabindranath. *Three Plays*. Translated by Ananda Lal. New Delhi: Oxford University Press, 2001. Contains a lengthy critical introduction to Tagore.

SECONDARY SOURCES

Baradi, Hasmukh. *History of Gujarati Theater*. New Delhi: National Book Trust, 2002.
Gokhale, Shanta. *Playwright at the Centre: Marathi Drama*. Kolkata: Seagull, 2000.
Kurtkoti, K. D., ed. *The Tradition of Kannada Theater*. Bangalore: IBH, 1986.
Lal, Ananda, ed. *The Oxford Companion to Indian Theater*. New Delhi: Oxford University Press, 2004.
Lal, Ananda, and Chidananda Dasgupta, eds. *Rasa: The Indian Performing Arts in the Last Twenty-five Years; Theater and Cinema*. Kolkata: Anamika Kala Sangam, 1995.

Narayana, Birendra. *Hindi Drama and Stage*. New Delhi: Bansal, 1981.

Perumal, A. N. *Tamil Drama*. Chennai: International Institute of Tamil Studies, 1981.

Raha, Kironmoy. *Bengali Theater*. New Delhi: National Book Trust, 1993.

Sarabhai, Mallika, ed. *Performing Arts of Kerala*. Ahmedabad: Mapin, 1994.

Vatsyayan, Kapila. *Traditional Indian Theater*. New Delhi: National Book Trust, 1980.

Yarrow, Ralph. *Indian Theater*. Richmond, U.K.: Curzon, 2001.

THEOSOPHICAL SOCIETY

The Theosophical Society was founded on 7 September 1875 in New York following a talk on ancient Egyptian spiritualism, by Helena Petrovna Blavatsky (1831–1891), a Russian occult medium, and Colonel Henry Steel Olcott (1832–1907), a U.S. Civil War veteran and abolitionist, who became the society's first president. Their goals were to study the spiritual truth underlying all religions, to reject materialism, and to do public service. The last aim enabled the society to establish schools, influence the Indian national movement, and act as the seedbed for India's first feminist association in Madras (Chennai) in 1917. Blavatsky claimed that a Rajput spirit "master" or "mahatma" had inspired her during her trip to Tibet and India in 1851. She met Olcott after writing a defense of his investigations into occult phenomena in an essay, "Rosicrucianism." In 1874 they claimed they had witnessed an apparition named Kitty King at a seance in Philadelphia. Their fascination with the occult led Blavatsky to start an Esoteric Section of the society in 1888 and to claim that her books were mystical revelations by "masters." Her first book, *Isis Unveiled* (1877) increased the society's membership worldwide.

In India

In 1879 Blavatsky and Olcott, who had corresponded with Dayananda Saraswati, the Vedic Hindu revivalist and founder of the Āryā Samāj, established their headquarters in his city, Bombay (Mumbai), calling it the Theosophical Society of the Ārya Samāj. However, theological disagreements separated them in 1882, the Theosophists moving south to Adyār, Madras. Blavatsky and Olcott's lectures across North India and Sri Lanka were reported extensively in the Allahabad *Pioneer* by A. P. Sinnett. The British kept them under surveillance as possible Russian spies.

In 1881 Blavatsky began publishing the journal the *Theosophist*, which C. W. Leadbetter edited when she moved to London due to ill health. There, in 1889, Annie Besant (1847–1933), who was to become her greatest disciple, visited her after reading *The Secret Doctrine* (1887) on the doctrine of karma (reincarnation).

Theosophist Annie Besant. Though a fervent advocate of Indian nationalism, she beseeched Hindu women not to emulate their materialistic Western counterparts, but to aspire to selflessness and the wisdom of the Upanishads. K. L. KAMAT / KAMAT'S POTPOURRI.

Blavatsky also soon published *The Key to Philosophy* (1889) and *The Voice of Silence* (1890). Besant joined the Theosophical Society in 1891, mesmerized by Hinduism and by Blavatsky's fervent appeal to "come among us!" (Besant, *Autobiography*, p. 311).

Olcott recorded the society's history in his *Old Diary Leaves* (1892). His interest in Buddhism led him to Sri Lanka and Japan in the 1880s. In *The Poor Pariah* (1902), Olcott urged the educational uplift of the Dalits, or the *panchamas*, "downtrodden, wretched human beings" who were shunned by the high castes as untouchables, and seduced by Christian zeal. In 1894 Olcott started a free school for "untouchables" in Urūr, near Adyār. He established the Panchama Education Society, starting five primary vocational schools in Madras and several others in Sri Lanka between 1898 and his death in 1907. The Olcott Schools remain in operation with the aid of government grants.

Annie Besant's Early Years

Annie Wood was born in 1847 in London to a middle-class Irish-English family that became impoverished by her father's death. She was educated by a wealthy Calvinist widow and was married at nineteen to Frank Besant, an Anglican vicar. Annie railed against her husband's rigid Christian Victorian values, eventually leaving the marriage. In 1879 she wrote the tract "Marriage as It Was, and as It Should Be," while fighting a legal battle for custody of her children. Thwarted from attaining a degree in science by misogynistic university rules, she became a vocal advocate of women's education. Her spiritual quest led her first to Unitarianism, then to atheism and Fabian Socialism, before she finally became a Theosophist and Hindu.

Besant became a labor activist due to the trade unionist William Roberts. Her affair with the atheist Charles Bradlaugh led to her joining his National Secular Society. In 1877 she and Bradlaugh were tried for "obscenity" for having published Dr. Charles Knowlton's tract on contraception. Their victory prompted Besant to write *Law of Population*, although later, as a Theosophist, she repudiated this work. As a Fabian Socialist, she supported democratic representation on municipal boards; fought successfully in 1888 for women who were on strike in match factories; wrote and published *The Unemployed, Why I Am a Socialist*, and *How Poverty May Be Destroyed*. Radical socialists criticized her "Modern Socialism," and her socialist convictions declined. She became estranged both from Bradlaugh and Bernard Shaw when she espoused Theosophy. In 1908 she declared that democratic socialism would not succeed in India.

Annie Besant in India

In 1893 she and her Theosophist "guru" Gyanandra Nath Chakravarti attended the Parliament of World Religions in Chicago, where Swami Vivekananda made his inspiring speech on Hinduism, predicting that it was destined to "conquer the world" with its philosophic wisdom. On 16 November 1893, at the age of forty-six, Besant reached India. Her appearance in a sari, and her passionate lectures, praising Hinduism and Indian nationalism, sparked interest in journals like *Amrita Bazaar Patrika*, winning avid followers. She resided first in Benares (Varanasi), learning Sanskrit from Bhagwan Das, with whom she founded the Central Hindu College.

In 1896 at Maharani Girls' School, Mysore, Besant addressed the students as Hindu girls who would "grow up to be Hindu wives and mothers." Noting that there was "nothing nobler than loving, unselfish, spiritual Indian women," Besant beseeched them not to emulate materialistic Western women, but to aspire to the wisdom of female Upanishadic sages like Gargi and Maitreyi, and to the selflessness of the Rāma's heroic wife, Sītā. Her 1904 pamphlet, *The Education of Indian Girls*, became the educational blueprint for Indian girls for decades. Olcott's death in 1907 brought Besant to

Adyār as the society's new president and head of the Theosophical Educational Trust's network of National Schools.

Besant joined the Indian National Congress in 1914, when she started the journal *Commonweal*. She and Lokamanya ("Friend of the People") Tilak each started Home Rule Leagues in 1916, also helping M. A. Jinnah to forge the Congress-League Lucknow Pact that year. Arrested in June 1917 under the Defence of India Act, Besant was released after intercession by U.S. President Woodrow Wilson. As the first European-born president of the Indian National Congress in 1917, Besant spoke about women activists in her inaugural address. In May 1917 at Adyār, she became president of the Women's Indian Association. On 18 December 1918, she led a delegation to Secretary of State Edwin Montagu, pleading for female suffrage in India.

In 1919 Besant was replaced as president of the National Home Rule League by Mahatma Gandhi, whom she had tried, without success, to convert to Theosophy when he first came to London. Her last years were clouded by scandals around Leadbetter's alleged homosexuality; and around her proclamation of Jiddu Krishnamurti, a brilliant student, as "the messiah" or "world teacher" through the Order of the Star with twelve apostles. Krishnamurti himself denied that he was a "savior" and dismantled the order, breaking free of Besant's ambitions for him. Annie Besant died in Adyār in 1933, but the Theosophical Society continues to flourish there.

Sita Anantha Raman

See also **Women's Education; Women's Indian Association**

BIBLIOGRAPHY

Besant, Annie. "Address to Maharani Girls' School," Mysore, 24 December 1896. In *Arya Bala Bodhini*. Adyār: Theosophical Society, January 1897.
———. "An Appeal: Higher Education for Indian Girls." Adyār: Theosophical Society, January 1915.
———. *An Autobiography*. 1893. Reprint, Adyār: Theosophical Publishing Society, 1984.

SECONDARY SOURCES

Chandra, Jyoti. *Annie Besant: From Theosophy to Nationalism*. Delhi: K. K. Publications, 2001.
Forbes, Geraldine. *Women in Modern India*. Cambridge, U.K., and New York: Cambridge University Press, 1996.
Jayawardena, Kumari. *The White Woman's Other Burden: Western Women and South Asia during British Rule*. New York: Routledge, 1995.
Kumar, Radha. *The History of Doing: An Illustrated Account of Movements for Women's Rights and Feminism in India, 1800–1900*. Delhi: Kali for Women, 1997.

Nethercott, Arthur H. *The First Five Lives of Annie Besant*, London: Rupert Hart-Davis, 1961.

———. *The Last Four Lives of Annie Besant.* London: Rupert Hart-Davis, 1963.

Raman, Sita Anantha. *Getting Girls to School: Social Reform in the Tamil Districts, 1870–1930.* Kolkata: Stree, 1996.

Ramusack, Barbara. "Catalysts or Helpers? British Feminists, Indian Women's Rights, and Indian Independence." In *The Extended Family: Women and Political Participation in India and Pakistan*, edited by Gail Minault. Delhi: Chanakya Publications, 1981.

Taylor, Anne. *Annie Besant: A Biography.* Oxford and New York: Oxford University Press, 1993.

Wolpert, Stanley. *Tilak and Gokhale.* Berkeley: University of California, 1962.

THUMRĪ A vocal (or sometimes instrumental) genre, *thumrī* (Hindustani, *thumaknā* "to walk with a jerky, mincing, or wanton gait"; possibly an onomatopoeic imitation of the sound of a stamp of a dancer's foot against the floor [*thumuk*]) features so-called light-classical *rāg*s and (in the case of vocal music) romantic texts. Most musicians associate the origins of the *thumrī* with the court of Wajid Ali Shah, the mid-nineteenth century ruler of Oudh, although the genre has numerous stylistic predecessors. Roughly parallel to the romantic storytelling genre *padam* of *bharata natyam* (dance idiom), *thumrī* has associations with the classical dance of northern India—*kathak*—and in a *kathak* program, dancers often mime their movements to *thumrī*.

Poets of *thumrī* texts have often drawn upon the legends of Krishna, particularly his amorous relationships with the milkmaids of Vraj. The gender of the voice of the text is usually feminine, although both men and women perform. Praise of the beloved, lament of the beloved's absence, and anticipation of the arrival of the beloved are among the favorite topics of *thumrī*, although explicitly erotic and obscene themes occasionally occur in special contexts. The dominant *rasa*s (emotions) of *thumrī* are *shringāra* (the erotic) and *karuna* (the pathetic).

Musical Characteristics

Musicians apply a select repertoire of *rāga*s and *tāla*s in *thumrī*. One characteristic of *thumrī rāga*s is the affective use of alternative notes to emphasize the *rasa* of the *rāga*. *Thumrī* singers also often temporarily introduce other *rāga*s in their renditions. As with most North Indian musical genres, the melody has two musical parts—*sthāyī* and *antarā*—in contrasting registers, each having two lines of poetry.

Musical ornaments in *thumrī* are generally quicker and lighter than in *khayal*. The principal type of elaboration in *thumrī* is the *boltān*, an improvised melodic rendering of the words of the song. These melismatic improvisations commonly function as "word-painting." Singers repeat text lines often, each time with new elaborations. At the conclusion, the singer returns to the first line and repeats it, while the drummer briefly solos in a sped-up section described as *laggi*. A *laggi* is often in a fast binary meter such as *kaharavā* (8 *mātra*s) or *tintāl*, even though the *thumrī* itself is in another *tāla* (such as the 14-*matra* Dīpcandī or the 6-*matra* Dādra). At the end of the solo, the drummer returns to the original *tāla*. Instrumentalists often perform *thumrī*s toward the end of their programs, in which context performers choose *rāga*s and *tāla*s typical of the genre. The mood of such performances is decidedly lighter than the more elaborate approach taken in *ālāp* and *gat-torā*, although devices such as *sawāl-jawāb* may still be part of the performance.

Gordon Thompson

BIBLIOGRAPHY

Bhatkhande, Visnu Narayan. *Krāmik Pustak-Mālika*, edited by Laksminarayan Garg. Hathras: Sangit Karyalay, 1969–1970.

Manuel, Peter. "Thumrī in Historical and Stylistic Perspective." Ph.D. diss., University of California, Los Angeles, 1983.

TIBETAN BUDDHISTS OF INDIA Since 1950, Tibetans escaping Chinese-occupied Tibet have resettled in numerous enclaves in India, including the community of Dharamsala in the foothills of the Himalayas, the headquarters of the Tibetan government-in-exile. In India, Tibetans have established new and stable communities, forged a united Tibetan identity, and created a democratic system of government under the leadership of the Dalai Lama, the spiritual and temporal leader of Tibetan people worldwide. The Tibetan population continues to establish a new, perhaps permanent home in India, the motherland of the Buddhist teachings through which Tibetan culture came to be uniquely defined.

History of Tibetan Buddhism

Tibetan Buddhism, or Tantric Buddhism, finds its roots in northern India, particularly in Nagarjuna's Mādhyamika (Middle Way) system. The Tibetan Buddhist tradition arose from a syncretism of the Indian Vajrayāna (Diamond Vehicle) and the indigenous, animistic Bön religion of Tibet, a religion of deities and spirits that some scholars link to the hierarchy of *bodhisattvas*, demons, and other figures of Tibetan Buddhism. Beginning under King Songsten Gampo's royal patronage in the seventh century A.D., Buddhism flourished, and it developed its unique Tibetan character in the centuries that followed. From the tenth

Worshiper Lights Candles at Monastery. Since 1980, Tibetans with the help of the Indian government have established almost 200 Buddhist monasteries and nunneries in India, housing nearly 20,000 monastics. FRANCOIS GAUTIER / FOTOMEDIA.

century onward, Buddhist masters in western Tibet held leadership positions alongside lay authorities, a governmental structure that soon spread throughout Tibet and became the norm. By the fifteenth century, the distinctive Tibetan Buddhist canon, consisting of the Kanjur (the teachings of the Buddha) and the Tanjur (commentaries on the teachings), and the complex monastic system, with its reincarnations of *bodhisattva*s, were established. The monastic system comprised four main orders, powerful in both political and religious spheres: the Nyingmapa, the Kargyupa, the Sakyapa, and the Gelugpa. It is from the Gelugpa (Yellow Hat) order that the Dalai Lamas of Tibet, the spiritual and political leaders of the Tibetan people, originated in 1391. The Dalai Lama ("ocean of wisdom," or "superior one") is understood to be the continual reincarnation of Avalokiteshvara, *bodhisattva* of compassion. He is a key figure in Tibetan Buddhism, the Tibetan government, and Tibetan identity in general.

The Community in Exile

Since the invasion of Tibet by the People's Republic of China on 7 October 1950, and the Tibetan revolt

against the Chinese occupation on 10 March 1959, India has provided a haven for Tibetan refugees and their families. By 1960, over 17,000 Tibetans resided in settlements established by the Indian government. The village of Mussoorie served as the headquarters of the Central Tibetan Administration until Jawaharlal Nehru offered Dharamsala in Himachal Pradesh to the Tibetan government-in-exile, headed by the Fourteenth Dalai Lama, in 1960. Dharamsala and numerous other bases in India are no longer simple refugee resettlement sites but developed, stable Tibetan communities. Over 8,000 Tibetans call Dharamsala, McLeod Gunj, and the surrounding Kangra Valley their home, while approximately 88,000 more reside in other communities in India. The majority of this population lives in Tibetan agricultural, agro-industrial, or handicraft-based settlements established with the assistance of the Indian government. Tibetan refugees continue to enter India at a steady rate of between 2,000 and 2,500 per year.

The Tibetan government-in-exile was restructured according to democratic principles in 1963 with the draft of a new constitution for an anticipated free Tibet in the future, as well as for the existing exiled government. While many leadership positions remain intact from the previous system, including the position of the Dalai Lama and his cabinet of ministers, the new democracy includes three branches of government, the executive, the legislature, and the judiciary, with clear separations of powers. The Kashag, the cabinet of ministers, incorporates departments of home, education, finance, and health, and consists of officials elected by the legislative branch of the government, the assembly of Tibetan People's Deputies. The assembly is diverse and represents Tibetans all over the world: two members currently represent Tibetans in Europe, and one represents Tibetans in the United States. The assembly, including the chief *kalon*, or chief executive officer, is elected by the Tibetan people living in India and in other countries outside Tibet. The Tibetan Supreme Justice Commission is the judicial branch of the government. Tibetans in India are subject to Indian law, but through India's arbitration law, the Justice Commission has some jurisdiction and can serve as an arbitrator in disputes. In this manner, Tibetans enjoy a modicum of self-power within the Indian judicial system.

According to the Government of Tibet in Exile, 44 percent of refugees from 1997 to 2002 were between the ages of fourteen and twenty-five. There are an estimated 30,000 Tibetan children in India. Education of Tibetan youth is thus a vital service provided by the government-in-exile, with efforts made toward accommodating the special needs of children orphaned during the arduous journey from Tibet. The Department of Education administers over eighty schools, not only in India but in Nepal and Bhutan as well. The Indian-run Central Tibetan Schools Administration funds and oversees approximately thirty of these schools in India. This has resulted in some tension between the Tibetan population and the Indian host culture: support is necessary and appreciated, but there is concern that the Tibetan schools, if run by non-Tibetans, will teach fewer Tibetan cultural values. Imbuing children with a Tibetan sense of respect and compassion, maintaining the Tibetan

The Fourteenth Dalai Lama, Tenzin Gyatso. To Tibetans in exile in India and other parts of the world, with no geographic link, the Dalai Lama remains an all-important symbol of continuity through generations. INDIA TODAY.

Buddhist Monks Gather at Ceremony. Saffron-robed Buddhist monks gathered at McLeod Gunj, home to the Dalai Lama, nestled high among the Himalyan forests. Maintaining the Tibetan language and culture, and especially its spiritual beliefs and rituals, are all vital aims for a people living in exile. FRANCOIS GAUTIER / FOTOMEDIA.

language, and teaching Tibetan cultural arts are all vital aims for a people living in exile.

Within the Kashag, the Department of Religion and Culture seeks to provide aid to Tibetan religious institutions and other cultural institutions. Monasteries and nunneries of the Tibetan Buddhist traditions are central to Tibetan Buddhist life. Since 1980 the population in Tibetan Buddhist monasteries and nunneries in India has more than doubled, resulting in overcrowded facilities. Thus, support for these institutions, as well as the construction of new monastic centers, is a priority for Tibetans in exile. Almost 200 monasteries and nunneries, with a population of nearly 20,000 monks and nuns, have been established in exile. Projects of the Department of Religion and Culture also include Tibet House in New Delhi, the Library of Tibetan Works and Archives and the Tibetan Institute of Performing Arts in Dharamsala, the Central Institute for Higher Tibetan Studies in Varanasi, and the Norbulinkha Institute for Tibetan Culture at Sidhpur. Numerous charitable organizations worldwide and the Indian government provide additional support.

Unity and Tibetan Identity

The occasionally divisive factors of Tibetan life, including regional or tribal loyalties, political rivalries, religious competition, and varying dialects of the Tibetan language, have been set aside since 1959 in favor of promoting unity in the face of the threat to Tibetan culture in general. The new identity forged by the Tibetans in their stateless condition emphasizes the Tibetan Buddhist values of compassion, patriotism, ethnic and linguistic unity, and a focus on what anthropologist Margaret Nowak identifies as the two main Tibetan rallying symbols, the Dalai Lama and *rangzen* (self-power). The Dalai Lama is a symbol of continuity through generations, representing stability for Tibetans in exile. The status as *bodhisattva* also makes him a living symbol of Buddhist reality. *Rangzen*, often defined as independence from China, is a hopeful concept for the possible Tibetan future. The Dalai Lama and *rangzen* both serve as symbols of Tibetan identity, ontological security, and empowerment. In them, religion, culture, political activism for the Tibetan cause, and even Tibet's history and future are encapsulated and advanced.

With no geographical union, Tibetans in India and in exile worldwide innovate a cultural, ethnic, and linguistic union, and the prominent symbols of Tibetan religion and culture emerge as rallying signs for the global Tibetan community. At the heart of the Tibetan project of identity and unity in exile is the conviction that being Tibetan means upholding a compassionate, active, and hopeful Tibetan Buddhist tradition and character.

Eve Mullen

See also **Buddhism in Ancient India**

BIBLIOGRAPHY

Gyatso, Tenzin (His Holiness the Dalai Lama). *Opening the Eye of New Awareness*, Translated by Donald S. Lopez Jr. Boston: Wisdom Publications, 1999.

Kapstein, Matthew T. *Reason's Traces: Identity and Interpretation in Indian and Tibetan Buddhist Thought*. Boston: Wisdom Publications, 2001.

Mullen, Eve. *The American Occupation of Tibetan Buddhism: Tibetans and Their American Hosts in New York City*. New York: Waxmann, 2001.

Nowak, Margaret. *Tibetan Refugees: Youth and the New Generation of Meaning*. New Brunswick, N.J.: Rutgers University Press, 1984.

Richardson, Hugh E. *Tibet and Its History*. Boston: Shambhala Publications, 1962.

Shakabpa, Tsepon W. D. *Tibet: A Political History*. New Haven, Conn.: Yale University Press, 1967.

Snellgrove, David L. *Indo-Tibetan Buddhism: Indian Buddhists and Their Tibetan Successors*. 2 vols. Boston: Shambhala Publications, 1987.

Stein, Rolf A. *Tibetan Civilization*. Stanford, Calif.: Stanford University Press, 1972.

TILAK, BAL GANGADHAR *(1856–1920), revolutionary Hindu nationalist leader, called Lokamanya ("Revered by the People")*.

Born to a venerable Chitpavan Brahman family in Maharashtra's Konkani village of Chikalgaon on 23 July 1856, Bal Gangadhar Tilak was married at fifteen to Tapi Bai, a Chitpavan girl of ten. A year later, he graduated from high school and immediately enrolled in Pune's Deccan College, where he focused on Sanskrit Vedic studies. Tilak later wrote books on the religious philosophy of the Bhagavad Gītā as well as Vedic astronomy and astrology. Unlike most modern Indian and Western scholars, Tilak believed that the Vedas were composed by ancient tribes, whose "Arctic home" was at the "North Pole" prior to the "Glacial Ice Age." He also studied law in Bombay (Mumbai), which he later found useful in his litigation-plagued career.

Cultural Nationalist

Tilak was one of Maharashtra's most popular cultural nationalists, publishing several important newspapers in

Portrait of Bal Gangadhar Tilak. In their extended discussions of self-rule for India, Tilak (widely regarded as a powerful figure as his penetrating gaze in this drawing and popular name, Lokamanya, attest) is purported to have told Gandhi, "There's no place in politics for saints or religious scruples." K. L. KAMAT / KAMAT'S POTPOURRI.

Pune, the *Mahratta* in English and *Kesari* (Lion) in Marathi, the latter read aloud in village centers to tens of thousands of illiterate peasants, as well as being subscribed to by urban intellectuals. Tilak thus became the cultural leader and political hero of Maharashtra's masses. Tilak denounced Sir Andrew Scoble's "Age of Consent" Bill, which tried to raise the "statutory rape" age for intercourse (with or without a child bride's consent) from ten to twelve years. He called it a "foreign Christian intrusion" in the private household affairs of Hindu Indians. Two years later he publicized the popular revival of annual religious festivals throughout Maharashtra to celebrate the "birthday" of the Hindu divinity Ganesha, whose elephant-headed statues were carried around every town and village for days before being raucously immersed in rivers or coastal waters. Ganpati festivities, which included paramilitary gymnastics by "Ganesh guards" dressed in khaki uniforms, are considered the birth of modern militant cultural Hindu nationalism. In 1895 Tilak inaugurated a second annual festival in Pune, to honor the birth of Maharashtra's greatest Hindu national hero, Shivaji Maharaj. The Shivaji festivals drew even larger crowds than those for Ganesha. Speeches in Marathi extolling Shivaji's heroic deeds in waging guerrilla warfare against, and defeating, the foreign Muslim Mughals, excited the most interest among young men, many of whom used their energies and time to make crude bombs in their basements, before long throwing them at British officers driving by in their carriages.

Tried and Transported for Sedition

Tilak's most popular mantra was "*Sva-raj* ('self-rule' or 'freedom') is my birthright, and I will have it!" At times, his Kesari editorials and powerful Shivaji festival speeches incited those who read or heard his words to violent actions against British officials or other foreigners. One of Tilak's Pune Brahman disciples assassinated an Englishman as he left the governor's Jubilee Ball honoring Empress Victoria in 1897, just half a century before another Maharashtrian Brahman was to assassinate Mahatma Gandhi. Tilak was tried for sedition for several editorials he wrote in his newspaper. He eloquently defended himself and pleaded innocent, but was found guilty in 1908 and was transported to Mandalay Prison in Burma (Myanmar) for six years. He was released at the start of World War I and cabled his "support" for the Allied cause to the king-emperor. He outlived Gopal Krishna Gokhale, his moderate Maharashtrian Brahman rival for leadership of the Indian National Congress, by five years.

Impact on Mahatma Gandhi

Gandhi first met Tilak when Gandhi returned to India from South Africa, while visiting Pune at his guru Gokhale's invitation. To Gandhi's mind, gentle Gokhale was like Mother India's greatest river, "the Ganges," which "invited one to its bosom." Tilak, on the other hand, was "the ocean" itself, forbidden to Hindus, who never knew what dreadful dangers lurked beneath its "dark waters." But Tilak's fearless insistence upon "freedom," his successful use of popular religious and cultural Hindu symbols, and his boycott of all things "foreign"— all of which lured India's illiterate peasant population into the nationalist movement—appealed powerfully to Mahatma Gandhi. But ever-scrupulous Gandhi insisted on nonviolence in all his *satyagraha* struggles. Tilak never feared or worried about violence. "There's no place in politics for saints or religious scruples," Lokamanya Tilak once told Mahatma Gandhi. Gandhi "begged to

differ," insisting that "religion (Hindu *dharma*) could no more be removed from 'politics' than from life itself." On 1 August 1920, the day Tilak died, Mahatma Gandhi launched his first nationwide *satyagraha* in Bombay.

Stanley Wolpert

See also **Congress Party; Gandhi, Mahatma M. K.; Gokhale, Gopal Krishna; Maharashtra**

BIBLIOGRAPHY

Athalye, D. V. *The Life of Lokamanya Tilak.* Poona: A. Chiploonkar, 1921.
Bhat, V. G. *Lokamanya Tilak: His Life, Mind, Politics and Philosophy.* Poona: R. B. Nigudkar, 1956.
Karandikar, S. L. *Lokamanya Bal Gangadhar Tilak. The Hercules and Prometheus of Modern India.* Poona, 1957.
Karmarkar, D. P. *Bal Gangadhar Tilak. A Study.* Mumbai: Popular Book Depot, 1956.
Tahmankar, D. V. *Lokamanya Tilak: Father of Indian Unrest and Maker of Modern India.* London: J. Murray, 1956.
Wolpert, Stanley A. *Tilak and Gokhale: Revolution and Reform in the Making of Modern India.* Berkeley and Los Angeles: University of California Press, 1953 and 1961.

TRADE LIBERALIZATION SINCE 1991 Import controls in India were originally imposed in May 1940 to conserve foreign exchange and shipping for World War II. But starting in 1947, regulation of the balance of payments became the central concern of the Indian government, which introduced restrictions on the rate at which foreign exchange could be depleted. From then on, India alternated between liberalization and tighter controls, until the beginning of the launch of the first Five-Year Plan. The period during that first plan, covering 1951– 1952 to 1955–1956, was one of progressive liberalization.

A balance-of-payments crisis in 1956–1957 led to a major policy reversal. India restored its comprehensive import controls, which remained in place until 1966. In June 1966, under pressure from the World Bank, it devalued the rupee from 4.7 rupees to 7.5 rupees per dollar, and took steps toward liberalizing import licensing and lowering import duties and export subsidies. But intense domestic reaction to the devaluation led to reversal of the policy within a year, and import controls were again tightened. By the mid-1970s, India's trade regime had become so repressive that the share of nonoil and noncereal imports in the Gross Domestic Product (GDP) fell from the already low 7 percent in 1957–1958 to an even lower level of 3 percent in 1975–1976.

In the late 1970s, two factors paved the way for yet another phase of liberalization. First, industrialists came to feel the adverse effect of the tight import restrictions

Finance Minister P. Chidambaram. One of the principal architects of economic liberalization and reforms. In early May 2005, the decidedly pro-business Chidambaram declared that India must open its doors to foreign investment in order to achieve faster economic growth, a position not supported by leftist leaders within and outside the government. INDIA TODAY.

on their profitability and lobbied for liberalization of imports of raw materials and machinery that did not have domestically produced substitutes. Second, improved export performance and remittances from overseas workers in the Middle East in the post–oil-crisis era led to the accumulation of a healthy foreign-exchange reserve, raising the comfort level of policy makers with respect to the effect of liberalization on the balance of payments.

Liberalization and Growth in the 1980s

The liberalization process was initiated in 1976 through the reintroduction of the so-called Open General Licensing (OGL) list that had been part of the original wartime regime but had become defunct as controls were tightened in the wake of the 1966 devaluation. The OGL operated on a positive-list approach, whereby the item placed on the list no longer required a license from the Ministry of Commerce. This did not necessarily mean that imports of the item on the list were free; the importer usually had to be the actual user of the imports, and could be subject to clearance from the industrial-licensing authority in the case of machinery imports.

Upon its introduction in 1976, the OGL list contained only 79 items. But by April 1990, the list covered 1,339 items, approximately one-quarter of all tariff lines and more than 30 percent of all imports. Though tariff rates were raised substantially during this period, with items on OGL given large concessions on those rates through "exemptions," they did not significantly add to the restrictive effect of licensing. The government also introduced several export incentives, especially after 1985, which partially neutralized the anti-trade bias of import controls. Above all, from 1985 to 1990, the effective nominal exchange rate was depreciated by a hefty 45 percent, leading to a real depreciation of 30 percent.

These and other liberalization measures relating especially to industrial licensing, improved agricultural performance, discovery of oil and expansionary fiscal policy combined to raise the growth rate in India from its traditional, so-called Hindu rate of approximately 3.5 percent during the years 1950 to 1980 to 5.6 percent during the period from 1981 to 1991. The jump in the average annual growth rate was particularly significant from 1988 to 1991, when it reached 7.6 percent.

Nevertheless, the external and internal borrowing that supported fiscal expansion was unsustainable and culminated in a balance-of-payments crisis in June 1991. This time, however, the government turned the crisis into an opportunity, and instead of reversing the course of liberalization, launched a truly comprehensive, systematic, and systemic reform program that continues to be implemented. The Soviet collapse, China's phenomenal economic rise following its adoption of outward-oriented policies, and India's own experience—first with protectionist policies for three decades and then liberalization in the second half of 1980s—convinced policy makers of the merits of the new policy approach that had been advocated for years by pro-market and pro–free-trade economists, most prominently Jagdish Bhagwati.

Systemic Reforms Beginning in 1991

The trade liberalization program, initiated in July 1991, was comprehensive but gradual and remains under implementation. It is useful first to consider the measures taken in the areas of trade in goods and services and then to discuss their impact.

Merchandise trade liberalization. The 1991 reforms did away with import licensing on virtually all intermediate inputs and capital goods. But consumer goods, accounting for approximately 30 percent of the tariff lines, remained under licensing. It was only after a successful challenge by India's trading partners in the Dispute Settlement Body of the World Trade Organization (WTO) that these goods were freed of licensing a decade later, starting 1 April 2001. Since that time—except for a handful of goods disallowed on environmental, health, and safety grounds, and a few others that are canalized (meaning they can be imported only by the government), including fertilizer, cereals, edible oils, and petroleum products—all goods can be imported without a license or other restrictions.

Tariff rates in India had been raised substantially during the 1980s to turn quota rents into revenue. For example, according to the Government of India (1993), tariff revenue as a proportion of imports went up from 20 percent in 1980–1981 to 44 percent in 1989–1990. According to the WTO (1998), in 1990–1991, the highest tariff rate stood at 355 percent, the simple average of all tariff rates standing at 113 percent and the import-weighted average of tariff rates at 87 percent. With the removal of licensing, these tariff rates became effective restrictions on imports. Therefore, a major task of the reforms in the 1990s and beyond has been to lower tariffs. This has been done in a gradual fashion by compressing the top tariff rate while rationalizing the tariff structure through a reduction in the number of tariff bands. The top rate fell to 85 percent in 1993–1994 and 50 percent in 1995–1996.

There were some reversals along the way in the form of new, special duties and the unification of a low and a high tariff rate to the latter, but the general direction has been toward liberalization, the top rate coming down to 20 percent in 2004–2005.

The 1990s reforms were accompanied by the lifting of exchange controls that had served as an extra layer of restrictions on imports. As a part of the 1991 reform, the government devalued the rupee by 22 percent against the U.S. dollar, from 21.2 rupees to 25.8 rupees per dollar. In February 1992 a dual exchange rate system was introduced, which allowed exporters to sell 60 percent of their foreign exchange in the free market and 40 percent to the government at the lower official price. Importers were authorized to purchase foreign exchange in the open market at the higher price, effectively ending exchange control. Within a year of establishing this market exchange rate, the official exchange rate was unified with it. Starting in February 1994, many current account transactions, including all current business transactions, education, medical expenses, and foreign travel, were also permitted at the market exchange rate. These steps culminated in India accepting the International Monetary Fund Article VIII obligations, which made the rupee officially convertible on the current account.

Liberalization of trade in services. Since 1991 India has also carried out a substantial liberalization of trade in services. Traditionally, services sectors have been subject to heavy government intervention. Public sector presence has been conspicuous in the key sectors of insurance, banking, and telecommunications. Nevertheless, considerable progress has been made toward opening the door wider to private-sector participation, including foreign investors.

Until recently, insurance was a state monopoly. On 7 December 1999, the Indian Parliament passed the Insurance Regulatory and Development Authority Act, which established an Insurance Regulatory and Development Authority and opened the door to private entry, including foreign investors. Up to 26 percent foreign investment, subject to obtaining a license from the Insurance Regulatory and Development Authority, is permitted.

Though the public sector dominates in banking, private banks are permitted to operate. Foreign direct investment (FDI) up to 74 percent in private banks is permitted under the automatic route. In addition, foreign banks are allowed to open a specified number of new branches every year. More than 25 foreign banks, with full banking licenses, and approximately 150 foreign bank branches are currently in operation. Under the 1997 WTO Financial Services Agreement, India committed to permitting 12 new foreign bank branches annually.

The telecommunications sector has experienced much greater opening to the private sector, including foreign investors. Until the early 1990s, the sector was a state monopoly. The 1994 National Telecommunications Policy provided for opening cellular as well as basic and value-added telephone services to the private sector, with foreign investors granted entry. Rapid changes in technology led to the adoption of the New Telecom Policy in 1999, which provides the current policy framework. Accordingly, in basic, cellular mobile, paging and value-added service, and global mobile personnel communications by satellite, FDI is limited to 49 percent subject to the granting of a license from the Department of Telecommunications. FDI up to 100 percent is allowed, with some conditions for Internet service providers not providing gateways (for both satellite and submarine cables) and infrastructure providers furnishing dark fiber, electronic mail, and voice mail. Additionally, subject to licensing and security requirements and the restriction that proposals with FDI beyond 49 percent must be approved by the government, up to 74 percent foreign investment is permitted for Internet service providers with gateways, radio paging, and end-to-end bandwidth.

FDI up to 100 percent is permitted in e-commerce. Automatic approval is available for foreign equity in software and almost all areas of electronics. One hundred percent foreign investment is permitted in information technology units set up exclusively for exports. These units can be set up under several programs, including Export Oriented Units, Export Processing Zones, Special Economic Zones, Software Technology Parks, and Electronics Hardware Technology Parks.

The infrastructure sector has also been opened to foreign investment. FDI up to 100 percent under automatic route is permitted in projects for the construction and maintenance of roads, highways, vehicular bridges, toll roads, vehicular tunnels, ports, and harbors. In construction and maintenance of ports and harbors, automatic approval for foreign equity up to 100 percent is available. In projects providing supporting services to water transport, such as operation and maintenance of piers, and loading and discharging of vehicles, no approval is required for foreign equity up to 51 percent. FDI up to 100 percent is permitted in airports, though FDI above 74 percent requires prior governmental approval. Foreign equity up to 40 percent, and investment by nonresident Indians up to 100 percent, is permitted in domestic air-transport services. Only railways remain off limits to private entry.

Since 1991 several attempts have been made to bring the private sector, including FDI, into the power sector but without perceptible success. The most recent attempt is the Electricity Bill 2003, which replaces three existing

power legislations dated 1910, 1948, and 1998. The new bill offers a comprehensive framework for restructuring the power sector and builds on experience in the telecommunications sector. It attempts to introduce competition through private-sector entry side by side with public-sector entities in generation, transmission, and distribution.

The bill fully de-licenses generation and freely permits captive generation. Only hydropower projects would henceforth require clearance from the Central Electricity Authority. Distribution licensees would be free to undertake generation, and generating companies would be free to take up distribution businesses. Trading has been recognized as a distinct activity, with the Regulatory Commissions authorized to fix ceilings on trading margins, if necessary. FDI is permitted in all three activities.

Impact of liberalization. The ratio of total exports of goods and services to GDP in India doubled from 7.3 percent in 1990 to 14 percent in 2000. The rise was less dramatic on imports because increased external borrowing was still financing a large proportion of imports in 1990, which was no longer true in 2000. But the rise was still significant, from 9.9 percent in 1990 to 16.6 percent in 2000. Within ten years, the ratio of total goods and services trade to GDP rose from 17.2 percent to 30.6 percent. Nevertheless, this is substantially lower than the corresponding ratio of 49.3 percent achieved by China in 2000.

The Road Ahead

Despite substantial progress, tariffs remain high and must be compressed further. At this stage, the best course will be to first unify all tariff rates applicable to industrial goods at 15 percent, and then to bring them down to 10 percent by 2006–2007. Tariff uniformity has the advantage of minimizing incentives to lobby and therefore makes future liberalization easier. It is also likely to create less distortion than a more variegated tariff structure.

In the Doha negotiations, India should press for complete elimination of industrial tariffs by 2015 in all developed countries and by 2025 in all developing countries. Such a stance may enable India to achieve its long-sought objective of eliminating tariff peaks in developed countries that apply to labor-intensive products such as clothing and footwear. At the same time, the elimination of tariffs at home is fully consistent with India's liberalization program.

Agricultural tariffs in India have risen in recent years, and there is considerable room for lowering them, but political constraints are daunting despite the potential benefit, so that change is unlikely. This makes it essential for India to adopt a more flexible approach in Doha negotiations.

A particularly disturbing development on the trade policy front in India has been the rise of antidumping duties, which started in January 1993. By 1998, 45 antidumping cases had been initiated, covering 18 products. Definitive duties had been imposed in 11 cases, and a ruling of no injury reached in 2. India has now replaced the United States as the premier user of this instrument. Between July and December 2001, it carried out 51 antidumping investigations, which only reverses the economic liberalization policies introduced since 1991.

India has also embarked upon preferential trade arrangements that liberalize trade with one or more trading partners on a discriminatory basis. On balance, this is an inferior strategy toward trade liberalization, but perhaps for political and strategic reasons India's government has essentially committed itself to it. To minimize the damage to itself from possible trade diversion, it is more important for India to lower its external barriers as well. From a strategic point of view, India's recent decision to forge free trade areas with the members of the Association of Southeast Asian Nations makes eminently good sense. Focusing on creating a South Asian Free Trade Area, on the other hand, offers no such benefits and is almost certain to impose economic costs associated with the diversion of trade from more efficient outside sources.

Arvind Panagariya

See also **Economic Reforms of 1991; Economy since the 1991 Economic Reforms**

BIBLIOGRAPHY

Bhagwati, Jagdish, and Padma Desai. *India: Planning for Industrialization*. London and New York: Oxford University Press, 1970.
Government of India. *Tax Reforms Committee: Final Report*, Part II. New Delhi: Ministry of Finance, 1993.
Pursell, Garry. "Trade Policy in India." In *National Trade Policies*, edited by Dominick Salvatore. New York: Greenwood Press, 1992.
World Trade Organization. *Trade Policy Review: India*. Geneva: WTO Secretariat, 1998 and 2002.

TRADE POLICY, 1800–1947 Defined either narrowly or broadly, the trade policy of the British government of India did not promote the interests of most Indian producers or consumers. Narrowly defined, trade policy refers to government rates of tariffs, duties, quotas, trade agreements, and other policy instruments that affect the price and quantities of goods exported and imported. Broadly defined, trade policy incorporates all government policies that influence a country's terms of trade, defined as the price of its exports relative to its imports. Such policies would include those targeting changes in exchange and interest rates, investment incentives, taxation and expenditure policies on tradable commodities, and nontariff barriers to trade, such as preferential treatment in government purchases. British imperial rule had many adverse consequences for India's international economic relations.

The British Raj had no consistent trade "policy" until the mid-nineteenth century. The three British East India Company presidencies of Bengal, Bombay, and Madras had operated largely independently and had adapted to a varying range of pre-colonial trade systems. For example, Mughal tariff rates often varied from 2.5 to 5 percent, depending on the region and the traders' community affiliation. Over time, the British consolidated the indigenous systems of inland and external customs rates of the eighteenth century.

By the time the East India Company's administration had solidified its hold over Indian territory, an all-India trade policy emerged. From 1846 the British Raj instituted a uniform tariff rate schedule: 3.5 percent on cotton twist and yarn, and 5 percent on all other goods imported from Britain. For imports from all other countries, the rates were double. The policy clearly favored Britain among India's numerous trading partners; yet it did not impose unique advantages to British industrial sectors over their Indian counterparts. However, what began as a simple, nonprotective tariff regime evolved during the late nineteenth century into a rigid reflection of the interests of British manufacturing and political interests.

Unlike many governments of the time, the British government of India did not rely upon import and export duties for the bulk of its revenues. In colonial India, the lion's share of revenues came from land taxes, a regressive tax regime retained from Mughal administrations. As fiscal expenditures outpaced revenues, the Raj looked to import duties as an expedient way of raising public revenues. In 1860 the rates on twists and yarn rose to 5 percent. For all other goods, the rates doubled. While this did provide additional income for the government, raising import tariffs also had the effect of raising the price Indian consumers paid for imported goods relative to those produced domestically. British cotton manufacturers cried foul. The Manchester Chamber of Commerce put enormous pressure on the Raj to lower rates, claiming that the government had unfairly favored Indian cotton goods producers to the disadvantage of British firms. Manchester's lobby found a sympathetic audience with Lord Salisbury, secretary of state for India in 1875. By 1882 all cotton import duties were abolished. When fiscal necessity prompted the reimposition of an import duty of 3.5 percent in 1894, the government again appeased British industrialists with an equivalent excise tax on Indian cotton textile production. These excise duties, which remained in place until 1925, galvanized political opposition to the notion that the imperial government could serve as a loyal steward of India's domestic economy.

For good reason, cotton textiles are symbolic of India's international trading relationships in the period. Between 1840 and 1865, the principal commodities of import included cotton twist and yarn, cotton goods, machinery, raw metals (particularly copper and iron), metal manufactures, and railway materials. Between 1870 and 1895, India was the biggest customer of Britain's Lancashire cotton industry. By 1920, imports included cotton manufactures, sugar, iron and steel, machinery and millwork, and mineral oils. Indian imports were more technologically advanced and had greater value-added than Indian exports. For basic industrial inputs—machinery, metals, and chemicals—India depended upon overseas production. Moreover, 90 percent of all India's imports in 1919–1920 originated from the United Kingdom. During the Great Depression, the British abandoned free trade orthodoxy and built huge tariff barriers to trade. In 1930 the British government of India passed the Cotton Textile Protection Act instituting duties of 15 percent for all British goods and 20 percent for all non-British imports. By 1931 both of these rates rose by 5 percent. The justification again was fiscal necessity, not protection of Indian industry. Most commentators, however, have concluded that the intent was simply to redirect India's foreign trade toward England. In the depressed economic environment of the 1930s, the Raj discouraged trade with other major textile producers such as Japan. The case of cotton textiles thus illustrates how the concerns of Indian consumers and producers were overridden by the special interest groups within the British Empire. British India's primary economic interests were abandoned in favor of overt "imperial preference" and bilateral agreements.

India's other major import was silver. Reportedly, Indian imports of silver accounted for a third of world silver production in the last three decades of the nineteenth century. According to the *Statistical Abstract relating to British India* (various years), precious metals accounted for approximately one-fifth of the value of India's total imports. Part of India's seemingly insatiable demand for silver was for private consumption purposes, sometimes called hoarding. Another part was converted into currency. In either case, the vast majority of the population preferred to accumulate their savings in the form of precious metals, which in times of distress could be easily converted into the official silver-based rupee. Government mints were open to the public until 1893 and charged modest commissions. Thus if the intrinsic value of the silver in the Indian rupee exceeded the exchange value of the coinage, then the government could anticipate a rise in the public's willingness to liquidate private stores. With a glut of silver on world markets, India's silver currency rapidly depreciated from 1876 to 1893. This illustrated the vulnerability of India's exchange rate, unmanaged by a central bank until 1935.

While the government of British India did have some policy instruments (in the form of counsel bills and reverse counsel bills) to affect the value of the rupee, the government developed no independent, central institution to integrate India's money markets and govern monetary policy. For most of the colonial period, the value of the rupee and its consequent impact on trade relations was left to world market forces. When the value of the rupee plummeted, Indian exports were given a huge boost.

Opium, indigo, sugar, and raw cotton were the major commodities exported by India in 1849. By 1920 exports remained overwhelmingly basic, unfinished commodities: raw cotton, jute manufactures (mainly gunny sacks), raw jute, raw skins and hides, and tea. Although from 1865 to 1920 Britain's share of Indian exports fell from 67 percent to 22 percent, on the eve of its independence India's economy resembled a classic third world economy, producing inelastic agricultural goods for a competitive world market and importing more expensive manufactured goods. Commodity imports exceeded exports by nearly 12 to 1.

Economic wisdom about protection and regulation of trade has changed considerably since the colonial period. While free trade has become the mantra for economic growth since around 1980, in the late nineteenth century many nations, including the United States, actively protected their industries. Protective duties on imports were considered essential for the nurturing of infant industries and at the same time provided a means for governments to reward important constituencies. Few economic historians would deny that India's nascent steel and paper industry got a healthy start thanks to interwar trade barriers. However, it remains an open question whether the absence of tariff protection before 1914 actually hurt the mature Indian textile sector. New research suggests that Indian craft industries, including hand-loom textile production, continued to thrive in the colonial period. Modern machine production was not always a substitute for traditionally processed textiles due to the breadth and segmentation of the textile market. It is possible that free trade may not have hurt Indian producers before 1914, but it certainly did help British producers compete on world markets. For the rulers of British India, free trade held ideological charm, but it often proved contradictory to the necessities of colonial administration.

Santhi Hejeebu

See also **Balance of Payments: Foreign Investment and the Exchange Rate; Economic Policy and Change, 1800–1947**

BIBLIOGRAPHY

Charlesworth, Neil. *British Rule and the Indian Economy, 1800–1914.* London: Macmillan, 1982.
Rothermund, Dietmar. *India in the Great Depression, 1929–1939.* Delhi: Manohar, 1992.
———. *An Economic History of India.* London: Routledge, 1993.
Roy, K. C. *The Sub-Continent in the International Economy, 1850–1900.* Hong Kong: Asian Research Service, 1988.
Roy, Tirthankar. *The Economic History of India, 1857–1947.* Delhi: Oxford University Press, 2000.

TRIBAL PEOPLES OF EASTERN INDIA

India's tribal population, about 83.6 million, constitutes 8 percent of the total population of the country. This population comprises about 461 distinct tribal communities. More than 90 percent of the tribals live in tribal minority states. The tribal minority states spread over a broad girdle in middle India from Gujarat to West Bengal. The tribal majority states like Arunachal Pradesh, Meghalaya, Mizoram, and Nagaland are all located in the northeast region of the country. But less than 10 percent of the total tribal population resides there.

Ethnically, the tribes in eastern India belong to two racial stocks, Proto-Austroloid and Mongoloid. The Proto-Austroloid group is found in Jharkhand, Orissa, and the southern districts of West Bengal, while the Mongoloid group covers the other tribes in Bengal and the Northeast.

The most important tribal communities are: Santhal, Munda, Oraon, and Ho in Jharkhand; the Bhumij, Bhuiya, Gond, Kandha, and Saora in Orissa; the Bhumij, Santhal, Kora, Lepcha, Bhutia, Munda, and Oraon in West Bengal; Kachari, Miri, and Rabha in Assam; the Adi, Nyishi, Apatani, Monpa, and Wancho in Arunachal Pradesh; the Naga in Nagaland; Garo and Khasi in Meghalaya; the Mizo in Mizoram; some Naga tribes, Mac, and Paite in Manipur; and Tripuri, Riang, and Chakma in Tripura.

All these tribes differ in population, levels of sociocultural and economic development, means of subsistence, religion, and language. However, 90 percent of tribal populations reside in villages. There are many tribes spread over more than one state, such as the Santal, Munda, Oraon, the Naga, and the Gond. All these tribes

Young Members of Naga Tribe Armed with Swords and Shields. In this c. 1930 photo, young Naga warriors from the northeast Assam region pose for the camera. HULTON-DEUTSCH COLLECTION / CORBIS.

are known as scheduled tribes (STs). This status gives them certain safeguards, as well as certain rights and privileges, and entitles them to additional development funds from the central government. It also provides for reservation in legislatures, services, and educational institutions. Some of these tribal communities have been identified as "primitive tribal groups," characterized as inhabiting preagricultural land and having extremely low levels of literacy. Some of them are found in Jharkhand and Orissa. India's government pays special attention to speeding up their development and saving them from extinction.

The literacy percentage among the STs in eastern India varies between 82 percent in Mizoram and 23 percent in Orissa. The literacy percentage in the middle Indian states is much lower than in the Northeast. Among women, the rates of literacy of the scheduled caste (SC) population are lowest in Jharkhand and Orissa.

PERCENTAGE OF TRIBAL POPULATION IN EASTERN INDIA STATES	
Arunachal Pradesh	63.7
Assam	12.8
Jharkhand	26.9
Manipur	34.4
Meghalaya	85.5
Mizoram	94.8
Nagaland	87.7
Orissa	22.2
West Bengal	5.6
Tripura	30.95

The work participation rate of the tribal population is about 50 percent, which is much higher than that of the general population, primarily due to very high rate of work participation among tribal women. The tribal population is largely concentrated in rural areas, which have higher female participation rates than the urban areas. In addition, women are employed in forestry operations, which are largely female-oriented. Since very few tribal girls go to school, they are available for taking up gainful economic activity. Ninety percent of the workers are engaged in the primary sector, about 4 percent in the secondary sector, and 6 percent in the tertiary sector.

Social Structure

Each tribal group is known by a distinct name. Some of these are divided into subtribes. Dual organization is also found among some tribes in Orissa. Almost all the tribes are made up of clans, which are exogamous. Of course, there are some exceptions, such as Maler and Parahiya in Jharkhand and Saora in Orissa. In northeast India, social stratification is found among some tribes, such as Monpa and Apatani in Arunachal Pradesh.

By and large, most of the tribes are patriarchal and patrilocal. Succession is from father to son. There are only two tribes that are matriarchal and matrilocal: the Khasi and Garo of Meghalaya. There is no polyandry among eastern Indian tribes, but polygyny is permitted and practiced among many tribes.

The basic unit of the tribal society is the family. Joint or extended families are very rare; in most places the family is nuclear. After marriage, both son and daughter leave the parental home. The son sets up a new household, while married girls go to live with their husbands, In most marriages, there is the practice of paying a bride price, either in cash or in kind, or in both. In some communities in the Northeast, the bride price consists of cattle.

Most of the marriages are negotiated by parents, but there are also other methods of mate selection. Most marriages are adult marriages, and in some cases there are love marriages that are later approved by the parents. In these tribal communities, marriages are a long process, punctuated by various rituals. However, unlike Hindu marriage, tribal marriage is not a religious sacrament, and no priests are involved at any stage in the entire process. Marriage rules prohibit marriage inside the clan and outside the tribe. Anyone breaking these rules invites social ostracism in addition to incurring divine displeasure. Divorce is allowed under certain conditions but must be approved by the village council, which provides for compensation to the aggrieved party. Widow remarriage is allowed. Polygyny is largely confined to affluent sections of the tribal society. It is also a status symbol. The eldest wife enjoys a privileged position in a polygynous family.

In matriarchal societies, among the Khasi and Garo, the family is headed by a woman who has full command over family resources and makes all important decisions regarding family matters. On her death, her position is inherited by her daughter. After marriage, a man must shift to his wife's family. A person inherits the clan title of his mother. In such a society, men play a secondary role.

In many tribal societies in eastern India, youth dormitories used to play an important role in the socialization of children. It was an effective economic organization for guests, a useful seminary of training for young men in the social and cultural duties, and was an institution for magico–religious observances calculated to secure success in hunting. It was also a place for training in music and dance. The organization was entirely managed by the youths, helping them to acquire organizational and leadership skills. It was indeed a "kingdom of the young." In Jharkhand, among the Oraon, it was known as *dhumkuria*. Although *dhumkuria* buildings are found in some villages, they have lost their functions. A similar organization known as the *ghotul* is functioning on traditional lines among the Muria Gond in the Bastar District of Chhatisgarh.

Among the northeastern tribes like the Naga, an organization of this nature, called *morung*, exists. It also functions as a community house where all the weapons of war and head-hunting trophies are placed, reminiscent of days when village raids were common. The Naga *morung* strengthens the sense of social unity, develops in boys a strong esprit de corps, and at the same time encourages competition between the *morung*, thus stimulating the activities of the whole village.

The position of women in tribal societies in eastern India is much better than in other societies, for they are independent and do not suffer any seclusion. They move about freely in the forest, farms, and agricultural fields. They work shoulder to shoulder with men. In the Northeast they also engage in small business and manage sales in small shops.

However, tribal custom prohibits giving a share to daughters in their fathers' property on the plea that after marriage they become members of another clan. She is entitled to a share in her husband's property after his death. In other matters, women do not suffer from any inequality. In matriarchal society, the status of women is higher than in patriarchal society, since all authority is vested in the head of the family, who is a woman.

Tribal Economy

Tribals in eastern India make a living by different means. There are some communities that are still in the hunting and gathering stage. The Birhor in Jharkhand are a classic example of such subsistence. Now a section of this tribe is engaged in settled cultivation. Some communities are pastoralists, engaged in sheep or cattle rearing, such as the Sulung of Arunachal Pradesh. The number of people engaged in hunting, food gathering, and pastoralism is very small. More than 90 percent of tribals subsist on agriculture, either shifting or settled. Shifting cultivation is generally carried out in areas where flat land is not available for plow cultivation. In Jharkhand, the Maler of Santal Pargana are still engaged in shifting cultivation. Many tribal communities in Orissa, particularly in the hilly regions, are engaged in shifting cultivation. In this process, a plot where vegetation has grown is set on fire, and then the ashes are spread all over. Seeds are sown with help of digging sticks. No plow is used. One plot is cultivated for a year or two. It is then left fallow for a number of years to allow vegetation to grow again. Shifting cultivation is regarded as wasteful by agronomists and foresters. Efforts are being made to introduce scientific horticulture. In many areas of Arunachal Pradesh, apples, oranges, pineapples, and potatoes are being grown on shifting cultivation sites.

The bulk of the tribals in other areas are engaged in settled cultivation and grow a large number of food crops, but the agricultural technology continues to be traditional. Efforts are being made to improve the situation by providing irrigation, improved seeds, and fertilizes and insecticides. This is extremely important, as the fertility of the soil is quite low in plateau and hill areas in comparison to river valleys, villages, and plains.

With the growth of education and the opening up of communication in tribal areas, both in middle India and the Northeast, some tribals have shifted to secondary and tertiary sectors of employment. In Jharkhand and Orissa, the growth of industry has attracted tribal people, who have joined largely as unskilled laborers in Jharkhand and Orissa and as contractors and small businessmen in the Northeast.

Religious Beliefs and Practices

Most tribal religions are animistic. Their deities are associated or named after natural objects like sun, moon, hills, forest, rivers, and so on. Most of them have a pantheon headed by a high god (God of Gods), such as Singbonga among the Munda of Chotanagpur. He is benevolent, omniscient, and omnipresent. Below the high god are clan and village gods. There are a number of deities associated with hill, forest, and rivers. In Chotanagpur they are known as Bonga. There are also ancestral spirits at home to whom worship is offered on certain occasions. In Jharkhand most villages have a common place of worship—known as *sarna*—where a number of village gods are propitiated by the village priest, known differently among different tribes. In recent times, *sarnaism* is a term that has been used for tribal religion in Jharkhand. However, in census reports, most tribals have been classified as Hindu.

In Arunachal Pradesh most of the tribals, except the Christians and Buddhists, are followers of the popular tribal deity Donyi Polo. In many tribal religions, there are both benevolent and malevolent spirits. The latter must be propitiated so that they do not cause any harm to man or cattle. Tribal society is also characterized by firm belief in totem and taboo. In fact, each clan has a totem fashioned after a natural object, animate or inanimate. This object is given all respect and is regarded as the protector of that totemic group. Taboo is observed in regard to certain items of behavior and ritual practices. Any breach of taboo attracts divine punishment.

All tribal societies in India observe many fairs and festivals. These are largely connected with agriculture, such as the sowing of seeds, first fruit rituals, and harvest. These festivals are spread throughout the year and are celebrated for several days. All the festivals are marked by dances, music, and community worship of deities. The fervor with which these festivals are celebrated is an assertion of tribal identity.

In Jharkhand, Orissa, and West Bengal, a large number of tribals observe Hindu festivals and worship Hindu gods and goddesses during festivals. Such practices do not clash with belief in tribal gods and goddesses. This spirit of accommodation is not evident when they come into contact with Christian missionaries.

Christian missionaries entered tribal areas in Chotanagpur and the Northeast at different times, under the patronage of British rulers. Christian missionaries belonging to various denominations entered interior tribal areas and started to convert people there. They met with greater success in the Northeast, particularly in Nagaland, Meghalaya, and Mizoram, where they converted large numbers of tribals to Christianity. These converts shed their old religious beliefs and practices and slowly adopted the norms and behavior patterns of the missionaries. This process was accelerated by the spread of education through the medium of the church, which came to play a guiding role in their sociocultural life.

Some tribes in Arunachal are Buddhist. The Monpa follow Mahayana Buddhism, while the Singpho belong to the Hinayana sect. Tawang, which is located close to the Chinese border in Arunachal Pradesh, has a very large monastery with three hundred monks. Some tribes follow the Bon religion, which is a mixture of Buddhism and tribal beliefs and practices.

Colonial Encounters with Tribal Communities

Studies in ancient and medieval Indian history have revealed several instances of continued interaction between the local population and indigenous (tribal) groups in different parts of India. The names of such groups (Bhil, Kol, Kirat, Kinar, Nishad, Asur, etc.) are found in historical literature. Indian rulers were satisfied if tribal chiefs acknowledged their sovereignty and never interfered with tribal customs or imposed tribute. During Mughal rule some revenue was realized, but tribal rights in forest and forest produce were not disturbed. With the establishment of British colonial rule in eastern India, things changed a great deal. The government acquired tribal lands, and different kinds of taxes were imposed on them. Tribal lands were acquired to lay down railways and roads, setting up townships with administrative offices, police stations, educational institutions, and hospitals. In areas where the *zamindari* system prevailed, they were placed under control of the *zamindar*. The exploitative and oppressive behavior of administrative officials and of the *zamindar*s forced the tribals to launch agitation for the removal of their grievances. Such unrest in tribal areas sometimes became violent revolts.

In the wake of famine of 1770, the Pahariya of Rajmahal hills in Santal Pargana rose in revolt against the government. Forced by starvation to come down from the hills, they engaged in theft and murder. The government tried to suppress the revolt but could not. Ultimately, it was an enlightened official, Agustus Cleveland, who solved the problem by introducing certain reforms for providing better administration. This was the first attempt at indirect rule. In 1821 the Ho of Singhbhum rose in a revolt against the incursion of British troops in their area. To solve this problem, Thomas Wilkinson, the agent of the governor-general, introduced a series of

rules by which the second example of indirect rule was put into practice. Again in 1831, the Kol rebellion forced the administration to take steps to curb exploitation and oppression by officials and others from outside the area. The Santal revolt of 1855 was mainly directed against up-country outsiders who came to Santal Pragana as shopkeepers and moneylenders. The exploitation by these elements led to a violent revolt, which continued for more than a year. After the rebellion was quelled, certain reform measures were enacted, the most important of which was the demarcation of Santal-dominated areas known as Damin–e–Koh, which were taken out of the general administration and were placed under special regulations. It is clear that all these movements originated from economic exploitation, encroachment on tribal land, infringement of tribal rights in land and forest, and interference with age-old customs.

Survival and Identity

The tribals are faced with a large number of problems emanating from land alienation, which has continued in spite of government legislation: the chronic deficit budget of the tribal family (leading to indebtedness and bonded labor), low productivity of the soil, traditional agricultural practices, poor marketing facilities due to lack of communication, low literacy, and unemployment. These problems are compounded by severe malnutrition, poor health, and lack of sanitation. In recent times many development projects in tribal areas resulted in large-scale displacement; building large industrial establishments resulted in ousting tribals from their homes. Irrigation projects in tribal-dominated areas have submerged a large number of villages by the construction of reservoirs. Reports of the commissioner for SCs and STs are replete with examples of the ravages of such projects. The tribals were displaced from the traditional sources of their livelihood and their places of habitation. The funds they received as "compensation" for their land were soon dissipated, and they joined the ranks of landless laborers. The establishment of vast industrial enterprises in tribal zones has led to the sacrifice of tribal interest at the altar of India's modernization.

In a cultural contact situation there is a greater likelihood of the smaller group losing its language and adopting the language of the economically stronger, culturally more advanced neighbor. In the past two centuries, tribal cultures have become the targets of assault from two sides. Interaction with Hindu society has led to the adoption of many norms and values that were foreign to tribals. This process has not only created prejudice against occupations such as leather working and butchering, but has introduced the dietary taboos, child marriage, and restrictions on remarriage of widows associated with

Hinduism. This is a part of the Sanskritization process, in which the norms and values of Hindu society became the reference model and principal criteria of social responsibility.

Hinduism is not the only ideological force that constitutes the cultural assault on tribal mores. With the advent of Christianity a large number of tribals in eastern India have been converted. Missionary influence has eroded much of their cultural heritage, including myths, beliefs, and rituals. Conversion of a part of any tribal community tends to destroy its social unity.

It is generally seen that not only physical survival but much of tribal social organization and its culture centers around access to land and control and management of natural resources, which is a basis of their life support system. Steady deprivation of these resources and of the traditional right of management and control of the same is reflected in the process of pauperization. The problems are compounded by the lack of diversification of occupations. Under these circumstances, some tribals in middle and eastern India began to suffer from threats to their identity. This is the result of the spread of education, exposure to urban influences, and entry into government service through job reservations. The resurgence of traditional religious identity, the creation of new literature, and the invention of scripts bear testimony to growing tribal identity assertion.

Christian missionaries, nongovernmental organizations, and tribal associations are all catalysts of social change in this regard. Tribal associations initiate social reforms in customary matters, like the reduction or abolition of bride price. Cultural movements launched by Ragunath Murmu among the Santals, focusing on education with a district script and culturally oriented curriculum, as well as social reform, continued for many decades. The Manki-Munda movement launched by the traditional headman of Singhbhum in Jharkhand emanated from an encroachment on traditional land rights but later assumed political overtones. Threats to traditional systems of control and management of resources and the search for a more satisfactory system of organization of community power leads to the creation of political platforms, launching movements that at times react with violence.

The assertion of tribal identity is more evident in tribal minority states. The tribals felt that changes initiated by the state or through market forces tended to erode their identity. In tribal majority states there is no such problem, since tribals can reshape their own future through a democratic process and legal constitutional means. They have never experienced any exploitation or discrimination at the hands of nontribals. In fact, as a result of the dispensation of "Inner Line" regulations, tribals are protected from incursions by nontribal elements. This creates a situation of exploitation in reverse, resulting in the exploitation of nontribals who go to the tribal states in search of small business jobs.

Some of the states in the Northeast are in the grip of sustained violent insurgency. The roots of that insurgency may be traced to hopes entertained among some tribal leaders that with the end of British rule in 1947, the tribal areas in the Northeast would revert to independent status. Thus insurgency is a struggle not so much for autonomy but for secession from India. In some parts of the Northeast, like Arunachal Pradesh, Meghalaya, and Mizoram, total peace prevails and people are reaping the fruits of peace through steady development and a rise in their standards of living.

In India the tribals do not face any problem of physical survival. There has been a steady rise in tribal population, from 30 million in 1961 to 67.8 million in 1991. The literacy percentage rose from 8.5 percent in 1961 to 30 percent in 1991. Ninety-two percent of tribals in the country live in rural areas, and the percentage of people below the poverty line in the rural areas is slightly over 50 percent, while that of general population is 37 percent. They have adequate representation in government service, in the Indian Parliament, and in *panchayati raj* institutions. In the tribal minority states, where the fifth schedule of the Constitution is in operation, adequate measures have been taken to safeguard their interests in all walks of life. Whenever money has to be allotted for the promotion of "total literacy" or Integrated Child Development Service projects, priority is given to tribal areas. Steps have also been taken to promote tribal culture through songs, dances, marketing of handicrafts, and the promotion of tribal languages.

The tribals in India, both in tribal majority and tribal minority states, have retained their identity and are proud of their cultural heritage. Their leaders' main concern is to see that their rights as citizens in India's democracy are well protected. They are striving, through the help of state and the wider society, to achieve a better quality of life while slowly moving toward social integration with other communities of their region.

Sachchidananda

See also **Scheduled Tribes**

BIBLIOGRAPHY

Furer-Haimendorf, C. von. *Highlanders in Arunachal Pradesh*. New Delhi: Vikas, 1982.
Ghurye, G. S. *Aborigines, So Called and Their Future*. Pune: Gokhale Institute of Politics and Economics, 1943.

Sachchidananda. *The Changing Munda*. New Delhi: Concept Publishing House, 1979.

Singh, Kumar Suresh. *The Scheduled Tribes*. Delhi: Oxford University Press, 1994.

TRIBAL POLITICS The "tribal" peoples or *adivasis* of India, according to the 2001 census, constitute roughly 8.1 percent of the country's population, some 83.6 million people, classified under 461 different communities. They occupy a belt stretching from the Bhil regions of western India through the Gond districts of central India, to Jharkhand and Bengal, where the Mundas, Oraons, and Santals predominate. There are also pockets of tribal communities in the south like the Chenchus, Todas, and Kurumbas, and very small endangered communities in the Andamans, like the Jarawas, Onge, and Sentinelese. Northeast India contains another major portion of the tribal population, including the different Naga subtribes, Khasis, Garos, Mizos, Kukis, Bodos, and others. The intellectual, political, and administrative rationale for treating all these communities together under a single "tribal" rubric remains unclear.

One feature common to all these communities, however, whether in central or northeastern India, is their division between different state and administrative boundaries, including national borders (e.g., the Chakmas are divided between Mizoram and Bangladesh, the Nagas and Kukis cross the Indo-Myanmar border). In central India, although communities like the Gonds and the Bhils number some 7.3 million people each (1991 census), none of them has been recognized as peoples, nor have they been given statehood, as have other linguistic communities. Even though the struggle for a tribal but multiethnic state of Jharkhand preceded that of many other linguistic states, it was finally achieved in truncated form in November 2000. In the Northeast, struggles for autonomy range from complete independence to statehood to autonomous district councils. Another common feature is the combination of special legal provisions for tribals on the one hand, and repression by the police and army on the other, when tribal peoples try to assert their own visions of the good life.

The "tribal question" in central India has traditionally been posed in two ways by academics and policy makers: the question of differentiating between tribes and castes on the one hand, and tribes and peasants on the other; and the question of how best to improve what is universally seen as a poverty-stricken condition among tribals. In the Northeast, struggles for autonomy, statehood, and secession have put the question of identity at center stage. For the government, the main issue there is law and order, and solutions are usually conceived in military terms, such as the draconian Armed Forces (Special Powers) Act of 1958, which gives armed personnel the right to shoot on sight on mere suspicion, arrest without warrant, and enter and search premises at will. To understand contemporary tribal politics, however, it is essential to start with the colonial period.

Colonialism

In the pre-colonial period, while hill and plains people occupied different ecological, social, and often political spaces, there was often considerable trade and even intermarriage between the two. Both in central and northeastern India, hills people would raid the plains, and were in turn looked down upon as savages. Yet categories were often fungible, and the balance of power was never fixed. Colonialism was a significant watershed, both in epistemological and material terms. The production of census records, gazetteers, official or semiofficial ethnographies, grammars, linguistic surveys, and land tenure records all served to create sociological and epistemological categories such as castes and tribes. The characterization of the tribal in India was similar to that in Africa, drawing on evolutionary classifications based on race and anthropometry, the denigration of any indigenous kingship or polity in favor of an acephalous, kinship-bound society, and the perceived primitiveness of modes of production. The categories "tribal," "primitive," "savage," or "wild" were also used interchangeably to characterize those peoples who resisted colonial rule, and formed part of the justifciation for particularly violent campaigns of "pacification," such as the burning of Kond villages in Orissa in the nineteenth century, ostensibly to suppress human sacrifice, or Naga villages in the twentieth century, to outlaw head-hunting.

But the Indian "tribe" was further understood to be differentiated by religion and culture from the Indian "caste." The census reports, with their agonizing over the distinction between animists and Hindus, in particular contributed to this objectification, which continues to fuel social science debates. There were of course dissenters from the conventional view, for example, sociologist André Beteille (1974), who pointed out that in terms of size, isolation, religion, and means of livelihood, it was often not possible to distinguish between castes and tribes.

In material terms, the colonial view of tribal communities as isolated, poor, and backward created conditions for their exploitation. Shifting cultivation, which was a widely practiced form of agriculture, was dismissed as wasteful and destructive of the forests. Reservation of the forests to make space for monocultures, which would contribute to the British shipbuilding, railway, and war efforts, was introduced in the guise of "scientific forestry." Restrictions were introduced on the collection and sale of nontimber forest produce, which was a major source of income for most tribal communities. These changes set off more than a century of conflict over access to the forests. Some of the major rebellions in tribal India, such as the Bastar Bhumkal of 1910 and the Jharkhand Sal Andolan of the late 1970s, have been over forest rights. In many places, the forest department claimed land that *adivasis* had been cultivating for generations but on which their rights had never been recorded. Forced evictions from such lands, and the precarious situation of forest villages, remains a central and burning issue for large numbers of forest communities. Similarly, colonial settlement policies that transformed community lands into individually owned plots, higher rents, and unfamiliar legal systems led to significant land alienation. Moneylenders, traders, and others found a foothold in tribal areas, which they progressively expanded into complete dominance. Industrialization has further transformed the demographics of several tribal regions. In Jharkhand for example, tribals were down to approximately 26 percent in 2001 from roughly 50 percent in 1901.

Despite this clear history of underdevelopment, official policy attributes *adivasi* poverty to the backwardness and primitiveness of *adivasis* themselves, or in other words, regards it as an internal condition of their society. In the 1930s and 1940s, there was considerable debate among "isolationists," "integrationists," and "assimilationists" about whether to leave tribals alone, integrate them with some perceived "mainstream," or attempt assimiliation as a path toward progress. In neither case was it acknowledged that they had already been integrated, but on disadvantageous economic terms, as labor and supplier of raw materials. While the official policy of the government of India, as reflected in Jawaharlal Nehru's five principles for tribal policy, or Panchsheel, is culturally "integrationist" and leaves space for *adivasis*' own distinctive customs, in practice, assimiliationist pressures predominate, especially in the sphere of schooling, language, and religion. For instance, the census automatically records *adivasis* as Hindus. The struggle to be recorded as followers of *sarna dharm* has been an important part of *adivasi* politics in Jharkhand in recent years.

Constitutional and Policy Provisions for Tribes

Like the scheduled castes, tribal communities are officially characterized as among the most vulnerable populations in the country, in need of special protective laws. In addition, however, tribal resistance to colonialism ensured that they were governed under distinctive administrative arrangements, some of which are now being rapidly eroded. Maintaining special tenure laws like the Chotanagpur Tenancy Act is now an important part of tribal politics in the state of Jharkhand. The constitutional provisions for scheduled tribes are inevitably a mixture of colonial legacy and fresh thinking at the time of the framing of the Constitution.

Following the various rebellions in *adivasi* areas in the eighteenth and nineteenth centuries, such as the Santal Hul of 1855–1856, the Birsa Ulgulan of 1895–1900, the Tana Bhagat Movement of 1914–1920, and the Bastar Bhumkal of 1910, the colonial government responded either by maintaining indirect rule (as in Bastar or the Dangs) or by setting up specific areas, under the direct rule of an agent to the governor-general, where the land, forest, and other laws applicable to the rest of the British province did not apply and where special administrative arrangements could be made that recognized, at least to some extent, community rather than private property (see, for example, the Bengal Regulation XIII of 1833 which followed the Kol rebellion of 1831–1832). This state of exceptionalism was continued in the Scheduled Districts Act (Act XIV) of 1874, which listed scheduled districts across British India. Special provisions for tribal areas were continued in the Government of India Act of 1919, which allowed for certain areas to be declared "backward tracts," followed by the Government of India Act of 1935 and the Government of India (excluded and partially excluded areas) Order of 1936. These excluded and partially excluded areas later became the scheduled areas of independent India.

There are two broad types of scheduling in the Indian Constitution: area-based and community-based. Under Article 244 of the Constitution (Part X), which deals with the "Administration of Scheduled Areas and Tribal Areas," there are two types of arrangements. The Sixth Schedule applies to tribal areas in the states of Assam, Meghalaya, Tripura, and Mizoram, while nine states have scheduled areas under the Fifth Schedule: Andhra Pradesh, Chhattisgarh, Gujarat, Himachal Pradesh, Jharkhand, Maharashtra, Madhya Pradesh, Orissa, and Rajasthan. While there is a strong overlap between the category of scheduled tribes and scheduled areas, the fit is imperfect. Some states that have the most vulnerable *adivasi* populations, like West Bengal, Karnataka, Tamil Nadu, and Kerala, have no scheduled areas at all, and even in the states where the Fifth Schedule is in operation, not all areas where *adivasis* constitute a majority are covered under the schedule.

Article 342 of the Constitution gives the president the power to schedule or list particular communities in order to render them special protection. These lists are state specific; for instance, the Santals and Mundas are a scheduled tribe in Jharkhand, but not so in Assam or the Andamans, where some of them migrated. Even in their states of origin and despite clear poverty, not all tribal communities are scheduled as tribes, for example the Kols of Sonbhadra and Mirzapur in Uttar Pradesh.

While the Fifth and Sixth Schedules of the Constitution have colonial antecedents, the detailed provisions were framed by three subcommittees of the Advisory Committee on Fundamental Rights and Minorities. The committee, which was to look at the tribal areas "other than Assam" and whose work resulted in the Fifth Schedule, was chaired by the Gandhian A. V. Thakkar, who believed in a policy of "uplift" rather than "rights." The basic assumption underlying the 1833 Bengal Regulation, the 1874 act, and the 1919 and 1935 acts, which has continued in the Fifth Schedule as well, is that tribal areas are best governed by a paternalistic and personalized administration with special and fewer rules than those that apply to nontribal areas. The Fifth Schedule makes provision for Tribes Advisory Councils and for certain laws to prevent alienation of land to nontribals and exploitation by moneylenders. The governor of the state has wide-ranging powers to modify or forbid existing laws or to propose special laws for these areas. In practice, experience with the Fifth Schedule has been very disappointing. The Tribes Advisory Councils have hardly any teeth, laws applicable to the rest of the state are routinely extended to scheduled areas, the governor rarely exercises the powers vested in him or her, and the net result is demonstrated by the miserable human development indicators for *adivasi*s.

The Sixth Schedule, pertaining to former Assam, gives greater recognition to the right to self-governance, through the formation of autonomous district and regional councils with legislative powers in a variety of important matters, including the management of forests, the regulation of shifting cultivation, the appointment of chiefs or headmen, property inheritance, and social customs. The District Councils also have the power to levy taxes, regulate money lending, establish and manage primary schools, dispensaries, and markets. However, it still falls short of the autonomy that many groups in the Northeast region were demanding at the time.

In a parallel stream, the 73rd Amendment Act of the Constitution (1993) made it mandatory for every state to constitute *panchayat*s, or councils, at the village, intermediate, and district levels. Past experience with elected *panchayat*s that supplanted traditional tribal systems, however, led to a legal challenge by *adivasi* groups, and in 1995 the Andhra Pradesh High Court ruled that a separate act was needed for scheduled areas. Accordingly, in December 1996, Parliament passed the Provisions of the Panchayats (Extension to the Scheduled Areas) Act (PESA). This act is applicable to Fifth Schedule areas, since the Sixth Schedule already contains many of its provisions regarding customary law. In fact, PESA explicitly aspires to implement Sixth Schedule–like arrangements in Fifth Schedule areas. PESA mandates that any "State legislation on the Panchayats . . . shall be in consonance with the customary law, social and religious practices and traditional management practices of community resources" and that "every Gram sabha [village assembly] shall be competent to safeguard and preserve the traditions and customs of the people, their cultural identity, community resources and the customary mode of dispute resolution." However, most states have not passed appropriate legislation to implement the act, and there is widespread and often purposeful ignorance of its provisions on the part of officials.

In addition to the Fifth and Sixth Schedules and PESA, a number of constitutional provisions are addressed to *adivasi*s as individual citizens. These include: Article 15 (4), which enables special provisions for the advancement of socially and educationally backward classes; Article 16 (4a), which enables reservations in government services; Article 275 (1), which relates to central grants-in-aid to states for the specific purpose of scheduled tribe welfare; Articles 330, 332, and 335, which stipulate seats for scheduled tribes in the Parliament, state assemblies, and services; and Article 339, which mandates the setting up of a commission to report on the administration and welfare of scheduled areas and scheduled tribes. Successive five-year plans have also created special plans for tribal development, in the shape of multipurpose tribal blocks (second plan), tribal development agencies (fourth plan), and tribal subplans (fifth plan).

Tribal Politics in Central India

However, even as the state created paternalist schemes and legal provisions for tribal "development," it contributed to their poverty and landlessness through land acquisition for mining, hydroelectric projects, defense projects, and other "development" activities, leading to massive displacement. The Bailadilla iron ore mine in Bastar, the Hirakud and Upper Indravati hydroelectric projects in Orissa, and the Sardar Sarovar dam in Gujarat are all examples. Apart from displacement, the two other axes of tribal politics are struggles over the forest and everyday encounters with the police.

Adivasi communities have responded to their situation in several ways: many of them have succumbed to the forces of industrialization and displacement, losing their lands and migrating to urban centers or other states in search of employment. A significant number, however, have joined communist struggles, like the Telengana movement and become members of the various "Naxalite" parties, such as the Communist Party of India (Maoist), to demand land reform and access to resources. They have also been active in various struggles against displacement by large dams led by organizations like the Narmada Bachao Andolan or the Koel Karo Andolan, as well as in the struggle against insensitive and overly exploitative mining as in Kashipur, Orissa. In each of these struggles, people have been arrested and killed by the police, their houses have been razed, and their crops destroyed.

Since the late 1990s several tribal groups have mobilized to retain rights to forest land, which are in danger of being usurped by the Supreme Court decision of 1996, in the Godavarman forest case, which gives the forest department the right to manage all "forests," as defined in the dictionary, regardless of their actual ownership. With one stroke, this judgment negates decades of struggle for more participatory forest management, as well as the specific rights provided by local tenurial acts like the Chotanagpur Tenancy Act.

Another major plank of *adivasi* politics today is to claim the rights promised by PESA. Many nongovernmental organizations and social movements have promoted the setting up of village assemblies (*gram sabha*s), on the grounds that they have a constitutionally recognized "competence" to manage their own resources. The government, however, does not recognize these assemblies. In Meghalaya, there has been a parallel move to revive Khasi *syiem*s, or chiefs. Several *adivasi* groups have also begun to make alliances with international networks of tribal and indigenous peoples.

Given the desperate situation in which many of the central Indian *adivasi*s live, survival issues have usually dominated over identity questions. Competitive proselytization by Christian and Hindu groups has also served to reduce the space for the expression of an autonomous *adivasi* culture, language, and religion. In recent years, while some *adivasi* communities have been mobilized by Hindutva (Hindu nationalist) political forces, primarily through the work of Rashtriya Swayamsevak Sangh fronts like the Vanvasi Kalyan Ashram, the Bajrang Dal, and the Vishwa Hindu Parishad, others have attempted to revive traditional *adivasi* religions like the *sarna dharm* (sacred grove religion).

Tribal Politics in the Northeast Region

Many of the movements in the Northeast date back to the colonial policy of excluded areas and inner line permits, which cut off existing links between the hills and plains peoples, creating isolated tribal areas and communities. Christian missionary activities in these areas, particularly what is now Nagaland, Mizoram, and Meghalaya initially resulted in a loss of indigenous identity, culture, and religion, but eventually led to the formation of new identities, like that of the Naga and the Mizo peoples out of different subtribes, and the emergence of an educated middle class, which could articulate nationalist aspirations.

The failure of the Indian state to recognize people's aspirations, forced accessions at the time of independence, as well as subsequent military action and repression further fueled secessionist politics.

The Northeast is marked by a multiplicity of insurgent outfits representing different ethnic groups, some of whom are engaged in interethnic warfare (e.g., the Naga-Kuki tensions) as well as conflict with the Indian state. Within the space demanded by larger nationalities like the Assamese or the Mizos, there are several minority groups that are also engaged in autonomy struggles, including the Bodos, Karbis, Dimasas, and Koch Rajbanshis in Assam, and the Hmars and Reangs in Mizoram. Some of them, like the Bodos, have been successful in negotiating accords with the Indian government, resulting in the Bodoland Territorial Council within Assam. Immigration by nontribals into tribal areas, especially Bangladeshis, is a major political issue in the area. Since it would be impossible to go into the histories of each movement, what follows here is simply a representative glimpse of two major nationality struggles, those of the Nagas and the Mizos.

Until the 1960s, Arunachal Pradesh (earlier known as North East Frontier Area or NEFA), Meghalaya, Nagaland, and Mizoram were part of the province of Assam. Manipur and Tripura, which were princely states, were absorbed into the Indian union as Part C states and then union territories, and were given separate statehood much later.

The Naga movement, which is the oldest and most powerful autonomy movement in the area, goes back to 1918, with the formation of the Naga club, in which ex-members of the World War I labor corps played a major role. In 1946 leadership of the Nagas was taken over by the Naga National Council (NNC), with representation from different subtribes. Apprehending that Indian independence and the absorption of Naga areas into India would mean a loss of autonomy, and yet with no clear alternative, the NNC wanted a ten-year interim agreement with India, during which it could decide whether it wanted complete independence. A nine-point agreement to this effect was signed between the NNC and the governor of Assam, Sir Akbar Hydari, in 1947. However, there was a dispute over the interpretation of the ninth clause, which stated that "at the end of this period (10 years) the Naga council will be asked whether they require the above agreement to be extended for a further period or a new agreement regarding the future of the Naga people arrived at." While the Nagas interpreted it to mean that they would be given the choice of independence, the Indian government interpreted it to mean that the Naga hills were now an integral part of India. The Nagas hills became a district of Assam, to be administered under the Sixth Schedule. This led to a split within the NNC, with A. Z. Phizo demanding complete independence. From about 1953, the NNC was forced into underground resistance by the presence of the Indian army. Since then, the Naga peoples have seen continued insurgency, as well as severe army repression involving rapes, killings, and the occupation of churches and schools, all of which is "legally" sanctioned under the Naga Hills Disturbed Areas Ordinance, the Assam Maintenance of Public Order Act, and the Armed Forces Special Powers Act 1858 (amended in 1972). Pressure by Naga moderates on both the insurgents and the Indian government bought some peace in the form of statehood for Nagaland in 1963. Like the Hydari Agreement, the 1974 Shillong Accord between the central government and the insurgents died a quick death, and in 1980 the National Socialist Council of Nagalim (NSCN) was formed. This in turn split into two factions, named after their leaders, the NSCN (Isak-Muivah) and NSCN (Khaplang). From 1997 onward, again due to pressure by civil society groups like the Naga Hoho, the Naga Peoples Movement for Human Rights, and the Naga Mothers Association, there have been talks between the NSCN (I-M) and the Indian government. However, the Indian government's proposal to extend a cease-fire to all Naga areas in 2001 created huge unrest in Manipur. The cease-fire was read as an initial step toward accepting the NSCN demand for a greater Nagaland, or Nagalim, which would incorporate the three northern districts of Manipur. Naga unification would also affect Assam and Arunachal Pradesh, creating resistance within those states.

Among the Mizos, the earliest social and political associations were the Young Lushai Association and the Mizo Union. The early struggles of the Mizos were against their own feudal chiefs, and around the time of independence, the left faction of the Mizo Union was in favor of merging with India as a way of abolishing the chiefship. Another faction, however, wanted independence or union with Burma (Myanmar). Eventually, in 1947, the Mizos became a part of India, but were split between Bangladesh (Chittangong Hill Tracts), and the Indian states of Tripura and Manipur. Unlike in Tripura, however, where there was a long struggle for the tribal areas to be brought under the Sixth Schedule in an Autonomous District Council, in Mizoram the Sixth Schedule was applied from the start. In 1958 the cyclic flowering of the bamboo led to a huge multiplication of rats and famine. Inadequate relief, the Assam government's imposition of the Assamese language, and the construction of a separate Christian and Mizo identity led to the formation of the Mizo National Front (MNF), led by Laldenga. The MNF carried out attacks on government offices and communication lines and on 1 March 1966 declared independence. The Indian government's response was to declare the Mizo hills a disturbed area, aerially strafing villages and forcibly regrouping several villages into concentrations along the highway. This effectively destroyed the Mizos' own subsistence economy, based on shifting cultivation and made them dependent on government rations. After episodic peace talks, an accord was signed in 1986 between Laldenga, the Mizoram government, and the government of India, whereby the MNF became part of the government in Mizoram.

Nandini Sundar

See also **Ethnic Conflict; Ethnic Peace Accords; Insurgency and Terrorism; Mizoram; Nagas and Nagaland; Northeast States, The; Tribal Peoples of Eastern India**

BIBLIOGRAPHY

Baruah, Sanjib. *India against Itself: Politics of Nationality in Assam.* Philadelphia: University of Pennsylvania Press, 1999.

Beteille, André. *Six Essays in Comparative Sociology.* New Delhi: Oxford University Press, 1974.

Furer-Haimendorf, Christoph von. *Tribes of India: The Struggle for Survival.* Berkeley: University of California Press, 1982.

Gadgil, Madhav, and Ramachandra Guha. *This Fissured Land: An Ecological History of India.* Delhi: Oxford University Press, 1992.

Ghurye, G. S. *The Scheduled Tribes.* Mumbai: Popular Press, 1963.

Grigson, W. V. *The Aboriginal Problem in the Central Provinces and Berar.* 1944. Bhopal: Vanya Prakashan, 1993.

Grove, R., V. Damodaran, and S. Sangwan, eds. *Nature and the Orient: The Environmental History of South and South East Asia.* Delhi: Oxford University Press, 1998.

Guha, Ranajit. *Elementary Aspects of Peasant Insurgency in Colonial India.* Delhi: Oxford University Press, 1983.

Guha, Sumit. *Environment and Ethnicity in India, 1200–1991.* Cambridge, U.K.: Cambridge University Press, 1999.

Munda, Ram Dayal, and Samar Bosu Mullick, eds. *The Jharkhand Movement: Indigenous People's Struggle for Autonomy in India.* Document no. 168. Copenhagen: International Work Group for Indigenous Affairs, 2003.

Nag, Sajal. *Contesting Marginality: Ethnicity, Insurgency, and Subnationalism in North-East India.* New Delhi: Manohar, 2002.

Nehru, Jawaharlal. "An Approach to Tribal Problems." In *Anthropology in the Development Process,* edited by H. M. Mathur. New Delhi: Vikas Publishing House, 1977.

Sharma, B. D. *Report of the Commissioner for Scheduled Castes and Scheduled Tribes: 28th Report, 1986–87.* Delhi: Government of India, 1988.

———. *Report of the Commissioner for Scheduled Castes and Scheduled Tribes: 29th Report, 1987–89.* Delhi: Government of India, 1990.

Sundar, Nandini. *Subalterns and Sovereigns: An Anthropological History of Bastar, 1854–1996.* Delhi: Oxford University Press, 1997.

TRIPURA Located in India's Northeast region, Tripura is the smallest of the seven hill states, the "Seven Sisters." The climate is generally hot and humid. Tripura is bordered by Bangladesh on the north, the south, and the west, Assam on the northeast, and Mizoram on the east. The monsoon usually begins in April and lasts until September. The population of nineteen tribes, led by Tripuris (over 50% of tribals), Reangs, and Chakma, who speak a variety of languages and dialects, and immigrant Bengalis, was about 3 million in 2004. The main languages spoken are Bengali, Kakbarak, and Manipuri, although Bengali is the official language. Animism plays a large part in the life of the tribals, but the largest number of people follow Buddhism, followed by Christianity and Hinduism.

The state is divided into the four districts of North, South, and West Tripura, where the capital Agartala is located, and Dhalai. Just over 50 percent of the state is covered by forest, and the landscape is composed of picturesque hills and dales and green, deep valleys. Less than 25 percent of the land is suitable for agriculture, with rice being the main crop. The main rivers are the Gomati, the largest and the one considered to be the most sacred, the Khowati, Manu, Haorah, and Muhari. Dunbar Falls is one of the most sacred places in the state.

The early history of the state is told in legend and is said to have played a role in the Battle of Kurukshetra. Some seventy-four Tripuri rajas ruled Tripura and were called "Manikya." In about 1280, Muslims invaded the state, and this was followed by settlers from Bengal and Burma. The Bengali sultan ruled until 1515, but in 1586, the Mughals defeated Jasodhara Manikya, and he ceded a part of the state to them. The state was ceded to the British in 1761.

The tribals followed *jhuming*, or slash-and-burn agriculture, or shifting irrigation, which has led to soil erosion and ecological degradation and depletion. Large-scale *jhuming* was banned by the government in 1952. The per capita income is well below the national average, and more than 80 percent of the people live below the poverty line. In addition, the state bore the brunt of massive immigration from East Pakistan and Bengal. The Bengalis brought with them plow cultivation and forced the tribals from the plains to the hills, where they fell into the clutches of Bengali moneylenders and traders.

On 15 October 1949 Tripura entered the Indian Union as a state. It became a Union Territory on 21 January 1972, and Ujjayanta Palace became the Legislative Assembly. Though the Communists had championed the cause of the Tripuris, they created the Tripura Upajati Juba Samiti, a separatist party, on 10 June 1967; their demands included more autonomy and the recognition of the Kakbarak language as an official language. In 1978 a secret military organization, the Tripura National Volunteers, was formed, aimed at achieving complete independence for the state, and they committed hit-and-run attacks and assassinations of Bengalis, who responded through their Amra Bengali. Communal tension has never dissipated.

Roger D. Long

See also **Assam; Ethnic Conflict; Mizoram**

BIBLIOGRAPHY

Pakem, B. *Regionalism in India: With Special Reference to North-East India.* New Delhi: Har-Anand Publications, 1993.
Ray, Syamal Kumar. *India's North-East and the Travails of Tripura.* Kolkata: Minerva Associates, 2003.

TYĀGARĀJA *(1767–1847), poet-composer.* The most influential poet-composer (*vāggēyakāra*) of South India, Tyāgarāja was born on 4 May 1767 in Tiruvārūr near Tanjāvūr, then a center of learning and culture. Between seven hundred and one thousand of his songs, mainly belonging to the genres known as *kīrtana* and *kriti*, have been preserved by several teacher-disciple lineages (*guru shishya parampara*). His Telugu lyrics are infused with Sanskrit and reveal a variety of literary and philosophical influences as well as a profound knowledge of music theory. Unlike his contemporaries, Muttusvāmi Dīkshitar and Shyāma Shāstri, with whom he forms the "Trinity" of South Indian music, Tyāgarāja often shares the joys and struggles of his personal life and worship with his public. Like Dīkshitar, he was an accomplished vina player (*vainika*) who succeeded in amalgamating the expressiveness (*bhāva*) of the voice and the aesthetic appeal (*rasa*) of instrumental music.

The fact that Tyāgarāja's father was an exponent of *harikathā* (musical discourse) explains the composer's aptitude for bringing the divine and heroic characters of the Rāmāyaṇa, the Purāṇas, and the Bhāgavatam to life. This art form has devotion (*bhakti*) for its subject, provides ample scope for variations on a given theme, and is based on India's ancient Hindu texts.

Tyāgarāja also composed two musical plays, titled *Naukachāritramu* (Boat story) and *Prahlāda bhakti vijayamu* (Victory of Prahlāda's devotion). These original versions of popular stories were told through the characters' singing as well as in narrative passages provided by a *sūtradhāra*, the conventional director of Indian drama. Both works have been adapted for Bhāgavatamēlam drama as well as for Kuchipudi and

Bharata Nātya dance-drama, although they were probably not written for the purpose of being so enacted. Similarly, some portions have long been included in musical concerts.

Tyāgarāja's fame spread during his lifetime and has steadily grown since his death in 1847, initially by way of *harikathā* performances. Since 1925, homage is annually paid to him at festivals known as *Tyāgarāja ārādhana*, primarily in Tiruvaiyāru, where he lived and where his *samādhi* (resting place) was erected, as well as in other locations. Some music societies (*sabhā*) maintain the tradition of reenacting Tyāgarāja's performance of *unchavritti*, the custom of collecting food alms while singing religious songs with his disciples, as he shunned the demands of worldly patrons. With the boldness of a creative genius and the authority of a sage advancing the art and science of music, he celebrates the very experience of music time and again in his songs.

Ludwig Pesch

See also **Music: South India**

BIBLIOGRAPHY

Bhagavathi, Y. *Tyāgarāja's Naukācaritramu.* Chennai: Sarvani Sangeetha Sabha Trust, 1995.
Jackson, William J. *Tyāgarāja: Life and Lyrics.* Chennai: Oxford University Press, 1991.
Pesch, Ludwig. *The Illustrated Companion to South Indian Classical Music.* Delhi: Oxford University Press, 1999.
Ramanujachari, C., and V. Raghavan. *The Spiritual Heritage of Tyāgarāja.* 1958. Chennai: Sri Ramakrishna Math, 1981.
Sambamoorthy, P. *Great Composers II: Tyāgarāja.* 2nd ed. Chennai: Indian Music Publishing House, 1970.

UNDERGROUND ECONOMY, DIMENSIONS OF

India's underground economy, or the "black" economy, as it is commonly referred to in India, has serious implications for India's social, political, and economic development. The underground economy is synonymous with illegality; incomes generated in the illegal sectors, on which direct taxes are evaded, constitute India's black economy. The underlying motives for generation of black income and its disposal in terms of consumption and investment usually differ from those of white incomes, but in some activities and in their convertibility, there are links between the two. The black economy, therefore, is not a parallel economy but one that is deeply intertwined with the white economy.

The level of tax compliance in India declined during the 1970s and 1980s, reflecting perhaps the growth of the black economy. Scams have become larger in magnitude and have increased in numbers. Despite being estimated at 40 percent of India's gross domestic product (GDP), the black economy has remained immune to precise mainstream analysis.

Black incomes are also identified as property incomes, profits, interest, rent, and dividends, rather than wage incomes as black incomes are generated through artificial escalation of costs or underreporting of production or sales or some combination of these; in other words, black incomes are generally generated by the propertied class. Illegal transfer payments such as bribes and tax-evaded incomes from capital gains are not to be included in the definition of black incomes, since that would lead to double counting.

The true economy of any country consists of a white and a black component. The importance of the black economy for a country can be gauged from its size relative to the size of the reported GDP. By its very nature, assessing the size of the black economy is a difficult task. Noteworthy studies giving estimates of the size of the black economy in India are not strictly comparable, owing to the differences in the underlying methodologies and the corresponding differences in its coverage. However, the size of the black economy relative to the size of the white economy has been growing since the 1950s.

Consequences

The impact of the black economy on India's economy, society, and polity is too significant to be ignored. It vitiates data, thereby making it difficult to get a true picture of the economy. It has resulted in higher levels of unemployment, lower levels of human development, more skewed distribution of income, poorer quality of infrastructure, subversion of the political system, weakening of the institutions of democracy, and increasing problems of law and order, which result in poor governance.

Macroeconomic linkages. The black economy has strong macroeconomic linkages affecting all the major macrovariables. The black economy has rendered the information base of India's economy unreliable, which is crucial for policy making, as the data collected for national income accounting from the producing units are fudged in the presence of tax evasion. Incomes are often shown to be originating in agriculture to avoid taxation; therefore the GDP is underestimated.

The propensity for black income generation is greater in the tertiary sector than in the secondary sector, and virtually negligible in the agricultural sector. Thus sectoral composition of income as revealed by the official statistics is distorted. Income distribution and employment figures are substantially biased by the black economy. Furthermore, the growth of black incomes, property incomes, and the size of India's service sector tend to boost each other and constitute a growing trinity.

At the macroeconomic level, the efficacy of fiscal policy has been severely dented. Government expenditure gets inflated due to leakages while the actual delivery of services suffers. The poor quality of education and health services provided by the government in the majority of cases is forcing people to move toward privately provided services. Revenues turn out to be lower so that the deficit becomes higher, resulting in inadequate allocations of infrastructure, both social and physical. Several studies indicate that revenues from tax and nontax sources are far below their potential at all tiers of the government, which results in rising borrowing and interest payments, fostering budgetary crises.

The rate of growth. In sharp contrast to the channels of white investment, many black channels of investment are generally unproductive and are in the nature of transfers. Speculation, hoarding of cash, smuggling, and capital flight abroad through fake invoicing of exports and imports are some such channels. These channels of black investments opened up the Indian economy even before the liberalization process began during the early 1990s, and the economy traversed along a lower trajectory of growth. The black economy can be shown to result in deficiency of demand, thereby slowing down the rate of growth. The high costs of conducting business because of poor infrastructure, bribery and kickbacks, and uncertainty have contributed to India becoming a high cost economy. The black economy has led to criminalization of India's society due to a nexus among politicians, bureaucrats, and businesspeople. It is often argued that funding of elections by big businesses helps entrench such an unholy relationship. Societal unrest mounts as disparities between groups widen, while growth and employment remain below that which should be achievable, and thus sound policies fail.

Remedies

There is no consensus concerning diagnosis or remedies for the menace of the black economy. The black economy continues to thrive, despite policy initiatives, because it is systemic, and there exists a nexus among the three groups: the corrupt politicians, the corrupt public functionaries, and the corrupt businesspeople.

The last of the Tax Reform Committees (Government of India, 2002) has suggested that the economics of tax evasion must be changed by reducing costs of complying with tax obligations, moderating tax rates, phasing out concessions, and increasing the use of technology in compiling information related to taxpayers,

reducing the scope for interface between taxpayers and tax administrators. The general perception has been to reduce government intervention in the economy and to rely more on market forces so as to reduce the incentives behind tax evasion.

In the wake of India's integration with the global economy, there is an urgent need for restoration of fiscal balance and improvement in the efficacy of economic policies to accelerate growth and reduce poverty. The government stands discredited regarding its ability to rein in corruption. The black economy is a serious issue that must be remedied, as it darkens India's image abroad and undermines the quality of public life at home.

Saumen Chattopadhyay

See also **Economic Development, Importance of Institutions in and Social Aspects of; Economic Reforms of 1991**

BIBLIOGRAPHY

Acharya, Shankar N., et al. *Aspects of Black Economy in India.* New Delhi: National Institute of Public Finance and Policy, 1985.

Bhattacharyya, Dilip K., and Susmita Ghosh. "Corruption in India and the Hidden Economy." *Economic and Political Weekly* 33 (31 October 1998): 2795–2799.

Chattopadhyay, Saumen. "Macroeconomic Dis-equilibrium and the Black Economy in the Context of Stabilization Policy in India." Ph.D. diss., Jawaharlal Nehru University, 2002.

Das-Gupta, Arindam. *Reports on Informal Credit Markets in India.* New Delhi: National Institute of Public Finance and Policy, 1989.

Das-Gupta, Arindam, and D. Mookherjee. "Design and Enforcement of Personal Income Taxes in India." In *Public Finance: Policy Issues for India*, edited by Sudipto Mundle. Delhi: Oxford University Press, 1997.

Government of India. *Report of the Comptroller and Auditor General for the Year Ended March 2000: Union Government (Direct Taxes), Number 12 of 2001.* New Delhi: Comptroller and Auditor General of India, 2001.

———. *Report of the Task Force on Direct Taxes.* New Delhi: Ministry of Finance and Company Affairs, 2002.

Gupta, Poonam, and Sanjeev Gupta. "Estimates of the Unreported Economy in India." *Economic and Political Weekly* 17 (16 January 1982): 69–75.

Gupta, Suraj B. *Black Economy in India.* New Delhi: Sage Publications, 1992.

Kaldor, N. *Indian Tax Reform: Report of a Survey.* New Delhi: Government of India, Ministry of Finance, 1956.

Kumar, Arun. *The Black Economy in India.* New Delhi: Penguin Books, 1999.

Shukla, Arvind. *Behaviour of the Velocity of Circulation of Money in India from 1980–1981 to 1993–1994: A Study of the Impact of the Structural Change in the Economy.* M.Phil. diss., Centre for Economic Studies and Planning, Jawaharlal Nehru University, 1992.

UNITED STATES, RELATIONS WITH India's relations with the United States since independence in 1947 have varied between diplomatic hostility and cordiality, though never bordering on armed conflict. Their foreign policy perspectives and priorities during the cold war did not always coincide, leading to periodic tensions despite their common democratic value systems. The collapse of the Soviet Union and the end of the cold war in 1991, marked by the end of socialism and the commencement of dramatic economic reforms in India, generated a new era in Indo-U.S. relations. This has been especially spectacular in the areas of U.S. investment in India, economic collaboration, and defense technology cooperation. At the beginning of the twenty-first century, the relationship is cordial and cooperative between the countries that are now widely referred to as the world's largest and most powerful democracies.

Non-alignment and the Cold War

Indo-U.S. relations had a promising beginning under Franklin D. Roosevelt's administration, when the United States supported India's struggle for independence from the British. During World War II, the Atlantic Charter called for freedom from Japanese and German aggression and occupations throughout Europe and China; Roosevelt would have extended this to the British imperial occupation of India, arguing that there could not be two different standards of freedom for nations. But Winston Churchill adamantly refused to agree. After the tragedy of partition that coincided with Indian independence in 1947, Indo-U.S. relations cooled. In the 1950s, following the commencement of the cold war, relations between India and the United States were weakened by India's refusal to join the U.S. alliance in the East-West cold war struggle. India also rejected the American capitalist system of free markets and unlimited private sector profit. Instead, India embarked on a policy of economic socialism in a series of five-year plans within a democratic political framework, allowing for only a limited, regulated private sector.

Resisting U.S. pressure to the join the proposed South-East Asia Treaty Organization (SEATO) in 1954, Prime Minister Jawaharhal Nehru declared that India would follow a policy of "non-alignment" between the Western bloc and the Soviet Communist bloc. India's most urgent need as a new state, Nehru insisted, was an era of peace unencumbered by military alliances. Nehru stated that it would be "a tragedy of infinite magnitude if we should be checked and baulked and our policy should be set at naught because of the troubles and quarrels of others" (cited in Thomas, *The Defence of India*, p. 34). India also refused to join the Baghdad Pact, expanded in 1955 to the Central Treaty Organization (CENTO), for the same reason.

I. K. Gujral and Madeleine Albright. Former Indian prime minister I. K. Gujral (left) and Madeleine Albright, then U.S. secretary of state, meet in September 1997, New York City, before the session of the UN Council of Foreign Relations. With Gujral's stateside visit (which also included a private meeting with former U.S. president Bill Clinton) came meaningful diplomatic exchange, and the hope of improved relations between the two countries, in recent years complicated by a number of sensitive issues. PRESS INFORMATION BUREAU / FOTOMEDIA.

India's refusal to join the U.S.-sponsored military pacts against the Communist bloc caused an adverse reaction in the United States, which was in the grip of a strong anti-Communist fervor, led by Senator Joseph McCarthy, in the mid-1950s. There was an immediate condemnation by Secretary of State John Foster Dulles and Vice President Richard M. Nixon. Dulles called India "immoral" and "shortsighted," and claimed that remaining non-aligned in the face of the Communist threat was inconsistent with the United Nations Charter provisions on Collective Security. The United States then proceeded to arm Pakistan, which immediately joined all these pacts.

Despite the tensions raised by Nehru's refusal to join the U.S.-sponsored military alliances, there was no likelihood of the United States going to war against India, or even following an aggressive military policy of encirclement, as some Indians feared. And since the Indian political system was modeled on the pattern of Western political ideas and institutions, there could be no question of parliamentary democracy being subverted from this direction. What had not been foreseen, however, was the indirect, and perhaps inadvertent, threat that would arise from the U.S.-Pakistan alliance. The military risk to India had escalated, not because of threats from the Soviet Union and China, but as a result of the American decision to arm Pakistan against these Communist giants. Nehru complained that Pakistan had not joined these pacts "because it expected some imminent or distant invasion or aggression from the Soviet Union. The Pakistan newspapers and the statements of responsible people in Pakistan make it perfectly clear that they have joined this Pact because of India" (cited in Thomas, *The Defence of India*, p. 37).

Through much of the cold war, relations between India and the United States were bedeviled by two sets of conflicting strains: There were common political values of democracy and freedom in both countries, but these were undermined by the tensions that arose from the U.S. arming of Pakistan. India insisted that these arms would only be used by Pakistan against India. The United States provided the most economic aid to India in the 1950s and 1960s, yet India pursued closer ties with China (until the Sino-Indian War of 1962) and with the Soviet Union. A sense of Indian "ingratitude" rankled many members of the U.S. Congress, as well as the State Department and the White House.

The United States and the Wars of India

American arms supplied to Pakistan under SEATO and CENTO included fighters, bombers, tanks, artillery, and other logistical facilities. India responded by purchasing similar weapon systems from Britain and France, escalating a major India-Pakistan arms race. The effect of these developments was that Indian perceptions of threat were almost exclusively riveted on Pakistan. Contingency defense plans were aimed at Pakistan and all defense purchases were undertaken with a view to offsetting the American arming of Pakistan.

The most serious repercussion of this preoccupation with the Pakistani threat was India's neglect of its northern Himalayan borders, even though India's relations with China were far from satisfactory because of oppressive Chinese actions in Tibet. Deteriorating Sino-Indian relations over the Tibetan question and disputes over their boundaries in the northeast and the northwest eventually led to a border war between the two countries in October 1962. Although the war occurred concurrently with the Cuban missile crisis between the United States and the Soviet Union, the Kennedy administration was quick to rush mountain guns and other non-lethal aid to India to help it fight at high altitudes. More substantial American military equipment to India was opposed by Pakistan, and consequently the United States called upon India to resolve the Kashmir conflict with Pakistan before substantial military assistance could be advanced.

Pakistan's wars with India in September 1965 over Kashmir, and in December 1971 over the demand for an independent Bangladesh out of East Pakistan, caused further tensions between India and the United States. U.S. arms, supplied to Pakistan only for use against potential Communist advances from the north, were used against India during the 1965 war. While this aging equipment was also used in the 1971 war, India had by then obtained substantial heavy Soviet artillery and tanks, and Pakistan was easily defeated in two weeks, leading to an independent Bangladesh. Events leading up to this two-week war in December 1971 caused substantial tension between India and the United States, aggravated by the conflicting personalities of Prime Minister Indira Gandhi and President Nixon. India wanted the United States to take swift action in ending the Pakistani military suppression of East Pakistan's Bengali revolt that had led to the deaths of an estimated million civilians and the flight of some 10 million refugees to India. However, the United States did not wish to alienate the military regime of General Yahya Khan, because Pakistan had provided a secret channel to pursue rapprochement with Communist China, Pakistan's ally.

This perceived emerging new triangular alliance among Pakistan, the United States, and China, and the need to take swift military action in East Pakistan, prompted India to sign a "Treaty of Peace and Friendship" with the Soviet Union in August 1971. The treaty carried some military clauses, which required the Soviet Union not to extend assistance to Pakistan in the case of military conflict, and that both sides would enter into consultations when either side was faced with immediate threats or armed conflict. With respect to the general purposes served, in the Indian case the treaty was primarily a response to the United States, an effort to neutralize its involvement in case of hostilities by making the consequences of any such involvement potentially a great power conflict. India then proceeded to resolve the East Pakistan conflict by armed force. In response to India's use of force, the United States sent its nuclear carrier, the U.S.S. *Enterprise*, into the Bay of Bengal, in a show of gunboat diplomacy—a warning that India should not venture beyond the liberation of Bangladesh to overrun West Pakistan.

The new regional and global alignments that occurred during the 1971 crisis subsided over the next few years. India's fears of an emerging Washington-Islamabad-Beijing alliance did not materialize. However, the aftermath of the 1971 Indo-Pakistan War generated discordant relations between the two countries during the prime ministership of Indira Gandhi. Her declaration of a "National Emergency" between June 1975 and March 1977, suspending the fundamental rights in India's democratic constitution, and her imposition of authoritarian rule in India caused new tensions in relations between the two countries, as these actions were widely condemned in the United States. An initial thaw began with a meeting between President Ronald Reagan and Indira Gandhi in Cancún, Mexico, in 1981, when a technology cooperation agreement was signed. The succession of Rajiv Gandhi as prime minister following the assassination of his mother in 1984 produced a further upswing in Indo-U.S. relations during the rest of the Reagan administration. These cordial ties continued to grow during successive Indian governments, headed first by the Congress Party, then the Janata Party, followed by two United Front coalitions, and then the Bharatiya Janata Party–led coalition government from 1998 to 2004.

India and the Wars of the United States

India supported various American diplomatic moves when North Korea invaded South Korea in June 1950. It voted for the United Nations Security Council's resolutions condemning the invasion and for military actions to drive back North Korean forces, which were about to occupy all of South Korea. The aggression was perceived as a test of United Nations (UN) credibility, but as U.S. forces under General Douglas MacArthur began to roll back the North Korean forces to the 38th parallel that divided South and North Korea, India warned the United States that moving further would provoke China to enter the war. After Chinese forces invaded and began to drive back American forces, India played an important diplomatic role at the UN and served as a mediator between the United States and China in helping to end the Korean War.

India opposed the U.S. war in Vietnam from 1964 to 1974. Frequent public and private criticism by Indian officials and the media became a source of irritation in the United States especially since India was then receiving substantial American economic aid. The United States perceived the Vietnam War as part of its policy of containing the advance of communism. India saw it as a civil war and a struggle against foreign military occupation. The withdrawal of American forces from Vietnam did not end Indo-U.S. differences on policy in the region. There were differences of policy and allegiance between India and the United States when China engaged in two short border wars with Vietnam in 1979 and 1984, and when Vietnam invaded Cambodia in 1979 to overthrow the Khmer Rouge regime of Pol Pot. The Khmer Rouge was responsible for the deaths of about a million Cambodians, who were massacred or worked to death, between 1975 and 1979. India and the Soviet

Union supported the Heng Samrin regime that was installed by the invading Vietnamese forces. The United States and China opposed the regime. These dissensions between India and the United States over Southeast Asian conflicts passed with the end of the cold war in 1991.

The Soviet invasion of Afghanistan in December 1979 was interpreted very differently in the United States and in India. The United States perceived the invasion as part of a wider Soviet strategy to seize the oil fields of the Persian Gulf and to gain warm water ports on the Indian Ocean. India perceived the invasion as an overreaction by Moscow, aimed at preventing the replacement of the pro-Soviet Marxist regime in Kabul by a pro-American regime. The American-supported insurgency against Soviet forces in Afghanistan between 1979 and 1989 was of great concern to India because the United States renewed massive arms shipments to Pakistan, which had been cut off after the 1971 war. India had preferred to see the more friendly Soviet-backed Marxist government remain in Afghanistan, fearing the possibility of a Pakistani-sponsored radical Islamic government coming to power. This concern became a reality when the zealous Islamic forces of the Taliban seized control of Afghanistan by armed force, following the Soviet withdrawal of its forces in 1989 and the subsequent collapse of the Soviet Union.

Subsequently, India differed with the United States in its use of force in the former Yugoslavia in 1999, in Afghanistan in 2002, and in Iraq in 2003. India joined Russia and China in opposing a U.S.-led North Atlantic Treaty Organization (NATO) air war against Serbian forces in Kosovo. India's permanent representative to the UN declared to the Security Council on 24 March 1999 that the attacks were in violation of the UN Charter and illegal because they were not authorized by the council. The problem in former Yugoslavia's Muslim-majority province of Kosovo was not unlike that in India's Muslim-majority state of Jammu and Kashmir, where an insurgency had raged for over a decade. The use of force in Kosovo in 1999 by an American-led NATO was invoked as an additional post hoc justification for India's decision to test nuclear weapons earlier in May 1998. This difference with U.S. policy was short-lived, however, as there appeared to be no further effort to dislodge Kosovo from Serbia, which would have set a precedent for Kashmir. Subsequently, India welcomed the American use of force in Afghanistan, which removed the Islamic extremist Taliban regime. But India opposed the U.S. war against Iraq in 2003. Like much of the rest of the world, India saw this war as counterproductive against the terrorism conducted by nonstate actors such as al-Qaeda. However, India joined the United States in its worldwide campaign to root out the sources of international and transnational terrorism.

The Aftermath of the Cold War

The intensified momentum for better Indo-U.S. relations was prompted by the end of the cold war. India rushed toward embracing the United States, particularly seeking military cooperation. This drive initially ran into some difficulties over India's failure to protect U.S. pharmaceutical patents, its purchase of cryogenic engines for its space program and nuclear reactors from Russia, both of which were perceived to advance India's nuclear weapons and missile programs, and India's testing of its short-range Prithvi and medium-range Agni missiles despite American opposition.

Such disputes generated lukewarm responses from the United States for establishing closer military ties, and growing suspicions in India that U.S. friendship with Pakistan was closer than that with India. By the turn of the twenty-first century, however, Indo-U.S. relations blossomed at all levels. A series of joint air, naval, and army exercises were conducted, and there has been close cooperation in the war against international terrorism by both sides, especially following al-Qaeda terrorist attacks on the World Trade Center in September 2001. India went through a similar experience on 13 December 2001, when the Laskhar-e-Toiba terrorist group, seeking independence for Kashmir, attempted to destroy India's parliament building in a suicide attack while it was in session. This experience strengthened India's commitment to the United States in its campaign against worldwide terrorism.

Meanwhile, Indo-U.S. economic ties continued to grow rapidly. The United States was India's main trading partner for more than two decades, and later became the leading foreign investor in India. Following liberalization and reforms in 1991, an avalanche of American corporations have rushed into India with newer investments. From the other side, India provides much of the software for American corporations and is the source of high-tech personnel for American industries. Further improvement in ties followed in the immediate aftermath of President Bill Clinton's visit to India in March 2000 and Prime Minster A. B. Vajpayee's trip to the United States in September 2000, and a number of new U.S. business investments in India were inaugurated during both visits. The volume of American trade with and investments in India, however, still remained overshadowed by U.S. economic ties with China.

A significant rift between the two countries followed India's decision to conduct a series of nuclear tests in May 1998. Those tests were swiftly followed in a tit-for-tat fashion by Pakistan. This led to a series of technology sanctions by Washington in areas that may have direct or indirect benefits to India's nuclear and missile programs. Prime Minister Vajpayee requested that the United States lift sanctions on dual-use technologies; these were partially lifted in 1999, and most of them were removed by 2004.

Overall, four basic policy concerns continue to characterize U.S. policies in South Asia and affect its relations with India. First, it has been a long-standing American policy to attempt to contain regional nuclear proliferation in South Asia, the Middle East, and East and Central Asia. This goal failed when India conducted five nuclear tests in May 1998 followed immediately by Pakistan. However, no further tests have been conducted, and further proliferation has been contained. Second, the United States made strenuous efforts to prevent an India-Pakistan nuclear war following their nuclear tests in 1998; since there has been no nuclear war between India and Pakistan, the American policy appears to have succeeded. Third, following the terrorist attacks on New York's World Trade Center in September 2001, the United States has conducted a campaign to root out global transnational terrorism from havens in South Asia, especially Pakistan. India has provided full cooperation on this front. Fourth, the United States has sought to facilitate a resolution of the Kashmir dispute with Pakistan which continued to plague Indo-U.S. relations. Occasional friction over this issue has been relegated to the margins of the relationship, which is now based primarily on common political and economic values. With a strong democracy and a free market economy, India's relations with the United States are now on very firm ground.

Economic Relations

The most spectacular change in the relationship has been on the economic front. Although India's share of U.S. imports and exports is only about 1 percent of the total volume of American trade, it represents a significant proportion of India's external trade. The United States is India's largest trading partner, the source of 9 percent of Indian imports and the destination of 21 percent of Indian exports. In 2002 total Indian exports to the United States were about $17 billion, of which about $6 billion consisted of software exports. Merchandise exports included diamonds and gold jewelry, woven and knit apparel, textiles, fish and seafood, machinery, carpets, iron and steel, and pharmaceuticals. Indian imports from the United States included machinery (computers and components, gas turbines, and telecommunications equipment), electrical machinery (recording/sound media), medical and surgical equipment and instruments, aircraft, spacecraft (small aircraft), precious stones (diamonds, not mounted or set), metals, jewelry, miscellaneous chemical products, organic chemicals, and plastic.

By 2003 several major American corporations had established subsidiaries and other facilities in India. A majority of General Electric's businesses worldwide have a presence in India, covering aircraft engines, broadcasting, capital services, lighting, medical systems. Some 19,000 General Electric professionals work in India, and the company set up its largest laboratory worldwide—the John Welch Technology Centre—in Bangalore. The multidiscipline laboratory covers research in hot-air gas paths, materials, design, and computer science. Other major U.S. corporations established in India include Whirlpool, Ford Motors, 3M, Microsoft, Intel, Texas Instruments, Sun Microsystems, Procter and Gamble, Oracle, IBM, Adobe Systems, and several others. They produce in India for the Indian and overseas markets. American banking and financial services such as Citicorp, GE Capital, and American Express have also established offices and operations in India. American corporations in the bioinformation and biotechnology fields have subsidiary operations in India.

India is the premier country for U.S. information technology (IT) services, with major corporations "outsourcing" its needs to Indian software engineers, who are able to perform the same tasks more cheaply than American software engineers. This business relationship has been aided by the large English-speaking high-tech workforce in India and the twelve-hour time difference between the two countries; software needs and problems can be sent to India at the end of the American working day to be resolved by highly qualified and less costly Indian technical staff by the end of their working day and the beginning of the next American workday. The arrangement has enabled round-the-clock collaborative operations between India and the United States. U.S. companies that have taken advantage of this unique outsourcing opportunity include American Express, Citicorp, Microsoft, Dell, Hewlett-Packard, HSBC, Morgan Stanley, AT&T, Reebok, GM, Boeing, Pepsi, and Coca-Cola. Outsourcing to India has caused some resentment within the U.S. labor force because of the loss of American jobs.

Investments by Indian companies in the United States grew rapidly in the 1990s. For example, India's United Breweries bought breweries in the United States, while companies such as Dr. Reddy's Laboratories and Ranbaxy bought pharmaceutical manufacturing units in the United States. Mahindra and Mahindra set up an automotive manufacturing unit. In the IT sector, Tata Infotech, Sathyam, Infosys, and WIPRO set up large operations in the United States.

Defense Cooperation

From strategic hostility and suspicion during the cold war, defense cooperation between India and the United States became the norm at the beginning of the twenty-first century. An India-U.S. Defense Policy Group, composed of senior defense officials and military officers, meets once a year in Washington to provide guidance and direction to potential collaborative efforts. A Joint Technical Group coordinates the transfer of technology and explores areas of scientific interaction between the two countries. An Executive Steering Group composed of the army, navy, and air force from both sides meets annually. Joint military exercises between the military services of the two countries have become commonplace.

While there is caution in the United States on the transfer of common civilian-military technologies in nuclear and space programs to India, defense technology cooperation has expanded in other areas. They include cooperation in three mission areas: aircraft technology, antitank systems, and technical manpower training.

The collaboration between Lockheed Martin Controls Systems of Binghamton, New York, and the Aeronautical Development Establishment of Bangalore, India, is one example of this growing cooperation in technology. Much of this revolves around the development of various systems for India's projected "Light Combat Aircraft." A Joint Technical Group, composed of members of the U.S. Department of Defense and the Indian Ministry of Defence, meets regularly to coordinate defense research and production and logistical support. Cooperation and technical exchanges now extend to defense research and development organizations in the United States and the Defence Research and Development Organization in India. Scientists from the latter regularly visit U.S. defense industries and military installations to update themselves on the state of art of defense technology.

The Role of Indian Americans

Indian Americans have contributed significantly to the growth of cordial ties between India and the United States. According to the U.S. census of 2000, there are approximately 1.7 million American citizens of Indian origin, representing the various languages, religions, and regions of India. They belong mainly to a highly educated class of academics, doctors, engineers, corporate executives, and businesspeople. Almost 60 percent of all Indian Americans are college educated and earn an average median family income of $60,000, compared to the national average of about $39,000. The average median income of Indians working in the Silicon Valley IT sector in the 1990s was about $125,000, with about 15 percent of the start-up companies there being initiated by Indian Americans.

With a vested interest in promoting close ties between their old and new homelands, Indian Americans have been active in supporting U.S. Congress members who support India in its various endeavors. In 2003 various Indian groups consolidated their political activities into an organization called the U.S. India Public Affairs Committee (USINPAC), modeled after the Jewish American lobbying group, the American-Israeli Public Affairs Committee. With financial contributions from the wealthy Indian American community, USINPAC has become a major factor in expanding the relationship between India and the United States. USINPAC lobbies to prevent policies that may have an adverse impact on India, and promotes exchange visits between American and Indian political leaders to foster mutual understanding. Indian Americans of various ethnic backgrounds, such as Gujaratis, Tamils, Maharashtrians, and Punjabis, also promote American trade and investments with their Indian states. Chief ministers and economic delegations from various Indian states visit the United States to advance the economies of their states. These lines of communication initiated by the Indian American community have further strengthened the India-U.S. relationship.

Prospects

The cordiality between India and the United States at the beginning of the twenty-first century appears irreversible. India is now part of the global economy, and its status has risen as a major diplomatic and economic player in world affairs. India's close relations with the United States have played an important part in the new, positive world image of India.

Raju G. C. Thomas

See also **Jammu and Kashmir; Nuclear Programs and Policies; Pakistan and India; Russia, Relations with**

BIBLIOGRAPHY

Brands, H. W. *India and the United States: The Cold Peace.* Boston: Twayne, 1990.

Harrison, Selig. *India and the United States.* New York: Macmillan, 1961.

Kux, Dennis. *India and the United States: Estranged Democracies.* Washington, D.C.: National Defense University Press, 1992.

Rubinoff, Arthur G., et al., eds. *India and the United States in a Changing World.* New Delhi: Sage Publications, 2002.

Sidhu, Waheguru Pal Singh. *Enhancing Indo–U.S. Strategic Cooperation.* International Institute for Strategic Studies, Adelphi Paper no. 313. Oxford and New York: Oxford University Press, 1998.

Subrahmanyam Raju, A. *Democracies at Loggerheads: Security Aspects of U.S.–India Relations.* Colorado Springs, Colo.: International Academic Publishers, 2002.

Thomas, Raju G. C. *The Defence of India: A Budgetary Perspective of Strategy and Politics.* Delhi: Macmillan, 1978.

———. *Indian Security Policy.* Princeton, N.J.: Princeton University Press, 1986.

UNTOUCHABLES. *See* **Dalits.**

UPANISHADIC PHILOSOPHY The Upanishads are one of the world's great repositories of spiritual insight and wisdom. Composed orally by Indian sages as early as the ninth century B.C., they have attracted the attention of scholars and spiritual seekers the world over. They signal a personal, experiential, and at times mystical understanding of the cosmos, the divine, and the human self, which over the centuries many have found profound. Much of Hindu thought self-consciously sees itself as a development of Upanishadic teaching, which is regarded as *shruti*, divinely revealed truth carrying supreme authority. And outside Hinduism, thinkers as diverse as Dara Shikoh (the great-grandson of the Mughal emperor Akbar), Roberto de Nobili, Arthur Schopenhauer, and Ralph Waldo Emerson have all sung the praises of these texts. In fact, Max Müller, the German Indologist, referring to the Vedānta philosophy based on the Upanishads, spoke of it as "a system in which human speculation seems to have reached its very acme" (cited in Radhakrishnan and Moore, p. 37).

Etymological and Historical Contexts

The term *upanishad* is composed of the Sanskrit roots *sad* (sit), *upa* (near), and *ni* (a closed group) and represents an esoteric teaching imparted by a teacher to a group of students in search of sacred knowledge. The term also connotes the positing of correlations between entities and powers belonging to different spheres, and, through such equivalences, the drawing out of deeper meanings. Thus, for example, equivalences drawn between the human body and the cosmos point to notions of order, hierarchy, and balance. These connections are more suggestive and speculative than strictly logical, and represent poetic speculation rather than a rigorously applied method. Indeed, the Upanishads are explicit that such spiritual truths are not attainable through logical processes. "Not by reasoning is this apprehension attainable" (Katha Up, 1.2.4), for "words return (from Brahman) along with the mind, not attaining it" (Taittiriya Up, 2.9.1).

Such speculation follows certain intellectual and religious developments. The Upanishads both chronologically and thematically come at the end (*anta*) of the Vedas, and thus the teachings based on them are called

Vedānta in both senses of the word "end": culmination, on the one hand, and the real meaning or fulfillment of Vedic teaching, on the other. What comes before them are the hymns and chants of the four Vedas: Rig Veda, Samur Veda, Yajur Veda, and Atharva Veda, collectively known as the Saṃhitās (collections). These are followed by the Brāhmaṇas, a set of ritual instructions having principally to do with the sacrifices offered to the gods. These sacrifices were elaborate and often expensive, and those who either could not afford them or were unwilling for various reasons to perform them retreated to the forest in order to meditate on the spiritual meanings of these hymns and rituals. These allegorical renderings came to be known as the Āraṇyakas, or forest books. It is out of this complex development that the Upanishads emerged as a set of philosophical reflections on the preceding Vedic literature. They denote a subjective and contemplative turn away from ritualism and priestcraft to ontological musings about the nature of reality and the place of humans within it. These reflections were often expressed in a set of pithy formulas like the famous "*tat tvam asi*" (that thou art), which by their very nature call out for explication. It was this explication that the gurus would provide to students whom they considered spiritually developed enough to absorb it. Hence the distinctly esoteric tone that the Upanishads bear, at least early in the pedagogical tradition, when they refer, for example, to the "truth of truth" (Bṛhad Up, 2.1.20) or "the supreme secret" (Kaṭh Up, 3.17). It is quite clear from many such passages that the teachings were not meant for the untutored.

Classification

So great was the prestige attached to the genre that over two hundred works call themselves Upanishads, including texts outside the Hindu tradition like the Christopanishad and the Allopanishad (secret teachings about Allah), which were composed in the medieval period. The Muktika Upanishad provides a list of 108 Upanishads, which has come to be regarded as canonical, although recent scholarship has increased that number slightly. These can be divided into two categories: the Vedic Upanishads and the later Upanishads. In the first group are the thirteen that are traditionally considered the principal Upanishads. In rough chronological order, they are: Bṛhadāraṇyaka, Chāndogya, Īsa, Kena, Aitareya, Taittirīya, Kauṣītakī, Kaṭha, Muṇḍaka, Shvetāshvatara, Prashna, Maitri, and Māṇḍukya. Further classification can be done on the basis of sectarian orientation, textual features, and ritual development, but for our purpose, it is important to mention again that these Upanishads are all, though not exclusively, regarded as *shruti*, or authoritative scripture, and as *apauruṣeya*, or authorless, hence, revealed. They are traditionally attached to specific

*sākha*s, or schools of Vedic interpretation. The former feature, that is, their revealed status, is not true—at least in terms of wide acceptance—of the later Upanishads, which are not as well known as the Vedic Upanishads, but are nonetheless important in their respective sectarian communities.

Central Teachings

Perhaps the most well-known teaching of the Upanishads is the equation of *brahman* and *ātman*, the ultimate reality with the transcendental self existing at the core of one's being. *Brahman*, derived from the root *bṛh* (to grow or burst forth), was first identified with prayer and, given the importance of prayer and sacrifice in maintaining the cosmos, was soon seen as the primary cause of the universe. *Ātman*, which originally meant breath, came to be identified with the essence of man, his self or soul. This divine or real self, however, is sharply distinguished from the *jīva*, the empirical or embodied self, which is finite. The speculative genius of Upanishadic thought is to effect the equivalence of two seemingly different ideas, one referring to the outer material world, the other to the inner psychic one. This in a sense is a continuation of the earlier Vedic habit of seeking homologies or correlations between the individual and the cosmos. Now, however, it pushes further to a "nondual" (*a-dvaitic*) unity. The conception of *brahman*, being objective and referring to the external world, is by its very nature hypothetical and lacking in certainty. The conception of *ātman*, by contrast, is free of these defects, but, as commonly understood, it is finite and hence cannot encompass the whole of reality. When the two conceptions are combined, however, a third conception is born, which is richer in significance and meaning than the two considered individually. Like *brahman*, this new notion of *ātman-brahman* encompasses the whole world, but unlike it, it now acquires the certainty of personal existence. Like *ātman*, it is spiritual, but unlike *ātman* considered by itself, *ātman-brahman* is infinite. "That is the Upanishadic absolute—neither *brahman* or *ātman* in one sense, but both in another. . . . The enunciation of this doctrine marked the most important advance in the whole history of Indian thought," says M. Hiriyanna (*Outlines of Indian Philosophy*, 1932, p. 58).

Various further accounts and descriptions are provided both of *brahman* and of *ātman*. *Brahman*, for example, may be regarded cosmically (*saguṇa*, with qualities) or acosmically (*nirguṇa*, without qualities). In the first case, *brahman* may be seen as evolving into the world, and the philosophical task becomes one of grasping the unity of the world in *brahman*. In the second, *brahman* is at most the logical ground of both subject and object, and the corresponding philosophical task becomes one of deconstruction, that is, of negating all qualities that may be ascribed to *brahman*, as in the famous doctrine of "*neti, neti*" (not this, not that), where the sheer indescribability of the Absolute in language is highlighted (Bṛhad Up, 3.8.8ff.).

It is also in this second (*nirgunic*) interpretation that the doctrine of *māyā* makes its appearance—*māyā* being the empirical world of space, time, causation, and substance, which is taken to be real by the ignorant, but is not really real. Opinion is divided about the degree of unreality attached to *māyā*—whether it is absolutely or only relatively unreal compared to *brahman*. Upanishadic thought is, however, firm in its insistence on going beyond the world of *māyā*.

The imagination of the Upanishadic sages moved thus in speculative and transcendental realms, rather than in empirical or natural-scientific ones. Underlying the flux of spatiotemporal reality is an eternal, immutable, and psychic reality, just as there is a deeper, timeless, and infinite self underlying the vicissitudes of the empirical ego. The equation of *ātman* and *brahman* is not a mere philosophical or dialectical move, but rather an intuitive one arising out of direct experience of ultimate reality. At this level, the ultimate is experienced as *sat* (existence as such), *cit* (pure consciousness), and *ānanda* (bliss). This experience also brings one *moksha*, or release from the *saṃsāric* world of phenomenal existence. The ultimate thrust of Upanishadic speculation is thus not so much theoretical as practical and soteriological—deliverance from the empirical world and from the cycle of karma and rebirth.

The path to such deliverance requires great moral and spiritual purification and preparation. To see the Self, one must become "calm, controlled, quiet, patiently enduring, and contented" (Bṛhad Up, 4.4.23). Most of the Upanishads concur that the best way to move toward *moksha* is through the practice of yogic meditation. The Vedic Upanishads often highlight the difference between such meditation and ratiocination, and emphasize the efficacy of the former and the poverty of the later (Katha Up, 6.9–11; Svet Up, 1.3). It is, however, in the later Yoga Upanishads that the details of yogic practice and ascesis are most clearly spelled out (see the Yogatattva and the Sandilya Upanishads).

The Upanishads touch on a great many other topics, from the different states of consciousness through death and rebirth processes to the cultivation of the virtues and attitudes needed for *moksha*. This is as one would expect from a heterogeneous collection of material culled from various sources at different times. Later philosophical systems and particularly the schools of Vedānta attempt to systematize them into more unified philosophies, but the Upanishads themselves are best regarded as spiritual texts, which, like the Bible in the Jewish and Christian traditions, serve as a wellspring for later developments. Even though in terms of composition they are remote in time, in terms of resonance and inspiration, they will always remain contemporary to spiritual seekers.

Joseph Prabhu

See also **Vedic Aryan India**

BIBLIOGRAPHY

Hiriyanna, M. *Outlines of Indian Philosophy*. London: George Allen & Unwin, 1932.
Hume, Robert E., trans. *The Thirteen Principal Upanishads*. 1931. Reprint, Delhi: Oxford University Press, 1995.
Keith, A. B. *The Religion and Philosophy of the Vedas and Upanishads*. 2 vols. 2nd ed. Westport, Conn.: Greenwood Press, 1971.
Nikhilananda, Swami, trans. *The Upanishads*. 4 vols. New York: Bonanza Books, 1949–1959.
Panikkar, Raimundo, ed. and trans. *The Vedic Experience: Mantramanjari*. Berkeley: University of California Press, 1977.
Radhakrishnan, S., ed. and trans. *The Principal Upanishads*. New York: Harper, 1953.
Radhakrishnan, S., and C. Moore, eds. *A Source Book in Indian Philosophy*. Princeton, N.J.: Princeton University Press, 1957.

URBANISM Soon after arriving in India in 1950 to build India's first planned capital city at Chandigarh, the architect Le Corbusier insightfully commented that "India hasn't yet created . . . architecture for modern civilization" (cited in Kalia, *Chandigarh*, p. 87). Even in the twenty-first century, nearly 70 percent of India's population still lives in over 500,000 villages, although about 300 million Indians currently live in cities, a number almost equal to the total population of the United States. Because of this urban-rural paradox, Jawaharlal Nehru, India's first prime minister, observed, "However well we may deal with the towns, the problem of the villages of India will remain for a long time" (cited in Kalia, *Chandigarh*, p. 30).

The Ancient Cities

The Indus Valley Civilization (c. 2600–1900 B.C.) had nevertheless achieved a measure of urban sophistication, best reflected in the twin capital cities of Mohenjo-Daro and Harappa, as well as several other cities. Displaying a remarkable uniformity in urban planning, covering a wide geographical spread that stretched from the Arabian Sea to the foothills of the Himalayas and from the eastern border of Iran to the Ganges Valley near Delhi, the

Chandni Chowk Bazaar. Not far from the Red Fort (in the background), Chandni Chowk (Moonlight Square), the largest bazaar in Old Delhi. In the Mughal ruler Shah Jahan's time (1592–1666), it was the central commercial thoroughfare of Shahjahanabad, the vast capital city he had built after abandoning his other great capital, Agra. Today, Chandni Chowk is equally alive with activity, hopelessly congested with buyers and sellers. JYOTI M. BANERJEE / FOTOMEDIA.

more than 150 sites of the Indus Valley Civilization attest to the sophistication of building skills, the arts, and, possibly, a written language that has yet to be deciphered. Among the excavated cities, Mohenjo-Daro is the most pristine. Built on the gridiron system on the flat, hot floodplain of the Indus, some 300 miles (483 km) north of present-day Karachi in Pakistan, the city was planned with a broad north-south boulevard 30 feet (9 m) wide that was crossed at right angles every 200 yards (185 m) or so by smaller east-west streets that were studded with shops and food stalls, the blocks between them served by narrow curving lanes 5 to 10 feet (1.5–3 m) wide. Urban Indus houses presented blank walls to the main streets, much like today, the main entrances located behind the main streets on service lanes; interior courtyards provided light, air, and space for socialization; and windows were screened with grills of terra-cotta or alabaster. Many houses had a second story and a flat roof that served as a sleeping space in the hot summer months—a practice that continues today, although that is beginning to change with the emergence of multistoried apartment

buildings in most high-density cities. India's fast-growing economy, which has been stimulated by the information technology revolution and buttressed by the expanding privatization of the public sector, has improved the urban infrastructure, including the supply of electrical power, allowing the use of air-conditioning and other electrical appliances for a modern urban lifestyle.

Perhaps the most impressive feature of the ancient Indus cities, unrivaled until much later in Greek and Roman times, was the use of a sophisticated open sewer system along the sides of the streets, with catch-basins dug below sewer level to trap debris that might otherwise have clogged the drainage. These sewers were connected to the houses by an open gutter, also made of brick, into which emptied the house drains, which were often made of an enclosed system of clay pipes. Several of the houses had sit-down toilets that were connected to the sewers, and practically all houses had bathrooms with waterproof brick floors fitted with drains leading to the sewer pipes. The Indus cities displayed other architectural marvels and

Fatehpur Sikri. Now a UN World Heritage site, Fatehpur Sikri (City of Victory) was built during the second half of the sixteenth century by the emperor Akbar. The capital of the Mughal empire for approximately fourteen years, it is a complex of monuments and temples, all constructed in a uniform, awe-inspiring architectural style. AMAR TALWAR / FOTOMEDIA.

feats of civil engineering: a Great Bath with a sunken bathing pool approached by wooden steps set into asphalt (much like the bathing *ghat*s at Varanasi), a granary, residences for high officials, and, of course, the citadel.

The next push toward urbanism in India was facilitated by the discovery of iron in modern Bihar around 1000 B.C., which accelerated the expansion of the Aryans by allowing them to clear the Gangetic forests, and facilitated their transition from a nomadic pastoral economy to a hybrid agricultural-pastoral one. A more enduring consequence of the Aryan expansion was that Brahmanical Hinduism was firmly implanted on Indian urban developments, the arts, and literature. Henceforth, all public works and architectural designs would be aimed at reinforcing the imperial authority of kings and celebrating gods and goddesses, invoking their blessings, depending on the royal religious preference. The Buddhist architects that preceded the Hindu architects provided historical continuity to temple architecture, which came to combine the best of traditions from the north and south. The resulting "free mixing" of ideas and cultures produced the miracle of temple architecture, which burst

into a passionate and almost frantic activity, raising temple after temple in classical India. Thirteenth-century India experienced the last of the best expressions of Hindu art before the force of Islam under the mighty Mughals swept across the subcontinent.

Islamic Influence

To celebrate the triumph of monotheistic Islam, the Delhi sultans and later the Mughals created an impressive complex of buildings outside Delhi, including the multistoried Qutb Minar, from whose rooftop the call for prayer was issued every day. Whereas Hindu buildings reflected nature in both their shapes and decorations, iconoclastic Islam prohibited Muslim artists and architects from using natural images, even though floral decoration was sometimes allowed. Instead, Islamic art and architecture produced pure geometric designs, reflecting the abstract definition of Allah. The Mughals, informed in their taste by Persian culture, produced the most impressive buildings, as well as erecting new cities to serve Allah and Islam in predominantly Hindu India. Mughal architecture received a new impetus during the reign of Akbar (r. 1556–1605), whose tolerant religious spirit, mystical disposition, and artistic sense inspired a synthesis of Persian and Indian styles of architecture— thereby producing the Indo-Saracenic style that would later influence the British in their construction of New Delhi. From the 1500s, the Mughal emperors continued to build, not only in Delhi but also in their other capital of Agra, and in Punjab's Lahore, producing remarkable buildings, including Delhi's Jama Masjid and the two Red Forts at Delhi and Agra. To combat the intense heat of the subcontinent, the Mughals created magnificent gardens with terraces, stairways, running streams carrying cool water from the mountains to nearby lakes, and a complex system of fountains and cascades. At Delhi and Agra, special channels carried cooling water through the interiors of imperial buildings. In the 1600s, Shah Jahan built mosques and other buildings within his Red Forts. These buildings were made of imported Italian white marble, as was the magnificent Taj Mahal, the tomb that Shah Jahan had built for his wife Mumtaz, beside the river Jamuna at Agra.

The British Period

The British began their building efforts in India when Sir Thomas Roe, King James's ambassador, secured permission in 1619 for the East India Company to build its first factory (trading post) at Surat, a bustling city and principal port of the Mughal empire at the mouth of the Tapti River, the western gateway to India. From these humble beginnings, the British would ultimately culminate their imperial construction in the building of the British capital at New Delhi, when King George V declared, on the occasion of his coronation durbar at the Red Fort on 12 December 1911, that British India's capital was being shifted from Calcutta to a new site on Delhi's historic plain.

Among many myths surrounding the British Empire was the myth of imperial unity. Their search for an elusive imperial identity through the medium of architecture occupied the imagination of many a British administrator. Although this imperial impulse never became pervasive, it nevertheless achieved its most eloquent expressions in the building of the first British capital city at Calcutta and, even more so, in their second capital city at New Delhi. At the heart of this impulse was the British illusion that if imperial unity could be achieved in brick and stone in heterogeneous India, then perhaps such unity could be attained globally.

The British East India Company's Francis Day bought land in 1638 from the Hindu Vijayanagar kingdom, near the South Indian village of Mandaraz; in 1642 he built Fort St. George there, which came to be called Madras, British India's premier city and urban port on the Coromandel coast. The archipelago of Bombay, which had been given to King Charles II as part of Catherine of Braganza's dowry in 1661, was handed over to the East India Company in 1668 for a nominal £10 annual rent. This transfer changed Bombay from a cluster of seven sleepy fishing villages into British India's western headquarters, displacing Surat and, in time, becoming a sprawling modern financial metropolis and the capital of Maharashtra. Soon after securing permission from Mughal emperor Alamgir in 1690 to trade in eastern Bengal, the British erected a factory on the Hugli River, a tributary of the Ganges that flowed into the Bay of Bengal. The site, located near a village shrine to the Hindu goddess Kālī, and from which *ghat*s (steps) descended to the river, was thus named Kalighat, later corrupted by the British to "Calcutta." The English merchant Job Charnock, a member of the Bengal Council, drew his urban plan for British India's first imperial capital there.

The creation of the British Company presidencies of Bombay, Calcutta, and Madras marked the beginning of British experiments in urban planning in India. Many imposing structures still stand in these cities, enduring testimony to the power of the British Raj: in Calcutta (present-day Kolkata), the Governor's Mansion, modeled by Viceroy Lord Curzon after his Kedleston Hall; its Gothic High Court; neoclassical Town Hall; and the Renaissance-inspired Victoria Memorial. In Bombay (present-day Mumbai), the Gateway to India, born of Anglo-Indian parenthood, commemorates the visit of King George V in 1911, while the Central Telegraph Office, High Court, General Post Office, and Victoria Terminus (present-day Chatrapati Shivaji Maharaj Railway Station) show Gothic features. In Madras (present-day Chennai), several civic and public buildings, including a banquet hall, a museum, and the legislative assembly, represent Western classicism. Thereafter, the British built hill stations, civil lines, and cantonments— all in their efforts to sanitize and segregate Europeans in India and to establish British authority in India. However, it is at New Delhi that the architectural experiments of British Raj in India find their resolution in a style of architecture that is neither Indian nor European, but a complete fusion of the two traditions. Architect Edwin Lutyens's New Delhi represents a mutated but monumental style born of European classicism and Indo-Saracenic influences, and the city itself offers a place where colonial life was sanitized in the spacious symphony of Garden City greenery (the influence of Ebenezer Howard) and imperial power was celebrated in the grouping of public buildings in a monumental center with radiating axial vistas, ending in areas of open space and imposing buildings. To Prime Minister Jawaharlal Nehru, New Delhi was the worst example of British sensibility and imperial arrogance; to British poet Lord Byron it was the Rome of "Hindoostan."

Independent India

New Delhi remains the capital of independent India, and also the most ostentatious expression of the British Raj. Shortly after independence, Nehru censored New Delhi as "most un-Indian." Nehru's nationalist remark, made at the outset of India's experiments in European modernist architecture, was to set the terms of the national debate on the character of India's new cities and its post-colonial architectural style. Nehru felt that the average American or English urban planner could not understand the social background of India. Still, he realized that modern India could not be built without technology, and consequently he supported the creation of the Indian Institutes of Technology and Indian Institutes of Management (modeled after the Massachusetts Institute of Technology and Harvard Business School, respectively). But he insisted that Western technology must be fused with Indian cultural traditions, just as he had fused the political ideologies of communism and democracy to create democratic socialism as a means for leading India on the path of planned economic development.

To a degree, the British who planned New Delhi also were influenced by the ideas of Beaux Arts city planning, American style, which tended to group monumental public buildings in the urban center, leaving the rest of the city to green spaces. What Nehru objected to in New Delhi was not the "leafy capital" per se, for that represented village India, but the monumentality of its official buildings, decorated with classical motifs, attesting to the roots of the British Raj. It therefore followed that in post-colonial India, a new paradigm of planning and architectural style had to be invented. Prime Minister Nehru provided the imaginative shape to the new urban vision at Chandigarh, Punjab's new capital: "Let this be a new town symbolic of the freedom of India, unfettered by the traditions of the past . . . an expression of the nation's faith in the future" (cited in Kalia, *Chandigarh*, p. 21)

Arguably, Nehru's greatest gift was his ability to bring to the surface, through his historical vision, images that fused traditional India with the modern world. He thus introduced a modernist discourse for the making of a nation state—a discourse that was to encourage his countrymen to develop a more encompassing sense of what constituted their world. Nehru said of Chandigarh: "It is the biggest example in India of experimental architecture. It hits you on the head, and makes you think" (cited in Kalia, *Chandigarh*, p. 29). The man who would deliver Nehru his urban dream was Le Corbusier, whose vision brought down old walls that had long imprisoned India, defying ancient prejudices. Le Corbusier opened the

doors of modernism's golden age, which stretched from the 1920s through the 1960s, promising to make the world a better place through design. This was to be achieved, according to the menu of modernism, by providing plenty of unadorned open space, abundant natural light through large expanses of glass, and an intimate connection with the outdoors. In the 1960s, the experiment in modernism was expanded by American architect Louis Kahn in his seminal work on the Indian Institute of Management (1962–1974) at Ahmedabad. Modernism's technological innovation and aesthetic self-expression were seen as the twin forces of urban design that could solve housing and other social problems. The ability of modernism to meet a surging housing demand and to revitalize decaying cities in postwar Europe was not lost on India, which itself was burdened with refugees as a result of the 1947 partition of the subcontinent.

From the struggle over rival visions of independent India's future emerged a new understanding of the confluence of history and memory for India's intellectuals, architects, urban planners, and political leaders. Partitioned India demonstrated two versions of history and ideology: Mahatma Gandhi's vexed, sometimes mystical, attachment to villages as the source of ideals for building a new India competed with Nehru's inclination toward modern cities. Nehru spent much of his career as a public figure trying to confront traditional India, and his Western training placed him in an oppositional—and sometimes advantageous—position to comment on the struggle over memory in Indian society. In his writings and speeches, Nehru presented a historical vision for India in which urbanism flourished and modern industry thrived.

Fifty years after its inception, the Chandigarh plan remains India's inspiration in urban planning and renewal, repeated with mantralike regularity in its application, always with idiosyncratic variations to legitimize the enterprise as truly Indian. Through this process of repetition, the Chandigarh plan has been absorbed into the assimilative Indian tradition, first in Orissa's capital of Bhubaneswar, then in Gujarat's new capital of Gandhinagar, as well in the other new cities and in rebuilding of the old ones. However, after its first impact, the modern movement lost its way in India, resulting in idiosyncratic building designs. Still, the best Indian architecture, which represented the thoughtful synthesis of old and new, the fusing of regional and universal, and the blending of local craft with modern technology, would evolve after the masters of modernism had been consigned to history. Indian architects such as Charles Correa, B. V. Doshi, Raj Rewal, and others in their youth had fervently sought answers from the masters of modernism to build a new India; they now truly belong in a new nation that is building monuments for the future and rapidly forgetting the burden of colonial rule and the deep religious and communal roots of the partition.

Ravi Kalia

See also **Agra; Bhubaneswar; Bombay; Calcutta; Chandigarh; Gandhinagar; New Delhi**

BIBLIOGRAPHY

Asher, Catherine B. *Architecture of Mughal India.* Cambridge, U.K., and New York: Cambridge University Press, 1992.
Davies, Philip. *Splendors of the Raj.* New York: Penguin, 1987.
Forrest, G. W. *Cities of India: Past and Present.* 1903. Reprint, New Delhi: Metropolitan, 1977.
Irving, Robert. *Indian Summer: Lutyens, Baker, and Imperial Delhi.* New Haven, Conn.: Yale University Press, 1981.
Kalia, Ravi. *Bhubaneswar: From a Temple Town to a Capital City.* Carbondale: Southern Illinois University Press; New Delhi: Oxford University Press, 1994.
———. *Chandigarh: The Making of an Indian City.* New Delhi: Oxford University Press, 1999.
———. *Gandhinagar: Building National Identity in Postcolonial India.* Columbia: University of South Carolina Press; New Delhi: Oxford University Press, 2004.
Land, Jon, Madhavi Desai, and Miki Desai. *Architecture and Independence: The Search for Identity—India, 1880–1980.* New Delhi: Oxford University Press, 1997.
Metcalf, Thomas. *An Imperial Vision: Indian Architecture and Britain's Raj.* Berkeley: University of California Press, 1989.
Tadgell, Christopher. *The History of Architecture: From the Dawn of Civilization to the End of the Raj.* London: Architecture Design and Technology Press, 1990.

URDU. *See* **Languages and Scripts.**

USHAS. *See* **Vedic Aryan India.**

UTTAR PRADESH. *See* **Geography.**

VAISHESHIKA According to Kanāda, the mythical founder of the system, *Vaisheshika* is the enumeration of everything in this world that has the character of being. Since the categories are numerous, the use of formal logic is essential to draw inferences, and in this respect *Nyāya* is its sister system.

Kanāda's Vaisheshika Sūtra presents a system of physics and metaphysics. Its physics is an atomic theory of nature, where the atoms are distinct from the soul, of which they are the instruments. Each element has individual characteristics (*vishesha*s), which distinguish it from the other nonatomic substances (*dravya*s): time, space, soul, and mind. The atoms are considered to be eternal.

There are six fundamental categories (*padārtha*) associated with reality: substance (*dravya*), quality (*guna*), motion (*karman*), universal (*sāmānya*), particularity (*vishesha*), and inherence (*samavāya*). The first three of these have a real objective existence, and the last three are products of intellectual discrimination. There are nine classes of substances (*dravya*), some of which are nonatomic, some atomic, and others all-pervasive. The nonatomic ground is provided by the three substances, ether (*ākāsha*), space (*dik*), and time (*kāla*), which are unitary and indestructible; a further four, earth (*prithivī*), water (*āpas*), fire (*tejas*), and air (*vāyu*) are atomic, composed of indivisible, and indestructible atoms (*anu*); self (*ātman*), which is the eighth, is omnipresent and eternal; and, finally, the ninth is the mind (*manas*), which is also eternal but of atomic dimensions, that is, infinitely small.

There are seventeen qualities (*guna*), listed in no particular order as color or form (*rūpa*), taste (*rasa*), smell (*gandha*), and touch (*sparsha*); number (*sankhyā*), size (*parimāna*), separateness (*prithaktva*), conjunction (*samyoga*), and disjunction (*vibhāga*); remoteness (*paratva*) and nearness (*aparatva*); judgment (*buddhi*), pleasure (*sukha*), pain (*duhkha*), desire (*ichchhā*), aversion (*dvesha*), and effort (*prayatna*). These qualities are either physical or psychological.

Two atoms combine to form a binary molecule (*dvyanuka*). Two, three, four, or more *dvyanuka*s combine into grosser molecules of *tryanuka, chaturanuka*, and so on. The other view is that atoms form dyads and triads directly to form the molecules for different substances. Atoms possess an incessant vibratory motion. The activity of the atoms and their combinations are not arbitrary but are based on laws that are expressed as the *adrishta*.

Molecules can also break up under the influence of heat. In this doctrine of heating of atoms, the impact of heat particles decomposes a molecule. Heat and light rays are taken to consist of very small particles of high velocity. The particles of heat and light may be endowed with different characteristics, and therefore heat and light can be of different kinds.

Ākāsha (ether), time, and space have no lower constituents. Of *ākāsha* the qualities are sound, number, dimension, separateness, conjunction, and disjunction. Thus, being endowed with qualities, and not being located in anything else, it is regarded as a substance. In as much as it has no cause, either homogeneous or heterogeneous, it is eternal. "Time" is the cause of the relative notions of priority, posteriority, or simultaneity and succession, and of late and soon, in as much as there is no other cause or basis for these notions. The Vaisheshika Sūtras clearly present the principle of cause (*kārana*) and effect (*kārya*). Time and space are the efficient cause for all phenomena.

It is stated that there are two kinds of universals: higher and lower. The higher universal is Being, which encompasses everything. Lower universals exclude as well as include, which means that the universals may be defined in a hierarchical fashion. The higher universal is akin to a superposition of all possibilities and it therefore anticipates the essence of the quantum theory.

Subhash Kak

See also **Vedic Aryan India**

BIBLIOGRAPHY

Matilal, B. K. *Nyāya-Vaisesika*. Wiesbaden, Germany: Otto Harrassowitz, 1977.
Phillips, Stephen H. *Classical Indian Metaphysics*. Chicago: Open Court, 1995.

VAJPAYEE, ATAL BIHARI *(1924–), prime minister of India (1996–1998 and 1998–2004).* A. B. Vajpayee was India's prime minister in the Bharatiya Janata Party–led coalition government of the National Democratic Alliance from March 1998 to April 1999. It fell in a vote of no-confidence in 1999 when the Dravida Munnetra Kazahgam (DMK) party refused to vote with its coalition partners. Vajpayee led the alliance to victory again in the general elections that followed in October 1999. He became prime minister when this coalition formed a government from October 1999 to May 2004. Vajpayee's coalition government lost the 2004 general elections to a Congress Party–led coalition government led by Sonia Gandhi, president of the party.

Vajpayee was born on 25 December 1924 in Gwalior, in what was then British India's Central provinces, now Madhya Pradesh. He attended college in Gwalior and Kanpur, and has a master's degree in political science. He first entered politics during the independence struggle as a member of the Rashtriya Swayamsevak Sangh (RSS), the extremist Hindu nationalist wing of the Hindu Mahasabha. He was a founding member of the Hindu right-wing Jana Sangh Party in 1951, a reconstituted version of the Hindu Mahasabha, which was banned from politics after one its members, Nathuram Godse, assassinated Mahatma Gandhi in 1948. Vajpayee was a member of India's lower house of parliament, the Lok Sabha, and briefly of its upper house, the Rajya Sabha, since 1957. He was elected to Parliament at various times from constituencies in Uttar Pradesh, Gujarat, Madhya Pradesh, and Delhi.

Vajpayee became leader of the revamped Bharatiya Janata Party (BJP), and a coalition member of the Janata Party government led by Prime Minister Morarji Desai. This newly constituted alliance of parties under the banner of the Janata Party had ousted Indira Gandhi's Congress Party government in a national election following

Atal Bihari Vajpayee. Vajpayee in a private moment of reflection, the festival of Holi, March 2003. During his two terms as prime minister, his was the moderate face of Hindu nationalism, insisting that India remain a secular state. REUTERS / CORBIS.

her twenty-two-month "National Emergency" rule that suspended the democratic process in India from June 1975 to March 1977. Vajpayee had been jailed by the Indira Gandhi government during the Emergency. After the defeat of the Congress Party, he became external affairs minister in the Janata Party government of Prime Minister Desai.

Following the victory of the BJP-led coalition over the Congress Party in March 1998, newly appointed prime minister Vajpayee immediately gave the go-ahead for a series of nuclear tests in early May 1998. Pakistan countered promptly with nuclear tests of its own. BJP rule also ushered in a wave of Hindu nationalism, pushed by more extreme Hindu parties, the Vishwa Hindu Parishad, the Rashtriya Swayamsevak Sangh, and the Shiv Sena. There were attempts to redefine India as a Hindu state called "Hindutva," against the opposition of the more secular parties, groups, and leaders in India. However, Vajpayee appeared as the moderate face of Hindu nationalism, insisting that India remain a secular state.

Vajpayee's tenure as prime minister is best known for his efforts to bring about reconciliation with Pakistan through what came to be called "bus diplomacy." In February 1999 he took a well-publicized bus trip from Amritsar in Indian Punjab to Lahore in Pakistani Punjab and was greeted warmly by Pakistani prime minister Nawaz Sharif. This gesture of Indian goodwill and reconciliation fell apart two months later, when Pakistan launched an attack on Kargil in Indian Kashmir. The peace initiative by Prime Minister Vajpayee collapsed. Relations appeared to suffer a further setback when the perceived mastermind of the Pakistani attack on Kargil, General Pervez Musharraf, overthrew Sharif's civilian government and imposed military rule. In early 2004, Vajpayee made further conciliatory gestures toward Pakistan, declaring that he would like to see peace between India and Pakistan during his lifetime.

Economic growth at averages of 6 to 8 percent of the gross national product continued under Vajpayee's BJP-led coalition government, drawing further on the reforms introduced in 1991 by Congress Party minister of finance, Dr. Manmohan Singh. Even during the global economic recession of 1998–1999, India's growth continued at 5.8 percent. However, the defeat of Vajpayee's government by the Congress Party is attributed largely to its excessive commitment to high-tech development in India and the welfare of the rising Indian middle class, and the neglect of the masses of India's rural poor.

Raju G. C. Thomas

See also **Bharatiya Janata Party (BJP); Hindutva and Politics**

BIBLIOGRAPHY

Bakshi, S. R. *Atal Behari Vajpayee.* New Delhi: Deep and Deep, 2002.
Raghavan, G. N. S. *New Era in the Indian Polity: A Study of Atal Behari Vajpayee and the BJP.* New Delhi: Gyam Publishing House, 1996.
Sondhi, M. L. *Vajpayee's Foreign Policy: Daring the Irreversible.* New Delhi: Har-Anand Publications, 1999.
Thakur, C. P., and Devendra P. Sharma. *India under Atal Behari Vajpayee.* New Delhi: UBS Publishing Company, 1999.

VALMIKI. *See* **Rāmāyaṇa.**

VANAPRASTHA. *See* Hinduism (Dharma); Saṃskāra.

VARANASI A city in the state of Uttar Pradesh, Varanasi (called Benares by the British) had a population of 1.1 million in 2001. The name Varanasi is derived from the two rivers, Varuna and Asi, that flow into the Ganga (Ganges) there. The city is located on the western bank of the Ganga, which flows from north to south in this area, and the city thus faces the morning sun. Many *ghat*s (steps) lead from the high bank down to the river, where pilgrims bathe; the Manikarnika Ghat and the Dasasvamedha Ghat are the most famous of these. Being the most sacred place of the Hindus, the city has many temples, including the Hanuman Temple, dedicated to the monkey god Hanuman, and the Durga Temple of the Mother Goddess Durgā. The most important of all is the Vishwanath Temple, dedicated to Lord Shiva, the patron of the city. The original Vishwanath Temple was destroyed by the Mughal emperor Aurangzeb, who had a mosque built at this site, which still occupies one of the most prominent locations of the city.

Many pious Hindus come to Varanasi when they believe they are near death, in order to be cremated on one of the "burning *ghat*s" in the northern part of the city. The ashes of the dead are swept into the river, which is believed to have a self-purifying quality. In recent years the river has been polluted by many industrial effluents.

This sacred city was earlier known as Kashi. Its origins can probably be traced back to the eighth century B.C. The Buddha preached his first sermon in neighboring Sarnath, which is marked by its ancient Dharam Eka stupa. In addition to its ancient religious traditions, Varanasi is also known for its silk saris, which are coveted by Indian women everywhere. The saris are usually decorated with borders containing gilded threads, some with beautifully embroidered patterns.

The city is also home to one of India's most famous universities, Banaras Hindu University. When the Muslim University at Aligarh was started, Pandit Madan Mohan Malaviya, a leading Hindu politician, advocated the establishment of a Hindu university in Varanasi and received a great deal of support for it. The university was inaugurated in February 1916. The humanities have played an important role in its curriculum, but it has also gained a reputation as a center of science and technology. It is one of India's national universities, which are under the direct supervision of the president of India.

Dietmar Rothermund

BIBLIOGRAPHY

Singh, Bhagwati Sharan. *Varanasi.* New Delhi: National Book Trust, 1988.
Singh, Rana P. B. *Cosmic Order, Sacred City, Hindu Traditions.* Varanasi: Tara Book, 1993.

Verma, T. P. *Varanasi through the Ages*. Varanasi: Bharatiya Itihas Sankalan Samiti, 1986.

VARṆA. *See* Caste System.

VARUṆA

A powerful deity, Varuṇa is known in the Rig Veda as the universal ruler in charge of *rita*, cosmic law and order, and the personification of moral authority. He is an all-seeing, omniscient, celestial controller and exacting punisher of those who transgress his commandments (*vrata*). In hymns he is frequently invoked in the compound Mitravaruṇa along with his brother, Mitra, also one of the Ādityas, the sons of the goddess Aditi, "the Unbounded." Mitra, a name cognate to ancient Iranian Mithra, meaning "friend," shares the major features of Varuṇa, including kingship, but appears as a benign, restoring, and contractual side of divine sovereignty. Varuṇa, on the other hand, is the wielder of occult power (*māyā*) and the severe binder of sinners, capturing with nooses (*pāsha*) those who infringe upon *rita*, often inflicting diseases upon them. Hymns to Varuṇa invariably include pleas for forgiveness and release from his wrath, judgment, and bondage for any moral offense (*āga*). Like Mitra, Varuṇa may extend grace to the penitent. Release from one or another of his hundred nooses means not only cessation of disease or physical pain but also removal of the sin that brought on punishment. He is the dominant side of the pair, Mitra being addressed alone in a single Rig Vedic hymn, whereas a dozen are directed solely to Varuṇa.

Satya, or truth and exactitude in sacrifice, are within Varuṇa's guardianship, and several Vedic sacrifices feature him, including *rājasūya* (consecration of a king), *ashvamedha* (horse sacrifice), and *varuṇapraghāsa* (second of three seasonal sacrifices, a rite in which the sacrificer's wife must confess sins). One of the priests essential to the Vedic soma cult is named Maitrāvaruṇa; he takes the pressed juice offered to Mitravaruṇa, the pair, as divine unity.

Sūrya, the sun, serves as eye of the all-observant Varuṇa, who as divine overseer also has spies (*spasha*); the same word occurs for Mithra's spies in the Avesta, indicating an Indo-Iranian antiquity for this feature of cosmic control. Since Varuṇa is associated with both the day and night sky, his spies are possibly stars. Cosmic waters above and below the earth, rivers, and rain are all within his domain.

During the Vedic period, Varuṇa as *samrāj* (king by his nature) gradually lost his position as all-powerful sovereign and greatest of deities to Indra, who is king by force,

by self-rule (*svarāj*). In the Sanskrit epics and Purāṇas, Varuṇa appears as a *lokapāla*, assigned to the west as one of the eight guardian deities. Still lord of the waters, now featuring the ocean, he is king of *nāga*s, or serpents. He may be seen in temple sculptures on his mount (*vāhana*), the *makara*, a crocodile-like composite creature. In addition to Varuṇānī, named in the Rig Veda, his legitimate wives in various Purāṇas include Gaurī and Jyeshthā, while Bhadrā, daughter of Soma and wife of Utathya, he captured by force. Among his sons were the *rishi* Vasishtha (fathered jointly with Mitra), Pushkara, and the great poet of the Rāmāyaṇa, Vālmīki, born according to one version when Varuṇa's semen fell on a termite mound (*valmīka*).

Today, Varuṇa's aide is sought when digging wells or in times of drought. If monsoon rains are late and crops are endangered, Vaidika Brahmans may be summoned to recite Rig Veda hymns in a Varuṇa *pūjā*. Although Varuṇa is now seldom credited, both *dharma* as cosmic law and *vrata* as human vow to observe *dharma* continue to be the focus of modern Hinduism, as they were for the development of the classical Dharma Sūtras and Dharma Shāstras.

David M. Knipe

See also **Agni; Hinduism (Dharma); Indra; Soma; Vedic Aryan India**

BIBLIOGRAPHY

Brereton, Joel P. *The Ṛgvedic Ādityas*. New Haven, Conn.: American Oriental Society, 1981. Discusses Varuṇa as well as Mitra, Aryaman, and other Ādityas in the Rig Veda.

Gonda, Jan. *Dual Deities in the Religion of the Veda*. Amsterdam: N. V. Noord-Hollandsche Uitgevers Maatschappij, 1974. Ch. 5 details Mitra and Varuṇa separately and as the compound Mitravaruṇa.

Parpola, Asko. "The Religious Background of the Sāvitrī Legend." In *Harānandalaharī*, edited by Ryutaro Tsuchida and Albrecht Wezler. Reinbek: Verlag für Orientalistische Fachpublikationen, 2000. Suggests Proto-Dravidian and Vedic connections regarding Varuṇa's noose, spies, heavenly banyan tree.

Rodhe, Sten. *Deliver Us from Evil: Studies on the Vedic Ideas of Salvation*. Lund: C. W. K. Gleerup, 1946. Ch. 2 illuminates passages on Varuṇa's noose (*pāsha*) in Rig Veda, Atharva Veda, Brāhmaṇas.

VEDĀNGA JYOTISHA

The earliest astronomical text from India, the *Vedānga Jyotisha* is attributed to Lagadha and has an internal date of approximately 1350 B.C. It is available in two recensions, one belonging to the Rig Veda and the other to the Yajur Veda (which, from the language used, appears to have been edited a few centuries later). The text is dated from the statement that the winter solstice was at the beginning of the asterism Shravishthā (beta Delphini) and the summer solstice at the midpoint of Ashleshā.

According to the *Vedānga Jyotisha*, in a *yuga* there are 5 solar years, 67 lunar sidereal cycles, 1,830 days, 1,835 sidereal days, 62 synodic months, 1,860 *tithi*s, 135 solar *nakshatra*s, 1,809 lunar *nakshatra*s, and 1,768 risings of the moon. It also provides ingenious rules to determine the positions of the *nakshatra*s, the sun, and the moon at any time.

A lunar month is divided into 30 *tithi*s. The solar day is divided into 124 parts and also into 603 *kalā*s. The measurement of time, by the use of a clepsydra, was in the unit of *nādikā*, which was the sixtieth part of a day. The units used were chosen to allow for the use of integers in various calculations.

The *Vedānga Jyotisha* is a lunisolar system in which the movements of the moon across the *nakshatra*s in the sky identify the days, and the position of the sun, tracked by its northward and southward course in the two halves of year (*ayana*), identifies the twelve months of the year. In this system, intercalary months need to be added and other corrections made in order to make the sun's northward course begin in the correct month.

Although the *Vedānga Jyotisha* says that the *yuga* of five years has 1,830 civil days and 62 lunar synodic months, actually the correct number of days is 1,826, and an additional day should be added to the 62 synodic months. The length of the year was measured from one winter solstice to another, and this was taken to be 366 days. Since the year was divided into six equal seasons of 61 days, the civil count of 1,830 was a convention. The number of civil days in the *yuga* was corrected in the two extra intercalary months that were employed.

Lagadha gives the ratio of the longest to the shortest day as 3:2. This is true for northwestern India, and one may conclude that he belonged to that region.

Subhash Kak

See also **Astronomy; Vedic Aryan India**

BIBLIOGRAPHY

Kak, Subhash. "The Astronomy of the Age of Geometric Altars." *Quarterly Journal of the Royal Astronomical Society* 36 (1995): 385–395.
Sastry, T. S. Kuppanna. *Vedānga Jyotisa of Lagadha.* New Delhi: Indian National Science Academy, 1985.

VEDĀNTA. *See* **Upanishadic Philosophy.**

VEDIC ARYAN INDIA The Saṃhitās—"collections" of hymns (*sūkta*) or, more comprehensively, ritual formulas (*mantra*)—constitute the oldest surviving literature of South Asia. They form the earliest category of texts belonging to the four divisions of the Veda (sacred knowledge), composed in the Sanskrit language. The Saṃhitās are the sources discussed in this article. (See the article "Brāhmaṇas" for a discussion of later Vedic texts, the Brāhmaṇas [in a broader sense comprising the Āraṇyakas and Upanishads], the subsequent category of Sūtras [Shrauta, Grihya, and Dharma Sūtras], and other auxiliary texts.)

The Saṃhitās and Brāhmaṇas came to be considered eternal, transcendental wisdom (*shruti;* literally, "hearing"), supernaturally "heard" or "seen" by ancient sages (*rishi*), the ultimate authority in Hinduism. Though each Veda thus comprises other texts besides (one or more) Saṃhitās, their plain names are often used to designate the respective Saṃhitās: Rig Veda = Rig Veda Saṃhitā. The fourfold division of the Veda results from the engagement of four groups of priests in the elaborate *shrauta* rites ("based on the *shruti*"), which first took their codified shape in Yajur Veda.

Rig Veda—"knowledge of praise stanzas"—was the domain of the *hotar* priest and his assistants, who praised deities by reciting specific stanzas of the Rig Veda. Its 1,028 hymns total 10,417 stanzas. Most hymns were probably composed in the thirteenth century B.C. and the whole corpus collected by about 1100 B.C. The final redaction took place around 700 B.C., whereafter the text was handed down with extraordinary fidelity. Preserving extant poems by oral repetition replaced a living tradition of composing new poems.

The Rig Veda is divided into ten books. The oldest are the nuclear "family books" (II–VII), each ascribed to a family of poets descended from a particular sage: II, Gritsamada; III, Vishvāmitra; IV, Vāmadeva; V, Atri; VI, Bharadvāja; and VII, Vasishtha. Almost equally old is Book VIII, with hymns of the Kanva (1–66) and Angiras (67–103) families, and its supplement, the Kanva hymns (1–50) of Book I, though the rest of Book I is more recent. Book IX was created by extracting all the hymns addressed to God Soma from Books I through VIII. Book X is the most recent addition.

Sāma Veda—"knowledge of the melodies"—is the domain of the *udgātar* and other chanter priests. The Saṃhitā, preserved in two versions (Kauthuma and Jaiminīya), consists of text books (*ārcika*) with stanzas mostly taken from the Rig Veda, and of extensive song books (*gāna*) with melodies (*sāman*) set to the (variously altered) texts.

Yajur Veda—"knowledge of the muttered formulas," largely in prose— belonged to priests performing practical operations. The earlier Saṃhitās of "Black Yajur Veda" (Maitrāyaṇīya, Katha, Kapishthala-Katha, and Taittirīya) include prose passages explaining the origin and symbolism of the *shrauta* ritual. In contrast, the younger "White Yajur Veda" separates its (Vājasaneyi) Saṃhitā from the ritual explanations in prose, which are collected in the most extensive of the existing Brāhmana texts, the Shatapatha-Brāhmana.

Atharva Veda—"knowledge of the *atharvan* priest"—contains charms for healing, love affairs, sorcery, and domestic (*grihya*) and royal rites. The next oldest collection after the Rig Veda, the Atharva Veda (and the latest hymns of the Rig Veda, which anticipate it) differs from the Rig Veda in language and content, and probably reflects the traditions of both earlier arrived Aryan immigrants and the indigenous population of India. It was initially excluded from the solemn ritual, but later became the Veda of the Brahman priest, whose main duty was to control that everything was done correctly and to "heal" eventual mistakes.

Background of the Vedic Aryans in South Asia and Beyond

The ancestry of the Vedic Aryans is understood today better than before. At the same time, it has become a heatedly debated and politicized issue. Opinions widely differing from the traditional "immigration hypothesis" are expressed especially by Hindu fundamentalists. These opponents maintain that the birthplace of the Aryan (and even other Indo-European) languages is India, and that Vedic Sanskrit was spoken in the Indus Valley, or Harappan, Civilization (2600–1900 B.C.). The forgotten Indus script is difficult to decipher in the absence of any translations, but its analysis leads to the conclusion that the language was Proto-Dravidian. This is supported by the presence of Dravidian loanwords in the Rig Veda and later Vedic texts and the survival of one Dravidian language (Brahui) in the Indus Valley. Most important, however, is the absence of the horse, both from excavated animal bones antedating 2000 B.C. in South Asia and from the otherwise rich gallery of animals in Harappan art. By contrast, the horse is frequently mentioned in the Rig Veda and was culturally important.

The Vedic language is archaic Sanskrit, or Old Indo-Aryan, the oldest phase of Aryan languages spoken in (ancient) India. *Ārya* (hospitable, noble) is the ethnic self-appellation of the authors of the Rig Veda, shared by the speakers of Avestan and Old Persian, the two varieties of Old Iranian (or "Irano-Aryan"), the oldest phase of Aryan languages spoken in (ancient) Iran. The original location of the Proto-Aryan or Proto-Indo-Iranian parent language is indicated by the many Proto-Aryan loanwords in the Finno-Ugrian protolanguage, which dispersed from

central Russia. The Rig Vedic hymns imply a long poetic tradition with refined style and metrics. They share numerous phrases with Zarathushtra's Old Iranian poems. Some poetic formulas go back even to Proto-Indo-European. The phrase *shrávas. . . . ákshitam* (imperishable fame) has an exact etymological counterpart in ancient Greek, in the Homeric phrase *kléos áphthiton.*

Several terms related to wheeled vehicles reconstructable to the Indo-European protolanguage indicate that its speakers knew ox-drawn carts and wagons, which were invented around 3500 B.C. This gives a firm starting point for identifying the chain of archaeological cultures through which the various Indo-European languages eventually reached their historical seats. On this basis, Proto-Aryan was spoken in the Sintashta-Arkaim culture (c. 2200–1800 B.C.) in southern Russia between the Volga and Ural rivers. The earliest known horse-drawn chariots are from aristocratic graves of this culture.

The Indo-Aryan branch seems to have broken off with the Andronovo culture (c. 1800–1300 B.C.) that spread to Siberia and Central Asia. In Central Asia, Indo-Aryan speakers apparently took over the rule in the Bactria and Margiana Archaeological Complex (BMAC) in the first quarter of the second millennium. A similar BMAC-related takeover of power happened in Syria, where the Mitanni kingdom, famed for its horse-drawn chariots, had rulers with Indo-Aryan names (c. 1500–1300 B.C.).

Entrance of the Vedic Aryans to South Asia

Ceramics with BMAC origin came to the Swat Valley of north Pakistan around 1600 and again around 1300 B.C. These two waves of immigration most probably brought the poetic tradition of the Rig Veda to South Asia. These dates agree with the fact that the Rig Veda mentions bronze (*ayas*) but not iron. Iron came to South Asia around the eleventh century B.C. and is mentioned in the Atharva Veda.

River names occurring in the Rig Veda connect its oldest parts with the northwest and the Punjab. The "seven streams" are repeatedly mentioned; in X, 75 all the major rivers of the Indus system are enumerated. Eastern rivers (Yamuna and Ganga) are mentioned only a few times. In later Vedic literature the geographical horizon widens eastward and southward. Several river names seem to have had their referents in Afghanistan. Thus Rasā, corresponding to Avestan Ranhā, probably denotes the Amu Darya and may have a Proto-Aryan background in the Volga River, called Rhā in Greek sources. Sarasvati mostly denotes the North Indian Ghaggar-Hakra, but in VI, 61 Sarasvati evidently refers to the Argandāb River in the Afghan province of Kandahar, called Harahvaiti in

Avestan and Harahuvati in Old Persian. This was the birthplace of King Divodāsa.

The Vedic Aryans did not come to an empty country when they entered South Asia. The Harappan population is estimated to have been around 1 million. The walled Indus cities collapsed around 1900 B.C., and the Aryan war god Indra and his protégé, King Divodāsa, have long been blamed for this: according to the Rig Veda, they vanquished "black-skinned" enemies called Dāsa, Dasyu, and Pani, and destroyed their numerous strongholds.

However, chronological reasons alone make it difficult to accept this popular hypothesis, as King Divodāsa probably did not come to the Indus Valley before 1300 B.C. Moreover, the Dāsa forts are described as having circular and often multiple, concentric walls, while the Indus cities had a square layout. In the 1970s, a "temple fort" with three round concentric walls was discovered at the BMAC site Dashly-3 in Afghanistan. The battles against the Dāsas may therefore have taken place west of the Indus Valley.

Later Iranian and Greek sources place a tribe called Dasa or Daha and its subtribe Parna in Afghanistan and southern Turkmenistan, the very area of the BMAC. Two East Iranian languages have preserved the word *daha* (from earlier *dasa*) in the meaning "man, hero, human being," which is often the basis of ethnic names. A wave of Early Proto-Iranian–speaking immigrants from the northern steppes may have preceded the Vedic Indo-Aryans in Central Asia (taking over the BMAC) and in South Asia. This earliest Aryan wave could be connected with the Late and Post-Harappan cultures in the Indus Valley ("Jhukar" in Sind, "Cemetery H of Harappa" in the Punjab), the Ganges-Yamuna Doab (the "Copper Hoards"), and with the early non-Vedic but Aryan languages of eastern India (Māgadhī). Their religion may have initiated Shākta Tantrism.

The Rig Veda mentions by name some thirty Aryan tribes and clans, major ones being the "five peoples." Four of these, paired as Yadu and Turvasha, and Anu and Druhyu, seem to represent the first wave of Rig Vedic immigrants (c. 1600 B.C.). The fifth tribe, Pūru, together with its ally or subtribe Bharata—which has given India its later native name, Bhārat(a)—appears have arrived later (c. 1300 B.C.), overpowering the earlier tribes. This immigration from Afghanistan over the Hindu Kush Mountains to the western side of the Indus was led by the Pūru king Purukutsa and the Bharata king Divodāsa.

Divodāsa's son or grandson Sudās defeated the Pūru king and his many allies in the celebrated "battle of ten kings" (Rig Veda VII, 18) on the Ravi River in the Punjab. Sudās became the supreme ruler in the easternmost realm of the Rig Vedic period, the area around Delhi later called Kurukshetra. The Pūrus stayed between the Jhelum and Ravi rivers, where Alexander conquered King Pōros ("descendant of Pūru").

Vedic History after the Rig Veda

Iron and a new luxury ceramic called painted gray ware appeared in the Punjab and Haryana around 1100 B.C. and remained cultural characteristics of this area until about 400 B.C. Iron probably came with Old Iranian–speaking horse riders from Central Asia. It is possible that the Kuru kings, who now assumed power in Kurukshetra, the center of Vedic civilization immediately after the Rig Veda, belonged to this wave of immigrants: they share the name "Kuru" with the founder of the Persian Empire, Cyrus.

Economy and Society

Cattle breeding was the basis of Vedic economy. The cow was the most important domestic animal as the provider of meat and milk products; others included the horse, donkey, mule, camel, goat, and sheep, as well as dog and cat, and in the Yajur Veda, also elephant. Agriculture (with plow) was practiced mainly by the indigenous sedentary population. The main crop was barley; rice is mentioned from the Atharva Veda onward.

Early Vedic Aryans were much on the move and continually at strife with each other, cattle rustling being a favorite pastime. Horse-drawn chariots with two spoked wheels served for fighting, hunting (wild boars and antelopes), and racing. Rivers were crossed with boats and floats. The word *grāma*, which later means "village," denotes in the Rig Veda "a group of wandering pastoralists and their camp," also "a warring band." People lived in their ox-drawn wagons, placed in a circle to provide a corral for the cattle at night. Actual buildings—called "house" (*griha*) or "hall" (*shālā*)—were lightly constructed with wooden beams and matted walls and roofs. Brick was not used for residential buildings, only for fire altars and hearths. Towns appear around 800 B.C. with the painted gray ware and start being referred to in Brāhmana texts.

Goods traded by barter included salt, metals and metal objects (weapons, tools and vessels), grain, wool, thread and garments, goatskins and plants (soma, herbs). Cattle was the main means of payment. Kings rewarded poets with gifts of cattle, horses, and golden ornaments.

Some specialized craftsmen are mentioned in the Rig Veda, including carpenters, smiths, merchants, and fishermen. Post–Rig Vedic texts speak of potters (*kulāla*) with potter's wheels, but they were considered non-Aryan and wheel-thrown dishes "demonic": ritual vessels were handmade by Aryans.

Vedic society consisted of extended families headed by patriarchal "masters of the house" (grihapati), clans (vish) headed by chieftains (vishpati), and tribes ruled by kings (rājan or kshatriya), war leaders like the war god Indra, and peacetime rulers like God Varuna, who guarded social rules and punished offenders. By the Brāhmana period, the administration was much more developed, with numerous dignitaries.

The Rig Veda distinguishes between the Ārya varna and the Dāsa varna, apparently a difference in skin color. In the late hymn X, 90, however, varna (color) denotes the four social classes—brāhmana (priests), rājanya (nobility), vaishya (commoners), and shūdra (serfs)—as originating from the mouth, arms, loins, and feet of the primeval man (purusha), whom the gods sacrificed in the beginning, creating the world out of his body. This seems to reflect the surfacing of earlier local developments. The priestly claim for superiority and monopolization of the sacrificial ritual probably started from the royal high priests (purohita) important in the Atharva Veda.

Religious Ideas and Forms of Worship

Contrasting with the systematic and detailed descriptions of rituals in the Brāhmanas and Sūtras, the Rig Veda repeats over and over a few central myths and cultic acts but leaves many others quite obscure, as poetics favored veiled and indirect references. The hymns mainly praise gods, invite them to a sacrificial meal, and pray to them for long life, sons, cattle, victory in battle, or fame. Verbal art and liturgy was most important in the uniconic worship of gods. The truthfully spoken word had magic power, brahman: by means of his poems, God Brihaspati (in later Hinduism, the chaplain of the gods and the planet Jupiter), helping Indra, opened the cave of the demon Vala who had imprisoned the cows of the Dawn.

The Rig Vedic worship or sacrifice (yajña), which was modeled on human hospitality, was a very important ceremony for the Aryans, as their ethnic name indicates; it was guarded by God Aryaman, "hospitality" personified. After the sacrificer and the priests (who represented particular deities) had become purified and initiated, the sacrificial fire was kindled. Gods were invited to come and seat themselves on the grass strewn near the fire. Agni, the god of fire, conveyed the offerings to them, or functioned as their mouth and priest. Agni is one of the principal Vedic deities, worshiped in every house as its master. Offerings consisted of cakes and of portions of slaughtered animals put into fire, while other parts were eaten by the priests.

The most important offering substance was soma, the deified sacrificial drink, pressed out of the stems of a plant previously soaked in hot water. The juice was purified with a woolen filter, and during this act lauded with Samur Vedic songs. The botanical identity of soma is controversial. Most likely, it was ephedra, still used as haoma by Zoroastrians, the followers of Zarathushtra. Ephedra contains ephedrine, a drug that enhances physical performance. Soma is the drink of the warrior. Poets, too, are inspired and kept awake by soma.

More than a quarter of the Rig Vedic hymns are addressed to Indra, the god of war and the principal drinker of soma. Indra's greatest feat is the killing of Dragon Vritra (Obstruction) who had imprisoned the waters. Maruts, the storm winds, assisted Indra. Indra also helps in finding cattle captured by the enemy and in breaking enemy forts. He is said to have created the sun, the heaven, and the dawns.

Indra, however, is not the only king of the gods. (He has this function also in Hinduism and other Indian religions.) Mitra (personified "treaty of friendship") and Varuna (personified "oath" or "true speech," upholder of cosmic order—rita, later dharma—and punisher of sinners) are worshiped as a dual deity of kingship. Mitra is associated with day (in Iran, Mithra was the sun god and the god of victory) and Varuna with night (conceived of as a heavenly ocean; in later Hinduism, Varuna is the god of ocean and the waters). As a dual divinity they represent the bright and the dark side of the single sun god, Savitar. Along with Aryaman, Bhaga (share [of booty], good fortune), and some other gods, they form a class of "abstract" deities called Ādityas, "sons of [Goddess] Aditi," possibly created by Proto-Indo-Aryans under the inspiration of the Assyrian religion, where similar deities are worshiped as aspects of the chief god Assur. Likewise, the "Holy Immortals" were aspects of Zarathushtra's Ahura Mazda "Lord Wisdom"—the Old Iranian counterpart of Varuna as the principal Asura.

As the title of Varuna, asura means "Lord," but in other Vedic contexts and in later Hinduism it means "Demon," an enemy of the "Gods," usually called deva in the Veda. Zarathushtra rejected most of the earlier Indo-Aryan gods, so daēva means "demon" in Avestan. There are traces of some rivalry between the cult of Indra (worshiped with soma) and the cult of the twin gods called Ashvin or Nāsatya (worshiped with gharma, an offering of heated milk, or with surā, a beer made from milk and honey). The Ashvins drive their flying horse chariot around heaven with their beautiful sister-wife, Ushas, the goddess of Dawn. They function as healers and saviors of gods and men, like their Greek counterparts, the horseman twins. The Dioskouroi, however, were also guardians of the dual kings of Sparta, so Mitra-and-Varuna may be partial doubles of the Ashvins, the original chariot gods. The horse sacrifice (ashvamedha) belonged to royal rites (in the Rig Veda as in the later epics and after). Mitra-and-Varuṇa, Indra, and the Nāsatyas were all invoked as oath deities by the Mitanni king in a treaty with the Hittite king in 1380 B.C.

The main gods of later Hinduism appear with a lower profile as early as the Rig Veda. Rudra (Shiva) is feared for his arrows, while Vishnu assists Indra and crosses the universe with his three strides.

The late books I and X of the Rig Veda differ considerably, in language as well as in content, from the rest of the collection but anticipate the Atharva Veda and Brahmanism. Philosophical speculation starts with the mighty hymn of creation (sat and asat, X, 129). Sorcery spells contain archaic Indo-European traditions, likewise the hymns associated with domestic rituals, which remain the most enduring part of the Veda in India today. Harappan heritage is preserved in Vedic calendrical astronomy, attested for the first time in the marriage hymn (X, 85). The Rig Veda speaks of both burial and cremation as current modes of disposing of the dead, but cremation became the standard method. The funeral hymns (X, 10–19) are related to Yama, "the twin (with his sister Yamî)," the first man and first mortal, and the king of the dead, who has an Old Iranian counterpart in the Avestan Yima, the first king and first mortal. Yama seems to be an earlier double of Manu (man), the ancestor of the Vedic Aryans; both descend from the solar god Vivasvat. Several cultural and cultic layers can thus be traced in the Veda.

Asko Parpola

See also **Ashvamedha; Brāhmaṇas; Harappa; Hinduism (Dharma); Indus Valley Civilization; Zoroastrianism**

BIBLIOGRAPHY

Erdosy, George, ed. *The Indo-Aryans of Ancient South Asia: Language, Material Culture, and Ethnicity.* Berlin and New York: Walter de Gruyter, 1995.
Gonda, Jan. *Vedic Literature (Samhitās and Brāhmanas).* Wiesbaden, Germany: Otto Harrassowitz, 1975.
Macdonell, A. A. *Vedic Mythology.* Strasbourg: Karl J. Trübner, 1897.
Macdonell, A. A., and A. B. Keith. *Vedic Index of Names and Subjects,* vols. I–II. London: John Murray, 1912.
O'Flaherty, Wendy Doniger, trans. *The Rigveda: An Anthology.* Harmondsworth, U.K.: Penguin, 1981.
Parpola, Asko. *Deciphering the Indus Script.* Cambridge, U.K., and New York: Cambridge University Press, 1994.
———. "Pre-Proto-Iranians of Afghanistan as Introducers of Shâkta Tantrism: On the Scythian/Saka Affinity of the Dāsas, Nuristanis and Magadhans." In *Iranica Antiqua* 37 (2002): 233–324.
Staal, Frits, ed. *Agni: The Vedic Ritual of the Fire Altar,* vols. I–II. Berkeley, Calif.: Asian Humanities Press, 1983.

VINA The South Indian vina is also called *Sarasvatī vīnā* due to its association with the goddess Sarasvatī, who embodies the respect for learning that characterizes South Indian culture. In song lyrics and paintings, the goddess is depicted as a beautiful lady who delights in playing the vina. The modern vina dates from the early seventeenth century and belongs to the category of long-necked lutes. Its main resonator (*kudam*) and neck (*dandi*) are carved from jackwood. A removable resonator (made from gourd, wood, fiberglass, plastic, or papier-mâché) mainly serves to support the vina on the left knee of its player. The neck holds twenty-four frets and seven tuning pegs, and it is decorated by a dragon head (*yāli*). The characteristic sound of the vina is the result of several factors, including the black wax layer on which the "bell metal" frets are placed, the convex shape of the brass plate covering the wooden bridge, and the optional use of wire plectra.

Of the seven strings, four are fitted on the top of the neck, and three along the side facing the player. The four melody strings are tuned to the tonic (middle and lower sā) and its fifth (lower pā and one octave below); these notes are arranged in the descending order from the player's point of view (sā-pā-sā-pā).

Three auxiliary strings constitute a kind of drone whenever the basic note (sā), its higher octave, and the fifth (pā) between them are sounded. In addition, these strings are used to indicate the cyclic pattern (*tāla*) that applies to any particular composition or improvisation. All these features and techniques account for the fact that in Sanskrit, this type of vina is referred to as a complete instrument (*sarva vādya*), one that is self-sufficient, as it expresses the melodic and rhythmic aspects of music even in the absence of an accompanist.

A few traditional vina exponents sing along with their instrument in order to highlight the lyrical aspect of a song. The repertoire of a vina player (*vainika*) is essentially the same as that of a vocalist, but unlike the human voice, a vina has a range of 3 1/2 octaves. Most performers prefer to tune it to a key note between E and F. Its playing technique involves slides (horizontal pull) and deflection (vertical pull) in order to produce subtle nuances such as microtonal shades (*shruti*) and a variety of embellishments. A fretless type of vina (*chitravīnā*) was earlier known as *gôttuvādyam*, which implies that it is played with a gliding "rod."

The *tānam* is a speciality of all vina players and involves the elaboration of a *rāga* in a pulsating manner. This musical expression of bliss (*ānantam*) during *tānam* is also achieved by singing the syllables "ā-nan-tam-tā-nam" in various combinations. Embellishments and grace notes (*gamaka*) serve to intertwine melodic phrases in a pleasing manner. Such continuity is greatly valued by the discerning listener (*rasika*). Although music of such high density requires much skill, a good vina performance conveys the legacy of composer-poets like Muttusvāmi Dīkshitar: his song (*kriti*) in praise of Mīnākshi invokes the beautiful goddess who plays music on the vina with ten different types of embellishments (*dashavidha gamaka*).

Ludwig Pesch

See also **Dīkshitar, Muttusvāmi**

BIBLIOGRAPHY

Beyer, Norbert: *Lautenbau in Südindien: M. Palaniappan Achari und seine Arbeit* (with English summary, photographs, and CD). Berlin: Museum für Völkerkunde, 1999.
Simon, Artur, ed., and Pia Srinivasan Buonomo (commentary). *Sambho Mahadeva: Musik für Vīnā, Südindien / Music for Vīnā, South India*. Double CD with commentary in German and English; performed by Rajeswari Padmanabhan and K. S. Subramanian (vinas), and Tanjore Upendran (*mridangam*). Berlin: Museum Collection Berlin, 2003.

VISHNU AND AVATĀRAS The god Vishnu, a relatively minor figure in the Vedas (which hold many but not all of the primary roots of Hindu tradition), emerges in the Sanskrit epics and Purāṇas to become one of the pair of most powerful male deities. As sectarian Shaivas are those whose primary devotional allegiance is to Shiva, Vaishnavas are worshipers of Vishnu in one or more of his manifestations. In many ways, Vishnu represents an entire pantheon of gods assembled under one name, a supreme being with multiple incarnations popularly known as *avatāra*s. Historically, these numerous divine beings had obscure but sometimes colorful origins in regional clan deities and cults of deified heroes. Gradually they were gathered under the umbrella designation of Vishnu and regarded as his appearances with various names, mythologies, and rituals. Alongside Shaivas on one hand and devotees of many forms of Devī, the goddess, on the other, Vaishnavas represent the core of the Hindu devotional tradition. Although many Hindus concentrate faith in one god as supreme deity, Hinduism has always been comfortable with devotees who worship in temples, shrines, and home altars that embrace more than one sacred being.

Vishnu in the Vedas

Of the more than one thousand hymns of the Rig Veda, Vishnu is addressed in only five, and his name appears fewer than a hundred times in all the others. Yet his most celebrated feat, the taking of three great strides, the last extending beyond human comprehension and presumably embracing the three cosmic levels of earth, midspace, and

Narasiṃha. Massive stone sculpture from Hampi depicting the fourth avatar of Vishnu, the all-powerful Narasiṃha (half-man, half-lion) sent to slay the errant ruler Hiranyakashipu. Regardless of what form his manifestation takes, Vishnu's pervasiveness in Indian culture is never far from mind. K. L. KAMAT / *KAMAT'S POTPOURRI*.

heaven, endows him with a permanent reputation for all-pervasiveness. He is associated with major Rig Vedic deities, including Indra, whom he assists in the conquest of the powerful demon of obstruction Vritra, and with whom he drinks the sacred soma offering. Detailing *yajña*, sacrifice, Brāhmaṇa texts direct the sacrificer to take three strides to reach heaven and the highest light. In so doing, the sacrificer becomes both Vishnu and the sacrifice (Shatapatha Brāhmaṇa 1.9.3.9–10). Such a homology of the god, worshiper, and sacrifice assures Vishnu a prominent and lasting role in a religion that focuses on ritual. Communication between gods in heaven and humans on earth is secured by identifying Vishnu with the *yūpa*, at once the sacrificial pole and a cosmic *axis mundi*.

In addition to myths featuring Indra, Soma, and Agni, Vishnu also plays a part in various accounts, from the Rig Veda to the Brāhmaṇas, of a boar and a dwarf, prefiguring two of the famous *avatāra*s narrated in greater detail in subsequent Sanskrit epics and Purāṇas. A central motif in these developing myths is cosmogony, the creation or rescuing of the earth from chaos or the Asuras (enemies of the gods) through sacrifice, often personified in the form of Prajāpati, Lord of creatures. For example, the Asuras, unaware of Vishnu's talent for a three-step across the universe, are fooled when they readily consent to give up as much of the earth as the dwarf can lie upon or cross in three strides. And the boar, called Emūsha in some variants, stars as an "earth-diver" type of creator who raises out of primeval waters the entire earth on his tusk. Two other early myths involve Prajāpati and either a fish or a tortoise, yet another pair of *avatāra*s of Vishnu that achieved widespread popularity in post-Vedic texts.

At the close of the Vedic textual period, most Upanishads paid scant attention to Vishnu. The early Brihadāraṇnyaka placed Vishnu in a creative role, alongside Prajāpati and other deities, as overseers of ritual impregnation. In the later Kaṭha Upanishad, Vishnu's highest step occurs with the first mention of the term for rebirth, *saṃsāra*: one with proper knowledge of the self attains that heaven from which he will not be reborn. But more significantly, by the third century B.C., the Mahā-Nārāyaṇa Upanishad, book 10 of the Taittirīya Āraṇyaka, connected Vishnu with cosmic Purusha, Prajāpati, time personified as Kāla, order, truth, the highest light, and in fact the Absolute, *brahman*. Among all these associations with supreme cosmic entities was inserted Nārāyaṇa, a Rishi and son of Dharma who became known as "Purusha Nārāyaṇa" in the Shatapatha Brāhmaṇa (e.g., 12.3.4.1). The identification of Vishnu with Nārāyaṇa proved to be momentous in post-Vedic theological circles that led to the establishment of sectarian Vaishnavism.

Vishnu in Epics and Purāṇas

In the last half of the first millennium B.C., Vishnu and Shiva came into prominence, each expressing a range of essential myths, rites, and symbols of the past, both Vedic and non-Vedic. Over the succeeding centuries, they were joined by an array of local, regional, and eventually pan-Indian goddesses who also achieved status in popular worship. Aspects of Vedic Vishnu that served best to highlight him in a new age that produced epic roles in the Sanskrit Mahābhārata, Harivaṃsha, and Rāmāyaṇa included his role as the sacrifice, and particularly as the sacrificial victim Purusha-Prajāpati, the primal person whose body became the distributed cosmos. As cosmic pole (*skambha*), Vishnu was everywhere present as essential cosmic energy. To the scattered earlier cosmogonic folklore of the boar, fish, tortoise, and dwarf were added weightier cycles of two great heroic figures, Krishna and Rāma, who became the most famous of all manifestations. In the system of *avatāra*s that emerged well into

Vishnu as Boar. Kavi mural of the third avatar, Vishnu's reincarnation as a boar to save the earth from raging flood waters. Hindus believe that whenever injustice or disorder rules the universe, God will assume an earthly form to reestablish *dharma* (balance). K. L. KAMAT / KAMAT'S POTPOURRI.

the first millennium A.D., these two, in widely separate ways, were considered to be descents of Vishnu into the human world to restore *dharma*, sacred order, in a time of lawlessness and chaos. Each appears at the shift of an age, or *yuga*, within the great cycle of time, and each is said to be the ideal king for the new age.

Multiple cults of regional clan leaders and deified heroes, some of them thought to be Rishis, appear to have formed, reformed, and coalesced during the period of composition of the Mahābhārata, about 500 B.C. to A.D. 200. The great epic reveals the names of Vāsudeva, Nārāyaṇa, Krishna, Bala-Rāma, Nara, and Hari, as well as communities known as Bhāgavatas (worshipers of Bhagavan, the

Vishnu Sanskarana. Carving of Vishnu, c. 1147. In Hinduism, the worship of Vishnu ("all preserving one") is frequently associated with *sanskar* (sacraments or rituals) that mark a new stage of life. NATIONAL MUSEUM / FOTOMEDIA.

Lord), Pāñcarātras, and others, but gives no transparent view of their developing relationships. The Nārāyaṇīya section in book 12 provides some degree of focus. But the words of Krishna in the Bhagavad Gītā (c. 200 B.C.)—verses often considered the essence of the Mahābhārata in its portion of the sixth book—declare a divine mission and provide a rationale employed later in the concept of *avatāra*s: "For the preservation of good and destruction of evil . . . I come into being in age after age" (Gītā 4.8). The relationship of the warrior Arjuna's charioteer, Krishna, to the god Vishnu is complex and certainly mystifying to Arjuna. In a crucial moment, transcendent Vishnu reveals his bodily form in the terrifying splendor of a thousand suns, and Arjuna beholds all the gods and the fiery dissolution of the universe. Quickly he begs for the mercy of normal human vision and then learns that it is only through steadfast devotion (*bhakti*) that such a theophany occurs and god himself may be entered (Gītā 11.3–55).

In other epic passages, including the Harivaṃsha, and in the Purāṇas, particularly the Vishnu and Bhāgavata, Krishna is portrayed quite differently, as a valiant warrior dispatching monsters and demons, and then again as the cowherd Gopāla and lover of *gopī*s, milkmaids who represent the adoring souls of humans, more often found languishing in separation from the god than relishing his embrace. In sculpture, wood carvings, and later medieval paintings, Krishna is seen conquering the serpent Kāliya, hoisting up Mount Govardhana in a rescue mission, or as a lithe, dark blue figure, surrounded by cattle and rolling hills, enchanting all with his flute, but crowned and still royal. The Gītā Govinda, a twelfth-century Sanskrit devotional poem by Jayadeva, provided a name for the *gopī* favored by the dark lord, and a cult of Rādhā and Krishna was born. Krishna's many heroic deeds are recited with great affection, and in fact his entire life fascinates his devotees, including his childhood antics. Bāla-Krishna stealing butter from the pantry is a favored scene. Another episode echoes the revelation to Arjuna: Krishna's mother looks into her child's mouth when she thinks he has been eating dirt and discovers the entire universe, earth, moon, and stars.

Rāma, prince of Ayodhya, is hero of the Rāmāyaṇa, perhaps the earlier of the two epics. His character is more focused and transparent than that of Krishna. Popularly known to Vaishnavas as Rāmacandra, he is portrayed as a handsome blue figure, crowned, an arrow in one hand, bow in the other. Vishnu's descent in this instance of the *avatāra* series is to restore the rightful kingdom to Rāma, who has been unjustly exiled, and to defeat the usurping demon Rāvaṇa, king of Lanka. The epic centers on Rāma and Sītā as ideal man and wife, each the model of virtue, truth, and beauty. Rāma's heroic younger brother, Lakshmaṇa, and monkey allies championed by Hanuman are crucial in a war to rescue the abducted Sītā. The Sanskrit Rāmāyaṇa traditionally attributed to Vālmīki was followed by other, substantially different regional versions in several languages, including Tamil, Hindi, and Bengali between the twelfth and sixteenth centuries. Before tens of thousands of devotees, the Hindi Rāmāyaṇa of Tulsīdās is dramatized annually as the Rām-Līlā.

Although some Purāṇas maintain longer catalogs, a classical list of ten *avatāra*s of Vishnu endures, often beginning with Matsya, the fish. A well-known myth in the Shatapatha Brāhmaṇa features an unnamed tiny fish, cared for by Manu, that grows into a giant fish strong enough to save Manu from a universal flood by towing him in a boat. In the Mahābhārata, the Matsya, and other Purāṇas, this fish is identified either as Brahmā or Vishnu, and rescue from world annihilation now entails all beings, with Manu in charge of a new creation in which the Vedas must be heard anew. Paintings illustrating Purāṇa manuscripts charmingly show four personified Vedas and seven Rishis alongside Manu and family, all bobbing in a boat on an endless sea that represents an interlude between destruction and a new creation.

Kurma, the tortoise incarnation of Vishnu, also has Vedic cosmogonic origins. In the *agnicayana* sacrifice, a live tortoise, symbol of the three worlds and life-sap, was buried as foundation for the fire altar. In epics and Purāṇas, Kurma lies at the bottom of the cosmic ocean with Mount Mandara based on his back like an *axis mundi*. In the myth of the churning of the ocean, warring gods and demons employ the great serpent Vāsuki as churning rope to twirl this pole and produce from an ocean of milk fourteen cosmic treasures, including *amrita*, the drink of immortality, and the goddess Lakshmī.

Again the Vedic tradition is one source for the boar *avatāra*, Varāha, widely represented in early iconography. The assimilation of indigenous myths and cults of a sacred boar into Vedic tradition and thence into the Vaishnava pantheon is illustrated in an association of Varāha with every aspect of the sacrifice. He is shown either upright on his hind legs or standing on all fours. Often a naked young girl is suspended from one tusk, a symbol of Prithivī, the goddess Earth, brought up by the boar who dove to the bottom of the sea to rescue her.

Unlike the other great male god, Shiva, who appears in at least as many fearful and demonic guises as gracious and benign ones, the incarnations of Vishnu are almost always benevolent. One exception is his descent as Narasimha, the man-lion. This curious mixture came about when a clever demon, Hiraṇyakashipu, extracted a boon from Brahmā that no weapon could harm him, that he could not be killed by man or beast, by day or night, inside or outside his dwelling. The demon's son, Prahlāda, a passionate devotee of Vishnu, enraged his father, who tried every means to kill the boy. Vishnu therefore dispatched this troublesome demon by his own hands, appearing as a man-lion, at twilight, on the threshold. Usually depicted with fierce lion face, Narasimha is often shown in a macabre scene, Hiraṇyakashipu stretched across his lap being disemboweled.

The dwarf in the Shatapatha Brāhmaṇa who tricked the Asuras into giving up the world by recapitulating Rig Vedic Vishnu's three great strides across the cosmos now receives a name, Vāmana. Yet another demon, Bali, is fooled by the innocent-looking but wide-striding dwarf. Vāmana is often pot-bellied as a dwarf but lithe and virile when conquering.

Parashu-Rāma, Rāma-with-battle-ax, presents the anomaly of a Brahman priest who is a fierce warrior wielding a deadly weapon. His myths center on the perpetual struggle for supremacy between the two primary classes, Brahmans and Kshatriyas, priests and warriors. Depicted with his right hand holding an ax given by Shiva, Parashu-Rāma recalls the mythic annihilation of a warrior class that temporarily usurped sovereignty and inverted cosmic order.

Even the Buddha was drawn into the orbit of Vishnu. Just as Buddhists co-opted several Hindu gods (Indra was said to have become a Buddhist convert), so did Vaishnavas submerge the Buddha into one more incarnation of Vishnu. According to one source, Vishnu deliberately deceived and punished those incapable of knowing god. The Mahābhārata and several Purāṇas list Hamsa, the goose, Brahmā's mount, instead of the Buddha.

These nine *avatāra*s are said to have descended in times of distress to rescue or re-create the world. That leaves only the tenth of the classic set, a Vishnu still to come. At the close of our current Kali *yuga*, worst of the four ages, Kalki will arrive to initiate the Krita *yuga*, the golden age restored once again. As an eschatological figure akin to both ancient Iranian Saoshyant and the Buddha Maitreya, he is to appear with flaming sword on a white horse, riding to end chaos, reestablish order, and reward or punish all according to their deeds.

Of the ten, it is Krishna and Rāma who emerged as such powerful magnets of devotion that worshipers often dismiss all others and think of one or the other instead of Vishnu. But regardless of manifestation, Vishnu's pervasiveness is never far from mind. Nammālvār, most famous of the twelve Tamil Vaishnava poet-saints of South India in the seventh to tenth centuries, spoke of Tirumāl (Vishnu) coming to him "happily, all grace, my lord who became fish, tortoise, man-lion, dwarf, wild boar, and who'll soon be Kalki, occupied me, became all of me, my lord dark as raincloud" (trans., A. K. Ramanujan).

The iconography of Vishnu that began with temple sculpture in the late centuries B.C. and flourished between the fourth and sixth centuries A.D. continued with coins and on to medieval paintings. Frequently he is youthful in appearance, dark blue, a *shrīvatsa* in his chest hair marking him as the favorite of Shrī-Lakshmī, his four hands holding a conch and lotus, with discus and mace as weapons. A prize from the churning of the ocean is the *kaustubha* jewel worn by Vishnu. Often he appears on Garuḍa, his eagle or hawk mount, a well-winged (*suparṇa*) figure in his own right, whose career echoes that of the Vedic eagle who carried a hero to steal soma. Garuḍa is known as the enemy of serpents, *nāga*s. But another theriomorphic mount for Vishnu is the cosmic serpent Shesha, known as Ananta, endless, a coil floating upon the ocean as foundation for the sleeping god. A recurrent scene depicts Vishnu lying asleep on Shesha, Lakshmī tending his feet, while a lotus sprouts from his navel to reveal the creator god Brahmā. In the late and synthetic Purāṇic theology of Trimūrti, a triune godhead, Brahmā creates, Vishnu preserves, and Shiva destroys each temporary world. Another conflation was Hari-Hara, Vishnu, and Shiva as one being performing all functions. The *shālagrāma* stone found in many home shrines is a fossil ammonite from a sacred river. It is pervaded by the god and therefore is Vishnu.

Lakshmī, at Vishnu's feet or by his side on Gupta coins, is his wife but also the famed goddess of good fortune, wealth, prosperity, and beauty. By the close of the Vedic texts, Lakshmī had merged with Shrī, an older Vedic goddess with similar characteristics. Vishnu's divine consort may also be known as Padmā, the lotus. In South Indian temples the god is often flanked by Shrī-Lakshmī and Bhū or Bhūmi, a variant of Prithivī, the earth. The goddess remained subordinate until such texts as the Lakshmī Tantra of the Pāñcarātra Āgamas promoted her to equality, even identity with Vishnu. Here, Lakshmī-Nārāyaṇa becomes as arresting and complicated a manifestation as Shakti-Shiva among other texts and rituals of Tantra. The Tamil Shrī Vaishnava treatises of the twelfth and later centuries and the emergence of Rādhā in the Gīta Govinda from Bengal, also in twelfth century, assured a permanent place for goddesses and feminine powers within Vaishnava tradition. In the fourteenth and later centuries, the popularity of openly erotic poems of Vidyāpati, Sūrdās, Caṇḍīdās, and the Sahajiyā mysticism of Bengal meant a more intricate demonstration of the Lord's love play (rāsa līlā) with the human soul, and a counterpoint to those such as Caitanya, who stressed his experience of Krishna's absence.

Vishnu in Faith and Practice

Vishnu as godhead and his principal avatāras, Krishna and Rāma, are most readily discernible in the context of bhakti, devotional movements in which the bhakta, devotee, fervently seeks the presence of god. To be with god—really to return to him, since the body of Purusha-Nārāyaṇa is the source of all being—is a desire that remains unqualified by time, as evidenced in the widespread belief in Vishnu's heaven, Vaikuṇṭha, on the Ganges River flowing from Mount Meru (or in variants, within the deepest ocean). Moksha is the sought-after release from further rebirths, but living for eternity in the presence of Lord Vishnu is a far higher reward for devotion. In funerary rituals Rāma may be invoked in several ways, including a chant "the name of Rāma is satya, truth!"

The mythology of manifestation according to the Bhagavad Gīta and several Purāṇas is one statement of Vishnu's pervasive nature. But the attempt to explain the relationship between the one and the many, a supreme being with multiple forms that do not exhaust his totality, was approached by different communities from several perspectives from the fifth century B.C. The highest being could be disclosed as unitary, two-, three-, four-, five-, or even sixfold, each expression supported by cosmology and mythology, including agricultural and pastoral symbols of sun, rain, earth, plows, pestles, and cattle. Vedic Purusha is again recalled, the primal being in four parts, three of them remaining unmanifest (Rig Veda 10.90.3). The doctrine of vyūhas emerged from the Pāñcarātra school, perhaps under the influence of Sāṃkhya philosophy, with its division of consciousness and matter, purusha and prakriti. An early branch envisioned four vyūhas, arrangements or emanations, proceeding from the supreme Vishnu as an aggregate of deified heroes: Saṃmkarshaṇa (Bala-Rāma), Vāsudeva, Pradyumna, and Aniruddha. Another perspective noted five by including Sāmba or Shāmba, and still another counted triads in pairs. Krishna devotees centered upon Vāsudeva as Krishna, the other four being his brother, two sons, and a grandson. By the time of the Vishnu and Bhāgavata Purāṇas, many of these cosmological perspectives had melded into a more uniform background for the doctrine of avatāras and proliferation of bhakti.

As Shankara was the great eighth-century monistic philosopher of Advaita Vedānta and impersonal brahman, so were Yāmuna, and in particular, his successor, Rāmānuja, the principal architects of what came to be known as Vishishtādvaita, the qualified nondualism school of Vedānta. Rāmānuja was an eleventh-century student of Vedānta whose personal experience of Vishnu and Shrī-Lakshmī brought realization of brahman as a limitless being with whom an individual soul could unite. Passionate devotion to the point of complete self-surrender, prapatti, later became the hallmark of many South Indian Shrī Vaishnavas. Eventually this movement split into northern and southern subsects. The former stressed Sanskrit texts and cooperative grace, whereas the latter relied on Tamil hymns and the irresistible grace of god, a conviction that one is rescued by god alone without human effort. As chief priest of the Ranganatha temple in Shrirangam, Rāmānuja systematized Vaishnava devapūjā, divine worship, and traveled widely to disseminate theological and liturgical reforms that became fundamental to the overall success of bhakti in Hinduism.

A list of 108 sacred sites for Vaishnava pilgrims includes Shrirangam, Tirupati, and even Vaikuṇṭha, heaven. Among celebrated festivals are birthdays for Krishna and Rāma, Holi, and special times to honor regional poet-saints who made manifestations of Vishnu accessible in Tamil, Kannada, Marathi, Braj, Bengali, or a score of other languages.

David M. Knipe

See also **Bhagavad Gīta; Bhāgavata Purāṇa; Devī; Hinduism (Dharma); Krishna in Indian Art; Rāmāyaṇa; Shiva and Shaivism**

BIBLIOGRAPHY

Archer, W. G. *The Loves of Krishna in Indian Painting and Poetry*. 1957. Reprint, Mineola, N.Y.: Dover, 2004. A brief classic study with 40 plates of late sixteenth- to early nineteenth-century paintings.

The Bhagavadgītā in the Mahābhārata. Chicago: University of Chicago, 1981. Romanized Sanskrit text, translation, introduction to the classic Gītā.

Bhattacharya, Deben, trans. *Love Songs of Vidyāpati*. London: George Allen & Unwin, 1963. Fourteenth-century Maithili songs of Krishna and Rādhā, edited with introduction by W. G. Archer; 31 plates of paintings from the seventeenth to early nineteenth centuries.

Biardeau, Madeleine. *Hinduism. The Anthropology of a Civilization*, translated by Richard Nice. 1981. Reprint, Delhi: Oxford University, 1989. Convincing synthesis explains the transformation of Vedic religion into "a universe of *bhakti*" able to sustain the Vaishnava tradition along with other options.

Buitenen, J. A. B. van. *Rāmānuja on the Bhagavadgītā*. 1953. Reprint, Delhi: Motilal Banarsidass, 1968. Abbreviated and annotated translation of the foremost Vaishnava philosopher's influential commentary on the Gītā.

Desai, Kalpana. *Iconography of Viṣṇu (in Northern India up to the Medieval Period)*. New Delhi: Abhinav, 1973. 104 plates of temple sculpture first century B.C. to fourteenth century A.D.

Dimock, Edward C. *The Place of the Hidden Moon: Erotic Mysticism in the Vaiṣṇava-Sahajiyā Cult of Bengal*. Chicago: University of Chicago, 1966. A careful analysis of poetry, doctrine, and ritual in a sixteenth-century movement that served as tantric counterpoint to Vaishnava orthopraxy.

Goldman, Robert P. *The Rāmāyaṇa of Vālmīki: An Epic of Ancient India*. Princeton, N.J.: Princeton University, 1984. General introduction to the history and critical edition of the Sanskrit epic; translation of the Bālakāṇḍa, first of a seven-volume series.

Gonda, Jan. *Viṣṇuism and Śaivaism: A Comparison*. London: Athlone, 1970. Concise, coherent depiction of myth, ritual, theology, and folklore; copious endnotes include further details.

Macdonell, A. A. *Vedic Mythology*. 1897. Reprint, Varanasi: Indological Book House, 1963. Detailed description of Vishnu in the Rig Veda and Brāhmaṇa texts.

Miller, Barbara Stoler, ed. and trans. *Love Song of the Dark Lord. Jayadeva's Gītagovinda*. New York: Columbia University, 1977. Introduction and translation of twelfth-century Sanskrit classic poetry about Krishna, Rādhā, and the *avatāra*s.

O'Flaherty, Wendy Doniger. *Hindu Myths*. Baltimore: Penguin, 1975. Excellent sampler of basic myths in translation from the Rig Veda, Brāhmaṇas, Rāmāyaṇa, Harivamsa, and Purāṇas.

Ramanujan, A. K. *Hymns for the Drowning*. Princeton, N.J.: Princeton University, 1981. Beautifully translated selections from Nammāḻvār, best-loved Tamil poet-saint, circa ninth century.

Richman, Paula, ed. *Many Rāmāyaṇas: The Diversity of a Narrative Tradition in South Asia*. Berkeley: University of California Press, 1991. Essays by twelve scholars on textual, oral, and dramatic versions in different regions and languages.

Schrader, F. Otto. *Introduction to the Pāñcarātra and the Ahirbudhnya Samhitā*. Chennai: Adyar, 1916. Slightly dated but still the best access to Vaishnava sources.

Soifer, Deborah A. *The Myths of Narasiṁha and Vāmana: Two Avatars in Cosmological Perspective*. Albany: State University of New York Press, 1991. Comparative study of these two *avatāra*s as respective representations of cosmic destruction and re-creation as well as two complementary *varṇa*s, Kshatriyas and Brāhmaṇas.

VISHWA HINDU PARISHAD (VHP) Established in 1964 by a Hindu nationalist party, the Rashtriya Swayamsevak Sangh (RSS), the Vishwa Hindu Parishad (VHP, or World Hindu Council) was created to campaign for an end to the slaughter of cows, a central demand of Hindu activists, who consider the cow a sacred embodiment of Hinduism. The VHP is also a religious and voluntary social service organization that espouses a broader agenda of reform to eradicate various perceived ills of Hindu Indian society. An important underlying ideological motif of the VHP's program is to unify Hindus politically throughout the world, in order to establish a powerful global Hindu voice.

The broader agenda of the VHP includes its stated desire to abolish the consequences of caste divisions in Indian society. It wishes to emulate other world religions by instituting greater rigor and homogeneity in religious practices, as well as to defend traditional Indian cultural values. A central dimension of the VHP's aims and sociopolitical activities is to oppose the conversion of Hindus to other faiths and to encourage the return of converts to the Hindu fold ("homecoming").

Individual VHP organizational service units (*sevakaryas*) adopt a holistic approach, combining religious and sociocultural activities, such as the study of Sanskrit, the classical language of the ancient Hindu texts. They organize gatherings of religious leaders and perform sacerdotal rites to propagate Hinduism. The VHP considers the participation of religious leaders (Dharmacharyas and Shankaracharyas) under its auspices as a crucial element of its activities, as it allows Hindu leaders to speak with a single voice on subjects like the ban on cow slaughter and the construction of a new Rāma temple. The VHP also provides voluntary social services and has pioneered one-teacher schools for deprived rural communities. It helps in the upkeep of rural Hindu temples and trains priests. The VHP operates in virtually all the 770 districts of India and more than two dozen countries abroad.

The VHP's opposition to religious conversion has brought it into sharp conflict with various Christian churches. The VHP is evidently willing to intervene physically to prevent Christian missionaries from undertaking religious or welfare activities that it construes as part of religious conversion. Missionary groups, who have been protesting the disruption of their activities, argue that the right to proselytize is fundamental to their faith and is guaranteed by India's Constitution. A turning point for the VHP was the mass conversion to Islam of India's deprived Dalit community (formerly called "untouchables") in the southern district of Meenaksipuram in 1992. That episode galvanized the VHP into action in a campaign to bring the converts to Islam and other faiths back to the Hindu fold.

During the 1990s the VHP acquired notoriety by spearheading the campaign to build a temple for the Hindu deity, Lord Rāma, at the site in Ayodhya of the Babri Masjid, a mosque constructed in the sixteenth century by the Mughal emperor Babur. The controversy over the site was revived in 1989 when Prime Minister Rajiv Gandhi reopened it for worship by Hindus, after decades of quarantine, hoping thereby to head off conflict between Muslims and Hindus. The conflict, however, escalated, and the mosque was demolished by a Hindu mob in December 1992.

The VHP and its allies argue that an ancient Rāma temple must have stood at the site, was destroyed to make way for the mosque, and must therefore be reinstated. Indians remain divided over the issue. Supporters of the previous coalition government led by the Bharatiya Janata Party (BJP), allied to the VHP, backed the claim, while critics, both secular and Muslim, regarded attempts to destroy any ancient historical monument as a real danger to Indian secularism and tolerance. At least two other mosques, known to have replaced significant temples, are regarded as potential flash points that could provoke religious passions. The VHP insists that few major Hindu temples in northern India survived Islamic rule and that the temples at Ayodhya, Varanasi, and Mathura must be "restored" to allow Hindus to worship there.

In 2001 fifty-nine Hindu pilgrims, including forty women and children, returning from the controversial Rām Janmabjoomi ("Rām birth") temple site in Ayodhya, were attacked and burned to death by a Muslim mob at Godhra station in Gujarat. Retaliatory Hindu mob violence against Muslims followed, and it is believed that various elements of the Sangh Parivar political organization, including the VHP, participated. More than one thousand Muslims were killed. Witnesses allege that members of the VHP, the Bajrang Dal (the youth wing of the RSS), BJP state legislators, and Gujarat state government ministers were involved in the murderous riots that resulted in the killing of innocent Muslims. The events in Gujarat polarized public opinion in India. Nevertheless, anxious Hindus in Gujarat voted overwhelmingly to ensure a resounding victory for the BJP in the state elections that year.

Critics of the VHP view their militant Hindu politics as responsible for instigating intolerance, as well as encouraging violence against religious minorities. The VHP also stands accused of active involvement in the demolition of the Babri Masjid in Ayodhya in 1992. The VHP dismisses its detractors as prone to "appeasement" of unjust demands from India's religious minorities, and it insists that the rise of Hinduism is irresistible after centuries of repression by monotheistic invaders.

Gautam Sen

See also **Ayodhya; Bharatiya Janata Party (BJP); Hindu Nationalist Parties; Hindutva and Politics; Shiv Sena**

BIBLIOGRAPHY

Hansen, Thomas Blom. *The Saffron Wave: Democracy and Hindu Nationalism in Modern India*. Princeton, N.J.: Princeton University Press, 1999.
Jaffrelot, Christophe, ed. *The Sangh Parivar: A Reader*. New Delhi and New York: Oxford University Press, 2005.

VIVEKANANDA, SWAMI *(1863–1902), Hindu religious leader.* Born Narendranath Dutta in Calcutta (Kolkata), Vivekananda studied philosophy at the Scottish Churches College of Kolkata and became a disciple of Sri Ramakrishna Paramhansa, the head priest of the Dakshineshwar Temple. Ramakrishna was a mystic who taught the unity of all religions, an idea that Vivekananda propagated worldwide. In 1893 Vivekananda was invited to attend the World Parliament of Religions, convened in Chicago, as a representative of Hinduism. In his opening speech on 11 September he expressed the hope that the bell which rang at the welcome ceremony had sounded the death knell of all fanaticism. He addressed the parliament several times. In one of his speeches he praised Buddhism as the fulfillment of Hinduism. He advocated a synthesis of the intellect of Hinduism's Brahman with the heartfelt message of the Buddha. Though a Hindu monk, Vivekananda did not stress the renunciation of this world or the quest for individual salvation. He instead made a plea for active social work, seeing God in the poor (*daridra narayan*). As a philosophical justification for this approach, he emphasized Karmayoga, that is, the path to salvation by active work in this world in selfless devotion, without looking to the fruits of one's actions.

The respect that Vivekananda had earned in the West made a great impact on his contemporaries in India, who had been used to the British denigration of Hinduism as a ragbag of superstitions. He thus became a national hero who fired the imagination of young India. Some of the Indian nationalists then also used the idea of Karmayoga as justification for terrorist attacks on the British colonial rulers, but Vivekananda had never intended to inspire violent methods. His main source of inspiration was the Vedānta philosophy of the Upanishads. He reinterpreted Indian traditions so as to fit with modern ideas. Praising the Brahman ideal of service and the spurning of the profit motive, he constructed an Indian socialism. In this way he influenced Indian politicians of various schools of thought, including the great Liberal, Gopal Krishna Gokhale, and the fervent socialist, Jawaharlal Nehru, who acknowledged his debt to Vivekananda in later years. Vivekananda praised the Hindu spiritual tradition but was an ardent critic of Hindu practices such as untouchability, which he characterized as a social custom not justified by religion.

As an instrument for both the propagation of his ideas and active social work, Vivekananda founded the Ramakrishna Mission, named after his spiritual mentor, in 1887. At that time Vivekananda and other followers of Ramakrishna had taken monastic vows. Although most Hindus do not believe in conversion, the Ramakrishna Mission did accept disciples from all over the world who were not born as Hindus. Vivekananda's trips to several Western countries paved the way for the global spread of the Ramakrishna Mission. The Mission has published the eight volumes of his collected works, which contain his books on Bhakti Yoga, Jnana Yoga, Raja Yoga, and Karma Yoga, as well as his numerous speeches.

Dietmar Rothermund

BIBLIOGRAPHY

Vivekananda, Swami. *Collected Works.* 8 vols. 10th ed. Kolkata: Advaita Ashram, 1957.

Women harvest the fiery red kernels of buckwheat. The grain is now almost exclusively cultivated in remote villages of the Himalayas. ASHOK DILWALI/ FOTOMEDIA

TOP: At day's end, still bustling camp-site of the annual cattle fair in Pushkar, Rajasthan. Every fall, thousands of dealers, villagers, tourists, and religious pilgrims (drawn to the city's 400 temples and a nearby lake) flock to this destination. SUDHIR KASLIWAL/FOTOMEDIA

BOTTOM: Surrounded by the heavenly peaks of the Himalayas, Sonmarg, Kashmir, rests in the valley of the Sindh River. With its almost painterly vistas, Sonmarg has become a popular getaway for adventurers. AMIT PASRICHA/FOTO-MEDIA

TOP: Munnar, a small but verdant station set high among the Kannan Devan hills in Kerala. AMIT PASRICHA/FOTOMEDIA

BOTTOM: To the man shown here and the largely agriculture-based economy in India, the monsoon season brings relief from the searing heat of summer. AMIT PAS-RICHA/FOTOMEDIA

TOP: Elephants from the Bandavgarh National Park in Madhya Pradesh calmly submit to a bath at the hands of their *mahouts* or trainers. TOBY SINCLAIR/ FOTOMEDIA

BOTTOM: Rolling dunes of the Thar in northwest India. The largest portion of this desert (which also extends into eastern Pakistan) may be found in Rajasthan. TOBY SINCLAIR/FOTOMEDIA

TOP: The peacock remains the beloved national bird of India and may be observed in large numbers in forested regions and sometimes even in the most unlikely of places: a front lawn of a home. This regal specimen was photographed at Kanha National Park, Madhya Pradesh. TOBY SINCLAIR/FOTOMEDIA

BOTTOM: "Tea pluckers" scour the land on an Assam estate in search of the "two leaves and a bud," the essential ingredient of fine teas. This plantation industry has its roots in British colonial rule. TOBY SINCLAIR/FOTOMEDIA

TOP: At Kaziranga National Park in Assam, tourists on "elephant back" descend on a one-horned rhinoceros. This is one of the few reserves where the rhino may still be found in abundance. TOBY SINCLAIR/FOTOMEDIA

BOTTOM: A wily leopard awaits his prey. These quick-witted cats are quite a common sight in India's jungles. TOBY SINCLAIR/FOTOMEDIA

TOP: A petite langur atop a tree at the Bandhavgarh National Park, Madhya Pradesh. With many different-sized and different-colored species throughout India, langurs are named for the Hindu monkey-god Hanuman. TOBY SIN-CLAIR/FOTOMEDIA

BOTTOM: Aerial view of terraced fields in the fertile, high-altitude Kulu Valley, Himachal. Rice- and wheat-growing fields such as these are commonly held, in small segments, by numerous families. ASHOK DILWALI/FOTOMEDIA

TOP: A cane suspension bridge over the Siyom River in Arunachal Pradesh, a remote and heavily forested state in the northeast of India. Without such bridges, some villages in the region would be entirely cut off from the rest of civilization as navigation is virtually impossible in the fast-flowing rivers of the hills. IPSHITA BARUA/FOTOMEDIA

MIDDLE: Winter view of Bhimakali, wooden palace and temple of the Rampur Bushahr kings. In Sarahan, Kinnaur, Himachal. ASHOK DILWALI/ FOTOMEDIA

BOTTOM: *Ghats* (landing places) along the banks of the Ganges in the holy pilgrim city of Varanasi. They and the many nearby temples and shrines daily reverberate with the sounds of Hindu religious practices. TOBY SINCLAIR/ FOTOMEDIA

WARS, MODERN India has fought four open wars and been involved in several near and minor armed conflicts with its neighbors. India has large standing armed forces and also possesses nuclear weapons. Arguably these are a result of insecurities arising from a history of conflicts that it has been involved in, some whose origins lie in forming a nation comprising scores of ethnic and linguistic groups. The disputes with Pakistan are said to center on Jammu and Kashmir, but as the record shows, the causes of disagreements between the two countries could be more elemental. In the case of China, the dispute is over their border and is yet to be resolved.

Indo-Pakistan War: The First Round

Britain's Independence of India Act of 1947 created the dominions of India and Pakistan, and while the rulers of the over five hundred princely states were asked to work out arrangements with the two new nations, none had the option of remaining independent. Pakistan assumed that the Muslim-majority Kashmir would accede to it, but witnessing the carnage of partition, the maharaja, a Hindu, vacillated. To force his hand, a tribal army attacked the state on 22 October, and the ruler decided to accede to India. India launched a massive airlift on the morning of 27 October, flying in troops to defend the state. Pakistani army regulars, allegedly on leave, led the attack, notwithstanding claims that they were Azad (free) Kashmir forces who had revolted against the maharaja.

The Valley of Kashmir was quickly cleared of the invaders, but through 1948, India and Pakistan were locked in combat across the entire state. In the north, British officers of the Gilgit Scouts handed over the territory to Pakistan. But the battle focused on Indian efforts to secure Ladakh in the northeast, while Pakistan attempted to prevent the Indians from recapturing a strategic sliver of territory stretching from Muzaffarabad to Mirpur, cushioning its Punjabi heartland. It was only in July 1948, when a United Nations commission reached the subcontinent, that Pakistan conceded that its regulars had been involved, but only since earlier that year.

The British generals and a unified British commander-in-chief, Field Marshal Claude Auchinleck, who still headed the two armies, were able to manipulate and moderate the conflict to some degree. Essentially it was an infantry war of mortars, machine guns, and some artillery. India used light tanks to capture the crucial Zoji La Pass and open the road to Leh and used the Indian air force continuously, but Pakistan could not use its air force because of the issue of its legitimacy as a combatant in Kashmir.

When it became clear that neither side could advance beyond what they held by the autumn of 1948, the two sides accepted a cease-fire that became operational at midnight on 31 December 1948.

The Sino-Indian Border War of 1962

The entire 2,520 miles (4,056-km) Sino-Indian border is considered disputed by Beijing, while New Delhi argued that a customary line defined it. Attempts by both sides to militarily establish the border as they perceived it have led to clashes since 1959. The ill-equipped and poorly led Indian army was ordered by the government to undertake a "forward policy" to establish posts behind the Chinese positions. The Chinese bided their time and launched an attack on Indian positions in the North-East Frontier Agency and in Ladakh on 22 October 1962.

Tiger of Mysore Mural. Wall mural depicting a battle between the British and Tipu Sultan (the "Tiger of Mysore") at the Daria Daulat Bagh, Srirangapattana, 1784. After a series of bloody skirmishes, the British finally killed Tipu Sultan in 1799 and took control of South India. T. S. SATYAN.

An Indian brigade readying to occupy the Thag La ridge across the Namka Chu River was wiped out and the monastery town of Tawang captured. On 16–17 November, after a lull of some three weeks, the Chinese moved against the supposedly strong Indian defenses at Se La and Bomdi La to the east, using infiltration tactics reminiscent of the Korean War. The Indian division was routed, bringing the Chinese within sight of the plains of Assam. Further east, the Indian forces fought with great determination in the Walong area, but were also forced to retreat in some disorder. The Indian army performed better in Ladakh, where they conceded ground to the Chinese only after a tough fight, on some occasions to the last man. Indians used light tanks here, but did not commit the combat strength of the Indian air force during the war for fear of Chinese retaliation.

India sought military help from the United States and the United Kingdom, but the Chinese shrewdly declared a unilateral cease-fire on 20 November and in most cases withdrew to their original positions before any significant assistance arrived. Though fighting was limited, the war, particularly the collapse in the east, was a major trauma that led India to embark on a major expansion and reequipment of its forces.

Indo-Pakistan War: The Second Round, August–September 1965

The second Indo-Pakistan war began with a clash in the southern extremity of their land border in the Rann of Kutch in February 1965, and through the summer there were heightened tension and clashes across the cease-fire line in Kashmir. But beginning in August, Pakistan initiated Operation Gibraltar, an invasion of the state by thousands of irregulars. Their aim was to converge on Srinagar and stage a "popular" uprising, which failed to take place; those guerrilla forces that did not retreat were captured or killed. The tough Indian reaction, which included the capture of the strategic Haji Pir Pass and several other Pakistani posts in Kashmir, compelled the Pakistanis to up the ante.

On 1 September, a Pakistani armored division moved toward Akhnur, to cut Indian forces in western Kashmir and threaten links with the valley. Pakistan hoped to localize the conflict within the Jammu and Kashmir state, as had been the case in the 1947–1948 war. But the Indians had other ideas; to relieve pressure in the north, they launched on 6 September a three-pronged attack toward Lahore and also moved against Sialkot. The Indian plans were, however, poorly executed. The Indian air force was not told of the Lahore thrusts, and the Pakistani air force disrupted the central Indian spearhead, striking at Indian air bases and causing considerable damage.

Pakistan had audacious plans of its own, and after blocking the southern thrust against Lahore, they counterattacked with the aim of capturing a vital bridge on the Beas River linking Amritsar with the rest of India. But the badly led Pakistanis floundered at Khem Karan, and the attacking force was trapped and destroyed. By mid-September, Pakistan had expended most of its ammunition, and India's advantage of size would have come into play; strong Chinese pressure and poor advice from army headquarters, however, persuaded India to accept a cease-fire on 22 September. Both sides returned the territory they had captured through an agreement signed at Tashkent in early 1966.

Indo-Pakistan War: The Third Round, The Bangladesh War of 1971

The refusal of Punjabi-dominated West Pakistan to accept the victory of the Awami League, the principal party of East Pakistan, in the first general election of the country in early 1971 led to the latter declaring itself as an independent Bangladesh. Beginning on 25 March 1971, the Pakistani army sought to restore authority through a brutal campaign, killing hundreds of thousands of people. Some 10 million refugees fled across the border to India, along with many Bengali leaders. Led by Bengali officers of the Pakistani army, a Mukti Bahini (Liberation Force) launched a guerrilla war against the Pakistani forces in East Pakistan/Bangladesh.

India began to assist this force and to prepare for a general war. As the battle lines were being drawn, India signed a friendship treaty with the Soviet Union on 9 August 1971; meanwhile, U.S. secretary of state Henry Kissinger's secret visit to China, via Pakistan in July 1971, cemented the already existing U.S. tilt toward Islamabad. By the end of November, fighting along the border intensified, and Indian forces entered East Pakistan/Bangladesh at several points.

On 3 December, in a bid to ease Indian pressure, the Pakistani air force launched a series of air strikes against Indian airfields in the west, leading to open war. The Pakistani commander in Bangladesh planned to keep screening forces on the border and build up cities as strong points that could hold out for two months or so.

The initial Indian plan was to advance on four fronts across the riverine terrain, occupying positions short of the capital, Dhaka. But as the confused Pakistanis pulled back, Indian generals sensed opportunity, and two of the thrusts reached the gates of the city by 14 December; two days later, the 91,000-strong Pakistani army surrendered. The dispatch of a nuclear-powered carrier group to the region by U.S. president Richard M. Nixon was to little avail.

The Pakistani army had vague plans for an offensive in the west to help the beleaguered forces in the east. The plan to capture Poonch failed, but Pakistani forces captured Chamb again. But the anticipated big offensive, however, did not take place. Indian forces were put off-balance by contradictory orders on whether they should take the offensive or remain on the defensive. The limited offensives that did take place yielded insignificant gains because of poor leadership. Unlike the war of 1965, this conflict saw considerable naval action. The Indian navy conducted two daring raids on Karachi, bombed Chittagong harbor, and sank a Pakistani submarine, though it lost a frigate off Gujarat.

Under the Simla Agreement in 1972, prisoners of war were exchanged and captured territory returned, except in Jammu and Kashmir, where the cease-fire line was replaced by a Line of Control (LOC), through which both sides kept their respective gains: Pakistan in Chamb, and India in Ladakh.

The Indian Peacekeeping Force in Sri Lanka, 1987–1990

India sent in a division-sized force in September 1987 as part of an accord with Sri Lanka. Their job was to enforce a peace with the Liberation Tigers of Tamil Eelam (LTTE), a separatist group that India had earlier backed. However, the effort soon involved India in combat operations against the LTTE, which expanded to a guerrilla war across the northern and eastern parts of the island and sucked in another three Indian divisions. A change in government led to a Sri Lankan request for an Indian withdrawal in March 1990, which took place after India had lost some 1,100 soldiers.

The Siachen War

The officials who determined the LOC in 1972 did not anticipate one problem when they terminated the line at a point NJ 9842: the agreement did not stipulate the location of the line for the remaining about 60 miles (100 kilometers) of glaciated terrain before it reached the border with China. In the early 1980s, Pakistan began to issue maps with the border running northeast to the Karakoram Pass, incorporating the Saltoro range and Siachen Glacier. India refused to accept this, sending reconnaissance parties to occupy the Saltoro range on the western side of the glacier in April 1985, thereby pre-empting a similar Pakistani plan. Since that time, an autonomous conflict has raged there, primarily in the form of artillery duels, though a greater proportion of Indian losses have been caused by avalanches, altitude sickness, and frostbite, since the forces occupy altitudes up to 20,000 feet (over 6,000 m). An agreement between the two sides to withdraw from the area has been pending implementation since 1989.

The Kargil War of May–July 1999

This miniwar, the first face-to-face conflict between two nuclear-armed powers anywhere, began when India discovered a shallow Pakistani incursion on the LOC near Kargil in early May 1999. India's initial efforts to push back the well-entrenched Pakistanis failed. After a buildup, a counteroffensive was launched in June with the help of massed artillery and the Indian air force, but the main thrust consisted of near-suicidal enveloping infantry attacks on Pakistani strong points. India strictly confined the area of fighting to the locale of the incursion. The Pakistanis maintained that the intruders were mujahideen (Muslim guerrilla fighters) and even refused to reclaim the remains of 279 soldiers buried by the Indians, who in turn lost 524 dead. A U.S.-brokered agreement persuaded Pakistan to pull out, and India declared the war to have ended on 26 July.

Minor Wars and Near Wars, 1947–2002

The 100-hour war to liberate Hyderabad in September 1948 was termed a "police action," but it was conducted as an orthodox military operation codenamed "Polo." Surrounded by Indian territory, the state was run by the Muslim nizam, who declared independence in 1947, despite being told by the British that this was not an option. The state had a fairly large army, including armored car regiments and a large levy of paramilitary *razakar*s, or Islamic volunteers. India used a roughly division-sized force as well as combat aircraft beginning 13 September 1948, and the state forces surrendered on 17 September.

After independence, remnants of the Portuguese empire—Goa, Dadra, and Nagar Haveli—were a sore point for Indian nationalists, who tried to use Gandhian tactics to liberate them, but failed. In 1961 Prime Minister Jawaharlal Nehru, despite pressure from the United Kingdom and the United States, gave the go-ahead for a military operation. Given the imbalance of forces, Operation Vijay was virtually uncontested. It began on 17 December and ended in a day, since the Portuguese put up only token resistance.

In 1986–1987, two major exercises nearly triggered conflicts with Pakistan and China, respectively. Exercise

Brasstacks, an Indian military exercise that concentrated a huge amount of armor in Rajasthan, led to precautionary Pakistani deployments in Punjab, setting off a train of events that nearly led to war, as well as a veiled Pakistani nuclear threat in January–February 1987. Exercise Chequerboard was designed to test Indian abilities to move forces from their bases in the plains to the Sino-Indian border in the east. Unsure of its purpose, the Chinese mobilized, and the two forces came face to face in the Tawang region, the site of the Indian disaster in 1962. Some deft diplomacy defused the crisis by May 1987.

In a show of force linked to a series of demands after the 13 December 2001 terrorist attack on its Parliament, India mobilized its army for a punitive strike against Pakistan. By the time the Indian forces were ready, however, Pakistani leader Pervez Musharraf delivered a speech, on 12 January 2002, outlining steps to break Islamabad's terrorist links. A second alarm came in May 2001, after terrorist killings of relatives of Indian army personnel at Kalu Chak, near Jammu; it was defused by U.S. intervention after Pakistani leaders declared that they would end infiltration across the LOC "permanently."

Manoj Joshi

See also **Armed Forces; Bangladesh; China, Relations with; Ethnic Conflict; Kargil Conflict, The; Military Interventions in South Asia; Nuclear Programs and Policies; Pakistan and India; Strategic Thought**

BIBLIOGRAPHY

Brines, Russell. *The Indo-Pakistan Conflict.* London: Pall Mall Press, 1968.
Jacob, Lt. Gen. J. F. R. *Surrender at Dacca: Birth of a Nation.* New Delhi: Manohar, 1998.
Maxwell, Neville. *India's China War.* London: Jonathan Cape, 1970.
Palit, Maj. Gen. D. K. *War in High Himalaya: The Indian Army in Crisis, 1962.* London: Hurst and Company, 1991.
Praval, Maj. K. C. *Indian Army after Independence.* New Delhi: Lancers, 1987.
Singh, Lt. Gen. Depinder. *Indian Peacekeeping Force in Sri Lanka.* Dehra Dun: Natraj, 2001.
Singh, Maj. Gen. Sukhwant. *India's Wars since Independence.* 3 vols. New Delhi: Vikas, 1981.

WAVELL, LORD *(1883–1950), viceroy of India (June 1943–March 1947).* Field Marshal Lord Archibald Wavell was commander-in-chief of British India's forces prior to his appointment as Britain's penultimate viceroy of India. Born at Colchester, the son of an army officer who first brought him to India as a child, Wavell was educated in Winchester College and also graduated from Sandhurst, returning to serve in India at the age of twenty. At the start of World War I, he worked in the War Office, but was soon shipped over to fight in Ypres, Belgium, where he lost an eye.

Wavell was assigned to Field Marshal Allenby's staff in 1918, and two decades later to the command of British forces in the Middle East, but he failed to anticipate the swift power of General Erwin Rommel's tank corps, and was ordered in June 1941 to switch his command in North Africa with Field Marshal Claude Auchinleck's in India. Since Wavell's India command included the British 18th division, which in the following year surrendered Singapore to the Japanese, he was blamed by many for that loss as well. His battlefield wounds and losses appear to have predisposed Wavell for the rest of his life to long, lugubrious interludes of silence. Jawaharlal Nehru and Mahatma Gandhi distrusted him; others considered him too "wooden."

Prime Minister Winston Churchill chose Wavell to be India's viceroy in 1943, when Lord Linlithgow finally stepped down after six years at that post, precisely for all the reasons that India's Congress leaders feared, mistrusted, and disliked him. Churchill wanted Wavell to hold the line against any and all political demands from Congress for concessions of any kind as long as the war lasted. He felt certain, of course, that good soldier Wavell agreed. But Wavell, whose intellectual interests included poetry and the classics, wanted, in fact, to try his hand at diplomacy, which as viceroy he thought only appropriate. He had ideas about bringing Mahatma Gandhi and M. A. Jinnah together for a summit meeting at his vice-regal mansion in Simla, hoping to persuade them to work out their differences and agree to a new formula he toyed with for Hindus and Muslims sharing power. Student of Herodotus and Thucydides that he was, and knowing well from his own bitter experience the painful cost of all combat, Wavell hoped to bring peace to sorely troubled and conflicted India. But when Churchill heard of Wavell's idea, he vowed that only "over his dead body" should any approach to Gandhi be made during the war.

By the end of 1943, Bengal's dreadful famine had claimed more than one and a half million lives. Wavell tried his best to secure shipments of grain to relieve that starving province, knowing as he did that 6 million tons of wheat were floating nearby inside a fleet of British storage vessels, their holds full of food for "emergency" British military needs only, as Churchill's tight-fisted minister of war transport, Baron Leathers, coldly informed Wavell.

In the summer of 1945, after Germany surrendered, Wavell released all his Congress prisoners from jail and convened the Simla summit he had dreamed of holding

two years before. Gandhi, Jinnah, and Nehru all went up, as did lesser party leaders, but no agreement could be reached. Then Britain held its first postwar elections and Churchill lost his seat, as did most of his Tory colleagues. Prime Minister Clement Attlee's Labour Party moved into London's halls of power, determined to end Britain's exorbitant imperial expenditures as quickly as possible. Now, however, instead of appearing too eager to launch a plan of peace and political reform, Wavell proved too cautious and outdated for both Attlee and Sir Richard Cripps, Attlee's Chancellor of the Exchequer, who looked for a much younger and more genial viceroy to effect the swift transfer of power they had in mind. Their choice was dashing Dickie Mountbatten, the king's cousin.

Stanley Wolpert

BIBLIOGRAPHY

Mansergh, N., and E. W. R. Lumby, eds. *The Transfer of Power, 1942–7*, vol. IV: *The Bengal Famine and the New Viceroyalty, 15 June–31 August 1944*; vol. V: *The Simla Conference, Background and Proceedings, 1 September 1944–28 July 1945*; vol. VI: *The Post-War Phase: New Moves by the Labour Government, 1 August 1945–22 March 1946*; vol. VII: *The Cabinet Mission, 23 March–29 June 1946*; vol. VIII: *The Interim Government, 3 July–1 November 1946*; vol. IX: *The Fixing of a Time Limit, 4 November 1946–22 March 1947*. London: Her Majesty's Stationery Office, 1973–1980.
Moon, Penderel, ed. *Wavell: The Viceroy's Journal*. London: Oxford University Press, 1973.
Wolpert, Stanley. *Shameful Flight: The Last Years of the British Empire in India*. New York: Oxford University Press, 2005.

WEAPONS PRODUCTION AND PROCUREMENT

All armed forces need to replace their aging weapons systems after they complete their life cycles. For India, the MiG-21 aircraft and T-59 tanks, and its sole aircraft carrier, need replacement. The problem of bloc obsolescence is acute in India because its major weapons systems, mainly ex-Soviet in origin, were procured in the 1960s and now require urgent replacement. Current generation weapons systems, incorporating the latest available technology, are naturally costlier than the equipment being replaced. The paucity of resources had inhibited long-term planning by the Indian defense establishment, leading to a "bunching" of expensive requirements. The MiG-21 variants, for example, were imported from the Soviet Union in the 1960s at around U.S.\$500,000 apiece; the MiG-29 fighters were obtained in the mid-1980s for \$14 million; and the Su-30 fighter bombers currently being inducted cost about \$30 million each.

Missiles on Display at Annual Republic Day Parade. Many accuse recent Indian leaders of an obsession with nuclear weapons and missile technology, at the expense of defense research and the adequate production of aircraft and other weaponry. INDIA TODAY.

Difficult decisions consequently need to be made whether the successor weapons systems should be indigenously developed or procured from abroad, or whether aging equipment should be refurbished, if possible, to extend its service life. Inadequacy of funds inhibits ideal acquisition decisions. The refurbishment option is therefore becoming more viable for India as the costs of state-of-the art equipment rise astronomically.

Issues Involved

Weapons acquisition decisions in India are not simple. Political factors restrict the choice of external suppliers. The initial unavailability of Western arms, due to political factors, led to India's dependence on the Soviet bloc; currently some 70 percent of the major weapons systems in India's armed forces are of Soviet origin. The end of the cold war, however, has created a buyer's market. Arms supplier nations are vying with each other to sell any type of armaments for purely commercial considerations. But problems remain, as occurred when the United States and other Western nations imposed sanctions on India after its nuclear tests in May 1998. Not only did they withdraw

from negotiations for supplying new equipment, but also from contractual obligations to supply spares and ancillaries and to undertake repairs to equipment already supplied. India had similar experiences in September 1965, during the second Indo-Pak War, when the United States stopped all supplies of military equipment to India.

Therefore, the achievement of a maximum degree of self-reliance and self-sufficiency has long been a hallowed goal of India's defense establishment. In furtherance of this objective, a decision was taken by the Government of India in the mid-1990s to launch a ten-year self-reliance plan, designed to raise defense expenditure on acquisitions from indigenous sources. A three-pronged approach, involving indigenization of vital spare parts, upgrading of existing systems by life-extension programs, and indigenous design and development of high-technology weapons systems, was launched.

The Indian Bureaucratic Process

A major problem in the Indian situation is that weapons equipment must perform in very different

230

terrains over wide temperature variations, ranging from −22° Fahrenheit (−30° C) in the Himalayan heights to 122° Fahrenheit (50° C) in the Rajasthan Desert. A make or buy decision has then to be made after consulting Defence Research and Development to ascertain whether they can develop the weapons system within an acceptable time frame. Extensive debates take place to arrive at a pragmatic solution. If the decision taken is to produce the equipment indigenously, the defense laboratory is identified and tasked to develop a model, freeze the design, develop a prototype, and conduct user trials.

Should it be decided, however, to procure the equipment from abroad, suitable suppliers must be identified by a literature search; the military attachés serving abroad are also tasked to identify suitable suppliers. The actual selection of a particular weapons system involves two stages. A technical evaluation of the various systems is made by Services Headquarters. Later, the short-listed suppliers are requested to send in price quotations. The commercial terms for inducting the equipment are then placed before a Price Negotiation Committee, which enters into negotiations and ultimately signs the contract with the selected supplier. These contracts often incorporate clauses for the transfer of technology and the indigenous manufacture of the equipment.

The Department of Defence Production was set up in 1962, following the Sino-Indian border conflict. In 1965 the Department of Defence Supplies was created to forge closer links with the civil sector, in order to promote the indigenous production of imported defense stores and new stores required by units in the public sector. This department was merged into the Department of Defence Production in 1984 to form the Department of Defence Production and Supplies.

Defense production in the public sector is organized in forty ordnance factories and eight public sector undertakings, incorporated as limited companies under the law. In addition to the armed forces, these units cater to the needs of the paramilitary forces and the police. The ordnance factories are divided into five operating divisions: ammunition and explosives; weapons, vehicles, and equipment; materials and components; armored vehicles; and ordnance equipment. They also produce items for the civil market, like textiles, leather goods, and sporting arms and ammunition. An aggressive effort is being made to export their products. The eight defense public sector undertakings produce a wide variety of goods for the armed forces, including aircraft, electronic goods, heavy vehicles, naval vessels, missiles, and special alloys.

The Defence Research and Development Organisation (DRDO) was created in 1958 by amalgamating the existing technical development establishments in the services. The Department of Defence Research and Development, established in 1980 to enhance self-reliance in defense systems, now has forty-nine laboratories engaged in developing defense technologies and covering disciplines like aeronautics, armaments, electronics, combat vehicles, engineering systems, instrumentation, missiles, advanced computation and simulation, special materials, naval systems, life sciences, training, information systems, and agriculture. It employs over 5,000 scientists and around 25,000 other scientific, technical, and supporting personnel, making it the largest scientific establishment in India. Some of its notable achievements are development of the Lakshya pilotless target aircraft, the Nishant remotely piloted vehicle, airborne electronic warfare systems, the Agni-I land/rail mobile missile, and the PACE parallel processing supercomputer. Its major projects under development include the Light Combat Aircraft and its Kaveri engine, the Trishul surface-to-air missile, different warheads for the Prithvi short-range missile, the BRAHMOS supersonic cruise missile, electronic warfare systems for the three services, and various types of sonars and battlefield surveillance radars. Several of the technologies developed by DRDO have civil applications, such as agricultural practices in high-altitude areas, malaria control, high-altitude medicine, nuclear medicine, and radio-pharmaceuticals.

A symbiotic linkage exists between the Defence Production and Supply Department and the DRDO; consequently, a weakness in one affects the other. The DRDO is headed by the scientific adviser to the defense minister, and the combination of advisory and line functions offends a basic principle of public administration. Quality control is also carried out in-house by the user services, which again offends a basic administrative principle that external checks are necessary to ensure integrity in any activity. How effective the newly constituted Defence Procurement Organisation will be to address these weaknesses remains to be seen. But the lack of accountability in the processes of indigenous research and development and defense production is worth highlighting, as it incorporates a single developer (DRDO), a single buyer (the armed forces) and a single funder (the government). There is regrettably no credible legislative oversight available over these activities. Parliamentary committees like the Public Accounts Committee, which undertakes examination of past procurement cases, or the Estimates Committee, which examines budget estimates, and the Standing Committee on Defence are unable to exercise any effective checks over defense acquisitions.

Role of Private Industry

A change in official Indian attitudes toward the private sector has occurred with the steady liberalization of the economy and the impact of globalization. Greater participation by Indian private industry is thus being sought, and such companies are now eligible to apply for licenses to manufacture a wide range of defense items and to seek foreign direct investment, to the extent of 26 percent of their business.

For indigenization of spares, a serious problem regarding all ex-Soviet equipment, the Department of Defence Production and Supplies has set up technical committees to identify the needs of the user services, take up indigenization activities, and ensure timely supply of defense equipment and stores. Sample rooms are also being maintained in metropolitan cities to familiarize the civil industry with the requirements of the armed forces. Civil industry clearly expects to play a larger role in future defense production.

Conclusions

India has been most fortunate, compared to other developing countries, in having internal stability and a democratic system of government that has taken deep roots; one of its manifestations is the firm control of the civilian leadership over the military apparatus. The civilian bureaucracy, however, is largely untutored in dealing with complex military issues, including defense acquisitions, research and development, and domestic production of weapons systems. The discovery of several major cases of corruption in the purchase of foreign weapons has led to great caution in the procurement process, which at times seems to be paralyzed. This has also resulted in the defense research and defense production establishments functioning below par and paying altogether too much attention to nuclear weapons and missile technology. Inadequate attention has been paid to the reform of the defense apparatus, despite a plethora of reports and sensible suggestions having been made to achieve this objective. Consequently the Indian weapons procurement and production processes are as yet performing less efficiently than they should.

P. R. Chari

See also **Ballistic and Cruise Missile Development; Ballistic Missile Defenses; Nuclear Programs and Policies; Nuclear Weapons, Testing and Development.**

BIBLIOGRAPHY

Government of India. *Ministry of Defence, Annual Report, 1999–2000.* New Delhi: GOI, 2000.
———. *Ministry of Defence, Annual Report, 2002–2003.* New Delhi: GOI, 2003.
———. *Defence Services Estimates, 2003–2004.* New Delhi: GOI, 2003.
Lok Sabha Secretariat. Ministry of Defence, Standing Committee on Defence. *Demand for Grants, 1994–1995.* Fourth Report. April 1995.
———. *Defence Research and Development: Major Projects.* Fifth Report. August 1995.

SECONDARY SOURCES

Chari, P. R. "India: The Policy Process." In *Defense Policy Formation: Towards Comparative Analysis,* edited by James M. Roherty. Durham, N.C.: Carolina Academic Press, 1980.
Ghosh, A. K. *India's Defence Budget and Expenditure Management in a Wider Context.* New Delhi: Lancer Publishers, 1996.
Rao, P. V. R. *Defence without Drift.* Mumbai: Popular Prakashan, 1970.
Singh, Jasjit. *India's Defence Spending: Assessing Future Needs.* New Delhi: Knowledge World, 2000.
Singh, R. P., ed. *Arms Procurement Decision Making,* vol. I: *China, India, Israel, Japan, South Korea, and Thailand.* New York: Oxford University Press, 1998.
Thomas, Raju G. C. *The Defence of India: A Budgetary Perspective of Strategy and Politics.* Delhi: Macmillan, 1978.

WELLESLEY, RICHARD COLLEY *(1760–1842), governor-general of India (1798–1805).* Richard Colley Wellesley, Earl Mornington and Marquess Wellesley, was born into the English "ascendancy" in Ireland. First elected to the British House of Commons in 1784, his introduction to Indian affairs came with his appointment in 1793 to the Board of Control, the link between the government and the East India Company. He became governor-general of the company's possessions in India in 1798. Before leaving for India he had been warned by the directors of the company not to get involved in wars, as they were too expensive and were arousing the Indian rulers against the British traders. Wellesley, an eighteenth-century pleasure-loving aristocrat, was contemptuous of the bourgeois merchants who controlled the company, but he was also the first of the great nineteenth-century imperialists who believed that territorial power in India would give Great Britain an enormous advantage over her European rivals. He was personally ambitious, in search of fame in India that would assure him a place in British politics. He had a degree of freedom from London to pursue his own policies in India that later governors-general did not have, since it took four months for an action in India to become known in England and another four or six months for approval or disapproval to reach Calcutta (Kolkata). Wellesley believed that the British position in India was threatened by an alliance between Tipu Sultan, the ruler of Mysore, with the French; by the Maratha chieftains who had established themselves in western and central India; and by the ruler of the state of Awadh, who realized that the British were becoming a threat to his power. Wellesley dealt with these hostile powers by defeating them in battle, then forcing them to give territory to the British, making them pay for the cost of the wars, forbidding them to have any dealings with foreign powers, and permitting British officials, or "Residents," to live in their territories to keep watch on what was happening. During these years of decisive action, Wellesley's brother, Arthur, later the great Duke of Wellington, was in charge of many of the important military campaigns. While bitterly criticized by the directors of the East India Company, Wellesley was supported by the British government, and he later became foreign secretary and lord-lieutenant of Ireland, but in neither post did he enjoy the success he had had in India, where he could correctly claim that he had created an empire for the British.

Ainslie T. Embree

BIBLIOGRAPHY

The Despatches, Minutes and Correspondence of the Marquess Wellesley during His Administration in India, 5 vols., edited by Robert M. Martin (reprint, New Delhi: Inter-India Publications, 1984), is a sampling of an immense correspondence. P. E. Roberts, *India under Wellesley* (London: G. Bell, 1929) provides a military and political history. Iris Butler, *The Eldest Brother: The Marquess Wellesley, the Duke of Wellington's Eldest Brother* (London: Hodder and Stoughton, 1973) is a biography.

WOMEN AND POLITICAL POWER Indian women became politically active in 1889 when some elite women started to attend meetings of the Indian National Congress. Inspired by the task of social rejuvenation, they established girls' schools and raised consciousness against child marriage and *purdah* (the seclusion of women), while expressing solidarity with male nationalists. These social goals were expanded by the Women's Indian Association (1918) and the All-India Women's Conference (1927) to include a demand for women's suffrage and the right to hold elected office. Idealists like Dr. Muthulakshmi Reddi introduced legal measures in the Madras Assembly to promote women's education and health care. Congress president Sarojini Naidu helped to pass a resolution in 1930 supporting female suffrage and equal rights. When thousands of women joined the *satyagraha* campaigns against colonial rule, they gained the respect of Mahatma Gandhi, Jawaharlal Nehru, and the entire nation. After India's independence in 1947, several women held powerful administrative positions. Rajkumari Amrit Kaur was appointed union minister for health; Sarojini Naidu was governor of Uttar Pradesh; Prime Minister Jawaharlal Nehru's sister, Vijaya Lakshmi Pandit, served as India's ambassador to the Soviet Union; and Shareefah Hamid Ali was a member of the United Nations commission on women's status.

Legislators and Administrators

In 1950 the Constitution of the Republic of India granted universal suffrage, allowing millions of women to vote without restrictions of any kind. While there have been many women cabinet ministers since 1947, women legislators have been seriously underrepresented in village councils (*panchayat*s), state assemblies, and Parliament. In 1967 women constituted 5.9 percent of the Lok Sabha (Parliament's lower house); thirty years later, they held only 7 percent of the seats. In 1974 the Committee on the Status of Indian Women declared this underrepresentation to be undemocratic and conducive to further gender inequality. However, no remedial action was taken until 1992–1993, when Constitutional Amendments 73 and 74 reserved one-third of *panchayat* and town council seats for women. In June 1996, Prime Minister Deve Gowda's United Front government introduced a bill reserving 33 percent of the seats in Parliament to women. However, due to differences amongst his coalition allies, the bill was not passed. Meanwhile, a Women's Reservation Bill was introduced in Parliament, supported by leftist and regional Dravidian parties. Polls showed that 75 percent of Indian voters supported affirmative action for women. Yet, the Bharatiya Janata Party (BJP) and its allied parties, especially the Shiv Sena, blocked its enactment; their anxiety over the prospect of a contingent of 180 women in Parliament was evident when Prime Minister Atal Bihari Vajpayee called the bill "revolutionary legislation." Twenty-five women's organizations staged mass demonstrations in favor of the Reservation Bill in May 2003, but it remained in limbo. In February 2005, the new government led by the Congress Party and its socialist allies announced that a revised bill would be introduced giving women 33 percent of the seats in central and state legislatures. Within this quota, the socialist parties support a further reservation for Dalit, backward caste, and minority women. Women's associations have also focused on increasing female representation in village *panchayat*s and other local bodies.

Despite women's comparative lack of leverage within India's state and central legislatures, they have been politically active through various parties, voluntary women's associations, a broad spectrum of nongovernmental organizations, as well as administrative services. Top-ranking women administrators have effected many reforms at the local level, and the number of mid-level female officials has increased steadily, with women scoring highly in the competitive examinations for the administrative services. As more talented women enter the bureaucratic "steel frame" that still governs India, they may provide fresh solutions to the country's ancient problems.

Women Supporters of the BJP Protest Rising Prices. Though most political parties in India now actively court the female vote, many feminist organizations accuse them of mere lip service, claiming they include women only in ways that do not fundamentally challenge their traditional roles within the family. INDIA TODAY.

Gender in Politics

In December 1974 the United Nations Committee for the Status of Women published their report *Towards Equality*, revealing that although professional Indian women had made strides, the vast majority of Indian women lagged behind men in nutrition, education, and employment, and that the female-male ratio in the population was alarmingly low. Census records show a continuing decline in the number of Indian women: in 1991 there were 945 females to every 1,000 males; in 2001 the ratio had dropped to 927 females to 1,000 males. This decline can be attributed to regressive manifestations of patriarchy in a modernizing society, and not simply to ancient traditions. New technologies, such as amniocentesis through which the sex of a fetus is revealed, have increased female feticide; and although sex-discriminatory abortion is illegal and expensive, it is practiced often by the educated and affluent in large cities. Unfortunately, *Towards Equality* coincided with Indira Gandhi's "National Emergency" (1975–1977), an era when all civil rights were curtailed in the name of national security. Women activists mobilized against the Emergency's harsh "voluntary" sterilization programs, as well as other common offenses such as "custodial rape" by police officers, marital rape, and instances of "bride burning" by in-laws angered by insufficient dowries.

Although Indira Gandhi was admired for being a powerful woman leader, she gave scant attention to women's issues. After the 1970s, the new feminists charged politicians with ignoring women's rights in their preoccupation with economic development. They accused all political parties, including left-wing groups with progressive views, of subsuming gender under the umbrella of "minority" rights. While women's issues are often addressed through various bureaucracies, they rarely receive adequate attention from politicians. Especially after 1989, gender has become of secondary interest to a nation focused on religious and caste controversies. Yet, these issues are interrelated, since minority women are more likely to be exploited and sexually abused than women of the Hindu upper castes. In the 2002 Gujarat riots, thousands of Muslim women were raped; and the widespread sexual exploitation of working class and Dalit women has been documented by the All-India Democratic Women's Association. Despite the seriousness of these problems,

Indira Gandhi's model of ungendered politics has become a blueprint for her male and female successors.

Women Politicians

Elite women have been elected to the highest positions, often carving out these spaces as chaste wives, widows, mothers, daughters, and daughters-in-law. Female politicians of many parties embrace these domestic identities in the public arena for electoral advantages. Most offer to "cleanse" the body politic, like Rabri Devi (Rashtriya Janata Dal, wife of Lalu Prasad Yadav) of Bihar, whose speeches were laced with colorful, domestic imagery. Only a few, like chief minister Sheila Dixit of Delhi, have conveyed an active interest in women's issues while participating in India's patriarchal political game.

Thus, Indira Gandhi rose to power as Jawaharlal Nehru's daughter, and Congress Party president Sonia Gandhi achieved popularity as the assassinated prime minister Rajiv Gandhi's widow and the daughter-in-law (*bahu*) of the Nehru-Gandhi clan. The BJP's moral arbiter, Sushma Swaraj, is the wife of Swaraj Kaushal, governor of Mizoram; Vasundhara Raje is a dutiful *bahu* of former Jaipur rani Gayatri Devi. All-India Dravida Munnetra Kazhagam chief minister Jayalalitaa advertises herself as "Amma," the loyal widow of the charismatic star and political Tamil Nadu idol M. G. Ramachandran. Madhya Pradesh chief minister Uma Bharti is a self-styled ascetic (*sadhvi*) and "daughter" of Hindutva. The same phenomenon is visible in Pakistan, where Benazir Bhutto rose to power after her father's hanging; in Bangladesh where Sheikh Hasina Wajed entered politics after her husband, Sheikh Mujibur Rahman, was assassinated; and in Sri Lanka, where Chandrika Kumaratunga follows her parents' ministerial footsteps.

Scandals around corruption are common in India, and a few women politicians have been notorious for complicity in nefarious schemes; among these are Tamil Nadu's Jayalalitaa and Uttar Pradesh's former chief minister Mayavati. Like their male counterparts, not all women politicians have proven trustworthy, due to the pervasive climate of opportunism in politics. Perhaps the solution to gender equality lies not in the public, corruptible centers of political power, but rather in the idealism of anonymous women administrators who honestly strive to serve India. One such leader is Sheila Rani Chunkatt, who in her short stint in 1988 as the collector of Pudukottai, Tamil Nadu, made her district 100 percent literate by working with the National Literacy Mission; retrained sex workers as diamond cutters; and organized unskilled women workers for higher wages. Indian women have learned to play the political game skillfully, but gender justice will be achieved only through the enduring work of honest women in political office.

Sita Anantha Raman

See also **Feminism and Indian Nationalists; Gandhi, Indira; Gender and Human Rights; Women's Education**

BIBLIOGRAPHY

Basu, Amrita. "Women's Activism and the Vicissitudes of Hindu Nationalism." *Journal of Women's History* 10, no. 4: 104–124.

Basu, Amrita, ed. *The Challenge of Local Feminisms: Women's Movements in Global Perspective*. Boulder, Colo.: Westview Press, 1995.

Bhatia, Krishan. *Indira: A Biography of Prime Minister Gandhi*. New York: Praegar, 1974.

D'Amico, Francine, and Peter R. Beckman, eds. *Women in World Politics*. Westport, Conn.: Bergin and Garney, 1995.

Dhanda, Meena. "Should Feminists Support Quotas?" *Economic and Political Weekly* 25, no. 33: 2969–2979.

Forbes, Geraldine. *Women in Modern India*. Cambridge, U.K.: Cambridge University Press, 1996.

Keddie, Nikki. "The New Religious Politics and Women Worldwide: A Comparative Study." *Journal of Women's History* 10, no. 4: 11–34.

Kishwar, Madhu. "Equality of Opportunities vs. Equality of Results: Improving Women's Reservation Bill." *Economic and Political Weekly* 35, no. 47: 4151–4156.

Kumar, Nita. *A History of Doing*. Delhi: Kali for Women, 1993.

Mazumdar, Vina, ed. *Symbols of Power: Studies on the Political Status of Women in India*. Mumbai: Allied Publishers, 1979.

Ramusack, Barbara, and Sharon Sievers. *Women in Asia: Restoring Women to History*. Bloomington: Indiana University Press, 1999.

WOMEN'S EDUCATION It is ironic that although Indians have deified knowledge as the goddess Sarasvatī, Indian women have been relegated to educational subservience throughout India's long history. Education means power, which in India remains largely in male hands. The earliest British educational surveys in Madras presidency in 1822 brought to official attention the relative absence of girls in formal schools. In 1881 the Hunter Educational Commission noted that a mere .2 percent of the women in British India were literate, although as in all early colonial surveys, investigators focused solely on school enrollment and failed to count the girls taught informally at home. On the eve of independence in 1947, literacy rates for both genders were abysmally low at 6 percent (female) and 22.6 percent (male). Since then, they have plodded forward slowly but surely, and there has been a noticeable improvement since the 1980s. Thus, in 1961 the literacy rates were 15.3 percent (female) and 40.4 percent (male); in 1981 they rose to 28.5 percent (female) and 53.5 percent

Literacy Classes for Rural Women in Rajasthan. A late-twentieth-century study by the U.S. Department of Commerce estimated that fewer than 40 percent of women in India were literate. Although the results of the study varied greatly among Indian states, they suggest that there are possibly upwards of 200 million illiterate women in India today. AMAR TALWAR / FOTOMEDIA.

(male); and in 2001 they had risen to 54.3 percent (female) and 76 percent (male). However, women's education still shuffles far behind that of men, with the disparities greater in a state like Bihar, where rates are 33.6 percent (female) and 60.3 percent (male), than in Kerala, where they are 87.9 percent (female) and 94.2 percent (male). The last century's goal for women was to educate better mothers and wives for the nation. However, some of the urban literate classes have begun to acknowledge that women are a national resource that India cannot squander away in this competitive era of globalization and computer technology.

Education in Early India

For much of Indian history, education involved the oral and written transmission of sacred texts, and the acquisition of survival and craft skills. Among some

*adivasi*s (aboriginals) like the Birhor of Jharkhand, for example, there was greater gender parity in learning the skill of toolmaking. However, Sanskritization and Westernization as "civilizing" agents have today marginalized women's vestigial rights among many tribal communities, which have been integrated into the mainstream society and economy. Artifacts from the literate Indus Civilization (6000–1650 B.C.) include icons of goddesses and the female genitalia (*yōni*), while some seals suggest that there may have been priestesses in an arboreal religion. The inhabitants clearly revered the female in nature, a vision of divinity that persists across India today. However, male power was also venerated, and no evidence exists of a matrilineal society. The absence of gendered spaces in the houses and public buildings do indicate that women had freedom of movement, but we have no information yet as to how and where education took place.

The arrival of patriarchal Aryan groups in the early second millennium B.C. profoundly shaped Indian notions of gender equity. Their most revered skill was the oral transmission of the Vedas (Books of knowledge) to propitiate the gods. Known as *shruti* (revelations that are heard), this form of oral learning became central to the acquisition of knowledge, although these Sanskrit hymns were later also written in the Devanāgari script. At first, some women initiates, who wore the sacred thread of the twice-born upper castes, recited the Vedas. The Rig Veda (1500–100 B.C.) attests to some *brahmavādini*s (women bard-poets) like Lōpamudra and Ghōsha. Even as late as 800 B.C., there were spirited female savants like Gārgi and Maitreyi in the Brahadaranyka Upanishad, and Sāvitri in the Mahābhārata.

From this point, due to geopolitical reasons leading to patriarchal ascendency, the Vedas became the exclusive preserve of male Brahman caste priests, and women's learning became subsidiary to that of men. However, women were permitted to know the "remembered" secondary scriptures (*smriti*), including the Mahābhārata and Rāmāyana epics, and later texts like the Dharma Shāstras (law books) and Purāṇas (Ancient tales), the latter containing myths about Hindu deities. Boys were taught in open air classes around a tree, or on the open verandas (*pyāl*s) of buildings. Meanwhile, higher caste girls often sat away from the public eye, in rooms adjacent to the *pyāl*s, where they studied the *smriti* and nonreligious subjects like arithmetic.

Thus, around 525 B.C., we hear of learned women such as Queen Mahāgotāmi, the Buddha's foster mother, who struggled to establish the first order of nuns. Learned female ascetics like Mitta and Patacāra composed the Thērigāthā, a revered hymnal section of the Buddhist Pali canon. Jainism's followers also revere an early female *tirthankara* (fjord crosser) or teacher, and Jainism

ENCYCLOPEDIA OF *India*

encouraged women ascetics. However, over time, misogyny crept into texts, which scorned female sexuality and downgraded women's intellect. South Indian Dravidian society appears to have respected accomplished women during the Tamil Sangam era (200 B.C.–A.D. 500). Sangam poetry was composed by some 470 poets, including 154 women sages like Auvaiyār. Moreover, despite male dominance, women's power is seen in three of the five Tamil epics, which revolve around learned women.

By the first century A.D., as society absorbed new immigrants across racial lines, Brahmans reinforced gender and caste hierarchies in texts like the Mānava Dharmashāstras (Laws of Manu). This work praised women's domestic duties and denounced their sexual proclivities. Artisan groups transmitted craft skills, and both working and elite castes transmitted their oral traditions across generations. However, the lowest castes were excluded from literacy, while women's education became largely informal and haphazard. After the sixth century, in the medieval climate of invasions, wars, and feudalism, elite women retreated further into the domestic arena, instructed informally at home until the nineteenth century.

Medieval Women's Education

Despite such patriarchal norms and prejudice, there were still scores of women poet-saints and writers in the medieval centuries. Thus, Āndāl, Kāraikkal Ammaiyār, Akkamahādēvi, Gangāsati, Lallā, and Mīra have left a legacy of devotional (bhakti) compositions in the regional languages. Moreover, one class of educated South Indian women attended schools in public with boys. They were the lower caste temple dancers (dēvadāsis) who were rarely Brahman women. Dēvadāsis were ritually married to the shrine's deity in South India during the first millennium A.D., and they were the repositories of Indian traditions of dance and music. By the seventeenth century, however, many became court dancers and courtesans outside the norms of female domesticity. Governor Munro's survey of schools in South India in 1822 revealed that, except for the dēvadāsis, no other girls studied on the pyals in the company of boys.

The prophet Muhammad's wife and daughter were literate and powerful, but despite this and the Islamic belief in salvation through the written Qur'an, Muslim women's educational lot in India was not substantially different. Islam was introduced into the subcontinent by patriarchal groups who kept their women in domestic seclusion within female quarters (zenānā). If women ventured outside, they wore a veil (purdah). Those women who defied the purdah were prevented from rising to power. Thus, Sultana Raziya (thirteenth century A.D.), the sole Muslim queen in India, was deposed quickly by men. Aristocratic women were often instructed by female teachers (ustād

bis) in the zenānā, and some have left records, like the Mughal princess Gulbadan (sixteenth century), who wrote an elegant royal biography in Persian. Like Hindu dēvadāsis, Muslim courtesans (tawaif) were taught to read and write. The tawaif Mahlaqa Bai Chanda (eighteenth century) wrote lyrical Urdu songs. Ordinary Muslim boys and girls studied the Qur'an at mosque schools (madrassas), but often this consisted of rote chanting of the sacred verses. In this era, conservative Muslim and Hindu patriarchs often feared that a literate girl would write love letters and become promiscuous.

In North India, Muslim and Hindu women wore the restrictive purdah. In South India, elite Muslim women wore purdah, while Hindu women lived in domestic seclusion but enjoyed greater freedom of movement. As an important deterrent to female attendance in formal schools, purdah became the subject of discussion among elite women reformers in the twentieth century. The other major obstacle to girls' education was the custom of early marriage among Hindus and Muslims. Muslim women reformers were divided on purdah and the extent to which it should be practiced. Shareefa Hamid Ali and Dr. Rahamatunnissa Begum felt that it injured girls' health and prevented their attendance in schools. Nazar Sajjad Hyder initially argued that parents would more readily send their veiled daughters to school, but she later opposed purdah. In 1914 the Begum of Bhopal convened a Muslim Women's Educational Conference in Allahabad, and philanthropists began schools for girls, raising the female literacy rate.

Colonial Era

European conquest led to the political decline of Indian states, and indigenous schools decayed. Catholic missionaries began schools to teach Christianity in Goa and elsewhere from the sixteenth century, while Protestant evangelicals founded schools in southern, eastern, and western India beginning in the eighteenth century, notable for their attempt to bring girls to school without caste distinctions. The early colonial state's interest in education was cursory, but it supported missionary endeavors, and British officials gauged educational competence through literacy and school enrollment. Henceforth, oral and informal learning became less significant. When the British Parliament gave the East India Company a large grant in 1813 to promote education in India, evangelicals arrived in droves to proselytize in schools. Women missionaries assiduously began elementary classes for girls, who learned English through the Bible and converted to Christianity. Indian rulers like the Rānis Lakshmibai and Parvatibai of Travancore gave financial support to missionaries for their educational work. In 1849 the government subsidized a Calcutta (Kolkata) girls' school, founded by J. E. D. Bethune, Ram Gopal Ghosh, and Jaikissen Mookherjee. In 1854 Charles Wood's Despatch on Education launched a new policy of granting aid to private schools. Promptly, Gopal Kistnah Pillai asked for a grant for his girls' school in Madras (Chennai). However, the first major breakthrough for girls' secular and high school education occurred in 1877. Mary Carpenter, the eminent educator, advised the government to establish secular teacher training centers in the presidency capitals of Calcutta, Bombay (Mumbai), and Madras. She used the guidelines of a similar school started in Madras by the Maharaja of Vijayanagaram.

Child marriages were a major impediment to girls' education. Among the higher Hindu castes, girls were married before puberty, until which time they might attend municipal or mission schools. After their nuptials, at the age of eleven or twelve, girls no longer attended public classes; if lucky, they were taught at home. Until the 1930 Sarda Act raised the age of marriage for girls to fourteen years, female literacy did not substantially improve. Christian converts educated their daughters, however, so their literacy rates were higher. This goaded Hindu reformers, whose daughters had not studied at mission schools, and they sent their daughters to schools with a secular curriculum. In 1904 Annie Besant wrote *The Education of Indian Girls*, which laid the curricular foundation for girls' schools. Reform organizations like the Prārthanā Samāj, Ārya Samāj, Rāmakrishnā Society, and the Theosophical Society started schools that taught Indian culture as well as Western subjects like geography and hygiene.

Indian nationalists worked to legalize compulsory education and to increase government funding for schools. The paucity of women teachers and doctors led to the establishment of teachers' training institutes and colleges such as the Lady Hardinge Medical College for Women in Delhi in 1916 and Queen Mary's College in Madras in 1914. Besant also worked to start a Women's University at Adyar in 1916, while women reformers started occupational training institutions for working-class women.

Independence Era

Since 1947 the Indian government has tried to provide incentives for girls' school attendance through programs for midday meals, free books, and uniforms. This welfare thrust raised primary enrollment between 1951 and 1981. In 1986 the National Policy on Education decided to restructure education in tune with the social framework of each state, and with larger national goals. It emphasized that education was necessary for democracy, and central to the improvement of women's condition. The new policy aimed at social change through revised texts, curricula, increased funding for schools, expansion

in the numbers of schools, and policy improvements. Emphasis was placed on expanding girls' occupational centers and primary education; secondary and higher education; and rural and urban institutions. The report tried to connect problems like low school attendance with poverty, and the dependence on girls for housework and sibling day care. The National Literacy Mission also worked through female tutors in villages. Although the minimum marriage age is now eighteen for girls, many continue to be married much earlier. Therefore, at the secondary level, female dropout rates are high.

Indian women's education has, however, certainly improved since independence. Many urban women are highly educated in the sciences, medicine, computer technology, and the social sciences. India now has missions of female doctors, nurses, teachers, and social workers. Yet, in most important fields, girl students are outnumbered, and women professionals do not often receive equal pay, even though Indian women scientists, for example, are among the world's most talented. Such gender disparities in education will continue until girls are valued as highly as boys; until patriarchy and sexual predation are reduced; and until female feticide and infanticide, reflected in the sex disproportion of India's population, disappear.

Sita Anantha Raman

See also **Feminism and Indian Nationalists; Subbalakshmi Ammal, R. S.; Theosophical Society; Women's Indian Association**

BIBLIOGRAPHY

Advani, Lal. "Women and the Widening Horizons in Education." In *The Position of Women: Proceedings of a Seminar Held in Srinagar, September 1972*, edited by Kamla Bhasin. Mumbai: Leslie Sawhny Programme of Training for Democracy, 1973.

Agarwal, Usha. *Indian Women, Education and Development*. Ambala: Indian Publication, 1995.

Basu, Aparna. *The Growth of Educational and Political Development in India, 1898–1920*. Mumbai: Oxford University Press, 1974.

Basu, Aparna, and Bharati Ray. *Women's Struggle: A History of the All India Women's Conference, 1927–2002*. New Delhi: Manohar, 2003.

Besant, Annie. *Higher Education in India*. Mysore: Theosophical Society, 1932.

Carpenter, Mary. *Six Months in India*, vol. 2. London: Longmans Green, 1868.

Chaudhary, Pratima. *Women's Education in India*. New Delhi: Har Anand Publications, 1995.

Cheriyan, P. *Malabar Christians and the Church Missionary Society, 1816–1856*. Kottayam: Church Missionary Society, 1935.

Jayawardena, Kumari. *The White Woman's Other Burden: Western Women and South Asia during British Rule*. New York: Routledge, 1995.

Kanwar, Asha, and Neela Jagannathan. *Speaking for Ourselves*. New Delhi: Manohar, 1995.

Mathur, Y. B. *Women's Education in India (1813–1966)*. Mumbai: Asia Publishing House, 1973.

Misra, Lakshmi. *Education of Women in India, 1921–1966*. Mumbai: Macmillan, 1966.

Raman, Sita Anantha. "From Chattrams to National Schools: Educational Philanthropy in South India, Eighteenth–Twentieth Centuries." In *Selected Papers in Asian Studies* 52. Association for Asian Studies, 1994.

———. *Getting Girls to School: Social Reform in the Tamil Districts, 1870–1930*. Kolkata: Stree, 1996.

———. "Walking Two Paces Behind: Women's Education in India." In *Ananya: A Portrait of India*, edited by S. N. Sridhar and Nirmal Mattoo. New York: Association of Indians in America, 1997.

Vaikuntam, Y. *Education and Social Change in South India: Andhra, 1880–1920*. Chennai: New Era, 1982.

WOMEN'S INDIAN ASSOCIATION

On 8 May 1917 in Adyār, Madras, a multiethnic group of women established the Women's Indian Association (WIA), India's first major feminist organization, which remains in operation today. The WIA's success can be attributed to its secular agenda for women of all sects, classes, and castes, and to its initial effective use of the organizational framework of the Theosophical Society, whose president, Annie Besant, was chosen as the first WIA president. The honorary secretaries were Margaret Cousins, a teacher and Irish suffragist; Dorothy Jinarajadasa, the Irish wife of a Sri Lankan Theosophist; Ammu Swaminathan and Malathi Patwardhan. Borrowing the idea of a cross-cultural association from the Tamil Māthar Sangam (Tamil Women's Organization) formed in 1906 by Indian and European women, Margaret Cousins sounded out her proposal to a gathering of Theosophists at Adyār after her arrival in 1915. The founders included S. Ambujammal, Dr. Muthulakshmi Reddi, Mangalammal Sadasivier, Saralabai Naik, Herabai Tata, Dr. Poonen Lukhose, Kamaladevi Chattopadhyaya, Begam Hasrat Mohani, and Dhanavanti Rama Rao. Describing themselves as the "daughters of India," its mothers and wives, their objectives were to guide the nation; serve the poor; promote women's education and compulsory universal primary education; abolish child marriage; raise the age of sexual consent to sixteen for women; win female suffrage; and attain the female right to elected office. The WIA was one of the first organizations to boldly connect Indian women's social and sexual subjugation with patriarchy, poverty, and political disenfranchisement.

Reform and Early Women's Groups

A primary goal of most women's *samāj*s (associations) in India has been to improve women's educational conditions and to remove customs like early marriage, enforced widowhood among Hindus, and the Muslim *purdah* (veil), all of which were mental and physical impediments to women's health. One of the earliest groups was the Ārya Mahila Samāj (Ārya Women's Association), founded by Pandita Ramabai (1858–1922) in 1881. Early Hindu reform organizations, like the Brahmo Samaj, Prārthana Samāj, and the Ārya Samāj promoted women's education, while condemning early marriage and enforced widowhood. In 1896 Justice M. G. Ranade (1842–1901) and his wife Ramabai (1862–1924) started the Ladies Social Conference, a secular forum for women's issues, within the Indian National Congress.

Effective changes in the status of women would occur only when educated women began their own associations. Sectarian groups included Stri Zarothoshti Mandal (Parsi Women's Organization) in 1900 in Bombay; the Young Women's Christian Association; and the Anjuman-e-Khawatin-e-Islam (Association for Muslim Women) in 1915, associated with the All-India Muslim Women's Conference. A regional women's group was the Andhra Mahila Sabha (Andhra Women's Club; 1910), founded by Virēsalingam Pantulu (1848–1919), a male reformer who worked to educate girls and to promote widow remarriage.

However, a truly national feminist organization was possible only with the emergence of a sizable number of educated women. Between 1902 and 1912, the girls' school enrollment doubled in Madras presidency, especially after reformers started schools that taught Indian culture. The Tamil Māthar Sangam (Tamil Women's Organization) met intermittently in Madras (Chennai) city (1906) and in Kanchipuram (1907, 1914). In 1908 its Tamil, Malayali, Telegu, Marathi, and English-speaking members attended an all-India Ladies' Congress (*parishad*) in Madras with a strong feminist agenda, according to Rajkumari Amrit Kaur, later president of the All-India Women's Conference (1927), India's third feminist organization. The WIA drew its initial membership from the Ladies' Congress, and its founders were doubtless aware of the Bharata Stree Mahāmandal (Great Society of Indian Women), which Sarladevi Chaudrani, a niece of Rabindranath Tagore, founded in Allahabad in 1910. However, the Mahāmandal's goals remained unfulfilled.

Women's Suffrage

On 18 December 1917, the WIA sent a delegation led by Sarojini Naidu (1879–1949) to Edwin Montagu, secretary of state for India. Representing themselves as Indian women who had awakened to their civic responsibilities, they requested female suffrage on a par with men in the expanded provincial legislatures as a part of the forthcoming Government of India Act of 1919. Naidu had earlier appealed for support from the Indian National Congress. She sought to calm male fears that women would try to usurp authority, emphasizing that their maternal instincts would inspire the nation's children. The imperial Southborough Franchise Commission in London did not sanction their request, although they won the support of Sir C. Sankaran Nair. Sarojini Naidu, Annie Besant, and Herabai Tata then appealed their case in London, and the provincial legislatures were later authorized to decide individually. Thus, with the help of some male nationalists on the councils, a few women were enfranchised, first in Madras in 1920, and in Bombay in 1921.

In 1926 the WIA sent five delegates to the Congress of International Women Suffrage Alliance in Paris. It encouraged its members to stand for election as magistrates and supported Muthulakshmi Reddi in 1928. She was elected to the Madras Legislative Council and was chosen as its deputy president. As India's first woman legislator, Reddi introduced legislation to improve women's education, raise the age of marriage to fourteen for girls through the Sarda Act of 1930, aid programs for women's health, and end the controversial system of *dēvadāsi* (slaves to the god) dedication to temples in 1929.

The second struggle to expand female suffrage began in 1930 in preparation for the Government of India Act of 1935. Unlike the new feminist organization, National Organization of Women of India (1925), the WIA followed the National Congress stand against separate electorates for minorities and women. In the next decades, WIA members spoke passionately about their agendas, and although they disagreed with individual Congress members, they joined in the struggle for India's independence led by Mahatma Gandhi.

Social Service

By the end of 1918, the WIA had thirty-three self-governing local branches, dedicated to the service of a sisterhood of women of all creeds, castes, and classes. Although its leaders aspired to attract women of all castes, it remained an elite organization for years; however, it finally became a significant national organization for women. In 1920 Margaret Cousins began to edit a quarterly newsletter, *Stri Dharma* (Women's duty), first in English, but later with Tamil and Hindi sections. The journal developed into a monthly after a few years. *Stri Dharma* publicized the WIA and its agenda against child marriages and the Muslim *purdah*. Its membership increased noticeably; by 1924 there were 51 branches and 2,500 members across India, and by 1926, it was the largest Indian women's organization, with over 4,000 members and 80 branches.

The WIA held free elementary classes, as well as classes on hygiene, child welfare, and vocational skills. Its ideals of service facilitated the establishment of the Avvai Home for girls, which Dr. Reddi started in 1930, and its members also worked with the vocational programs in Madras Seva Sadan. The WIA provided the framework for medical help to the poor by Drs. Reddi, Lukhose, and Rahamatunissa Begam. Since independence, the WIA has continued to serve India's women through numerous regional branches.

Sita Anantha Raman

See also **Feminism and Indian Nationalists; Theosophical Society**

BIBLIOGRAPHY

Basu, Aparna, and Bharati Ray. *Women's Struggle: A History of the All India Women's Conference, 1927–2002*. New Delhi: Manohar, 2003.
Chatterjee, Partha. "The Nationalist Resolution of the Women's Question." In *Recasting Women: Essays in Colonial History*, edited by Kumkum Sangari and Sudesh Vaid. Delhi: Kali for Women, 1989.
Forbes, Geraldine. *Women in Modern India*. Cambridge, U.K. and New York: Cambridge University Press, 1996.
Jayawardena, Kumari. *The White Woman's Other Burden: Western Women and South Asia during British Rule*. New York: Routledge, 1995.
Kumar, Radha. *The History of Doing: An Illustrated Account of Movements for Women's Rights and Feminism in India, 1800–1990*. Delhi: Kali for Women, 1997.
Lateef, Shahida. *Muslim Women in India: Political and Private Realities, 1890s–1980s*. Delhi: Kali for Women, 1990.
Naravane, Vishwanath S. *Sarojini Naidu: Her Life, Work, and Poetry*. Delhi: Orient Longman, 1980.
Raman, Sita Anantha. "Crossing Cultural Boundaries: Indian Matriarchs and Sisters in Service." *Journal of Third World Studies* 18, no. 2 (Fall 2001): 131–148.
———. *Getting Girls to School: Social Reform in the Tamil Districts, 1870–1930*. Kolkata: Stree, 1996.

WORLD BANK (WB), RELATIONS WITH

India was one of the forty-four original signatories to the agreements reached at Bretton Woods that established the International Bank for Reconstruction and Development (IBRD) and the International Monetary Fund (IMF). It was also one of the founding members of the International Finance Corporation (IFC) in 1956 and the International Development Association (IDA) in 1960. India later became a member of the Multilateral Investment Guarantee Agency in January 1994.

IBRD lending to Indian commenced in 1949 with a loan to the Indian railways; the first investment by the IFC in India took place in 1959, and by IDA in 1961 (a highway construction project). The World Bank has been India's largest source of external capital and, in turn, India has been the largest borrower from the World Bank, with loans accounting for 11.4 percent of total lending by June 2003. During this period, the World Bank had lent India a total of $60 billion in 441 projects, almost equally divided between the IBRD and the IDA, which constituted nearly 8 percent of IBRD lending and 20.7 percent of IDA lending. India's share of IFC loans has been somewhat less: $2.7 billion for 162 enterprises; 4.6 percent of total lending, including syndications.

During the 1950s, the IBRD was India's sole source of World Bank borrowings. By the end of the decade, India's mounting debt problems became an important factor in the launch of the IDA, the soft loan affiliate of the World Bank (WB) group. As India increasingly turned to a state-dominated economic model, the WB was skeptical, but mindful of the hypersensitivity of Indian policy makers, it refrained from overt criticism. These reservations notwithstanding, the imperatives of the cold war and India's pivotal position as a democratic role model for newly independent countries, distinct from Communist China, as well as the high quality of India's interlocutors ensured continuous support by the industrialized countries.

By the mid-1960s, India's economic problems were compounded by back-to-back failures of the monsoons. With the specter of famine looming, the WB mounted an ambitious mission in 1966 (in conjunction with the U.S. Agency for International Development [U.S. AID] and the IMF) to persuade India to undertake sweeping policy reforms. This attempt, popularly known as the "Bell mission," recommended both internal and external liberalization, currency devaluation, and a focus on agriculture. Except for agriculture (which was instigated by U.S. AID and even more by some Indians themselves), this highly visible attempt at policy reform by the WB proved to be a singular failure. The episode left a deep mark on both Indian policy makers and the WB. While the latter became much more deferential to India's sensibilities in the next two decades, Indian policy makers also became much more cautious in undertaking ambitious policy reforms.

By the end of the 1960s, the United States, until then India's largest source of external resources, sharply cut its bilateral aid program. Since then, the WB emerged as the most important source of official long-term finance. During the 1960s and 1970s, the IDA accounted for nearly three-fourths of all WB lending to India and, in turn, India was by far the largest recipient of IDA funds, accounting for more than two-fifths of all its lending. The subsequent decade, with China joining the WB in 1980 and accordingly entering its own claims to limited IDA resources, the worsening economic fortunes of

Africa, and India's better performance, saw a sharp decline in India's share in IDA. Instead, its share of IBRD lending grew sharply in the 1980s, buoyed by its improving creditworthiness and the Indian government's waning inhibitions with regard to nonconcessional borrowing. Prior to the launch of the economic liberalization program in 1991, the WB accounted for nearly a third of India's long-term debt and 60 percent of official debt.

The share of WB debt in India's total external debt has been around a quarter since 1980. Non-concessional IBRD debt peaked at about 37 percent of total WB debt in 1990, in part due to faster repayment schedules of IBRD debt and a postliberalization drop in IBRD lending. The latter was the result of several factors: sanctions imposed after India conducted nuclear tests in 1998, which curbed new IBRD loans; the slow pace of policy reforms that reduced the supply of new loans in certain sectors; and mounting transaction costs of IBRD lending that reduced the demand for new loans in other sectors.

Despite India's salience in the WB's loan portfolio and the WB's importance in India's external borrowings, these financial flows were, in the aggregate, modest for India's economy, comprising less than 1 percent of gross national product and seldom more than a couple of dollars per capita. However, their relative importance has been greater in certain sectors and time periods. In particular, the WB has been one of India's most reliable sources of external financing when the country suffered balance of payments problems, such as in the 1960s, after the first and second oil shocks, and in 1990–1991.

Lending Portfolio

In its early decades, WB lending to India was largely in support of India's five-year plans that concentrated on infrastructure (railways, dams) and development finance companies. The heyday of WB lending to India was during the 1970s and 1980s. More than three-fourths of lending in this period was in energy, agriculture and rural development, and industry. In the 1970s, India's emphasis on agriculture and poverty rhetoric dovetailed well with the WB's own lending priorities. India's large size and its need for external capital also meshed well with the WB's emphasis on expanding lending volumes. With many of the WB's other poor borrowers plagued by political instability and weak administrative capacity, India offered a convenient sponge to absorb WB resources and meet its annual lending targets.

The early 1980s were pivotal years for the WB. Its greater emphasis on liberal economic policies, however, did not lead to any significant changes in its stance toward India. Even though, as the decade progressed, India's dirigiste economic policies were increasingly at odds with those espoused by the WB, India's standing as a valued customer of the IBRD grew. The outset of the debt crisis meant there were few large creditworthy borrowers in the IBRD's portfolio. Indeed, the WB even increased its overall lending volume for the industrial sector, with some of its largest loans to public sector manufacturing enterprises (e.g., $545 million in two loans to Indian Petrochemicals Limited), science and technology development, and sectoral and subsectoral industrial restructuring. The WB also continued to pour money into sectors with unsound policies and corrupt institutions, especially irrigation and power.

Near the end of the decade, India's bargaining position weakened as the strains in India's political and economic fabric became more pronounced. The absence of alternative sources to service India's external debt, coupled with the emergence of Eastern Europe as a region deserving of the WB's resources, altered the relationship. The WB pressed India to take more loans in social sectors, especially education and health, as well as to implement policy reforms, but was rebuffed.

The lending portfolio changed sharply after the 1991 macroeconomic crisis. In the immediate aftermath, India became one of the last important WB borrowers to partake of structural adjustment lending, which supported policy reforms in finance, taxation, and the investment and trade regime. With the abatement of the crisis, lending shifted away from public enterprises in electricity and irrigation to a focus on health and education. By the late 1980s, the WB had begun to warn India that its level of IDA lending would depend on its receptivity to loans in the social sectors. In the second half of the 1980s, the social sectors accounted for barely 7 percent of total WB lending. A decade later, between 1996 and 2000, they accounted for nearly a third of all lending. Communicable diseases (particularly HIV/AIDS and tuberculosis) emerged as a new focus of lending.

A second shift occurred in sharply reduced lending for "hard" infrastructure projects. In part, this was due to the decidedly lackluster outcomes in infrastructure sectors where the WB long had involvement, such as irrigation, railways, and power. The precipitating factor was the protracted controversy surrounding the WB's support of the massive Narmada irrigation project, which involved the construction of dams and irrigation canals and concomitant large-scale resettlement of displaced people. The project became a cause célèbre for international nongovernmental organizations (NGOs), thus forcing the WB to have its first ever external review of an ongoing project. The resulting report was strongly critical of the project's implications for displaced populations and the

environment. The WB ceased disbursements in 1993, and eventually the Indian government simply canceled the loan in 1995. An important consequence was that the WB became much more risk averse with regard to infrastructure projects. Although infrastructure-related lending revived by the end of the 1990s (especially for roads), its attempts to implement innumerable safeguards multiplied transaction costs, dampening demand for such loans.

Another change occurred in the level of lending, with a greater focus on subnational lending through state-level adjustment loans. These loans sought to improve the fiscal health of states, by improving expenditure priorities and taxation. This shift was facilitated in part by the decision of the central government to give the states a greater share in external loans, unlike the past, when the money went into a central pool, and concerned states received only a marginal increase in additional resources. The WB's increasing poverty focus and its recognition that the locus of poverty-related policies and implementation was situated at the state level were additional factors.

The World Bank's Impact on India

As with any borrower, it is not easy to get a simple bottom line on the WB's effects on India. At the most fundamental level, it has contributed to augmenting India's foreign exchange resources and level of investment. Although most attention is placed on the transfer of resources (especially long-term concessional resources), these are just one element of a multifaceted relationship. Much of the WB's lending to India has been for investment projects, and it was through these projects that it played an active technical assistance role, improving the quality of engineering and training, propagating new technical doctrines (such as the Training and Visit system in agricultural extension), developing strategies to reduce the incidence of corruption, setting up organizational competencies, and so on. The WB nurtured and supported organizations that have emerged as some of India's strongest, be it in finance (Industrial Credit and Investment Corporation of India) or power (National Thermal Power Corporation, or NTPC). In other cases, as with the Indian railways, despite an extensive long-term commitment that spanned over four decades and loans totaling $1.5 billion (the most made by the WB to a single entity), the WB's influence on policies was limited, and it finally gave up. Similarly, although its lending to NTPC and Indian Farmers Fertilizers Cooperative built excellent organizational capabilities in the power and fertilizer sectors respectively, these were undermined by the inability to change the policy environment. While its protracted involvement in agriculture did produce some good results (such as in agriculture extension and the dairy sector), the substantial lending for irrigation and agricultural credit through National Bank for Agricultural and Rural Development produced few results.

For most of its history, the WB's project performance in India outperformed its global portfolio. However, and somewhat paradoxically, in recent years, even as India's growth rate accelerated, the performance of the WB's India portfolio fell below its global average. The mediocre project performance was particularly apparent in sectors like water supply, power, and environment, while social sectors and industry did better. There has also been a substantial opportunity cost of nonlending (especially in infrastructure), the result of increasing transaction costs in borrowing from the WB as a result of the "Christmas tree"–like profusion of lending criteria over the 1990s.

There are four areas in which the WB made important but less heralded contributions. First, externally it played an important role as an advocate for India and a coordinator of aid flows. It organized, and has since coordinated, the Aid India Consortium since 1958, the sole institutional mechanism coordinating official flows to India. The Aid India Consortium was renamed the India Development Forum in 1993, signaling that official flows had become less important for India, and thus the importance of this institution waned. The WB played a critical diplomatic role in settling a major dispute between India and Pakistan regarding the sharing of the waters of the Indus River, and the resulting Indus Water Treaty of 1960 has stood the test of time despite the fractious relationship between the two countries. In recent years, the WB (along with the Asian Development Bank) has attempted to build epistemic communities of policy makers in South Asia through conferences and workshops, which might also help build bridges across the region.

Second, the WB also frequently played an important coordinating role within India, both among central government agencies as well as between central government agencies and state governments. The lack of strong central coordinating mechanisms in India and the inevitable interagency rivalries of bureaucracies have meant that as an outsider with seemingly deep pockets, the WB has often been a constructive informal peacemaker, while advancing its own interests. Third, the WB has also acted as an "agency of restraint." The covenants and conditionalities in many of its loans—at times at the urging of its Indian counterparts—often helped limit welfare-reducing political discretion in areas such as procurement to tariffs and expenditure priorities. Of course, in some cases, these restraints also served to advance the interests of the institution's major shareholders.

Finally, the WB also provided India with a range of public goods, both directly from its own substantial research, as well as indirectly for agricultural research through the Consultative Group on International Agricultural Research system. Moreover, it played a socialization role as an ideas intermediary, helping push advances in knowledge from the mundane (bidding procedures) to the ideological, reflecting its intrinsic ethos and governance. It has been an important contributor to applied economics research in India, although for many years the government of India did not allow its reports to be publicly circulated. By not investing more in vernacular languages, the WB severely circumscribed the dissemination (and influence) of its intellectual products. On the other hand, an important mechanism that enhanced the diffusion of the WB's ideas was the number of Indian economic reformers who worked in the WB and then returned home. In fact, there have always been steady numbers of Indian civil servants working with or in the WB for short to medium periods, who collectively serve as a mechanism of influence.

Evaluating the Relationship

While many in India (especially on the left) have always been suspicious about the WB and its ideological baggage, the overall relationship between the WB and India has been characterized by symmetry and equality (despite some notable exceptions). The relationship was particularly symbiotic in the first quarter century. As the first history of the WB put it in 1971, "No country has been studied more by the World Bank than India, and it is no exaggeration to say that India has influenced the Bank as much as the Bank has influenced India." The reality has been that the WB has treated India more favorably than most other borrowers. The perceived sophistication of Indian policy makers, their ability to articulate programs (as distinct from their ability or willingness to implement them), and the caution that inevitably comes in dealing with a large country all played a role. India's democracy, the exigencies of the cold war, extreme poverty, and eloquent political and economic interlocutors long made India the best argument for foreign aid for many years. On the flip side, criticisms of India would have weakened the general case for development aid. India's assigned role as an aid showcase added to the constraints the WB felt in pressing India for policy change.

The WB's limited leverage were also due to the reality that its resources were quite modest relative to the size of Indian economy, whether that money was seen in per capita terms or as a percent of both total government expenditures and gross domestic investment. This insignificance was due to both demand and supply. On the demand side, India's economic policies always relied primarily on domestic resources. The rare episodes when this was not the case (such as the mid-1960s and 1990–1991) simply reaffirmed these policies subsequently. As for the supply side, the IBRD side of WB lending was limited by concerns over India's creditworthiness. At the same time, IDA lending was both constrained by the IDA's own limited resources and by politically imposed limits on India's share of those same resources.

However, even within the confines of these limited resources, there were reasons internal to the WB that may have limited the institution's leverage. In particular, until well into the 1980s, the WB's anxiousness to commit the annual tranches of IDA availabilities by the end of each fiscal year frequently limited its leverage on Indian policy. A view that the foreign exchange gap and aid shortages contributed to India's growth also played into this. When it came to balancing lending against policy insistence the WB acted as if foreign exchange was critical and therefore untouchable. During the 1980s, while the WB shifted its emphasis to stress policy reforms and greater economic liberalization, it continued to lend to poorly governed public sector institutions in India and was muted in its criticism of India's closed economy. The WB itself admitted that throughout the 1980s its management did not address "India's disappointing policy record for fear of jeopardizing a strong lending relationship with a sensitive client." Internally, however, the WB's senior management had been concerned about India's policies and launched a series of collaborative reports with the Indian government on trade and industrial reform. These reports laid the groundwork for India's later policy reform agenda and were an important factor in the relatively smooth implementation of trade and industrial reforms in the early 1990s.

The WB's relationship with India has also been affected by India's federal system. As with other international organizations, its dealings were principally with the central government. Of course many of its projects were at the state level. However, selection of state projects was done largely on project and sector grounds, rather than on the basis of the overall policy stance of the state itself. WB loans were part of overall plan resources; hence a state with a WB project received only a small fraction of additional resources. And the central government's preoccupations—getting more foreign exchange—mattered little to state governments. Cash-strapped states therefore did not put a priority on their contributions of counterpart resources to WB projects, leading to projects delays and poor disbursement rates.

Changes in the 1990s led the WB to focus on state-level adjustment loans. This led to a paradox: even as the WB's overall resources became much less important for India, they became much more important for cash-strapped states, leading to an increase in the WB's influence. However, by 2004, outcomes in the three states where the WB focused its efforts—Andhra Pradesh, Karnataka, and Uttar Pradesh—were modest. Indeed, the WB's showcase, the Chandrababu Naidu–led government in Andhra Pradesh, performed poorly on the very fiscal criteria that had been the raison d'être of these loans, and its electoral defeat in 2004 dealt a blow to the WB's reform strategies.

Ultimately, the sheer size and complexity of India and its democratic polity means that there are limits to what any outside actor can do—for better or for worse. Both its critics and the WB itself give the institution too much importance. The dilemma faced by the WB is exemplified by its involvement with the notorious Narmada project or its cessation of lending to the Indian railways, or nonlending to states like Bihar. In the first case, although the WB earned the opprobrium of NGOs, much of the problems lay with the borrowers, especially the concerned state governments. The fact that WB financing was barely a fifth of overall cost reduced its leverage. As NGOs, who had been severely critical of the WB, realized after India canceled the loan in 1995, their actual targets were more vulnerable to pressure when there was external funding through the WB than when there was not. In the case of Indian railways or Bihar, the WB has struggled with two competing pressures—lend to sectors and regions where the need is greatest and potential economic and social rates are highest or lend to where implementation outcomes are likely to be most successful. In the past, well-intentioned efforts to stay engaged and try for incremental change have often simply exacerbated the problem. Perhaps the single biggest error the WB has made in India has been its failure to realize that nonlending might serve the country better.

Devesh Kapur

See also **Asian Development Bank (ADB), Relations with; International Monetary Fund (IMF), Relations with**

BIBLIOGRAPHY

Guhan, S. "The World Bank's Lending in South Asia." In *The World Bank: Its First Half Century*, vol. 2: *Perspectives*, edited by Devesh Kapur, John Lewis, and Richard Webb. Washington, D.C.: Brookings Institution, 1997.

Kapur, Devesh, John Lewis, and Richard Webb, eds. *The World Bank: Its First Half Century*, vol. 1: *History*. Washington, D.C.: Brookings Institution, 1997.

Lewis, John P. *India's Political Economy: Governance and Reform*. Delhi: Oxford University Press, 1995.

Mason, Edward, and Robert Asher. *The World Bank since Bretton Woods*. Washington, D.C.: Brookings Institution, 1973.

Morse, Bradford. *Sardar Sarovar: Report of the Independent Review*. Ottawa: Resources International Review, 1992.
World Bank. *India: Country Assistance Evaluation*. Washington, D.C., 2001.

WORLD TRADE ORGANIZATION (WTO), RELATIONS WITH

India is one of the twenty-three original contracting parties to the General Agreement on Tariffs and Trade (GATT). It thus automatically became a member of the World Trade Organization (WTO), which replaced GATT on 1 January 1995, following the completion of the Uruguay Round of negotiations in 1994.

India has been an active participant in all rounds of GATT negotiations, notwithstanding its declining share in world trade through most of the post–World War II period. In the post-WTO era, India continues to be an important voice in discussions to launch a new round of multilateral trade negotiations. The thrust of India's position has been to ensure a fair distribution of rights and obligations between developed and developing countries and to address the developmental concerns of poor countries. Its negotiating strategy has, however, evolved with its overall trade and development strategy and policy orientation. Its earlier strategy was largely defensive, in line with its import substitution policies. But the initiation of economic reforms following the balance of payments crisis of 1991 altered India's views on the opportunities, benefits, and threats of engaging in the multilateral trading system and has led to the adoption of a more forward-looking negotiating strategy.

GATT and India: The Pre–Uruguay Round Years

India played an important role in international trade negotiations under the auspices of GATT. Time and again it played the role of a leader and spokesperson for developing countries, along with Brazil. For instance, as early as 1963, India initiated an action program to expand exports by less developed countries to the developed countries. This program called for a standstill on all new tariff and nontariff barriers, the elimination of all GATT illegal Quantitative Restrictions (QRs), the removal of all duties on tropical primary products, and a schedule for reducing and eliminating tariffs on semiprocessed and processed products. But often such efforts bore little success.

However, India's overall approach to the multilateral trading system during the pre–Uruguay Round period was ambivalent and protectionist. It was driven by an ideology of import substitution and foreign exchange conservation and was underpinned by its belief in a new international economic order. India was an advocate of special and differential treatment to developing countries and unilateral concessions by developed countries. This defensive approach was evident in the continued high levels of tariff and nontariff protection in India, despite successive rounds of GATT negotiations. In 1990 India's import weighted average tariff rate stood at 87 percent, its unweighted average tariff at 128 percent, and its highest tariff rate at 355 percent, much higher than rates in other developing countries. In addition, 65 percent of all its imports and 90 percent of its manufacturing imports were subject to nontariff barriers in 1990. Moreover, India repeatedly invoked GATT Article 19(B), which permitted the maintenance of QRs for balance of payments reasons. Agriculture and textiles, which were two major sectors of export interest to India, remained outside GATT agreements. Concessions given under special and differential treatment arrangements like the Generalized System of Preferences were heavily qualified, discriminatory, and often nonsubstantive. Overall, India viewed GATT as an international forum to address asymmetries in the balance of economic power between developed and developing countries rather than a forum to liberalize its trade policies and integrate with global trade.

The Uruguay Round of Negotiations

The Uruguay Round of negotiations introduced textiles and agriculture as well as several new issues like intellectual property rights, services, and trade-related investment measures into the multilateral trading system. India, along with Brazil, led a group of developing countries against the inclusion of these new issues. It feared that industrialized countries would make commitments in textiles and agriculture subject to developing country concessions in such areas. However, India eventually had to agree to negotiate on these new issues as part of the Uruguay Round.

India made far more substantive commitments to reduce tariff and nontariff barriers on merchandise trade under the Uruguay Round than in all earlier rounds. Its relatively more liberal approach in this round was made possible by the far-reaching trade reforms introduced in the country beginning in 1991. In its Uruguay Round commitments, India increased the percentage of bound tariff lines for all products from a mere 6 percent in the pre–Uruguay Round period to 67 percent following the Uruguay Round. It bound its tariffs on 62 percent of all nonagricultural tariff lines, which included a large number of important products like iron and steel, chemicals, and machinery. It further committed to reduce its bound rate on all industrial products by 40 percent, from an import weighted average tariff rate of 71.4 percent to 32.4 percent, and committed to reduce tariffs on 2,701 industrial product lines. In agriculture, India bound 81.4 percent of its agricultural imports from the rest of the world. However, India remained largely defensive in the agricultural sector owing to food security and livelihood concerns. The bindings in agriculture were set at very high levels, at rates of 100 percent for primary products, 150 percent for processed products, and 300 percent for edible oils. Moreover, some tariffs that had been bound at zero before the Uruguay Round were renegotiated and were set at higher levels to afford a greater degree of protection to sensitive products. Inclusive of industrial and nonindustrial products, India offered to reduce its basic duty by roughly 30 percent. The duty reductions were to be made over a period of six years.

India has thus far adhered to its tariff binding and reduction commitments. It brought down its applied import-weighted average tariff rate on industrial products from 54 percent in the pre–Uruguay Round period to 33 percent in 1996–1997, further to 30.3 percent in 1998, and to 29 percent in 2001–2002 and most recently to around 20 percent. It has reduced its applied tariffs for a large number of industrial products and has brought them close to their bound levels. However, in agriculture, tariff reductions have been less substantive, with the difference between bound and applied rates remaining at more than 50 percent for 656 out of 673 tariff lines as late as 2000. The slower pace of trade liberalization in this sector has been due to concerns about potential adverse effects on rural employment, livelihoods, and food security.

India also made substantive commitments to reduce nontariff protection in the Uruguay Round. It agreed to phase out QRs on all goods except for some 600 items or product lines for security reasons. As per the Agreement on Agriculture, it also committed to tariff its nontariff barriers on agricultural imports. But due to concerns about the potential adverse impact on domestic producers and on the balance of payments, India took recourse to GATT Article 18:B to maintain QRs on some products. The latter was, however, ruled inconsistent with India's WTO obligations following a dispute filed against India by the United States in 1996, and India had to agree to phase out all its QRs (on 1,429 product lines) by 31 March 2001, earlier than originally scheduled. In line with the WTO decision, India removed QRs on 714 items by 1 April 2000 and the rest by 1 April 2001, covering both bound and unbound products.

Under the General Agreement on Trade in Services (GATS), India's approach was highly conservative. It scheduled only a few services for negotiations and did not table important services, such as energy and distribution services, where there is great interest on the part of developed countries to enter the Indian market. Even within the scheduled sectors, India's market access and national treatment commitments were very limited in scope and more restrictive than prevailing policies. The revised offers made by India in January 2004 as part of the ongoing GATS negotiations are not substantively different and remain subject to numerous restrictions. Today, the wedge between India's GATS commitments and existing policies is even greater, given the considerable autonomous liberalization undertaken in the 1990s in many of India's service sectors. India's main market access interest within services has been the movement of service suppliers; India wants to secure increased and predictable market access for the temporary movement of its service providers and was earlier influential in developing the GATS annex on this mode of supply. More recently, India has been pushing for secure market access for the cross-border supply of services, a mode which covers trade in services through business process outsourcing, which is of growing interest to India. It has formed developing country coalitions and presented bold proposals on both these GATS modes of supply.

The issue of intellectual property rights and the resulting agreement on Trade-Related Aspects of Intellectual Property Rights (TRIPs) aroused much debate in India. While the agreement had no major implications for India in the area of copyrights, trademarks, and designs, as domestic legislation in the latter areas were already in conformity with the TRIPs agreement, in the area of patents India had several concerns. The foremost concern was about the likely impact of amendments in domestic patent legislation due to the TRIPs agreement (given differences between the two in terms of coverage, duration, working of patents, and compulsory licensing provisions) on the Indian pharmaceutical sector and on public health and equity objectives. It was feared that the introduction of product patents for pharmaceuticals (as opposed to process patents, which was the case in India) would lead to higher drug prices and benefit developed country pharmaceutical firms at the expense of domestic generic drug manufacturers in developing countries. Moreover, in the Indian view, there was no convincing link between stronger intellectual property rights legislation and innovation, investment, technology transfer, and quality. A second concern was that patent protection to plant varieties and microorganisms under the TRIPs agreement would lead to "bio-piracy" and plundering of the ecological wealth of developing countries like India as well as monopoly over seed and fertilizer trade and production by Western multinationals. The fear was that such protection would ultimately raise input prices for developing country agricultural producers, would limit their ability to indigenize to suit local conditions, and could potentially have adverse environmental effects.

Notwithstanding such concerns and much domestic opposition, India has taken steps to bring its domestic legislation into conformity with the TRIPs agreement. India's Patents Act of 1970 has undergone three amendments, the latest being at the end of 2004. The main changes include the extension of patent protection to a period of twenty years for all inventions, the specification of a list of nonpatentable innovations, including seeds, plants, species, traditional knowledge, and other items for which innovations may not classify as inventions, clarification of what constitutes the working of patents, conditions for the grant of compulsory license, including on grounds of national and public health emergencies, and introduction of product patents. India has also introduced the Protection of Plant Variety and Farmer's Right Act as a sui generis system for protecting plant and animal life. However, the basic concerns and debates over the TRIPs agreement continue in India, and have also shaped India's position on this agreement in the post–Uruguay Round discussions.

According to various studies, India was expected to be among the main developing-country beneficiaries of the Uruguay Round agreement, mainly due to the elimination of nontariff barriers. The coverage ratio for nontariff barriers on Organization for Economic Cooperation and Development (OECD) countries' imports from India was estimated to decline from 29.4 percent to 5.1 percent across all products. The bulk of this reduction was due to improved market access in textiles and clothing and agriculture, following the phasing out of the Multi Fibre Agreement (MFA) by 2005 and the elimination of nontariff barriers in agriculture. Quantitative exercises indicated an increase in exports of .3 percent of the value of India's 1992 exports due to liberalization of agricultural trade and of 7.4 percent due to elimination of the MFA. The gains were not as significant in other areas. For instance, committed tariff reductions averaged a mere 2.4 percent and affected only 5 percent of all merchandise exports by India to OECD countries. In the area of services, the gains were limited, given the lack of substantive commitments by all countries in India's main area of export interest, namely, movement of service suppliers. Any gains were, however, finally contingent on the implementation of commitments by the developed countries and on India's ability to capitalize on the improved market access opportunities by introducing domestic structural and policy reforms to remove supply-side constraints and compete more effectively in world trade.

Post–Uruguay Round Developments

In the various Ministerial Conferences that have taken place since the Uruguay Round, India's focus has been on three issues. These are: the implementation of the Uruguay Round commitments in agriculture and textiles to ensure that the gains promised to developing countries in that round are realized; ensuring greater sensitivity to equity and developmental concerns of developing countries in the context of TRIPs; and preventing further widening of the WTO mandate. In the course of these Ministerials, India has also been very influential in shaping the outcome of discussions and the introduction of new frameworks and proposals.

In agriculture, India has pushed strongly for the implementation of subsidy reduction commitments made in the Uruguay Round by the developed countries. In preparation for the Cancún Ministerial in September 2003, India was instrumental in forming a new alliance of developing countries (G-22), including important developing countries like Brazil, South Africa, China, and Egypt, which rejected the framework on agriculture that was put forward by the European Union and the United States just prior to the Cancún meetings. The collapse of the talks at Cancún was in large part due to the G-22's insistence on implementation issues in agriculture. India was a key player in this coalition, fostering unity among the group despite the divergent interests of its member countries and despite divisive tactics by the developed countries to fragment the coalition. It also helped in framing an alternative proposal by the developing countries on agriculture and garnered the support of the smaller and poorer developing country coalition, the G-90 grouping.

In the July 2004 discussions in Geneva to develop a framework agreement, India again played a leading role within the G-22 alliance. It pushed for provisions such as safeguard measures, the adoption of less than full reciprocity in tariff reductions, exemptions from *de minimis* subsidy reductions for resource-constrained farmers in poor countries, and explicit recognition in the framework on agriculture of the food security, livelihood, and rural and social development concerns of developing countries. India was also one of the members of a new group that emerged during the July 2004 discussions, the Five Interested Parties Group (including Brazil, the United States, the European Union, and Australia), which consisted of countries with both offensive and defensive interests in agriculture. India played an important role within this group in helping forge a last-minute consensus on the July framework agreement, particularly in the context of agriculture, thus keeping the Doha Round alive.

India has also voiced implementation concerns in textiles. It criticized the fact that during the 1995–2005 transition period of this agreement, developed countries had phased out quotas on textile and clothing products which did not face binding quotas and that over 95 percent of

India's textile and clothing trade would remain unintegrated until the final year of transition. Moreover, India also voiced concerns about unilateral changes introduced by certain importing countries on rules of origin, repeated antidumping investigations on India's textile exports, and selective liberalization of quotas under preferential bilateral arrangements, which further eroded any market access gains realized in this sector by India. It pushed successfully for the scheduled elimination of the MFA on 1 January 2005. Its textile and clothing exports are expected to grow significantly in the post-MFA regime.

There has also been some concern in India with regard to the nonagricultural market access negotiations. Although India has not opposed these discussions, it has expressed concerns about the formula that will be adopted for reductions in industrial tariffs from the Uruguay Round levels. It has opposed proposals for larger reductions on industrial products that are subject to higher tariffs, and proposals for zero duties on selected products. This opposition stems from concerns about possible adverse effects on certain emerging manufacturing sectors and on labor-intensive small-scale industries, with implications for employment and poverty. India has also lobbied for credit to be given to developing countries for autonomous liberalization in recognition of the fact that significant reductions in applied tariffs have been undertaken unilaterally by many developing countries since the Uruguay Round in the context of trade reforms.

With the backing of developing countries like South Africa and Brazil, India has argued the need to interpret and implement the TRIPs agreement in a manner that gives member countries the right to protect public health and promote acccess to medicines for all. India lobbied actively to introduce flexibility provisions under the TRIPs agreement in the area of public health and medicines and was finally successful in realizing the Declaration on TRIPs and Public Health at the Doha talks. This declaration gives members the right to grant compulsory licenses, to determine the grounds on which to grant these licenses, and to determine what constitutes a national health emergency. Before the Cancún Ministerial, India, along with the United States, Brazil, South Africa, and Kenya, also succeeded in introducing a provision under the TRIPs agreement that would allow developing countries to import generics from earmarked countries in case of public health emergencies. This was seen as a major victory for developing countries and their generic manufacturers, although how such a provision will operate in practice and its implications for the Indian pharmaceutical industry are not yet clear.

India has also made two other demands in the post–Uruguay Round discussions on TRIPs. The first is to extend geographic indicators to products other than wines and spirits in view of India's export interests in products like basmati rice. The second is to introduce restrictions on the misappropriation of biological and genetic resources and traditional knowledge from developing countries. However, its primary focus under TRIPs has been the issue of affordable access to medicines and equity in public health.

India differs from the major developed countries concerning the scope of future WTO negotiations. It has insisted that the scope of WTO negotiations be restricted to the built-in agenda of the Uruguay Round and the implementation of commitments made in the previous round. It strongly opposed the inclusion of labor and environmental standards and the four Singapore issues of investment, competition policy, transparency in government procurement, and trade facilitation under the WTO framework. As part of the G-22 alliance, it was instrumental in the dropping of three of the four Singapore issues as part of the July 2004 framework agreement.

Future Strategies and Policy Directions

India's approach to the WTO negotiations has been largely issue- and cause-based and very much driven by coalition dynamics and alliances, often at the expense of its own strategic interests. On several occasions, India's firm public stand on issues has attracted criticism from developed country negotiators and the media. For instance, it was widely blamed for "scuttling" the launch of a new round at Doha, and was termed by one observer as the "fallen hero of a lost third world cause" (Panagariya).

Overall, critics contend that India has often espoused the cause of developing countries at the expense of its own interests in WTO negotiations. In future WTO negotiations, India needs to adopt a more strategic approach. It must dovetail its negotiating strategy into its overall economic liberalization and trade reform program. It needs to use its multilateral engagement in the WTO to facilitate meaningful policy reform, such as by ensuring that domestic opening generates payoffs in terms of increased market access abroad. The latter would also enhance India's credibility as a bargainer. Given the extent of trade liberalization and market opening that has occurred in India since the Uruguay Round, India needs to solidify these policies through multilateral commitments to lock in its reforms and to signal the credibility of its policy orientation.

Rupa Chanda

See also **Brazil–India Relations; Economic Reforms of 1991; Intellectual Property Rights; Trade Liberalization since 1991**

BIBLIOGRAPHY

Bhattacharya, B., ed. *Seattle and Beyond: The Unfinished Agenda*. New Delhi: Indian Institute of Foreign Trade, 2000.

Bhattacharya, B., and A. K. Sengupta, eds. *Trade in Agriculture: The Uruguay Round and After*. New Delhi: Indian Institute of Foreign Trade, 1995.

Debroy, D. *Beyond the Uruguay Round: The Indian Perspective on GATT*. New Delhi: Sage Publications, 1996.

Martin, W., and A. Winters, eds. *The Uruguay Round and the Developing Economies*. World Bank Discussion Papers, no. 307. Washington, D.C.: World Bank, 1995.

Mattoo, A., and R. Stern, eds. *India and the WTO*. Washington, D. C.: World Bank and Oxford University Press, 2003.

Mehta, P., ed. *WTO and India: An Agenda for Action in Post Doha Scenario*. Jaipur: CUTS, 2002.

Mehta, R. *WTO, Liberalization and the Industrial Sector: The Case of Market Access*. New Delhi: Research and Information System for the Non-Aligned and Other Developing Countries, 2001.

Panagariya, A. "India at Doha: Retrospect and Prospect, Commentary." *Economic and Political Weekly* (26 January 2002): 279–284.

Singh, R. "Agriculture, India, and the WTO." *Vision: The Journal of Business Perspective* (January–June 2002): 45–50.

Srinivasan, T. N. "Global Trading System, the WTO, and the Developing Countries." Golden Jubilee Seminar Series, 6th Lecture. New Delhi: NCAER, 24 July 1998.

Srinivasan, T. N., and S. Tendulkar. *Reintegrating India with the World Economy*. New Delhi: Oxford University Press, 2003.

World Trade Organization. "Trade Policy Review: India." Press release. Geneva: WTO, 17 April 1998.

———. "Trade Policy Review: India." First press release, Secretariat and Government Summaries. Geneva: WTO, 21 June 2003.

WORLD WAR I AND WORLD WAR II, IMPACT ON INDIA. *See* **History and Historiography.**

X

XAVIER, FRANCIS *(1506–1552), Jesuit missionary to India.* Francis Xavier was born in 1506 in the Pyrenees kingdom of Navarre. At eighteen he went to the University of Paris, where nine years later he joined the faculty and came under the influence of Ignatius Loyola, who was planning to start the Society of Jesus. Xavier was one of the first six to join Loyola.

Eventually Xavier was commissioned by King John III of Portugal to Christianize his eastern colonies. Xavier left for India on 7 April 1541. As papal nuncio, he was given supreme authority over all missions and churches already in existence. He landed in Goa on 6 May 1542.

Late in 1542, he went to Madras (Chennai), converting the Parava fisher people in great numbers. though their acquiescence was not necessarily spiritually motivated. Harassed by pirates at sea and powerful vested interests on the land, they readily agreed to become Christians in return for the protection of the king of Portugal. Xavier had no fluency in any of the local vernacular languages, so he memorized the Creed, the Lord's Prayer, the Ave Maria, and the Ten Commandments. His method was to gather the people of a village together on Sundays. "We begin," Xavier wrote, "with a profession of faith." He would then recite the Creed and the Commandments and the people would respond in a "mighty chorus . . . with their arms folded on their breasts in the form of a cross," affirming that they believed (Firth, p. 59). In such a fashion, in one month, he baptized as many as ten thousand. After a year, Xavier turned his attention to the west coast, journeying through Travencore to Cochin. Here he repeated his efforts. Everywhere he went he endeavored, but without much success, to train Indian workers, both ordained and lay, to provide for the spiritual nurture of the young Christian community. In addition, he instructed his fellow Jesuits to "build schools in every village, that the children may be taught daily." Remarkably, the Parava remain Christian to this day.

Subsequent to his work in India, Xavier attempted, but failed, to enter China, and he died of a fever on 2 December 1552 off the south coast of China. He

St. Francis Xavier. St. Francis Xavier's remains as preserved at the Catholic Basilica of Bom Jesus in Goa. Xavier is regarded as one of the greatest of Christian missionaries; his travels covered many thousands of miles in a dozen years. TIME LIFE PICTURES / GETTY IMAGES.

was eventually buried in Goa and was canonized to saint-hood in 1622.

Graham Houghton

BIBLIOGRAPHY

Amaladoss, Anand. *Jesuit Presence in Indian History*. Anand, India: Gujurat Sahitya Prakash, 1988.

Firth, Cyril Bruce. *An Introduction to Indian Church History*. Chennai: Christian Literature Society, 1968.

Neill, Stephen. *The Story of the Christian Church in India and Pakistan*. Grand Rapids, Mich.: Eerdmans, 1970.

Ogilvie, J. N. *The Apostles of India*. London: Hodder and Stoughton, 1915.

YAJÑA "Sacrifice," or *yajña*, is the key word in a Vedic worldview that dominated South Asian religion for the entire first millennium B.C. Derived from *yaj* (to sacrifice, worship), *yajña* has an Avestan counterpart *yasna*, indicating an Indo-Iranian pre-Vedic origin. In the highly influential Purusha hymn, Rig Veda 10.90, the self-sacrificing cosmic being Purusha creates not only the world and classes of beings but also the institution of *yajña* and the first cosmic laws. Sacrifice for Vedic poets and ritualists became the crucial link between human and divine worlds. *Karman*, ritual "work" in *yajña*, was declared a human responsibility, and sacrifice evolved into a complex, highly sophisticated instrument by which the cosmos itself was ritually renewed.

Early in the first millennium B.C., Vedic tradition divided ritual activity into *shrauta* sacrifices based on *shruti*, the revealed Vedas, and *grihya* ceremonies based on *smriti*, or human tradition. The former apparently had priority, and Shrauta Sūtras of numerous Vedic schools systematized sacrifices already described in the Saṃhitās, Brāhmaṇas and Āraṇyakas of the orally transmitted Vedic texts. Grihya Sūtras of the same schools provided domestic guidelines. These Sūtras listed sacrifices that could be performed on one fire in the home, some with assistance from a *purohita* (domestic priest), or great sacrifices requiring three fires and as many as sixteen or seventeen priests. The latter included soma sacrifices, with the *agnishtoma*, an initial soma offering, as paradigm. Once a sacrificer (*yajamāna*) and his wife (*patnī*) performed the five-day *agnishtoma* (known today among Vaidika Brahmans of Andhra simply as *yajña* to declare its priority), the couple may then go on to further soma *yajña*s such as the *agnicayana* and *vājapeya*. When one of the pair dies, all of the dozen or more implements, *yajñapātra* or *yajñāyudha* (literally, "sacrificial weapons") go to the fire-god Agni in the funeral pyre.

Beginning with Brāhmaṇa texts (e.g., Shatapatha Brāhmaṇa 11.5.6.1) and continuing on to the authoritative law code of Manu (3.67–74), an important reduction of sacrifice to a manageable yet spiritually satisfying scale arrived with stipulation of five daily "great" *yajña*s (*mahāyajña*) to be made by a householder without priestly assistance. *Yajña*s to *deva*s (gods), *brahman* (the Veda), *pitri*s (ancestors), *manushya* (humans), and *bhūta*s (supernatural beings) could be accomplished simply by adding a stick to the ritual fire, reciting a Vedic verse, offering water, giving alms to a Brahman or beggar, scattering leftover grains for crows or ants.

In the post-Vedic era of classical Hinduism, the solemn *shrauta* schedule of *yajña* gradually gave way to *devapūjā*, the worship of images of deities in households, roadside shrines, and increasingly elaborate public temples with priestly staff. Aside from innumerable goddesses of rural and urban theistic Hinduism, the two principal male deities, Vishnu and Shiva, both demonstrate strong connections with *yajña*. Vishnu is pervader of the universe, like the sacrificial pole (*yūpa*), and Shiva is Sthāṇu, that same *axis mundi*. Both gods also have mythic links to the cult of soma, although it is only Shiva, famously excluded from Daksha's *yajña*, who succeeds in destroying the sacrifice.

In contemporary India, elaborate sectarian rituals, often labeled "Vedic" *yajña*s or *yāga*s to acquire prestige, have little to do with authentic Vedic ritual.

David M. Knipe

See also **Agni; Devī; Hinduism (Dharma); Shrauta Sūtras; Soma; Vedic Aryan India; Yajur Veda**

BIBLIOGRAPHY

Kane, P. V. *History of Dharmasāstra*, vol. II, parts I–II. Poona: Bhandarkar Oriental Research Institute, 1941. Detailed overview of Vedic sacrifices and their texts.

Smith, Brian K. *Reflections on Resemblance, Ritual and Religion.* New York: Oxford University Press, 1989. Good theoretical perspective on the meanings of Vedic sacrifice.

Staal, Frits. *Agni. The Vedic Ritual of the Fire Altar.* 2 vols. Berkeley, Calif.: Asian Humanities, 1983. Monumental study of 1975 Agnicayana sacrifice in Kerala and its historic context; excellent plates.

YĀJNAVALKYA, *Indian astronomer, perhaps of the second millennium B.C.* Yājnavalkya is one of the foremost figures in the earliest period of Indian astronomy. There is no unanimity about his time, which has been estimated in an indirect manner. His time was considered to have been around 800 B.C., based on the dating of the Shatapatha Brāhmana—a voluminous prose text from his school, which serves as a commentary on Vedic ritual— by nineteenth-century philologists. These philological theories have been called into question by new archaeological data, and his true period may be the second millennium B.C.

Yājnavalkya's parents were Brahmaratha and Sunandā. He studied first in the hermitage of Vaishampāyana and later with Bāshkala and Uddālaka. He is credited with the authorship of the Shukla (White) Yajurveda. He is also credited with the school that put together the Shatapatha Brāhmana. Many dialogues of Yājnavalkya with his disciples and with rival sages are preserved in the Vedic literature. Legends connect him to the sun; this may be a slanted reference to his discovery of two important facts about the motions of the sun.

In the Shatapatha Brāhmana, Yājnavalkya advances two important theories: first, that a cycle of ninety-five years is required to reconcile the lunar and the solar years (indicating that the length of the year was known to a great degree of accuracy); second, that the circuit of the sun is asymmetric in its four quarters. The proportion for the two halves of the year described by him is 176:189. It is interesting that this proportion is also used in describing the asymmetry of the two halves in the Angkor Wat temple in Cambodia (c. 1150). Yājnavalkya's astronomy is very important in the history of ideas because it pushes the recognition of the ninety-five-year lunisolar cycle and the asymmetry of the year to a much earlier time than has been supposed.

Yājnavalkya's astronomy belongs to a period in which astronomical knowledge was part of ritual. Complicated geometrical altars were built to represent the year, with facts about the year expressed in terms of number or area within the altar design. Yājnavalkya is a major figure in early Vedic thought, renowned for his stress on the correspondence between the outer world and the inner world. Many of his dialogues form a part of the narrative of the Brihad-Āranyaka-Upanishad, in which he mentions a preliminary version of the Purānic system of cosmology.

Subhash Kak

See also **Astronomy; Science; Vedic Aryan India**

BIBLIOGRAPHY

Kak, Subhash. "The Orbit of the Sun in the Brahmanas." *Indian Journal of History of Science* 33 (1998): 175–191.
———. "Birth and Early Development of Indian Astronomy." In *Astronomy across Cultures: The History of Non-Western Astronomy*, edited by H. Selin. Dordrecht: Kluwer Academic Publishers, 2000.
Millar, G., and Subhash Kak. "A Brahmanic Fire Altar Explains a Solar Equation in Angkor Wat." *Journal of the Royal Astronomical Society of Canada* 93 (1999): 216–220.

YAJUR VEDA The Yajur Veda is one of four primary Samhitās (anthologies) of Vedas, India's most ancient textual authority. The oldest, decidedly seminal Veda, the Rig Veda—1,028 hymns composed in the final centuries before 1000 B.C.—became a source of mantras, cited with additional material in three later Vedas: Yajur, Samur, and Atharva Veda, all compiled within two or three centuries. An "inside" perspective of Vedic heritage, including those Vedic Brahmans still tasked today with memorizing and reciting Vedas as oral traditions, understands the four Samhitās as unitary ("the Veda"), eternal, without human or divine origin, and therefore without literary chronology as recognized by "outside" historians and linguists.

The great system of sacrifices at the heart of Vedic religion depended upon invocations of deities and ritual prescriptions of the Yajur Veda, literally "knowledge of the *yaju*s (sacrificial formulas)," and the melodies of the Samur Veda, literally "knowledge of the *saman* (chant)." Together with the Rig Veda, they form a "triple Veda," following a traditional predilection for triads. A fourth Samhitā, the Atharva Veda, was added as an important ancient compendium of hymns regarding popular religious practices not directly related to the sacrificial calendar. Four major priests were assigned to these four Vedas, the *hota, adhvaryu, udgata,* and *brahman*, for the Rig, Yajur, Samur, and Atharva Vedas, respectively. Each has essential ritual roles, but it is the *adhvaryu*, reciting from the Yajur Veda, who functions as executive priest, assigning sacrificial duties and mantras to the *yajamana* (sacrificer-patron) and other priests. In great *shrauta* sacrifices, including paradigmatic soma and animal offerings, the *adhvaryu* may direct sixteen or seventeen priests in an arena outside the sacrificer's home. Or the *adhvaryu* may direct actions inside the home in new- and full-moon-day sacrifices, with the *yajamana* alone or with one to three other priests in the *grihya* (domestic) schedule patterned after that of the *shrauta*. In either case, portions of the Yajur Veda are incorporated into ritual handbooks for procedures.

Over the centuries, the four Vedas were orally transmitted and edited by numerous schools known as *shakhas* (branches). The Yajur Veda text generated the largest number of schools in two divisions: the older Krishna (Black) Yajur Veda, with four Saṃhitās (Taittiriya, Maitrayani, Kathaka, and Kapishthala-Katha); and the younger Vajasaneyi Saṃhitā, also known as the Shukla (White) Yajur Veda, with two closely related schools, Madhyamdina and Kanva. Whereas the texts of the latter were composed, and are still recited today, in verse only, those of the various Krishna Yajur Veda schools are mixed, with prose passages among metrical ones. Almost the same rites are provided by each school, although length of coverage, schedule order, and even emphasis in the subcontinent vary considerably.

The major difference between the two Yajur Vedas, Krishna (Black) and Shukla (White), concerns *brāhmaṇa*s. Every Veda has a prose genre known as *brāhmaṇa*, a discourse with rules concerning particular mantras or ritual actions, along with explanations of their meanings. For example, in his schedule of memorized texts, a Vedic student born into the Taittiriya *shakha* first learns the Taittiriya Saṃhitā (= Krishna Yajur Veda), which includes numerous *brāhmaṇa* passages throughout (although he then goes on to memorize an equally lengthy text known as the Taittiriya Brāhmaṇa, followed by the briefer Taittiriya Aranyaka and Taittiriya Upanishad). On the other hand, a student born into the Madhyamdina *shakha* learns the metrical Shukla Yajur Veda (= Vajasaneyi Saṃhitā) without any *brāhmaṇa* explanations, those having been collected in a separate text known as the Shatapatha Brāhmaṇa, the next assignment for memorization.

David M. Knipe

See also **Agni; Hinduism (Dharma); Shrauta Sūtra; Soma; Vedic Aryan India; Yajña**

BIBLIOGRAPHY

Gonda, Jan. *Vedic Literature*. Wiesbaden, Germany: Harrassowitz, 1975. Best detailed overview.

Keith, Arthur B. *The Religion and Philosophy of the Veda and Upanisads*. 2 vols. 1925. Reprint, Westport, Conn.: Greenwood Press, 1971. Knowledgeable overview by English translator of Taittiriya Saṃhitā (Krishna Yajur Veda).

Renou, Louis. *Vedic India*, translated by Philip Spratt. 1947. Reprint, Delhi: Indological Book House, 1971. Concise summary by a leading authority on Vedic *shakha*s.

YOGA The Yoga tradition is extremely old. Yogic postures are depicted on the third millennium B.C. seals of the Harappan period. The Rig Veda speaks of the visions (*dhi*) of harmony stretched on the loom of cosmic existence.

Yoganarayana Stone Sculpture. Narasiṃha, the fourth avatar of Lord Vishnu, who cast off his fiery nature in deep meditation or yoga mudra. From remains of Hampi, capital of the Hindu kingdom of Vijayanagar, c. sixteenth century. NATIONAL MUSEUM / FOTOMEDIA.

This task was compared to harnessing of the plow (*yuga*). The mind is compared to the flutterings of a bird, indicating its union in the heart with the divine. The Rig Veda asserts that the universe is stationed within the heart, suggesting the yoking of it with the individual's body.

The goal of Yoga is self-transformation and transcendence, achieved by yoking the body and mind with the spirit within. This yoking may be viewed as an interiorization of the ritual that is more commonly done externally.

By the time of the Bhagavad Gītā, the most popular text of Yoga, the teachings are already very ancient. The Mokshadharma section of the Mahābhārata has a longish description of Yoga. Other texts that may belong to the first part of the first millennium B.C. and that also describe Yoga are the Katha, the Shvetāshvatara, and the Maitrāyanīya Upanishads. Around 150 B.C., the teachings were codified by Patanjali in his Yoga Sūtra (Aphorisms of Yoga), which is now termed Classical Yoga. An important early commentary on this text is Vyāsa's Yoga Bhāshya.

The Purāṇas (Ancient tales) also teach Yoga. Another encyclopedic work is the Yoga Vāsishtha, which teaches a nondualistic Jnāna Yoga of seven stages. Yoga teachings are a part of the Tantras of Shakti, the Āgamas of Shiva, and the Saṃhitās of Vishnu worship.

Hatha Yoga is a later development within the Yoga tradition, credited to Gorakshanātha of the eleventh century. The major texts of this Yoga, which has become very popular in the West, are the Hatha Yoga Pradīpikā, the Gheranda Saṃhitā, and the Shiva Saṃhitā. An important early Tamil text on Yoga is Tirumandiram.

Patanjali's Yoga Sūtra speaks of a system of eight limbs:

1. Moral restraint (*yama*), comprising nonharming (*ahimsā*), truthfulness (*satya*), nonstealing (*asteya*), chastity (*brahmacharya*), and noncovetousness (*aparigraha*)
2. Discipline (*niyama*), consisting of purity (*shaucha*), contentment (*santosha*), asceticism (*tapas*), self-study (*svādhyāya*), and devotion to the Lord (*īshvara-pranidhāna*)
3. Posture (*āsana*)
4. Breath control (*prānayāma*)
5. Sense withdrawal (*pratyāhāra*)
6. Concentration (*dhāranā*)
7. Meditation (*dhyāna*)
8. Absorption (*samādhi*).

Several kinds of Yoga are described in the texts. These include Jnāna-Yoga, or the path of knowledge; Sānkhya-Yoga, or the path of union through transformation of the elements within the psychical person; Karma-Yoga, the path of selfless action; Bhakti-Yoga, the path of devotion; Mantra-Yoga, the path of sacred sound; and Hatha-Yoga, the path of self-transformation using the arduous path of physical purification.

Breath control, or *prānāyāma*, is fundamental to yogic practice. Vedic books speak of five kinds of breath (*prāna*) that mediate the various processes in the body. These may be viewed not only as inhalation and exhalation but also as electric and chemical currents coursing through the body. The five main breaths are: *prāna*, associated with inhalation and with the regions of heart and head; *apāna*, associated with exhalation and with the navel and the lower abdomen; *udāna*, located at the throat and associated with speech and other functions; *samāna*, the midcurrent located at the abdomen and chiefly responsible for digestion; and *vyāna*, the diffuse current pervading the entire body.

The Hatha Yoga texts speak of seven (in some texts, as many as thirteen) *chakra*s (centers of energy) in the body:

1. *Mūlādhāra chakra*, at the bottom of the spine, is associated with the coiled energy of *kundalini* and is portrayed as a lotus of four petals. This *chakra* is associated with the earth element, the sense of smell, and the lower limbs.
2. *Svādhishthāna chakra*, at the genitalia, is associated with the water element, the sense of taste, and the hands. It is shown as having six petals.
3. *Manipūra chakra*, at the navel, is associated with the fire element, the sense of sight, and the digestive tract. It is portrayed as having ten petals.
4. *Anāhata chakra*, at the heart, is associated with the air element, the sense of touch, and the reproductive organs. It is shown with twelve petals.
5. *Vishuddhi chakra*, at the throat, is associated with the ether, the sense of hearing, the skin and the mouth, and is shown as having sixteen petals.
6. *Ājnā chakra*, at the center of the eyebrows, is associated with the mind and the sense of individuality (*ahamkāra*). It has two petals.
7. *Sahasrāra chakra*, at the crown of the head, is viewed as having a thousand spokes or petals. It is associated with pure consciousness.

The exertions of the yogi make it possible for the kundalini (representing the natural energy of the individual) to rise up and ultimately pierce through to the highest *chakra*. This joining of the kundalini at the *sahasrāra chakra* is called the union of Shakti and Shiva, respectively representing body and consciousness. Before reaching the top, the kundalini must pierce through three particularly difficult knots or hurdles (*granthi*) at the first (at the base of the spine), the third (at the navel), and the fifth (at the throat) *chakra*s. These points are called Brahmā, Vishnu, and Rudra *granthi*s.

The physical body is supposed to be enveloped in an energy sheath, which is the subtle body (*sūkshma sharīra*). The energy flows around through 72,000 channels (*nādi*s) that are described in the Upanishads. The three main pathways down the spine are the *sushumnā* at the center, with the *idā* and the *pingalā* to the left and right of it. The *idā* is associated with cooling (and the moon) and the *pingalā* with heating (and the sun).

In recent decades, the popularity of Yoga has spread around the world. It is practiced for its health benefits as well as its promise of mastery of mind and body through the advanced practice of meditation.

Subhash Kak

See also **Science**

BIBLIOGRAPHY

Feuerstein, Georg. *The Essence of Yoga*. London: Rider, 1974.
Radhakrishnan, Sarvepalli. *Indian Philosophy*. London: Unwin Hyman, 1989.
Woodroffe, John. *The Serpent Power*. Chennai: Ganesh & Co., 1981.

ZOROASTRIANISM A religion founded on the teachings of the prophet Zoroaster, who lived in ancient Persia (now Iran), Zoroastrianism is practiced by about 100,000 people worldwide. Most of its adherents live in India (and are also called Parsis). A smaller number are in Iran; and many Indian and Iranian Zoroastrians migrated to and now live in Britain, the United States, Canada, Australia, South Africa, and other countries. One of the world's oldest monotheistic religions, Zoroastrianism has influenced other monotheistic religions. Its main tenets are rather simple—it espouses three virtues of good thoughts, good words, and good deeds, realization of which enables one to win the battle between good and evil.

Zoroaster, or Zarathustra, is believed to have lived around 1500 B.C. in eastern Iran, in what is now the Russian steppes. Like the Buddha after him, Zoroaster sought to understand the reasons for death and suffering and the origin of evil. He had a deep longing for justice and for a moral law that would allow humankind to lead a good life in peace. In search of answers, he meditated in a mountain cave for ten years. When he received enlightenment, he descended from the mountain and sought to promote a new way of life among his tribesmen. He preached monotheism in a land that followed an aboriginal polytheistic religion, and he was therefore attacked for his teaching. Zoroaster eventually gained the royal patronage of King Vishtasp, resulting in a substantial following for his faith. Zoroastrianism was already over a millennium old when the first Persian Empire was established by Cyrus of the Achaemenid dynasty. It was propagated in various Persian empires by the Achaemenids, then the Parthians who ruled from 247 B.C. onward, and the Sassanians who overthrew the Parthians in A.D. 224. When Muslim invaders entered Persia around A.D. 650, a small number of Zoroastrians fled to India. Zoroastrians were free to practice their religion in India and, though small in number, made important contributions to Indian society.

The sacred text of the Zoroastrians is the Zend-e-Avesta. One part of the Avesta consists of the Gathas, which are songs or hymns composed by Zoroaster. The Gathas are abstract sacred poetry, directed toward the worship of the one God, the understanding of righteousness and cosmic order, the promotion of social justice, and individual choice between good and evil. The Gathas have a general, even universal vision. The remaining parts of the Avestas were written perhaps centuries after the Gathas, and they deal with laws of ritual and practice and with the traditions of the faith.

One central theme in Zoroastrianism is the battle between good and evil in human life. In nature, there exist two opposing forces—*spenta-mainyu* (the good mind) and *angre-mainyu* (the wicked mind)—which are in continuous conflict. A person's soul is caught between them and is pulled by each side. To help the soul balance itself between these two forces, it is given a rudder in the form of a tail. This tail has three layers of feathers, which reminds one of the path of good thoughts, words, and deeds, by which the soul is able to make spiritual progress. Every soul has a free will to choose either to obey divine universal natural laws or to disobey them. If these divine laws are obeyed, the soul will be able to attain union with God. This remote event, toward which all creation moves, is called *frasho-kereti*.

In short, every individual has the twin spirits of good and evil in his or her mind, forming a dual nature. When individuals exercise the better mind, they create life and draw God and his divine powers toward themselves. When they choose to use the evil mind, they enter a state of spiritual death. Confusion descends upon them and they rush toward wrath and bloodlust. An individual's duty is to play his or her part in this great cosmic battle between good and evil, with each individual's life serving as the battlefield. Every decision made and every choice of thought, word, and deed, is weighed in the balance.

Upon physical death (which is seen as the temporary triumph of evil), the soul will be judged at the "Bridge of the Separator," where the soul, it is believed, will receive either its reward or punishment, based upon the balance of its thoughts, words, and deeds. If found righteous, the soul will ascend to the abode of joy and light. If wicked, it will descend into the depths of darkness and gloom. The latter state, however, is a temporary one, as there is no eternal damnation in Zoroastrianism. Thereafter, there is a promise of a series of saviors who will appear in the world to complete the triumph of good over evil. Evil will be rendered ineffective. There will then be a general last judgment of all the souls awaiting redemption, followed by the resurrection of the physical body, which will once again meet its spiritual counterpart, the soul. Time, as we know it, will cease to exist, and life, it is believed, will remain in a perfect state of joy.

Individual responsibility is another key theme in Zoroastrianism. Salvation for the individual depends on the sum of his or her thoughts, words, and deeds, and no intervention by any divine being may alter this. No costly material sacrifices or rituals will change the way the individual is judged. Making their own choices, individuals alone must bear responsibility for their souls. A life of active good toward others (people, animals, nature) is critical, giving individuals a simple creed to follow—good thoughts, good words, and good deeds.

Further, adherents are encouraged to lead a good and prosperous life, and monasticism, celibacy, fasting, and the mortification of the body are anathema to the Zoroastrian faith. Such practices are believed to weaken the individual and thereby lessen his or her power to fight evil. Zoroaster saw pessimism and despair as sins, in fact, as a submission to evil. In his teachings, the individual is encouraged to lead an active, industrious, honest, and above all, a happy and charitable life. Since this world created by God (Ahura Mazda) is essentially good, the individual should live well and enjoy its bountiful gifts, though always in moderation (as the states of excess and deficiency are deemed to be the workings of a hostile spirit).

It is perhaps difficult to appreciate the originality and courage of Zoroaster's thought today. Many prophets have appeared in later times with similar proclamations. But Zoroaster's religion was radically different from anything humankind had previously believed. Instead of a religion based on fear, Zoroaster's religion exalted the free and rational mind. Later religions—Judaism, Christianity, and Islam—all borrowed from Zoroaster's teachings. They all grew to attract millions of believers, while Zoroastrianism declined. Today, the Zoroastrian religion is probably familiar only to scholars of religion and to its adherents in South Asia, Iran, and the West.

In terms of customs, Zoroastrians have been incorrectly called fire worshipers. They do not worship fire, but fire has special significance. It is regarded as giving light, warmth, and energy and is therefore vital to life. Parsi places of worship (temples) have altars that contain fire and are called fire-temples. Eight principal fire-temples in India include four in Mumbai and four in the State of Gujarat (two in Surat, one in Udwada, one in Navsari). There are no caste divisions and no religious restrictions concerning food for Zoroastrians. A Zoroastrian child is formally initiated into the religion at a *navjote* or thread ceremony, which takes place between the ages of seven and nine. Zoroastrians continue to debate whether a child with one non-Zoroastrian parent can be initiated into the religion—orthodox members oppose this, while reformists favor the issue. Conversion is not practiced, and though some reformists suggest allowing children of non-Zoroastrian parents to be initiated into the Zoroastrian religion, this issue has not been seriously considered.

Zoroastrianism is one of the world's oldest religions, and the influence of its core tenets may be detected in all three Abrahamic religions. Though Zoroastrians (Parsis) have been prominent in Indian society, the number of Zoroastrians has been declining at the beginning of the twenty-first century.

Dinshaw Mistry

See also **Parsis**

BIBLIOGRAPHY

Boyce, Mary. *Zoroastrians: Their Religious Beliefs and Practices.* London: Routledge, 1979.

Boyce, Mary, and Frantz Grenet. *A Persian Stronghold of Zoroastrianism.* Oxford: Oxford University Press, 1977.

———. *A History of Zoroastrianism.* 3rd ed. Leiden and New York: E. J. Brill, 1996.

Federation of Zoroastrian Associations of North America. *Zoroastrians: Followers of an Ancient Faith in a Modern World.* Hinsdale, Ill.: Federation of Zoroastrian Associations of North America.

Hinnells, John. *Zoroastrianism and the Parsis.* London: Ward Lock Educational, 1981.

Mehr, Farhang. *The Zoroastrian Tradition: An Introduction to the Ancient Wisdom of Zarathushtra.* Costa Mesa, Calif.: Mazda, 2003.

Mistree, K. P. *Zoroastrianism: An Ethnic Perspective.* Mumbai: Zoroastrian Studies, 1982.

Nigosian, S. A. *The Zoroastrian Faith: Tradition and Modern Research.* Montreal: McGill-Queen's University Press, 1993.

Writer, Rashna. *Contemporary Zoroastrians: An Unconstructed Nation.* Lanham, Md.: University Press of America, 1993.

Zoroastrian Association of Greater New York. *The Good Life: An Introduction to the Religion of Zarathushtra.* New Rochelle, N.Y.: Zoroastrian Association of Greater New York, 1994.

primary sources

Table of Contents:

Selected Edicts of King Ashoka

Introduction

King Ashoka (r. 268–231 B.C.), Priyadarśī in the Edicts, the third of the Mauryan kings, left behind on rock and pillar edicts the oldest Indian written documents of any historical significance. In addition to their historical importance, the edicts also contain a number of personal statements believed to have been drafted by Ashoka himself. For this reason, more is known about the personality of Ashoka and his administration and policy than any other ancient Indian ruler. His story was a remarkable one. After a decade as a typical Indian king he had, after the Battle of Kalinga, a change of heart and embarked on a new policy. While not abjuring force entirely, he established a social policy marked by high ethical content. To enforce this policy he created a class of officials called *dharma-mahāmātra*, "Officers of Righteousness." It is believed that Ashoka became a Buddhist, although he supported other religious sects. The Pāli canon was codified at a great Buddhist council held at Ashoka's capital, Pataliputra, and he sent missionaries to Ceylon. It was during his reign that Buddhism ceased to be an Indian sect alone and began to be a universal religion. Rock Edict VIII tells of how Ashoka was converted to his new policy and how his life changed. Rock Edict VI explains how he was available to officials day and night, no matter what he was doing, as his highest calling was the welfare of his subjects.

Rock Edict VIII

SOURCE: *The Edicts of Aśoka.* Edited and translated by N. A. Nikam and Richard McKeon. Chicago: The University of Chicago Press, 1959, p. 37.

In the past, kings used to go on pleasure tours (*vihār-yātrās*). On these tours, they hunted and indulged in other pastimes.

King Priyadarśī, however, became, enlightened in wisdom (*sambuddha*) ten years after his coronation. Since then his tours have been moral-tours (*Dharma-yātrās*).

He visits priests and ascetics and makes gifts to them; he visits the aged and gives them money; he visits the people of rural areas, instructing them in Dharma and discussing it with them.

King Priyadarśī takes great pleasure in these tours, far more than could result from other tours.

Rock Edict VI

SOURCE: *The Edicts of Aśoka.* Edited and translated by N. A. Nikam and Richard McKeon. Chicago: The University of Chicago Press, 1959, pp. 37–38.

King Priyadarśī says:

In the past, state business was not transacted or reports made at all hours of the day. I have therefore made arrangements that officials may have access to me and may report on the affairs of my people at all times and in all places—when I am eating, when I am in the harem or my inner apartments, when I am tending to the cattle, when I am walking or engaged in religious exercises. I now attend to the affairs of the people in all places. And when a donation or a proclamation that I have ordered verbally, or an urgent matter which I have delegated to my high officials, causes a debate or dispute in the Council, this must be reported to me immediately, at all hours and in all places. These are my orders.

I am never completely satisfied with my work or my vigilance in carrying out public affairs. I consider the promotion of the people's welfare my highest duty, and its exercise is grounded in work and constant application.

No task is more important to me than promoting the well-being of all the people. Such work as I accomplish contributes to discharging the debt I owe to all living creatures to make them happy in this world and to help them attain heaven in the next.

I have ordered this edict on Dharma inscribed in order that it may endure forever and in order that my sons, grandsons, and great-grandsons may follow it for the welfare of all. This is difficult to do, however, without devoted and sustained work.

Selections from the Autobiography of Mahatma M. K. Gandhi

Introduction

Mohandas Karamchand Gandhi was born on October 2, 1869, at Porbandar in what is now the state of Gujarat, India. He was married to Kasturbai and they had four sons. From 1888 until 1891 he studied law in England and was called to the bar but traveled to South Africa in May 1893 to practice law. Subsequently, he developed his strategy of nonviolent noncooperation, *Satyagraha* (truth force), to fight government policies. He returned to India in January 1915 and in 1917 he started a *Satyagraha* movement against the indigo growers of Champaran in Bihar and then against the mill owners of Ahmedabad. In 1919 he called for a national *hartal* (strike) against the British and supported the Khilafat Movement. By 1920 he had become the most important leader of the Indian National Congress. His *An Autobiography: The Story of My Experiments with Truth,* written in the 1920s, is one of the enduring records of a political leader. Gandhi was not only a political leader, he was also a social reformer.

One of Gandhi's concerns was the institution of child marriage, which he opposed. This was courageous as he had been married at the age of thirteen. The passage "Child Marriage" recounts Gandhi's marriage to

Kasturbai of which, in retrospect, Gandhi felt ashamed. He relished the marriage when it occurred but in the fullness of time came to regard it as a shameful event and he later became highly critical of his father for his childhood marriage. He criticized the extravagent way Hindus were married but, above all, he was tormented by his carnal lust in his early years. This was especially so when Gandhi left his sick father to engage in sex with his pregnant wife. During that time his father died. His newborn child also died and the death of his father and the death of his child became linked in his mind. In "Playing the Husband" he recounts his early relationship with his wife and how he had to establish his authority as a husband. Gandhi believed he was saved from the sin of carnal pleasure by his separation from his wife due to his sojourn to England and the Indian custom of the wife spending time with her family.

For Gandhi the most important aspect of his *Satyagraha* strategy was *ahimsa*, or nonviolence. When he began the *Satyagraha* struggle in Kheda district, Gujarat, on 22 March 1918 he expected the campaign for nonpayment of taxes to be conducted in a disciplined manner on the basis of his credo of love and justice. He was not satisfied with the way the campaign was carried out by the peasants, and accordingly he realized he had made a "Himalayan miscalculation." He decided, therefore, to raise a corps of disciplined *satyagrahi* who would spearhead any future civil disobedience movement strictly on the basis of discipline and nonviolence.

The Indian National Congress, which had been founded in 1885, was led by Western-trained lawyers who took a constitutional path in their fight for independence. It was remarkable that Gandhi became the recognized leader of the Congress in such a short period of time and that he changed the ethos of the organization and the whole independence movement to reflect his own nativist mores. In "Congress Initiation" he relates how he was responsible for the creation of a new constitution for the party and in "The Birth of Khadi" he recounts the way in which he and the members of his ashram learned how to spin *khadi* and how an untouchable, Gangabehn Majumdar, searched for a spinning wheel for him. One was located in Vijapur in Baroda State as recounted in "Found at Last." In "An Instructive Dialogue" Gandhi presents the mill owners' viewpoint about *khadi* through a reported conversation with Umar Sobani, a mill owner. Gandhi explained his rationale for the production of *khadi* and how it would provide work for women.

In "Its Rising Tide" Gandhi reports his success in establishing noncooperation and nonviolence as the official policies of a number of organizations, such as regional Congress parties and the Khilafat movement, where he had to discuss whether Islam forbade its adherents from following nonviolence. At the 1920 special session of the Congress at Calcutta the Congress supported noncooperation but also adopted a controversial

resolution calling for independence, *Swaraj*, a resolution that was adopted "At Nagpur" where Gandhi also discusses Hindu–Muslim unity, untouchability, and *khadi*.

In "Farewell" he recounts his relationship with the Congress and how all his major activities were conducted through the Congress. He reaffirms his belief that there is no other God than Truth and that Truth is *ahimsa*. It reveals how idealistic Gandhi was and how committed he had become to his ideals of purity of heart. For him this entailed his belief in "Ahimsa in mind, word, and deed."

Child Marriage

SOURCE: Gandhi, Mohandas K. *An Autobiography: The Story of My Experiments with Truth*. Translated by Mahadev Desai. Boston: Beacon Press, 1957, pp. 8–11.

Much as I wish that I had not to write this chapter, I know that I shall have to swallow many such bitter draughts in the course of this narrative. And I cannot do otherwise, if I claim to be a worshipper of Truth. It is my painful duty to have to record here my marriage at the age of thirteen. As I see the youngsters of the same age about me who are under my care, and think of my own marriage, I am inclined to pity myself and to congratulate them on having escaped my lot. I can see no moral argument in support of such a preposterously early marriage.

Let the reader make no mistake. I was married, not betrothed. For in Kathiawad there are two distinct rites,— betrothal and marriage. Betrothal is a preliminary promise on the part of the parents of the boy and the girl to join them in marriage, and it is not inviolable. The death of the boy entails no widowhood on the girl. It is an agreement purely between the parents, and the children have no concern with it. Often they are not even informed of it. It appears that I was betrothed thrice, though without my knowledge. I was told that two girls chosen for me had died in turn, and therefore I infer that I was betrothed three times. I have a faint recollection, however, that the third betrothal took place in my seventh year. But I do not recollect having been informed about it. In the present chapter I am talking about my marriage, of which I have the clearest recollection.

It will be remembered that we were three brothers. The first was already married. The elders decided to marry my second brother, who was two or three years my senior, a cousin, possibly a year older, and me, all at the same time. In doing so there was no thought of our welfare, much less our wishes. It was purely a question of their own convenience and economy.

Marriage among Hindus is no simple matter. The parents of the bride and the bridegroom often bring themselves to ruin over it. They waste their substance, they waste their time. Months are taken up over the preparations—in making clothes and ornaments and in preparing budgets for dinners. Each tries to outdo the other in the number and variety of courses to be prepared. Women, whether they have a voice or no, sing themselves hoarse, even get ill, and disturb the peace of their neighbours. These in their turn quietly put up with all the turmoil and bustle, all the dirt and filth, representing the remains of the feasts, because they know that a time will come when they also will be behaving in the same manner.

It would be better, thought my elders, to have all this bother over at one and the same time. Less expense and greater *eclat*. For money could be freely spent if it had only to be spent once instead of thrice. My father and my uncle were both old, and we were the last children they had to marry. It is likely that they wanted to have the last best time of their lives. In view of all these considerations, a triple wedding was decided upon, and as I have said before, months were taken up in preparation for it.

It was only through these preparations that we got warning of the coming event. I do not think it meant to me anything more than the prospect of good clothes to wear, drum beating, marriage processions, rich dinners and a strange girl to play with. The carnal desire came later. I propose to draw the curtain over my shame, except for a few details worth recording. To these I shall come later. But even they have little to do with the central idea I have kept before me in writing this story.

So my brother and I were both taken to Porbandar from Rajkot. These are some amusing details of the preliminaries to the final drama—*e.g.* smearing our bodies all over with turmeric paste—but I must omit them.

My father was a Diwan, but nevertheless a servant, and all the more so because he was in favour with the Thakore Saheb. The latter would not let him go until the last moment. And when he did so, he ordered for my father special stage coaches, reducing the journey by two days. But the fates had willed otherwise. Porbandar is 120 miles from Rajkot,—a cart journey of five days. My father did the distance in three, but the coach toppled over in the third stage, and he sustained severe injuries. He arrived bandaged all over. Both his and our interest in the coming event was half destroyed, but the ceremony had to be gone through. For how could the marriage dates be changed? However, I forgot my grief over my father's injuries in childish amusement of the wedding.

I was devoted to my parents. But no less was I devoted to the passions that flesh is heir to. I had yet to learn that all happiness and pleasure should be sacrificed in devoted service to my parents. And yet, as though by way of punishment for my desire for pleasures, an incident happened, which has ever since rankled in my mind and which I will relate later. Nishkulanand sings: 'Renunciation of objects, without the renunciations of desire, is short-lived, however hard you may try.' Whenever I sing this song or hear it sung, this bitter untoward incident rushes to my memory and fills me with shame.

My father put on a brave face in spite of his injuries, and took full part in the wedding. As I think of it, I can even today call before my mind's eye the places where he sat as he went through the different details of the ceremony. Little did I dream then that one day I should severely criticize my father for having married me as a child. Everything on that day seemed to me right and proper and pleasing. There was also my own eagerness to get married. And as everything that my father did then struck me as beyond reproach, the recollection of those things is fresh in my memory. I can picture to myself, even today, how we sat on our wedding dais, how we performed the *Saptapadi*, how we, the newly wedded husband and wife, put the sweet *Kansar* into each other's mouth, and how we began to live together. And oh! that first night. Two innocent children all unwittingly hurled themselves into the ocean of life. My brother's wife had thoroughly coached me about my behaviour on the first night. I do not know who had coached my wife. I have never asked her about it, nor am I inclined to do so now. The reader may be sure that we were too nervous to face each other. We were certainly too shy. How was I to talk to her, and what was I to say? The coaching could not carry me far. But no coaching is really necessary in such matters. The impressions of the former birth are potent enough to make all coaching superfluous. We gradually began to know each other, and to speak freely together. We were the same age. But I took no time in assuming the authority of a husband.

Playing the Husband

SOURCE: Gandhi, Mohandas K. *An Autobiography: The Story of My Experiments with Truth*. Translated by Mahadev Desai. Boston: Beacon Press, 1957, pp. 11–14.

About the time of my marriage, little pamphlets costing a pice, or a pie (I now forget how much), used to be issued, in which conjugal love, thrift, child marriages, and other such subjects were discussed. Whenever I came across any of these, I used to go through them cover to cover, and it was a habit with me to forget what I did not like, and to carry out in practice whatever I liked. Lifelong faithfulness to the wife, inculcated in these booklets as the duty of the husband, remained permanently imprinted on my heart. Furthermore, the passion for truth was innate in me, and to be false to her was therefore out of the question. And then there was very little chance of my being faithless at that tender age.

But the lesson of faithfulness had also an untoward effect. 'If I should be pledged to be faithful to my wife, she also should be pledged to be faithful to me,' I said to myself. The thought made me a jealous husband. Her duty was easily converted into my right to exact faithfulness from her, and if it had to be exacted, I should be watchfully tenacious of the right. I had absolutely no reason to suspect my wife's fidelity, but jealousy does not wait for reasons. I must needs be for ever on the look-out regarding her movements, and therefore she could not go anywhere without my permission. This sowed the seeds of a bitter quarrel between us. The restraint was virtually a sort of imprisonment. And Kasturbai was not the girl to brook any such thing. She made it a point to go out whenever and wherever she liked. More restraint on my part resulted in more liberty being taken by her, and in my getting more and more cross. Refusal to speak to one another thus became the order of the day with us, married children. I think it was quite innocent of Kasturbai to have taken those liberties with my restrictions.

How could a guileless girl brook any restraint on going to the temple or on going on visits to friends? If I had the right to impose restrictions on her, had not she also a similar right? All this is clear to me today. But at that time I had to make good my authority as a husband!

Let not the reader think, however, that ours was a life of unrelieved bitterness. For my severities were all based on love. I wanted to *make* my wife an ideal wife. My ambition was to *make* her live a pure life, learn what I learnt, and identify her life and thought with mine.

I do not know whether Kasturbai had any such ambition. She was illiterate. By nature she was simple, independent, persevering, and with me least, reticent. She was not impatient of her ignorance and I do not recollect my studies having ever spurred her to go in for a similar adventure. I fancy, therefore, that my ambition was all one-sided. My passion was entirely centred on one woman, and I wanted it to be reciprocated. But even if there were no reciprocity, it could not be all unrelieved misery because there was active love on one side at least.

I must say I was passionately fond of her. Even at school I used to think of her and the thought of nightfall and our subsequent meeting was ever haunting me. Separation was unbearable. I used to keep her awake till late in the night with my idle talk. If with this devouring passion there had not been in me a burning attachment to duty, I should either have fallen a prey to disease and premature death, or have sunk into a burdensome existence. But the appointed tasks had to be gone through every morning, and lying to anyone was out of the question. It was this last thing that saved me from many a pitfall.

I have already said that Kasturbai was illiterate. I was very anxious to teach her, but lustful love left me no time. For one thing the teaching had to be done against her will, and that too at night. I dared not meet her in the presence of the elders, much less talk to her. Kathiawad had then, and to a certain extent has even today, its own peculiar useless and barbarous *Purdah*. Circumstances were thus unfavourable. I must therefore confess that most of my efforts to instruct Kasturbai in our youth were unsuccessful. And when I woke from the sleep of lust, I had already launched forth into public life, which did not leave me much spare time. I failed likewise to instruct her through private tutors. As a result Kasturbai can now with difficulty write simple letters and understand simple Gujarati. I am sure that, had my love for her been absolutely untainted with lust, she would be a learned lady today; for I could then have conquered her dislike for studies. I know that nothing is impossible for pure love.

I have mentioned one circumstance that more or less saved me from the disasters of lustful love. There is another worth noting. Numerous examples have convinced me that God ultimately saves him whose motive is pure. Along with the cruel custom of child marriages, Hindu society has another custom which to a certain extent diminishes the evils of the former. Parents do not allow young couples to stay together long. The child-wife spends more than half her time at her father's place. Such was the case with us. That is to say, during the first five years of our married life (from the age of 13 to 18), we could not have lived together longer than an aggregate period of three years. We would hardly have spent six months together, when there would be a call to my wife from her parents. Such calls were very unwelcome in those days, but they saved us both. At the age of eighteen I went to England, and this meant a long and healthy spell of separation. Even after my return from England we hardly stayed together longer than six months. For I had to run up and down between Rajkot and Bombay. Then came the call from South Africa, and that found me already fairly free from the carnal appetite.

'A Himalayan Miscalculation'

SOURCE: Gandhi, Mohandas K. *An Autobiography: The Story of My Experiments with Truth.* Translated by Mahadev Desai. Boston: Beacon Press, 1957, pp. 469–471.

Almost immediately after the Ahmedabad meeting I went to Nadiad. It was here that I first used the expression 'Himalayan miscalculation' which obtained such a wide currency afterwards. Even at Ahmedabad I had begun to have a dim perception of my mistake. But when I reached Nadiad and saw the actual state of things there and heard reports about a large number of people from Kheda district having been arrested, it suddenly dawned upon me that I had committed a grave error in calling upon the people in the Kheda district and elsewhere to launch upon civil disobedience prematurely, as it now seemed to me. I was addressing a public meeting. My confession brought down upon me no small amount of ridicule. But I have never regretted having made that confession. For I have always held that it is only when one sees one's own mistakes with a convex lens, and does just the reverse in the case of others, that one is able to arrive at a just relative estimate of the two. I further believe that a scrupulous and conscientious observance of this rule is necessary for one who wants to be a Satyagrahi.

Let us now see what that Himalayan miscalculation was. Before one can be fit for the practice of civil disobedience one must have rendered a willing and respectful obedience to the state laws. For the most part we obey such laws out of fear of the penalty for their breach, and this holds good particularly in respect of such laws as do not involve a moral principle. For instance, an honest, respectable man will not suddenly take to stealing, whether there is a law against stealing or not, but this very man will not feel any remorse for failure to observe the rule about carrying head-lights on bicycles after dark. Indeed it is doubtful whether he would even accept advice kindly about being more careful in this respect. But he would observe any obligatory rule of this kind, if only to escape the inconvenience of facing a prosecution for a breach of the rule. Such compliance is not, however, the willing and spontaneous obedience that is required of a Satyagrahi. A Satyagrahi obeys the laws of society intelligently and of his own free will, because he considers it to be his sacred duty to do so. It is only when a person has thus obeyed the laws of society scrupulously that he is in a position to judge as to which particular rules are good and just and which unjust and iniquitous. Only then does the right accrue to him of the civil disobedience of certain laws in well-defined circumstances. My error lay in my failure to observe this necessary limitation. I had called on the people to launch upon civil disobedience before they had thus qualified themselves for it, and this mistake seemed to me of Himalayan magnitude. As soon as I entered the Kheda district, all the old recollections of the Kheda Satyagraha struggle came back to me, and I wondered how I could have failed to perceive what was so obvious. I realized that before a people could be fit for offering civil disobedience, they should thoroughly understand its deeper implications. That being so, before restarting civil disobedience on a mass scale, it would be necessary to create a band of well-tried, pure-hearted volunteers who thoroughly understood the strict conditions of Satyagraha. They could explain these to the people, and by sleepless vigilance keep them on the right path.

With these thoughts filling my mind I reached Bombay, raised a corps of Satyagrahi volunteers through the Satyagraha Sabha there, and with their help commenced the work of educating the people with regard to the meaning and inner significance of Satyagraha. This was principally done by issuing leaflets of an educative character bearing on the subject.

But whilst this work was going on, I could see that it was a difficult task to interest the people in the peaceful side of Satyagraha. The volunteers too failed to enlist themselves in large numbers. Nor did all those who actually enlisted take anything like a regular systematic training, and as the days passed by, the number of fresh recruits began gradually to dwindle instead of to grow. I realized that the progress of the training in civil disobedience was not going to be as rapid as I had at first expected.

Congress Initiation

SOURCE: Gandhi, Mohandas K. *An Autobiography: The Story of My Experiments with Truth*. Translated by Mahadev Desai. Boston: Beacon Press, 1957, pp. 486–488.

I must regard my participation in Congress proceedings at Amritsar as my real entrance into the Congress politics. My attendance at the previous Congresses was nothing more perhaps than an annual renewal of allegiance to the Congress. I never felt on these occasions that I had any other work cut out for me except that of a mere private, nor did I desire more.

My experience of Amritsar had shown that there were one or two things for which perhaps I had some aptitude and which could be useful to the Congress. I could already see that the late Lokamanya, the Deshabandhu, Pandit Motilalji and other leaders were pleased with my work in connection with the Punjab inquiry. They used to invite me to their informal gatherings where, as I found, resolutions for the Subjects Committee were conceived. At these gatherings only those persons were invited who enjoyed the special confidence of the leaders and whose services were needed by them. Interlopers also sometimes found their way to these meetings.

There were, for the coming year, two things which interested me, as I had some aptitude for them. One of these was the memorial of the Jalianwala Bagh Massacre. The Congress had passed a resolution for it amid great enthusiasm. A fund of about five lakhs had to be collected for it. I was appointed one of the trustees. Pandit Malaviyaji enjoyed the reputation of being the prince among beggars for the public cause. But I knew that I was not far behind him in that respect. It was whilst I was in South Africa that I discovered my capacity in this direction. I had not the unrivalled magic of Malaviyaji for commanding princely donations from the potentates of India. But I knew that there was no question of approaching the Rajas and Maharajas for donations for the Jalianwala Bagh memorial. The main responsibility for the collection thus fell, as I had expected, on my shoulders. The generous citizens of Bombay subscribed most liberally, and the memorial trust has at present a handsome credit balance in the bank. But the problem that faces the country today is what kind of memorial to erect on the ground, to sanctify which, Hindus, Musalmans and Sikhs mingled their blood. The three communities, instead of being bound in a bond of amity and love, are, to all appearance, at war with one another, and the nation is at a loss as to how to utilize the memorial fund.

My other aptitude which the Congress could utilize was as a draftsman. The Congress leaders had found that I had a faculty for condensed expression, which I had acquired by long practice. The then existing constitution of the Congress was Gokhale's legacy. He had framed a few rules which served as a basis for running the Congress machinery. The interesting history of the framing of these rules I had learnt from Gokhales' own lips. But everybody had now come to feel that these rules were no longer adequate for the ever increasing business of the Congress. The question had been coming up year after year. The Congress at that time had practically no machinery functioning during the interval between session and session, or for dealing with fresh contingencies that might arise in the course of the year. The existing rules provided for three secretaries, but as a matter of fact only one of them was a functioning secretary, and even he was not a whole-timer. How was he, single-handed, to run the Congress office, to think of the future, or to discharge during the current year the obligations contracted by the Congress in the past? During that year, therefore, everybody felt that this question would assume all the more importance. The Congress was too unwieldy a body for the discussion of public affairs. There was no limit set to the number of delegates in the Congress or to the number of delegates that each province could return. Some improvement upon the existing chaotic condition was thus felt by everybody to be an imperative necessity. I undertook the responsibility of framing a constitution on one condition. I saw that there were two leaders, *viz.*, the Lokamanya and the Deshabandhu who had the greatest hold on the public. I requested that they, as the representatives of people, should be associated with me on the Committee for framing the constitution. But since it was obvious that they would not have the time personally to participate in the constitution-making work, I suggested that two persons enjoying their confidence should be appointed along with me on the Constitution Committee, and that the number of its personnel should be limited to three. This suggestion was accepted by the late Lokamanya and the late

Deshabandhu, who suggested the names of Sjts. Kelkar and I. B. Sen respectively as their proxies. The Constitution Committee could not even once come together, but we were able to consult with each other by correspondence, and in the end presented a unanimous report. I regard this constitution with a certain measure of pride. I hold that, if we could fully work out this constitution, the mere fact of working it out would bring us Swaraj. With the assumption of this responsibility I may be said to have made my real entrance into the Congress politics.

The Birth of Khadi

SOURCE: Gandhi, Mohandas K. *An Autobiography: The Story of My Experiments with Truth.* Translated by Mahadev Desai. Boston: Beacon Press, 1957, pp. 489–491.

I do not remember to have seen a handloom or a spinning wheel when in 1908 I described it in *Hind Swaraj* as the panacea for the growing pauperism of India. In that book I took it as understood that anything that helped India to get rid of the grinding poverty of her masses would in the same process also established Swaraj. Even in 1915, when I returned to India from South Africa, I had not actually seen a spinning wheel. When the Satyagraha Ashram was founded at Sabarmati, we introduced a few handlooms there. But no sooner had we done this than we found ourselves up against a difficulty. All of us belonged either to the liberal professions or to business; not one of us was an artisan. We needed a weaving expert to teach us to weave before we could work the looms. One was at last procured from Palanpur, but he did not communicate to us the whole of his art. But Maganlal Gandhi was not to be easily baffled. Possessed of a natural talent for mechanics, he was able fully to master the art before long, and one after another several new weavers were trained up in the Ashram.

The object that we set before ourselves was to be able to clothe ourselves entirely in cloth manufactured by our own hands. We therefore forthwith discarded the use of mill-woven cloth, and all the members of the Ashram resolved to wear hand-woven cloth made from Indian yard only. The adoption of this practice brought us a world of experience. It enabled us to know, from direct contact, the conditions of life among the weavers, the extent of their production, the handicaps in the way of their obtaining their yarn supply, the way in which they were being made victims of fraud, and, lastly, their ever growing indebtedness. We were not in a position immediately to manufacture all the cloth for our needs. The alternative therefore was to get our cloth supply from handloom weavers. But ready-made cloth from Indian mill-yarn was not easily obtainable either from the cloth-dealers or from the weavers themselves. All the fine cloth woven by the weavers was from foreign yarn, since Indian mills did not spin fine counts. Even today the outturn of higher counts by Indian mills is very limited, whilst highest counts they cannot spin at all. It was after the greatest effort that we were at last able to find some weavers who condescended to weave Swadeshi yarn for us, and only on condition that the Ashram would take up all the cloth that they might produce. By thus adopting cloth woven from

mill-yarn as our wear, and propagating it among our friends, we made ourselves voluntary agents of the Indian spinning mills. This in its turn brought us into contact with the mills, and enabled us to know something about their management and their handicaps. We saw that the aim of the mills was more and more to weave the yarn spun by them; their cooperation with the handloom weaver was not willing, but unavoidable and temporary. We became impatient to be able to spin our own yarn. It was clear that, until we could do this ourselves, dependence on the mills would remain. We did not feel that we could render any service to the country by continuing as agents of Indian spinning mills.

No end of difficulties again faced us. We could get neither spinning wheel nor a spinner to teach us how to spin. We were employing some wheels for filling pearns and bobbins for weaving in the Ashram. But we had no idea that these could be used as spinning wheels. Once Kalidas Jhaveri discovered a woman who, he said, would demonstrate to us how spinning was done. We sent to her a member of the Ashram who was known for his great versatility in learning new things. But even he returned without wresting the secret of the art.

So the time passed on and my impatience grew with the time. I plied every chance visitor to the Ashram who was likely to possess some information about handspinning with questions about the art. But the art being confined to women and having been all but exterminated, if there was some stray spinner still surviving in some obscure corner, only a member of that sex was likely to find out her whereabouts.

In the year 1917 I was taken by my Gujarati friends to preside at the Broach Educational Conference. It was here that I discovered that remarkable lady Gangabehn Majmundar. She was a widow, but her enterprising spirit knew no bounds. Her education, in the accepted sense of the term, was not much. But in courage and commonsense she easily surpassed the general run of our educated women. She had already got rid of the curse of untouchability, and fearlessly moved among and served the suppressed classes. She had means of her own, and her needs were few. She had a well seasoned constitution, and went about everywhere without an escort. She felt quite at home on horseback. I came to know her more intimately at the Godhra Conference. To her I poured out my grief about the charkha, and she lightened my burden by a promise to prosecute an earnest and incessant search for the spinning wheel.

Found at Last!

SOURCE: Gandhi, Mohandas K. *An Autobiography: The Story of My Experiments with Truth.* Translated by Mahadev Desai. Boston: Beacon Press, 1957, pp. 491–494.

At last, after no end of wandering in Gujarat, Gangabehn found the spinning wheel in Vijapur in the Baroda State. Quite a number of people there had spinning wheels in their homes, but had long since consigned them to the lofts as useless lumber. They expressed to Gangabehn their readiness to resume spinning, if someone promised to provide them with a regular supply of slivers, and to buy the yarn spun by them. Gangabehn communicated the joyful news to me. The providing of slivers was found to be a difficult task. On my mentioning the thing to the late Umar Sobani, he solved the difficulty by immediately undertaking to send a sufficient supply of slivers from his mill. I sent to Gangabehn the slivers received from Umar Sobani, and soon yarn began to pour in at such a rate that it became quite a problem how to cope with it.

Mr. Umar Sobani's generosity was great, but still one could not go on taking advantage of it for ever. I felt ill at ease, continuously receiving slivers from him. Moreover, it seemed to me to be fundamentally wrong to use mill-slivers. If one could use mill-slivers, why not use mill-yarn as well? Surely no mills supplied slivers to the ancients? How did they make their slivers then? With these thoughts in my mind I suggested to Gangabehn to find carders who could supply slivers. She confidently undertook the task. She engaged a carder who was prepared to card cotton. He demanded thirty-five rupees, if not much more, per month. I considered no price too high at the time. She trained a few youngsters to make slivers out of the carded cotton. I begged for cotton in Bombay. Sjt. Yashvantprasad Desai at once responded. Gangabehn's enterprise thus prospered beyond expectations. She found out weavers to weave the yarn that was spun in Vijapur, and soon Vijapur Khadi gained a name for itself.

While these developments were taking place in Vijapur, the spinning wheel gained a rapid footing in the Ashram. Maganlal Gandhi, by bringing to bear all his splendid mechanical talent on the wheel, made many improvements in it, and wheels and their accessories began to be manufactured at the Ashram. The first piece of Khadi manufactured in the Ashram cost 17 annas per yard. I did not hesitate to commend this very coarse Khadi at that rate to friends, who willingly paid the price.

I was laid up in bed at Bombay. But I was fit enough to make searches for the wheel there. At last I chanced upon two spinners. They charged one rupee for a seer of yarn, i.e., 28 tolas or nearly three quarters of a pound. I was then ignorant of the economics of Khadi. I considered no price too high for securing handspun yarn. On comparing the rates paid by me with those paid in Vijapur I found that I was being cheated. The spinners refused to agree to any reduction in their rates. So I had to dispense with their service. But they served their purpose. They taught spinning to Shrimatis Avantikabai, Ramibai Kamdar, the widowed mother of Sjt. Shankarlal Banker and Shrimati Vasumatibehn. The wheel began merrily to hum in my room, and I may say without exaggeration that its hum had no small share in restoring me to health. I am prepared to admit that its effect was more psychological than physical. But then it only shows how powerfully the physical in man reacts to the psychological. I too set my hand to the wheel, but did not do much with it at the time.

In Bombay, again, the same old problem of obtaining a supply of hand-made slivers presented itself. A carder twanging his bow used to pass daily by Sjt. Revashankar's residence. I sent for him and learnt that he carded cotton for stuffing mattresses. He agreed to card cotton for slivers, but demanded a stiff price for it, which, however, I paid. The yarn

thus prepared I disposed of to some Vaishnava friends for making from it the garlands for the *pavitra ekadashi*. Sjt. Shivji started a spinning class in Bombay. All these experiments involved considerable expenditure. But it was willingly defrayed by patriotic friends, lovers of the motherland, who had faith in Khadi. The money thus spent, in my humble opinion, was not wasted. It brought us a rich store of experience, and revealed to us the possibilities of the spinning wheel.

I now grew impatient for the exclusive adoption of Khadi for my dress. My *dhoti* was still of Indian mill cloth. The coarse Khadi manufactured in the Ashram and at Vijapur was only 30 inches in width. I gave notice to Gangabehn that, unless she provided me with a Khadi *dhoti* of 45 inches width within a month, I would do with coarse, short Khadi *dhoti*. The ultimatum came upon her as a shock. But she proved equal to the demand made upon her. Well within the month she sent me a pair of Khadi *dhotis* of 45 inches width, and thus relieved me from what would then have been a difficult situation for me.

At about the same time Sjt. Lakshmidas brought Sjt. Ramji, the weaver, with his wife Gangabehn from Lathi to the Ashram and got Khadi *dhotis* woven at the Ashram. The part played by this couple in the spread of Khadi was by no means insignificant. They initiated a host of persons in Gujarat and also outside into the art of weaving handspun yarn. To see Gangabehn at her loom is a stirring sight. When this unlettered but self-possessed sister plies at her loom, she becomes so lost in it that it is difficult to distract her attention, and much more difficult to draw her eyes off her beloved loom.

An Instructive Dialogue

SOURCE: Gandhi, Mohandas K. *An Autobiography: The Story of My Experiments with Truth.* Translated by Mahadev Desai. Boston: Beacon Press, 1957, pp. 494–496.

From its very inception the Khadi movement, Swadeshi movement as it was then called, evoked much criticism from the mill-owners. The late Umar Sobani, a capable mill-owner himself, not only gave me the benefit of his own knowledge and experience, but kept me in touch with the opinion of the other mill-owners as well. The argument advanced by one of these deeply impressed him. He pressed me to meet him. I agreed. Mr. Sobani arranged the interview. The mill-owner opened the conversation.

'You know that there has been Swadeshi agitation before now?'

'Yes, I do,' I replied.

'You are also aware that in the days of the Partition we, the mill-owners, fully exploited the Swadeshi movement. When it was at its height, we raised the prices of cloth, and did even worse things.'

'Yes, I have heard something about it, and it has grieved me.'

'I can understand your grief, but I can see no ground for it. We are not conducting our business out of philanthropy. We do it for profit, we have got to satisfy the shareholders.

The price of an article is governed by the demand for it. Who can check the law of demand and supply? The Bengalis should have known that their agitation was bound to send up the price of Swadeshi cloth by stimulating the demand for it.'

I interrupted: 'The Bengalis like me were trustful in their nature. They believed, in the fullness of their faith, that the mill-owners would not be so utterly selfish and unpatriotic as to betray their country in the hour of its need, and even to go the length, as they did, of fraudulently passing off foreign cloth as Swadeshi.'

'I knew your believing nature,' he rejoined; 'that is why I put you to the trouble of coming to me, so that I might warn you against falling into the same error as these simple-hearted Bengalis.'

With these words the mill-owner beckoned to his clerk who was standing by to produce samples of the stuff that was being manufactured in his mill. Pointing to it he said 'Look at this stuff. This is the latest variety turned out by our mill. It is meeting with a widespread demand. We manufacture it from the waste. Naturally, therefore, it is cheap. We send it as far North as the valleys of the Himalayas. We have agencies all over the country, even in places where your voice or your agents can never reach. You can thus see that we do not stand in need of more agents. Besides, you ought to know that India's production of cloth falls far short of its requirements. The question of Swadeshi, therefore, largely resolves itself into one of production. The moment we can increase our production sufficiently, and improve its quality to the necessary extent, the import of foreign cloth will automatically cease. My advice to you, therefore, is not to carry on your agitation on its present lines, but to turn your attention to the erection of fresh mills. What we need is not propaganda to inflate demand for our goods, but greater production.'

'Then, surely, you will bless my effort, if I am already engaged in that very thing,' I asked.

'How can that be?' he exclaimed, a bit puzzled, 'but may be, you are thinking of promoting the establishment of new mills, in which case you certainly deserve to be congratulated.'

'I am not doing exactly that,' I explained, 'but I am engaged in the revival of the spinning wheel.'

'What is that?' he asked, feeling still more at sea. I told him all about the spinning wheel, and the story of my long quest after it, and added, 'I am entirely of your opinion; it is no use my becoming virtually an agent for the mills. That would do more harm than good to the country. Our mills will not be in want of custom for a long time to come. My work should be, and therefore is, to organize the production of handspun cloth, and to find means for the disposal of the Khadi thus produced. I am, therefore, concentrating my attention on the production of Khadi. I swear by this form of Swadeshi, because through it I can provide work to the semi-starved, semi-employed women of India. My idea is to get these women to spin yarn, and to clothe the people of India with Khadi woven out of it. I do not know how far this movement is going to succeed, at present it is only in the incipient stage. But I have full faith in it. At any rate it can do no harm. On the contrary to the extent that it can add to

the cloth production of the country, be it ever so small, it will represent so much solid gain. You will thus perceive that my movement is free from the evils mentioned by you.'

He replied, 'If you have additional production in view in organizing your movement, I have nothing to say against it. Whether the spinning wheel can make headway in this age of power machinery is another question. But I for one wish you every success.'

Its Rising Tide

SOURCE: Gandhi, Mohandas K. *An Autobiography: The Story of My Experiments with Truth.* Translated by Mahadev Desai. Boston: Beacon Press, 1957, pp. 497–500.

I must not devote any more chapters here to a description of the further progress of Khadi. It would be outside the scope of these chapters to give a history of my various activities after they came before the public eye, and I must not attempt it, if only because to do so would require a treatise on the subject. My object in writing these chapters is simply to describe how certain things, as it were spontaneously, presented themselves to me in the course of my experiments with truth.

To resume, then, the story of the non-co-operation movement. Whilst the powerful Khilafat agitation set up by the Ali Brothers was in full progress, I had long discussions on the subject with the late Maulana Abdul Bari and the other *Ulema*, especially, with regard to the extent to which a Musalman could observe the rule of non-violence. In the end they all agreed that Islam did not forbid its followers from following non-violence as a policy, and further, that, while they were pledged to that policy, they were bound faithfully to carry it out. At last the non-co-operation resolution was moved in the Khilafat conference, and carried after prolonged deliberations. I have a vivid recollection how once at Allahabad a committee sat all night deliberating upon the subject. In the beginning the late Hakim Saheb was skeptical as to the practicability of non-violent non-co-operation. But after his skepticism was overcome he threw himself into it heart and soul, and his help proved invaluable to the movement.

Next, the non-co-operation resolution was moved by me at the Gujarat political conference that was held shortly afterwards. The preliminary contention raised by the opposition was that it was not competent to a provincial conference to adopt a resolution in advance of the Congress. As against this, I suggested that the restriction could apply only to a backward movement; but as for going forward, the subordinate organizations were not only fully competent, but were in duty bound to do so, if they had in them the necessary grit and confidence. No permission, I argued, was needed to try to enhance the prestige of the parent institution, provided one did it at one's own risk. The proposition was then discussed on its merits, the debate being marked by its keenness no less than the atmosphere of 'sweet reasonableness' in which it was conducted. On the ballot being taken the resolution was declared carried by an overwhelming majority. The successful passage of the resolution was due not a little to the personality of Sjt. Vallabhbhai and

Abbas Tyabji. The latter was the president, and his leanings were all in favour of the non-co-operation resolution.

The All-India Congress Committee resolved to hold a special session of the Congress in September 1920 at Calcutta to deliberate on this question. Preparations were made for it on a large scale. Lala Lajpat Rai was elected President. Congress and Khilafat specials were run to Calcutta from Bombay. At Calcutta there was a mammoth gathering of delegates and visitors.

At the request of Maulana Shaukat Ali I prepared a draft of the non-co-operation resolution in the train. Up to this time I had more or less avoided the use of the word non-violent in my drafts. I invariably made use of this word in my speeches. My vocabulary on the subject was still in process of formation. I found that I could not bring home my meaning to purely Moslem audiences with the help of the Samskrit equivalent for non-violent. I therefore asked Maulana Abul Kalam Azad to give me some other equivalent for it. He suggested the word *ba-aman*; similarly for non-co-operation he suggested the phrase *tark-i-mavalat*.

Thus, while I was still busy devising suitable Hindi, Gujarati and Urdu phraseology for non-co-operation, I was called upon to frame the non-co-operation resolution for that eventful Congress. In the original draft the word 'non-violent' had been left out by me. I had handed over the draft to Mauland Shaukat Ali who was traveling in the same compartment, without noticing the omission. During the night I discovered the error. In the morning I sent Mahadev with the message that the omission should be made good before the draft was sent to the press. But I have an impression that the draft was printed before the insertion could be made. The Subjects Committee was to have met the same evening. I had therefore to make the necessary correction in the printed copies of the draft. I afterwards saw that there would have been great difficulty, had I not been ready with my draft.

None the less my plight was pitiable indeed. I was absolutely at sea as to who would support the resolution and who would oppose it. Nor had I any idea as to the attitude that Lalaji would adopt. I only saw an imposing phalanx of veteran warriors assembled for the fray at Calcutta, Dr. Besant, Pandit Malaviyaji, Sjt. Vijayaraghavachari, Pandit Motilalji and Deshabandhu being some of them.

In my resolution non-co-operation was postulated only with a view to obtaining redress of the Punjab and the Khilafat wrongs. That however, did not appeal to Sjt. Vijayaraghavachari. 'If non-co-operation was to be declared, why should it be with reference to particular wrongs? The absence of Swaraj was the biggest wrong that the country was labouring under; it should be against that that non-co-operation should be directed,' he argued. Pandit Motilalji also wanted the demand for Swaraj to be included in the resolution. I readily accepted the suggestion and incorporated the demand for Swaraj in my resolution, which was passed after an exhaustive, serious and somewhat stormy discussion.

Motilalji was the first to join the movement. I still remember the sweet discussion that I had with him on the resolution. He suggested some changes in its phraseology which I adopted. He undertook to win the Deshabandhu for the movement. The Deshabandhu's heart was inclined towards it, but he felt sceptical as to the capacity of the people to carry out the programme. It was only at the Nagpur Congress that he and Lalaji accepted it whole-heartedly.

I felt the loss of the late Lokamanya very deeply at the special session. It has been my firm faith to this day that, had the Lokamanya been then alive, he would have given his benedictions to me on that occasion. But even if it had been otherwise, and he had opposed the movement, I should still have esteemed his opposition as a privilege and an education for myself. We had our differences of opinion always, but they never led to bitterness. He always allowed me to believe that the ties between us were of the closest. Even as I write these lines, the circumstances of his death stand forth vividly before my mind's eye. It was about the hour of midnight, when Patwardhan, who was then working with me, conveyed over the telephone the news of his death. I was at that time surrounded by my companions. Spontaneously the exclamation escaped my lips, 'My strongest bulwark is gone.' The non-co-operation movement was then in full swing, and I was eagerly looking forward to encouragement and inspiration from him. What his attitude would have been with regard to the final phase of non-co-operation will always be a matter of speculation, and an idle one at that. But this much is certain—that the deep void left by his death weighed heavily upon everybody present at Calcutta. Everyone felt the absence of his counsels in that hour of crisis in the nation's history.

At Nagpur

SOURCE: Gandhi, Mohandas K. *An Autobiography: The Story of My Experiments with Truth.* Translated by Mahadev Desai. Boston: Beacon Press, 1957, pp. 500–502.

The resolutions adopted at the Calcutta special session of the Congress were to be confirmed at its annual session at Nagpur. Here again, as at Calcutta there was a great rush of visitors and delegates. The number of delegates in the Congress had not been limited yet. As a result, so far as I can remember, the figure on this occasion reached about fourteen thousand. Lalaji pressed for a slight amendment to the clause about the boycott of schools, which I accepted. Similarly some amendments were made at the instance of the Deshabandhu, after which the non-co-operation resolution was passed unanimously.

The resolution regarding the revision of the Congress constitution too was to be taken up at this session of the Congress. The sub-committee's draft was presented at the Calcutta special session. The matter had therefore been thoroughly ventilated and thrashed out. At the Nagpur session, where it came up for final disposal, Sjt. C. Vijayaraghachariar was the President. The Subjects Committee passed the draft with only one important change. In my draft the number of delegates had been fixed, I think at 1,500; the Subjects Committee substituted in its place the figure 6,000. In my opinion this increase was the result of hasty judgment, and experience of all these years has only confirmed me in my view. I hold it to be an utter delusion to believe that a large number of delegates is in any way a help to the better conduct of the business, or that it safeguards the principle of democracy. Fifteen hundred delegates, jealous of the interests of the people, broad-minded and truthful, would any day be a better safeguard for democracy than six thousand irresponsible men chosen anyhow. To safeguard democracy the people must have a keen sense of independence, self-respect and their oneness, and should insist upon choosing as their representatives only such persons as are good and true. But obsessed with the idea of numbers as the Subjects Committee was, it would have liked to go even beyond the figure of six thousand. The limit of six thousand was therefore in the nature of a compromise.

The question of the goal of the Congress formed a subject for keen discussion. In the constitution that I had presented, the goal of the Congress was the attainment of Swaraj within the British Empire if possible and without if necessary. A party in the Congress wanted to limit the goal to Swaraj within the British Empire only. Its viewpoint was put forth by Pandit Malaviyaji and Mr. Jinnah. But they were not able to get many votes. Again the draft constitution provided that the means for the attainment were to be peaceful and legitimate. This condition too came in for opposition, it being contended that there should be no restriction upon the means to be adopted. But the Congress adopted the original draft after an instructive and frank discussion. I am of opinion that, if this constitution had been worked out by the people honestly, intelligently and zealously, it would have become a potent instrument of mass education, and the very process of working it out would have brought us Swaraj. But a discussion of the theme would be irrelevant here.

Resolutions about Hindu–Muslim unity, the removal of untouchability and Khadi too were passed in this Congress, and since then the Hindu members of the Congress have taken upon themselves the responsibility of ridding Hinduism of the curse of untouchability, and the Congress has established a living bond of relationship with the 'skeletons' of India through Khadi. The adoption of non-co-operation for the sake of the Khilafat was itself a great practical attempt made by the Congress to bring about Hindu–Muslim unity.

Farewell

SOURCE: Gandhi, Mohandas K. *An Autobiography: The Story of My Experiments with Truth.* Translated by Mahadev Desai. Boston: Beacon Press, 1957, pp. 503–505.

The time has now come to bring these chapters to a close.

My life from this point onward has been so public that there is hardly anything about it that people do not know. Moreover, since 1921 I have worked in such close association with the Congress leaders that I can hardly describe any episode in my life since then without referring to any relations with them. For though Shraddhanandji, the Deshabandhu, Hakim Saheb and Lalaji are no more with us today, we have the good luck to have a host of other veteran Congress leaders still living and working in our midst. The history of the Congress, since the great changes in it that I have described above, is still in the making. And my principal experiments during the past seven years have all been made through the Congress. A reference to my relations with the leaders would therefore be unavoidable, if I set about describing my experiments further. And this I may not do, at any rate for the present, if only from a sense of propriety. Lastly, my conclusions from my current experiments can hardly as yet be regarded as decisive. It therefore seems to be my plain duty to close this narrative here. In fact my pen instinctively refuses to proceed further.

It is not without a wrench that I have to take leave of the reader. I set a high value on my experiments. I do not know whether I have been able to do justice to them. I can only say that I have spared no pains to give a faithful narrative. To describe truth, as it has appeared to me and in the exact manner in which I have arrived at it, has been my ceaseless effort. The exercise has given me ineffable mental peace, because, it has been my fond hope that it might bring faith in Truth and Ahimsa to waverers.

My uniform experience has convinced me that there is no other God than Truth. And if every page of these chapters does not proclaim to the reader that the only means for the realization of Truth is Ahimsa, I shall deem all my labour in writing these chapters to have been in vain. And, even though my efforts in this behalf may prove fruitless, let the readers know that the vehicle, not the great principle, is at fault. After all, however sincere my strivings after Ahimsa may have been, they have still been imperfect and inadequate. The little fleeting glimpses, therefore, that I have been able to have of Truth can hardly convey an idea of the indescribable luster of Truth, a million times more intense than that of the sun we daily see with our eyes. In fact what I have caught is only the faintest glimmer of that mighty effulgence. But this much I can say with assurance, as a result of all my experiments, that a perfect vision of Truth can only follow a complete realization of Ahimsa.

To see the universal and all-pervading Spirit of Truth face to face one must be able to love the meanest of creation as oneself. And a man who aspires after that cannot afford to keep out of any field of life. That is why my devotion to Truth has drawn me into the field of politics; and I can say without the slightest hesitation, and yet in all humility, that those who say that religion has nothing to do with politics do not know what religion means.

Identification with everything that lives is impossible without self-purification; without self-purification the observance of the law of Ahimsa must remain an empty dream; God can never be realized by one who is not pure of heart. Self-purification therefore must mean purification in all the walks of life. And purification being highly infectious, purification of oneself necessarily leads to the purification of ones' surroundings.

But the path of self-purification is hard and steep. To attain to perfect purity one has to become absolutely passion-free in thought, speech and action; to rise above the opposing currents of love and hatred, attachment and repulsion. I know that I have not in me as yet that triple purity, in spite of constant ceaseless striving for it. That is why the world's praise fails to move me, indeed it very often stings me. To conquer the subtle passions seems to me to be harder far than the physical conquest of the world by the force of arms. Ever since my return to India I have had experiences of the dormant passions lying hidden within me. The knowledge of them has made me feel humiliated though not defeated. The experiences and experiments have sustained me and given me great joy. But I know that I have still before me a difficult path to traverse. I must reduce myself to zero. So long as a man does not of his own free will put himself last among his fellow creatures, there is no salvation for him. Ahimsa is the farthest limit of humility.

In bidding farewell to the reader, for the time being at any rate, I ask him to join with me in prayer to the God of Truth that He may grant me the boon of Ahimsa in mind, word and deed.

Jawaharlal Nehru's Speech on the Assassination of Mahatma M. K. Gandhi

Introduction

Jawaharlal Nehru (1889–1964) was one of Mahatma Gandhi's most devoted followers and this speech he gave on Air India Radio on the day that Gandhi was assassinated is one of his most sensitive and one of his finest. Along with his "Tryst with Destiny" speech, given to mark India's independence in August 1947, this talk must rank as one of his most memorable and one of the elevated speeches of history. At this time of tragedy, when Nehru was visibly brokenhearted, he called for the continuation of Gandhi's teachings of love for others, for nonviolence, and for living up to the great principles by which he lived his life. Nehru and Gandhi were so different in many ways, not least of which was their attitude toward modernization. Nehru was a Utopian Marxist who believed in socialistic planning and industrialization while Gandhi had little faith in either. Yet Nehru, like so many people, was devoted to Gandhi from the time that he first followed Gandhi in "National Week" in 1919 to protest the Black Acts. For Nehru as well as for many others, Gandhi was an enigma and his ways and methods were sometimes hard to comprehend. But time and again, as during the Salt March of 1930, Nehru recognized the brilliance of Gandhi's tactics in Indian eyes and followed him devotedly. For some thirty years Nehru would seek Gandhi out or, as he put in his broadcast, he would "run to him and seek solace from him." This devotion of Nehru (himself one of the great figures of history) to Gandhi, and his depiction of the role that Gandhi played for him and for India and the world is sensitively portrayed in this broadcast.

The Light Has Gone Out

SOURCE: Norman, Dorothy, ed. *Nehru: The First Sixty Years.* Vol. 2. London: The Bodley Head, 1965, pp. 364–366.

Broadcast, New Delhi, 30 January 1948.

Friends and comrades, the light has gone out of our lives and there is darkness everywhere. I do not know what to tell you and how to say it. Our beloved leader, Bapu as we called him, the Father of the Nation, is no more. Perhaps I am wrong to say that. Nevertheless, we will not see him again as we have seen him for these many years. We will not run to him for advice and seek solace from him and that is a terrible blow, not to me only, but to millions and millions in this country. And it is a little difficult to soften the blow by any other advice that I or anyone else can give you.

The light has gone out, I said, and yet I was wrong. For the light that shone in this country was no ordinary light. The light that has illumined this country for these many many years will illumine this country for many more years, and a thousand years later, that light will still be seen in this county and the world will see it and it will give solace to innumerable hearts. For that light represented something more than the immediate present, it represented the living, the eternal trusts, reminding us of the right path, drawing us from error, taking this ancient country to freedom.

All this has happened when there was so much more for him to do. We could never think that he was unnecessary or that he had done his task. But now, particularly, when we are faced with so many difficulties, his not being with us is a blow most terrible to bear.

A madman has put an end to his life, for I can only call him mad who did it, and yet there has been enough of poison spread in this country during the past years and months, and this poison has had an effect on people's minds. We must face this poison, we must root out this poison, and we must face all the perils that encompass us, and face them not madly or badly, but rather in the way that our beloved teacher taught us to face them.

The first thing to remember now is that none of us dare misbehave because he is angry. We have to behave like strong and determined people, determined to face all the perils that surround us, determined to carry out the mandate that our great teacher and out great leader has given us, remembering always that if, as I believe, his spirit looks upon us and sees us, nothing would displease his soul so much as to see that we have indulged in any small behaviour or any violence.

So we must not do that. But that does not mean that we should be weak, but rather that we should, in strength and in unity, face all the troubles that are in front of us. We must hold together and all our petty troubles and difficulties and conflicts must be ended in the face of this great disaster. A great disaster is a symbol to us to remember all the big things of life and forget the small things of which we have thought too much. In his death he has reminded us of the big things of life, that living truth, and if we remember that, then it will be well with India. . . .

It was proposed by some friends that Mahatmaji's body should be embalmed for a few days to enable millions of people to pay their last homage to him. But it was his wish, repeatedly expressed, that no such thing should happen, that this should not be done, that he was entirely opposed to any embalming of his body, and we so decided that we must follow his wishes in this matter, however much others might have wished otherwise.

And so the cremation will take place on Saturday in Delhi city by the side of the Jumna river.... I will trust that [there will be] silence [and no] demonstrations. That is the best way and the most fitting way to pay homage to this great soul. Also, Saturday should be a day of fasting and prayer for all of us.

Those who live elsewhere out of Delhi and in other parts of India will no doubt also take such part as they can in this last homage. For them also, let this be a day of fasting and prayer. And at the appointed time for cremation, that is 4 P.M. on Saturday afternoon, people should go to the river or to the sea and offer prayers there. And while we pray, the greatest prayer that we can offer is to take a pledge to dedicate ourselves to the truth, and to the cause for which this great countryman of ours lived and for which he has died. That is the best prayer that we can offer him and his memory. That is the best prayer that we can offer India and ourselves.

Selections from Hindu Texts

Introduction

The Rig Veda, consisting of 1,028 hymns, is the oldest of the four collections of the Vedas, from the Sanskrit word *vid* (to know). The other Vedas are the Yajur Veda, the Sama Veda, and the Arthava Veda. Each of the four Vedas consists of two parts, the Saṃhitā, consisting of hymns and incantations used in rituals and sacrifices, and the Brāhmaṇa, offering exegeses on ritual. The Rig Veda, composed over several centuries by generations of poets, marks the beginning of Hindu religious–philosophical thought. From the worship of many gods such as Usha and Indra, the concept of monism—as represented by the Upanishads—arises. Hinduism offers guidance to every aspect of life and for every stage of life. The special characteristic of Hinduism is the concept of the transmigration of souls. Doing one's duty is the key to living a virtuous life and this can be expressed in devotion to god. These ideas are expressed in the readings that follow.

The poems dedicated to the Goddess Usha, the Goddess of Dawn, are among the most beautiful in the Vedas. She is the subject of twenty hymns and her name is invoked 300 times in the Saṃhitā. In Rig Veda I:48 she is referred to as "Daughter of the Sky, the Lady of Light." She was also called the mother of the gods. She tends to everything, rouses man and animals to activity, encourages them, and assures them of her largess. She drives away bad dreams and opens the gates of darkness. In another hymn, Rig Veda VI:6,7 Usha delivers men from the power of curses. She is a young maiden dressed gaily and reveals her bosom to mortals. The sun follows her as a lover and she is known as the wife and beloved of Sūrya, the sun god. The lovely goddess brings wealth, long life, fame, and glory.

Rig Veda I:113 Usha the Dawn

SOURCE: Embree, Ainslee T., *The Hindu Tradition*. New York: The Modern Library, 1966, pp. 16–17.

This light has come, of all the lights the fairest:
The brilliant brightness has been born effulgent.
Urged onward for god Savitar's uprising,
Night now has yielded up her place to morning.
Bringing a radiant calf she comes resplendent:
To her the Black One has given up her mansions.
Akin, immortal, following each the other,
Morning and Night fare on, exchanging colours.
The sisters' pathway is the same, unending:
Taught by the gods alternately they tread it.
Fair-shaped, of form diverse, yet single-minded,
Morning and Night clash not, nor do they tarry.
Bright leader of glad sounds she shines effulgent:
Widely she has unclosed for us her portals.
Pervading all the world she shows us riches:
Dawn has awakened every living creature.
Men lying on the ground she wakes to action:
Some rise to seek enjoyment of great riches,
Some, seeing little, to behold the distant:
Dawn has awakened every living creature.
One for dominion, and for fame another;
Another is aroused for winning greatness;
Another seeks the goal of varied nurture:
Dawn has awakened every living creature.
Daughter of heaven, she has appeared before us,
A maiden shining in resplendent raiment.
Thou sovereign lady of all earthly treasure,
Auspicious Dawn, shine here to-day upon us....
Gone are those mortals who in former ages
Beheld the flushing of the early morning;
We living men now look upon her shining:
Those will be born who shall hereafter see her.
Dispelling foes, observer of world order,
Born in due season, giver of enjoyment,
Wafting oblations, bringing wealth and fortune,
Shine brightly here to-day, O Dawn, upon us....
In the sky's framework she has gleamed with brightness;
The goddess has cast off the robe of darkness.
Rousing the world from sleep, with ruddy horses,
Dawn in her well-yoked chariot is arriving.
She brings upon it many bounteous blessings;
Brightly she shines and spreads her brilliant lustre.
Last of innumerable morns departed,
First of bright morns to come, has Dawn arisen.
Arise! The vital breath again has reached us:
Darkness has gone away and light is coming.

She leaves a pathway for the sun to travel:
We have arrived where men prolong existence.

(from *Rig Veda* I: 113, in A.A. Macdonnell, *Hymns from the Rigveda*, p. 38)

Rig Veda I:32 Indra

SOURCE: Embree, Ainslee T., *The Hindu Tradition*. New York: The Modern Library, 1966, pp. 18–20.

Introduction

The God Indra is one of the oldest in the Aryan pantheon and found along with Mitra, Varuṇa, and Nasatra as one of the gods of the Mitanni. He is the greatest god in the Rig Veda with the single exception of Varuṇa, who equals him in power. Indra is the subject of 250 hymns, almost one-quarter of the collection, and he is mentioned in over fifty more. He is regarded as the War God and is associated with thunderstorms and lightning. He is particularly associated with the intoxicating drink soma, and known as "soma-drinker." His great belly is so filled with soma that it is likened to a lake. Like other miraculous births he is born through his mother's side. His most famous feat was the slaying of the demon Vritra. This myth has been interpreted as the defeat by the Aryans of the people of the Indus Valley.

Indra's heroic deeds, indeed, will I proclaim, the first ones which the wielder of the thunderbolt accomplished. He killed the dragon, released the waters, and split open the sides of the mountains.

He killed the dragon lying spread out on the mountain; for him Tvashtar fashioned the roaring thunderbolt. Like bellowing cows, the waters, gliding, have gone down straightway to the ocean.

Showing off his virile power he chose soma; from the three bowls he drank of the extracted soma. The bounteous god took up the missile, the vajra; he killed the first-born among the dragons.

When you, O Indra, killed the first-born among the dragons and further overpowered the wily tricks (māyā) of the tricksters, bringing forth, at that very moment, the sun, the heaven, and the dawn—since then, indeed, have you not come across another enemy.

Indra killed Vritra, the greater enemy, the shoulderless one, with his mighty and fatal weapon, the thunderbolt. Like branches of a tree lopped off with an axe, the dragon lies prostrate upon the earth.

For, like an incapable fighter, in an intoxicated state, he [Vritra] had challenged the great hero [Indra], the mighty overwhelmer, the drinker of soma to the dregs. He did not surmount the onslaught of his fatal weapon. Indra's enemy, broken-nosed, was completely crushed.

Footless and handless he gave battle to Indra. He [Indra] struck him with the vajra upon the back. The castrated bull, seeking to become a compeer of the virile bull, Vritra lay shattered in many places.

Over him, who lay in that manner like a shattered bull flowed the waters for the sake of man. At the feet of the very waters, which Vritra had once enclosed with his might, the dragon now lay prostrate.

Vritra's mother had her vital energy ebbing out; Indra had hurled his fatal weapon at her. The mother lay above, the son below; Dānu, his mother lay down like a cow with her calf.

In the midst of the water-streams, which never stood still nor had any resting place, the body lay. The waters flow in all directions over Vritra's secret place; Indra's enemy lay sunk in long darkness.

With the demon as their lord and with dragon as their warder, the waters remained imprisoned. . . . Having killed Vritra, [Indra] threw open the cleft of waters which had been closed.

You became the hair of a horse's tail, O Indra, when he [Vritra] struck at your sharp-pointed vajra—the one god though you were. You won the cows, O brave one, you won soma; you released the seven rivers, so that they should flow.

Neither did lightning nor thunder, nor mist nor hailstorm, which he [Vritra] had spread out, prove efficacious when Indra and the dragon fought. And the bounteous god remained victorious for all time to come.

Whom did you see, O Indra, as the avenger of the dragon, that fear entered into your heart, after you had killed the dragon, and frightened, you crossed nine and ninety rivers and the aerial regions like the falcon?

Indra, who wields the thunderbolt in his hand, is the lord of what moves and what remains rested, of what is peaceful and what is honored. He alone rules over the tribes as their king; he encloses them as does a rim the spokes.

(from Rig Veda, I:32, in *Sources of India Tradition*, pp. 13–25)

Rig Veda X:90 Sacrifice as Creator

SOURCE: Embree, Ainslee T., *The Hindu Tradition*. New York: The Modern Library, 1966, pp. 25–26.

Introduction

Rig Veda X:90, The "Purushasukta," or "Sacrifice of the Cosmic Man," appears in the tenth and final book of the Rig Veda and is one of the most renowned hymns of the Vedas. It is a mystical account of the origin of the four classes (varṇa) of Aryan society, and, therefore, an account of the genesis of mankind. These four classes originated from the sacrifice of the god Purusha. From the mouth first sprang the Brahmans, the priestly class; second from the arms came the Kshatriyas, the warriors; third emerged the Vaishyas, the traders and other "middle class" professions, from the thighs; and finally, from the feet came the Shudras, the peasants or workers. From this sacrifice the Brahmans claimed the highest rank in Indian society and it was they alone who could bestow divinity to kings and give religious sanction to caste distinctions. The hymn also gave sanction to caste as the basis of social control. This resulted in prohibitions on commensality and exogamy, with the ritual observance and the hierarchy of the four castes maintained by the Brahmans.

Thousand-headed Purusha, thousand-eyed, thousand-footed—he having pervaded the earth on all sides, still extends ten fingers beyond it.

Purusha alone is all this—whatever has been and whatever is going to be. Further, he is the lord of immortality and also of what grows for food.

Such is his greatness; greater, indeed, than this is Purusha. All creatures constitute but one quarter of him, his three quarters are the immortal in heaven. . . . Being born, he projected himself behind the earth as also before it.

When the gods performed the sacrifice with Purusha as the oblation, then the spring was its clarified butter, the summer the sacrificial fuel, and the autumn the oblation.

The sacrificial victim, namely, Purusha, born at the very beginning, they sprinkled with sacred water upon the sacrificial grass. With him as oblation the gods performed the sacrifice, and also the Sādhyas [a class of semidivine beings] and the rishis [ancient seers].

From that wholly offered sacrificial oblation were born the verses and the sacred chants; from it were born the meters; the sacrificial formula was born from it.

From it horses were born and also those animals who have double rows of teeth; cows were born from it, from it were born goats and sheep.

When they divided Purusha, in how many different portions did they arrange him? What became of his mouth, what of his two arms? What were his two thighs and his two feet called?

His mouth became the brāhman; his two arms were made into the rājanya; his two thighs the vaishyas; from his two feet the shūdra was born.

The moon was born from the mind, from the eye the sun was born; from the mouth Indra and Agni, from the breath the wind was born.

From the navel was the atmosphere created, from the head the heaven issued forth; from the two feet was born the earth and the quarters (the cardinal directions) from the ear. Thus did they fashion the worlds.

Seven were the enclosing sticks in this sacrifice, thrice seven were the fire-sticks made, when the gods, performing the sacrifice, bound down Purusha, the sacrificial victim.

With this sacrificial oblation did the gods offer the sacrifice. These were the first norms (*dharma*) of sacrifice. These greatnesses reached to the sky wherein live the ancient Sādhyas and gods.

(from Rig Veda X:90, in *Sources of Indian Tradition*, pp. 16–17)

Rig Veda X:129 The One as Creator

SOURCE: Embree, Ainslee T., *The Hindu Tradition.* New York: The Modern Library, 1966, pp. 26–27.

Introduction

This hymn is the first clear presentation in Hindu texts of the concept of monism. There is no explicit reference to *Atman* (self or soul) in the hymn although some orthodox Brahmans believe the idea is implied. In the hymn the monistic principle is known as "That One," the Brahman, a power which was invoked through prayer. The universe arose out of darkness and chaos and the calm of nature was the result of a conscious and intelligent will. Prior to this late hymn, nature was apportioned to different gods. The creator breathed calmly in the beginning and was developed by the power of *tapas*, warmth or heat—"by the great power of Warmth was born that One." Heat has two opposed forms: *kama*, the heat of sexual desire, and *tapas*, the heat generated by ascetic practices, especially chastity. *Tapas*, for many people, is a sign of spirituality. It was *tapas* that led to Desire, the primal seed and the germ of Spirit, which in turn led to the world's creation.

Then was not non-existent nor existent; there was no realm of air, no sky beyond it.

What covered in, and where? and what gave shelter? Was water there, unfathomed depth of water?

Death was not then, nor was there aught immortal: no sign was there, the day's and night's divider.

That One Thing, breathless, breathed by its own nature: apart from it was nothing whatsoever.

Darkness there was: at first concealed in darkness this All was undifferentiated chaos.

All that existed then was void and formless: by the great power of Warmth was born that One.

Thereafter rose Desire in the beginning, Desire, the primal seed and germ of Spirit.

Sages who searched with their heart's thought discovered the existent's kinship in the non-existent.

Transversely was their severing line extended: what was above it then, and what below it?

There were begetters, there were mighty forces, free action here and energy up yonder.

Who verily knows and who can here declare it, whence it was born and whence comes this creation?

The Gods are later this world's creation. Who knows then whence it first came into being?

He, the first origin of this creation, whether he formed it all or did not form it,

Whose eye controls this world in highest heaven, he verily knows it, or perhaps he knows not.

(from Rig Veda X:129, in Griffith, *The Hymns of the Rig Veda*, II, pp. 575–76)

The Four Stages of Life

SOURCE: Embree, Ainslee T., *The Hindu Tradition.* New York: The Modern Library, 1966, pp. 84–93.

Introduction

In Hinduism there are four stages of life: the student, the householder, the hermit, and the homeless wanderer. The duties for each stage of life are spelled out and the good Hindu will do his duty and follow each in turn.

The Student

He who has been initiated shall dwell as a religious student in the house of his teacher . . .

Twelve years (should be) the shortest time (for his residence with his teacher).

A student who studies the sacred science shall not dwell with anybody else than his teacher.

Now (follow) the rules for the studentship.

He shall obey his teacher, except when ordered to commit crimes which cause loss of caste.

He shall do what is serviceable to his teacher, he shall not contradict him.

He shall always occupy a couch or seat lower than that of his teacher.

He shall not eat food offered at a sacrifice to the gods or the Manes,

Nor pungent condiments, salt, honey, or meat.

He shall not sleep in the day-time.

He shall not use perfumes.

He shall preserve chastity.

He shall not embellish himself by using ointments and the like.

He shall not wash his body with hot water for pleasure.

But, if it is soiled by unclean things, he shall clean it with earth or water, in a place where he is not seen by a Guru.

Let him not sport in the water whilst bathing; let him swim motionless like a stick. . . .

Let him not look at dancing.

Let him not go to assemblies for gambling, &c., nor to crowds assembled at festivals.

Let him not be addicted to gossiping.

Let him be discreet.

Let him not do anything for his own pleasure in places which his teacher frequents.

Let him talk with women so much only as his purpose requires.

Let him be forgiving.

Let him restrain his organs from seeking illicit objects.

Let him be untired in fulfilling his duties;

Modest;

Possessed of self-command;

Energetic;

Free from anger;

And free from envy.

Bringing all he obtains to his teacher, he shall go begging with a vessel in the morning and in the evening, and he may beg from everybody except low-caste people unfit for association with Aryas.

(from *Apastamba Dharma Sūtra*, I:1,2,3, and 6, *passim*, in *Sacred Books of the East*, II, pp. 7–8, 10–11)

The Householder and Family Life

One should first examine the family [of the intended bride or bridegroom], those on the mother's side and on the father's side. . . . One should give his daughter in marriage to a young man endowed with intelligence. One should marry a girl who possesses the characteristics of intelligence, beauty, and good character, and who is free from disease. . . .

(from *Āśvalāyana Grihya Sūtra*, I:5, *passim*, in *Sources of Indian Tradition*, p. 230)

A householder should perform every day a Smriti rite [i.e., a domestic rite prescribed by the Sacred Law, Smriti] on the nuptial fire or on the fire brought in at the time of the partition of ancestral property. He should perform a Vedic rite on the sacred fires.

Having attended to the bodily calls, having performed the purificatory rites, and after having first washed the teeth, a twice-born [Aryan] man should offer the morning prayer.

Having offered oblations to the sacred fires, becoming spiritually composed, he should murmur the sacred verses addressed to the sun god. He should also learn the meaning of the Veda and various sciences. . . .

He should then go to his lord for securing the means of maintenance and progress. Thereafter having bathed he should worship the gods and also offer libations of water to the manes.

He should study according to his capacity the three Vedas, the *Atharva* Veda, the Purānas, together with the Itihāsas [legendary histories], as also the lore relating to the knowledge of the Self, with a view to accomplishing successfully the sacrifice of muttering prayers.

Offering of the food oblation, offerings with the proper utterance, performance of Vedic sacrifices, study of the sacred texts, and honoring of guests—these constitute the five great daily sacrifices dedicated respectively to the spirits, the manes, the gods, the Brahman, and men.

He should offer the food oblation to the spirits [by throwing it in the air] out of the remnant of the food offered to the gods. He should also cast food on the ground for dogs, untouchables, and crows.

Food, as also water, should be offered by the house-holder to the manes and men day after day. He should continuously carry on his study. He should never cook for himself only.

Children, married daughters living in the father's house, old relatives, pregnant women, sick persons, and girls, as also guest and servants—only after having fed these should the householder and his wife eat the food that has remained. . . .

Having risen before dawn the householder should ponder over what is good for the Self. He should not, as far as possible, neglect his duties in respect of the three ends of man, namely, virtue, material gain, and pleasure, at their proper times.

Learning, religious performances, age, family relations, and wealth—on account of these and in the order mentioned are men honored in society. By means of these, if possessed in profusion, even a shūdra deserves respect in old age.

(from *Yājnavalkya Smriti*, I:97-116, *passim*, in *Sources of Indian Tradition*, pp. 231–32)

I will now propound the eternal laws for a husband and wife who keep to the path of duty, whether they be united or separated.

Day and night must women be kept in dependence by the males of their families, and, if they attach themselves to sensual enjoyments, they must be kept under one's control.

Her father protects her in childhood, her husband protects her in youth, and her sons protect her in old age; a woman is never fit for independence.

Reprehensible is the father who gives not his daughter in marriage at the proper time; reprehensible is the husband who approaches not his wife in due season, and reprehensible is the son who does not protect his mother after her husband has died.

Women must particularly be guarded against evil inclinations, however trifling they may appear; for, if they are not guarded, they will bring sorrow on two families.

Considering that the highest duty of all castes, even weak husbands must strive to guard their wives.

He who carefully guards his wife, preserves the purity of his offspring, virtuous conduct, his family, himself, and his means of acquiring merit. . . .

No man can completely guard women by force; but they can be guarded by the employment of the following expedients:

Let the husband employ his wife in the collection and expenditure of his wealth, in keeping everything clean, in the fulfillment of religious duties, in the preparation of his food, and in looking after the household utensils.

Women, confined in the house under trustworthy and obedient servants, are not well guarded; but those who of their own accord keep guard over themselves, are well guarded.

Drinking spirituous liquor, associating with wicked people, separation from the husband, rambling abroad, sleeping at unseasonable hours, and dwelling in other men's houses, are the six causes of the ruin of women. . . .

Thus has been declared the ever pure popular usage which regulates the relations between husband and wife; hear next the laws concerning children which are the cause of happiness in this world and after death.

Between wives who are destined to bear children, who secure many blessings, who are worthy of worship and irradiate their dwellings, and between the goddesses of fortune who reside in the houses of men, there is no difference whatsoever.

The production of children, the nurture of those born, and the daily life of men, of these matters woman is visibly the cause.

Offspring, the due performance of religious rites, faithful service, highest conjugal happiness and heavenly bliss for the ancestors and oneself, depend on one's wife alone.

She who, controlling her thoughts, speech, and acts, violates not her duty towards her lord, dwells with him after death in heaven, and in this world is called by the virtuous a faithful wife.

(from *Manu Smriti* IX:1–7, 10–13, 25–29, *Sacred Books of the East*, XXV, pp. 328–29, 332)

The Hermit

When a householder sees his skin wrinkled, and his hair white, and the sons of his sons, then he may resort to the forest.

Abandoning all food raised by cultivation, and all his belongings, he may depart into the forest, either committing his wife to his sons, or accompanied by her.

Taking with him the sacred fire and the implements required for domestic sacrifices, he may go forth from the villages into the forest and reside there, duly controlling his senses.

Let him offer those five great sacrifices according to the rule, with various kinds of pure food fit for ascetics, or with herbs, roots, and fruit.

Let him wear a skin or a tattered garment; let him bathe in the evening or in the morning; and let him always wear his hair in braids, the hair on his body, his beard, and his nails being unclipped.

Let him perform the food offering with such food as he eats, and give alms according to his ability; let him honour those who come to his hermitage with alms consisting of water, roots, and fruit.

Let him be always industrious in privately reciting the Veda; let him be patient of hardships, friendly towards all, of collected mind, ever liberal and never receiver, and compassionate toward all beings. . . .

He should live without a fire, without a house, a silent sage subsisting on roots and fruit. . . .

(from *Manu Smriti* VI:2–8, 25, in *Sacred Books of the East* XXV, pp. 198–200)

The Homeless Wanderer

But having thus passed the third part of a man's natural term of life in the forest, he may live as an ascetic during the fourth part of his existence, after abandoning all attachment to worldly objects.

He who after passing from order to order, after offering sacrifices and subduing senses, becomes, tired with giving alms and offerings of food, an ascetic, gains bliss after death.

When he has paid the three debts, let him apply his mind to the attainment of final liberation; he who seeks it without having paid (his debts) sinks downwards.

Having studied the Vedas in accordance with the rule, having begat sons according to the sacred law, and having offered sacrifices according to his ability, he may direct his mind to the attainment of final liberation.

A twice-born man who seeks final liberation, without having studied the Vedas, without having begotten sons, and without having offered sacrifices, sinks downwards. . . .

Departing from his house fully provided with the means of purification, let him wander about absolutely silent, and caring nothing for enjoyments that may be offered to him.

Let him always wander alone, without any companion, in order to attain final liberation, fully understanding that the solitary man, who neither forsakes nor is forsaken, gains his end.

He shall neither possess a fire, nor a dwelling, he may go to a village for his food, (he shall be) indifferent to everything, firm of purpose, meditating and concentrating his mind on Brahman.

A potsherd instead of an alms-bowl, the roots of trees for a dwelling, coarse worn-out garments, life in solitude and indifference towards everything, are the marks of one who has attained liberation.

Let him not desire to die, let him not desire to live; let him wait for his appointed time, as a servant waits for the payment of his wages.

Let him put down his foot purified by his sight, let him drink water purified by straining with a cloth, let him utter speech purified by truth, let him keep his heart pure.

Let him patiently bear hard words, let him not insult anybody, and let him not become anybody's enemy for the sake of this perishable body.

Against an angry man let him not in return show anger, let him bless when he is cursed, and let him not utter speech, devoid of truth, scattered at the seven gates.

Delighting in what refers to the Soul, sitting in the postures prescribed by the Yoga, independent of external help, entirely abstaining from sensual enjoyments, with himself for his only companion, he shall live in this world, desiring the bliss of final liberation.

(from *Manu Smriti*, VI, *passim*, in *Sacred Books of the East*, XXV, pp. 204–07)

Bhagavad Gītā II:11–30, 55–59

SOURCE: Embree, Ainslee T., *The Hindu Tradition*. New York: The Modern Library, 1966, pp. 120–122.

Introduction

One of the fundamental ideas of Hinduism is the belief in *karma*, the notion that each act carries a result, and another is the belief in the transmigration of souls. From the middle of the first millenium B.C. a number of religions and sects arose in Hinduism which developed two important ideas: an intense devotion to a god, *bhakti*, which was an end in itself, and the belief that the god would grant salvation to his devotees. Through *bhakti* the devotee could escape from rebirth. Krishna and Rāma became particular objects of devotion and

Shiva and Vishnu inspired very large numbers of devotees. All Hindu gods had images created in their honor and visual representations, especially in carved images, are a distinguished feature of Hinduism. Shiva, whose worship may be associated with the Indus Valley civilization, attracted followers in the south of India. Vishnu, or one of his incarnations (avatāras), was especially considered to be loving and beneficent and to offer salvation to his followers. Light and the life-giving sun were associated with him. Vishnu is prominent in the Bhagavad Gītā, or "the Lord's Song," the most famous work of literature dedicated to the worship of an individual god, and composed sometime between the fourth and second centuries B.C. (the Gītā is part of the Mahābhārata but was a separate composition). Near the beginning of the Bhagavad Gītā is a description of man's nature wherein Arjuna, one of the five Pandava princes and the hero of the epic, is horrified by the thought of the consequences, his *karma*, that will arise from his killings on the battlefield. He is therefore reluctant to engage in a fratricidal war. Vishnu's incarnation, Krishna, is his charioteer and his statement to Arjuna wherein he discusses the nature of man is one of the most famous in the Gītā and one of the most renowned passages in the Hindu religion. Krishna explains to Arjuna that the death of the body does not mean the death of the soul. The body is comparatively unimportant.

The Blessed Lord said:

You grieve for those who should not be mourned, and yet you speak words of wisdom! The learned do not grieve for the dead or for the living.

Never, indeed, was there a time when I was not, nor when you were not, nor these lords of men. Never, too, will there be a time, hereafter, when we shall not be.

As in this body, there are for the embodied one [i.e., the soul] childhood, youth, and old age, even so there is the taking on of another body. The wise sage is not perplexed thereby.

Contacts of the sense-organs, O son of Kuntī, give rise to cold and heat, and pleasure and pain. They come and go, and are not permanent. Bear with them, O Bhārata.

That man, whom these [sense-contacts] do not trouble, O chief of men, to whom pleasure and pain are alike, who is wise—he becomes eligible for immortality.

For the nonexistent there is no coming into existence; nor is there passing into nonexistence for the existent. The ultimate nature of these two is perceived by the seers of truth.

Know that to be indestructible by which all this is pervaded. Of this imperishable one, no one can bring about destruction.

These bodies of the eternal embodied one, who is indestructible and incomprehensible, are said to have an end. Therefore fight, O Bhārata.

He who regards him [i.e., the soul] as a slayer, and he who regards him as slain—both of them do not know the truth; for this one neither slays nor is slain.

He is not born, nor does he die at any time; nor, having once come to be will he again come not to be. He is unborn, eternal, permanent, and primeval; he is not slain when the body is slain.

Whoever knows him to be indestructible and eternal, unborn and immutable—how and whom can such a man, O son of Pritha, cause to be slain or slay?

Just as a man, having cast off old garments, puts on other, new ones, even so does the embodied one, having cast off old bodies, take on other, new ones.

Weapons do not cleave him, fire does not burn him; nor does water drench him, nor the wind dry him up.

He is uncleavable, he is unburnable, he is undrenchable, as also undryable. He is eternal, all-pervading, stable, immovable, existing from time immemorial.

He is said to be unmanifest, unthinkable, and unchangeable. Therefore, knowing him as such, you should not grieve [for him].

And even if you regard him as being perpetually born and as perpetually dying, even then, O long-armed one, you should not grieve for him.

For, to one who is born death is certain and certain is birth to one who has died. Therefore in connection with a thing that is inevitable you should not grieve. . . .

Unmanifest in their beginnings are beings, manifest in the middle stage, O Bhārata, and unmanifest, again, in their ends. For what then should there be any lamentation?

Someone perceives him as a marvel; similarly, another speaks of him as a marvel; another again hears of him as a marvel; and, even after hearing of him, no one knows him.

The embodied one within the body of everyone, O Bhārata, is ever unslayable. Therefore, you should not grieve for any being. . . .

When one renounces all the desires which have arisen in the mind, O son of Pritha, and when he himself is content within his own Self, then is he called a man of steadfast wisdom.

He whose mind is unperturbed in the midst of sorrows and who entertains no desires amid pleasures; he from whom passion, fear, and anger have fled away—he is called a sage of steadfast intellect.

He who feels no attachment toward anything; who, having encountered the various good or evil things, neither rejoices nor loathes—his wisdom is steadfast.

When one draws in, on every side, the sense-organs from the objects of sense as a tortoise draws in its limbs from every side—then his wisdom becomes steadfast.

(from *Bhagavad Gītā*, II:11–30, 55–59, in *Sources of Indian Tradition*, pp. 284–85, 298)

Bhagavad Gītā, The Way of Salvation: Duty

SOURCE: Embree, Ainslee T., *The Hindu Tradition*. New York: The Modern Library, 1966, pp. 122–124.

Introduction

After explaining the nature of the human body, Krishna then informs Arjuna of the proper activity of human beings. A human being should not shy away from life, he should not try to be a mendicant or a reclusive sage. He should, instead, engage in life's activities but he should do so—and this is one of the most important messages of Hinduism—without a feeling of attachment, without thoughts of personal advantage or desire. That is, he should act dispassionately, without thinking of the consequences. The most important thing a human being can do is do his duty, *dharma,* dispassionately. The cardinal point, therefore, was to do one's duty without thought of the consequences and without sentiment interfering with duty. A brahman's duty was to teach and preach; a kshatriya's, to fight; a vaishya's, to his profession; and a shudra's, to service. Arjuna was a warrior, so it was his duty to fight and, if necessary, to kill his own kinsmen on the battlefield.

Not by nonperformance of actions does a man attain freedom from action; nor by mere renunciation of actions does he attain his spiritual goal.

For no one, indeed, can remain, for even a single moment, unengaged in activity, since everyone, being powerless, is made to act by the dispositions of matter.

Whoever having restrained his organs of action still continues to brood over the objects of senses—he, the deluded one, is called a hypocrite.

But he who, having controlled the sense-organs by means of the mind, O Arjuna, follows without attachment the path of action by means of the organs of action—he excels.

Do you do your allotted work, for action is superior to non-action. Even the normal functioning of your body cannot be accomplished through actionlessness.

Except for the action done for sacrifice, all men are under the bondage of action. Therefore, O son of Kuntī, do you undertake action for that purpose, becoming free from all attachment. . . .

But the man whose delight is in the Self alone, who is content with Self, who is satisfied only within the Self—for him there exists nothing that needs to be done.

He, verily, has in this world no purpose to be served by action done nor any purpose whatsoever to be served by action abnegated. Similarly, he does not depend on any beings for having his purpose served.

Therefore, without attachment, always do the work that has to be done, for a man doing his work without attachment attains to the highest goal. . . .

Better is one's own dharma [class duties] which one may be able to fulfill but imperfectly than the dharma of others which is more easily accomplished. Better is death in the fulfillment of one's own dharma. To adopt the dharma of others is perilous. . . .

The fourfold class system was created by Me in accordance with the varying dispositions and the actions [resulting from them]. Though I am its creator, know Me, who am immutable, to be a non-doer.

Actions do not cling to Me, for I have no yearning for their fruit. He who knows Me thus [and himself acts in that spirit] is not bound by actions.

So knowing was action done even by men of old who sought liberation. Therefore do the same action [i.e., your class duties] which was done by the ancients in ancient times.

What is action? What is inaction?—as to this even the wise sages are confounded. I will expound action to you, knowing which you will be liberated from evil.

One has to realize what is action; similarly, one has to realize what is wrong action; and one has also to realize what is inaction. Inscrutable, indeed, is the way of action.

He who sees inaction in action and action in inaction, he is discerning among men, expert in the technique of karma-yoga, the doer of the entire action [enjoined by his dharma].

He whose undertakings are all devoid of motivating desires and purposes and whose actions are consumed by the fire of knowledge—him the wise call a man of learning.

Renouncing all attachment to the fruits of actions, ever content, independent—such a person even if engaged in action, does not do anything whatever.

(from *Bhagavad Gītā*, III:3–9, 17–19, IV:13–20, in *Sources of Indian Tradition*, pp. 286–87, 289)

Gītā Govinda

SOURCE: Embree, Ainslee T., *The Hindu Tradition*. New York: The Modern Library, 1966, pp. 169–170.

Introduction

The Gītā Govinda, or the "Song of the Cowherd," is an erotic poem written in Bengali by the court poet Jayadeva (12th century). The song describes the love of Krishna for Rādhā and the *gopīs*, or milkmaids. It begins with invocations to the ten incarnations of Vishnu and then describes Krishna's longing for Rādhā and the joy of his lovemaking with her and the *gopīs*. The special characteristic of the poem is that unlike most other classical Sanskrit poetry Jayadeva's poem was rhymed. The love of Krishna for the *gopīs* is allegorized as the desire of the soul for God and Krishna's response of love is God's answer. One of the ends of life in the Hindu tradition is the enjoyment of physical love. The Gītā Govinda is one of the highest expressions of passion one finds in the whole corpus of Sanskrit literature.

Sandal and garment of yellow and lotus garlands upon his body of blue,

In his dance the jewels of his ears in movement dangling over his smiling cheeks.

Hari here disports himself with charming women given to love!

The wife of a certain herdsman sings as Hari sounds a tune of love

Embracing him the while with all the force of her full and swelling breasts.

Hari here disports himself with charming women given to love!

Another artless woman looks with ardour on Krishna's lotus face

Where passion arose through restless motion of playful eyes with sidelong glances.

Hari here disports himself with charming women given to love!

Another comes with beautiful hips, making as if to whisper a word,

And drawing close to his ear the adorable Krishna she kisses upon the cheek

Hari here disports himself with charming women given to love!

Another on the bank of the Jamna, when Krishna goes to a bamboo thicket,

Pulls at his garment to draw him back, so eager is she for amorous play.

Hari here disports himself with charming women given to love!

Hari praises another woman, lost with him in the dance of love,

The dance where the sweet low flute is heard in the clamour of bangles on hands that clap.

Hari here disports himself with charming women given to love!

He embraces one woman, he kisses another, and fondles another beautiful one,

He looks at another one lovely with smiles, and starts in pursuit of another woman.

Hari here disports himself with charming women given to love!

May all prosperity spread from this, Shri Jayadeva's famed and delightful

Song of wonderful Keshava's secret play in the forest of Vrindāvana!

Hari here disports himself with charming women given to love! . . .

With his limbs, tender and dark like rows of clumps of blue lotus flowers,

By herd-girls surrounded, who embrace at pleasure, any part of his body,

Friend, in spring beautiful Hari plays like Love's own self

Conducting the love sport, with love for all, bringing delight into being.

(from Jayadeva, *Gītā Govinda*, trans. by George Keyt)

Selections from the Upanishads

Introduction

The Upanishads, literally "to sit down in front of," are philosophical ideas of the Vedic Indo-Europeans created in dialogue form and transmitted by gurus to students. They were memorized by rote learning, hence they are called *smritis* as opposed to the *srutis,* which were Vedic texts to be recited and heard. Collectively, they are also called Vedānta, "the end of the Vedas." They are not concerned with rituals or sacrifices but with abstract speculations about truth and reality, the knowledge of which would enable a person to attain release (*moksha*) from the cycle of birth and rebirth. They revolve around the concepts of *Brahman* (the Absolute) and *ātman* (the Self or individual soul). They are mostly written in prose although a few are in verse. They are pre-Buddhist and the earliest were written in archaic Sanskrit but some are later compositions. There are 108 extant dialogues but Shankara (8th century), who expounded the monism of Vedānta through his "Brahman is reality, the world is illusion, and the soul is God," wrote commentaries on twelve of the thirteen Upanishads considered to be the original treatises. Each Upanishad was attached to a Brāhmaṇa, a supplement of a Veda. Representing different philosophic schools, some of the Upanishads expound monistic ideas, some stress the worship of a personal god, and others focus on the practice of yoga.

Yājnavalkya the sage had two wives, Maitreyi and Katyayani, and when—in the "Fourth Brāhmana"—he wished to make a settlement on them and depart on another phase of his life as an ascetic, his favorite wife Maitreyi asked him whether she would be immortal if the settlement he made on her would make her wealthy. When he replied that wealth would not bring immortality she asked him, therefore, what was the good of wealth? Instead he should give her knowledge. He was touched by this reply and informed her that she should see, know, perceive, and hear the *ātman*. Once she had understood that there was only consciousness of the Self and that nothing else was real then she would achieve immortality. With that he departed, content that his message—that the only reality was the one when the soul had joined in unity with the Absolute—had been understood.

Throughout the Upanishads the soul of the individual is identified with the soul of the universe and is considered the only reality. There were many ways to achieve understanding of this and renunciation was one of them. A life of asceticism was not absolutely necessary to achieve salvation—even rulers could realize Brahman—but if a mind was filled with material cares then it was very difficult. Thus, the renouncing of all pleasures, including the joy of family, was one of the ways to achieve salvation. This is the message of the "Fifth Brāmana."

In the "Sixth Brāhmana," the delightful conversation between the learned lady Gārgī and Yājnavalkya instructs her not to think too much and not to ask too many questions. This offers the Upanishadic message that salvation comes through an abstract and instinctual understanding of the reality of Brahman and not through sacrifices and good works. This reflects the Upanishadic method of explanation of the path to salvation. The nature of the *ātman* was not expressed in concrete terms but in negative ones as "not this, not that" (*neti, neti*). It was a totally abstract entity that could not be assailed. This is seen in the "Seventh Brāhmana," which heralded that an understanding of the path of salvation would lead to the freedom from all desires and that, in turn, would lead to unity with Brahma in a state of bliss that existed before creation itself.

Śvetataku is one of the most familiar interlocutors in the Upanishads and his dialogues in the ninth through fourteenth khandu are some of the most endearing, most celebrated, and most cited. Śvetataku was a conceited youth who had studied with brahmans for twelve years. In one renowned dialogue he was instructed to fetch a fig, to divide it, to divide the seeds, and to explain what he saw. When he said nothing, he was informed that what he missed was the essence of the fig and that the whole world had it as its soul. That was reality, *ātman,* and that too was Śvetataku. In the parable of the salt in the water he was asked to place some salt in water and come back the next morning and explain where the salt was. When he said he could not find it he was asked to sip the water from two ends and the middle. He said that it was always the same but was told that it contained the finest essence which was the whole world, which was *ātman,* which was Śvetataku.

The Fourth Brāhmana

SOURCE: *The Thirteen Principal Upanishads. Translated from the Sanskrit with an outline of the philosophy of the Upanishads and an annotated bibliography by Robert Ernest Hume. With a list of recurrent and parallel passages by George C. O. Haas.* 2d ed., rev. London: Oxford University Press, 1931, pp. 98–102.

The conversation of Yājñavalkya and Maitreyī concerning the pantheistic Soul

1. 'Maiteryī!' said Yājñavalkya , 'lo, verily, I am about to go forth from this state. Behold! let me make a final settlement for you and that Kātyāyanī,'

2. Then said Maiteryī: 'If now, sir, this whole earth filled with wealth were mine, would I be immortal thereby?'

'No,' said Yājñavalkya. 'As the life of the rich, even so would your life be. Of immortality, however, there is no hope through wealth.'

3. Then said Maiteryī: 'What should I do with that through which I may not be immortal? What you know, sir—that, indeed, tell me!'

4. Then said Yājñavalkya: 'Ah (*bata*)! Lo (*are*), dear (*priyā*) as you are to us, dear is what you say! Come, sit down. I will

explain to you. But while I am expounding, do you seek to ponder thereon.'

5. Then said he: 'Lo, verily, not for love of the husband is a husband dear, but for love of the Soul (*Ātman*) a husband is dear.

Lo, verily, not for love of the wife is a wife dear, but for love of the Soul a wife is dear.

Lo, verily, not for love of the sons are sons dear, but for love of the Soul sons are dear.

Lo, verily, not for love of the wealth is wealth dear, but for love of the Soul wealth is dear.

Lo, verily, not for love of Brahmanhood (*brahma*) is Brahmanhood dear, but for love of the Soul Brahmanhood is dear.

Lo, verily, not for love of Kshatrahood (*ksatra*) is Brahman dear, but for love of the Soul Kshatrahood is dear.

Lo, verily, not for love of the worlds are the worlds dear, but for love of the Soul the worlds are dear.

Lo, verily, not for love of the gods are the gods dear, but for love of the Soul the gods are dear.

Lo, verily, not for love of all is all dear, but for love of the Soul all is dear.

Lo, verily, it is the Soul (*Ātman*) that should be seen, that should be hearkened to, that should be thought on, that should be pondered on, O Maitreyī. Lo, verily, with the seeing of, with the hearkening of the Soul, this world-all is known.

6. Brahmanhood has deserted him who knows Brahmanhood in aught else than the Soul.

Kshatrahood has deserted him who knows Kshatrahood in aught else the Soul.

The Worlds have deserted him who knows the worlds in aught else than the Soul.

The gods have deserted him who knows the gods in aught else than the Soul.

Beings have deserted him who knows beings in aught else than the Soul.

Everything has deserted him who knows everything in aught else than the Soul.

This Brahmanhood, this Kshatrahood, these worlds, these gods, these beings, everything here is what this Soul is.

7. It is—as, when a drum is being beaten, one would not be able to grasp the external sounds, but by grasping the drum or the beater of the drum the sound is grasped.

8. It is—as, when a conch-shell is being blown, one would not be able to grasp the external sounds, but by grasping the conch-shell or the blower of the conch-shell the sound is grasped.

9. It is—as, when a lute is being played, one would not be able to grasp the external sounds, but by grasping the lute or the player of the lute the sound is grasped.

10. It is—as, from a fire laid with damp fuel, clouds of smoke separately issue forth, so, lo, verily, from this great Being (*bhūta*) has been breathed forth that which is

Rig-Veda, Yarjur-Veda, Sāma-Veda, [Hymns] of the Atharvans and Aṅgirases, Legend (*itihāsa*), Ancient Lore (*purāṇa*), Sciences (*vidyā*), Mystic Doctrines (*upaniṣad*), Verses (*śloka*), Aphorisms (*sūtra*), Explanations (*anuvyākhyāna*), and Commentaries (*vyākhyāna*). From it, indeed, are all these breathed forth.

11. It is—as of all waters the uniting-point is the sea, so of all touches the uniting-point is the skin, so of all tastes the uniting-point is the tongue, so of all smells the uniting-point is the nostrils, so of all forms the uniting-point is the eye, so of all sounds the uniting-point is the ear, so of all intentions (*saṁkalpa*) the uniting-point is the mind (*manas*), so of all knowledges the uniting-point is the heart, so of all acts (*karma*) the uniting-point is the hands, so of all pleasures (*ānanda*) the uniting-point is the generative organ, so of all evacuations the uniting-point is the anus, so of all journeys the uniting-point is the feet, so of all Vedas the uniting-point is speech.

12. It is—as a lump of salt cast in water would dissolve right into the water; there would not be [any] of it to seize forth, as it were (*iva*), but wherever one may take, it is salty indeed—so, lo, verily, this great Being (*bhūta*), infinite, limitless, is just a mass of knowledge (*vijñāna-ghana*).

Arising out of these elements (*bhūta*), into them also one vanishes away. After death there is no consciousness (*na pretya samjñā 'sti*). Thus, lo, say I.' Thus spake Yājñavalkya.

13. Then spake Maitreyī: 'Herein, indeed, you have bewildered me, sir—in saying (*iti*): "After death there is no consciousness"!'

Then spake Yājñavalkya: 'Lo, verily, I speak not bewilderment (*moha*). Sufficient, lo, verily, is this for understanding.

14. For where this is a duality (*dvaita*), as it were (*iva*), there one sees another; there one smells another; there one hears another; there one speaks to another; there one thinks another; there one understands another. Where, verily, everything has become just one's own self, then whereby and whom would one smell? then whereby and whom would one see? then whereby and whom would one hear? then whereby and to whom would one speak? then whereby and on whom would one think? then whereby and whom would one understand? Whereby would one understand him by whom one understands this All? Lo, whereby would one understand the understander?'

The Fifth Brāhmana

SOURCE: *The Thirteen Principal Upanishads. Translated from the Sanskrit with an outline of the philosophy of the Upanishads and an annotated bibliography by Robert Ernest Hume. With a list of recurrent and parallel passages by George C. O. Haas.* 2d ed., rev. London: Oxford University Press, 1931, pp. 112–113.

The practical way of knowing Brahma—by renunciation

Now Kahola Kaushītakeya questioned him. 'Yājñavalkya,' said he, 'explain to me him who is just the Brahma present and not beyond our ken, him who is the Soul in all things.'

'He is your soul, which is in all things.'

'Which one, O Yājñavalkya, is in all things?'

'He who passes beyond hunger and thirst, beyond sorrow and delusion, beyond old age and death—Brahmans who know such a Soul overcome desire for sons, desire for wealth, desire for worlds, and live the life of mendicants. For desire for sons is desire for wealth, and desire for wealth is desire for worlds, for both these are merely desires. Therefore let a Brahman become disgusted with learning and desire to live as a child. When he has become disgusted both with the state of childhood and with learning, then he becomes an ascetic (*muni*). When he has become disgusted both with the non-ascetic state and with the ascetic state, then he becomes a Brahman.'

'By what means would he become a Brahman?'

'By that means by which he does become such a one. Aught else than this Soul (*Ātman*) is wretched.'

Thereupon Kahola Kaushītakeya held his peace.

The Sixth Brāhmana

SOURCE: *The Thirteen Principal Upanishads. Translated from the Sanskrit with an outline of the philosophy of the Upanishads and an annotated bibliography by Robert Ernest Hume. With a list of recurrent and parallel passages by George C. O. Haas.* 2d ed., rev. London: Oxford University Press, 1931, pp. 113–114.

The regressus to Brahma, the ultimate world-ground

Then Gārgī Vācaknavī questioned him. 'Yājñavalkya,' said she, 'since all this world is woven, warp and woof, on water, on what, pray, is the water woven, warp and woof?'

'On wind, O Gārgī.'

'On what then, pray, is the wind woven, warp and woof?'

'On the atmosphere-worlds, O Gārgī.'

'On what then, pray, are the atmosphere-worlds woven, warp and woof?'

'On the worlds of the Gandharvas, O Gārgī.'

'On what then, pray, are the worlds of the Gandharvas woven, warp and woof?'

'On the worlds of the sun, O Gārgī.'

'On what then, pray, are the worlds of the sun woven, warp and woof?'

'On the worlds of the moon, O Gārgī.'

'On what then, pray, are the worlds of the moon woven, warp and woof?'

'On the worlds of the stars, O Gārgī.'

'On what then, pray, are the worlds of the stars woven, warp and woof?'

'On the worlds of the gods, O Gārgī.'

'On what then, pray, are the worlds of the gods woven, warp and woof?'

'On the worlds of Indra, O Gārgī.'

'On what then, pray, are the worlds of Indra woven, warp and woof?'

'On the worlds of Prajāpati, O Gārgī.'

'On what then, pray, are the worlds of Prajāpati woven, warp and woof?'

'On the worlds of Brahma, O Gārgī.'

'On what then, pray, are the worlds of Brahma woven, warp and woof?'

Yājñavalkya said: 'Gārgī, do not question too much, lest your head fall off. In truth, you are questioning too much about a divinity about which further questions cannot be asked. Gārgī, do not over-question.'

Thereupon Gārgī Vācaknavī held her peace.

The Soul of the Unreleased after Death

SOURCE: *The Thirteen Principal Upanishads. Translated from the Sanskrit with an outline of the philosophy of the Upanishads and an annotated bibliography by Robert Ernest Hume. With a list of recurrent and parallel passages by George C. O. Haas.* 2d ed., rev. London: Oxford University Press, 1931, pp. 140–141.

3. Now as a caterpillar, when it has come to the end of a blade of grass, in taking the next step draws itself together towards it, just so this soul in taking the next step strikes down this body, dispels its ignorance, and draws itself together [for making the transition].

4. As a goldsmith, taking a piece of gold, reduces it to another newer and more beautiful form, just so this soul, striking down this body and dispelling its ignorance, makes for itself another newer and more beautiful form like that either of the fathers, or of the Gandharvas, or of the gods, or of Prajāpati, or of Brahma, or of other beings.

5. Verily, this soul is Brahma, made of knowledge, of mind, of breath, of seeing, of hearing, of earth, of water, of wind, of space, of energy and of non-energy, of desire, of anger and of non-anger, of virtuousness and of non-virtuousness. It is made of everything. This is what is meant by the saying "made of this, made of that."

According as one acts, according as one conducts himself, so does he become. The doer of good becomes good. The doer of evil becomes evil. One becomes virtuous by virtuous action, bad by bad action.

But people say: "A person is made [not of acts, but] of desires only." [In reply to this I say:] As is his desire, such is his resolve; as his resolve, such the action he performs; what action (*karma*) he performs, that he procures for himself.

6. On this point there is this verse:—

Where one's mind is attached—the inner self
Goes thereto with action, being attached to it alone.
Obtaining the end of his action,

Whatever he does in this world,
He comes again from that world
To this world of action.

—So the man who desires.

The Soul of the Released

SOURCE: *The Thirteen Principal Upanishads. Translated from the Sanskrit with an outline of the philosophy of the Upanishads and an annotated bibliography by Robert Ernest Hume. With a list of recurrent and parallel passages by*

George C. O. Haas. 2d ed., rev. London: Oxford University Press, 1931, pp. 141–144.

Now the man who does not desire.—He who is without desire, who is freed from desire, whose desire is satisfied, whose desire is the Soul—his breaths do not depart. Being very Brahma, he goes to Brahma.

7. On this point there is this verse:—

When are liberated all
The desires that lodge in one's heart,
Then a mortal becomes immortal!
Therein he reaches Brahma!

As the slough of a snake lies on an ant-hill, dead, cast off, even so lies this body. But this incorporeal, immortal Life (*prāṇa*) is Brahma indeed, is light indeed.'

'I will give you, noble sir, a thousand [cows],' said Janaka, [king] of Videha.

8. [Yājñavalkya continued:] 'On this point there are these verses:—

The ancient narrow path that stretches far away
Has been touched by me, had been found by me.
By it the wise, the knowers of Brahma, go up
Hence to the heavenly world, released.

9. On it, they say, is white and blue
And yellow and green and red.
That was the path by Brahma found;
By it goes the knower of Brahma, the doer of right
    (*punya-kri*),
and every shining one.

10. Into blind darkness enter they
That worship ignorance;
Into darkness greater than that, as it were, they
That delight in knowledge.

11. Joyless are those worlds called,
Covered with blind darkness.
To them after death go those
People that have not knowledge, that are not awakened.

12. If a person knew the Soul (*Ātman*),
With the thought "I am he!"
With what desire, for love of what
Would he cling unto the body?

13. He who has found and has awakened to the Soul
That has entered this conglomerate abode—
He is the maker of everything, for he is the creator of all;
The world is his: indeed, he is the world itself.

14. Verily, while we are here we may know this.
If you have known it not, great is the destruction.
Those who know this become immortal,
But others go only to sorrow.

15. If one perceives Him
As the Soul, as God (*deva*), clearly,
As the Lord of what has been and of what is to be—
One does not shrink away from Him.

16. That before which the year
Revolves with its days—
That the gods revere as the light of lights,
As life immortal.

17. On whom the five peoples
And space are established—
Him alone I, the knowing, I, the immortal,
Believe to be the Soul, the immortal Brahma.

18. They who know the breathing of the breath,
The seeing of the eye, the hearing of the ear,
(The food of food), the thinking of the mind—
They have recognized the ancient, primeval Brahma.

19. By the mind alone is It to be perceived.
There is on earth no diversity.
He gets death after death,
Who perceives here seeming diversity.

20. As a unity only is It to be looked upon—
This indemonstrable, enduring Being,
Spotless, beyond space,
The unborn Soul, great, enduring.

21. By knowing Him only, a wise
Brahman should get for himself intelligence;
He should not meditate upon many words,
For that is a weariness of speech.

22. Verily, he is the great, unborn Soul, who is this [person] consisting of knowledge among the senses. In the space within the heart lies the ruler of all, the lord of all, the king of all. He does not become greater by good action nor inferior by bad action. He is the lord of all, the overlord of beings, the protector of beings. He is the separating dam for keeping these worlds apart.

Such a one the Brahmans desire to know by repetition of the Vedas, by sacrifices, by offerings, by penance, by fasting. On knowing him, in truth, one becomes an ascetic (*muni*). Desiring him only as their home, mendicants wander forth.

Verily, because they know this, the ancients desired not offspring, saying: "What shall we do with offspring, we whose is this Soul, this world?" They, verily, rising above the desire for sons and the desire for wealth and the desire for worlds, lived the life of a mendicant. For the desire for sons is the desire for wealth, and the desire for wealth is the desire for worlds; for both these are desires.

That Soul (*Ātman*) is not this, it is not that (*neti, neti*). It is unseizable, for it cannot be seized. It is indestructible, for it cannot be destroyed. It is unattached, for it does not attach itself. It is unbound. It does not tremble. It is not injured.

Him [who knows this] these two do not overcome—neither the thought "Hence I did wrong," nor the thought "Hence I did right." Verily, he overcomes them both. What he has done and what he has not done do not affect him.

23. This very [doctrine] has been declared in the verse:—

This eternal greatness of a Brahman
Is not increased by deeds (*karman*), nor diminished.
One should be familiar with it. By knowing it,
One is not stained by evil action.

Therefore, having this knowledge, having become calm, subdued, quiet, patiently enduring, and collected, one sees the Soul just in the soul. One sees everything as the Soul.

Evil does not overcome him; he overcomes all evil. Evil does not burn him: he burns all evil. Free from evil, free from impurity, free from doubt, he becomes a Brahman.

This is the Brahma-world, O king,' said Yājñavalkya.

[Janaka said:] 'I will give you, noble sir, the Videhas and myself also to be your slave.'

24. [Yājñavalkya continued:] 'This is that great, unborn Soul, who eats the food [which people eat], the giver of good. He finds good who knows this.

25. Verily, that great, unborn Soul, undecaying, undying, immortal, fearless, is Brahma. Verily, Brahma is fearless. He who knows this becomes the fearless Brahma.'

The Ninth Khaṇḍa

SOURCE: *The Thirteen Principal Upanishads. Translated from the Sanskrit with an outline of the philosophy of the Upanishads and an annotated bibliography by Robert Ernest Hume. With a list of recurrent and parallel passages by George C. O. Haas.* 2d ed., rev. London: Oxford University Press, 1931, p. 246.

The unitary World-Soul, the immanent reality of all things and of man

1. 'As the bees, my dear, prepare honey by collecting the essences of different trees and reducing the essence to a unity,

[2.] as they are not able to discriminate "I am the essence of this tree," "I am the essence of that tree"—even so, indeed, my dear, all creatures here, though they reach Being, know not "We have reached Being."

3. Whatever they are in this world, whether tiger, or lion, or wolf, or boar, or worm, or fly, or gnat, or mosquito, that they become.

4. That which is the finest essence—this whole world has that as its soul. That is Reality. That is Ātman (Soul). That art thou, Śvetaketu.'

'Do you, sir, cause me to understand even more.'

'So be it, my dear,' said he.

The Tenth Khaṇḍa

SOURCE: *The Thirteen Principal Upanishads. Translated from the Sanskrit with an outline of the philosophy of the Upanishads and an annotated bibliography by Robert Ernest Hume. With a list of recurrent and parallel passages by George C. O. Haas.* 2d ed., rev. London: Oxford University Press, 1931, pp. 246–247.

1. 'These rivers, my dear, flow, the eastern toward the east, the western toward the west. They go just from the ocean to the ocean. They become the ocean itself. As there they know not "I am this one," "I am that one"—[2] even so, indeed, my dear, all creatures here, though they have come forth Being, know not "We have come forth from Being." Whatever they are in this world, whether tiger, or lion, or wolf, or boar, or worm, or fly, or gnat, or mosquito, that they become.

3. That which is the finest essence—this whole world has that as its soul. That is Reality. That is Ātman (Soul). That art thou, Śvetaketu.

'Do you, sir, cause me to understand even more.'

'So be it, my dear,' said he.

The Eleventh Khaṇḍa

SOURCE: *The Thirteen Principal Upanishads. Translated from the Sanskrit with an outline of the philosophy of the Upanishads and an annotated bibliography by Robert Ernest Hume. With a list of recurrent and parallel passages by George C. O. Haas.* 2d ed., rev. London: Oxford University Press, 1931, p. 247.

1. 'Of this great tree, my dear, if some one should strike at the root, it would bleed, but still live. If some one should strike at this middle, it would bleed, but still live. If some one should strike at its top, it would bleed, but still live. Being pervaded by Atman (Soul), it continues to stand, eagerly drinking in moisture and rejoicing.

2. If the life leaves one branch of it, then it dries up. It leaves a second; then that dries up. It leaves a third; then that dries up. It leaves the whole; the whole dries up. Even so, indeed, my dear, understand,' said he.

3. Verily, indeed, when life has left it, this body dies. The life does not die.

That which is the finest essence—this whole world has that as its soul. That is Reality. That is Ātman (Soul). That art thou, Śvetaketu.'

'Do you, sir, cause me to understand even more.'

'So be it, my dear,' said he.

The Twelfth Khaṇḍa

SOURCE: *The Thirteen Principal Upanishads. Translated from the Sanskrit with an outline of the philosophy of the Upanishads and an annotated bibliography by Robert Ernest Hume. With a list of recurrent and parallel passages by George C. O. Haas.* 2d ed., rev. London: Oxford University Press, 1931, pp. 247–248.

1. 'Bring hither a fig from there.'

'Here it is, sir.'

'Divide it.'

'It is divided, sir.'

'What do you see there?'

'These rather (*iva*) fine seeds, sir.'

'Of these, please (*aṅga*), divide one.'

'It is divided, sir.'

'What do you see there?'

'Nothing at all, sir.'

2. Then he said to him: 'Verily, my dear, that finest essence which you do not perceive—verily, my dear, from that finest essence this great Nyagrodha (sacred fig) tree thus arises.

3. Believe me, my dear,' said he, (3) 'that which is the finest essence—this whole world has that as its soul. That is Reality. That is Ātman (Soul). That art thou, Śvetaketu.'

'Do you, sir, cause me to understand even more.'

'So be it, my dear,' said he.

The Thirteenth Khaṇḍa

SOURCE: *The Thirteen Principal Upanishads. Translated from the Sanskrit with an outline of the philosophy of the Upanishads and an annotated bibliography by Robert Ernest Hume. With a list of recurrent and parallel passages by George C. O. Haas.* 2d ed., rev. London: Oxford University Press, 1931, p. 248.

1. 'Place this salt in the water. In the morning come unto me.'

Then he did so.

Then he said to him: 'That salt you placed in the water last evening—please bring it hither.'

Then he grasped for it, but did not find it, as it was completely dissolved.

2. 'Please take a sip of it from this end,' said he. 'How is it?'

'Salt.'

'Take a sip from the middle,' said he. How is it?'

'Salt.'

'Take a sip from that end,' said he. 'How is it?'

'Salt.'

'Set it aside. Then come unto me.'

He did so, saying. 'It is always the same.'

Then he said to him: 'Verily, indeed, my dear, you do not perceive Being here. Verily, indeed, it is here.

3. That which is the finest essence—this whole world has that as its soul. That is Reality. That is Ātman (Soul). That art thou, Śvetaketu.'

'Do you, sir, cause me to understand even more.'

'So be it, my dear,' said he.

The Fourteenth Khaṇḍa

SOURCE: *The Thirteen Principal Upanishads. Translated from the Sanskrit with an outline of the philosophy of the Upanishads and an annotated bibliography by Robert Ernest Hume. With a list of recurrent and parallel passages by George C. O. Haas.* 2d ed., rev. London: Oxford University Press, 1931, p. 249.

1. Just as, my dear, one might lead away from the Gandhāras a person with his eyes bandaged, and then abandon him in an uninhabited place; as there he might be blown forth either to the east, to the north, or to the south, since he had been led off with his eyes bandaged and deserted with his eyes bandaged; [2] as, if one released his bandage and told him, "In that direction are the Gandhāras; go in that direction!" he would, if he were a sensible man, by asking [his way] from village to village, and being informed, arrive home at the Gandhāras—even so here on earth one who has a teacher knows: "I shall remain here only so long as I shall not be released [from the bonds of ignorance]. Then I shall arrive home."

3. That which is the finest essence—this whole world has that as its soul. That is Reality. That is Ātman (Soul). That art thou, Śvetaketu.'

'Do you, sir, cause me to understand even more.'

'So be it, my dear,' said he.

Liberation into the Real Brahma By Relinquishment of All Desires, Mental Activity, and Self-Consciousness

SOURCE: *The Thirteen Principal Upanishads. Translated from the Sanskrit with an outline of the philosophy of the Upanishads and an annotated bibliography by Robert Ernest Hume. With a list of recurrent and parallel passages by George C. O. Haas.* 2d ed., rev. London: Oxford University Press, 1931, pp. 442–443.

30. *Om*! One should be in a pure place, himself pure (*śuci*), abiding in pureness (*sativa*), studying the Real (*sat*), speaking of the Real, meditating upon the Real, sacrificing to the Real. Henceforth, in the real Brahma which longs for the Real, he becomes completely other. So he has the reward (*phala*) of having his fetters cut; becomes void of expectation, freed from fear in regard to others [as fully] as in regard to himself, void of desire. He attains to imperishable, immeasureable happiness, and continues [therein].

Verily, freedom from desire (*niṣkāmatva*) is like the choicest extract from the choicest treasure. For, a person who is made up of all desires, who has the marks of determination, conception, and self-conceit, is bound. Hence, in being the opposite of that, he is liberated.

On this point some say: "It is a quality (*guṇa*) which by force of the developing differentiation of Nature (*prakṛti*) comes to bind the self with determination [and the like], and that liberation results from the destruction of the fault of determination [and the like]."

[But] it is with the mind, truly, that one sees. It is with the mind that one hears. Desire, conception, doubt, faith, lack of faith, steadfastness, lack of steadfastness, shame, meditation, fear—all this is truly mind.

Borne along and defiled by the stream of Qualities, unsteady, wavering, bewildered, full of desire, distracted, one goes on into the state of self-conceit. In thinking "This is I" and "That is mine" one binds himself with himself, as does a bird with a snare! Hence a person who has the marks of determination, conception, and self-conceit is bound. Hence, in being the opposite of that, he is liberated. Therefore one should stand free from determination, free from conception, free from self-conceit. This is the mark of liberation (*mokṣa*). This is the pathway to Brahma here in this world. This is the opening of the door here in this world. By it one will go to the farther shore of this darkness, for therein all desires are contained. On this point they quote:—

When cease the five
[Sense-] knowledges, together with the mind,
And the intellect stirs not—
That, they say, is the highest course.'

glossary

Sanskrit and Hindi Pronunciation Guide

Long vowels have lines above them: ā, ī, and ū are pronounced as the "a" in *bar* or *calm*, the "i" in *machine*, and the "u" in *rule* or *soon*.

Diphthongs e, o, ai, and au are also long, pronounced: "e" as the "a" in *take* or the "e" in *prey*; "o" as in *so* or *go*; "ai" as "ai" in *aisle* or "i" in *time*; "au" as in "ow" in *how* or *cow*.

Short vowels are a, i, and u and pronounced: "a" as "u" in *up* or *cut*; "i" as "i" in *sin* or *bit*; and "u" as "u" in *pull* or *bull*.

Consonants

    Pronounce "c" as "ch" in *chin* and "g" as "g" in *gun*.

    Aspirates "dh," "gh," and "bh" pronounce as in *roundhouse*, *doghouse*, and *clubhouse*.

    Aspirates "th" and "ph" pronounce as in *pothole* and *shepherd*.

    Ś and ṣ are both pronounced as "sh" in *shape*.

abhisheka: Ancient Brahman ritual to consecrate a king.

Ādityas: Early Vedic deities.

adivasis: Tribal peoples.

Agni: Vedic Aryan god of fire.

ahimsa: Nonviolence.

Ajivika: Early monastic sect, similar to Jains.

Akbar: "Great" Mughal emperor.

amir: Muslim prince or commander of troops.

aparigraha: Hindu vow of poverty.

arhat: Buddhist monk who has achieved great wisdom.

Arjuna: Brave Aryan Pandava brother, whose charioteer was Krishna.

Artha Shāstra: "Science of Material Gain," ancient Brahman textbook on polity.

Aryan: Indo-European linguistic group or early tribal invaders of North India.

Aryavarta: Land of the Aryans; North India's Punjab to Delhi.

asat: Ancient Rig Vedic "Unreal," or untrue; nebulous or demonic.

Ashoka: Mauryan emperor.

Ashrama: One of four stages in a good Hindu's life; also a rural community.

ashvamedha: Vedic royal horse sacrifice.

Ashvins: Vedic Hindu twin gods.

Atharva Veda: Late Vedic Saṃhitā, containing medicinal remedies.

ātman: Ancient Vedic breath, later self; finally Soul, identical to Vedāntic Brahman.

Aurangzeb: Mughal emperor.

avatāra: Earthly emanation of Vishnu, nine of which have appeared, the tenth yet to come.

avidya: Ignorance.

Ayodhya: Ancient North Indian Hindu Temple city, recent center of communal conflict.

azad: Free.

Babur: First great Mughal emperor.

bagh: Garden.

Bande Mataram: "Hail to thee, mother!," first national anthem of India.

Bania: Hindu merchant caste of Gujarat.

Bhadralok: Bengali intellectuals, "gentle learned people."

Bhagavad Gītā: "Song of the blessed one," philosophic dialogue between Arjuna and Krishna from the longer epic Mahābhārata.

bhakti: Hindu devotion to a personal god.

Bharata: Sanskrit name for India; name of an ancient Aryan tribe and of Rāma's brother.

Bharatiya Janata Party (BJP): "Indian People's Party," a political party.

Bhīma: Ancient Pandava brother hero.

Bhoodan: "Gift of land," original appeal launched by Vinoba Bhave.

Bimbisara: Buddha's royal patron, king of Magadha.

Bindusara: Second Mauryan emperor, father of Ashoka.

bodhi: Enlightenment.

bodhisattva: Mahayana Buddhist heavenly being, whose "essence is True Enlightenment."

Brahmā: Vedic god of creation.

Brahmacharya: Celibate studenthood *ashrama*, the first "stage" of a devout Hindu's life.

Brahman: Sacred utterance; hence, Hinduism's highest class of priests who control religious mantras, reciting Vedic texts from memory; also transcendental Brahman, the Upanishadic divine principle, equated to *ātman* in Vedānta texts.

Brāhmaṇas: Ancient commentaries on Vedic Saṃhitās.

Brahmi: Ancient alphabet and script in which Sanskrit Vedic and Hindu texts were first written.

Brihadāraṇyaka Upanishad: "Great Forest" Upanishadic text, perhaps the most ancient to survive.

Buddha: The Enlightened One.

caste: Portuguese term for India's *jati* (birth) and *varṇa* (class) systems.

chaitya: Sacred spot, or shrine, carved into ancient Buddhist and Jain caves.

chakra: Wheel, found in the middle white band of India's flag; Ashoka's "Wheel"; also Mahatma Gandhi's cotton hand-spinning "wheel."

chakravartin: Universal Hindu emperor, for whom the "Wheel of Law" turns.

Chalukya: Ancient Central and South Indian Hindu dynasty; later period.

Chandragupta I and II: First and third emperors of the later Gupta dynasty.

Chandragupta Mauryan: First emperor of the ancient Mauryan dynasty.

Charaka: Ancient Indian physician, author of an important medical text.

Chatrapati: Ancient Hindu monarch of the "Four Quarters" of the universe.

Cholas: Ancient South Indian maritime dynasty, greatest Hindu bronze artists.

Dalits: Formerly "Untouchables," or "Outcaste" peoples, named Harijans by Mahatma Gandhi.

danda: "Rod" used to punish lazy students or neighboring kingdoms, ancient India's weapon for retaining and expanding a raja's power.

dandaniti: Art of government.

Darshana: "View" or "vision" of an icon of a Hindu god, saintly being, or mahatma; also the term used for each of the classical schools of Hindu philosophy.

Dasa: Initially pre-Aryan "dark-skinned" peoples of the Indus Valley, later "slave."

Deva: Vedic Aryan god—"Shining One."

dēvadāsi: "Slave of the God," temple dancers, orphan girls abandoned, left to be reared by Brahman priests, for whom they danced and performed other services.

Devanagari: "City of god"—the script in which most modern Indo-European languages, including India's national language, Hindi, are written.

Devī: Hindu goddess.

Dharma: Hindu religion, law, duty, truth, or responsibility; a Sanskrit term of many meanings.

Dharma Shāstra: Ancient Hindu legal textbook, among which the Manava Dharma Shāstra (Manu's law text) is most famous.

Dhimmis: "Peoples of the Book," including Jews and Christians, specially protected by Muslim monarchs as long as they paid the extra *jizya* "head tax."

dhruva-pada: Rhythmic musical form.

dhyana: Yogic meditation.

diwan: Prime minister to a Muslim sultan or emperor, originally "court."

diwani: Revenue-collection powers granted by Mughal emperors to provincial officers.

Draupadi: Epic polyandrous wife of all five Pandava brothers.

Dravidian: Family of South Indian languages that include Tamil, Telugu, Malayalam, and Kanarese; a South Indian "nationalist" movement which has tried to unite all peoples who speak those tongues.

dukkha: Sorrow or suffering, the Buddha's first noble truth of universal human pain.

Durgā: Mother goddess, Hinduism's fiercest "Mother," who wears a necklace of skulls.

Dyaus: Rig Vedic "Father Sky," one of the most ancient Hindu gods.

Elephanta: Ancient Hindu rock-carved caves on an island off Mumbai (Bombay).

Epic Age: Hinduism's great epics, Mahābhārata and Rāmāyaṇa, were composed in North India between about 1000 B.C. and the dawn of the common era.

Eucratides: Early Bactrian Greek king who invaded Northern India.

Euthydemus: Bactrian Greek king who invaded India's North-West Frontier.

Fahsien: Chinese Buddhist monk who traveled through India during the Gupta era.

feringi: "Polluted" foreigner, a term often used by high caste Hindus.

Gaṇesha: One of the most popular Hindu gods, the elephant-headed son of Shiva and Pārvatī.

Gaṅgā: River goddess.

Gayatri: Rig Vedic morning sacred verse to the rising Sun god.

ghats: "Steps," usually of stone, leading into a river's water from Hindu temples along its bank, where worshipers bathe before praying, or as in Varanasi, the "burning *ghats*" where corpses are consumed by flame; also used for the mountain ridge along Southwest India, the "Western Ghats."

gopī: Milkmaid, usually a Hindu cowherd's daughter, devoted to fluting Krishna, the most perfect and beloved of Vishnu's *avatāra*s.

gōpura: South Indian Hindu temple gate tower, usually high enough to be seen for miles.

gotra: Hindu Brahman exogamous sect.

grama: Village.

Gupta dynasty: Classical "Golden Age" of Hindu unification (c. A.D. 320–550).

Gurjara-Pratiharas: One of the last great Hindu dynasties of North India.

Gurmukhi: Unique cursive script used by Sikhs.

guru: Hindu teacher or preceptor; semidivine leader of the Sikhs, starting with Guru Nanak and ending with Guru Govind Singh.

Guru Granth Sahib: Sikh scripture, kept in Amritsar's Golden Temple.

Hara: Great Hindu god Shiva; ancient northern "capital" of Indus Valley, Harappa.

Hari: Great Hindu god Vishnu, disciples of whom are called Vaishnavites.

Harihara: Sculptural syncretism of Vishnu and Shiva, classical Hindu attempt to integrate artistically its two most popular male gods; royal founder of South India's Vijayanagar dynasty (Harihari I, r. A.D. 1336–1357).

Harijan: "Child of God," the term used by Mahatma Gandhi for "Untouchables."

Harsha Vardhana: Powerful king of Kanauj (r. A.D. 606–647).

Hastinapura: Ancient Vedic Aryan city.

Hinayana: "Lesser Vehicle" early form of Buddhism.

Hsieun Tsang: "Master of the Law," Chinese Buddhist pilgrim.

Hyder Ali: Muslim ruler of Mysore.

Indra: Great Vedic god of war.

Isha Upanishad: One of the most sacred Upanishads, of "the Lord-Isha."

Islam: Faith of the prophet Muhammad; Arabic, "surrender" to the will of Allah.

Jahangir: Great Mughal emperor (r. A.D. 1605–1627).

Jain: A follower of the faith of Mahāvīra, Jainism.

Jajmani system: A rural Hindu Indian system of exchange based on patronage and barter.

Jallianwala Bagh: A garden in Punjab's Amritsar, where some 400 Indian nationalist Sikhs and Hindus were massacred by British-led troops in April 1919.

Jana: Ancient Aryan tribe.

Jatakas: Mythical "birth" stories and folktales of previous "lives" of the Buddha.

Jati: "Birth" group, misnamed "caste," within which Hindus traditionally marry.

jina: "Conqueror," one of the titles given to the founder of Jainism, Mahāvīra.

jiva: Soul, very important to the Jain faith.

jizya: Head tax imposed by Muslim rulers on Dhimmis ("Peoples of the Book").

Kailasanatha Temple: Shiva's celestial palace carved out of the rock mountain at Ellora.

Kālī: Mother goddess ("Black") worshiped by millions of Hindus.

Kālidāsa: Greatest ancient Indian poet-dramatist, author of *Shakuntala*.

kalpa: A period within traditional Hindu-Jain cyclical cosmic aeons of time.

Kāma: Hindu god of love.

karma: To "do," or "act," actions bearing fruit similar to, or based upon, parent deeds.

Karma Yoga: "Discipline of Action," a Hindu path to salvation expounded in the Bhagavad Gītā.

khadi: Hand-spun cotton and woven cotton cloth, such as Mahatma Gandhi made.

khalifa: Muslim caliph or emperor, whose restoration was demanded by pan-Islamic leaders.

Khalsa: Sikh army of the "Pure."

Krishna: Most popular *avatāra* of Vishna, pastoral Hindu god, whose name means "Black."

Kshatriya: Hindu warrior; the second highest Hindu "class" (*varṇa*) among four.

Lakshmaṇa: Brother of Rāma.

Lakshmī: Mother goddess.

lok: People.

Lok Sabha: "House [Assembly] of the People"—Lower House of Parliament in New Delhi.

Madhya Pradesh: "Middle Province," a large state of Central India.

Mahābhārata: "Great-Bharata," the longer epic Sanskrit poem of ancient India.

maharaja: "Great-King," the title taken by monarchs who conquered several rajas.

mahatma: "Great-Soul," the only title Mahatma Gandhi ever had.

Mahāvīra: "Great Hero," the title name of the founder of Jainism.

Mahayana: "Greater Vehicle" of later Buddhism, post–common era.

Maheshvara: "Great God," the term often used for Shiva.

mandala: "Circle" or ring.

mansabdar: Mughal official, whose rank was usually associated with a number of horsemen for whom he was responsible, obliged to bring ready for battle, whenever the emperor called.

mantra: A sacred utterance, e.g., a syllable, "*Om*," or god's name, "*Ram, Ram*," or phrase, as the Upanishadic equation of *ātman* and Brahman, "*Tat tvam asi*"—"thou art That One."

Maurya dynasty: North Indian Jain–Buddhist imperial unification, (c. 324–184 B.C.).

maya: Illusion, used for material things of this world by Vedāntic philosophers.

moksha: "Liberation" or "release" from worldly pains of the here and now and reincarnation, a devout Hindu's ultimate goal; sometimes called "*neti, neti*," ("not this, not that").

mudra: Hand gesture, hundreds of which are used as one code of classical Indian dance.

nabob: British corruption of Mughal *nawāb*.

Naga: Snake-spirit or tribe.

Nanak: Guru founder of Sikhism.

Narasimha: Man-lion *avatāra* of Vishnu.

Nataraja: Shiva depicted in bronze sculpture or other art forms as "King of Dance."

Nātya Shāstra: Classic Hindu textbook of music, dance, and drama, attributed to the ancient sage Bharata.

nawāb: Mughal provincial governor, or viceroy, or deputy.

netaji: "Leader," the title used by Subhash Chandra Bose.

nirvāna: "Blowing out," the ultimate goal of "extinction" for Buddhist monks.

Nyāya: Ancient Hindu school of philosophy focusing on salvation through "logic."

om: Sacred Sanskrit syllable of cosmic unity.

Ophir: Ancient West Indian port or region from which ivory, gold, and peacock feathers were shipped to King Solomon.

Orissa: Indian state, named Kalinga during the Mauryan era, conquered by Ashoka.

padishah: Mughal "emperor."

padmāsana: Classical dance and Yogic lotus position.

Pallavas: South Indian "robber" dynasty, from fourth century B.C.

Panchamas: "Fifths," a term used for "Untouchables," who fall below the four-class Hindu system.

panchayat: Village "council of five," usually Brahman, Kshatriya, or Vaishya elders.

panchayati raj: Ideal of rural democracy, an experiment launched in 1959 in India's Rajasthan state, to help in its economic planning for agricultural development.

Panch Shila: "Five principles," including peaceful coexistence, Prime Minister Nehru's ideal foreign policy, initially agreed upon in a 1954 treaty with China regarding Tibet.

Pandavas: Five virtuous sons of Pandu—Yudhishtira, Bhīma, Arjuna, Nakula, and Sahadeva, the heroes of the epic Mahābhārata, who defeat their Kaurava cousins at Kurukshetra.

Parsis: A small, enlightened Zoroastrian community, expelled from Persia in the seventh century A.D., settling mostly in Bombay (Mumbai), leaders in politics, law, and the arts.

Pārvatī: Shiva's consort, popular Hindu mother goddess.

Pashupati: Shiva as "Lord of Beasts."

Pataliputra: Ancient capital of the Mauryan empire, modern Patna, capital of Bihar.

peshwas: Chitpavin Brahman prime ministers of Poona (Pune).

pir: Muslim holy Sufi.

prakriti: "Woman"; also primeval "matter," in the Sāṃkhya school of Hindu philosophy.

Punjab: "Land of Five Rivers."

Pur: Ancient fortified city.

Purāṇas: Ancient "tales," mythical stories of many incarnations of popular Hindu gods.

purdah: Hiding female Muslim faces and bodies behind usually dark cloth veils and robes.

purusha: "Man," the original Vedic sacrificial Being from which the four Hindu *varṇa*s emerged, Brahmans from his mouth, Kshatriyas from his arms, Vaishyas from his thighs, Shudras from his feet; in the Sāṃkhya ("Numbers") school of classical Hindu philosophy, Purusha ("Man" or "Spirit") is the first of 25 numbered "matters," the other 24 emerging from Prakriti ("Woman").

Purva Mimansa: "Early inquiry" school of ancient Hindu philosophy, focuses on re-creating the ancient Vedic fire altar and performing its annual ritual sacrifice.

Pushyamitra Shunga: Martial founder of the Shunga dynasty (184–72 B.C.).

Quaid-i-Azam: "Great Leader," honorific title reserved for M. A. Jinnah, father of Pakistan.

Qurʿan: Sacred "book" of Islamic scripture, Arabic message of God heard by the prophet Muhammad.

Rādhā: Krishna's most beloved consort.

rāga: Series of five or more musical notes on which a classical Indian melody is based.

Raj: "Rule," hence government, used for the British Empire of India, "The Raj."

raja: Ancient Indian king, later exalted to "Great King," maharaja, and "King of Kings," rajaraja.

Rajaraja Chola: "King of Kings" of the South Indian dynasty (r. A.D. 985–1016).

Rāma: Ideal heroic Hindu king; popular incarnation (*avatāra*) of Vishnu.

Rāmāyaṇa: The shorter Sanskrit epic poem, the story of Raja Rāma and his beloved wife Sītā.

Ram Rajya: Hinduism's mythical "Golden Age," when Raja Rāma ruled over Ayodhya.

Rashtrakuta: "Country Lord" dynasty established in eighth century A.D. in Central India.

Rishi: Rig Vedic sage.

rita: Vedic cosmic order of the true.

Rudra: Rig Vedic ("Howler") god, later associated with Shiva.

Rukmini: Krishna's consort.

ryot: Agricultural laborer.

sabha: Council chamber or assembly.

Salt March: Led by Mahatma Gandhi in opposition to the British tax on salt, March–April 1930.

Samadhi: Deep Yoga meditation.

Sāma Veda: Vedic prayer hymnal, probably the third Saṃhitā compilation.

Saṃhitā: Four ancient compilations of Vedic prayers: Rig, Yajur, Sāma, Atharva.

Sāṃkhya: "Numbers" school of classical Hindu philosophy.

saṃsāra: Cycle of birth and death; life in this world of pain and sorrow.

Samudra Gupta: Second Guptan emperor (r. A.D. 335–375).

sangha: Buddhist monastic order.

Sarasvatī: Goddess of the Sarasvati River, sister of Gaṅgā.

sarkar: District; later expanded to mean the entire British administration.

Sarvodaya: "The uplift of all," Gandhian socialism.

sat, satya: Vedic "Real," and "True" or "Truth."

sati: "True One," euphemism used for a Hindu widow immolated on her husband's funeral pyre, abolished by the British in 1829, but recently revived in Rajasthan.

satyagraha: "Hold fast to truth," Mahatma Gandhi's term for his nonviolent, noncooperation movements, first launched in South Africa, later as nationwide protests in India.

sepoy: Indian "police" first hired by Portuguese, later by the British, also used as soldiers.

Shah Jahan: Mughal emperor (r. A.D. 1628–1658).

Shaivism: Hindu worship of Shiva, the "Great God" (Maheshvara).

Shakti: Mother goddess "Power," whose undying force invigorates all male gods, each of whom thus needs a female consort; Shiva's first consort.

Shakuntala: Kālidāsa's greatest Sanskrit drama; its heroine's name.

Shariʿa: Islamic law.

shastri: Teacher.

Shi'i: Heterodox Islamic sects, followers of Ali.

Shiva: Hinduism's "Great God," "King of Dance," "Lord of Beasts," master of Yogic power.

shreni: Hindu merchant or artisan guild.

shruti: "Heard"—sacred Vedic texts, from the Rig Veda through Brāhmaṇa commentaries, and Upanishadic Vedānta.

Shudra: One of the lowest *varṇa* (class) of Hinduism's four Ashramas, usually a landless menial laborer.

Sikh: "Disciple," of the gurus (great teachers) of Sikhism.

Sītā: Rāma's consort, the ideal Hindu wife.

sitar: Classic stringed musical instrument, usually made of lacquered gourds.

Soma: Vedic god of divine nectar.

stupa: "Gathered" mound of earth and brick over some of the Buddha's ashes, worshiped by monks who circumambulate it in a clockwise direction.

Sufism: Mystical "third" sect of Islam, most appealing to lower class or outcaste Hindus.

Sunni: Orthodox Islamic faith of the majority of Muslims.

swadeshi: "Of our own country," goods made by Indian nationalists, rejecting British imports.

swaraj: "Of our own rule," the battle cry for independence, demanding "home rule" or "freedom," raised by early revolutionary leaders of India's National Congress.

tabla: Classic Indian musical drum set, covered with tightly drawn hide, the fast-moving fingers of skilled drummers tapping out rhythmic tālas to accompany a sitar player's *rāga*.

tāla: Rhythmic figure, the second most important element (after *rāga*) of classic Indian music.

Tamil Nadu: South India's "Land of the Tamils" state, formerly Madras.

Tantrism: Esoteric form of Hinduism, sexually orgiastic in nature, obscure in its ancient origins.

tapas: Heat generated during Yogic meditation.

tapasya: Self-purification through intense prolonged "suffering."

Tat: "That One," the transcendental monistic essence, Brahman, of Upanishadic Vedānta.

Theravada: "Teachings of the Elders," the earliest form of Buddhism.

Thugi: Ritual murder by strangulation, performed by gangs of Thugs, Hindu worshipers of Mother goddesses Kālī and Durgā, outlawed by the British in 1828.

Tipu Sultan: Enlightened Muslim ruler of Mysore, defeated by Lord Wellesley in 1799.

Tīrthānkara: "Ford-crosser," worshiped by Jains, the last (24th) of whom was Mahāvīra.

ulama: Muslim learned elite, plural of *alim*.

Umā: Hindu Mother goddess.

Umma: Universal Islamic brotherhood of Muslims.

untouchables: Lowest class of Hindus, also called Outcastes, or Harijans, now Dalits.

Upanishad: "To sit down in front of," esoteric teachings of Vedānta philosophy.

vaidya: Āyurvedic traditional Hindu physician.

Vaisheshika: "Atomic" or "individual characteristics" school of traditional Hindu philosophy.

Vaishnavism: Hindu worshipers of Vishnu, whose many *avatāra*s include Krishna, Rāma, and the Buddha.

Vaishya: Merchant or landowning third "class" (*varṇa*) in Hinduism's social hierarchy.

Varṇa: Hindu "class," traditionally only four, though an outcaste fifth was later added.

Varuṇa: Rig Vedic god of "Universal Law and Order" (initially *rita*, later *dharma*).

vazir: Muslim ruler's premier.

Vedānta: "End of Vedas," Upanishadic philosophy, last of six classical schools of Hindu philosophy.

Vedas: Earliest Sanskrit ritual prayers and sacred books of "knowledge" (*vid*).

vihara: Monastic cells for living quarters carved out of mountain escarpments by Buddhist and Jain monks in Northeast India, in the state for which they are named—Bihar.

vina: "Lute," classic Hindu musical instrument, with a long fingerboard and gourd body.

Vishnu: Shares with Shiva the greatest popularity among a majority of Hindu worshipers of male divinities; devotees often marking their foreheads with a chalk or lime-white V.

Yajur Veda: Probably the second compilation (Saṃhitā) of ancient Vedic prayers.

Yama: Vedic god of death.

Yoga: "Discipline," probably the most ancient Indian school of philosophy, pre-Aryan in its Indus Valley origins, emerging later as the unifying discipline of all six classical schools of traditional Hindu philosophy, always associated with Shiva.

Yogis: Hindu, Buddhist, and Jain practitioners of Yoga, known to have sat in lotus positions from very ancient times, meditating deeply in the forests of North India.

zakat: Islamic tax imposed on all Muslims.

zamindar: Initially temporary Mughal land-revenue collectors, later made more wealthy and powerful as permanent landlords throughout Bengal by the British.

zenānā: Hindu women's secluded quarters in rural as well as urban homes, usually completely hidden from the eyes of strangers passing on lanes or roads outside.

Zoroastrianism: Religion of India's Parsis, most of whom still live in Mumbai.

general bibliography

Ahmed, Akbar S. *Islam under Siege.* Cambridge, U.K.: Polity Press, 2003. One of the most insightful studies of Islam by one of Pakistan's most brilliant scholar-diplomats, a living bridge between superficially incompatible civilizations.

Allchin, B., and F. R. Allchin. *The Birth of Indian Civilisation: India and Pakistan before 500 BC.* Harmondsworth, U.K.: Penguin, 1968. Very good general introduction to the Indus Valley culture and its archaeological excavations and treasures.

Anand, Mulk Raj. *Untouchable.* New Delhi: Orient Paperback, 1970. Also: *Coolie.* Delhi: Hind Pocket Books, 1972. Two excellent novels by one of India's greatest writers of the last century.

Anderson, Walter K., and Shridhar D. Damle. *The Brotherhood in Saffron: The Rashtriya Swayamsevak Sangh and Hindu Revivalism.* Boulder, Colo.: Westview Press, 1987. A history of the growth of the paramilitary RSS and its powerful impact on modern India.

Ballhatchet, Kenneth. *Race, Sex and Class under the Raj: Imperial Attitudes and Policies and Their Critics, 1793–1905.* New York: St. Martin's Press, 1980. One of the best scholarly studies of this important subject.

Barnett, Richard B. *North India between Empires: Awadh, the Mughals and the British, 1720–1801.* Berkeley: University of California Press, 1980. Illuminating history of a relatively ignored era of great importance and conflict.

Basham, A. L. *The Wonder That Was India.* 3rd ed. New York: Grove, 1967. Excellent general introduction to early Indian history and to Indian civilization.

Bayly, C. A. *Indian Society and the Making of the British Empire,* pt. 2 of vol. 1: *New Cambridge History of India,* edited by Gordon Johnson. Cambridge, U.K.: Cambridge University Press, 1987. Comprehensive study of the making of British India. Also see his excellent *The Local Roots of Indian Politics: Allahabad, 1880–1920.*

Bhagwati, Jagdish. *India in Transition: Freeing the Economy.* Oxford: Oxford University Press, 1993. Excellent introduction to the recent opening of India's economy that has led to such rapid growth and development.

Bittansen, Thomas. *The Saffron Wave.* Princeton, N.J.: Princeton University Press, 1999. One of the best introductions to the emergence and alarming growth of India's Hindutva politics.

Bose, Subhas Chandra. *The Indian Struggle.* Kolkata: Chuckervertty, Chatterjee, 1952. The autobiography of Bengal's greatest revolutionary nationalist and one of India's nationalist heroes, elected twice to serve as president of the Indian National Congress.

Brass, Paul. *Ethnicity and Nationalism.* Newbury Park, Calif.: Sage, 1991. An excellent introduction to an important aspect of India's complex history.

Brown, Judith M. *Gandhi: Prisoner of Hope.* New Haven, Conn.: Yale University Press, 1989. An insightful biography of India's greatest saintly leader and social reformer.

Brown, Percy. *Indian Architecture.* 3rd ed. Vol. I: *Buddhist and Hindu Periods.* Vol. II: *Islamic Period.* Mumbai: Taraporevala's, 1956. Brilliantly comprehensive text with splendid photographs.

Brown, W. Norman. *The United States and India, Pakistan, Bangladesh.* 3rd ed. of *The United States and India and Pakistan.* Cambridge, Mass.: Harvard University Press, 1972. Still among the best single volume introductions to South Asia since the emergence of India and Pakistan as independent states, with an excellent chapter on the birth of Bangladesh.

Chadda, Maya. *Building Democracy in South Asia.* Boulder, Colo.: Lynne Rienner, 2000. Excellent analysis of this important subject.

Chaudhuri, Nirad C. *The Autobiography of an Unknown Indian.* Berkeley: University of California Press, 1968. A classic memoir of life in British India's Bengal by one of young India's most precocious Anglo-Indian authors.

Coomaraswamy, Ananda K. *The Dance of Shiva.* Rev. ed. New York: Noonday Press, 1957. A brilliant brief survey of India's artistic riches and cultural genius.

Copland, Ian. *The British Raj and the Indian Princes: Paramountcy in Western India, 1857–1930.* London: Longman, 1982. Excellent analysis of a regal subject.

Davies, Philip. *The Penguin Guide to the Monuments of India,* vol. 2: *Islamic, Rajput, European.* Penguin: London, 1989. Vol. 1, by George Mitchell, covers Buddhist, Jain, and Hindu monuments of India. Both volumes are very clear architectural guides.

Edgerton, Franklin, trans. *The Bhagavad Gita.* Cambridge, Mass.: Harvard University Press, 1972. Wonderful translation of Hinduism's most famous religio-philosophic text.

Embree, Ainslie T., ed. *The Hindu Tradition.* New York: Modern Library, 1966. An excellent primary source book of Hinduism with brief introductions to each text by its editor. Dr. Embree has also edited *Sources of Indian Tradition.* 2nd ed. New York: Columbia University Press, 1988. The best comprehensive primary source book of India's great traditions.

Forster, E. M. *A Passage to India.* New York: Harcourt, Brace & World, 1952. Brilliant fictional account of Indo-British relations and racial conflict during the Raj. Also see the fascinating memoir of his service to an Indian prince, *The Hill of Devi,* New York: Harcourt Brace, 1953.

Gandhi, Mohandas K. *An Autobiography: The Story of My Experiments with Truth.* Translated by Mahadev Desai. Boston: Beacon Press, 1957. Fascinating primary source insight into the mind of India's greatest religious and political leader, and the history of his evolution.

Gandhi, Rajmohan. *Rajaji: A Life.* New Delhi: Penguin, 1997. The best biography of C. Rajagopalachari, the only Indian to serve as governor-general, written by his grandson, also a grandson of Mahatma Gandhi, whose brief biography he wrote as well: *The Good Boatman,* New Delhi: Viking, 1995.

Gandhi, Sonia, ed. Vol. I: *Freedom's Daughter: Letters between Indira Gandhi and Jawaharlal Nehru, 1922–39.* London: Hodder & Stoughton, 1989. Vol. II: *Two Alone, Two Together: Letters between Indira Gandhi and Jawaharlal Nehru, 1940–1964.* London: Hodder & Stoughton, 1992. These two volumes of primary sources of recent Indian history are sensitively introduced by the editor, who, as of 2005, presides over India's Congress Party. They provide insights into the lives of Nehru, India's first prime minister, and his daughter, Indira, India's third prime minister, each of whom led India's Congress Party governments for more than fifteen years.

Hambly, Gavin. *Cities of Mughul India.* Photographs by Wim Swaan. New York: G. P. Putnam's Sons, 1968. Beautiful photos of Delhi, Agra, and Fatehpur Sikri accompany excellent descriptions of those great Mughal capitals.

Hardy, P. *The Muslims of British India.* Cambridge, U.K.: Cambridge University Press, 1972. An illuminating study of an important chapter in recent South Asian history.

Hawley, John Stratton, ed. *Sati, the Blessing and the Curse: The Burning of Wives in India.* New York: Oxford University Press, 1994. Excellent anthology of articles on *sati.*

Hume, Robert Ernest, trans. *The Thirteen Principal Upanishads.* 2nd ed. London: Oxford University Press, 1979. Excellent translation of the most important sources of Vedāntic Indian philosophy.

Ikram, S. M. *Muslim Civilization in India.* Edited by A. T. Embree. New York and London: Columbia University Press, 1964. Valuable introduction to Islam in India and its powerful impact.

Inden, Ronald. *Imagining India.* Oxford: Basil Blackwell, 1990. An excellent and insightful study.

Irving, Robert Grant. *Indian Summer: Lutyens, Baker and Imperial Delhi.* New Haven, Conn., and London: Yale University Press, 1981. A fine history of New Delhi with beautiful photographs.

Jaffrelot, Christophe. *The Hindu Nationalist Movement in India.* New York: Columbia University Press, 1996. A scholarly study of modern India's populist Hindutva movement.

Kālidāsa. *Shakuntala and Other Writings.* Translated by Arthur W. Ryder. New York: E. P. Dutton, 1959. Translations of Kālidāsa's greatest play and several of his beautiful poems.

Karve, D. D., trans. *The New Brahmans: Five Maharashtrian Families.* Berkeley: University of California Press, 1963. Insightful primary source of recent social history of Maharashtra and changes brought by British rule to its old Brahman families.

Kopf, David. *British Orientalism and the Bengal Renaissance: The Dynamics of Indian Modernization, 1773–1834.* Berkeley: University of California Press, 1969. Valuable history of the early impact of the British East India Company on India's Bengal.

Kramrisch, Stella. *Manifestations of Shiva.* Philadelphia: University of Pennsylvania Art Museum, 1981. A remarkable study of ancient Indian art by one of its greatest scholars.

Low, D. A., ed. *Soundings in Modern South Asian History.* Berkeley: University of California Press, 1968. An excellent compilation of scholarly studies on recent Indian history. Dr. Low has also edited *Congress and the Raj*, London: Macmillan, 1977.

Ludden, David. *Contesting the Nation: Religion, Community and the Politics of Democracy in India.* Philadelphia: University of Pennsylvania Press, 1996. A very fine scholarly study.

Madan. T. N. *Modern Myths, Locked Minds: Secularism and Fundamentalism in India.* New Delhi: Oxford University Press, 1997. An illuminating study of India's most important intellectual conflict.

Majumdar, R. C., H. C. Raychaudhuri, and K. K. Datta, eds. *An Advanced History of India.* London: Macmillan, 1961. Comprehensive history of Indian politics and culture. Professor Majumdar et al. also edited a much more detailed and comprehensive eleven-volume *History and Culture of the Indian People*, Mumbai: Bharatiya Vidya Bhavan, 1951–1966.

Marshall, P. J. *Bengal: The British Bridgehead, Eastern India, 1740–1828*, pt. 2 of vol. 2: *New Cambridge History of India*, edited by Gordon Johnson. Cambridge, U.K.: Cambridge University Press, 1987. Excellent scholarly history of Greater Bengal under the British East India Company's Raj.

Martin, Briton. *New India, 1885.* Berkeley: University of California Press, 1969. Excellent history of the origins and emergence of India's National Congress.

McLeod, Hew. *Sikhism.* Harmondsworth, U.K.: Penguin, 1997. An excellent summary of Sikhism and its history.

Mistry, Rohinton. *A Fine Balance.* London: Faber and Faber, 1995. A fictional account of India (Bombay) in the mid-1970s under Indira Gandhi's "State of Internal Emergency."

Naipaul, V. S. *India: A Wounded Civilization.* New York: Vintage Books, 1978. A sensitive appreciation of India's many problems by one of her greatest diaspora authors. His *India: A Million Mutinies Now*, London:

Heinemann, 1990, is even more insightful and provocative.

Narayan, R. K. *Swami and Friends.* East Lansing: Michigan State College Press, 1954. *Bachelor of Arts.* Mysore: Indian Thought Publications, 1965. *My Days.* New York: Viking, 1974. *The Financial Expert.* East Lansing: Michigan State College Press, 1953. *The Guide.* New York: Viking, 1958. Some of the best novels by South India's greatest author of the last century.

Nayar, Kuldip, and Khushwant Singh, eds. *Tragedy of Punjab: Operation Bluestar and After.* New Delhi: Vision Books, 1984. A brilliant anthology of Punjab's recent political traumas and tragedy.

Nehru, Jawaharlal. *Toward Freedom.* New York: John Day, 1941. Nehru's brilliantly written autobiography, a primary source of India's freedom struggle and recent history by its first prime minister. His *Discovery of India*, also published in New York by John Day in 1946, is a rich and wide-ranging history by one of recent India's best authors, as well as its greatest premier-statesman.

O'Flaherty, Wendy D. *Hindu Myths.* Harmondsworth, U.K.: Penguin, 1975. Fascinatingly original study of Hinduism's mythology. Also see her *Asceticism and Eroticism in the Mythology of Siva*.

Pearson, M. N. *The Portuguese in India*, pt. 1 of vol. 1: *New Cambridge History of India*, edited by Gordon Johnson. Cambridge, U.K.: Cambridge University Press, 1987. Excellent scholarly account of this important chapter in Indian history.

Perkovich, George. *India's Nuclear Bomb.* Berkeley: University of California Press, 1999. Accurate history of India's development as a nuclear-armed power.

Raychaudhuri, Tapan. "The Mughal Empire," in "The State and the Economy," in *The Cambridge Economic History of India*, vol. I, edited by T. Raychaudhuri, and I. Habib. Cambridge, U.K.: Cambridge University Press, 1982. A brilliant history of the Mughal economy.

Robinson, Francis. *Separatism among Indian Muslims: The Politics of the United Provinces' Muslims, 1860–1923.* London: Cambridge University Press, 1974. An excellent study of a difficult subject.

Rothermund, Dietmar. *An Economic History of India.* London: Croom Helm, 1988. A good general survey of India's economic history. Also see his *The Phases of Indian Nationalism and Other Essays*, Mumbai: Popular Prakashan, 1970.

Rowland, Benjamin. *The Art and Architecture of India. Buddhist, Hindu, Jain.* Harmondsworth, U.K.: Penguin, 1953. Classic work of India's early art history with remarkable plates.

Rushdie, Salman. *Midnight's Children.* New York: Knopf, 1981. Brilliant novel of partition's aftermath.

Scott, Paul. *The Raj Quartet:* Book I: *The Jewel in the Crown.* London: Heinemann, 1966. Book II: *The Day of the Scorpion.* 1968. Book III: *The Towers of Silence.* 1971. Book IV: *A Division of the Spoils.* 1975. Vivid, compelling, broad-ranging account of the last decades of the British Raj, which though written as fiction is truly historic in its content.

Seal, Anil. *The Emergence of Indian Nationalism.* Cambridge, U.K.: Cambridge University Press, 1968. A very fine scholarly study.

Sen, Amartya, and J. Dreze. *India: Development and Participation.* New Delhi: Oxford University Press, 2002. A brilliant study of India's recent economic development and many flaws.

Seth, Vikram. *A Suitable Boy.* New York: Harper Perennial Library, 1993. Set in post-partition India in the 1950s, this expansive novel traces the lives of four extended families.

Singh, Khushwant. *A History of the Sikhs.* 2 vols. Princeton, N.J.: Princeton University Press, 1963. An excellent general history of the Sikhs, written by one of its most brilliant authors.

Sisson, Richard, and Stanley Wolpert, eds. *Congress and Indian Nationalism: The Pre-Independence Phase.* Berkeley: University of California Press, 1988. Edited papers initially presented at a centenary celebration of the birth of India's National Congress at the University of California, Los Angeles, in 1985.

Spear, Percival. *Twilight of the Moghuls.* Cambridge, U.K.: Cambridge University Press, 1951. An excellent history of Delhi during the decline of Mughal power. See also his *The Nabobs: A Study of the Social Life of the English in Eighteenth-Century India.* London: Oxford University Press, 1963.

Stewart, Gordon. *The Marathas 1600–1818*, pt. 2 of vol. 4: *New Cambridge History of India,* edited by Gordon Johnson. Cambridge, U.K.: Cambridge University Press, 1993. Wonderful account of Maratha history.

Tagore, Rabindranath. *Gitanjali and Fruit-Gathering.* New York: Macmillan, 1919. The poems for which India's first Nobel Prize winner, and greatest Bengali author and dramatist, won his Nobel Prize in literature.

Talbott, Strobe. *Engaging India: Diplomacy, Democracy and the Bomb.* Washington, D.C.: Brookings Institution, 2004. A frankly refreshing memoir of a difficult diplomatic engagement.

Thapar, Romila. *A History of India,* vol. 1 of 2 vols. Harmondsworth, U.K.: Penguin, 1966. A very fine early history by one of India's greatest historians. Professor Thapar's later works include: *Interpreting Early India,* Delhi: Oxford University Press, 1992; her edited *Recent Perspectives of Early Indian History,* Mumbai: Popular Prakashan, 1995; and *Ancient Indian Social History: Some Interpretations,* London: Sangam, 1996.

Thomas, Raju G. C. *Democracy, Security and Development in India.* New York: Palgrave Macmillan, 1996. A most astute study of three interrelated aspects of modern India's power.

Trautmann, Thomas R. *Kautilya and the Arthashāstra.* Leiden: Brill, 1971. Excellent translation and history of India's most ancient text on imperial administration and power politics.

Tully, Mark, and Satish Jacob. *Amritsar: Mrs. Gandhi's Last Battle.* London: Jonathan Cape, 1985. Very fine historical account of the tragic attack in Punjab that triggered Prime Minister Gandhi's assassination.

Wallace, Paul, ed. *Regions and Nations in India.* New Delhi: Oxford University Press, 1985. An excellent compendium of scholarly articles, edited by a brilliant historian.

Wheeler, Mortimer. *Civilizations of the Indus Valley and Beyond.* New York: McGraw-Hill, 1966. A good introduction to the Indus Valley digs, with excellent photos of the major sites and artifacts.

Wiser, William H., and Charlotte Viall Wiser. *Behind Mud Walls, 1930–1960*, with a sequel: *The Village in 1970.* Berkeley: University of California Press, 1971. Classic anthropological study of village India.

Wolpert, Stanley. *A New History of India.* 7th ed. New York and Oxford: Oxford University Press, 2004. *India,* 3rd ed. Berkeley: University of California Press, 2005. *Nehru: A Tryst with Destiny.* New York and Oxford: Oxford University Press, 1996. *Gandhi's Passion: The Life and Legacy of Mahatma Gandhi.* New York and Oxford: Oxford University Press, 2001. *Tilak and Gokhale: Revolution and Reform in the Making of Modern India.* Berkeley: University of California Press, 1962.

index

Note: **Bold** page numbers indicate main discussions. *Italic* page numbers indicate figures and tables. Colons separate volume numbers from page numbers. Color inserts are abbreviated as "col. ins." plus the volume number.

A

Abbas, K. A., films of, 1:255

Abbasid dynasty, and Ghaznavid sultanate, 3:200

Abbinaya (expression), 1:286, 288, 289, 291, 292

Abdali, Shah, Mughal empire threatened by, 3:295

'Abd al-Rahīm, manuscripts commissioned by, 3:400

'Abd al-Samad, art of, 3:184, 185

Abduh, Muhammad, 1:6

Abdülhamid II (Ottoman sultan), 1:6

Abdul Kalam, Avul Pakir Jainulabdeen (A. P. J.), **1:1**, 3:*311*
  election of, 3:332, 333
  in missile development, 1:1, 4:94–95
  in nuclear program, 1:1, 4:116
  as president of India, 1:1, 3:334
  as scientist, 1:1

Abdullah, Mohammad
  Dogra rule opposed by, 3:12
  in Kashmir conflict, 3:12, 13

Abdullah Qutb Shah (sultan of Golconda), paintings of, 1:300

Abdur Rahman (Afghan amir)
  in Anglo–Afghan War, Second, 1:47
  British relations with, 1:47, 3:57, 411
  Kafirs under, 1:111
  Lansdowne and, 3:57
  Ripon recognizing, 3:411

Abhai Singh, painting under, 3:131, 382

Abhaneri, monuments in, 3:178–179

Abhayakaragupta (Buddhist scholar), 4:135, 136

Abhaya pose, in Buddha bronzes, 1:196

Abhijñānashākuntala (Kālidāsa), 3:2, 72, 72, 4:163

Abhinava Gupta (philosopher)
  on aesthetic experience, 1:5
  on *rasa*, 1:3, 4, 2:334

Abortion
  of female fetuses, 1:306, 3:317, 318, 4:234
  legislation on, 1:305

Abu, Mount, temples on, 3:180

Abu-al-Fazl
  on metalware, 3:115
  on portraits, 3:187
  on Tansen, 4:134

Abu al-Hasan, art of, 3:186, 187

Abu'l Hasan Qutb Shah (sultan of Golconda), paintings of, 1:300

Accommodation
  in Congress Party, 1:271–272
  in Pakistani–Indian relations, 3:266, 268

Achyutarāya temple (Hampi), 3:171

Acquired immuno deficiency syndrome. *See* AIDS/HIV

Adalaj stepwell, 3:181, 4:111

Adarang (musician), 3:34

ADB. *See* Asian Development Bank

Adhirājendra (Chola king), 1:247

Adi Granth (Sikh text), 4:65
  in Amritsar, 1:40, 4:66
  compilation of, 4:66

Guru Nanak's verses in, 2:167, 4:68
  hymns in, 4:68, 69
  Kabir's poems in, 3:1
  as source of authority, 4:67

'Adil Shahi dynasty, paintings under, 1:299

Adinatha temple (Mount Abu), 3:180

Adinatha temple (Ranakpur), 4:153

Adinath Temple (Aravali Hills), col. ins. v1

Ādityas (abstract deities), 4:214

Adivasis, Prasad (Rajendra) on, 3:330

*Adivasi*s. *See* Tribal peoples of India

Administrative Service, Indian (IAS)
  in defense department, 3:219
  establishment of, 3:288
  Indian Civil Service members moving to, 1:171
  Patel (Sardar Vallabhbhai) and, 3:288

ADMK. *See* Anna Dravida Munnetra Kazhagam

Adolescents, gender ratio of, 3:317–318

ADRs. *See* American depository receipts

Advani, Lal Krishna, 1:*2*, **1:2–3**, 2:*204*
  in Bharatiya Janata Party, 1:2, 144
  in Bharatiya Janata Sangh Party, 1:2
  in Hindutva movement, 1:2–3, 2:198
  and Indo–Israeli relations, 2:*312*
  on Nagaland, 3:242
  in National Democratic Alliance government, 1:2, 3
  on pilgrimage, 2:206
  political career of, 1:2–3

Baluchistan (province of Pakistan)
(*continued*)
economy of, 1:111
future of tribes in, 1:111–112
geography of, 1:110, 111
Hinduism in, 1:111
mountains in, 2:137
in Neolithic period, 3:229–230
Pakistani policies on, 1:110–111
passes into India from, 1:110
Pukhtun tribes in, 1:109–112
religious political parties in, 1:112
rock art in, 3:413
social structure in, 1:111
Tribal Areas of, 1:111, 112
U.S.-led fight against Taliban and,
1:112
Baluch tribes
in Baluchistan, 1:109–112
British agreements with, 1:109–110
British opinion of, 1:110
chief of, 1:111
code of behavior in, 1:111
future of, 1:111–112
in Great Game, 1:110
in North-West Frontier, 1:109–112
politicians from, 1:111
social structure of, 1:111
Balwant Singh, Nainsukh's paintings
of, 3:213–214, 387
Ba Maw, 1:211
Bāna (poet), 2:172
Banaras, *jamdani* from, 2:329
Bandaranaike, Sirimavo
Indian military intervention
requested by (1971), 3:118
in Sino–Indian War (1962), 1:243
Sirimavo-Shastri Pact of 1964 signed
by, 4:97
Bandavgarh National Park, col. ins. v4
"Bande Mataram" (Chatterji),
1:112–113, 1:237–238
in *Anandamath*, 1:112
as anthem, 1:113, 2:67, 4:127
ban on, 1:112
set to music, 1:112–113, 135, 237, 2:67
Bande Mataram (daily), Aurobindo
writing in, 1:76
Bandhani (dyeing technique),
1:113–115, 1:*114*
Bandhavgarh National Park, col.
ins. v4
Bandung Conference (1955), and
Chinese–Indian relations, 1:241
Bandyopadhyay, Manik, *Putul nācher
itikathā*, 3:66
Banerjea, Surendranath N., **1:115–116**
in civil service, 1:115
in Congress Party, 1:115, 268

decline in popularity of, 1:116
in Indian Association, 1:115, 136
nationalism of, 1:115–116, 136
opponents of, 1:116
Banerjee, Bibhuti Bhushan, *Pather
pānchāli*, 3:66, 406
Banerjee, Krishna Mohan, 4:164
Banerji, R. D., Mohenjo-Daro discovered by, 3:140
Bangadarsham (Journal), Chatterji in,
1:112, 238
Bangalore (city in Karnataka), **1:116**
establishment of, 1:116
Indian Institute of Science in, 1:116,
4:139
industries in, 1:116
information technology in, 1:116,
2:270, 273
Bangladesh, **1:116–118**
agriculture in, 1:118, 2:138, 140
constitution of, 1:117
coups in (1975), 1:117
coups in (1976), 1:117–118
coups in (1982), 1:118
education in, 2:144–145
foreign investment in, 2:143
geography of, 1:118, 4:106
hydroelectric power in, 4:88
independence for (1971), 1:117,
2:117, 308, 309, 3:259, 4:105
Indian recognition of, 1:117
Indian relations with, 3:245
insurgencies in, 3:245
linguistic diversity in, 2:40
migration from, 3:245
Muslims in, number of, 2:309
natural gas from, 4:88, 89
and Northeast Indian states, 3:245
Rahman (Mujibur) in creation of,
3:372
rainfall in, 2:139
river traffic in, 2:144
settlement patterns in, 2:142
urbanization in, 2:145
Bangladesh Nationalist Party (BNP),
1:118
Bangladesh war (1971). *See* Indo–
Pakistani war (1971)
Banigrama (merchant guild), 2:2
Banker, Ashok, 2:74
Bank failures
1913–1946, 3:*149*
in 1960s, 1:312
during and after World War II,
1:311
Banking, **1:118–125**. *See also* Saving
in Bengal, 1:311
central (*See* Central banking; Reserve
Bank of India)

commercial (*See* Commercial
banking)
competition in, 1:123
under economic planning, 2:16
future of, 1:124–125
legislation on, 1:118–120, 311–312
linkages with non-banking financial
institutions, 3:239–240
performance of system, 1:124
private sector, 1:*120*, 121, 123, 4:175
public sector, 1:123–124, 2:149
in Punjab, 1:311
reforms since 1991, **1:120–125**, 2:97,
98, 147, 256, 4:175
by *shreni*s, 4:60
supervision of, **1:118–120**, 1:*119*,
123
Banking Companies Act of 1949,
1:119, 311
Banking Laws Provisions Act of 1963,
1:120
Banking Regulation Act of 1949,
1:118, 119
Banking Sector Reforms, Committee
on, 1:120–121
Bansri (musical instrument), 1:327
Bapu (film director), 1:256
Barabar Hills excavations (Bihar), 4:28,
149
Barahmasa (paintings of seasons),
1:125–126
in Bundi miniatures, 3:121, 122
in Kotah miniatures, 3:129
Bara Imambara hall (Lucknow), col.
ins. v1
Barani, on paper use, 3:276
BARC. *See* Bhabha Atomic Research
Centre
Bardhan, Pranab, 3:61
Bardoli *satyagraha*, 3:286
Bargha, Operation, 3:48, 49
Baroda (city in Gujarat), **1:126–128**
architecture of, 1:126, 127, *127*
art in, 1:128, 3:137–138
as candidate for capital, 2:126
modernization of, 1:127–128
under Sayajirao Gaekwad III,
1:126–127
Baroda (princely state)
Aurobindo in, 1:75–76
reforms in, 3:344
Baroda School of Art, 3:137–138
Baroli, temples in, 3:179–180
Barua, Jahnu, films of, 1:257
Barua, P. C., 1:254
Basavanna (saint), in Vīrasaiva sect,
1:32
Basel banking standards, 1:119, 121,
124

Chahamana dynasty, monuments of, 3:177

Chaitanya (mystic), **1:231**
  as incarnation of Krishna and Rādhā, 1:231
  influence of, 1:231
  and Krishna in art, 3:40
  life of, 1:231

Chait Singh (raja of Benares), Hastings deposing, 2:173–174

Chakkarai, V.
  as Christian leader, 3:60
  in Congress Party, 3:60
  education of, 3:60
  in nationalist movement, 1:250, 251, 3:60

Chakma tribe, 3:245

*Chakra*s (nerve centers), 2:200, 201, *201*, 4:256

Chakravartin, in Buddhist art, 1:208, 4:26, 27

Chalcolithic (Bronze) Age, **1:232–235,** 2:259
  Early, 1:234
  Kot Diji Phase in, 1:232, 233–234
  Late, 1:234
  Mature, 1:234
  metalware in, 3:113
  Ravi Phase in, 1:232–233
  rock art in, 3:413

Chalukya dynasty
  architecture in, 3:165–167
  block-printed textiles in, 4:156
  in Gujarat, 2:160
  Harsha's conflict with, 2:172
  in Karnataka, 3:11
  paper used in, 3:275
  temples of, 3:165–167, 4:151, 152, 153

Chamarajendra Wodeyar, Sayajirao Gaekwad III and, 1:127

Chamber of Princes, 3:344–345

Champaran, *satyagraha* in, 3:329

Chāmundā (deity), 2:201–202

Chanda, love stories about, 3:74

Chandala (caste), 1:283
  eyewitness accounts of, 1:224
  Hindu texts on, 1:224

Chandarnagar, Dupleix as governor of, 1:345, 2:105

Chanda Sahib, in Nabob Game, 3:210

Chandavarkar, Anand, 3:411

Chandbibi (queen of Ahmednagar), in miniature paintings, 3:127

Chandella Rajputs, in Khajuraho, 3:26, 27

Chanderi, Paithani weaving in, 3:257, 258

Chandigarh (city), **1:235–237**
  architecture of, 1:149, *236*, 236–237, 4:200, 204
  as capital of Punjab and Haryana, 1:237, 2:46
  hospital in, 2:*175*
  population of, 1:237
  Secretariat Building in, 1:*236*

Chandra, Harish, 4:22

Chandragupta I (Guptan emperor)
  Chandragupta Maurya's influence on, 2:164
  Guptan empire established by, 2:163, 211

Chandragupta II (Guptan emperor)
  Kālidāsa and, 2:164, 211, 3:2
  military campaigns of, 2:163, *163*, 166
  as patron of Udayagiri cave, 2:166

Chandragupta Basti temple, 3:168

Chandragupta Maurya (Mauryan emperor), 3:103
  Alexander the Great as inspiration for, 1:35, 2:210
  Artha Shāstra and, 1:55, 2:210
  Bengal under, 1:130
  Chandragupta I admiring, 2:164
  expansion of empire under, 3:103, 4:28
  Jainism of, 3:103
  Kauṭilya as minister under, 1:130, 2:210, 4:114

Chandralekha (film), 1:254

Chandrasekhar, Subrahmanyan (Chandra), 4:22

Chandrasekhara Rao, K., in Telengana Rashtra Samiti, 1:43

Chandrasekhar limit, 4:22

Chaplevé enameling technique, 3:115

Charaka (physician), 1:82, 85, 4:19

Charaka Samhitā, 1:82
  Patanjali as author of, 3:283

Chariots
  bronzes of, 1:193
  Krishna in sculptures of, 3:39

Charles II (king of England), Bombay under, 1:158

Charnock, Job
  in Bengal, 1:132
  Calcutta founded by, 1:132, 214

Chateri Gumani, 3:384

Chatterji, Bankim Chandra, 1:237, **1:237–238**
  Anandamath, 1:112, 237
  "Bande Mataram," **1:112–113,** 1:135, 237–238, 2:67
  in *Bangadarsham,* 1:112, 238
  in Bengali intellectual tradition, 1:135

  in civil service, 1:112, 135, 237
  Durgeshnandini, 1:135
  nationalism of, 1:112–113, 135, 238
  novels of, 1:112, 237, 3:65
  poetry of, 1:112–113
  Rajani, 1:239
  Rajmohan's Wife, 1:237

Chattopadhya, Kamaladevi, and Paithani weaving, 3:258

Chau (dance), 2:91

Chaudharani, Sarladevi Ghoshal, 2:67

Chaudhurani, Sarat Kumari, 2:67

Chaudhuri, Amit, *The Vintage Book of Modern India Literature,* 3:70

Chaudhuri, Haridas, 1:76

Chaudhuri, Nirad C., **1:238–239**
  Autobiography of an Unknown Indian, 1:238, 3:67
  on British rule, 1:238
  The Continent of Circe, 1:238
  education of, 1:238
  languages studied by, 1:238
  Passage to England, 1:238

Chaudhury, Praveen, 4:23

Chaulukya dynasty, monuments of, 3:177

Chaurapanchasika group, 3:379–380, 381

Chauri Chaura tragedy, 2:123

Chausa, bronzes from, 1:195

Chavan, S. B., 2:109

Chawand *Rāgamālā* painting (Nisardi), 3:371, 381

Chelmsford, Lord, **1:239–240**
  in Government of India Act of 1919, 1:239, 2:156
  Jallianwala Bagh Massacre and, 1:239
  Montagu and, 1:239
  as viceroy of India, 1:239, 2:172

Chemistry
  contributions in, 4:21, 23
  development of, 4:18

Chenchiah, P.
  as Christian leader, 3:60–61
  education of, 3:60

Chenda (musical instrument), 1:290

Chennai. *See* Madras

Cheraw (bamboo dance), in Mizoram, 3:134

Chettiar jewelry, 2:*341*

Chhandah-shāstra (Pingala), 3:297

Chhatrapatis (kings), relationship with *peshwas,* 3:294

Chhatris (pavilions), in Mughal architecture, 3:157, 158, 160

Chhattisgarh, human development indicators of, 2:217, *218*

Chhota Nagpur (region), 2:138, 143

in Nepal, 3:232, 233

in Pakistan, 3:261, 262

presidential, 3:310–311, 312, 332

Electoral college, in presidential elections, 3:310–311, 332

Electricity Act of 2003, 2:257, 281, 4:176

Electricity Supply Act of 1948, 2:280

Electronics, Department of, 2:272

Elephanta (island), 2:28

Elephanta caves, *2:28*, **2:28–29**

  Ellora caves compared to, 2:29, 30

  Gaṇesha images in, 2:129

Elephant-headed deity. *See* Gaṇesha

Elephants, col. ins. v4

  Artha Shāstra on, 1:57

  bronzes of, 1:193, 194

  in miniature paintings, 3:122, 129

  in *patola* design, 3:290

Elipattayam (film), 1:257

Elizabeth I (queen of England), British East India Company charter granted by, 1:176

Ellenborough, earl of, **2:29–30**

  in Anglo–Afghan War, First, 1:46, 2:29

  in conquest of Sind, 2:29–30

  as governor-general of India, 2:29

Elliot, Gilbert. *See* Minto, Lord

Ellora (Elura) caves, **2:30–31**, *2:31*

  Ajanta caves compared to, 2:30

  Elephanta caves compared to, 2:29, 30

  Jain sanctuary in, 2:31, 328

Elphinstone, Mountstuart, **2:32**

  as governor of Bombay, 1:159, 2:32

Emeralds, 2:343

Emergencies. *See also* National Emergency

  suspension of fundamental rights in, 2:107–109

Emergent Genetics India Pvt. Ltd. v. Shailendra Shivam, 2:291

Emotion, *rasa* as, 1:5

Employee Pension Scheme (EPS), 3:292–293

Employee Provident Fund (EPF), 3:292–293

Employee Provident Fund Organisation (EPFO), 3:291, 292–293

Employees' State Insurance (ESI) Act of 1948, 2:177

Employment

  agricultural (*See* Agricultural workers)

  under British Crown Raj, 2:32–33

  under British East India Company, 2:32

  for Dalits, 1:40

economic reforms of 1991 and, 2:22

food security through, 2:95

and gender ratios, 3:318

globalization and, 2:144

and health insurance, 2:177

in independent India, 2:33

industrial (*See* Industrial labor force)

in Kerala, 3:24

in manufacturing, 2:11, 33, 252, 253

in private sector, 2:252, 253

in public sector, 2:252, 253–254

in rural areas, 2:252

in services, 2:33, 252

structure of, **2:32–33**

in urban areas, 2:145, 252

of women, 2:131, 132

Employment Guarantee Scheme (EGS), 2:95

Emusha Varāha (boar), 1:78, 4:217

Enamel decoration

  on metalware, 3:115

  techniques for, 3:115

Enemy of the People (film), 3:407

Energy politics and policy, **2:33–37**

  under British rule, 2:278–279, 280

  dependence on oil and, 2:33–34, 35

  economic reforms of 1991 and, 2:34, 36, 280, 281

  and environmental damage, 2:38

  projected energy needs and, 2:35, 280, 4:88–89

Energy sector

  Asian Development Bank and, 1:64

  electric generation capacity of, 2:35, 36

  in Pakistan, 4:88

  per capita electricity consumption, 2:280–281

  in private sector, 2:280, 4:109, 176

  in public sector, 2:36, 257, 280

  regional disparities in, 2:280, 4:109

  in South Asia, 4:88

  World Bank loans in, 4:241, 242

Energy sources, 2:34–36, 142–143, 278–279

  for households, 1:267

  nuclear, under Nehru (Jawaharlal), 3:247–249

  thermal, 2:34, 35, 143, 279

Engineering, in Bangalore, 1:116

England. *See also* Britain

  Bonnerji in, 1:135, 159, 160

  Chaudhuri (Nirad C.) in, 1:238

  Gandhi (Mahatma) studying in, 2:119–120

  Iqbal studying in, 2:296–297

  Jinnah as barrister in, 2:351, 352

  Patel (Sardar Vallabhbhai) in, 3:285

  Sayyid Ahmed Khan in, 4:12

England, Bank of, Reserve Bank of India modeled on, 3:149

England, Church of, Andrews in, 1:44

English alphabet, 3:55

English language, 3:53

  in Assam, 1:68–69

  dominance of, as British legacy, 1:185

  in education, 1:139, 172–173, 185, 248, 2:25, 307

  literature written in, 3:65, 66, 68–70

  as national unifier, 2:213

  newspapers in, 3:105–106

Enlightenment (spiritual state)

  of Buddha, 1:200–201

  in Jainism, 2:323

Environment, col. ins. v4

Environmental consciousness, **2:37–39**

  under British rule, 2:37

  in independent India, 2:37–39

Environmental protection

  Asian Development Bank in, 1:64, 65

  on common land, 1:267

  legislation on, 2:38

Environment and Forests, Ministry of (MoEF), 2:38, 39

EPF. *See* Employee Provident Fund

EPFO. *See* Employee Provident Fund Organisation

Ephedra, 4:84, 214

Epicycle theory, 4:18

Epidemics

  in colonial era, 1:302, 303–304, 307

  famines and, 2:58, 60

  goddesses and, 1:322, 323

  in independent India, 1:305

EPS. *See* Employee Pension Scheme

Equality. *See* Inequality

Equilibrium, computable general, 4:42–43

Eri (variety of silk), in brocade weaving, 1:190

Ericsson building, col. ins. v1

Eroticism, in Khajuraho sculpture, 3:28

Erotic love, Kāma Sūtra on, 3:2–3

Ershad, Hussain Muhammad

  coup led by (1982), 1:118

  as president of Bangladesh, 1:118

Erskine, William

  in Asiatic Society of Bombay, 1:67

  Rajagopalachari and, 3:374

Esoofally, Abdulally, rise of, 1:253

Espionage, *Artha Shāstra* on, 1:56

Essential Commodities Act of 1956, 2:82

Estate duty, 2:83

Ethics

  in Ashoka's inscriptions, 1:203, 3:103

  of Buddhism, 1:203

Forward Markets Commission (FMC),
1:265
Foster, William, 3:375
France
British rivalry with, 3:79 (*See also*
Nabob Game)
Burmese relations with, 1:210
impact of, **2:103–106**
Indian community in, 1:334
Indian indentured labor used by,
1:331–332
Kashmir shawls in, 3:20, 21
nuclear energy in, 2:36
secularism in, 4:37, 39
Francis Mary of Toure, 1:249
Frauwallner, Erich, 2:187
Free contract, principle of, 2:8
French East India Company,
2:101–103
armies of, 1:179
block-printed textiles traded by,
4:158, 159–160
British East India Company in con-
flict with, 1:176, 179, 345, 346,
2:213, 3:210
Dupleix as governor-general of,
1:344–345, 2:103, 105, 106
Dutch East India Company in com-
petition with, 2:102
establishment of, 2:101–102
and Madras, 3:79
Nabob Game in, 3:209–210
problems of, 2:102
French impact, **2:103–106**
French West India Company, 2:103,
104
Friendship and Cooperation, Treaty of
(1993), 3:421
Friezes, Krishna in, 3:39
Fry, Maxwell, 1:236
FTII. *See* Film and Television Institute
of India
Fuller, Sir Bampfylde, "Bande
Mataram" banned by, 1:112
Fundamentalism. *See* Hindu nationalism; Islamic fundamentalism
Fundamental rights, **2:106–109**. *See
also* Food security; Human rights
Constitution on, 2:106–109,
219–220, 354
and family law, 2:56
gender and (*See* Gender and human
rights; Women's rights)
legislation on, 2:108–109, 219–220
suspension of, 2:107–109, 220–221,
222–223
Furlan, Luiz Fernando, 1:167
Futures trading, in commodity markets, 1:264–265

G
G-3. *See* Group of 3
Gadwal, Paithani weaving in, 3:257,
258
Gaekwad dynasty, Baroda under,
1:126–127
Gaitonde, V. S., art of, 3:137
Gajasurasamharamurti, Baroli temple
to, 3:179–180
Gajendragadhar Commission (1967),
2:336
Gaj Singh, painting under, 3:121, 382,
383
Galaganātha temple, 3:165
Galbraith, John Kenneth, *2:111,*
2:111–112
Gama, Vasco da, **2:112–113,** 2:233
atrocities of, 3:322
in Calicut, 3:319–322
explorations in India, 3:319–322
sea route to India "discovered" by,
3:319
Gaṇapati. *See* Gaṇesha
Gandamak, Treaty of (1879), 1:46
Gandharan art and architecture,
2:113–117
Chinese pilgrims to, 2:116
classical features of, 2:115
Nikāya-Mahayana Buddhism affiliated with, 2:116
patronage of, 2:116
sculptures, 2:113, *115,* 115–116,
4:24, 26, 27
temples, 2:113, *114,* 115, 116
Gandhara region, bronzes from, 1:195
Gandhi, Devadas, 3:374
Gandhi, Feroze, 2:117
as Parsi, 3:282
Gandhi, Indira, **2:117–119,** *2:118,*
3:314
and Asiatic Society of Bengal, 1:67
and Assam separatism, 1:70
assassination of, 1:41, 273, 2:43, 119,
125, 4:65, 68
and Bhindranwale's capture of
Golden Temple, 1:41, 2:119, 288
Bhutto (Zulfikar Ali) and, 1:150–151
Brazil visited by, 1:167
cabinet of, 3:301, 314–315
centralization by, 2:63
civil-military relations under, 1:260
in Congress Party, 1:272, 273, 2:134
decline and fall of, 2:117–119
Desai as minister under, 1:311, 2:118
development politics of, 1:316, 318
economy under, 2:117–118
education of, 2:117
on European relations, 2:48
father of (*See* Nehru, Jawaharlal)

foreign policy of, 2:117, 3:316, 4:194,
195
Golden Temple and, 1:41, 273,
2:119, 288, 4:65, 68
Gujral under, 2:161–162
in Indo–Pakistani war (1971), 2:117,
3:372
intelligence agencies under,
3:315–316
marriage of, 2:117
military interventions by, 3:116
Narayan (Jaya Prakash) and, 3:216
national emergency declared by (*See*
National Emergency)
and National Security Act of 1980,
2:108
in national security decision-making,
3:220
nuclear program under, 1:151, 2:118,
3:247, 251, 253
on Palestine, 2:313
Pandit (Vijaya Lakshmi) and, 3:272
in Parliament, 3:313
political power of, 2:117
in presidential elections, 3:312
as prime minister, 3:338
and princely states, 3:346
in Punjab, 3:358
Punjab under, creating new states
from, 2:43
Rajagopalachari and, 3:375
rise of, 3:315
and rural credit, 3:417
under Shastri, 3:315
and Sikhs, 2:118–119, 4:64–65
and Simla Agreement of 1972, 4:70
Socialism of, 2:117
on Soviet invasion of Afghanistan, 1:8
Soviet relations under, 2:117, 3:420
and Sri Lanka, 4:98
Vajpayee imprisoned by, 4:208
women's rights ignored by, 4:234
Gandhi, Kasturbai, Gandhi (Mahatma)
on, 4:264–265
Gandhi, Mahatma M. K., **2:119–125,**
2:120
on *ahimsa,* 2:121, 124, 4:7, 8, 9
in Ahmedabad, 1:25
Ambedkar's approach to Dalits *vs.*,
1:39, 2:123
Anand's commitment to, 1:41
Andrews' friendship with, 1:44, 251
ashrams founded by, 1:25, 2:121, 122,
123
assassination of, 1:175, 2:124, 194,
199, 205, 214, 4:272–273
on atomic bomb, 3:253
autobiography of, 3:67, 4:262–272
Āyurveda fascinating, 2:119

Government of India Act of 1935,
2:157–158
and All-India Muslim League, 1:37
on Bengal, 1:136
on Burma, 1:211
Congress Party against, 2:158
Constitution influenced by,
3:302–303
and Council of India, 1:189
on Dalits, 1:284
events leading up to, 2:157–158
Federal Court of India established
by, 2:356
Indian response to, 2:158
and India Office, 2:232
Linlithgow's role in, 3:64
princely states in, 3:345
on provinces, 2:158
on scheduled tribes, 4:14, 16
Government of India bonds,
1:296–297
Governor-generals. *See also specific
officials*
in British Raj administrative structure, 1:169
after independence, 3:333
Gowariker, Aamir Khan-Ashutosh,
films of, 1:259
Gowda, H. D. Deve
as prime minister, 3:338
Russian relations under, 3:421
Gramdan (village gift), 1:147
Grammar, 4:19
Ashtādhyāyī (Pānini) on, 1:61–62,
3:273–274, 4:19
Mahābhāshya (Patanjali) on,
3:283–284
Granth Sahib. *See* Adi Granth
Grass mats, col. ins. v3
Grazing, in common property
resources, 1:266
Great Britain. *See* Britain
Great Depression
fiscal deficit during, 2:79
and price fluctuations, 3:335, 336
Great Game (Russian–British rivalry)
Bactria region in, 1:90
Baluch tribes in, 1:110
definition of, 1:110
Persia in, 1:45
Pukhtun tribes in, 1:110
Great Mutiny. *See* Struggle of 1857
Great Stupa (Amaravati), 1:208–209
Great Stupa (Nagarjunakonda),
1:209
Greco-Bactrian kingdom, 2:210
Greece, ancient
India's impact on, 2:233
music of, 3:189

Greene, Graham, Narayan (R. K.) and,
3:218
Green Revolution (1966–1980)
and agricultural wages, 1:23
in Punjab, 3:*356*, 358
technical change in, 4:145–146
Green Revolution, second
biotechnology as, 1:155
rural credit and, 3:418
Grocery stores, 1:16–17
Gromyko, Andrey, visit to India, 3:420
Gross domestic product (GDP)
agriculture's share in, 1:17
balance of payments as percentage of,
2:21
defense expenditure as percentage of,
2:4, 7, 3:219
domestic savings as percentage of,
4:*10*
external debt as percentage of, 2:52,
53, 83, 84
foreign investment as percentage of,
2:149, 4:10
growth in, 1:14, 2:21, 22, *22*
internal debt as percentage of, 2:293
per capita, growth of, 2:21
public spending as percentage of,
2:82
small-scale industry's share in, 4:82
underground economy as percentage
of, 4:191
Group 1890, 3:138
Group of 3 (G-3), establishment of,
1:168
Group of Ministers (GOM), on
national security, 1:261
Grow More Food Campaign, 4:143,
144
Growth Centre Scheme (1988), 2:242
GSLV. *See* Geostationary satellite
launch vehicle
Guerrilla war, 2:287
Guilds. *See* Shrenis
Gujarat (state), **2:159–161**
Ahmedabad in (*See* Ahmedabad)
architectural patronage in, 4:124
bandhani in, 1:113, 114
Baroda in (*See* Baroda)
Bharatiya Janata Party in, 2:160, 161,
196, 198, 206–207
block-printed textiles from, 4:155,
156, 157, 158, 159
under Bombay presidency, 2:126, 160
under British rule, 2:160
brocade weaving in, 1:191
capital of (*See* Gandhinagar)
in Chalcolithic Age, 1:234
Congress Party in, 2:160
creation of, 2:43

development in, 1:318
economic growth in, 4:107
famine in, 2:122
festival in, 2:91, *91*
fire-temples in, 4:258
folk art in, 2:87, col. ins. v3
folk dance in, 2:90–91, *91*
in Guptan empire, 2:159
Hindu–Muslim conflict in,
2:160–161, 206, 303, 4:222, 234
Indus Valley civilization in, 2:159,
258, 260, 265
informal credit markets in, 2:267
Jainism in, 2:322, 328
Jain temples in, 2:329
jewelry in, 2:344
manuscript painting in, 4:121
Marathas in, 2:160
maritime trade in, pre-colonial, 2:1,
3, 159
migrants from, 1:328, 333, 334,
336
monuments in, 3:176–181
in Mughal empire, 2:160, 224
Muslim architectural remains in,
4:122
in Neolithic period, 3:231
*panchayat*s in, 4:*2*
paper in, 3:275
Parsis in, 2:160
Patel's *satyagraha* movement in, 3:286
*patola*s in, 3:289, 290
population of, 2:159
railroads in, 2:285
road construction in, 2:283
settlement patterns in, 2:142
step-wells in, 4:110, 111
sultanate of, 2:160
temples in, 4:153
textile industry in, 4:79
theater in, 4:164
tribes living in, 4:186
women abused in, 2:222
women on pilgrimage to obtain
water in, 2:*132*
Gujarati language, 2:40, 43
Gujral, Inder Kumar, 2:*161*,
2:161–163
in Congress Party, 2:161
on democracy, 1:318
economic policy of, 2:21
foreign policy of, 2:162, 4:*193*
under Gandhi (Indira), 2:161–162
on military interventions, end of,
3:119
in national security decision-making,
3:221
as prime minister, 3:338
Sharif's (Nawaz) meeting with, 3:*263*

Gujral, Satish, art of, 3:137
Gulab Singh, Jammu and Kashmir
  princely state created by, 3:340
Gulbadan (Mughal princess), 4:237
Guler painting, 3:386–387
Gulshan-e-ishq (love story), 3:74
Gunas (constituent qualities), 4:5
Gunga Jumna (film), 1:255
Gupta, Prem Chand, *2:9*
Guptan empire, *2:163*, **2:163–164,**
  2:211. *See also specific rulers*
  Alexander the Great as inspiration
    for, 1:35
  architecture in, 2:164–167
  Bengal in, 1:130
  Bihar in, 1:152
  bronzes from, 1:195–196
  Buddhist temples in, 4:*149*
  collapse of, 1:130
  Deccan in, 2:211
  decline of, 2:164, 3:109
  education in, 2:25
  feudalism in, 2:71, 72, 73, 164, 211
  Gujarat in, 2:159
  Hinduism in, 2:190–191
  Hindu temples in, 2:164, 165–166,
    167
  Jain sculptures in, 2:327–328, *328*
  Kashmir in, 2:211
  Krishna in sculpture of, 3:38–39
  legacy of, 1:130, 2:164
  literature in, 2:164
  Magadha in, 3:82
  Maharashtra in, 2:211
  metalware of, 3:113
  origins of, 2:163
  Pataliputra in, 3:289
  political culture of, 2:164
  religions coexisting in, 1:130
  Sanskrit language used in, 2:164
  Shaivism in, 2:164, 4:51
  state formation by, 4:103
  temple kingdoms after, 3:108–109
  Vaishnavism in, 2:164
Guptan period art, **2:164–167**
  bronzes, 1:195–196
  coins, 2:163, 165
  sculptures, 2:164, 165, *165*, 166, 167,
    4:33, 34
Gupta script, 3:55
Gupta-Vakataka art, 1:196
Gurdwara (door of the Guru), 4:69
Gurgaon, Ericsson building in, col.
  ins. v1
Gurkha dynasty, rise of, 3:231, 233
Gurkha soldiers, 3:233
Gurmata (decision), 4:63
Gurmukh (realized individual), 4:69
Gurmukhi script, 3:55, 4:66

Gurpurbs (Sikh festivals), 4:69–70
Gurudwaras (Sikh temples)
  in Canada, 1:335
  in United Kingdom, 1:333
  in United States, 1:334
Guru Granth Sahib. *See* Adi Granth
Gurukula schools, 1:60
Guru Nanak, **2:167–168,** 2:*168*
  accounts on life of, 4:65–66
  commune established by, 4:62, 66
  education of, 2:168
  hymns of, 2:167, 4:68, 69
  legends about, 2:168
  on violence, 4:62
Gurus, 4:62–63, 66–67. *See also*
  Sikhism; *specific gurus*
Guwahati (city in Assam), Indian Institute of Technology at, 2:229
Guyana, Indian community in, 1:335
Gwalior Fort, col. ins. v1
  rock art at, 3:*413*
Gyanendra (king of Nepal), 3:232, 233

H

Haasan, Kamal, films of, 1:256
Habibollah (Afghan amir)
  assassination of, 1:47
  British relations with, 1:47
  in World War I, 1:47
Hada Rajputs, and Kotah miniature
  paintings, 3:128–129
Haffkine, Waldemar Mordecai, 2:350
Hahnemann, Samuel, homeopathy
  founded by, 3:108
Hairpins, ivory, 2:316
Haldi (tumeric), 1:157
Haḷebīḍ, Hoysaleshvara Temple at,
  3:*109,* 167
Hamidullah (ruler of Bhopal), 1:147
Hampi (village in Karnataka), col.
  ins. v1
  Narasiṃha sculpture in, 4:*216,*
    255
  temples in, 3:169–171
Hamumān, in Rāmāyaṇa, 3:394–397
Hamzanāma, Akbar's commission of,
  3:185
Hanafi school of Islamic law, 2:300
  under British rule, 3:196
Handicrafts, col. ins. v3
Hand ornament, *2:343*
Hanuman Ghat (Varanasi), 1:*163*
Haoma (substance), 4:84
Haq, A. K. Fazlul, **2:169–170**
  coalition government led by, 1:136,
    2:170
  dismissal of, 1:137, 2:170
  education of, 2:169
  in Lucknow Pact (1916), 2:169

  Muslims working with, 1:136,
    2:169–170
  Rahman's (Mujibur) confrontation
    with, 3:371
Haq, Raja Zafarul, in Kargil conflict
  (1999), 3:9
Haraoti. *See* Bundi
Harappa (city), **2:170–171**
  archaeological excavations at,
    2:170–171
  architecture of, 2:170–171, *171,* 262
  burials in, 2:171
  in Chalcolithic Age, 1:232–234, 2:259
  as independent city-state, 2:263
  pre-colonial maritime trade in, 2:1
  script found at, 2:262, 263
  sculpture found at, 2:263
  textiles from, 4:157
  urban planning in, 4:200–201
  water in, 2:261
Harappan civilization. *See* Indus Valley
  civilization
Harappa Phase, 2:170, 171, 259
Hardinge, Lord, **2:171–172**
  attack on life of, 2:171
  Chelmsford replacing, 1:239, 2:172
  and Delhi as capital, 3:235
  in Mespot disaster (1916), 2:171, 172
  replacing Minto, 3:132
  reunification of Bengal proposed by,
    3:132
  as viceroy of India, 2:171
  in World War I, 2:171–172
Hard-stone beads, 2:342
Hardy, G. H., 4:21
Hare Krishna groups, in United
  States, 2:235
Harems
  of Akbar, 3:125, 126
  artistic activities in, 3:125
  hierarchy within, 3:125–126
  Kāma Sūtra on, 3:3
  in miniature paintings, **3:125–127**
Hargobind (Sikh guru)
  Akal Takht established by, 4:63
  in Amritsar, 1:40
  army of, 4:66
Harichandra (Partihara ruler), 3:176
Harihara temples (Osian), 3:179
Harijan (children of God), 1:285
Harimandir temple. *See* Golden Temple
Harisena (Vakataka emperor), Ajanta
  caves under, 1:28, 29, 3:378
Hari Singh, and Pukhtuns' invasion of
  Kashmir (1947), 2:331–332, 3:12–13
Hariti (deity), 2:154
Harivaṃsha (Hindu epic), Vishnu in,
  4:217, 218
Har Krishan (Sikh guru), 4:66

Iron
in Atharva Veda, 4:212
in Vedic Aryan India, 4:212, 213
Iron Age, metalware in, 3:113
Iron ore
in Goa, 2:150
in Jamshedpur, 2:337, 338
Irrigation, agricultural
Asian Development Bank in, 1:64
under British rule, 2:274–275
in Buddhist archaeological sites,
1:203, 204
expansion of, 1:20–21, 4:146
in famine policy, 2:60, 274, 275
in Indo-Gangetic Plain, 2:138
major projects of, 4:144, 146
mechanization of, 4:144, 145, 147
need for, 1:20
overexploitation of groundwater in,
2:39, 4:146
in peninsular massif, 2:139
in Punjab, 2:274, 275, 3:357
"watershed" technology of, 4:146
World Bank loans for, 4:242–243
IRS. *See* Indian Remote Sensing (IRS)
satellite
Irwin, Lord, **2:299**
and Gandhi (Mahatma), 2:299
and Gandhi-Irwin Pact, 2:157, 299
as governor-general of India, 2:299
on India's constitutional progress,
2:299
Paul (K. T.) meeting with, 3:291
on Round Table Conference, 2:299
ISA. *See* Islamic State of Afghanistan
ISI. *See* Import-substitution industrial
strategy; Inter Services Intelligence
Islam, **2:299–304, 3:198–205**. *See also*
Muslims
under Akbar, 1:31, 2:304
architecture of, 2:302, 305, 309,
4:202–203
art in, 2:302
Ārya Samāj in conflict with, 1:61
bandhani in, 1:114
in Bengal, 1:131, 136–137
bigamy in, 2:56, 57, 3:196
branches of, 2:300
under British rule, 2:305–306
conversion to, 3:200
criticism of, 2:305
divorce in, 2:56, 57, 3:195–198, 4:40,
44, 45
education in, 2:307 (*See also* Aligarh
movement)
family law in, 2:55, 56–57, 66, 4:40,
44–45
Five Pillars of, 2:299
folk art in, 2:88

fundamentalism in, 1:11, 12, 2:44
and Hinduism, 2:191–192, 301, 302,
304–305 (*See also* Hindu–Muslim
relations)
impact of, on India, 2:211–212,
301–303, **2:304–311**
Iqbal on, 2:297, 303, 305
of Jinnah, 2:352
jinn in, 1:149
judicial system in, 2:355
Kabir in, 3:1
in Ladakh, 2:331, 334, 337
languages in, 2:301–302
meaning of term, 2:299
modernism in, 2:302–303, 307–308
in Mughal empire, 2:305–306
music in, 2:302, 3:189–190
mysticism in (*See* Sufism)
in northwestern India, 3:200
origins in India, 3:198–200
origins of, 2:299
in Pakistani–Indian relations, 3:264
renaissance of, 2:309–310
rosaries in, 2:341
Sayyid Ahmed Khan on, 4:13–14
schools of law in, 2:300
of Shah Jahan, 4:45, 46
under Shivaji, 4:55
society in, 2:307
in South India, arrival of,
3:198–200
spread of, 2:300–301, 304
step-wells in, 4:110, 111
texts in, 2:*300* (*See also* Qur'an)
trends in, 2:310–311
women in, 2:310, 4:237
Islamabad (Pakistan), 3:*261*
Islamic fundamentalism
in Kashmir conflict, 2:44
in Pakistan, 1:11, 12
of Taliban, 1:11
Islamic law. *See* Muslim law
Islamic State of Afghanistan (ISA)
Indian recognition of, 1:9
Indian support for, 1:9–10
Isma'ili (Seveners) Shi'ism, 2:300, 301
Israel
consulate of, in Bombay, 2:311–312,
313
embassy of, in New Delhi, 2:313
establishment of, 2:311
Indian community in, 1:333
Indian nationalists on, 2:311
Indian recognition of, 2:311
Indian relations with, **2:311–315,**
2:*312*
as military supplier to India, 2:314
national security advisers from, 2:314
Pakistan compared with, 3:265

in Sri Lankan ethnic conflict, 2:313
trade with, 2:314
ISRO. *See* Indian Space Research
Organization
IT. *See* Information technology
ITBP. *See* Indo–Tibetan Border Police
I'timad-ud-Daulah, tomb of, 3:160
Itsing (Chinese pilgrim), on bronzes,
1:195
Itwari v. Asghari, 3:196
Ivory carving, **2:315–317,** 2:*316*
decorative, 2:315, 316–317
plaques, 2:315
sculptures, 2:315
socioeconomic importance of, 2:316
trade of, 2:316
Iyengar, Chakravarti, 3:372
Iyengar, K. R. Srinivasa, 3:376
Iyengar, P. K., 3:253, 4:23
Iyer, Palghat Mani, drum solos of,
3:195
Iyer, Semmangudi Srinivasa, Karnātak
music of, 3:191, 192

J

Jacob, J. F. R., 2:350
Jacquard, 1:190
Jagannath, in Rath Yatra, col. ins. v3
Jagat, temple in, 3:180
Jagat Singh (Rajput ruler, 1657–1684),
painting under, 3:129, 384
Jagat Singh I (Rajput ruler,
1628–1655), painting under, 3:381,
400–401
Jagat Singh II (Rajput ruler,
1734–1751), painting under,
3:381–382
Jaggayyapeta, Buddhist art in, 1:208
Jahan, Shah. *See* Shah Jahan
Jahanara (Mughal princess), 3:204
Jahangir (Mughal emperor),
2:319–320
Agra under, 1:14
Akbar's tomb built by, 3:159–160
architectural projects of, 3:156,
159–160
birth of, 1:31
father of (*See* Akbar)
gardens at Agra under, 3:156
memoirs of, 3:186, 188
metalware under, 3:114
music under, 3:190
Nur Jehan as wife of, 2:310, 319
painting under, 3:186–188
portraits of, 3:187
regulations by, 2:319
Sikhism under, 4:66
sons of, 2:319
wives of, 1:30, 2:310, 319

Jahangīrī Mahal (palace), miniature painting in, 3:124
Jain art. *See also* Jain manuscript painting; Jain sculpture
  Guptan, 2:166–167
Jain Committee (1966), 2:176
Jainism, **2:323–326**. *See also*
  Tīrthānkaras
  Agni in, 1:13
  ahimsa in, 2:210, 325, 326
  art of (*See* Jain art)
  Ayodhya in, 1:82
  Bihar in, 1:153
  books treasured in, 2:320, 322
  and Buddhism, 2:323
  of Chandragupta Maurya, 3:103
  enlightenment in, 2:323
  goddesses in, 2:152, 326
  in Gujarat, 2:322, 328
  and Hinduism, 2:323
  *jina*s in, 2:323, 326
  in Jodhpur, 2:354
  karma in, 1:202, 2:323–324, 325
  in Karnataka, 3:11
  in Khajuraho, 3:27
  in Kushan empire, 2:327, *327*, 328
  in Magadha, 3:82
  monasteries of, 2:*327*, 3:154
  monuments of, 3:153–154
  number of followers of, 2:*324*
  origins of, 2:323
  paper used in, 3:275
  pilgrimage in, 2:328, 329
  principles of, 2:325
  in Rajasthan, 2:322
  rasa in, 1:5
  rebirth in, 2:323–324
  *rishi*s in, 3:412
  rituals in, 2:*324*
  sects of, 2:324–325, 327
  stupas in, 3:153
  symbols in, 2:324
  temples of (*See* Jain temples)
  vegetarianism in, 2:323
  women in, 4:236–237
Jain manuscript painting, 2:*321*, **2:322**
  development of, 2:322, 3:379
  historical background of, 2:322, 3:379
  Sirohi school of, 4:76
Jain sculpture, **2:326–329**
  bronzes, 1:197, 2:328
  donation of, 2:*327*
  early history of, 2:327
  Guptan, 2:327–328, *328*
  Kushana, 4:27
  Mauryan, 4:29, 30
  of Tīrthānkaras, 2:326–327, 328, 329, 4:27

in rock art, 3:*413*
and temple architecture, 2:328–329
for veneration, 2:326, *327*
Jain temples, col. ins. v1
  architecture of, 3:154
  Ellora caves, 2:31, 328
  library of, 2:322
  Nāgara style of, 4:153
  remains of, 4:149
  sculptures in, 2:328–329
  in southern India, 3:167–169
  in western India, 3:179, 180, 181
Jaintia people, in Meghalaya, 3:111
Jaipur (city)
  block-printed textiles from, 4:159
  contemporary life in, col. ins. v2
  handicrafts in, col. ins. v3
  Hawa Mahal in, col. ins. v1
  metalware from, 3:*113*
  observatory in, 1:*71*, col. ins. v1
Jaipur (princely state)
  Rajput painting in, 3:383
  under Rajputs, 3:339, 383
Jaipur school of dance, 1:289
Jairazbhoy, N. A., on *rāga*s, 3:368
Jai Santoshi Maa (film), 1:255
Jai Singh
  observatories of, col. ins. v1
  painting under, 3:383
Jajmani system, 3:46
Jallianwala Bagh Massacre (1919), 1:40–41
  Chelmsford's response to, 1:239
  Dyer in, 1:40, 136, 173
  events of, 2:122
  Gandhi (Mahatma) on, 1:40–41, 2:122
  Prasad (Rajendra) influenced by, 3:329
  victims of, 2:122
Jama'at-i Islami, 3:15, 203
Jamdani (muslin), **2:329–331**
  British trade of, 2:330
  in Mughal empire, 2:329–330
  origin of, 2:329
  technique of weaving, 2:329, *330*, 330–331
James I (king of England), and Mughal painting, 3:187–188
James, William, 3:377
James Raj Committee, 1:313–314
Jamia Millia Islamia, 3:203
Jamid Masjid (Delhi), col. ins. v1
Jami Masjid (Agra), 3:162
Jami Masjid (Delhi), 3:162–163
Jami Masjid (Fatehpur Sikri), 3:158
Jammu (region), **2:334–337**
  block-printed textiles from, 4:155
  Hinduism in, 2:331, *332*, 334, 335–336

Hindu nationalism in, 2:335, 336, 3:13
human rights abuses in, 2:223
in Jammu and Kashmir, 2:331, 334, 3:12
languages in, 2:334
painting in, 2:333
Sikhs in, 2:334
Jammu and Kashmir (state), **2:331–334**, 3:11–16. *See also* Kashmir (region)
  accession to India, 3:12–13
  British transfer of territories of, 2:289, 3:12
  census in, 1:308
  citizenship in, 3:14
  constitution of, 3:14
  Constitution of India on, 2:335, 336, 3:13–14
  counterinsurgency operations in, 2:290
  creation of, 3:12
  de facto integration into India, 3:14–15, 287–288
  economy of, 3:15
  elections in, 3:15–16
  history of, 2:331–332
  Indian–Pakistani conflict over, 2:288–289, 3:11–16
  in Kargil conflict (1999), 3:6
  legislature of, 3:14–15
  map of, 3:*12*
  opposition parties in, 3:15
  Pakistani *vs.* Indian view of, 3:12, *12*
  paramilitary forces in, 3:277, 278, 279
  patronage in, 3:15
  plebiscite in, 2:332, 337, 3:13, 14
  population of, 2:334
  as princely state, 3:340
  Pukhtun invasion of (1947), 2:331–332, 3:12–13
  regional disparities in development in, 2:336
  regions within, 2:331, 3:12
  religious and cultural influence of, 2:332–333
  state government of, 3:14–15
  United Nations on, 2:289, 332, 3:13
Jammu and Kashmir Liberation Front (JKLF), 2:289, 3:15–16
Jammu and Kashmir Praja Parishad (Hindu nationalist party), 2:336
Jamshedpur (city in Jharkhand), **2:337–338**
  as modern industrial city, 4:139
  steel industry in, 2:337–338
Jamuna river, monuments on, 3:156, 157, 160, 163

migration to, 3:4
Muslims in, 3:4
as port city, 2:278
trade in, 3:4
Karachi Agreement (1949), 3:6
Karachi Resolution (1931), 1:271
Karaikkāl Ammaiyār, **3:4–5**
in *bhakti* movement, 3:4–5
devotion to Shiva, 3:4–5
marriage of, 3:5
poetry of, 3:4–5
Kāraka theory, 1:62
Karakoram Range, 2:137
*Karana*s (astronomical texts), 1:72
Karan Singh (Rajput ruler,
1620–1628), painting under, 3:381
Karan Singh (Rajput ruler,
1631–1669), painting under, 3:120,
385
Karanth, B. V., films of, 1:257
Karanth, Prema, films of, 1:258
Karen people, and Indian military
intervention, 3:117
Kargil (town), in Indo–Pakistani war
(1947–1948), 3:6
Kargil conflict (1999), **3:5–11**, 4:228
causes of, 3:6–7
cease-fire in, 3:8
China in, 1:245
India's strategy in, 3:7–8
Indo–Pakistani war of 1947 and, 3:6
international reaction to, 3:8, 9, 10
Kashmir conflict and, 3:6–7
nuclear weapons in, threat of, 3:6,
8–10, 4:228
outcome of, 3:5, 8
Pakistan's plan for, 3:7
paramilitary forces in, 3:279
political aspects of, 3:8
Russia in, 3:422
start of, 3:5, 7, 4:228
as war *vs.* conflict, 3:6
Kargil Review Committee, 3:9
Kārkota dynasty, 2:331, 4:34, 35
Karma
Buddha on, 1:202
in Jainism, 1:202, 2:323–324, 325
Upanishadic philosophy on, 1:202,
2:190
Karma (film), 1:254
Karma Yoga. *See also Bhagavad Gītā*
nationalists using, 4:223
Vivekananda on, 4:222
writings on, 4:256
Karmayogin (weekly), Aurobindo
writing in, 1:76
Karṇa, in *Mahābhārata*, 3:87–89
Karnad, Girish, films of, 1:257
Karṇāṭa-Andhra style of temple, 3:169

Karnataka (state), **3:11**
Bangalore in (*See* Bangalore)
Bijapur in (*See* Bijapur)
Congress Party in, 3:11
economic growth in, 4:107
folk art in, 2:89
folk dance in, 2:92
human development indicators of,
2:218, *218*
informal credit markets in, 2:269
Jainism in, 3:11
Jain sculptures from, 2:328
Jain temples in, 2:328
Kannada language in, 3:11
as linguistic state, 3:11
monuments in, 3:11
Mysore in, **3:207**
in Neolithic period, 3:230–231
paramilitary forces in, 3:278
road construction in, 2:283
Shaivism in, 4:52
step-well in, 4:111
tax reform in, 4:141
temples in, 3:11, *168*, 4:151, 152, 153
World Bank loans to, 4:244
Karnāṭak music, **3:190–195**
and dance, 3:194
of Dīkshitar, 1:337
education in, 3:192
vs. Hindustani music, 3:190, 193
history of, 3:190–192
instruments used in, 3:191, 194–195
kriti in, 3:43
modern, 3:191, 194–195
patronage of, 3:190–191, 192
performance of, 3:191, 192–193
*rāga*s in, 3:191, 193–194, 365
structure of, 3:191
*tāla*s in, 3:191, 193, 194, 4:130
women in, 3:194, 4:118
Karoṣṭhī script, 3:54
Kartikeya (deity), sculpture of, 4:27
Karun, Shaji N., films of, 1:257
Karuppur textiles, **4:160–161**
Karve, Irawati, on caste system,
1:227
Karzai, Hamid, as president of
Afghanistan, 1:10
Kasaravalli, Girish, films of, 1:257
Kashi (city). *See* Varanasi
Kashmir (region), **3:11–17**. *See also*
Jammu and Kashmir
architecture of, 2:333
art in, 2:333–334
bronzes in, 2:333
Buddhism in, 2:331, 333
conflict over (*See* Kashmir conflict)
dance in, 2:333
disappearance of relic in (1964), 3:15

discriminatory actions against
Ladakh, 2:336, 337
Emergency in the States invoked on,
2:107
environment of, col. ins. v4
in Guptan empire, 2:211
Hindu nationalist movement on,
2:196, 197, 199, 206
human rights abuses in, 2:223
independence movement in,
3:13
Indian army in, 1:*48*, 52
in Indo–Pakistani war (1947–1949),
4:225
in Indo–Pakistani war (1965),
4:226–227
in Purāṇic geography, 2:331
in Kargil conflict (1999), 3:5
in Kushan empire, 2:331, 333
literature in, 2:334
music in, 2:333, 334
Muslims in, 2:331, *332*, 3:15
painting in, 2:333, 3:*17*, **3:17–18**
papermaking in, 3:275, 379
paramilitary forces in, 3:279
in partition of India, 3:345
poetry in, 2:334
political boundaries of, 2:332
preventive detention in, 2:109
Pukhtun invasion of (1947),
2:331–332, 3:12–13
science in, 2:334
sculpture and bronze images from,
2:333, **4:33–36**
secessionist movement in, 3:11–12,
15–16
Shaivism in, 2:332–333, 4:52
shawls of, **3:18–21**, 3:*19*
stupas in, 4:35
Tantric Buddhism in, 2:333, 4:135
Tantric Hinduism in, 2:332–333
tourism in, 2:144
trade in, 2:331
Kashmir conflict, 3:11–16
Abdullah (Mohammad) in, 3:12, 13
Afghanistan in, 1:7, 9, 11, 12
Ayub Khan in, 3:261
China in, 1:243, 245
and defense budget, 2:5
factors of, 2:43
historical background for, 3:12–13
India's strategy in, 3:16, 269
and Indo–Israeli relations, 2:312
Islamic fundamentalism in, 2:44
Kargil conflict in (1999), 3:6–7
Khan (Liaquat Ali) in, 3:33
nuclear weapons in, 3:254
Pakistan sponsoring insurgencies in,
2:42, 44, 289

Kashmir conflict (*continued*)
  Pakistan's view of, 3:6–7, 12, 262, 269
  paramilitary forces in, 3:277
  Siachen Glacier in, 4:227–228
  Soviet position on, 3:419
  Taliban in, 1:11, 12
  terrorism in, 2:289
  United States in, 3:13, 4:194
Kashmiri, Agha Hashr, films written by, 1:253
Kashmiriyat, origins of concept, 3:12
Kashmir Line of Control (LOC)
  in Indo–Pakistani war (1947–1948), 3:6
  in Kargil conflict (1999), 3:5–9
Kashmir painting, 2:333, 3:*17*, **3:17–18**
Kashmir shawls, **3:18–21**, 3:*19*
  decline and revival of, 3:21
  design of, 3:20
  manufacture of, 3:18–20
  motifs of, 3:20
  origins of, 3:20–21
Kashmir War, First. *See* Indo–Pakistani war (1947–1948)
Kashmir War, Second. *See* Indo–Pakistani war (1965)
Kashrut (dietary law), in Bene Israel, 1:128
Kasi vastra (muslin), 2:329
Kasuri, Ahmad Raza, death of, 1:151
Kathak (dance), **1:288–289**, 1:*289*, 2:90
Kathakali (dance), **1:289–291**, 1:*290*, 2:90, 4:*162*
  Krishna in, 3:42
Kātyāyana, *Mahābhāshya* on, 3:283–284
Kaul, Mani, films of, 1:257
Kaur, Rajkumari Amrit, on Chandigarh, 1:236
Kauravas
  in Bhagavad Gītā, 1:140
  in Mahābhārata, 3:86–92
Kaushika (Jain king), Akkamahā dēvi and, 1:32
Kauṭilya
  as author of *Artha Shāstra*, 1:55–56, 2:24, 210, 4:15, 114
  as minister of Chandragupta Maurya, 1:130, 2:210, 4:114
Kavipriya (Keshavadasa), 1:126
  Rajput paintings for, 3:380
Kayasths (caste), **3:22–23**
  folk art by, 2:87
  myth of origin, 3:22
  regional divisions in, 3:22
  as writing caste, 3:22
Kaziranga National Park, col. ins. v4
Kehimkar, Haeem Samuel, 1:129

Kehimkar, Joseph Samuel, 1:129
Kellogg, S. H., 1:249
Kempe Gowda, Bangalore founded by, 1:116
Kennedy, John F.
  Galbraith under, 2:111
  Rajagopalachari's meeting with, 3:375
  in Sino–Indian War (1962), 1:243
Kerala (state)
  airport in, 1:*329*
  astronomy in, 1:73
  Christian missionaries in, 3:25
  coalition politics in, **3:23–24**
  Communist Party of India in, 3:23, 25
  contemporary life in, col. ins. v2
  creation of, 3:24
  dance forms of, 1:289–291, 293–294, 4:*162*
  development in, 1:315, 318, **3:24–25**
  economic growth in, 4:107
  Emergency in the States invoked on, 2:107
  environment of, col. ins. v4
  film in, 1:256, 257
  financial remittances to, 1:330
  folk art in, 2:89, col. ins. v3
  folk dance in, 2:91, 92
  Gama (Vasco da) in, 3:319–320
  infant mortality rate in, 4:108
  Jews in, 2:347, *347*, 348–349, 3:363
  literacy in, 1:305, 2:144, 3:24, 106
  megalithic constructions in, 2:153
  *patola*s in, 3:290
  population growth in, 1:306, 3:24
  road construction in, 2:283
  settlement patterns in, 2:142
  temples in, 4:151, 152
  theater in, 4:162, *162*
  trade in, 2:349
  women's education in, 4:236
Kerala Kala Mandalam, 1:290, 294
Kerala school of astronomy, 1:73
Kerkar, Kesarbai, **3:25–26**
Keshavadasa (poet), 1:126, 3:380
Kettle drums, 4:125–126
Keynes, J. M.
  on central banking, 3:149
  on gold exports from India, 3:102
  on monetary system weaknesses, 3:335
Khadi movement
  Gandhi (Mahatma) on, 4:267–269
  Prasad (Rajendra) in, 3:329
Khajuraho (city in Madhya Pradesh), **3:26–29**
  architecture of, 3:27–29
  religions in, 3:27
  sculpture in, 3:28–29
  temples in, 2:328–329, 3:*26*, 26–29, 4:152–153

Khalaji dynasty, Malwa under, 3:123
Khalili, Massoud
  as ambassador to India, 1:9, 10
  al-Qaeda attack against, 1:10
Khalistani insurgency, in Punjab, 3:358, 4:64–65, 68
Khalji, Ala'ud-Din Muhammad
  Khusrau and, 3:35
  Maharashtra under, 3:94
  music in court of, 3:189–190
  patola for, 3:289
Khalsa (Sikh institution), 4:63, 67
Khan, Abdul Ghaffar, **3:29–31**, 3:*30*
  education of, 3:30
  Gandhi (Mahatma) and, 3:30, 203
  imprisonment of, 3:29, 30
  nonviolence advocated by, 3:30–31, 203
  Pakhtun state called for by, 3:30–31
  partition of India opposed by, 3:203
  wives of, 3:30
Khan, Abdul Jabbar, education of, 3:30
Khan, Abdul Karim, 3:25
Khan, Ahmed, 4:44
Khan, Ali Akbar, **3:31**
  music of, 3:31
Khan, Alladiya, 3:25
Khan, Allaudin, 3:31, 4:46, 47
Khan, Bande Hasan, 3:33
Khan, Barkatullah, 3:25
Khan, Behram, 3:29–30
Khan, Bismillah, 3:33
Khan, Imrat, 3:33
Khan, Inayat, 3:33
Khan, Liaquat Ali, **3:31–33**, 3:*32*
  in All-India Muslim League, 1:37, 38, 3:31–33
  assassination of, 3:33, 259
  education of, 3:31
  as finance minister of India, 1:38
  Jinnah (Mohammad Ali) and, 2:352, 353, 3:32–33
  in Kashmir conflict, 3:33
  as prime minister of Pakistan, 1:38, 3:33
Khan, Mehboob, films of, 1:255
Khan, Nasrat Fateh Ali, *qawwāli* by, 3:361, *362*
Khan, Sayyid Ahmed. *See* Sayyid Ahmed Khan
Khan, Shahrukh, 1:*256*
Khan, Shujaat, 3:33
Khan, Sikander Hayat, in All-India Muslim League, 1:37
Khan, Ustad Asad Ali, music of, 3:*367*
Khan, Vilayat, **3:33–34**
  music of, 3:33
  Ray (Satyajit) working with, 3:33
  sitar playing of, 3:33, 4:77–78

under economic planning, 2:241
international comparison of, 4:78
labor in, in independent India, 2:253, 254
labor in, under British rule, 2:249–250
Large taxpayer unit (LTU), 4:142
Laski, Harold, 3:219
Lasya (dance), 1:286, 287, 292
Late Harappa Phase, 2:171, 259–260
Latina (tower), 4:152, 153
Laurak, love stories about, 3:74
Laur-Chanda (love story), 3:74
Lava, in Rāmāyaṇa, 3:390–391
Law. *See also* Family law; *specific laws*
on abortion, 1:305
Artha Shāstra on, 1:57
on banking, 1:118–120, 311–312
in Buddhism (*See Dharma*)
on child marriage, 1:187, 250, 2:67, 69, 4:238, 240
environmental, 2:38
family (*See* Family law)
on film industry, 2:76–77
on fundamental rights, 2:108–109, 219–220
on intellectual property rights, 2:290–291, 292
Islamic schools of, 2:300
labor, 2:10, 253, 254, 257
usury, 2:268
Law, John, 2:103–104
Law Commissions, Muslim law ignored by, 3:196
Lawrence, Stringer, army founded by, 1:50
Lawyers, in British Crown Raj, 1:171
Laxman, R. K., 3:217
Laxmi Villas Palace (Baroda), 1:127, 127, 128
Lazarus, John, as Christian leader, 3:60
Leadbeater, Charles, Krishnamurti (Jiddu) and, 3:42
Leaders
Christian, **3:59–61**
demonization of, in Pakistani–Indian relations, 3:266
Lee-Warner, William, on usage, 3:343
Left Democratic Front, in Kerala, 3:23
Legal Aid, 2:357
Legal system. *See also* Judicial system
in British Crown Raj, 1:171
in British East India Company, 1:171, 181, 225–226
British impact on, 1:187, 3:77
caste system and, 1:225–226
in contract farming, 1:276
Dharma Shāstra in, 1:325–326
Macaulay's impact on, 3:77

Legends, love stories inspired by, 3:73
Legislative Assemblies (state)
All-India Muslim League in, 1:37–38
of Jammu and Kashmir, 3:14–15
Khan (Liaquat Ali) in, 3:32
in presidential elections, 3:310–311
Reddi (Muthulakshmi) in, 3:409
Legislative Council (British)
in British Raj administrative structure, 1:169
Burma in, 1:211
Chelmsford in reforms to, 1:239
Indian members of, 1:169, 4:12
Morley in reforms to, 3:183
Muslim members of, 1:169
Sayyid Ahmed Khan as member of, 4:12
Lehria (dyeing technique), 1:114
Leibniz, Gottfried, 3:297
Leiter, Mary, 1:279
Leopards, col. ins. v4
Leprosy, Christian impact on, 1:250
Liberalization. *See also* Economic reforms of 1991
and enlargement of states' area of activities, 2:16, 17
"look east" policy in, 4:91–92
political economy of, **3:61–64**
Liberation. *See Moksha*
Liberation Tigers of Tamil Ealam (LTTE)
Gandhi (Rajiv) assassinated by, 2:125, 4:96
Indian war against, 3:118, 4:227
peace negotiations with, 4:96, 99
ruthlessness of, 4:96
LIC. *See* Life Insurance Corporation of India
Licchavi people, monuments of, 3:153
Licensing
foreign technology, 2:13, 247
import, 4:173, 174, 175
industrial (*See* Industrial licensing)
Life
contemporary, col. ins. v2
stages of, Rig Veda on, 4:275–278
Tree of (*See* Tree of Life)
Life Divine, The (Aurobindo), 1:76
Life expectancy
in colonial era, 1:302
as human development indicator, 2:216
in independent India, 1:305, 2:175
for women, 1:306, 315
Life insurance, 2:285–286
Life Insurance Corporation of India (LIC), 2:285–286
Lifestyle diseases, 2:178

Line of Control. *See* Kashmir Line of Control (LOC)
Liṅga (phallus), 4:49, 52
Lingaraja temple (Bhubaneswar), 3:156
Linguistic diversity, 2:39–40
and reorganization of provinces, 2:41, 43, 62, 288
Linguistic states
Andhra Pradesh as, 1:43
Karnataka as, 3:11
Kerala as, 3:24
Linlithgow, Lord, **3:64**
in Government of India Act of 1935, 3:64
Patel (Sardar Vallabhbhai) and, 3:286–287
as viceroy of India, 3:64
Lion(s)
bronzes of, 1:194–195
Narasimha as, 1:79, 4:*216*, 219
on pillars, 4:29–30
Lipai (dyeing technique), 1:114
Li Peng, India visited by, 1:244, 245
Literacy, col. ins. v2
under British rule, 4:235
census-based, 2:216
definition of, 3:105
as development criteria, 1:315
and fertility rates, 1:305–306
in Goa, 2:150
as human development indicator, 2:216, 4:108
in Kerala, 1:305, 2:144, 3:24, 106
and media, 3:105
regional disparities of, 4:108
in Sind, 4:71
in Sri Lanka, 2:144
in Tamil Nadu, 4:235
of tribal people, 4:179, 183
of voting population, 2:133
of women, 2:67, 4:235–236, 238
Literary Society of Bombay, 1:67. *See also* Asiatic Society of Bombay
Literature, **3:65–71**. *See also* Poetry; *specific writers*
autobiographical, 3:67
Bengali, 1:134–135
British, tribes in, 1:110
British impact on, 1:186, 3:65
under British rule, 1:186, 3:65–67
Christian impact on, 1:249
Dalit, 1:40, 3:67
in English language, 3:65, 66, 68–70
independence as theme of, 3:67–68
in Indian languages, 3:65, 69–70
in Kashmir, 2:334
love stories in, **3:71–75**
modern, **3:65–71**
Premchand on aim of, 3:331

*Madrasah*s (religious schools), and Taliban, 1:12

Madras Artists Corporation, 1:254

Madras Christian College
Chakkarai at, 3:60
Chenchiah at, 3:60
Mādhaviah at, 3:78

Madras Christo Samaj
Chakkarai in, 3:60
Chenchiah in, 3:61

Madras Government Museum
bronzes in, 1:195
Buddhist art in, 1:208

Madras Native Christian Association, 3:60

Madras presidency
in Andhra Pradesh state, 1:43
Bentinck as governor of, 1:138
British East India Company in, 1:177
languages spoken in, 1:43
Rajagopalachari as prime minister of, 3:374

Madras School of art, 3:137, 138

Madura. *See* Madurai

Madurai (city in Tamil Nadu), **3:80–81**
bandhani in, 1:113
design of, 3:80–81, 175
Kadal Alagar temple in, col. ins. v1
Minakshi Temple complex in, 3:80–81, *81*, 175–176, col. ins. v1
Nobili as missionary in, 3:239

Mafia (Indian)
film industry infiltrated with, 2:76
Shiv Sena involved in, 4:58

Magadha (ancient kingdom), **3:81–82**
under Ajatashatru, 1:154, 3:82
Anga incorporated by, 1:130, 3:82
under Bimbisara, 1:154, 3:82
Guptan empire in, 3:82
Mauryan empire in, 3:82, 103
Pataliputra in, 3:288

Mahābalipuram, temples of, 3:171–172

Mahābhārata (Hindu epic), **3:82–93**
Aryan tribes in, 2:209
Bhagavad Gītā as part of, 1:140, 2:190
Bharat in, 1:143
Bhīshma in, 3:84–85
book-by-book description of, 3:85–91
categorization of content, 3:85
on Chandala, 1:283
genre of, 3:83–84
goddesses in, 1:322
illustrations for, *3:83*
as love story, 3:71–72, 87
Narasimha in, 1:79
as narrative, 3:83–84
paintings illustrating, **3:399–402**

Pune Critical Edition of, 3:82, 83, 390

Rāmāyaṇa compared with, 3:390–392, 399

*sabha*s and *samiti*s in, 4:2

scientific speculation in, 4:19

Shiva in, 4:49, 50

size of, 3:82, 84

tapas in, 4:138

as textual archetype, 3:83

tribes in, 4:15

*upākhyāna*s (subparts) of, 3:83–85, 91–93

Vishnu in, 4:217, 219

Vyāsa as author of, 3:82–93

yoga in, 4:255

Mahābhāshya (Patanjali), 3:283–284

Mahādevī (deity), 1:322

Maha-Gurjara style of temple, 3:177–179

Mahakali Treaty (1996), 3:232

Mahakuta (Karnataka)
Sangamesvara temple in, 4:152, 153
step-well in, 4:111

Mahalanobis, Prasanta
and economic policy, 2:10
in statistics, 4:22

Mahal-i-Ilahi (Fatehpur Sikri), 3:159

Mahalwari system, 3:47

Maham Anga, Akbar's government led by, 1:29

Maha-Maru style of temple, 3:177–179

Mahanaleshvara temple (Menal), 3:181

Mahanama (Buddhist monk), 1:205

Maharaj, Birju, 1:289

Maharaj, Siyaji, 1:325

Maharaja Sayajirao University, art division of, 3:137

Maharashtra (state), **3:93–96**
Ahmednagar in, Deccani paintings at, 1:298, *298*
Bene Israel in (*See* Bene Israel)
bhakti movement in, 3:93, 94
Bombay in (*See* Bombay)
British East India Company's conquest of, 2:32
creation of, 2:43
development in, 1:318
economic growth in, 4:107
Ellora caves in, **2:30–31,** *2:31*
folk art in, 2:87
food security in, 2:95
Gaṇesha worship in, 2:129, 4:172
geography of, 3:93
in Guptan empire, 2:211
minimum wage legislation in, 2:253
nationalist movement in, 3:93–94
new states created in, 2:62
origin of name, 3:93

Paithani weaving in, 3:257, 258
road construction in, 2:283
Shaivism in, 4:52
under Shivaji, 3:93–95, 4:53
Shiv Sena in, 4:56, 57
tax reform in, 4:141

*Mahari*s (dancers), 1:294

Mahars (caste), Ambedkar and, 1:39

Mahāvamsa (Pali text), 1:205

*Mahavihara*s (monasteries), 3:154

Mahāvīra (Jain teacher)
in Bihar, 1:152
in Kshatriya caste, 1:223
lion representing, 2:327
as perceived founder of Jainism, 2:323, 327
sects organized by, 2:324
suicide of, 2:325

Mahāvīra temple (Kumbhariya), 3:181

Mahavira temple (Sewadi), 3:180

Mahayana Buddhism, 4:134
book cult in, 2:321
foundation of, 2:331
Gandharan Buddhism affiliated with, 2:116
other schools in relation to, 1:206
sculptures in, 4:24

Mahendra (king of Nepal), 3:231–232, 233

Maheshamurti, Baroli temple to, 3:179

Mahīpāla I (Pala ruler), 2:320

Mahiravana, in miniature painting, 3:124

Mahisasura (mythic figure), 3:207, 4:27

Mahisha (demon), 1:322, 2:154

Mahiwal, love stories about, 3:75

Mahmud I Begada (sultan of Gujarat), 2:160

Mahmud of Ghazni, 3:200

Mahmud Shah I Bigarha (sultan of Gujarat), manuscripts of, 3:379

Mahtab, Harekrushna, on Bhubaneswar as capital, 1:148

*Maibi*s (priestesses), dance dedicated to, 1:292

Mainframe computers, 2:270, 271

Maino, Sonia. *See* Gandhi, Sonia

Maintenance of Internal Security Act (MISA) of 1971, 2:108, 221

Maistry system, 1:328, 331

Maitrāyaniya Brāhmaṇa Upanishad, astronomy in, 1:70

Maitreya, 4:36, col. ins. v1

Maize, 2:141
high-yielding, 4:146, *146*
trends in output of, 4:*147*

Majumdar, Kshitindra Nath, 3:135

and famines, 1:301–302
first (1775–1782), 3:296
Hastings in, 2:174, 3:296
Maratha victories in, 3:296
Marathi language, 2:40, 43
Bhagavad Gītā translated into, 1:147
drama in, 4:164
feminist works in, 2:67
Maravani, love stories about, 3:73
Marconi, Guglielmo, 4:20
Marici (deity), 4:*136*, 136–137
Maritime commerce
from 1750 to 1947, **3:100–103**
with Britain, 3:102
under British rule, 2:278
with China, 3:101–102
cotton and textiles in, 3:100–102
in independent India, 2:281, 282
with Portugal, 3:319
pre-colonial (*See* Maritime contacts,
early)
with Sri Lanka, 4:96
with United States, 3:101
Maritime contacts, early, **2:1–3**
archaeological data on, 2:1
commodities in, 2:2, 3
in Gujarat, 2:1, 3, 159
map of, 3:*321*
organization of, 2:2–3
settlements in, 2:1, 2–3
transactions of, 2:2
Market economy
economic reforms of 1991 and,
2:16–17, 20
free contract principle in, 2:8
Marriage. *See also* Divorce; Weddings
between Arab Muslims and South
Indians, 3:198–199
in *brahmacarya*, 1:162
child (*See* Child marriage)
cross-cousin, 1:225
Gandhi (Mahatma) on, 4:262–265
and jewelry, 2:342
Kāma Sūtra on, 3:3
among Parsis, 3:282–283
in tribal society, 4:180
for widows, 1:187, 2:66, 68, 155
Marriage laws
in caste system, 1:223, 282, 2:66, 69,
4:60
on child marriage, 1:187, 250, 2:67,
69, 4:238, 240
Muslim, reform of, 3:195–198
Parsi, 3:282–283
reform of, 2:55, 57, 66–67
on widow remarriage, 1:187, 2:66, 155
Marshall, John, excavations at
Mohenjo-Daro by, 3:140
Martin, François, 2:102

Martyn, Henry, 1:249
Maru-Gurjara style of temple,
3:177–178, 180
Marumalarchchi Dravida Munnetra
Kazhagam (MDMK), 1:342
Maruts (spirits), 4:48–49
Marwar (princely state)
Mughal empire and, 3:382
under Rajputs, 3:339, 382
Marwari people, 2:354
Marwar painting, **3:130–131,**
3:382–383
Marx, Karl
on British economic impact on India,
1:184–185
on Indian feudalism, 2:71
on Indian thought, 2:234
Marxism
on colonial impact on small-scale
industry, 4:81
on feudalism, 2:70–73
and insurgency, 2:287
of Nehru (Jawaharlal), 2:9–10
Marxist-socialist movement, literature
influenced by, 3:66
Masala films, 1:254
Masani, Minoo, 3:375
Mashru fabric, 1:192
Masood, Syed Ross, 2:101
Massage, Āyurvedic, 1:*84*
Massoud, Ahmad Shah
alliance created by, 1:12
assassination of, 1:10, 11, 12
Mastaka, 3:155
Masters, John, on tribesmen, 1:110
Mastershare mutual fund, 3:206
Mataṅga, in Rāmāyaṇa, 3:395
Mātaṅgī (deity), 2:202
Materialism, Afghani's attack on, 1:6
Mathematics
Āryabhata in, 1:58, 59
contributions in, 4:19–20, 21, 22
Pingala in, 3:297–298
Vedic, 4:18–19, 20, 61
Mathura (city in Uttar Pradesh)
as birthplace of Krishna, 4:26
block-printed textiles from, 4:155
bronzes from, 1:195
Jain sculptures from, 2:327
sculptures from, 2:327, 4:26
Shaivism in, 4:26
Mathura Buddha image, 2:167, 4:24
Matilal, Bimal Krishna, 2:187
Mātra (beat), 4:129, 130, 131, 132, 133
Matrimonial law. *See* Marriage laws
Matsya (*avatāra* of Vishnu), 1:77–78
in the flood, 1:77
images of, 1:78
writings on, 4:218

Maududi, Abu'l 'Ala, 2:297, 303
on partition of India, 3:203
Mauritius, Indian community in, 1:332
Mauryan empire, 2:210, **3:103–105.**
See also specific rulers
art in, 2:113
Bengal in, 1:130
Bihar in, 1:152
census in, 1:308
expansion of, 3:103, 4:28
goddess images in, 2:153
Magadha in, 3:82, 103
map of, 3:*104*
political culture of, 2:164
political structure of, 3:105
sculpture in, **4:28–33**
sources of history of, 3:103,
104–105
state formation by, 4:103
temples in, 4:149
Mavalankar, G. V., on Patel (Sardar
Vallabhbhai), 3:285
Māyā (concept)
Shankara on, 4:47
in Upanishadic philosophy, 4:200
Varuṇa as wielder of, 4:210
Maya (mother of Buddha), 1:200
Mayer, Albert, and Chandigarh, 1:236
Mayer, Peter, on *jajmani* system, 3:46
Mazumdar-Shaw, Kiran, 1:*155*
McMahon Line, 1:242–243
MDGs. *See* Millennium Development
Goals
MDMK. *See* Marumalarchchi Dravida
Munnetra Kazhagam
Meat production, by smallholders,
1:16
Media, **3:105–107**. *See also specific types*
Medical science education, **3:107–108**
in Āyurveda, 1:83–84, 3:107
Medical tourism, 2:179, 182
Medications
generic, 2:177–178, 292, 4:246, 248
in Āyurveda, 1:85
intellectual property rights on, 2:292,
4:246, 248
pharmaceutical patents for, 2:292,
4:196, 246, 248
for tourists, 2:180
Medicine. *See also* Ayurveda; Health
care
Andy (S. Pulney) in, 1:44–45
Christian impact on, 1:250
education in, **3:107–108**
preventive, 2:178
Reddi (Muthulakshmi) in, 3:408–409
Medieval temple kingdoms, **3:108–
111**
Meditation. *See* Yoga

in Morley–Minto Reforms, 3:131, 183

Muslim delegation meeting with (1906), 1:36, 3:132

as viceroy of India, 3:131–132

Minyan (quorum required for public prayer), 2:349, 350

Mīrabai (saint), **3:132–133**, 3:*133*
on attributes of God, 3:133
devotion to Krishna, 3:132–133
life of, 3:133
poetry of, 3:132

Miracles, of Buddha, 1:201

*Mirasidar*s (village elites), land owned by, 3:45

Mirgavat (love story), 3:74

Mir Hasan, Sayyid, 2:296

Mir Jaffir (ruler of Bengal)
British installation of, 1:133, 215, 262
overthrow of, 1:263

Mir Kasim (ruler of Bengal)
in Battle of Buxar (1764), 1:133, 263
British relations with, 1:133

Mir Musavvir, art of, 3:184

Mir Sayyid 'Ali, art of, 3:184, 185

Mirza, Saeed, films of, 1:257

MISA. *See* Maintenance of Internal Security Act (MISA) of 1971

Mishra, Brajesh
in Chinese–Indian relations, 1:245
in Kargil conflict (1999), 3:9

*Misl*s (Sikh collective), 4:63, 67

Missile defense systems. *See* Ballistic missile defenses

Missiles. *See also* Ballistic missiles; Cruise missiles; Nuclear weapons
Abdul Kalam and, 1:1, 4:94–95
army's use of, 1:49
defenses against, **1:105–108**
development of, **1:101–105**
on display, at parade, 4:*230*
navy's use of, 1:54
of Pakistan, 1:104, 244

Missile Technology Control Regime (MTCR), China and Pakistan violating, 1:244

Missionaries, Buddhist, 1:205–206
across Bay of Bengal, 1:205–206
in Sri Lanka, 1:205

Missionaries, Christian, 1:247–250
Andy on limitations of, 1:45
Azariah organizing, 1:87
British East India Company and, 1:185–186
Catholic, 1:342–343, 2:185, 3:238–239, 4:251
Dalits and, 1:248–249
in education, 1:247–249, 3:59
impact of, 1:247–250

Jesuit, 1:248, 2:185, 3:238–239, 4:251
in Kerala, 3:25
in Konkan region, 2:348
leaders among, 3:59–60
in medicine, 1:250
and modernity, 1:251
and Mughal painting, 3:186
Nobili as, 3:238–239
tribal people converted by, 4:181–182, 183, 187
in women's education, 4:237

Missionaries, Muslim, 2:301

Mistry, Rohinton, literature of, 3:70

Mitra (deity), 4:210, 214–215

Mitra, Asok, 3:317

Mitra, Kumudini, 2:67

Miyan Tansen. *See* Tansen

Mizhava (musical instrument), 1:291

Mizo Accord of 1976, 2:45–46, 47

Mizo Accord of 1986, 2:47, 288, 4:188

Mizo Hills, 3:134

Mizo National Army (MNA), 2:45–46, 47

Mizo National Front (MNF), 2:45–46, 47, 3:134, 242, 4:188

Mizo people, 3:134
ethics of, 3:134
insurgency of, 3:134, 242–243
social structure of, 3:134

Mizoram (state), **3:134**
under British rule, 3:134
dance in, 3:134
famine in, 2:288
geography of, 3:134
insurgencies in, 2:288, 3:134, 242–243, 244, 4:183
Jews in, 2:350
peace accords with, 2:45–46, 47, 288, 3:242–243
statehood for, 3:134
tribes living in, 3:134, 4:179, 182, 187

Mizo Union, 4:188

MNA. *See* Mizo National Army

MNF. *See* Mizo National Front

Mobile phones, 2:*17*, 279, 280

Modeling careers, col. ins. v2

Modern and contemporary art, 2:154, **3:134–140**
artists' collectives and, 3:136–137
British influence on, 3:134
in diaspora, 3:138–139
gender in, 3:139
nationalism in, 3:134–135

Modernity, Christian impact on, 1:251

Modern Theaters (film studio), 1:254

Modhera, temple in, 3:180

Modi, Narendra, 2:198, 206–207

Modi, Sohrab, films of, 1:253

Modified value-added tax (MODVAT), 4:140

Mody, Jivanji, in Asiatic Society of Bombay, 1:67

MoEF. *See* Environment and Forests, Ministry of

Mohammad Ahmed Khan v. Shah Bano Begum, 3:197

Mohammad Shah Abdali (Afghan amir), Akbar challenged by, 1:29

Mohanty, Jitendranath, 2:187

Mohapatra, Nirad, films of, 1:257

Mohapatra, Robindra, 4:23

Mohenjo-Daro (archaeological site), **3:140–142**
brick wall and drain at, 2:*259*
bronzes from, 1:192–193
discovery of, 3:140
excavations at, 3:140
as independent city-state, 2:263
mortar and pestle found at, 2:*265*
mounds at, 3:140, *141*
pottery of, 3:140, 141
public buildings in, 2:262
script found at, 2:262, 263
sculpture found at, 2:263, 3:141
seal found at, 2:263, 264
textiles found at, 4:154
urban planning in, 4:200–201
water in, 2:261

Mohini Attam (dance), **1:293–294**

Moksha (liberation)
bhakti as path to, 1:143
Gandhi (Mahatma) on, 4:8
Shankara on, 4:48
in Tantric Hinduism, 2:200
in Upanishadic philosophy, 4:200
in Vedism, 2:209
Vishnu and, 4:220

Molecules, 4:18, 207

Mompa people, 3:*242*

Monasteries
architecture of, 3:154
Brahmanical, 3:153
Buddhist, 2:24, 25, 115, 320, 3:154
in eastern India, 3:154
Jain, 2:*327*, 3:154
Shankara establishing, 4:47
Tibetan Buddhist, 4:169, *169*, 171, *171*

Monasticism, Buddhist, 1:28, 29, 201, 202, 204, 206

Monetary policy
from 1952 to 1991, **3:142–143**
after 1991, 2:97, **3:143–148**
and agricultural prices, 1:21
and financial markets, 3:151
framework for, 3:142

ENCYCLOPEDIA OF *India*

in Purāṇas, 4:49–50, 51

in Rāmāyaṇa, 4:49

roots of, 4:48–49

and Satī, 1:321, 2:202

sexuality of, 4:49–50

Shankara on, 4:52

shivling as symbol of, 2:189

as supreme being, 4:50

in Tantric Hinduism, 2:203, 4:51

temples dedicated to, 4:49, 209

and Trailokyavijaya, 4:136

in Vedas, 4:48–49

vs. Vishnu, 4:219

Shivaji Bhonsla (Maratha king), 3:94, **4:53–56**

Akbar inspiring, 4:55

Aurangzeb's army attacked by, 1:75, 4:54–55

childhood of, 4:53–54

coronation and administration of, 4:55

historical accounts on, 4:54

Islam under, 4:55

in Maharashtra, 3:93–95, 4:53

military strategy of, 4:54, 55

peshwas after, 3:293–294

successors of, 4:55–56

Shivaji festivals, 4:53, 173

Shiva Nataraja, bronzes of, 1:197

Shiva saints. *See Nayanārs*

Shivling (state of eternity), 2:189

Shiv Sena, **4:56–58**

agenda of, 4:56–57

on Ayodhya temple issue, 4:57–58

Bharatiya Janata Party allied with, 2:135, 136

in Bombay, 4:56, 57, 58

involved in mafia, 4:58

in Maharashtra, 4:56, 57

origin of name, 4:53, 57

on Women's Reservation Bill of 1996, 4:233

Sholay (film), 1:256

Shore, Sir John, **4:58**

on Cornwallis' settlement of land revenues, 1:277, 4:58

as governor-general of India, 4:58

revenue reforms by, 4:58

Short stories, 3:66–68

Shrada ritu (spring), depiction of, 1:125

Shrāddha (ancestor cult), 2:183, 189

Shraddhananda

in ārya Samāj movement, 1:60

nationalism of, 1:60

Shrauta (sacrifice), 4:59, 253, 254

Shrauta Sūtras (ritual manuals), **4:58–59**, 4:84

Shravakayana Buddhism. *See* Hinayana Buddhism

Shravana Beḷgoḷa

monuments in, 3:167–169

temples in, 3:167–169

Shree 420 (film), 1:252

*Shreni*s (occupational guilds), **4:59–61**

as banks, 4:60

in caste system, 4:60–61

communities of, 4:59–60

organization of, 4:60

wealth of, 4:60

writings on, 4:59, 60–61

Shrī (deity), in Vedas, 1:320

Shringāra (amorous sentiment), 1:4–5

*Shruti*s (microtones), Nātya Shāstra on, 3:222, 364–365

Shudras (caste), 2:192

creation of, 1:281, 4:14–15

deprived of education, 2:24

Dubois on, 1:284

eyewitness accounts of, 1:225

Kayasths as, 3:22

occupations of, 1:223, *223*, 282

Rig Veda on, 1:223

as slaves of Brahmans, 1:282

Shuja Sadozai

in Anglo–Afghan War, First, 1:45–46, 73

assassination of, 1:46

Dost Mohammad Barakzai's struggle with, 1:45

Shuja-ud-Dawla, Clive and, 1:263

Shuka, in Mahābhārata, 3:92–93

Shukla Yajur Veda. *See* "White" Yajur Veda

Shulba Sūtras (Vedāngas), **4:61–62**

geometry in, 4:61

style of, 4:61

Shunga dynasty, 2:210

sculpture in, **4:28–33**, *4:29*

Shvetambara sect (Jainism)

bronzes in, 1:196–197

establishment of, 2:324–325

sculptures in, 2:327

Shyāma Shāstri, **4:62**

Karnātak music of, 3:191, 193

*kriti*s of, 3:43, 44

lyrics of, 4:62

*rāga*s by, 4:62

*tāla*s by, 4:62

Siachen Glacier (Kashmir), 4:227–228

Siddhamatrika script, 3:55

Siddha naturopathy, 2:179

*Siddhānta*s, astronomical, 1:72–73, 4:18

Siddhartha Gautama. *See* Buddha

Sidi Saiyad Mosque (Ahmedabad), 1:24

Sikandara Agra, Akbar's tomb at, 3:159–160

Sikandar Lodi, Agra as capital of, 1:13

Sikandar Sur, Akbar challenged by, 1:29

Sikh Gurdwaras Act of 1925, 4:68

Sikh institutions and parties, **4:62–65**

guru period, 4:62–63

post-guru period, 4:63–65, 67–68

Sikhism, **4:65–70**. *See also* Sikhs

under British rule, 4:64, 67–68

code of conduct in, 4:64, 67, 68

external symbols of, 4:67

festivals in, 4:69–70

Guru Nanak as founder of, 2:167–168, 4:62, 65–66

guru period of, 4:66–67

initiation in, 4:67

Kabir in, 3:1

in Mughal empire, 4:63, 66–67

pilgrimage in, 4:65

post-guru period of, 4:67

reform movements in, 4:67–68

temples in, 1:333, 334, 335, 4:66, 69, col. ins. v1

worship and customs in, 4:68–70

Sikh Rabit Maryada (Sikh Code of Conduct), 4:64, 67, 68

Sikhs. *See also* Sikhism

army of, 4:63, 66, 67

Bahadur Shah I fighting, 1:90

Delhi riot targeting, 2:288, 4:68

Gandhi (Indira) and, 2:118–119, 4:64–65

in Jammu, 2:334

population of, 4:65

as presidents, 3:332, 333

as prime ministers, 4:74

in Punjab, 2:42, 43, 46, 118–119, 288, 3:356, 358, 359, 4:68

Ramananda's sect influencing, 3:388

recruited in British army, 2:41, 213, 4:74

separatist movement of, 2:42, 43, 46, 288, 3:358, 4:64–65, 68

terrorist activities of, 3:358

and Vajpayee, 2:168

women, 4:67

Sikh Wars, 1:281, 3:356

Sikkim (state)

China and, 3:246

incorporation into India (1975), 3:244

Nepalis in, 3:244

northeast states and, 3:244

papermaking in, 3:275

Sikri. *See* Fatehpur Sikri

Sikri Commission (1979), 2:336

Silk

brocade, 1:189–192

Chinese, 1:190

refugees from Sri Lanka in, 4:98
settlement patterns in, 2:142
temples in, 4:151, 152
Tamil people
    bronzes of, 1:197–199
    Shaivism of, 4:52
    in Sri Lanka, 4:95, 96, 97–98
    in Sri Lanka, in ethnic conflict,
        2:125, 3:118, 4:96, 98–100, 227
Tamil script, 3:55
Tamil Tigers. *See* Liberation Tigers of
    Tamil Ealam
Tamil United Liberation Front, 4:96
Tanchoi (textile), **4:133–134**
    colors of, 4:133–134
    technique of weaving, 4:133
Tandabo, Treaty of (1826), 1:210
Tanda muslin, 2:329, 330
Tandava (dance), 1:286, 292
Tandon, Purushottam Das, in
    Congress Party, 3:315
Tanjāvūr, temples in, 3:173
Tanjore
    block-printed textiles from, 4:158
    Brihadīshvara temple at, 1:246, 247
    as folk art center, 2:89
    Karuppur textiles made for,
        4:160–161
    music at, 3:191
Tanks, stepped, 4:110, 111
Tansen (musician), **4:134**
    music of, 3:190, 4:134
    *rāga*s of, 3:366, 4:134
Tantric Buddhism. *See also* Tibetan
    Buddhism
    images in, 4:25, 25, **4:134–138,**
        4:135, 136, 137
    in Kashmir, 2:333, 4:135
    in Nepal, 4:135, 137
    in Tibet, 4:136, 137
Tantric Hinduism
    deities in, 2:153, 200, **2:200–203**
    emergence of, 2:191
    Gaṇesha in, 2:129
    goddesses in, 2:153, 200, 200–202
    goddess images in, 2:153, 200
    in Kashmir, 2:332–333
    rituals in, 2:200, 203
    Shiva in, 4:51
    spread of, 2:191
    yoga in, 2:200, 201
Tantrism
    sexuality in, 1:162
    tapas in, 4:138
Tapas, **4:138**
    meanings of, 4:138
    and *rishi*s, 3:412
    of soma, 4:138
    in yoga, 4:138

Tapasya (self-suffering), 4:8
Tapestry weave, 1:190–191. *See also*
    Paithani weaving
    in Kashmir shawls, 3:19–20
Tārā (deity)
    dharani of, 4:135
    images of, 4:135–136
    power of, 2:153
    and Shiva, 2:202
Tarabai (Maratha queen), 4:56
Targeted Public Distribution System,
    2:94
Tariffs
    by British Raj, 4:177–178
    current levels of, 2:258, 4:176
    decrease in, 2:10, 19, 146, 256, 4:175,
        245–246
    under economic planning, 2:255,
        4:245
    future of, 4:176–177
    increase in, 4:174, 175
    in Mughal empire, 4:177
Tarjuman al-Qur'an (Azad), 1:87
Tashkent Agreement (1966)
    Bhutto (Zulfikar Ali) in, 1:150
    Soviet Union in, 3:420
Tassar (variety of silk), in brocade
    weaving, 1:190
Tata, Dorabji J., 4:139
Tata, Herabai, 4:240
Tata, J. R. D., Narayanan and,
    3:219
Tata, Jamsetji N., **4:138–139**
    accomplishments of, 3:281–282
    city named after, 2:337
    cotton mills of, 4:139
    education of, 4:139
    Indian Institute of Science endowed
        by, 1:116, 4:139
    in steel industry, 2:337, 4:139
Tata, Jamsetji R. D., accomplishments
    of, 3:282
Tata, Mehribai, 2:68
Tata Airlines, 3:282
Tata Chemicals, 3:282
Tata Consultancy Services, 2:270
Tata Engine and Locomotive Co.
    (TELCO), 2:338, 3:282
Tata Group, 3:281–282
Tata Institute of Fundamental
    Research (TIFR), 1:140, 3:248, 253,
        282, 4:22, 23
Tata Iron and Steel Company
    (TISCO), 2:337–338
Tata Iron and Steel Works, 3:347
Tata Sons, 3:282
Tata Sons Limited v. Fashion ID,
    2:292
Tattva (basic principle), 4:4–5

Tavernier, Jean Baptiste, on caste
    system, 1:225
Tawaif (courtesans), 4:237
Taxation. *See also specific taxes*
    under Akbar, 1:31
    under Aurangzeb, 1:74
    in Bengal, 1:180
    under British Crown Raj, 1:172,
        4:177
    of British East India Company, by
        British government, 1:133, 2:32
    under British rule, 2:79–80
    census for, 1:308, 309
    central government collecting, 2:65,
        77, 4:101, 139, 140–141
    distribution of (*See* Finance
        Commission)
    evasion of, 4:142 (*See also* Under-
        ground economy)
    famines caused by, 2:58
    globalization and, 4:140
    in Indus Valley civilization, 2:265
    on manufacturing, 4:141
    under Mughal empire, 1:31, 74, 180
    on pre-colonial maritime trade, 2:2
    progressive, 2:83
    by states, 2:16–17, 83, 84, 4:100–101,
        139, 140, 141–142
Taxation policy since 1991 economic
    reforms, 2:84, **4:139–143.** *See also*
    Value-added tax
    administration in, 4:142–143
    excise tax/duties in, 2:84, 4:140–141,
        142
    income tax in, 2:84, 4:140, 142
Taxila (city)
    Alexander the Great in, 1:35
    Buddhist temple at, 2:113, 114,
        115
Tax Reform Committees, 4:192
TCSP. *See* Traditional civil servants
    pension
TDP. *See* Telugu Desam Party
Tea plantations, col. ins. v4
    in Assam, 1:68, 69
    in Sri Lanka, 2:141, 4:96
Technical change in agriculture
    (1952–2000), **4:143–148**
    economic reforms of 1991 and, 4:148
    fertilizer use, 4:145
    high-yielding varieties (*See* High-
        yielding varieties)
    irrigation, 4:144, 145, 146, 147
    mechanization, 4:144–145, 147
    package of practices, 4:143, 145
Technology. *See also* Information
    technology
    EU-India cooperation in, 2:50–51
    foreign, licensing, 2:13, 247

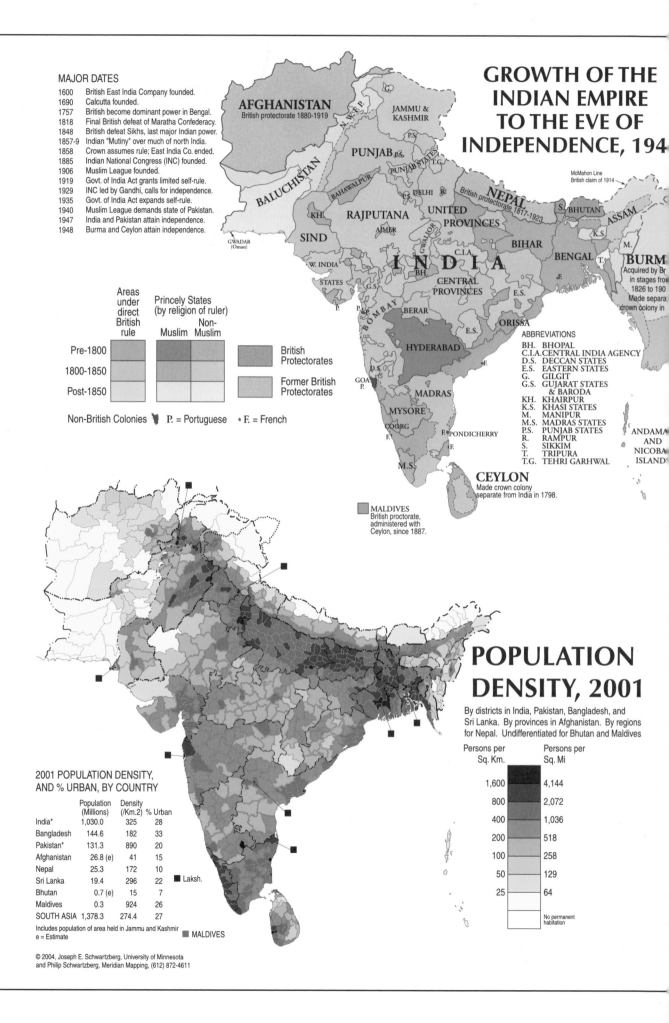

GROWTH OF THE INDIAN EMPIRE TO THE EVE OF INDEPENDENCE, 194[7]

MAJOR DATES

1600	British East India Company founded.
1690	Calcutta founded.
1757	British become dominant power in Bengal.
1818	Final British defeat of Maratha Confederacy.
1848	British defeat Sikhs, last major Indian power.
1857-9	Indian "Mutiny" over much of north India.
1858	Crown assumes rule; East India Co. ended.
1885	Indian National Congress (INC) founded.
1906	Muslim League founded.
1919	Govt. of India Act grants limited self-rule.
1929	INC led by Gandhi, calls for independence.
1935	Govt. of India Act expands self-rule.
1940	Muslim League demands state of Pakistan.
1947	India and Pakistan attain independence.
1948	Burma and Ceylon attain independence.

McMahon Line
British claim of 1914

BURM[A]
Acquired by Br[itish]
in stages from
1826 to 190[?]
Made separat[e]
crown colony in [?]

Legend

Areas under direct British rule | Princely States (by religion of ruler)
Muslim | Non-Muslim

Pre-1800
1800-1850
Post-1850

British Protectorates
Former British Protectorates

Non-British Colonies   P. = Portuguese   F. = French

ABBREVIATIONS

BH. BHOPAL
C.I.A. CENTRAL INDIA AGENCY
D.S. DECCAN STATES
E.S. EASTERN STATES
G. GILGIT
G.S. GUJARAT STATES & BARODA
KH. KHAIRPUR
K.S. KHASI STATES
M. MANIPUR
M.S. MADRAS STATES
P.S. PUNJAB STATES
R. RAMPUR
S. SIKKIM
T. TRIPURA
T.G. TEHRI GARHWAL

CEYLON
Made crown colony
separate from India in 1798.

MALDIVES
British proctorate,
administered with
Ceylon, since 1887.

GWADAR (Oman)

PONDICHERRY

ANDAMA[N] AND NICOBA[R] ISLAND[S]

AFGHANISTAN
British protectorate 1880-1919

JAMMU & KASHMIR

PUNJAB

BALUCHISTAN

BAHAWALPUR

SIND

RAJPUTANA

NEPAL
British protectorate 1817-1923

BHUTAN

ASSAM

UNITED PROVINCES

BIHAR

BENGAL

I N D I A

CENTRAL PROVINCES

BERAR

ORISSA

HYDERABAD

BOMBAY

GOA

MADRAS

MYSORE

COORG

W. INDIA STATES

POPULATION DENSITY, 2001

By districts in India, Pakistan, Bangladesh, and Sri Lanka. By provinces in Afghanistan. By regions for Nepal. Undifferentiated for Bhutan and Maldives

Persons per Sq. Km.	Persons per Sq. Mi
1,600	4,144
800	2,072
400	1,036
200	518
100	258
50	129
25	64
No permanent habitation	

2001 POPULATION DENSITY, AND % URBAN, BY COUNTRY

	Population (Millions)	Density (/Km.2)	% Urban
India*	1,030.0	325	28
Bangladesh	144.6	182	33
Pakistan*	131.3	890	20
Afghanistan	26.8 (e)	41	15
Nepal	25.3	172	10
Sri Lanka	19.4	296	22
Bhutan	0.7 (e)	15	7
Maldives	0.3	924	26
SOUTH ASIA	1,378.3	274.4	27

*Includes population of area held in Jammu and Kashmir
e = Estimate

■ Laksh.

■ MALDIVES

© 2004, Joseph E. Schwartzberg, University of Minnesota
and Philip Schwartzberg, Meridian Mapping, (612) 872-4611